Do It Yourself

Yourself

Visual Basic for MS-DOS

Do It Yourself

Visual Basic® for MS-DOS®

William J. Orvis

SAMS
PUBLISHING

A Division of Prentice Hall Computer Publishing
11711 North College, Carmel, Indiana 46032 USA

For my parents,
You got me here,
and did a great job in the process.

Trademark Acknowledgments

Sams Publishing has made every attempt to supply trademark information about
company names, products, and services mentioned in this book. Trademarks
indicated below were derived from various sources. Sams Publishing cannot
attest to the accuracy of this information.

Apple and Macintosh are registered trademarks of Apple Computer, Inc.

BASICA, Excel, GW-BASIC, Microsoft, Microsoft BASIC, MS-DOS, and Visual
Basic are registered trademarks of Microsoft Corporation, and OS/2 is a
registered trademark licensed to Microsoft Corporation.

IBM is a registered trademark of International Business Machines Corporation.

Pac-Man licensed to Atari by Namco-America, Inc.

Composed in Carmel, Indiana, by Prentice Hall Computer Publishing
Printed in the United States of America

About the Author

William Orvis is an electronics engineer at the University of California's Lawrence Livermore National Laboratory, where he is involved in the large scale numerical modeling of solid-state devices, development of micron-sized vacuum microelectronic devices, and computer security research. (He describes himself as a computer virus smasher.) Orvis received both his B.S. and M.S. degrees in Physics and Astronomy at the University of Denver in Colorado. He is the author of *Do It Yourself Visual Basic* (for Windows) (Sams Publishing, 1992), *ABC's of GW-BASIC* (Sybex, 1990), *Excel Instant Reference* (Sybex, 1989), *1-2-3 for Scientists and Engineers* (Sybex, 1987, 2nd ed. 1991), and *Electrical Overstress Protection for Electronic Devices*, (Noyes Data Corporation, 1986). His books have been translated into Japanese, Italian, and Greek. He also has written for *Computers in Physics* and *IEEE Circuits and Devices* magazine.

Overview

Contents

Part II: Opening Up Visual Basic

3 Understanding Forms   59

4 Using Strings · 81

5 Using Numbers and Control Structures · 107

6 Using Controls 141

7 Creating Custom Menus 167

8 Writing Custom Procedures 189

9 Using Sequential Files 217

Part III: Visual Basic Reference

Appendixes

Acknowledgments

I thank Joe Wikert, Greg Croy, Ella Davis, and Andy Saff from Sams Publishing, who kept the pressure on to get this work done, fixed my English, and kept me on track, and, of course, all the others at Sams Publishing who got this book from manuscript to print. Without them, you wouldn't be looking at anything now. I want to thank BJ, Skye, Sierra, and Shane for not being too upset as I shut myself away every evening to write this book. And I want to thank Julie for keeping just about everything else going, and holding the house together while I worked at the computer.

Preface

When Visual Basic for Windows came out, I was an immediate enthusiast. Nowhere else could I so quickly and easily create a Windows application in a language as familiar and easy-to-use as BASIC. Earlier this year, I was thinking that, because not everybody has Windows (yet), it would be nice to be able to use the same visual program development methods in DOS machines.

Then Visual Basic for MS-DOS arrived, and it's as thorough a development environment as I could imagine. Visual Basic for MS-DOS also is as compatible with Visual Basic for Windows as is possible.

I'm used to writing many lines of code to create the visual interface of a program—to define what it looks like on the screen and how it receives and responds to commands. Visual Basic takes much of that work into its own hands, and lets you draw the visual interface with a mouse. No longer do I have to guess where a button goes; I draw it exactly where I want it. No longer do I have to write code to determine when an event has occurred; I only have to write code to handle the events themselves. (An *event* is something that happens to a program, such as the user clicking a button with the mouse or pressing a key at the keyboard.) Visual Basic takes care of everything else. Now, if Microsoft will only create a Macintosh version (hint, hint), I could move applications from machine to machine without having to completely recode them.

When Visual Basic for MS-DOS arrived, Joe Wikert of Sams Publishing called and asked if I would write this book. Well, sure, I thought, I just wrote a book on Visual Basic for Windows, so one on Visual Basic for MS-DOS should be a cinch. However, he said he needed the manuscript in five weeks instead of the normal three to six months. I said okay in a shaky voice, went home, said goodbye to my family, and secluded myself with my computer.

Creating this book and redeveloping old applications in this new implementation of an old language was interesting and fun. It's really an ego boost to create a polished, windowed application in only a few minutes. Programs that look and work like commercial products are only

hours away. And, with windowed applications, everyone can more easily use what I have developed. Even my three year old, Shane, can move the mouse and click a button. (He wants more games.)

It's now two o'clock in the morning, and this is the last of the manuscript. Tomorrow, I'll see if I still have a family. Well, maybe the day after—I'm going to sleep tomorrow.

William J. Orvis
Livermore, California

Introduction

Computer languages and the programs they create have progressed over the last few years from elementary, text-mode applications to modern Graphical User Interface (GUI, pronounced "gooey") programs. This is a great boon for the users of computers, because the interface now is much simpler both to learn and to use. Unfortunately, creating GUI software often is a real headache for programmers. This is because the programs and their results are essentially text files. The program is text, the results are text, and most of the output is text. Even on the Macintosh, where the GUI is a well-defined art, programs created with BASIC interpreters and compilers still are text files that write or draw on a window rather than the whole screen. You can create GUI applications for Microsoft Windows, as for the Macintosh operating system, but the process is long and painful. Mountains of code must be written to create and draw windows on the screen, draw buttons and other controls on the windows, and track the keyboard and mouse.

You might think that Visual Basic for MS-DOS would be a step backward. By operating in the DOS environment, it has no GUI environment to work with—and even must contend with systems that have no graphics at all. However, Visual Basic for MS-DOS creates programs with windowed interfaces in text mode, and does it well. The windows and controls are drawn with text and graphics characters, and are so well done that you might not realize that you aren't using a graphics-mode interface. And Visual Basic includes the windowed interface from the very beginning of project development.

Visual Basic for MS-DOS is patterned after Visual Basic for Windows. You start a project with a window (called a *form*) and draw buttons or controls on it. Visual Basic generates the code to create buttons and controls on the screen, and to track the interactions of the mouse and keyboard with them. In fact, you never see any of that code; it's all handled in the background.

When a program is running, and something happens to a form or control (that is, when an event occurs), the Visual Basic runtime system passes control to the program or code you have written to handle that event. For example, you may "press" a button by clicking it with the mouse. You don't have to worry about writing code to track the mouse, or to determine whether the button has been pressed or not. You just write code that tells the computer what to do if the button is pressed.

In the past, up to 90 percent of the code I have written for large applications dealt with the user interface, with only about 10 percent going to the meat of the application. Switching to a programming environment that automatically handles the user interface for me—although I still have to create and draw the interface—results in a major change in my program-development time. Now, in minutes, I can create a professional-looking, windowed application, complete with interface, buttons, check boxes, and windows. Rather than spending my time figuring out how to make a button work, I spend it making the meat of the program work, and work efficiently.

If you've programmed before, I think you will find this an exhilarating experience. If you have never programmed before, may you never have to find out what it's like not to have a Visual Basic-like environment.

Compatibility

Visual Basic for MS-DOS is more than a DOS version of Visual Basic for Windows. It is the most complete, catch-all package I've seen in a long time. Not only does it run windowed code created with Visual Basic for Windows (with little modification), but it runs most code developed with Microsoft QuickBASIC and the BASIC Compiler in a nonwindowed mode. It even runs GW-BASIC and BASICA programs.

Because of this, Visual Basic has many built-in functions with overlapping capabilities. There also are many obsolete functions that have been included for compatibility. These functions are for use in importing existing code into the Visual Basic environment; you shouldn't use them if you're creating new code. I therefore have limited the functions I use in this book to those considered part of the modern BASIC language. The result is that the code developed in this book is almost completely compatible with Visual Basic for Windows.

The only area that has problems is graphics. Because the Visual Basic for MS-DOS interface is created in text mode, you cannot draw real graphics on Visual Basic forms. Graphics are done only in full-screen mode with all forms hidden. However, the statements for creating graphics in Visual Basic for MS-DOS are nearly identical in function and syntax to the methods used for drawing on forms in Visual Basic for Windows. Thus, converting code written in Visual Basic for MS-DOS to Visual Basic for Windows requires merely that you switch your graphics from the whole screen to a form.

The Need for Speed

As a programmer, you might be put off by the thought of using BASIC to create a serious application. Traditional BASIC, as an interpreted language, has never been known for creating speedy applications; however, a fully compiled Visual Basic application is as fast as those created for any other language but assembly language. In addition, if you still insist on coding the core of your application in some other language, that core code can be compiled into a library function, and then linked to a user interface created with Visual Basic.

In This Book

This book teaches the novice programmer the elements of the Visual Basic environment, the BASIC language, programming conventions and methods, and the development of a windowed user interface. Using the different controls as a vehicle, the book guides you through the modern BASIC language and the Visual Basic enhancements to it.

Many books develop simple, trivial examples to demonstrate programming and the language. These examples are fine for demonstrating a piece of the language, but they don't show how larger applications work, and they aren't useful later on. The example programs used in this book are not only vehicles for learning the language, but are usable additions to your programming library. Some are slightly longer than you might be used to seeing in an elementary programming book. However, I think you will find that the increased functionality of the programs is well worth the effort. As you develop each example, consider how you would modify it to suit your particular needs.

 Throughout this book, I've inserted sidebars that direct you toward variations and more-advanced versions of the applications. The sidebars are indicated by a light-bulb icon that looks like this:

Part I is an introduction to both windowed user interfaces, and Visual Basic programming. In this part, I explain what a windowed user interface is, and the role of objects in object-oriented programming. I examine the Visual Basic programming environment, and present an overview of the Visual Basic program development process.

Part II is a tutorial on Visual Basic programming. In Part II, I examine in more detail each Visual Basic object introduced in Part I. Visual Basic objects are the forms, buttons, and text boxes that make up the visual interface of a Visual Basic program. In addition, as I examine these objects, I also present the elements of the BASIC programming language.

Part III is a complete Visual Basic reference. Parts II and III complement each other, with Part II supplying the common usage of the language elements and objects and Part III supplying the details. In Part III, I explain each of the functions, statements, and methods that comprise the Visual Basic language, along with its syntax and an example showing its usage. In addition to the language elements, each object has properties that control how it looks and works, and events to which it responds. Each of these properties and events is explained in detail, with a description of what part of an object's character a property controls, how to change that property, and which events an object responds to.

Part IV is an appendix to Visual Basic, containing installation instructions, a table of the ASCII (ANSI) character codes, a table of the keycodes, and a table of advanced library functions. ASCII character codes are the standard codes used to represent characters in a computer. Keycodes are used to identify the specific keys on the keyboard.

Who Can Use This Book?

This book is for the novice computer programmer who wants to learn Visual Basic programming, and for the advanced and not-so-advanced computer user who wants to learn about programming in general. It's also for the programmer who wants to learn about programming a windowed user interface without the mass of code needed in other languages, and which tends to obscure an understanding of the environment. Advanced programmers probably will find this book too slow for them, but if they glance at the language syntax in each chapter and work through the examples, they'll get a useful understanding of the language.

This book is directed to both the home and small business computer user, though large business and technical computer users will have no problem adapting the techniques to their own work. The examples are all somewhat generic in their application, so they can be readily applied to a particular situation. I often indicate extensions to or variations of an example, and point you in the direction needed to achieve them.

What You Must Know

You must be familiar with DOS, and with running and using DOS applications. If you know how to use Windows and Windows methods, this material will be quite familiar to you because the windows in Visual Basic for MS-DOS are quite similar in functionality and control to windows in Windows. You don't have to be an expert, but you must at least be able to launch the Visual Basic application.

What You Must Have

Visual Basic requires some specific hardware and software:

- You must have an MS-DOS compatible computer with an 8086 processor (IBM-XT compatible) and 640K of memory. More memory and a more advanced processor would be better.

- Although Visual Basic will run with a text-mode monitor, you need a graphics monitor and card (such as the CGA, EGA, VGA, 8514, Hercules, or compatible) if you want to create graphics.

- You need a hard disk with about 11 megabytes (11M) free for the complete Visual Basic Pro package. The standard version requires about 8 megabytes (8M) of disk space. You can get away with about 4.5 megabytes (4.5M) if you leave out the libraries, the examples, the tutorial, and the help files.

- You also need a mouse. I know the documentation says you don't need a mouse, and perhaps you can operate everything without one, but get a mouse anyway. It makes things much simpler.

- You must have DOS version 3.0 or later. DOS version 5.0 is useful because it can move much of the operating system code and drivers into high memory (above 640K), making more memory available for Visual Basic. The software created by Visual Basic should run on machines with DOS 2.2 or later.

- If you want to translate applications between Visual Basic for Windows and Visual Basic for MS-DOS, you need Microsoft Windows 3.0 or later, and Visual Basic for Windows 1.0 or later. Both of these softwares need more powerful hardware than that previously listed for Visual Basic for MS-DOS. You don't need this software if you are not planning to translate programs to or from the Windows environment.

- You must install Visual Basic before you can use it. Appendix A, "Installing Visual Basic," describes the installation process.

Disk Offer

If you don't feel like typing all the examples in this book, they are available on disk directly from me for $20. In addition to the examples from this book, the disk includes some simple applications and pieces of test code for some of the advanced methods not covered in this book. To get the disk, use the coupon at the end of this book. Note that Prentice Hall Computer Publishing is not involved in the sale of this disk, and makes no warranty for it.

Conventions

As I develop language elements, I often use syntax statements to describe the syntax of that element. In Part III, every function, statement, and method includes a syntax statement. A syntax statement is an expression of the grammar of the computer language, showing where the commas go and how the words are spelled. The format of a syntax statement is as follows:

- Words and symbols that must be typed exactly as they are shown in the syntax statement are in `monospace bold.`

- Placeholders for variable names or constant values are in `monospace italic` and, where appropriate, are followed by the variable type suffix characters. These variable type suffix characters indicate the type of variable or number that is expected at this location. The types are

Suffix	Type
%	Integer
&	Long integer
!	Single-precision floating point
#	Double-precision floating point
@	Currency
$	String

Chapter 5, "Using Numbers and Control Structures," explains these types in more detail.

- Alternate entries—from which you must make a choice—are separated with vertical bars (¦) and surrounded by braces ({}).

- Optional entries are surrounded by square brackets([]).

- Repeated clauses are followed by an ellipsis (...).

For example:

```
ON [LOCAL] ERROR {GOTO line¦RESUME NEXT¦GOTO 0}
```

In this example, you must type the keywords ON, LOCAL, ERROR, GOTO, RESUME, and NEXT exactly as shown, so they are in monospace bold. The words ON and ERROR are required, but [LOCAL] is optional, so it is surrounded by square brackets. At the end of the statement are three clauses, from which you must select one, so these clauses are surrounded with braces and separated by vertical bars. The word *line* is a placeholder for a variable or a literal constant, so it is in monospace italic. A *literal* is the actual number or string rather than a variable containing the value of the number or string.

Here is a second example:

```
MSGBOX(msg$[,type%[,title$]])
```

In this example, the keyword MSGBOX, the two parentheses, and the two commas must be typed exactly as shown, so they are bold. The first argument, *msg$*, is a placeholder for a string. The argument *type%* is a placeholder for an integer, and *title$* is a placeholder for another string.

The first argument is required, but the second two are optional. The bracket-within-bracket arrangement indicates that if the third argument *title$* is used, the second argument *type%* also must be included.

Outside of the syntax statements, the following conventions are used to highlight different items:

- Words that you must type exactly as they are written, such as the code in programming examples, are in **monospace bold**.

- Access keys (*hot keys* for keyboard access to menu items) are bold in the text of this book—the **F**ile menu, for example.

- Some keyboards have Return keys and others have Enter keys. I use Enter in this text, but these keys are interchangeable. Use the one on your keyboard whenever I use Enter.

- Visual Basic keywords, variable names, methods, procedures, functions, events, properties, and objects are in monospace—for example, `END`, `OPEN`, and `MSGBOX`.

- The length of a line in Visual Basic occasionally is longer than can be printed in this book. Visual Basic statements cannot be arbitrarily split into two lines, because the program would not continue working. Therefore, when a line must be split in this book, it is prefaced with the following continuation arrow character:

⤿ Note that when you type a line followed by one that starts with this character, the two lines must be joined for the program to work. For example, in the following procedure, the first and second lines must be typed as a single line in a Visual Basic program or you will receive a syntax error:

```
⤿ SUB LeftArrow_MouseDown (BUTTON AS INTEGER,
    SHIFT AS INTEGER, X AS SINGLE, Y AS SINGLE)
LeftArrow.BackColor = BLACK
END SUB
```

Occasionally, a piece of information or advice does not fit within the current tutorial. A note of this type is separated from the rest of the text of the chapter into a boxed note, as shown here:

This an example of a boxed note.

Programming tips and shortcuts also are separated from the examples in a tip, as shown here:

Holding down the Ctrl, Alt, Shift, and Caps Lock key with the right hand while pressing Shift, Enter and Backspace with the left hand is guaranteed to get you strange looks.

Tips and notes that warn of problems or possibly unwanted results are inserted as cautions:

If you try the last tip, you may look dumb.

Finally, all the examples represent fairly basic applications that can be expanded and modified to show much more functionality. In these cases, I describe some of the possible changes that you can make and briefly point you in the right direction to make those changes. These suggestions appear in an FYI-Idea box:

Wow! I just had a great idea and I want to share it with you!!

Where Are You Going?

You're going on a wonderful trip, where you create your own worlds, travel among friends or enemies, win battles, and become the master of your computer. You are going to teach this machine who is boss, and make it politely carry out your wishes.

Part I

Visual Basic
Basics

Windows Programming

Early versions of high-level computer languages, such as BASIC and FORTRAN, were largely text oriented. The program was a text file typed on cards or at a Teletype, and the results were printed on a line printer or Teletype. With the help of special libraries and graphic output devices such as plotters and film recorders, these languages could do graphics—but not in real time. The graphics usually arrived on a roll of microfilm an hour or two after the program completed running.

With the advent of glass-fronted terminals (terminals that output to a CRT rather than to paper), programmers started drawing graphics online. However, such graphics still were a part of the output—they merely got to you faster than by the microfilm method.

The Graphical User Interface (GUI) actually originated at the Xerox Palo Alto Research Center (Xerox PARC), where engineers developed a graphical interface complete with icons and a mouse. Unfortunately, that project was not a commercial success, and largely disappeared. However, a visit to Xerox PARC by Steve Jobs, one of the founders of Apple Computer, provided the inspiration for the Macintosh's GUI. Responding to the popularity of the Macintosh interface, Microsoft developed Windows, and

Microsoft and IBM developed OS/2 for the PC and PC-compatible computers.

The graphical user interface used on the Macintosh, with Windows and with OS/2, is based on windows (called *forms* in Visual Basic). However, computers with graphics capabilities aren't the only computers that can have windowed input and output. Many modern applications that run under DOS have a windowed interface, even when running in text mode. Visual Basic for DOS is such a program as are the applications you create with it.

One of the basic tenets of modern operating systems is the concept of reusable blocks of code. In modern programming languages, that tenet is exemplified by the software object. A software object is an abstraction where a block of code and data is viewed as if it were a physical thing. This software object is more than a reusable block of code; it is both a container of data, and a software engine for manipulating that data. Objects consist of such things as windows, buttons, and menus. For example, a button object consists of several parameters—the data— describing where and how large to draw the button on the screen, and the code—the engine— that actually does the drawing and that initiates an event when the drawing of the button is pressed (clicked) with the mouse.

A modern operating system consists largely of libraries of these reusable objects, the use of which significantly reduces the amount of time you need to develop a new application. When you want a button for your application, you no longer have to spend several days coding it from scratch. Instead, you spend a few minutes attaching a button object to your program and passing it the information about the location and size of the button. The button object actually draws the button on the screen and changes the image of the button to simulate a pressed button.

In This Chapter

This chapter gives you some background on windowed user interfaces and the object-oriented programming (OOP) methods used in Visual Basic.

This is not a detailed discussion of windows or object-oriented programming, but a brief overview of these topics. This chapter covers

- Using a windowed user interface
- Object-oriented programming
- Object-oriented programming with Visual Basic

Using a Windowed User Interface

A window in Visual Basic for DOS is similar to a window in Windows 3.0, or OS/2. The similarity is intentional, to make it simple for a user to switch from one environment to the other. It also was done to make porting a program from one environment to another much less difficult. Traditionally, porting a program from DOS to Windows required a complete rewrite of the user interface. With Visual Basic, this no longer is necessary. With care, a program will work in both environments with few or no changes.

A window in Visual Basic for DOS contains several distinct parts, as shown in Figure 1.1. Figure 1.2 shows a Windows window for comparison. Along the top is a title bar. The title in the center of the title bar can be several different things. The usual choices are the name of the running application or the filename of the document the application is working on. On the right side of the window are two buttons. The left button is the Minimize button. The right one is the Maximize/Restore button, which is a Maximize button when a window is normal size and a Restore button when a window is maximized. A Maximize button has a single vertical arrow on it and a Restore button has a vertical double arrow on it.

On the left side of the title bar is the Control button that opens the Control menu, as shown in Figure 1.3. To open the Control menu, click the button with the mouse or press Alt– (that is, the Alt key and the minus key together).

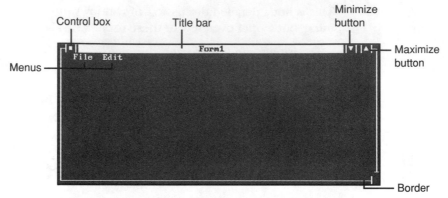

Figure 1.1. *A normal-sized Visual Basic for DOS window.*

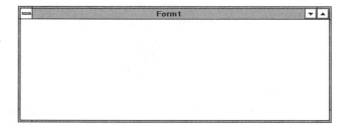

Figure 1.2. *A Windows window.*

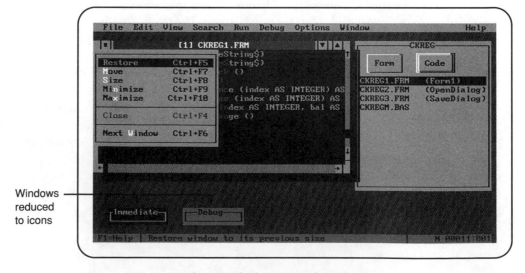

Figure 1.3. *A window with the Control menu open.*

The **Control** menu contains the **R**estore, **M**ove, **S**ize, Mi**n**imize, Ma**x**imize, **C**lose, and Next **W**indow commands. These commands are primarily used to run windows without a mouse. To select a command without a mouse, press the bold letter (called the *hot key*) or the indicated function key, or move the focus with the arrow keys and press Enter when the command is selected. To select a command with the mouse, click the command. Table 1.1 describes the operation of the buttons on the title bar and the commands on the Control menu.

Table 1.1. Operation of the controls on the Control menu.

Command	Keystrokes	Function
Restore	Ctrl-F5	Returns a maximized or minimized window to its initial size. To restore a maximized window with the mouse, click the Restore button, double-click the title bar, or click the **R**estore command on the Control menu. To restore a minimized window, double-click it.
Move	Ctrl-F7	Moves the window with the arrow keys. Press Enter when you have the window where you want it. To move the window with the mouse, place the mouse pointer on the title bar, press down on the left mouse button, and drag the window to its destination.
Size	Ctrl-F8	Resizes the window with the arrow keys. To resize the window using the mouse, place it on the border of the window (the pointer should change to double-ended arrow); then press the left mouse button and drag the border to the new position.

continues

7

Table 1.1. continued

Command	Keystrokes	Function
Minimize	Ctrl-F9	Reduces the window to an icon, such as those along the bottom of Figure 1.3. To minimize a window with the mouse, click the Minimize button.
Maximize	Ctrl-F10	Expands the window to fill the screen. To maximize the window with the mouse, click the Maximize button or double-click the title bar.
Close	Ctrl-F4	Closes the window; if the window is an application window, this action ends the application. To close the window with the mouse, double-click the button that opens the Control menu.
Next Window	F6/Ctrl-F6	Switches to the next open window.

Language Types

There basically are two different types of languages available on a computer: interpreted languages and compiled languages. These two language types differ in how they execute a program, not in the physical structure of their languages.

When a code is first written, it resides in a file in text form. An interpreter reads each line of that code, converts the line into machine language commands, and then executes them. The machine language commands are the numeric codes that the computer's hardware understands. When the code for one line completes, the interpreter moves to the next line, converts it, and executes it. The benefits of an interpreted language are the almost-immediate execution of code after a change, the ability to modify a running application, and simplified error detection and correction.

A compiler, on the other hand, first converts a whole program into machine language codes and then stores those codes in a file. That file now is an executable program that can be run directly without further interpretation. The benefits of a compiled code over interpreted code are increased speed and stand-alone execution. Compiled code runs faster than interpreted code because the lines of code already are in machine language form and don't have to be reinterpreted each time they're executed. The increase in speed can be by a factor of 100 or more over interpreted codes. Interpreted code also must have the interpreter in memory along with the code. After compilation, the compiler no longer is needed and the code runs by itself.

Visual Basic is both an interpreter and a compiler. The interpreter is used to speed code development, and the compiler is used to increase the speed of the code, and to make it portable (that is, a user does not have to own a copy of Visual Basic to be able to run the compiled code) after development is complete.

Object-Oriented Programming

Object-oriented programming (OOP) is the current development in programming methodology. This method bundles code and data into somewhat autonomous objects. The idea is that when you create an object to do something, you no longer have to know how it works—you simply pass it messages. That way, an object created in one program can easily be reused in another.

Objects

With the introduction of Visual Basic, Microsoft made a large advance in the field of object-oriented programming. Not only does Visual Basic have objects, but the objects are real, visible things such as buttons and boxes. Other object-oriented languages create objects with an Object command of some sort, which defines a block of code and data as an object. You then are supposed to imagine that object as a "thing" with features you can use. Visual Basic makes it easier by making the object a visible thing rather than a coding abstraction.

The main object in a Visual Basic program is the *form*. A form is the foundation of your application's user interface. All your controls—command buttons, option buttons, check boxes, text boxes, labels, and scroll bars—are attached to a form, which becomes the application window that you see when you run your program. Each of these controls is a Visual Basic object. To attach an object to a form, you draw the object on the form with the mouse. The whole visual interface of a Visual Basic program is drawn rather than coded.

Events

Objects communicate with each other, with the system, and with the program by means of events. Events are actions to which an object might respond. When the mouse is moved and a mouse button clicked, the system keeps track of the mouse pointer's location and what object was at that location when the mouse button was clicked. If that object was a button, the system sends a Click event to the button object. The button object then visually simulates a pressed button and passes a button_click event to the program. If the programmer writes a procedure to handle button_click events, that procedure gets control and performs its function. When that function is complete, control passes back to the system to wait for the next event.

As a programmer, you have the option to respond to numerous events passed to you by the objects that make up your program. These events include such things as clicking or double-clicking an object, or pressing a key while the object has the focus. Chapter 17, "Events," lists all the events to which you can respond. To respond to an event, you create an event procedure with the name

```
object_event
```

This event procedure then is executed whenever the object passes on that event.

Objects don't pass all events to the program; many events are handled by the object itself or by Visual Basic. For example, you can change the size of a window by dragging the window's edge. Resizing the window is handled by Visual Basic; although you, the programmer, don't have to do a thing, a Resize event is passed to your code to inform you that a change has taken place.

Methods

Objects are not simple, bundled code blocks, but a bundling of data and the code that manipulates it. Every object contains one or more code segments, known as *methods,* that manipulate that object's own data. To invoke a method, type the object name, a dot, then the method name. Following the method name are any arguments the method needs. For example:

```
Form1.PrintForm
```

This statement executes the PRINTFORM method of the form object named Form1. The PRINTFORM method prints the contents of the Form1 form object to a printer. Another example is

```
Form2.Print "Good Morning"
```

PRINT is another method contained in the form object. Here, PRINT prints the text "Good Morning" on the Form2 form object.

Properties

The data contained in an object are its *properties*. Properties contain not only the data stored in an object, such as the text to be printed in the PRINTER object, but also the object's dimensions, color, and numeric codes that

specify its capabilities. For example, the form object has a property called `BorderStyle`. Setting the `BorderStyle` property to `1 - Fixed Single` prevents the form from being resized by having its borders dragged. By changing `BorderStyle` to `2 - Sizable`, you can change the size of the form by dragging its borders. Chapter 16, "Properties," lists all the properties of the different objects.

Inheritance

Inheritance is the property of OOP in which an object inherits the methods of the objects from which it is made. When you draw a label on a form, that form inherits the label's properties. For example, the `Caption` property of a label object contains the text printed on the label. If the label is named Label1 (all objects have names), and it is drawn on Form1, then Form1 inherits the `Caption` property, which is accessed as follows:

```
Form1.Label1.Caption
```

All properties of objects drawn on the form are accessed in this manner.

Forms also inherit the methods of the objects, so when a form has a picture box drawn on it, that form inherits the picture box's `PRINT` method. The form now can print on a picture box.

Visual Basic: The Next Step

Visual Basic represents the next step in object-oriented programming. In Visual Basic, not only is code and data encapsulated, it even looks like the object it represents. In most object-oriented languages, you access a button object and tell it its location and size with lines of code. Only after you run your program can you actually see what it looks like. In Visual Basic, button objects look like buttons rather than lines of code. No longer do you have to imagine what it will look like; you draw it on a form with a button-drawing tool. Check boxes, option buttons, list boxes, scroll bars, and all code objects now look like the object they represent.

What You Have Learned

This chapter presented a brief overview of the windowed user interface and the use of object-oriented programming in Visual Basic. The intent here is to give you a feeling for the methods and procedures discussed in the rest of this book. For more information on Windows methods, see the *Microsoft Windows User's Guide,* included with Microsoft Windows. For more information on programming with Visual Basic, read on; an adventure begins.

Learning the Visual Basic Environment

Visual Basic is more than a programming language—it's a complete environment for developing a windowed DOS application. This environment includes

- A program editor to create and modify the code you write

- An interpreter to execute an application within the environment

- A compiler to turn an application into stand-alone code

- A Forms Designer to create forms

- A debugger to determine why an application does not work

Visual Basic is unique in that only a few lines of code are needed to create a complete, working, windowed application. In most programming languages, it takes a hundred or so lines of code simply to open a window, let alone do anything with it.

In This Chapter

In this chapter, you learn the application and operation of all the different commands and windows of the Visual Basic environment. The purpose of this chapter is to give you the flavor of the Visual Basic environment and teach you how to develop programs in that environment. Don't be concerned when you find that many of the descriptions are superficial; the following chapters cover the individual parts more completely. For now, get a feel for the overall structure of Visual Basic and how the windows and commands work together to make a program. Specifically, this chapter shows you how to

- Use the Programming Environment
- Navigate the windows and menus
- Use the Forms Designer
- Create forms and controls
- Create a windowed application
- Save and retrieve an application
- Compile an application

Starting Visual Basic

Like most DOS applications, Visual Basic is extremely simple to start. First, use the DOS command CD (change directory) to switch to the directory where you installed Visual Basic. Then type **VBDOS**. Visual Basic opens to the Programming Environment, as shown in Figure 2.1. Visual Basic actually consists of several programs, all of which are coordinated by the Programming Environment. You can run the different parts separately (see Appendix F, "Program Command Lines and Options"), but it's much simpler to let the Programming Environment do it for you.

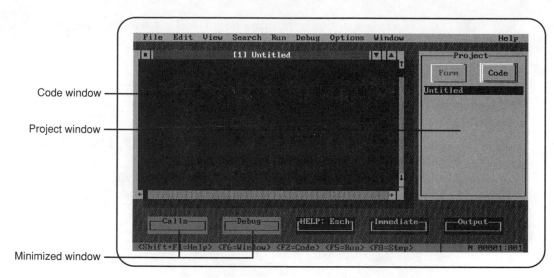

Code window

Project window

Minimized window

Figure 2.1. *The Visual Basic screen at startup, showing the Programming Environment.*

The two main visual parts of Visual Basic are the Programming Environment (Figure 2.1) and the Forms Designer (shown in Figure 2.2). The Programming Environment contains the program editor, the interpreter, and the debugger. It also is the launcher for all the other parts of Visual Basic. The Forms Designer (FD) is a drawing program for creating the visual parts of the forms that make up an application. The other parts of Visual Basic are

- BC, the basic compiler
- LINK, the linker
- LIB, the library manager
- FT, the forms translator
- TRANSLAT, which automatically translates Visual Basic for Windows to and from Visual Basic for DOS

There are several options that you can use when starting the Programming Environment. The syntax of the command line is

`VBDOS [options] [program] [/CMD string]`

where *program* is the name of a program to load when VBDOS is started, and *string* is a string passed to the program, which can be accessed with the COMMAND$ function. The *options* are one or more option switches, of which

the /L *libname* option is the only one you will use regularly. See Appendix F, "Program Command Lines and Options," for a complete list of the options.

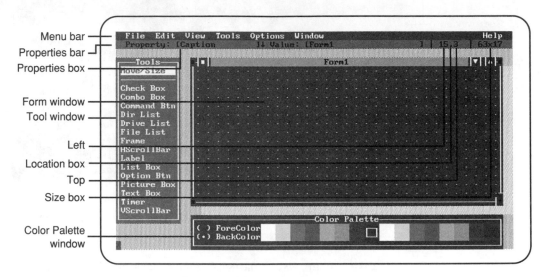

Figure 2.2. The Visual Basic Forms Designer.

Navigating the Programming Environment Windows

The first things you see when Visual Basic opens in the Programming Environment are two windows: Project and Code. Using the Window menu, you can open five other windows: Debug, Calls, Help, Immediate, and Output. When you switch to the Forms Designer you have the Form, Toolbox, Color Palette, and Menu Design windows.

The Project Window

The Project window is home for the Visual Basic application. The names of all the files and modules that comprise an application reside in the Project window. It's also the gateway to an application's windows. By selecting a form or module in the Project window and pressing either the Form or Code button, you can either bring the code into view for editing or switch to the Forms Designer to edit the visual appearance of the form.

The Code Window

The Code window is a text editing window in which you create all the code for an application. Each Code window is associated with a specific procedure in a form module or code module, and contains all the code for that procedure. You select existing procedures for editing in the Code window by clicking the Code button on the Project window, or executing the Code command of the View menu. Create a new procedure on a module with the New Sub, New Function, and Event Procedures commands of the Edit menu.

The New Sub and New Function commands ask for a procedure name and create a skeleton procedure in the current Code window. The Event Procedures command opens a large dialog box that contains all the controls on a form and all the events to which each control responds. Select a form, a control, and an event to create a skeleton event procedure in the Code window. A skeleton event procedure consists only of the first declarations line and the End line. You must enter all the code between these two lines.

The Debug Window

You cannot type in the Debug window, but it receives the results of the Watch variables. A Watch variable is a variable whose value you are interested in for debugging purposes. You create a Watch variable by selecting it in the Code window and then executing the Add Watch command of the Debug menu. While a program is running, the value of the Watch variable is shown on the Debug window.

The Calls Window

The Calls window is used like the Debug window, but shows the name of the currently executing procedure and a list of the last few procedure calls rather than the values of variables.

The Help Window

The Help window is a window into the Help database for Visual Basic. To move around in the Help window, you use the scroll bars and the left mouse button. To look up a word, click it with the right mouse button. The Help window is available in both the Programming Environment and the Forms Designer.

The Immediate Window

The Immediate window is used to test the operation of commands and statements, to test the value of statements, and to change the values of variables in a stopped application. Any basic statement or command typed into the immediate window is immediately executed.

The Output Window

The Output window shows a view of the currently visible forms in a stopped application. To see the whole output window, press the F4 function key.

Navigating the Forms Designer Windows

The following windows are on the Forms Designer. Switch to the Forms Designer by clicking the Form button of the Project window, or by executing the **Form** command of the **View** menu. Use Form1 as the form name when you are asked to supply one.

The Form

The form is the foundation of your application's user interface. All your buttons, text boxes, and lists are attached to a form, which becomes the application window that you see when you run your program. The simplest application usually consists of at least one form, although an application can contain as many forms as are necessary to complete the application. Although all forms are visible when you design your application, your application can make them visible or invisible at runtime. Consequently, only those forms that have to be seen are visible on screen when your application runs.

The Toolbox Window

The Toolbox window contains all the objects that can be placed on a form. An object is a programming abstraction relating a physical object and the code attached to it. That is, an object is something that has physical presence on the screen, or at least corresponds to a physical presence in a computer application, such as a timer. Table 2.1 lists all the objects on the Toolbox window that can be attached to a form.

Table 2.1. Objects available on the Toolbox window and the Tools menu.

Command	Function
Check Box	A button for setting nonexclusive options
Combo Box	A combined text box and list box
Command Button	A push button that causes the application to take an immediate action

continues

Table 2.1. continued

Command	Function
Dir List Box	A list box that contains all the subdirectories in the current directory
Drive List Box	A list box that contains all the disk drives available
File List Box	A list box that contains all the files in the current directory
Frame	Provides a visual frame for combining controls, and for grouping option buttons
HScrollBar	An input device for setting a value visually with a horizontal scale
Label	Displays text that the user cannot edit
List Box	A box containing a list of items
Option Button	A radio button for setting mutually exclusive options
Picture Box	Displays text or a picture created with graphics characters.
Text Box	Displays or inputs text that the user can edit.
Timer	An alarm clock that causes an event to take place at a certain time.
VScrollBar	An input device for setting a value visually with a vertical scale.

Other vendors using the Custom Control Toolkit included with the Pro version of Visual Basic have created additional objects that can be added to the Toolbox window and used in your programs.

To attach an object, follow these steps:

1. Select an object on the Toolbox window by clicking it with the mouse pointer.

2. Move the pointer to where you want the object's upper-left corner to be positioned and press and hold down the left mouse button.

3. Continue holding down the left mouse button and drag (move while holding down the mouse button) the pointer down to the lower-right corner of the object. While you drag the pointer, a rectangle appears showing you the size of the object being created.

4. When the rectangle is the correct size, release the mouse button and the object is drawn.

To reshape an object, follow these steps:

1. Select the object to be reshaped by clicking it.

2. Place the pointer on one of the black selection rectangles that surround the object and press and hold down the left mouse button.

3. Drag the rectangle until the object is the desired shape then release the mouse button.

To move an object, follow these steps:

1. Select the object to be moved by clicking it with the mouse.

2. Place the pointer on the object, hold down the left mouse button, and drag the object to the desired location.

3. Release the mouse button.

Create a few controls on Form1 and experiment with them a little. You can't hurt anything by doing so.

The Color Palette Window

The Color Palette window, shown in Figure 2.3, is used to select colors visually. The Color Palette window normally is not visible, so you must activate it with the Color Palette command of the **Window** menu. Colors and patterns are defined in Visual Basic with the unintuitive numbers 0 through 15. The Color Palette window makes selecting a color much more straightforward.

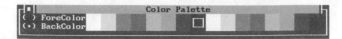

Figure 2.3. *The Color Palette window.*

The Color Palette window changes the colors of the front-most form, or the colors of the active object on the front-most form. The Color Palette window also is activated by the Settings box on the Properties bar when a color property is being set. (The "Understanding the Properties Bar" section of this chapter discusses the properties bar in more detail later.)

The two option buttons on the left side of the Color Palette window control where your color selection is applied. If you click the top option button, your next color selection becomes the foreground color. The foreground of a form usually includes any text or objects drawn on the window. If you click the bottom option button, the next color selection becomes the background color of the selected object. Experiment with the Color Palette window. Select Form1, or one of the controls you placed on Form1. Then select the Color Palette window and change the colors. Any foreground or background change immediately appears on that form or object.

The Menu Design Window

The Menu Design window normally is hidden. You activate it by clicking the **M**enu Design command of the **W**indows menu. The Menu Design window attaches one or more menus to the front-most form, as shown in Figure 2.4. You can experiment with the Menu Design window, but it's not as simple to figure out as the Color Palette window. You will learn about it in more detail in Chapter 7, "Creating Custom Menus."

Understanding Modules

When code is stored on disk, it normally is one of two different types of files known as *modules*. Form modules (.FRM files) contain both code and the description of a form with all its attached controls. Code modules (.BAS files) contain only code. Code is stored in modules in blocks known as *procedures*. A procedure is an autonomous unit of code that performs a specific task such as controlling what happens when a button is pressed. At the minimum, the code contained in a form module consists of all the procedures attached to the form and its controls. Code modules can contain only those procedures that are not attached to a form or control. Thus, a form is stored on disk in a form module along with all the procedures attached to that form and its controls. Although you can store unattached procedures in a form module, it's good programming practice to modularize a code by placing the unattached procedures in one or more separate code modules, especially if you have many unattached procedures.

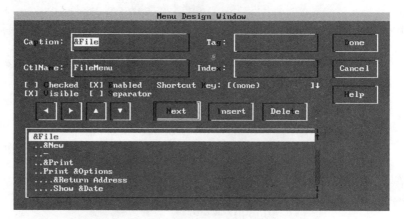

Figure 2.4. *A Menu Design window.*

In this book I often discuss code attached to a form. In this case, I am discussing that code contained in a form's form module. It is more intuitive to describe the code as attached to a form as though the form were a real, physical object rather than to discuss files containing form descriptions and code. In addition, if I discuss code stored in a module, I am usually referring to code in a code module.

There is a third type of file that can contain code—the include file (.BI file.) An include file is simply a file of code or definitions that can be included at one or more locations in form and code modules. Include files are used to reduce the clutter in procedures and to ensure that declarations and definitions used in different parts of a code are identical.

Procedures in code modules are available for use by any other procedure in an application. Procedures on a form, on the other hand, are available only to the other procedures on the same form. For example, a procedure that clears all printed text from a form could be attached to the form it clears, but a procedure to convert text strings into binary numbers would go into a code module, where any other procedure could use it. Note that these locations are not absolute; they depend on your particular application.

Unattached procedures stored in a module or form are reusable. If several parts of your program must execute an identical procedure, you can store one copy of the procedure in a code module and access it again and again. This not only saves space, but also makes maintaining your code easier because you have to make corrections only to one copy of a procedure.

Each form or code module has a declarations section at the beginning for definitions and declarations. A *definition* is a name that is assigned a constant value. For example, the name True usually is defined as –1, the value of a logical True. You can then use the name True in a program rather than –1, making the program much more readable. A *declaration* defines the type of value that can be stored in a variable. For example, the phrase INDEX AS INTEGER in a DIM or COMMON statement declares the variable Index as the numeric type INTEGER. Chapter 4, "Using Strings," and Chapter 5, "Using Numbers and Control Structures" discuss definitions and declarations in more detail.

CONSTANT.BI is an include file that contains a large list of useful definitions that you can load into the declarations section of a form or module and use in your application. Note that you can put only definitions and declarations, not code, in the declarations section of a form, but a code module may also have executable code in that section.

Using the Menus

The Visual Basic Programming Environment has nine menus: **File**, **Edit**, **View**, **Search**, **Run**, **Debug**, **Options**, **Window**, and **Help**. If you have used Windows applications, you probably are already familiar with the **File**, **Edit**, and **Help** menus. If you are still in the Forms Designer, you can switch back to the Programming Environment by executing the **Code** command on the **View** menu, and answering yes to the questions.

File, Edit, and Help are usually available in some form on most Windows applications, and are becoming more prevalent on other types of applications as well. The Code menu contains commands for working with Code windows. As you might expect, the Run menu contains commands for running an application. Run also contains the debugging commands. You already used the Window menu to open or select closed or hidden windows.

The File Menu

As in most Windows applications, the File menu (see Figure 2.5) contains those commands listed in Table 2.2 to open and close files. The first command is New Project, which clears the current project and creates empty Code and Project windows. If you haven't saved the old project, Visual Basic gives you one last chance to do so before deleting the project.

Table 2.2. The File menu commands.

Command	Shortcut Key	Function
New Project		Clears memory and opens a blank project and code window
Open Project		Clears memory and displays a file open dialog box to select a new project to open
Save Project		Saves all changes in the current project on disk
New Form		Adds a new blank form to a project
New Module		Adds a new blank code module to a project
Add File		Displays a file open dialog box to select a file to attach to a project

continues

Table 2.2. continued

Command	Shortcut Key	Function
Remove File		Removes a file from a project, but does not delete it from disk
Save File		Saves the file displayed in the code window
Save File **As**		Displays a file save dialog box to save the file displayed in the code window with a different name or in a different directory
Load Text		Loads a text file into the file displayed in the code window
Save **T**ext		Saves the file in the code window as a text file
Print		Prints the file in the code window
MS-DOS S**h**ell		Exits to the DOS prompt without exiting Visual Basic
E**x**it	Alt-F4	Quits Visual Basic

Figure 2.5. *The File menu.*

Visual Basic programs actually are stored in several files that are brought together in the Project window. The contents of the Project window are stored in a .MAK file. Forms are stored in .FRM files, including any code attached to the form or its controls. Modules are stored in .BAS files, and included files are stored in .BI files.

If you're familiar with other languages and operating systems, such as UNIX, you will notice that the .MAK files are similar in function to *makefiles*. A makefile contains all the information necessary to recreate a compiled program. When a program is compiled, the Make program examines the makefile to determine what files to compile and combine to create the final application. Visual Basic uses a similar process in that the Project file contains the names of all the files necessary to recreate an application.

You use the Open Project and Save Project commands to open or save all the files in a project. When you open a project, you only have to open the .MAK file. Loading the .MAK file automatically opens the rest of the .FRM and .BAS files that make up the project.

To change the name of every file in a project, or to save them in a different directory, select a file in the Project window, then use the Save File As command from the File menu. Once all the files are saved, use the New Project command to create a new project. Use the Add File command to attach the newly created files, then use the Save Project command to give the project file a new name.

Don't save the new file names in the old project file when it asks you to. If you do, your old project file will forget about the old files and think the new files belong to it. Nothing is lost, though, because the old files are still there. You just have to create a new Project file that includes them.

The New Form and New Module commands add either a new blank form or a new blank module to the list of files in the Project window. The Add File command adds a form or module file existing on disk to the current Project window. The Save File and Save File As commands copy a current Form or module to a disk file. You thus can share useful pieces of code between different programs simply by attaching previously written forms and modules.

The **R**emove File command deletes a Form or module from the Project window and removes the Form or module from your application. Note that **R**emove File removes a Form or module only from the current project. It does not delete the file from the disk. You must use the File Manager to do that. The **P**rint command lets you print the contents of the active Form or module. The MS-DOS **S**hell command creates a new MS-DOS shell and exits to the DOS prompt without exiting Visual Basic. Use it for file management or running small programs without exiting Visual Basic. To return to Visual Basic from a shell, type EXIT and press return.

The **L**oad Text and **S**ave Text commands either load the contents of a text file into the Code window or save the contents of the Code window in a text file. You can create or edit text files with most word processing programs, although you must save them in the word processing applications as plain text files, without any formatting information.

The last command on the File menu is the Exit command, which quits the application. As with the New Project command, you have another chance to save the current project before Visual Basic quits.

The Edit Menu

The Edit menu, shown in Figure 2.6 and described in Table 2.3, is standard among windowed applications. It contains the Undo, Cut, Copy, and **P**aste commands. In addition, the Visual Basic Edit menu contains the **D**elete, New **S**ub, New **F**unction, and E**v**ent Procedures commands.

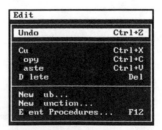

Figure 2.6. The Edit menu.

Table 2.3. The Edit Menu commands.

Command	Shortcut Key	Function
Undo	Ctrl-Z	Reverses the last edit
Cut	Ctrl-X	Cuts the selected item and stores it on the clipboard
Copy	Ctrl-C	Copies the selected item onto the clipboard
Paste	Ctrl-V	Pastes the contents of the clipboard at the cursor position
Delete	Del	Deletes the selected item
New Sub		Adds a new Sub procedure to the file in the code window
New Function		Adds a new Function procedure to the file in the code window
Event Procedures	F12	Opens the event procedures dialog to create a new event procedure

The Undo command, as its name suggests, undoes or reverses your previous change. Because Undo applies only to the last change you made, stop and consider what you want to do if you think you might want to reverse the change. If you make any other change, you will not be able to reverse the first change.

The Cut, Copy, and Paste commands move data between the clipboard and your Visual Basic project. The clipboard is a storage area containing the last item cut or copied. After you copy something to the clipboard, you can paste it to another location in your project, or paste it to a completely different project.

To cut or copy data, select it with the cursor and execute the Cut or Copy command. The Copy command places a copy of the selected text or object on the clipboard without deleting it from its original location. The Cut command removes the selected text or object from its original location and places it on the clipboard. The Paste command inserts the contents of the clipboard at the cursor.

The last three commands on the Edit menu control the creation of new procedures. New Sub creates a new subprocedure. New Function creates a new function procedure, and Event Procedures creates a new event procedure.

The View Menu

The View menu, shown in Figure 2.7 and described in Table 2.4, contains the commands for switching between the Forms Designer and the Programming Environment. The first command, Code, opens the Code window associated with the currently selected object. You can open a Code window also with the Code button in the Project window.

Table 2.4. The View menu commands.

Command	Shortcut Key	Function
Code	F2	Switch to the Programming Environment
Form	Shift-F12	Switch to the Forms Designer
Next Statement		Highlight the next statement to be executed in a stopped application
Output Screen	F4	Toggle between the output screen and Visual Basic
Included File		Open the currently selected include file for editing
Included Lines		Insert the contents of the currently selected include file
Menu Bar	F10	Hides the menu bar in the Forms Designer
Grid Lines		Toggles the grid on and off on a form in the Forms Designer

Figure 2.7. The View menu.

The **Form** command enables you to select a form to edit and switches to the Forms Designer. The **Next Statement** command highlights the next statement to be executed in a stopped application. The **Output Screen** command switches the view to the output screen of the stopped application. If a code window contains an $INCLUDE statement, the **Included File** command opens the include file for editing, or the **Included Lines** command displays the contents of an included file after the $INCLUDE statement.

The Search Menu

Ths **Search** menu is shown in Figure 2.8 and described in Table 2.5. The **Find**, **Selected Text**, **Repeat Last Find**, and **Change** commands locate specific strings of text in the Code window. First, use the **Find** or the **Selected Text** commands to set the string to be located. Then use the **Repeat Last Find** command to search again. To find and replace a string, use the **Change** command.

Table 2.5. The Search menu commands.

Command	Shortcut Key	Function
Find		Find a string in the code window
Selected Text	Ctrl-\	Make the selected text the text to find
Repeat Last Find	F3	Search again for the same text
Change		Search for a string and replace it with another

***Figure 2.8.** The Search menu.*

The Run Menu

The **Run** menu, shown in Figure 2.9 and described in Table 2.6, contains the commands for running, stopping, and compiling a project. The **Start** command begins executing the current program with the interpreter. You can stop an interpreted program any time by pressing Ctrl-Break. A program also stops if it encounters an error, a STOP statement, or a breakpoint set with the Toggle **Breakpoint** command on the **Debug** menu. Use the **Continue** or **Restart** commands to resume execution of a stopped program. The **Continue** command continues execution from where it was stopped. The **Restart** command restarts a program from the beginning.

Table 2.6. The Run menu commands.

Command	Shortcut Key	Function
Start	Shift-F5	Begins executing the program currently in memory
Restart		Restart a stopped program from the beginning
Continue	F5	Continue a stopped program from the point where it was stopped
Modify COMMAND$		Change the value of the string returned by the COMMAND$ function
Make EXE File		Compile the program currently in memory and create an executable program

Command	Shortcut Key	Function
Make Library		Compile the procedures currently in memory and create .QLB and .LIB library files
Set Start-up File		Select the form or module to execute first

Figure 2.9. *The Run menu.*

Some programs are designed to use command lines when you run them. For example, when starting a word processing program, you can usually follow the program name with the name of a file to start editing. The **Modify COMMAND$** command is used to modify the string returned by the COMMAND$ BASIC function. Use this command to test a program with different command lines. After a program is compiled, set the command line in the normal way by following the program name with the command line.

The **Make** .EXE File command compiles the current project into a stand-alone, executable application. Once compiled, a program is independent of the Visual Basic program. The Make Library command takes all the code currently open in Visual Basic, including any libraries loaded when you started Visual Basic with the /L switch, and makes it into a new library. Actually, two new libraries are made: one a .QLB Quick Library for use with Visual Basic, and a .LIB library to use when compiling an application.

Normally, execution of a program starts with the first form defined. To change the form or module executed first when Start is executed, execute the Set Start-up File command.

The Debug Menu

The commands of the **Debug** menu (Figure 2.10 and Table 2.7) are for debugging code. The **Add** Watch and **Instant** Watch commands create watch variables, whose value is displayed in the Debug window. The **Watchpoint** command sets a condition on a variable, which, when True, causes the program to stop. The **Delete** Watch and **Delete All Watch** commands delete either the selected watchpoint or watch variable, or all of the watchpoints and watch variables.

Table 2.7. The Debug menu commands.

Command	*Shortcut Key*	*Function*
Add Watch		Displays the value of the selected variable or expression on the Debug window
Instant Watch	Shift-F9	Displays the value of the current selection
Watchpoint		Sets an expression to cause a program to stop when the expression becomes True
Delete Watch		Deletes a watch variable or watchpoint
Delete All Watch		Deletes all watch variables and watchpoints
Trace On		Starts tracing program execution
History On		Saves the values of the variables for the last 20 statements
Toggle Breakpoint	F9	Toggles the current line as a breakpoint
Clear All Breakpoints		Removes all breakpoints

Command	Shortcut Key	Function
Break On Errors		Causes a program to stop at the first statement of an error handler
Set Next Statement		Sets the next statement to be executed in a stopped program

Figure 2.10. The Debug menu.

The **Trace On** command causes the program to run in slow motion and highlight each line of code when it is executed. The **History On** command causes Visual Basic to remember the state of the system for the last 20 statements executed, so you can back up through your code (by pressing Shift-F8) and see how the values of the variables changed.

The Set Next Statement command changes the execution order of a program that was paused by Ctrl-Break, a STOP statement, or a breakpoint. Normally, when you use the Continue command or press one of the step keys—F8 (single step) or F10 (procedure step)—Visual Basic starts executing at the next executable statement. The step keys, which enable you to step through a program one step at a time, are examined in more detail in Chapter 13, "Debugging and Error Trapping." The Set Next Statement command is used to start execution at a different statement. In a paused program, place the cursor in the statement at which you want execution to continue, then execute the Set Next Statement command. Now, when you execute Continue or press one of the Step keys, execution continues at that statement. Use the Set Next Statement command to run the same piece of code repeatedly to see the effect of changes.

If you know approximately where a code is having problems, insert either a STOP statement or a breakpoint directly before the problem code. You insert and remove breakpoints with the Toggle Breakpoint command or by pressing F9. When the execution of a code reaches a breakpoint, it halts execution and pauses as if you had pressed Ctrl-Break. The Clear All Breakpoints command is used to remove all breakpoints that were inserted with the Toggle Breakpoint command. Breakpoints also disappear when you close a project. You must edit the program to remove the STOP statements. The Break on Errors command causes a program to stop at the first statement of any error handler set with the ON ERROR statement (see Chapter 13, "Debugging and Error Trapping," for more information on error handlers).

The Options Menu

The Options menu (Figure 2.11 and Table 2.8) enables you to set options and conditions for the Visual Basic environment. Set the default display colors with the Display command, and set the default paths for locating the program files with the Set Paths command. Reverse the mouse buttons with the Right Mouse command. Set the save and file backup options with the Save command, and control automatic syntax checking with the Syntax Checking command.

Table 2.8. The Options menu commands.

Command	Function
Display	Sets the default display colors
Set Paths	Sets the default directories
Right Mouse	Switches the sense of the left and right mouse buttons
Save	Sets the save options
Syntax Checking	Toggles automatic syntax checking

Figure 2.11. The Options menu.

When the Syntax Checking command is checked, Visual Basic looks for syntax errors in each line of code as you type it. If Syntax Checking is unchecked, Visual Basic won't check for syntax errors until you run the program.

The Window Menu

The Window menu, shown in Figure 2.12 and described in Table 2.9, activates the different windows listed in the menu. In a windowed environment, it's easy to "lose" a window behind other windows. Executing any of the Window menu commands brings the window to the screen if it already is open, or opens it if it is not yet open. The New Window command opens another Code window. The Arrange All command tiles all the open windows on the screen.

Table 2.9. The Window menu commands.

Command	Function
New Window	Opens a new blank code window
Arrange All	Sizes and arranges all the open windows so they are all showing
Calls	Shows the Calls window
Debug	Shows the Debug window
Help	Shows the Help window
Immediate	Shows the Immediate window
Output	Shows the Output window
Project	Shows the Project window

continues

Table 2.9. continued

Command	Function
Color Palette	Shows the Color Palette window
Menu Design Window	Shows the Menu Design window
Toolbox	Shows the Toolbox window
Form	Shows the current form

Figure 2.12. *The Window menu.*

On the Window menu in the Forms Designer, you will find the **Color** Palette, **M**enu Design Window, **T**oolbox, **H**elp, and **F**orm commands. As with the Programming Environment, each of these commands displays the indicated window.

The Help Menu

The **H**elp menu, shown in Figure 2.13 and described in Table 2.10, contains the standard help commands **I**ndex, **C**ontents, **K**eyboard, **T**opic, Using **H**elp, **T**utorial, and **A**bout. The **I**ndex command opens the help index for Visual Basic. The **C**ontents command opens help to its table of contents. The **K**eyboard command lists the key combinations that you can use to select commands from the keyboard rather than with the mouse. The **T**opic command opens to the help window for the currently selected command or object. The Using **H**elp command describes how to use the online help. The **T**utorial command starts the Visual Basic tutorial. The **A**bout command gives the current version, copyright notice, licensing information, and serial number.

Table 2.10. The Help menu commands.

Command	Shortcut Key	Function
Index		Displays the Help index
Contents		Displays the table of contents
Keyboard		Displays help for the keyboard shortcuts
Topic	F1	Displays help for the currently selected language element
Using Help	Shift-F1	Displays help on help
Tutorial		Starts the Tutorial
About		Displays copyright information about Visual Basic

Figure 2.13. The Help menu.

The Tools Menu

The Tools menu is only found in the Forms Designer and contains the same tools shown on the Toolbox window, described in Table 2.1. When you use the Tools menu rather than the Toolbox window, the Tools menu always places the selected control on the form. If you have a frame on the form, you must use the Toolbox window to select the control and draw it on the frame. If you use the Tools menu, the control is placed on the form instead.

Understanding the Properties Bar

The Forms Designer, shown in Figure 2.2, is used to draw and set the properties of the form. The properties are set with the Properties bar, which is a unique feature of Visual Basic. All the forms and controls have properties such as color, size, and location. With the Properties bar, you select a property and change its value. The Properties bar consists of two list boxes: the Properties list and the Settings box. When you pull down the Properties list by clicking the arrow, you see a list of all the properties of the currently selected form or control that can be set at this time.

Figure 2.14 shows the Properties list with the form's Caption property selected. The Caption of a form is the title in the title bar, which appears at the top of the form. When a property is selected, its current value is displayed in the Settings box. If a property has a fixed set of allowed values, you can drop a list down from the Settings box and select the value from that list. Otherwise, you must type the value of the property. In Figure 2.14, the value of the Caption property is Form1. Because the value of this property is a title, you must type it in the Settings box.

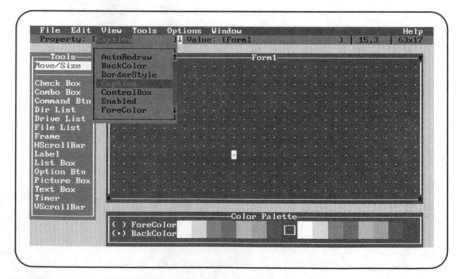

Figure 2.14. *The Properties bar with the Properties list dropped down.*

In Figure 2.15, the BorderStyle property is selected, and the arrow to the right of the Settings box was clicked to show the available options. To change the form's BorderStyle, simply select the new style from the list.

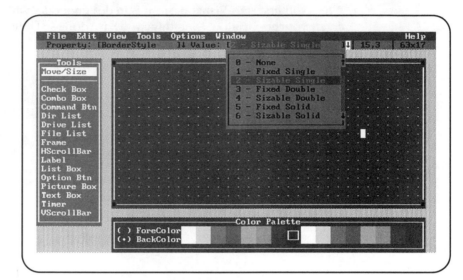

Figure 2.15. *Using the Settings box.*

The properties listed in the Properties bar are only those properties that can be set at design time—that is, when you are writing your program. Forms and controls also have other properties that your program can set only at runtime. A Visual Basic program can set or change most of the properties at runtime. Chapter 3, "Understanding Forms," discusses this topic in more detail.

Understanding the Running Modes

As you switch between editing a program and running it, Visual Basic switches its mode of operation and behaves differently toward user interaction. There are three operating modes: design, interpreted running, and compiled running.

Design Mode

When you first start Visual Basic, it is in design mode, which is where you create your application. Everything you have done so far has been in design mode. In design mode, you can

- Create files
- Open projects
- Close projects
- Save projects
- Copy code
- Cut code
- Paste code

In short, you can change your project in just about any way you want.

Interpreted Running Mode

When you select the **Start** command from the **R**un menu, or press F5 or Shift-F5, the Visual Basic interpreter takes over and begins running your program. First the screen is cleared, then the interpreter displays the first form that you have defined. The interpreter then executes your program one line at a time.

The interpreter reads a line of code, *converts* (interprets or compiles) it into microprocessor commands (*machine codes*), and executes those commands. Machine codes are numbers that your microprocessor interprets as commands to do something. Because the microprocessor commands are not saved, each time a line of code is executed it must be interpreted again. A benefit of this process is that you can make a change and run your program immediately without having to compile it. Unfortunately, the program runs more slowly than compiled code because each statement must be interpreted before it can be executed.

Visual Basic actually partially interprets every line as you input it and converts it into an intermediate code. That intermediate code can be more quickly converted into machine language and executed, which quickens the execution by the interpreter.

While your program is running, you cannot change your code, open project files, or save project files. For the most part, the only command available (other than those you defined in your program) is Ctrl-Break. When you press Ctrl-Break, Visual Basic returns to a mode state similar to design mode. You can edit some parts of your code in this state and then continue it from where it stopped. You cannot edit everything in your program and still be able to continue it. If you edit something that makes the code inconsistent, such as a variable definition, you get a warning that you won't be able to continue the execution of your code but must start it over. You can choose whether or not to continue.

Compiled Running Mode

Compiled mode isn't actually a Visual Basic mode, although it is a different state of operation for your program. When you compile a program, Visual Basic reads the statements in your program, interprets them, converts them into microprocessor commands, and stores the commands in an .EXE file (an *executable program file*). The increase in speed originates at this point. Because all your code already has been interpreted and converted into microprocessor commands, the statements do not have to be interpreted each time they are executed, which saves a step.

When you execute the .EXE file, your processor reads and executes the microprocessor commands independently of Visual Basic. At this point, the only commands available are those that you built into your program, or that already exist on the form (the Control box, the Minimize button, and the Maximize button).

Building Your First Program: The Good Morning Program

Now that you have a basic idea of how the Visual Basic environment works, you can go through the steps to build a program. This first program doesn't do much; however, when you create it, you use many of the commands and procedures discussed in this chapter. It also uses some language elements that have not been discussed so far. Don't worry about the new language elements now. You learn about them in more detail later in this book.

The "Good Morning" program, MYONE.EXE, displays a window with two text boxes and two buttons. You type your name in one box. "Good Morning" appears in the second box, followed by the name you typed in the first box. ("Good Morning" changes to "Good Afternoon" or "Good Evening," depending on the time of day.) MYONE.EXE isn't an exciting program, but it does exercise many of the options in Visual Basic. As you make your changes, use Figure 2.16 as a guide.

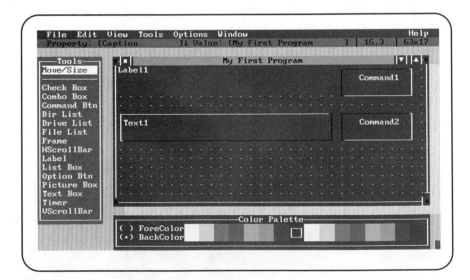

Figure 2.16. *The layout for the My First Program form.*

To create the Good Morning program, follow these steps:

1. Start Visual Basic or execute the New Project command on the **File** menu to get new Project and Code windows.

2. Execute the New **F**orm command on the **File** menu and use MYONE.FRM for the filename. You are then switched to the Forms Designer to create your form.

3. Execute the Save Project command on the **File** menu and use MYONE.MAK as the project filename.

First, change the caption of the Form1 form. The Caption property is the name displayed at the top of the form. The current caption is Form1. That's not terribly informative, so change it to My First Program.

4. Click the form to select it. The Properties list box should show the Caption property. If not, click the arrow to the right of the box and select Caption from the list.

5. In the Settings box, select the text MYONE and type My First Program in its place. Press Enter to make the change in the Caption property.

Now that you have a blank form, put the controls and text boxes on it.

6. In the Toolbox window, select the Label tool and draw a label on the form. Make the label about 3/4 of an inch tall and 5 inches wide.

> The two boxes on the right side of the Properties bar contain the location of the upper-left corner of the selected object, and its current width and height, all measured in character widths and character heights.

7. In the Toolbox window, select the text box tool and draw a text box of about the same size as the label. Place it directly below the label.

8. In the Toolbox window, select the command button tool and draw a button to the right of the label. Select the command button tool again and draw a second button below the first.

The next step is to change the properties of the boxes and buttons you just drew on the form. Change the Caption properties of the buttons to reflect their use. Change the CtrlName properties to make your program more readable. The Caption property of a button is the text displayed on top of thc button. The Caption property of a label is the text displayed in the label. The CtrlName property is the name that the object is referred to in the code.

9. Select the first button (marked Command1) and change its Caption property to OK. Change its CtrlName property to OKButton.

10. Select the second button (marked Command2) and change its Caption property to Exit and its CtrlName property to ExitButton. Your form now should look like Figure 2.17.

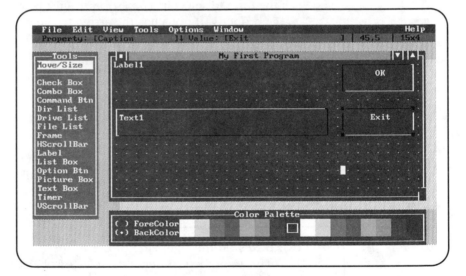

Figure 2.17. The edited form for My First Program.

The next step is to attach code to the different objects on the screen. Attach code to the Exit button first. When the Exit button is pressed, you want the program to end. When you open the Code window, it already has a template in it for the selected object and event.

11. Switch to the Programming Environment by executing the Code command of the View menu. Create an ExitButton_Click event procedure by executing the Event Procedures command of the Edit menu. In the Event Procedures dialog box (shown in Figure 2.18), select the ExitButton object, the Click event, and press the Edit in Active button. The code template for the ExitButton_Click

procedure appears in the Code window. The template consists of the header and footer for the procedure. The code in this procedure is executed whenever you click the button marked Exit. Type an END statement between the procedure header and footer. Your Code window now should look like Figure 2.19.

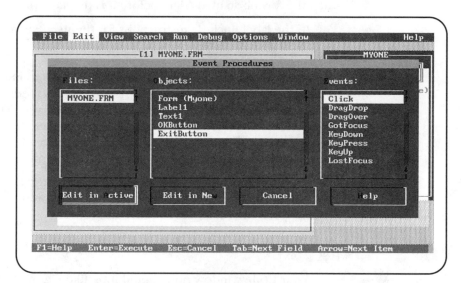

Figure 2.18. *The Event Procedures dialog box.*

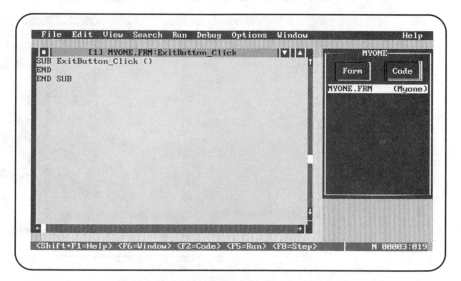

Figure 2.19. *The* ExitButton_Click *procedure.*

When the program starts up, you want the contents of the label and the list box to have some initial values. You could set these values at design time, as you did for the Caption properties of the command buttons, or you could do it in code that is executed when the application starts. A good place to put startup code is in the Form_Load procedure, which is executed when the form is loaded (right before it is displayed).

In the label, include instructions for the user, such as

```
Please type your name below.
```

To access the Caption property of the Label1 label, combine the CtrlName (Label1) and the property (Caption), separated with a period (Label1.Caption). All properties are accessed in this way. The visible text in a text box is contained in the Text property rather than in the Caption property (as it is with the label and command buttons). You want the text box to be blank, so set its Text property to the empty string.

12. Execute the Event Procedures command on the Edit menu and select the Form object and the Load event. Type the following code between the Form1_Load header and footer:

```
Label1.Caption = "Please type your name below."
Text1.Text = ""
```

Your Code window now should look like Figure 2.20.

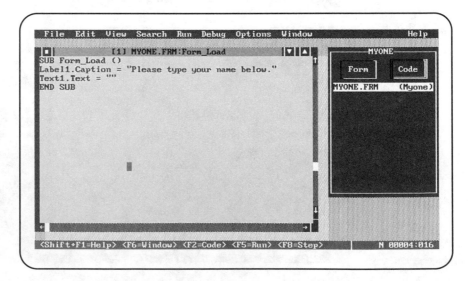

Figure 2.20. *The* Form1_Load *procedure.*

The code that does all the work in this program is attached to the OK button. When that button is pressed, you want the code to check the time of day to see whether it's morning, afternoon, or evening. The code then should combine the text Good Morning, Good Afternoon, or Good Evening with what the user typed in the text box, displaying the result in the label.

13. Execute the Event Procedures command of the Edit menu, select OKButton (from the Object list) and the Click event. Type the following code between the OKButton_Click header and footer:

```
IF VAL(Time$) > 0 AND VAL(TIME$) < 12 THEN
  Label1.Caption = "Good Morning " + Text1.Text
ELSEIF VAL(Time$) >= 12 AND VAL(TIME$) < 18 THEN
  Label1.Caption = "Good Afternoon " + Text1.Text
ELSE
  Label1.Caption = "Good Evening " + Text1.Text
END IF
```

Don't forget to type the space that follows the words, Morning, Afternoon, and Evening in this code block.

Your Code window now should look like Figure 2.21. The TIME$ function gets the time of day. It returns a string of text that contains the current time. The format of that string is *hh*:*mm*:*ss*, in which *hh* is the hour, *mm* is the minute, and *ss* is the seconds. Applying the VAL() function to this string returns the first number in the string, which is the current hour (on a 24-hour clock).

Use the IF THEN ELSE statement to test the hour to see what time it is. The first IF statement checks whether the time is between 0 and 12 (midnight and noon). If it is, the next statement is executed, which combines the text "Good Morning " with the contents of the text box (Text1.Text). The result is assigned to the Caption of the label (Label1.Caption). If the time isn't between 0 and 12, the ELSEIF statement checks whether it is between 12 and 18 (noon and 6:00 p.m.). If it is, "Good Afternoon " is used rather than "Good Morning ". If the time isn't between 0 and 12 or 12 and 18, the statement following the ELSE statement is executed, which uses "Good Evening " rather than "Good Morning " or "Good Afternoon ".

51

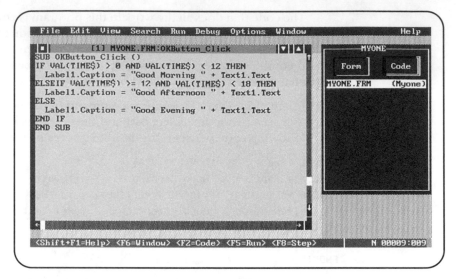

Figure 2.21. *The* `OKButton_Click` *procedure.*

Actually, you can have fun with this program by making changes to it. You can add more `ELSEIF` statements between the `IF` statement and the `ENDIF` statement to test for different ranges in the time and to print an appropriate message. For example, you could test for the range 9:00 a.m. to 10:00 a.m. and display a rude comment about being late. Or you could test for 6:00 p.m. to 7:00 p.m. and display `Go Home, it's dinner time`. When you complete this chapter, come back to this point and experiment a little.

Running Your Program

Your program is ready to be run in interpreted mode, so select **S**tart from the **R**un menu. If you made no typing errors, your screen looks like Figure 2.22. Your form waits for you to use it.

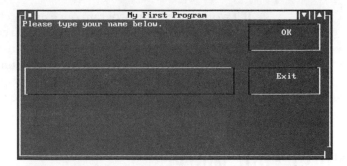

Figure 2.22. *My First Program after startup.*

Type your name in the text box and click the OK button to see your message appear in the label, as in Figure 2.23. If you made a typing mistake somewhere, Visual Basic probably will give you a syntax error and show you the offending statement. Fix it, and try to run your program again.

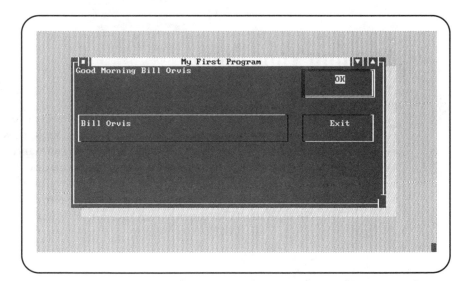

Figure 2.23. *My First Program after the OK button is pressed.*

To test your code for different times of day, run the code and press Ctrl-Break to break the program. Then open the Immediate window, type `TIME$="9:00"`, and press Enter. This sequence changes the setting of your system clock to 9:00 a.m. Select the Continue command of the **R**un menu to make your program start running again. See what it prints when you type your name and press the OK button.

If it works, break the program once more, change the system clock to a different time, and run the program again. You can continue changing the time and testing the program until you're satisfied that it works. Don't forget to reset the system clock to the correct time when you are done. If your program runs but doesn't do what it is supposed to do, check your code and properties settings until you find the error.

Saving Your Work

Now that you have a running program, you should save it. When you work on longer programs, save them frequently so you don't risk losing all your work if your system hangs or crashes. To save your program, select the Save Project command from the File menu.

Retrieving Your Work

Retrieving your work is easier than saving it. You retrieve only the project file; all the other files are retrieved automatically. Right now, your program is still in memory. Delete it with the New Project command in the File menu. Select the Open Project dialog from the File menu and a File Open dialog box appears. In the dialog box, set the directory by double-clicking the disk letters and directory names until you get into the directory that contains the MYONE.MAK file. Click the MYONE.MAK file and click the OK button. Your program is loaded back into memory.

Compiling Your Program

The last step is to compile your program into a stand-alone application. With your program in memory, select the Make .EXE File command from the Run menu. The dialog box shown in Figure 2.24 appears so that you can select the directory and name for your application. When you click OK, your program is compiled and stored on disk.

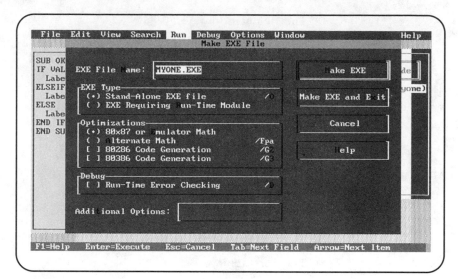

Figure 2.24. The Make .EXE File dialog box.

To run your program, exit Visual Basic and type MYONE at the DOS prompt. Your program will run. You can stop it by clicking the Exit button.

This completes all the steps necessary to create and compile a Visual Basic program. If you want, go back now and try to change some of the properties of the form, buttons, and text boxes. Try changing the colors of the form and controls with the ForeColor and BackColor properties. Go ahead and experiment with the code. Have some fun with it.

What You Have Learned

In this chapter, you examined the Visual Basic environment and its capabilities, including the commands, menus, controls, and windows. You also built your first application, performing all the steps from designing it to compiling it into a stand-alone application. Specifically, you examined

- The Project window
- The Code window
- The Debug window
- The Calls window

- The Help window
- The Immediate window
- The Output window
- The form
- The Toolbox window
- The Color palette window
- The **File** menu
- The **Edit** menu
- The **View** menu
- The **Search** menu
- The **Run** menu
- The **Debug** menu
- The **Options** menu
- The **Window** menu
- The **Help** menu
- The Properties bar
- The running modes of operation

In addition, you learned how to

- Create and run a first application
- Compile an application
- Save and retrieve a program

Part II examines each of the objects of Visual Basic in more detail so that you will understand the capabilities and limitations of each. I also continue to use the Visual Basic environment and examine more closely its different parts.

Part II

Opening Up
Visual Basic

Understanding Forms

This chapter discusses forms, the windows of Visual Basic. Pay close attention to forms; they are the foundation of most Visual Basic programs.

In This Chapter

This chapter shows you how to

- Create a form
- Change the appearance of a form
- Print on a form
- Print to a printer
- Draw objects on a form

- Create custom-printed forms
- Print a form to a printer

Creating a Form

Forms are the visual background for all the controls and boxes that make up an application. When you first create a form, it appears as a standard, blank window. It has a title bar showing its name, and draggable borders to change its size and shape. The form also has a Control menu in the upper-left corner and Maximize and Minimize buttons in the upper-right corner.

A form is like an adjustable drawing board on which you draw objects (such as buttons and labels) to form the visual interface of a project. Most of what you want to see when your application is running is attached to a form. In addition to being the place where the visual parts of objects are attached, forms also contain the code that is attached to the objects. Although nearly every Visual Basic project has at least one form attached to it, you can run older BASIC programs without forms. Older BASIC programs read directly from the keyboard, and write directly to the screen. Any new BASIC program should confine its output to the forms, if possible, to make use of the modularity afforded by forms and the portability to Visual Basic for Windows.

You can attach as many forms to a project as you want to create your application. I suspect there's a limit to the number of forms you can attach to a single project; I haven't run into it yet, however. To avoid cluttering the screen, you can hide forms that are not being used and make them visible only when you want them.

When you start Visual Basic, you're in the Programming Environment. The first form in a project is created by executing the New Form command from the File menu. When you do this, a dialog box will ask you for a filename for the form and switch to the Form Designer for you to create your form. To add more forms to a project, execute the New Form command again.

Printing on a Form with the Print Method

In addition to drawing buttons and boxes on a form, you can print on a form by using the PRINT method. Text printed on a form starts in the upper-left corner and continues down the form with each successive execution of PRINT.

> Printing on a form in this manner is similar to printing on the screen in other versions of BASIC, with one important difference: a form does not scroll when your printed text goes off the screen. It simply disappears off the bottom as your application continues printing. If you continue printing off the bottom of the form, an overflow error results after approximately 100 lines. You also can print on the screen, as with older versions of BASIC, but no forms can be visible when you do so. This capability is not transferrable to Visual Basic for Windows.

The PRINT method prints text on forms, on picture boxes, and on the printer. Its syntax is

```
[object.]PRINT [expression][{;¦,}]
```

where *object* is the name of the object on which to print and *expression* is the text you want printed. Ending the method with a comma, a semicolon, or nothing controls where the cursor is left after *expression* is printed; the cursor position determines where printing starts the next time you execute PRINT. Appending nothing to the end of a PRINT method causes the insertion point to move down one line and left to the margin. A comma moves the insertion point to the next print field (every 14 spaces). A semicolon leaves the insertion point at the end of *expression*.

A Print Method Example

Follow these steps to print a few lines on a form. Don't delete this example, because you will use variations of it throughout this chapter.

1. Start with a new project by opening Visual Basic. If Visual Basic already is open and in the Programming Environment, execute the

New Project command of the File menu. If Visual Basic is in the Forms Designer, switch to the Programming Environment and then execute the New Project command.

2. Execute the New Form command on the File menu and name it FORM1.FRM in thc dialog box.

3. You now should be in the Forms Designer, so switch back to the Programming Environment by executing the Code command from the View menu. Click Ok to exit to the Programming Environment and Yes to save the current form.

4. When the Programming Environment opens, you will be presented with a dialog box listing the procedures that can be edited in this project (only one so far.) Select Form1 and press the Edit in Active button.

5. Execute the Event Procedures command on the Edit menu. Select the FORM object, the Click event, and press the Edit in Active button. You now should see the Form_Click() procedure template.

6. Add one line of code to the procedure template so that it reads

```
Sub Form_Click ()
Print "Hello "
End Sub
```

7. Execute the Start command of the Run menu. A blank form appears.

8. Click the form to execute the procedure. "Hello" is printed on the form, as shown in Figure 3.1.

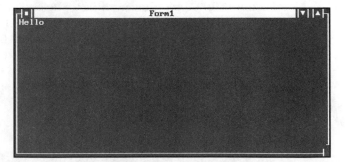

Figure 3.1. Printing a single line on a form.

9. Click several times on the form. "Hello" is repeated as shown in Figure 3.2. Eventually, if you continue to click the form, the text runs off the bottom.

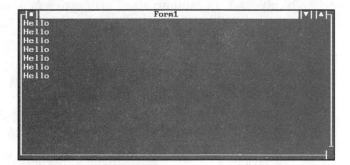

Figure 3.2. *Printing several times on a form.*

10. Press Ctrl-Break or click **Close** in the form's control box to end the program and go back to the Programming Environment.

> Try printing other text on the form. Also, try placing a comma or semicolon after the expression and see what happens.

Don't delete this program yet, because you will use it again later to examine some of a form's properties.

Changing the Appearance of Forms

The appearance of a form (its size, shape, color, border style, and so forth) is controlled by its properties. In addition, properties control how a form reacts to certain events, such as the redrawing of a form's contents when it's uncovered. Three different classes of properties are associated with objects: those that can be changed only at design time, those that can be changed only at runtime, and those that can be changed at any time. The majority of a form's properties can be changed at any time. Most design-time-only properties are readable at runtime, even though they can't be changed.

Table 3.1 lists some of the more commonly used properties of a form. See Chapter 15, "Command Reference," for a complete list.

Table 3.1. Commonly used properties of a form.

Property	Description
Runtime and Design-time Properties	
BackColor	The background color
Caption	The title displayed at the top of the form
ForeColor	The foreground color
FormName	The name of the form to use in code
Height	The height of the form in characters
Left	The distance from the left side of the form to the left side of the screen in characters
Top	The distance from the top of the form to the top of the screen in characters
Visible	Determines whether the form is visible at runtime (set to True or False)
Width	The width of the form in characters
Design-Time-Only Properties	
BorderStyle	The thickness of the form's border, and whether the form's size is adjustable
ControlBox	Whether the form has a control box (set to True or False)
MaxButton	Whether the form has a Maximize button (set to True or False)
MinButton	Whether the form has a Minimize button (set to True or False)

The Properties Bar

To change a form's properties at design time, select the form, switch to the Forms Designer, and change its properties with the Properties bar. The Properties bar contains two list boxes and four numbers. The first list box on the left is the properties list. It contains all properties that can be changed at design time. It does not contain properties that can be changed only at runtime. To the right of the properties list is the Settings box, which contains the value of the current setting for the property displayed in the Properties bar, as shown in Figure 3.3.

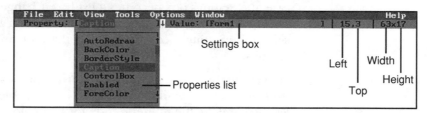

Figure 3.3. *The Properties bar with the properties list dropped down.*

Four numbers in two groups of two appear on the right side of the Properties bar. The two numbers on the left show the location of the upper-left corner of the currently selected object. The position is measured down and to the right of the upper-left corner of the screen if the object is a form. The position is measured down and to the right of the upper-left corner of the drawing area of the form if the object is on the form. The drawing area of a form is everything below the title bar. The right pair of numbers displays the width and height of the current object.

Both the location and the size of an object are measured in characters; that is, vertical measures are in character heights and horizontal scales are in character widths.

Changing Properties with the Settings Box

To change the appearance of a form (or any object on a form), you must change the value of its properties. At design time, you change the values of properties in two ways. For properties such as the size and location of a form, dragging the form or its borders automatically changes the Top, Left,

`Width`, and `Height` properties. You can also change these and other design time properties by using the Settings box.

To use the Settings box on the Properties bar, follow these steps:

1. Select the form or other object that has properties you want to change.

2. Pull down the properties list and select the property you want to change. At this point, the current value of the property is displayed in the Settings box.

3. Type a new value in the Settings box. Some properties have a fixed list of possible values (for example, True or False). If this is the case, the Settings box becomes a list box. Change the property by pulling down the list of settings (click the down arrow on the right side of the Settings box). Then select the value from the list of settings.

For setting the `ForeColor` or `BackColor` properties, you can also use the Color Palette window. When you select a color in the Color Palette window, the numeric code for that color is automatically inserted in the Settings box.

You can now return to the print method example and experiment with changing some properties:

1. If you made any changes in the procedure you created in the earlier example, remove them before continuing. You should be in the Forms Designer. If you aren't, click the Form button on the project window, or select Form from the View menu.

2. Select Form1. Then select the `BackColor` property on the Properties bar.

3. Pull down the Settings list. Select `9-Bright Blue`.

4. Select the `ForeColor` property and change it to `12-Bright Red` in the Settings list.

5. Run the program and click the form a few times. It should look like Figure 3.4, with a bright blue background and bright red text.

6. Quit the program by pressing Ctrl-Break.

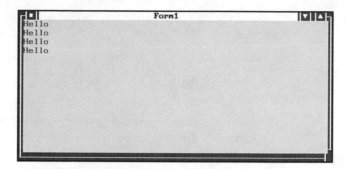

Figure 3.4. *Printing on a form with the* FontSize *property set to 24 points.*

Try changing some of the other properties of the form (such as BorderStyle), and run the example again. Don't be afraid to experiment with the properties or code. Although the manual might tell you what will happen, it could be ambiguous or, occasionally, wrong. The only way to see exactly what a property or code segment does is to try it.

Dynamically Changing Properties in a Running Application

To change properties in a running application, use a statement with the following format:

```
[object.]property = value
```

in which *object* is the name of the object having the property to be changed (in this case, the form name), *property* is the name of the property, and *value* is a new value for that property. If *object* is omitted, the attached orm is assumed to be the object. If the construction [*object.*]*property* is used on the right side of a formula rather than on the left side, it returns the current value of that property.

For example, the following code changes the foreground color to 12, the color attribute for red:

```
ForeColor = 12
```

For example, add a line to the print example to change the ForeColor each time "Hello" is printed, as follows:

1. Continue from the point at which you left off with the preceding example. If you've made any changes in the procedure, remove them before continuing. If you are in the Programming Environment, switch to the Forms Designer.

2. Select Form1 and change the ForeColor property to 0 - Black.

3. Switch back to the Programming Environment and edit the Form_Click procedure so that it reads as follows:

```
Sub Form_Click ()
ForeColor = ForeColor + 1
Print "Hello "
End Sub
```

4. Run the program and click the form a few times. It should look like Figure 3.5. Eventually, if you continue clicking, you get an Invalid Property Value error message because the value of ForeColor is limited to the range 0 through 15.

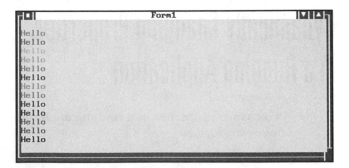

Figure 3.5. *Setting properties with code.*

Printing to the Printer

In addition to printing on forms, you can print to the printer by using PRINTER as the object in the PRINT method. For example, to change the last example so it prints to the printer rather than on the form, follow these steps:

1. In the Programming Environment, select the form and open its Click event code window.

2. Change the object in the PRINT method to the PRINTER object. Remove the line that changes the ForeColor so that the procedure reads

```
SUB Form_Click ()
Printer.Print "Hello."
END SUB
```

3. Run the program and click the form.

   The program doesn't seem to be doing anything. However, the printer is printing "Hello."

4. End the program by pressing Ctrl-Break.

Printing on a Text Box

Often you have to print a list of items on the screen, and you want the items to be in a scrollable box. Word processors and telecommunication programs are examples of programs that write on scrollable lists. To create a scrollable list, use a text box, and add any new text to its Text property.

To add text to a text box, you first need a large text box on a form. Clear any text already on the text box, and set the MultiLine property to True. If MultiLine is False, only one line of text is printed on the text box. Turn on the vertical scroll bar with the ScrollVertical property. Let's try creating a form with a scrollable list, and then add text to that list:

1. Clear the old project by executing the New Project command of the File menu; then create a new form (Form1) and switch to the

Forms Designer by executing the New Form command of the File menu.

2. Select the text box tool in the Toolbox window. Draw a text box nearly as large as the interior part of the form. Leave enough space at the right so you can still click the form.

3. With the text box selected, select the MultiLine property in the Properties list. Set its value to True in the Settings box.

4. Select the Text property and delete the contents of the Settings box. This clears the text inside the text box.

5. Select the ScrollBars property and set it to 2-Vertical.

   In the Form_Click procedure, append the new text to the text currently in the text box. Also append a carriage return and a line feed to move down to the next line.

6. Switch to the Programming Environment. Select the FORM object and the Click procedure. Then insert a line to add the text Hello to the contents of the text box. The procedure should look like the following:

```
SUB Form_Click ()
Text1.Text = Text1.Text + "Hello " + Chr$(13) + Chr$(10)
END SUB
```

   Note that the CHR$(13) function inserts a carriage return and the CHR$(10) function inserts a line feed.

7. Run the program and click several times part of the form that the text box doesn't cover. Your form now should look like Figure 3.6.

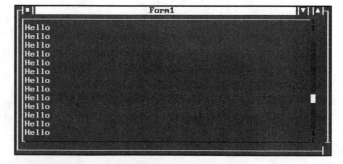

***Figure 3.6.** Printing in a text box.*

Drawing Your User Interface

Forms most commonly are used as backgrounds for the user interface to your application. In Chapter 2, "Learning the Visual Basic Environment," you learned that you draw the different controls and boxes on your form to create the interface you want. The Toolbox window is the source of the drawing tools for creating your interface. You use each of these tools by following these steps:

1. Select a tool in the Toolbox window.

2. Move the mouse pointer to where you want the upper-left corner of your object.

3. Hold down the left mouse button and drag the mouse pointer down to where you want the lower-right corner of your object to be, and release the mouse button. The object appears where you drew it. Its location, height, and width appear on the right side of the Properties bar.

Some objects, such as the timer, have a fixed size. No matter how large you draw them, they always appear the same size. Other objects (such as labels or text boxes) are the size you drew them. If an object you've drawn is the wrong size or in the wrong location, you can adjust it as follows:

- To move an object, select it and do one of the following:

  Edit the object's Top and Left properties.

  Place the mouse pointer on the object, and hold down the left mouse button. Drag the object to its new location, and release the button.

- To change the size of an existing object, you can do one of the following:

  Edit the Height and Width properties.

  Select the object and drag one of the small black squares that appear around it until the object is the shape you want.

Creating a Custom Form

In business situations, you often have to either fill out or create a paper form. You can buy a form-generation program, or you simply can use Visual Basic to create an online form you can fill out on the screen. The form's contents are then either printed or stored on a disk for use by another program.

One evening, my wife, who is a veterinarian, told me that she was out of vaccination certificates. She had just vaccinated Jessie, a dog we were giving away in the morning, and she needed a blank certificate. Her suppliers take a week or two to get forms to her; however, she needed a form right away so the new owners would have the correct paperwork when they picked up Jessie.

Using Visual Basic, I created the following vaccination certificate as a stand-alone application. You run the application, fill in the form, and press a button to print it. Creating the custom form took only about an hour. Of course, to be able to sign it legally requires about eight years of college and a license, so don't try to use this form for your own pets (unless you're a veterinarian, too).

The first step is to design the form. Sketch the different fields and labels you want so you have a rough idea where they go.

Frames have to go behind any objects that are on them. The first time I created the form described here, I forgot to put a frame around the outside. I tried to put it on at the end but, rather than being in the background, it covered everything else. Because the physical ordering of objects on the form cannot be changed, I had to redo the form from scratch.

Something else to consider at this time is the tab ordering of the text boxes. When you're filling out the form, you can press Tab to move from object to object. The order in which the objects are selected is determined by the order in which they are drawn on the form. However, you can change that ordering by changing the TabIndex property. The TabIndex property, which is incremented each time a new object is drawn on a form, determines the tab order. If you change the value of the TabIndex property of an object, it moves to that position in the tab order. The TabIndex properties of all the other objects on the form are automatically adjusted to make room for the inserted object. In the vaccination certificate example, you want to tab from one text box to the next, so you need to put all the text boxes on the form first.

I give you the exact positions and sizes of all the objects on this form, so you can create a form identical to the one in Figure 3.7. Alternatively, you can look at the figure and draw the objects to make your form similar to mine. It might not be identical, but you will see how to create a custom form.

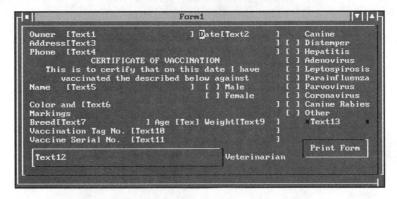

Figure 3.7. *The vaccination form in progress.*

1. Start with a blank form by executing the **New** Project command on the **File** menu, then the New **Form** command. This time name the form VETFRM.FRM and switch to the Forms Designer.

2. Enlarge the form until it is 74 characters wide by 20 characters high.

3. Select the Frame tool and draw a frame that's about the same size as the form. Set the following properties of the frame:

   Top   =   0

   Left   =   0

   Width   =   72

   Height =   18

   Caption =   " "

4. Table 3.2 lists 13 text boxes and their properties. Look at Figure 3.7 and draw the boxes first. Then, adjust their properties to match those in the table. Set the Text property for each text box to a blank (" ").

It's easiest to draw all the boxes on the form first in roughly the right location and size. Then select one property and adjust it on all the boxes rather than setting all the properties for a single box before going on to the next. To do this, select the first box and select the property to be adjusted. Change the property and press Enter to accept the change. Then press Tab to move to the next box. Using this procedure, you can go down the list of boxes, then change to the next property and do it again. Continue this process for all the properties that have to be adjusted.

Table 3.2. Text box properties for the custom form.

Control Name	Left	Top	Width	Height
Text1	8	0	26	1
Text2	39	0	12	1
Text3	8	1	43	1
Text4	8	2	43	1
Text5	8	6	26	1
Text6	11	8	40	1
Text7	6	10	19	1
Text8	30	10	5	1
Text9	42	10	9	1
Text10	21	11	30	1
Text11	21	12	30	1
Text12	1	13	39	3
Text13	56	10	13	1

5. There are 15 labels on the form. Using Figure 3.7 and Table 3.3, attach them to the form.

Table 3.3. Label box properties of the custom form.

Control Name	Left	Top	Width	Height	Caption
Label1	1	0	6	1	Owner
Label2	35	0	4	1	Date
Label3	1	1	7	1	Address
Label4	1	2	7	1	Phone
Label5	1	3	50	1	CERTIFICATE OF VACCINATION*
Label6	1	4	51	1	This is to certify that on this date I have vaccinated the described below against*
Label7	1	6	5	1	Name
Label8	1	8	10	1	Color and Markings
Label9	1	10	5	1	Breed
Label10	26	10	4	1	Age
Label11	36	10	6	1	Weight
Label12	1	11	20	1	Vaccination Tag No.
Label13	1	12	21	1	Vaccine Serial No.
Label14	40	14	13	1	Veterinarian
Label15	56	0	8	1	Canine

* *For Label5 and Label6, set* Alignment *to* 2 - Center.

6. Place 11 check boxes on the form, using Figure 3.7 and Table 3.4 as guides. Draw the smallest box that shows the entire check box.

Table 3.4. Check box properties of the custom form.

Control Name	Left	Top	Width	Height	Caption
Check1	36	6	11	1	Male
Check2	36	7	12	1	Female
Check3	52	1	16	1	Distemper
Check4	52	2	14	1	Hepatitis
Check5	52	3	15	1	Adenovirus
Check6	52	4	20	1	Leptospirosis
Check7	52	5	20	1	Parainfluenza
Check8	52	6	20	1	Parvovirus
Check9	52	7	20	1	Coronavirus
Check10	52	8	20	1	Canine Rabies
Check11	52	9	20	1	Other

7. Using the command button tool, insert a button on the lower-right corner of the form. Give the button the following properties:

```
Left     =  55
Top      =  12
Width    =  14
Height   =  3
Caption  =  Print Form
CtlName  =  PrintIt
```

Your form now should look like Figure 3.8. All that remains is to add some code that automatically fills in the current date and prints the form when the user presses the command button.

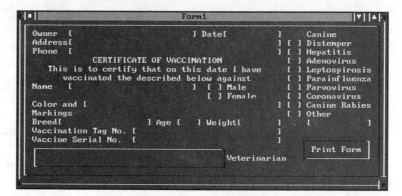

Figure 3.8. The user interface for the vaccination certificate custom form.

Using the PRINTFORM Method

Rather than having to draw the contents of the form on the PRINTER object, you can use a special method. The PRINTFORM method prints a form to the printer as it appears on the screen. The format of this method is

```
[Form.]PRINTFORM
```

If you leave out the *Form* argument, it prints the current form.

Continuing with the vaccination certificate program, add some code to the program to invoke the PRINTFORM method when the Print Form button is pressed.

8. Open the code window for the form. Select the PRINTIT object and the Click procedure. Insert code into the procedure template until it appears as follows:

```
SUB PrintIt_Click ()
PrintIt.Visible = 0
PRINTFORM
PrintIt.Visible = -1
END SUB
```

Setting the PrintIt.Visible property of the command button to 0 (False) makes the button disappear before printing the form with the PRINTFORM method. After the form is printed, setting PrintIt.Visible equal to -1 (True) makes the button visible again.

9. Select the FORM object and the Load procedure, and insert the following code:

```
SUB FORM_LOAD ()
Text2.Text = DATE$
END SUB
```

The DATE$ function always returns a string containing the current date. Setting the Text property of the Text2 text box with the DATE$ function causes the current date to be inserted in the box at the time the form is loaded. The box is editable, so the user can change the date if necessary.

10. Save the project with the name VETFRM.MAK.

11. Run the program with the **Start** command from the **Run** menu.

If you were a veterinarian, you would type the name of the dog's owner and a description of the dog. You also would click the check boxes to select the vaccines you gave to the dog. When you completed filling out the form, you would click the Print Form button to output it to the printer.

If everything works correctly, you now can compile the custom form into an .EXE file that can be given to anyone who needs to create the form.

> In addition to printing the form, you could write data to a file that a database program could read to keep a record of what animal has received what vaccinations. (Chapter 9, "Using Sequential Files," explains how to use disk files.) An accounting program also could read the file and print a bill for the patient's owner. I'm sure you can imagine many other uses for custom forms developed in this way.

Printing on a Preprinted Form

Printing on a preprinted form takes much trial and error. To do so, create a custom form that has the text box fields in the same place as the fields on the preprinted form. In the PrintIt_Click procedure, make all the field descriptions invisible (in this example, the label boxes) during printing, in the same manner as was done with the Print Form button. Then fill out the form with dummy text and print it. If it doesn't fit the preprinted form, move things around and print it again. Continue this trial-and-error procedure until you're satisfied with the result.

What You Have Learned

In this chapter you learned about forms, which are the foundation of most Visual Basic programs. Specifically, you learned how to

- Create new forms with the **New Project** and **New Form** commands

- Print text on a form and to the printer by using the PRINT method

- Change the appearance of a form and the text printed on it by modifying its properties both in design mode and dynamically in a running program

- Create a custom form-filling program

- Print the contents of a form to the printer using the PRINTFORM method

Using Strings

The primary method of communication with Visual Basic objects and with the user of a Visual Basic program is with strings of text. Although numbers are used internally for calculations, indices, and counters, they must be converted to strings before they can be displayed in a text box or label. Thus, manipulating strings and converting numbers to strings are some of the most important aspects of any Visual Basic program.

In This Chapter

Most of what you've read so far in this book has dealt with strings of text. List boxes and labels display text on the screen. Many object properties are defined as strings of text. This chapter formally defines strings and string formulas, and expands on the details of using strings in programs. This chapter shows you how to

● Define variables and determine their scope

● Define strings

● Create string formulas

● Manipulate strings with string functions

● Create an envelope-addressing program

Variables

To understand strings and string formulas, you must first consider the concept of variables and their scope. Variables are where you store information in a computer program. Later in this chapter, you learn about strings and how to manipulate them.

A *variable* is a descriptive name used to store information and the results of calculations. Actually, the information is stored in the computer's memory, and the variable name names that location. Whenever a variable name is used in a program, it's replaced by the contents of that memory location. A variable name is an abstraction that makes computer programs more readable. For example, `Label1.Caption` is a string variable that names the location of the string of text used for the caption of Label1. If I used an address such as `9FC80` for that location rather than the variable name, no one, including me, would have any idea what the program was doing. Using variable names makes reading a computer program understandable.

A variable name can contain up to 40 characters, including letters, numbers, and the underscore (_). The first character of a variable name must be a letter, and you cannot use a reserved word such as `Print` as a variable. However, a reserved word can be contained within a variable name, as in the variable `PrintIt`. Although you can use as many as 40 characters for a variable name, don't do it. Use enough characters to make it obvious what the variable is, but not so many that you spend all day typing 40-character variable names. A good rule of thumb is to imagine that you must give your program to someone else (your mother, for example), and she must be able to read your program and understand what it is doing. Then, when you come back to your program in a year or so, the odds are good that you still will understand it as well.

The Scope of Variables

The scope of a variable is determined by where and how the variable is defined, and determines where in a program the variable can be accessed. Figure 4.1 is a graphic representation of the scope of different variables. Each box in the diagram represents a part of a program such as a form or code module. At the top of each box, different BASIC statements are used to define some variables. Just below the definitions, is a list of the variables that are accessible everywhere within the box. As stated before, form modules or forms (.FRM files) contain both code and the description of a form with all its attached controls. *Code modules*, or just *modules* (.BAS files), contain only code. Code is stored in modules in blocks known as *procedures*, and a procedure is an autonomous unit of code that performs a specific task such as controlling what happens when a button is pressed.

Variables associated with the properties of objects, such as `Label1.Top`, are predefined and available to any code within the form containing that object. If some other form or module needs access to the properties of an object attached to a form (such as variable H in Figure 4.1), a `$FORM` statement must be inserted at the highest level in the form or module that needs access, giving the name of the form to access. For example, the following line, placed at the top- or module-level of a module, gives that module access to all the properties in Form1:

```
REM $FORM Form1
```

You define user variables (those variables that you create for your own use) by simply using them in a procedure, or by explicitly defining them with the `DIM`, `COMMON`, or `SHARED` statements.

If you place an `OPTION IMPLICIT` statement at the beginning of a module, then you can no longer define a variable in that module by using it, but must define it before using it with a `DIM`, `COMMON`, or `SHARED` statement. It's good practice to use the `OPTION IMPLICIT` statement, because it forces you to define explicitly all variables in your program. That way, misspelled or out-of-place variables show up as syntax errors at design time rather than as a program crash at runtime.

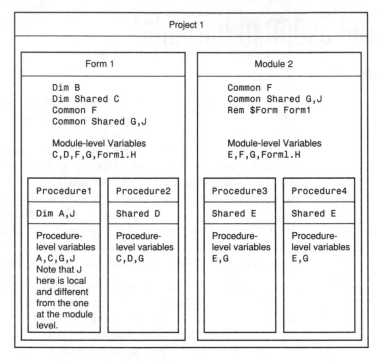

Figure 4.1. The scope of variables.

The scope of a variable is determined by which statement is used to define it, and where it is defined. At the highest level are variables defined at the module level with the COMMON SHARED statement (variable G in Figure 4.1). Variables defined at the module level are available to any procedure in that particular module, and to all other modules containing identical COMMON SHARED statements. For example, the following statement shares the variable G with all other modules that contain a COMMON SHARED statement:

```
COMMON SHARED G
```

Note that the names of the variables in two COMMON or COMMON SHARED statements in two different modules do not have to be the same. The values of the variables are associated by position in the two statements, not by name. This rule applies only to the COMMON statements, not to the DIM and SHARED statements, which associate variables by name.

Next are the COMMON statements defined at the module level (such as variable F in Figure 4.1). Variables defined there are available to the module-level code, and to the module-level code of any other module with an identical COMMON statement. COMMON and COMMON SHARED statements also may be named. The variables in named COMMON statements are shared only with COMMON statements with the same name. For example, the following statement shares the variable MyName with all modules that contain COMMON statements named PDat:

```
COMMON /PDat/ myName
```

Following the COMMON statements are the DIM SHARED statements at the module level (variable C in Figure 4.1). Variables defined there are available anywhere in a module and to all the procedures within that module. Variables defined in a DIM statement at the module level (variable B in Figure 4.1) are available only to code at the module level. For example, the following statement defines YourName as a string variable, which is available to all code at the module

```
DIM YourName AS STRING
```

Finally come the procedure level declarations. Variables defined in a DIM statement at the procedure level (variables A and J in Figure 4.1) are local variables, which are available only within that procedure. Variables defined with a SHARED statement at the procedure level (variables D and E in Figure 4.1) are available to both the procedure and the module-level code of the module that contains the procedure. Two procedures in the same module can share a variable if both include it in a SHARED statement (variable E in Figure 4.1).

Local variables are available only within the procedure in which they are used or defined, and nowhere else. When the procedure ends, local variables go away and their old values are unavailable the next time the procedure is called. To let local variables survive the end of a procedure, define them in the procedure with the STATIC statement. Variables defined with the STATIC statement persist until the next time the procedure is called. The STATIC statement has the same syntax as the DIM statement. The following code defines OurName as a static string variable:

```
STATIC OurName AS STRING
```

The declaration of a local variable always overrides the global declaration of a variable with the same name; see Figure 4.1, in which J is defined globally in a COMMON SHARED statement but also is defined as a local variable in Procedure1. The global variable and the local variable are two different

variables. Changing one has no effect on the other. The variable G also is defined globally in Form1 and used in Procedure1. However, because G is not defined in Procedure1, the global variable and the local variable are the same. Changing one changes the other.

The Variable Scope Example

To experiment with the scope of variables, create a setup like that shown in Figure 4.1. Create two forms and, as in Figure 4.1, define the variables as strings, and then try changing the values in different places to see what happens:

1. Start with a new project. Create a form with the New For command of the File menu and switch to the Forms Designer.

2. Draw two command buttons on Form1.

3. Create a second form with the New Form command on the File menu.

4. Draw two command buttons on Form2.

5. Switch to the Programming Environment, select Form1—you're now at the module level—and add the following lines to the module level of Form1:

```
DIM B AS STRING
DIM SHARED C AS STRING
COMMON F AS STRING
COMMON SHARED G AS STRING, J AS STRING
```

6. Select the Form_Click procedure for Form1 and type

```
SUB Form_Click ()
PRINT J
END SUB
```

7. Select the Form_Load procedure and type

```
SUB Form_Load ()
J = "Bill"
Form2.Show
END SUB
```

You need the Form2.Show method to make the second form appear on the screen when the program is run.

8. Select the Command1_Click procedure and type

```
SUB Command1_Click ()
DIM J AS STRING
PRINT J
END SUB
```

9. Select the Command2_Click procedure and type

```
SUB Command2_Click ()
PRINT J
END SUB
```

10. Select Form2, open its Code window, select the Command1_Click procedure, and type

```
SUB Command1_Click ()
SHARED E
PRINT J
END SUB
```

11. Select the Command2_Click procedure and type

```
SUB Command2_Click ()
SHARED E
END SUB
```

By clicking the buttons or the form, you now see the values of the variable J, which is defined globally and given a value in Form_Click on Form1. Note that when you run this program, Form2 may be hiding behind Form1, so if necessary move Form1 over a little to see Form2.

12. Run the program. Click first on Form1, then on the Command2 button on Form1, and finally on the Command1 button on Form2. All these procedures print "Bill" on the form, so they know the value of MyName because it's a global variable.

13. Click the Command2 button on Form1 and notice that the global value of MyName is not printed on the form. It is not available here because MyName is a local variable in that procedure, and currently is an empty, or null, string.

14. End the program. Open `Command2_Click` on Form1 and change it to

```
SUB Command2_Click ()
DIM J AS STRING
J = "Shane"
PRINT J
END SUB
```

15. Run the program again, pressing all the buttons.

Notice that J has the value `Shane` only when the Command2 button on Form1 is pressed, that is, in the `Command2_Click` procedure. The value of J is `Bill` everywhere else. Thus, the global definition persists everywhere but in the procedure `Command2_Click`, in which the local variable definition overrides the global definition.

Experiment with this code. Try changing and printing the values of the other variables in different places to see what happens.

Strings and String Formulas

Now that you have a feel for variables and their scope, you can begin examining strings and string variables.

Defining Strings

A *string* is a sequence of text characters. Although most strings consist of printable characters, they also can contain any of the nonprinting control characters, such as the carriage return and line feed. A string also can be the null or empty string, which has a length of zero and doesn't contain any characters. All the text boxes in Chapter 3's vaccination certificate program initially contain null strings.

A *substring* is an ordinary string that is contained in another string. In other words, it's a piece of another, longer string.

Characters actually are stored in the computer's memory and on disk as *ASCII* codes (ASCII stands for American Standard Code for Information Interchange). The standard set of ASCII codes ranges from 0 to 127 and includes all the standard typewriter symbols (see Appendix B, "ASCII/ANSI Code Chart"). Codes from 128 through 255 are the extended character set, which contains many symbols and foreign characters. The first 32 ASCII characters are *control characters,* which are used to control data flow in communication programs, and line and page control on printers or on the screen. The control codes you frequently use are for the Backspace (8), the Tab (9), the line feed (10), the form feed (12), and the carriage return (13).

The extended characters (128 through 255) for DOS and Windows are different. DOS follows the IBM standard character set. Windows follows the ANSI standard.

There are two functions for converting between characters and ASCII codes: ASC() and CHR$(). You might wonder why you would want to use the codes at all when you can use the more readable characters. A simple example is inserting end-of-line characters (carriage return and line feed) within a string in a program. If you try to type a carriage return in a program, the program editor moves you down to the next line in the program rather than inserting that character in the string you were typing. (It probably will give you a syntax error, too.) To insert a carriage return in a string, you must create one with the function CHR$(13) and add it to your string. You do this a little later in this chapter.

The syntax of the ASC() function is

ASC(*string$*)

Here, *string$* is a string. ASC() returns the ASCII code of the first character of *string$*.

The syntax of the CHR$() function is

CHR$(*code*)

Here, *code* is an ASCII code. CHR$() returns a one-character string containing the character represented by *code*.

Declaring String Variables

There are several ways to declare a string variable. As I mentioned previously, all the string variables in the properties of objects are predefined, so they do not have to be defined explicitly before they are used. User variables can be used without being defined; however, it's a much better programming practice to declare everything first in the appropriate procedure or module. Doing so ensures that if you use the name of a global variable as a local variable, the two variables are kept separate. The OPTION IMPLICIT statement helps enforce this by forcing you to define all variables before you use them. Another way to define a string variable is to append a $ to it. For example:

```
MyName$
```

also is a string variable. Notice that it's the same variable as the string variable MyName, defined previously with the DIM statement. That is, the $ is not included as part of the variable name.

Using String Formulas

After you define a variable, you have to create a string and store it in the variable. You assign a value to a string by using an assignment statement. The syntax of an assignment statement is

```
variable = formula
```

In this case, *variable* is a string variable and *formula* is a string formula or constant. The equals sign makes this an assignment statement. When it is executed, the formula on the right is evaluated and the string result is assigned to the variable on the left. You already have used assignment statements in this book to change the values of the properties of objects.

A string formula consists of a combination of quoted strings of text and string functions linked with the *concatenation operator* (+). Concatenation is the act of combining two short strings into a long string by placing the strings end to end. For example, the formula

```
Name = "Bill " + "Orvis"
```

combines the strings `"Bill "` and `"Orvis"` into the longer string `"Bill Orvis"` and assigns the result to the string variable `MyName`. Here's another example:

```
DIM MyName AS STRING, YourName AS STRING
MyName = "Bill"
YourName = "Julie"
OurName$ = MyName + " Loves " + YourName
```

This example combines the two string variables with the string `" Loves "` to create the string `"Bill Loves Julie"`, which is assigned to the string variable `OurName$`. Here, `MyName` and `YourName` are defined as string variables with a `DIM` statement. `OurName$` is defined as a string variable because it has the $ suffix.

Strings Displayed in Labels and Text Boxes

After you have created a string, you usually want to display it. Printing it on a form is an adequate way to display the string; however, in this age of dialog boxes and windows, inserting the string in a label or text box is more modern. Both labels and text boxes dynamically display text on the screen. The difference between them is that the user can edit the text in a text box, but cannot edit the text in a label.

Setting the Text with the Properties Bar

The simplest way to display text in a label or text box is to use the Properties bar at design time. For a label, select the `Caption` property and type the text into the Settings box. For a text box, find the `Text` property and, again, type the text into the Settings box. Although it's simple to do, setting the text in a box by using the Properties bar is good only for static text (text that won't change), or to set an initial string for a `Text` or `Caption` property that the program changes later.

Setting the Text with a Formula

To change the text in a box dynamically, use assignment statements in your program. The assignment statement that changes a property of an object has the following format:

```
object.property = formula
```

in which the *formula* must evaluate to a value consistent with the property being changed. The construct *object.property* is treated like any other variable defined at the form level and refers to the contents of the property of the object. For text properties such as Text and Caption, *formula* must evaluate to a string of text.

The Loves Program

Take the preceding example and turn it into the Loves program by following these steps:

1. Start with a new project by executing the **New Project** command of the **File** menu.

2. Execute the New Form Command of the File menu. Name the form LOVES1.FRM.

3. Draw two text boxes on the form.

4. Add one label on the form, as shown in Figure 4.2.

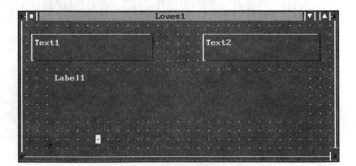

Figure 4.2. *Layout for the Loves application.*

5. Select the Text properties of the two text boxes and set them to the null string.

6. Select the Caption property of the label and set it to the null string.

7. Switch back to the Programming Environment and select the module-level code window. Then type

```
Dim Shared MyName As String, YourName As String
```

This statement makes MyName and YourName global definitions in the form. Thus they are available to any procedure on the form.

8. Select the Text1_Change procedure and type

```
SUB Text1_Change ()
MyName = Text1.Text
END SUB
```

This step stores the value of the Text property of the Text1 text box in the string variable MyName.

9. Select the Text2_Change procedure and type

```
SUB Text2_Change ()
YourName = Text2.Text
END SUB
```

This step does the same for the Text property of the Text2 text box.

10. Select the Form_Click procedure and type

```
SUB Form_Click ()
Label1.Caption = MyName + " Loves " + YourName
END SUB
```

Here the two string variables are combined with the string " Loves " and are stored in the Caption property of the Label1 label.

11. Run the program. Type your name in the first text box. Type the name of someone special in the second box, and click the form.

Your program now should look like Figure 4.3 (with your names replacing mine and Julie's, of course).

12. End the program by pressing Ctrl-Break. Save the project as LOVES1.MAK.

4

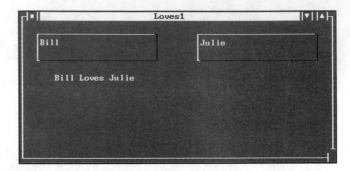

Figure 4.3. *The running Loves application.*

Try this program again, but without the declarations in the module-level code (step 7). The program won't work because the `Form_Click` procedure won't know the value of `MyName` or `YourName`. `MyName` and `YourName` now are local to the procedures that contain them.

Changing Label Properties

The properties of a label or text box are changed in exactly the same manner as those of a form. You change them either at design time with the Properties bar or at runtime with assignment statements. As an example, create version 2 of the Loves program, by copying version 1 of the program and then modifying it:

1. Start with a new project. Execute the **N**ew Project command of the **File** menu.

2. Attach the old form. Execute the **A**dd File command of the **File** menu and select LOVES1.FRM.

3. Change the name of the attached form. Select LOVES1.FRM on the Project window, execute the Save File **A**s command of the **File** menu, and save the file as LOVES2.FRM.

4. Click the form button on the Project window to switch to the Forms Designer.

5. Select the label and change the following properties:

```
Label1.Alignment = 2 - Centered
Label1.ForeColor = 7 - White
Label1.BackColor = 13 - Pink
```

6. Select the form, and change the following property:

```
Form.Caption = Loves2
```

7. Run the program again. It should now look like Figure 4.4.

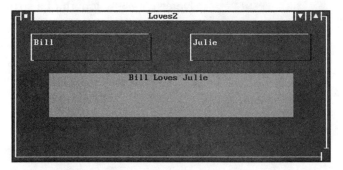

Figure 4.4. *The Loves program with changed* Text *properties in the label.*

8. Press Ctrl-Break to end the program, and then save it with the Save Project command on the File mcnu. Use LOVES2.MAK as the name for the project file.

Manipulating Strings

As you might expect, you can do more to strings than simply concatenate them. Visual Basic has a set of functions that deal exclusively with strings. This set includes functions that locate substrings, and others that extract a substring from a string. Table 4.1 contains a complete list of the string functions available in Visual Basic. See Chapter 15, "Command Reference," for descriptions of the individual functions.

Table 4.1. String functions.

Function	Description
ASC()	Converts a character to an ASCII code
CHR$()	Converts an ASCII code to a character
FORMAT$()	Converts a number to a string with a specific format
INSTR()	Locates a substring in a string
LCASE$()	Converts a string to all lowercase letters
LEFT$()	Extracts the left side of a string
LEN()	Determines the length of a string
LSET	Left-justifies a string
LTRIM$()	Removes leading spaces from a string
MID$()	Extracts a substring from a string
RIGHT$()	Extracts the right side of a string
RSET	Right-justifies a string
RTRIM$()	Removes trailing spaces from a string
SPACE$()	Returns a string of spaces
STRING$()	Returns a string of a specific character
UCASE$()	Converts a string to all uppercase letters

If your program has to deal with a string typed by the user or sent by another program, the first thing you usually do is test whether it's the one you expected to receive. You can calculate its length with the LEN() function, or search for a specific substring with INSTR(). If the LEN() function returns a length of 0, the string is empty—a situation that your program must be able to handle. The INSTR() function searches for a specific substring within another string and returns the character location of the start of that substring. If it doesn't find the substring, it returns a zero. The syntax of the LEN() function is

LEN(*string$*)

The syntax of the INSTR() function is

INSTR([*start-position,*]*string$,substring$*)

After you find a substring, you might want to extract it or some other substring. Do this with the MID$(), LEFT$(), and RIGHT$() functions. The MID$() function extracts any substring within a string. The LEFT$() and RIGHT$() functions are special cases of MID$() that extract some number of characters from the left or right side of a string. The syntaxes of these functions are

MID$(***string$,start-character[,length]*)**
LEFT$(***string$,length*)**
RIGHT$(***string$,length*)**

Here, *string$* is the string from which to extract a substring, *start-character* is the number of the first character to include in the substring, counting from the first character in *string$*, and *length* is the length of the substring to extract from *string$*. In MID$(), if you omit the *length* argument, the entire right side of the string is extracted.

You can also write MID$() as a statement (on the left side of a formula rather than on the right) that replaces a substring in a string with another string of equal length. That syntax is

MID$(***string$,start-character[,length]*)** = *substring$*

Here, the substring in *string$* that starts at *start-character* and is *length* long is replaced with *length* characters from *substring$*. If you omit *length*, all *substring$* is used. In both cases, the resulting length of *string$* is the same length as the original *string$*.

The Envelope Addresser Program (Version 1)

The Loves application is cute, but you can make something more useful. Often, when you write a letter, you have to type an envelope to go with it. Here's a program that prints addresses on envelopes. The program has a built-in return address. It accepts the address that is to be typed in a text box. When your address is ready, click the form to print the address. To create the envelope addresser program, follow these steps:

1. Execute the **New Project** command on the File menu.

2. Execute the New **Form** command on the **File** menu and name the form ADDR11.FRM.

3. Draw a text box on Form1 large enough to hold an address.
   Reduce the size of the form by dragging its borders until it looks

like Figure 4.5. Set the property MultiLine = True so the text box can contain more than one line of text. Set the Text property to null.

Figure 4.5. *The AddrBox setup for the envelope addresser.*

4. Select the form and change the following properties:

    ```
    Caption = Address Box
    FormName = AddrBox
    ```

5. Create a second form with the New Form command and name it ADDR12.FRM. Drag its borders until it looks like Figure 4.6.

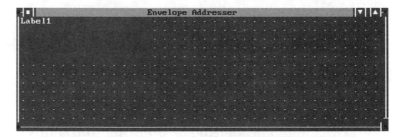

Figure 4.6. *The AddrFrm setup for the envelope addresser.*

6. Draw a label in the upper-left corner for the return address.

7. Select the form and set the following properties:

    ```
    AutoRedraw = True
    Caption = Envelope Addresser
    FormName = AddrFrm
    ```

    AutoRedraw must be turned on so the form remembers text that is printed on it. Otherwise, when the text is printed on the printer, only the text in the label and text box is printed. AutoRedraw also makes it possible to cover a form with another form, uncover the first form, and still have the text appear.

You need AutoRedraw only for forms and picture boxes, because text boxes and labels already store the text printed on them in one of their properties.

8. Switch to the Programming Environment, execute Event Procedures from the Edit menu, select the AddrBox form and the Form_Load procedure, and type

```
SUB Form_Load ()
AddrFrm.Show
END SUB
```

This procedure is executed when the AddrBox form loads. The procedure loads the AddrFrm form and makes it visible.

9. Select the Text1_Change procedure and type

```
SUB Text1_Change ()
TheLine = Text1.Text
END SUB
```

This procedure extracts the text from the text box as it is typed and stores it in the string variable TheLine. The Change event causes this procedure to be executed every time the user types a character into the text box. To pass the value of TheLine from Form1 to Form2, where it is printed, define TheLine in COMMON statements at the module level of both forms.

10. Press the Code button on the Project window and select the module-level code window for the AddrBox form. Type the following:

```
COMMON SHARED TheLine AS STRING
```

11. Press the Code button on the Project window and select the module-level code window for the AddrFrm form. Type the following:

```
COMMON SHARED TheLine AS STRING
DIM SHARED EOL$
```

The string EOL$ is a constant needed in two routines on Form2. By defining it here, you must define its value only once. You can't give it a value here with the CONST declaration because you can't type

the carriage return and line feed control characters in the editor, and functions such as CHR$(13) are not allowed in the module-level section of a form module.

12. Select the Form_Load procedure and type the following text. Substitute your own return address for the one I use here.

```
SUB Form_Load ()
EOL$ = CHR$(13) + CHR$(10)
Label1.Caption = "William J. Orvis" + eol$
Label1.Caption = Label1.Caption + "123 Some St." + eol$
Label1.Caption = Label1.Caption + "Anywhere, CA  91234"
END SUB
```

This routine inserts the return address into the label. This must be done with code because you can't type a carriage return in the editor. The routine first defines EOL$, the end-of-line string, as a carriage return (CHR$(13)) and a line feed (CHR$(10)). Next it combines the text of the return address into a single string with the end-of-line separating each line. This string is stored in the Caption property of the Label1 label.

13. Select the Form_Click procedure and type

```
SUB Form_Click ()
start = 1
AddrFrm.Cls
PRINT EOL$ + EOL$ + EOL$ + EOL$ + EOL$
PRINT SPACE$(40); MID$(TheLine, start,
   INSTR(start, TheLine, EOL$) - start)
start = INSTR(start, TheLine, EOL$) + 2
PRINT SPACE$(40); MID$(TheLine, start,
   INSTR(start, TheLine, EOL$) - start)
start = INSTR(start, TheLine, EOL$) + 2
PRINT SPACE$(40); RIGHT$(TheLine, LEN(TheLine) - start + 1
AddrFrm.PrintForm
AddrBox.Show
END SUB
```

This procedure uses the end-of-line character EOL$, which was given a value in the Form_Load procedure and passed to this procedure through the declarations placed in the form's module-level section. The procedure then initializes the variable start, and clears the form. The first PRINT statement prints five end-of-line characters to move the print location down five lines. The subsequent PRINT statements then use the SPACE$() function to move the print location right by 40 characters.

The second PRINT statement contains the MID$() function, which extracts the first line of the address stored in TheLine. TheLine was passed to AddrFrm from AddrBox by the COMMON SHARED statement in the module-level section. The number of characters to extract is determined with the INSTR() function, which searches for the first end-of-line character after the character whose character number is stored in start. The character number is the number of a character counting from the leftmost character in a string.

Next, the value of start increased to equal the character number of the character following the end-of-line character, which was just found with the INSTR() function. Thus, start now points to the first character of the second line of the address stored in TheLine. The next PRINT statement extracts and prints the second line of the address, in the same manner as the previous PRINT statement. The value of start is increased again to point to the first character of the last line of the address. The last PRINT statement extracts and prints the last line of the address, this time with the RIGHT$() function. Finally, this procedure uses the PRINTFORM method to print the form on the printer (on your envelope) and then redisplays AddrBox so you can address a second envelope.

While developing this program, change the statement that contains the PRINTFORM method into a comment. Do this by placing REM or a single quotation mark (') at the beginning of the statement. This enables you to test your program without wasting paper. When you think you have the program right, change the comment back into a statement by removing REM or '.

One limitation of this procedure is that it must receive a three-line address. It does not allow addresses with two lines, four lines, or any number of lines other than three. Later in Chapter 5, "Using Numbers and Control Structures," where logical statements are discussed, this book discusses putting protections in programs.

14. Save the project as ADDR1.MAK.

15. Run the program. Type the address for your letter in the text box on AddrBox. When you're ready, insert an envelope in your printer (or leave the paper in it if you just want to experiment), and click AddrFrm.

Your address and return address now should be printed on the envelope.

Using INPUTBOX$

In the envelope-addressing program, you created a small form to use when inputting the address to be printed on the envelope. In effect, you created an input box. The INPUTBOX$ function performs a similar function, although you can input only one line of text at a time. The syntax of the function is

```
INPUTBOX$(prompt$[,title$[,default$[,xpos%,ypos%]]])
```

Here, $xpos\%, ypos\%$ is the location of the top-left corner of the input box, $default\$$ is a default string of text placed in the box, $title\$$ is a string to be used as the title of the box, and $prompt\$$ is a string of text describing what you're supposed to do with the box. When you execute this function, it presents the user with an input box with the specified prompts, titles, and OK and Cancel buttons. When you click OK, the function returns what you typed in the box.

The Envelope Addresser (Version 2)

You can modify the envelope addresser to use an INPUTBOX$ to get the address. To do so, follow these steps:

1. Execute the **New Project** command of the **File** menu.

2. Execute the **Add File** command of the **File** menu and select ADDR12.FRM.

3. Execute the **Save File As** command of the **File** menu and use the filename ADDR2.FRM.

4. Execute the **Save Project** command of the **File** menu and use the filename ADDR2.MAK.

5. Press the Code button on the Project window and select the
   Form_Click procedure. Change the procedure to

```
SUB Form_Click ()
AddrFrm.Cls
PRINT EOL$ + EOL$ + EOL$ + EOL$ + EOL$
PRINT SPACE$(40); INPUTBOX$("Name", "Mailing Address")
PRINT SPACE$(40); INPUTBOX$("Address" , "Mailing Address")
PRINT SPACE$(40); INPUTBOX$("City, State and Zip" ,
   "Mailing Address")
AddrFrm.PrintForm
END SUB
```

Here you first replace the MID$() function with an INPUTBOX$, with
the string Name as the prompt and the string Mailing Address as the
box title (see Figure 4.7). When you run this program, what the
user types into the input box is printed immediately on AddrFrm
before moving to the next line of the address. The second and
third lines of the address are done the same way, then the procedure prints the form using the PRINTFORM method.

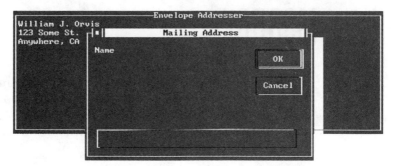

Figure 4.7. *The first Input box requesting the name.*

6. Press the Code button again and select the module-level code.
   Check whether the Programming Environment has automatically
   inserted the following statement (called a *metacommand*):

```
'  $FORM ADDR11.FRM
```

If it has, delete that line. This line was inserted as part of version 2
of the envelope addresser to give access to the other form in a
compiled version of this code. This version of the code does not
have that form, so to avoid confusing the compiler, you need to

remove the line. Metacommands are special compiler directives that tell the compiler where to look for values accessed by a program. In most cases, Visual Basic handles this automatically. Note that the metacommand is inserted as a comment (the leading single quote) so it will have no effect on how the code runs.

7. Save the changes with the Save Project command of the File menu.

8. Run the program, and click the form. The input box shown in Figure 4.7 appears. Type the name and press Enter.

9. After you press Enter, a similar input box appears. Type the address in the Input box.

10. After you press Enter, a third similar input box appears. Type the city and state and press Enter.

At this point, AddrFrm is filled out and is automatically printed on the printer.

Using MSGBOX

If you simply want to send a message to the user rather than requesting input, you can use the MSGBOX function. A message box is similar to an input box, except that there is no place to type a value. With a message box, the only input you can get from users is which button they pressed. The syntax of the MSGBOX function is

```
MSGBOX(msg$[,type[,title$]])
```

in which *msg$* is the message to be shown, *type* is a number indicating the number and type of buttons on the box (see Chapter 15, "Command Reference," for a complete list), and *title$* is a string title for the box. If you omit *type*, a simple message box with a single OK button is used. | The function returns a number indicating which button the user pressed. You can also write MSGBOX as a statement (by omitting the parentheses), but in that case nothing is returned.

Add this to the envelope addresser program so the program pauses before printing and the user has time to insert the envelope in the printer. Create version 2B of the envelope addresser by performing the following steps:

1. Execute the New Project command of the File menu.

2. Execute the Add File command of the File menu and select ADDR2.FRM.

3. Execute the Save File **As** command of the File menu and use the filename ADDR2B.FRM.

4. Execute the Save Project command of the File menu and use the filename ADDR2B.MAK.

5. Press the Code button on the Project window and select the Form_Click procedure. Change the procedure to

```
SUB Form_Click ()
Form2.Cls
PRINT EOL$ + EOL$ + EOL$ + EOL$ + EOL$
PRINT SPACE$(40); INPUTBOX$("Name", "Mailing Address")
PRINT SPACE$(40); INPUTBOX$("Address", "Mailing Address")
PRINT SPACE$(40); INPUTBOX$("City and State", "Mailing Ad-
dress")
MSGBOX ("Insert an envelope in the printer and click OK")
AddrFrm.PrintForm
END SUB
```

6. Run the program again. After you enter the city and state, the message box shown in Figure 4.8 appears.

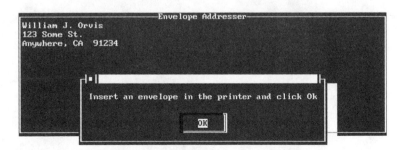

Figure 4.8. Using a message box for a pause in the envelope addresser.

7. End the program. Save the project by executing Save Project of the File menu.

What You Have Learned

Now you know the fundamentals about strings and string functions. As you have seen, strings are important in Visual Basic because all communication with the user is done with them. Keyboard input starts as a string, which then is turned into numbers and commands. Output to the screen or printer can start as numbers, but must be converted to strings to be printed. In this chapter you learned how to

- Define variables as storage locations for information

- Examine the scope of variables

- Define strings and string variables

- Create string formulas

- Manipulate strings by using the string functions

- Use Input and Message boxes

- Create an envelope addresser

5

Using Numbers and Control Structures

In most computer language books, numeric variables are discussed first and strings are mentioned almost as an afterthought. However, in this book about Visual Basic, I have reversed that order and placed string variables first in a chapter of their own, because they play such an important part in communicating with the user. Now that you know the fundamentals about strings, it's time to look at the numeric types. In addition, this chapter examines control structures that use the values of numeric types and strings to control the order of execution of a program.

In This Chapter

This chapter describes numeric variables and control structures. Numeric variables are variables that contain a number rather than a string of characters. Although you can only display or store strings, you can perform real numeric operations with numeric variables. In addition, control structures make it possible to examine the value of a variable and alter the order of execution of a program based on that value. In this chapter you learn to

- Compare the different numeric types
- Examine integers
- Examine floating-point numbers
- Examine currency format
- Define numeric variables
- Create formulas using numeric variables
- Examine array variables
- Examine control arrays
- Create logical formulas
- Control program flow with loops and logical variables

The Numeric Types of Visual Basic

There are six different data types in Visual Basic: five numeric types—INTEGER, LONG, SINGLE, DOUBLE, and CURRENCY—and the String type. I discussed the String data type in the previous chapter. INTEGER and LONG data types are used for storing whole numbers (numbers with no fractional parts). SINGLE and DOUBLE data types are used for storing real numbers (numbers with fractional parts). CURRENCY is a special data type designed to do calculations with decimal numbers rather than binary numbers.

This data type is used to eliminate the round-off errors caused by converting binary numbers to decimal notation. Table 5.1 lists the data types available in Visual Basic and describes their properties.

Table 5.1. Data types in Visual Basic.

Type	Preface Character	Memory Usage	Range	Description
INTEGER	%	2 bytes	–32,768 to 32,767	Two-byte integer.
LONG	&	4 bytes	–2,147,483,648 to 2,147,483,647	Four-byte integer.
SINGLE	!	4 bytes	–3.37E–38 to 3.37E+38	Single-precision floating-point number. This is the default for unspecified variables.
DOUBLE	#	8 bytes	–1.67D–308 to 1.67D+308	Double-precision floating-point number.
CURRENCY	@	8 bytes	–9.22E+14 to 9.22E14	Fixed-point number with two digits after the decimal. Math is done in decimal to eliminate round-off errors when convert ing from binary to decimal.
String	$	1 byte + 1 byte per character		String of characters.

5

Integers

The INTEGER and LONG data types represent whole numbers only. They cannot be used to represent fractions. As a result, they take less storage space than floating-point numbers. Mathematical operations that involve INTEGER and LONG types are much faster than those involving floating-point numbers. Use INTEGER data types when you know you do not have a fractional number. Use LONG data types when you have to store values larger than those allowed by the INTEGER data type.

> You might wonder why the limits in Table 5.1 are such odd numbers. Why should a type have a limit of 32,767 rather than a nice round number like 33,000? The fact is they *are* nice round numbers—in binary. The INTEGER data type is stored in two bytes (16 bits) of memory. The first bit is used as the sign bit (+ or -), and the rest represent the number in binary notation. The largest number that a sequence of n bits can represent is 2^n, which in this case is $2^{15} = 32,767$.

Floating-Point Numbers

Single- and double-precision floating-point numbers are used to represent real numbers (numbers with fractional parts). The single-precision floating-point number is the default numeric type for variables that are not defined with the prefix characters or with COMMON, DIM, or CONST statements. Single-precision numbers have about 7-digit precision, whereas double-precision numbers have about 15-digit precision. The *precision* of a data type is its capability to store a certain number of digits. If you try to store a number with more digits than the precision allows, the extra digits are lost. The number of digits of precision are approximate because the binary numbers stored in a variable do not convert into an even number of decimal digits.

On input and output, large floating-point numbers are expressed in E or D format as

```
1.94E+04 = 19,400.
9.2279E-28 = 0.00000000000000000000000000092279
0.3141592653589793D+01 = 3.141592653589793
```

in which E represents the single-precision floating-point, D is the double-precision floating-point, and the numbers following the E or D are the powers of 10 used to multiply the number on the left.

Currency

The CURRENCY numeric type is a fixed-point type used to calculate money values. In most cases, calculations are done in binary. The result is converted to decimal when it is printed or displayed on the screen. In the conversion process, round-off errors often are caused by the fact that some decimal numbers cannot be represented exactly in binary. As a result, you often get results such as 0.99999 rather than 1.00. In many cases, this is no problem. However, if you're dealing with money, you usually want the results to be exact to the penny. A number like 0.99999 is not acceptable when 1.00 is expected. The CURRENCY numeric type takes care of this by doing calculations in decimal rather than in binary, albeit decimal calculations are somewhat slower than binary calculations. CURRENCY type numbers have 14-digit precision.

Defining Numeric Variables

Numeric variables are defined in the same manner as the String data type. Moreover, all the arguments about the range of a variable apply equally to numeric types. For example, the following statements define the numeric variables Width, Account, RoadLen, and Counter:

```
COMMON Width AS SINGLE
DIM Account AS CURRENCY
DIM RoadLen AS DOUBLE, Counter AS INTEGER
```

5

In addition, you can use the variable prefix characters listed in Table 5.1 to define the type of any local variable, or to override the type of a global variable.

One defining statement you have not looked at so far is the CONST statement. You use the CONST statement anywhere you want to give a constant value a name. This is different than defining a variable and assigning it a value, because once defined, the value of a constant cannot be changed. The syntax of the CONST statement is

```
CONST variable = value [,variable = value ...]
```

Here, *variable* is the name of the constant, and *value* is the value to assign to it. The value of *value* can consist of simple numbers, other constants, or a simple formula of numbers and constants using any of the operators except those for exponentiation and concatenation. A *value* formula cannot include any functions. The numeric type of *variable* is determined either by the value assigned to it or by a variable prefix character. Strings also can be constants. However, as I mentioned previously, they cannot be concatenated, and you cannot use the CHR$() function to insert carriage returns or line feeds in your constant string. For example:

```
CONST RED = 4
```

defines the constant RED as the value of the color attribute for the red color. The constant then is used in the different procedures of the program rather than the numeric value, making the procedures much more readable.

Using Arrays

An array isn't actually a different numeric type. It is an indexed group of variables of the same type that can be referenced as a single object. An array variable must be defined with a SHARED or DIM statement; it cannot be defined in a COMMON statement. The syntax is

```
DIM ArrayName([lower TO] upper[,[lower TO] upper])[ AS type]
```

Here, each set of *lower* and *upper* is a dimension of the array, with *lower* as the lower limit of the index and *upper* as the upper limit. If you leave out the lower limit, its default value is 0. The range of array limits is the same as the range of the integer data type (–32,768 to –32,767). The maximum number of dimensions for a single array is 60. For example:

```
DIM TaxRate(5)
```

```
DIM CostTable(2,5 To 8)
```

The first example defines `TaxRate` as a one-dimensional array variable with five elements. Each element is accessed by placing an index within the parentheses. The value of the index then identifies the array element to be used. For example, the elements of `TaxRate` are

```
TaxRate(0)
```

```
TaxRate(1)
```

```
TaxRate(2)
```

```
TaxRate(3)
```

```
TaxRate(4)
```

```
TaxRate(5)
```

The second example, `CostTable(2,5 to 8)`, defines a two-dimensional, three-cell-by-three-cell array named `CostTable`. A two dimensional array is like the two-dimensional grid of cells in a spreadsheet. The first number is the row index, and the second is the column. The array elements are accessed as

```
CostTable(0,5) CostTable(0,6) CostTable(0,7)
CostTable(1,5) CostTable(1,6) CostTable(1,7)
CostTable(2,5) CostTable(2,6) CostTable(2,7)
```

You can imagine a three-dimensional array as a cube of cells with a row, column, and depth index. Higher-dimensional arrays than these are a little difficult to imagine, but they occasionally are useful.

Arrays are used for storing large blocks of similar data. For example, imagine you're working on your super stock estimator, which needs the average daily value of a stock over several months. You don't want to create a program with several hundred variables to hold all these values (`Day1`, `Day2`, `Day3`, ...). Instead, create a single array variable to hold them, such as `Day(Index1)`. Then the value of `Index1` selects the value of the stock for any specific day.

You can use this process for three different stocks as well; just create a two-dimensional array with three elements on one direction and a few hundred in the other. An example is Day(1 To 300, 1 To 3), with the values retrieved with

```
Day(Day_Index,Stock_Index)
```

where Day_Index selects the day and Stock_Index selects the stock. If you want to store the high and low values as well as the average, add another dimension to the array when you define it, such as

```
Day(1 To 300, 1 To 3, 1 To 3)
```

then access the elements with

```
Day(Day_Index,Stock_Index,HLA_Index)
```

where Day_Index selects the day, Stock_Index selects the stock and HLA_Index selects high, low, or average.

Inputting Numbers

Chapter 4, "Using Strings," explained how to input strings of text from the user. But what about inputting numbers? You get numbers from the user the same way you get strings. In fact, you input the number as a string, using the methods of the previous chapter, and then convert it into a number. You convert strings into numbers by using the VAL() function, which has the syntax

```
VAL(string$)
```

Here, *string$* is any string representation of a number. The string can have leading whitespace (spaces, tabs, and line feeds). It cannot, however, have nonnumeric leading characters. The function converts the numeric characters into numbers. The function continues until it encounters a character it cannot convert; then it stops. For example:

```
VAL("     456abs") = 456
VAL("456 789") = 456
VAL("a345") = 0
VAL(" 0 ") = 0
```

As you can see by the previous two examples, you must be careful what strings you give to the VAL() function. A string with a mistyped leading character—in this example, it's a—causes the result to be 0, even when the rest of the string contains a number. No error is generated if the function can't find a number in a string.

Displaying Numbers

Again, numbers are displayed in the same manner as strings. They are converted to a string first. Then the string is either printed or displayed in a label or text box. The simplest routine for converting numbers to text is the STR$() function. The STR$() function takes a number as an argument and converts it into a string. The format of the string is the simplest format that can display the full precision of the number. If you want the number formatted in a specific format, use the FORMAT$() function. The syntaxes of these functions are

STR$(*number*)

FORMAT$(*number*[,*format-string$*])

in which *number* is the value to be converted to a string and *format-string$* is a formatting string that controls how the string is converted. In the formatting string

- Place zeros or pound signs (0 or #) where you want the digits of the number to go. If you use pound signs, the space in the output string of the FORMAT$() function is reserved for a number. If you use zeros rather than pound signs, leading and trailing zeros are included at those positions, if necessary.

- Insert commas and the decimal point where you want them.

- Insert +, -, $, (,), and spaces in the string, as desired; these characters are included in the output where they were placed in the formatting string.

- Specific formatting strings exist for dates and times. See Chapter 15, "Command Reference," for a complete list.

- To insert any other characters in the output, surround them with double quotation marks (use CHR$(34), not "). For example:

5

```
ANumber = 1234.567
STR$(ANumber) = " 1234.567"
FORMAT$(ANumber,"#####.") = "1235."
FORMAT$(ANumber,CHR$(34)+"Balance = "+CHR$(34)+"$00000.00") =
    "Balance = $01234.57"
FORMAT$(ANumber,"##.##") = "1234.57"
ANumber2 = 0.123
FORMAT$(ANumber2,"##.#####") = ".123"
FORMAT$(ANumber2,"00.#####") = "00.123"
```

Users of other versions of BASIC should recognize the formatting capabilities of the `PRINT USING` statement contained in the `FORMAT$()` function. Visual Basic for MS-DOS includes the `PRINT USING` statement, but its use is not compatible with Visual Basic for Windows.

Calculating Mathematical Formulas

Mathematical formulas in Visual Basic look much like the equivalent algebraic formula for the same calculation. In other words, they are assignment statements such as those discussed for strings, with a numerical variable on the left and a formula that evaluates to a numeric result on the right. Visual Basic has a complete set of operators and mathematical functions to use when constructing a mathematical formula.

Arithmetic Operators

The arithmetic operators available in Visual Basic are listed in Table 5.2. They include the standard set of addition, subtraction, multiplication, division, and powers (such as 10^4), as well as modulus arithmetic and integer division. The precedence of the operators tells you which operation is done first in an expression involving more than one operator.

Table 5.2. The Visual Basic arithmetic operators and precedences.

Operator	Operation	Precedence
^	Power	1
–	Negation (unary operation)	2
*	Multiplication	3
/	Division	3
\	Integer division	4
MOD	Modulus	5
+	Addition	6
–	Subtraction	6

Addition, subtraction, multiplication, and powers operate, as you would expect, in the algebraic sense. The modulus operator is defined as the remainder of an integer division. The operands are rounded to integers first. Then the modulus operation is performed. For example, if you had 6.9 MOD 2, 6.9 would be rounded to 7 and then divided by 2. The remainder (the MOD) would be 1. The integer division operator also rounds the operands to integers, performs a normal division operation, and then truncates the result to an integer. For example, if you had instead specified 6.9\2, 6.9 again would be rounded to 7, then divided by 2. The answer would be 2. Table 5.3 shows more examples.

Table 5.3. Modulus and integer division.

Modulus Division	Integer Division
5 MOD 3 = 2	5\3 = 1
–5 MOD 3 = –2	–5\3 = –1
5.8 MOD 3 = 0	5.8\3 = 2

As you can see, the modulus and integer division operators perform a complementary set of operations. The modulus operator most often is used to unwind cyclical events, such as the actual angle between two lines when it is specified as a number greater than 360 degrees. It also can be

used to determine the day of the week (or the year) when the number of days between now and then is greater than a week (or a year). For example, to find the day of the week 138 days from now you could use

```
138 MOD 7 = 5
```

If today is a Monday, 138 days from now would be Monday plus five days, or Saturday.

Relational Operators

The relational operators shown in Table 5.4 compare two values and return a logical result. If the relationship between the two values is the same as the one expressed by the operator, the expression returns True (–1), otherwise it returns False (0). All relational operators have the same precedence, so use parentheses to ensure the correct comparisons are done.

Table 5.4. The Visual Basic relational operators.

Operator	Operation
=	Equals
>	Greater than
<	Less than
<>	Not equal to
<=	Less than or equal to

Logical Operators

The logical operators shown in Table 5.5 apply a logical operation to one or two logical values, and return a logical value. In addition, if they are applied to numeric values rather than logical values, the operation is performed bit-by-bit to each bit in the numeric values. All logical operators have the same precedence, so use parentheses to ensure the operations are performed in the order you want. The logical operators are explained in more detail later in this chapter.

Table 5.5. The Visual Basic logical operators.

Operator	Operation
NOT	Negation
AND	Logical AND
OR	Logical OR
XOR	Logical exclusive OR
EQV	Logical equivalence
IMP	Logical implies

Precedence of the Operators

As I previously stated, the precedence of the operators tells you which operation is done first in an expression involving more than one operator. When the computer has a choice between two operations, the operation with the highest precedence is performed first. When two operations have the same precedence, they are evaluated left to right. Parentheses always override the precedence of operators, so use them to control the order of calculation. If you are unsure what the order is, use parentheses to specify the order in which you want the formula to be calculated. Inserting unnecessary parentheses won't hurt anything, and they ensure that the calculations are being done in the order you want. Some examples are

```
A * B^C + D

A*B + C

A*(B + C)
```

In the first example, the power, B^C, is done first. Then this result is multiplied by A and added to D. In the second example, the multiplication, A*B, is done first. Then the result is added to C. The third example uses parentheses to reverse the order of the second: the addition, (B + C), is done first. The result is then multiplied by A.

5

Numeric Functions

The numeric functions consist of arithmetic functions, trigonometric functions, and logarithms. Table 5.6 lists the numeric functions available in Visual Basic.

Table 5.6. The numeric functions in Visual Basic.

Function	*Result*
Arithmetic Functions	
ABS()	Absolute value
CCUR()	Convert to CURRENCY
CINT()	Convert to INTEGER
CDBL()	Convert to DOUBLE
CLNG()	Convert to LONG
CSNG()	Convert to SINGLE
FIX()	Truncate to an integer
INT()	Round to an integer
RANDOMIZE()	Initialize the random-number generator
RND()	Generate a random number
SGN()	The sign of the argument
SQR()	Square root
Trigonometric Functions	
SIN()	Sine
COS()	Cosine
TAN()	Tangent
ATN()	Arctangent
Logarithmic Functions	
EXP()	Exponential
LOG()	Natural logarithm

There are four functions for converting a floating-point number to an integer: CINT(), CLNG(), FIX(), and INT(). The first two, CINT() and CLNG(), force the result to be an INTEGER or LONG type by rounding the floating-point number to an integer. For example, CINT(6.8) equals the integer 7. FIX() forms an integer by truncating the fractional part of the floating-point number. INT() returns the largest integer that is less than or equal to the argument. For example:

```
CINT(4.7) = 5     CLNG(4.7) = 5    FIX(4.7) = 4     INT(4.7) = 4
CINT(4.3) = 4     CLNG(4.3) = 4    FIX(4.3) = 4     INT(4.3) = 4
CINT(-4.7) = -    CLNG(-4.7) = -5  FIX(-4.7) = -4   INT(-4.7) = -5
CINT(-4.3) = -4   CLNG(-4.3) = -4  FIX(-4.3) = -4   INT(-4.3) = -5
```

The RANDOMIZE() and RND() functions initialize and return random numbers. The numbers are not truly random, but are generated by a pseudo-random function. The RANDOMIZE function normally is executed inside a program to initialize the *seed* (starting number) of the random number generator. By setting the seed of that generator, you can either repeat a set of random numbers or give the generator a random starting place. If you execute RANDOMIZE with no argument, the random number generator uses the TIMER function to get a random starting point. If you use a numeric argument with RANDOMIZE, the generator uses it as the seed, and RND(1) returns the same set of numbers every time. A new random number is generated every time the RND() function is executed with a positive argument.

The available trigonometric functions are sine, cosine, tangent, and arctangent. Use these built-in functions and the well-known rules of trigonometry to calculate the rest of the common trigonometric and hyperbolic functions.

The logarithmic functions available in Visual Basic calculate the natural logarithm (base $e = 2.71828$) and the exponential (power of e). To calculate the common logarithm (base 10), use

```
LOG10(x) = LOG(x)/LOG(10)
```

Type Conversion

Because five different numeric types are available in Visual Basic (INTEGER, LONG, SINGLE, DOUBLE, and CURRENCY), some type of conversion must occur when you create a formula that contains different types. Before a

calculation takes place, Visual Basic converts all the values on the right side of the formula into the most precise numeric type before performing the actual calculations. For example, if a formula combines single-precision floating-point numbers and integer numbers, Visual Basic converts everything to single-precision floating-point before performing the calculation. After the result is calculated, it is converted to the type of the variable on the left side of the formula.

The Self-Paced Learning Program (Version 1)

My son is learning mathematics and needs to practice for his weekly tests. The following program automatically creates a test for him to use for practice:

1. Execute the **New Project** command of the **File** menu.

2. Execute the New **Form** command of the **File** menu and use the filename MATH1.FRM for the form.

3. Draw five labels (four characters by two characters) on Math1, as shown in Figure 5.1.

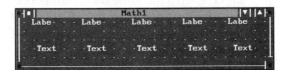

Figure 5.1. The initial form layout of the self-paced learning program.

4. Draw five text boxes (four characters by one character).

5. For each text box set the following. Note that `" "` stands for the empty or null string; therefore, delete the contents of the `Text` property as follows:

```
BorderStyle = 0 - None
Text = ""
```

6. Draw another five labels, each with a width of six characters and a height of one character. Use `BorderStyle = 1 - Single` to create the five horizontal lines between the labels and the text boxes, as shown in Figure 5.2.

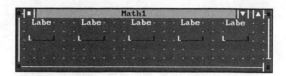

Figure 5.2. Modified form layout for the self-paced learning program.

7. Execute the Code command on the View menu to switch back to the Programming Environment. Select the module-level code window for the form and type the following:

```
DIM SHARED Probs(2, 5) AS SINGLE
```

This line defines the array Probs, which has three rows and six columns, as a single-precision array. The array holds two numbers for each addition problem. I define it here so the numbers are available for other routines to use. In the following step, don't forget that you can use the Copy and Paste commands on the Edit menu to make multiple copies of a line, then go back and edit the difference.

8. Execute the Event Procedures command on the Edit menu, and select the Form object and Load event. Type the following:

```
SUB Form_Load ()
REM Initialize the random number generator
RANDOMIZE
REM Define the end-of-line character
eol$ = CHR$(13) + CHR$(10)
REM Fill the probs array with 2 sets of 5 values
REM between 0 and 100
Probs(1, 1) = INT(RND(1) * 100)    'line 8
Probs(1, 2) = INT(RND(1) * 100)
Probs(1, 3) = INT(RND(1) * 100)
Probs(1, 4) = INT(RND(1) * 100)
Probs(1, 5) = INT(RND(1) * 100)
Probs(2, 1) = INT(RND(1) * 100)
Probs(2, 2) = INT(RND(1) * 100)
Probs(2, 3) = INT(RND(1) * 100)
Probs(2, 4) = INT(RND(1) * 100)
Probs(2, 5) = INT(RND(1) * 100)    'line 17
```

123

```
REM Insert the random numbers into the labels
Label1.Caption = FORMAT$(Probs(1, 1), " 00") + eol$
   + FORMAT$(Probs(2, 1), "+00")
Label2.Caption = FORMAT$(Probs(1, 2), " 00")
   + eol$ + FORMAT$(Probs(2, 2), "+00")
Label3.Caption = FORMAT$(Probs(1, 3), " 00")
   + eol$ + FORMAT$(Probs(2, 3), "+00")
Label4.Caption = FORMAT$(Probs(1, 4), " 00")
   + eol$ + FORMAT$(Probs(2, 4), "+00")
Label5.Caption = FORMAT$(Probs(1, 5), " 00")
   + eol$ + FORMAT$(Probs(2, 5), "+00")
END SUB
```

The second line of code contains a REM (remark) statement used to store remarks about what your code is doing. Visual Basic ignores anything following the REM keyword at the beginning of a line or a single quotation mark anywhere in a line. I use remarks of this type to mark lines of code as I describe them.

Use REM statements liberally in your code. They don't slow things down much, and they immensely improve the comprehensibility of your code. If you can remember every word you have ever written and why you wrote it, and your code is never going to be read by anyone else, you can forget about including REM statements. If, however, you're like me, you should use many REM statements to remind you what you have done and why.

Line 3 initializes the random number generator. Line 5 creates an end-of-line string, as you have done before. Lines 8 through 17 fill the array Probs() with random numbers between 0 and 100. The RND(1) function generates random numbers between 0 and 1. Multiplying by 100 extends the range of the numbers to 0 through 100. RANDOMIZE uses the random number generator and should be called at least once in a program that uses random numbers.

Lines 19 through 23 insert the numbers into the five Label boxes. First the numbers are converted to strings with the FORMAT$() function. Then those strings are combined with an end-of-line character and stored in the Caption property of the Label boxes.

There's a bug in the first version of Visual Basic that should be fixed in later versions. The # placeholder does not hold a place as it is supposed to do. Even if you use two #s in the FORMAT statement, numbers less than 10 won't align correctly with numbers greater than 10. Using the "00" format instead is a simple way to work around the bug. This format prints 01 through 09 for the numbers 1 through 9. Another option is to use the Alignment property to right-justify the text in the Label.

9. Run the program. A form like that shown in Figure 5.3 appears on the screen (although your numbers will be different). Type the first answer. Then press Tab to go to the next problem.

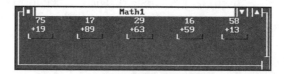

Figure 5.3. Running the self-paced learning program (version 1).

10. End the program by pressing Ctrl-Break, and save the project as MATH1.MAK.

My son now can take this math test by typing his answers in the text boxes below the problems. Maybe he'll think this is another computer game and spend hours practicing his math problems.

This test was purposely made into a five-problem test so it would be less confusing to explain. You can increase the number of problems to 10 or 20 easily by increasing the number of labels and text boxes, enlarging the Probs() array, and filling in the extra elements. Now you can exercise a young mind—or an old one, for that matter.

Using Loops and Control Arrays

If you look closely at the code in step 8 of the last example, you may notice two blocks of nearly identical statements. You shouldn't have to write the same statement repeatedly when the only difference is the value of an index. Loops are a good way to shorten the length of a program (and the amount of typing you have to do). They repeatedly execute a single block of statements so you can avoid including multiple copies of that block.

There are three types of loops in Visual Basic: FOR/NEXT, WHILE/WEND, and DO/LOOP. The FOR/NEXT loop is a counted loop, which executes a block of statements a fixed number of times. I use this type of loop most often. The WHILE/WEND loop executes a block of statements until some condition no longer is satisfied. The DO/LOOP loop executes a block of statements as long as a condition is satisfied, or until one condition becomes satisfied. The syntaxes of the loops are

```
FOR counter = start TO end [Step stepsize]
    block of statements
[EXIT FOR]
    block of statements
NEXT [counter[,counter]]

WHILE condition
    block of statements
WEND

DO [{WHILE¦UNTIL} condition]
    block of statements
[EXIT DO]
    block of statements
LOOP

DO
    block of statements
[EXIT DO]
    block of statements
LOOP [{WHILE¦UNTIL} condition]
```

Here, *counter* is a variable used to count the number of times the FOR/NEXT loop is iterated, *start* is the beginning value of the counter, *end* is the stopping value of the counter, and *stepsize* is the increment given to the counter at each step. If the STEP phrase is omitted, STEP 1 is assumed. For the WHILE/WEND and DO/LOOP loops, *condition* is a numeric formula that results in the value True (–1) or False (0). The WHILE and UNTIL keywords determine how the condition is used. WHILE continues executing the block until *condition* becomes False. UNTIL continues executing the block as long as *condition* is False. With the EXIT FOR and EXIT DO statements, you can terminate a loop prematurely and go on to the next statement after the NEXT or LOOP statement.

The Self-Paced Learning Program (Version 2)

A FOR/NEXT loop is made for the code in the self-paced learning program, because you want things done exactly two times in five places. The data used in the program is stored in an array, so the individual elements are accessible with an index value. To use a loop here, you also must be able to select one of the five text boxes by using an index. Do this by combining the text boxes into a single control array. A control array is one or more controls with the same name. Individual controls in the control array are accessed with an index, as is an array variable.

You create a control array by giving all the controls (text boxes in this case) the same CtlName and then setting the Index property to 1, 2, 3, and so on, to identify the individual control.

1. Execute the New Project command of the File menu.

2. Execute the Add File command of the File menu and select MATH1.FRM.

3. Execute the Save File **As** command of the File menu. Use the new filename MATH2.FRM.

4. Execute the Save Project command of the File menu and use the name MATH2.MAK.

5. Press the Form button on the Project window to switch to the Forms Designer.

6. Select the form and change the Caption property to Math2.

7. Select the Label1 box and set the Index property to 1.

8. Select the Label2 through Label5 labels, and set the CtlName property of each to Label1. Increment the value of the Index property of each label to 2, 3, 4, and 5.

9. Execute the Code command of the View menu to switch back to the Programming Environment. Select the Form object and the Load event, and change the code to

```
SUB Form_Load ()
REM Initialize the random number generator
RANDOMIZE
REM Define the end-of-line
eol$ = CHR$(13) + CHR$(10)
REM Fill the probs array with 2 sets of 5 values
REM between 0 and 100
FOR I = 1 TO 2        'line 8
  FOR J = 1 TO 5
    Probs(I, J) = INT(RND(1) * 100)
  NEXT J              'line 11
NEXT I
REM Insert the random numbers into the labels
FOR J = 1 TO 5        'line 14
Label1(J).Caption = FORMAT$(Probs(1, J), " 00")
+ eol$ + FORMAT$(Probs(2, J), "+00")
NEXT J
END SUB
```

10. Run the program. The results should be similar to those in Figure 5.3, but with different numbers.

As you can see, this is much simpler than the code in step 8 of the previous version of this program, but performs the same functions. Lines 8 and 9 start two nested FOR/NEXT loops that surround line 10. They're called *nested loops* because the loop for the counter J is within the loop for counter I. When line 8 is executed, I is set to 1. In line 9, J is set to 1. In line 10, Probs(1,1) is loaded. When the execution reaches line 11, the bottom of the J loop, it returns to line 9, where J is set to 2, and lines 10 and 11 are executed again. This continues until J equals 5, at which point the J loop is finished.

Execution now moves to line 12. Line 12 is the bottom of the I loop, so execution returns to line 8, where I is set to 2. Line 9 is executed again, starting up the J loop again to go through five more iterations. At this point, both the I loop and the J loop are done, so execution moves to line 14, where another J loop is started to load the Caption properties of the labels. The five labels now are a control array of labels named Label1(). Inserting an integer between the parentheses selects the particular label to access.

Something else you should notice in this piece of code is the use of indentation. The indentation is purely for visual delineation of the blocks of code associated with the FOR/NEXT loops. It has no effect on the actual execution of the code, although it does make the code much more readable. Everything between the FOR I = ... and the NEXT I statements is indented two spaces, which makes it easy to see the block iterated by that loop. The statements between the FOR J = ... and the NEXT J statements are indented an additional two spaces. Again, the use of indentation has no effect on the operation of the code, but it greatly improves the readability.

When modifying a project and saving it with a new name, be sure to save the forms and modules first with the File Save As command of the File menu, then save the Project with the Save Project command. If you save the project first, it is saved with the form and module names of the previous version. Be sure to save everything before you modify it, or you may end up modifying the previous version of your program rather than the current version. To save a project with a new name:

1. Save the old project with the Save Project command of the File menu.

2. Execute the New Project command of the File menu.

3. Execute the Add File command of the File menu for each of the forms and modules that need to be attached to this project.

4. Select a form or module in the Project window and execute the File Save As command of the File menu to save the form or module with a new name.

5. Continue this process until you have saved all the forms and modules.

6. Execute Save Project command of the File menu to save the project with a new name.

Creating Logical Formulas

Logical formulas (or *conditionals*) are formulas that have a numerical result of –1 (True) or 0 (False). You create them by relating two formulas with one of the relational operators from Table 5.5. If the two formulas fit the relation specified by the operator, the value of the formula is True. Otherwise, the value of the formula is False. For example:

```
(3 > 5) = 0 (False)
(3 + 1 = 4) = -1 (True)
A = 4: B = 5: (A <= B) = -1 (True)
```

Logical formulas are the conditions used to determine when to terminate the DO/LOOP and WHILE/WEND loops previously discussed. They also are the arguments of the IF THEN ELSE branching statements I discuss in the next section. You use logical formulas in a program to make decisions that control what the program does.

The logical operators listed in Table 5.5 have two functions. Most commonly, they're used to connect two or more logical formulas into a more complicated logical formula. A second function is to perform bitwise operations on one or two numbers. A bitwise operation on one number is an operation applied to each bit in that number as if each bit were a separate entity. Bitwise operations are used only for specialized applications that must access the individual bits in a computer word. For example, if you want to know whether the fourth bit in an integer is 0 or 1, create a mask with only that bit set to 1, then AND it with the integer. If the result is 0, the bit is 0; otherwise the bit is 1.

Table 5.7 is a *truth table* for the logical operators. A truth table shows the result for all combinations of True and False inputs.

- The NOT operator switches True to False and False to True.
- The AND operator returns True only when both operands are true.
- The OR operator returns True when either of the operands is true.
- XOR is the exclusive OR operator, which returns True when either of the operands is true, but not both.

- EQV is the equivalence operator, which returns True whenever both operands are the same.

- IMP is the implies operator, which always returns True, except when the first operand is true and the second is false. For example:

```
(3 > 2) AND (5 <= 7) = True
(2 = 2) XOR (5 > 3) = False
```

Table 5.7. Truth table of the logical operators T = True (–1), F = False (0).

A	*B*	NOT *A*	*A* AND *B*	*A* OR *B*	*A* XOR *B*	*A* EQV *B*	*A* IMP *B*
T	T	F	T	T	F	T	T
T	F	F	F	T	T	F	F
F	T	T	F	T	T	F	T
F	F	T	F	F	F	T	T

Logical operators all have the same precedence, so you must use parentheses to control the order of evaluation. Otherwise, you might not get the results you expect. For example, the only difference in the following statements is the placement of parentheses; however, each statement gives a different result.

```
False AND True OR True = True

(False AND True) OR True = True

False AND (True OR True) = False
```

Branching—Controlling Program Flow

The programs created in this book so far are relatively linear in function. Every step in the program is executed in order from the first to the last. *Branching* changes the order in which statements are executed.

The simplest branch is the unconditional GOTO. The GOTO statement has the following syntax:

```
GOTO label
```

in which *label* is a line label or number. In older versions of BASIC, all lines in a program had to be numbered. Visual Basic supports this numbering but does not require it. Modern programming languages use line labels only on those lines that require special access. A label consists of an alphabetic name that follows the same rules as a variable name and ends with a colon. When a GOTO statement is executed, execution branches immediately to the statement following the label. Although the GOTO statement is extremely powerful, it's better programming practice not to use it. A program with many GOTO statements rapidly becomes unmanageable. You should use structured branches, such as the loops or IF THEN ELSE statements, whenever possible.

A *conditional branch* uses a logical formula to decide which block of code to execute. The most heavily used conditional branch statement is the IF THEN ELSE statement, which examines a condition and branches accordingly. The IF THEN ELSE statement has two forms: a simple, one-line form and the block IF statement. The syntax of the simple IF statement is

```
IF condition THEN iftrue [ELSE iffalse]
```

Here, *condition* is a logical formula that results in a True (–1) or False (0) value, and *iftrue* and *iffalse* are statements that are executed if *condition* is True or False. *iftrue* and *iffalse* are Visual Basic statements, such as assignment or GOTO statements.

The preferred form of the IF THEN ELSE statement is the block IF. In a block IF statement, the statements comprising the THEN and ELSE clauses are visually separated from the IF statement, making it simpler to see what's going on. The syntax of the block IF statement is

```
IF condition1 THEN
  block of statements
[ELSEIF condition2 THEN]
  block of statements
[ELSE]
  block of statements
END IF
```

Here, if *condition1* is True, the block of statements between the IF and ELSEIF statements is executed and control passes to the statement after the END IF statement. If *condition1* is False, control passes to the first ELSEIF statement, where *condition2* is tested. If *condition2* is True, the statements between the ELSEIF statement and the ELSE statement are executed.

There can be multiple ELSEIF statements to test for different conditions. Visual Basic tests each one in turn until it finds one with a True condition. If none of the conditions are True, control passes to the ELSE statement and the block of statements between the ELSE and END IF statements is executed.

The Self-Paced Learning Program (Version 3)

Something that's missing from the self-paced learning program is a test of the answers. The computer can calculate the correct answers for the math problems easily and compare them to the answers my son types. In addition, the computer can keep track of the number of correct and incorrect answers and produce a percentage score at the end of the test. This is a modification of version 2 of the self-paced learning program.

1. Execute the New Project command of the File menu.

2. Execute the Add File command of the File menu and select MATH2.FRM as the file.

3. Execute the Save File **As** command of the File menu and save it as MATH3.FRM.

4. Execute the Save Project command of the File menu and use the filename MATH3.MAK.

5. Press the Form button on the Project window to switch to the Forms Designer.

6. Select the Text1 text box and set the Index property to 1 to start a control array.

7. Select Text2 through Text5 and set the CtlName properties of each to Text1 to create the rest of the control array. In subsequent text boxes, set the Index property to 2, 3, 4, and 5 respectively.

8. Enlarge the form as shown in Figure 5.4. Add three labels (seven characters by one character) and set their Caption properties to Wrong, Right, and Score.

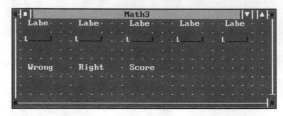

Figure 5.4. *Layout for the self-paced learning program (version 3).*

9. Below the word Wrong, place a label (seven characters by one character); set CtlName to NumWrong and Caption to "".

10. Below the word Right, place a label (seven characters by one character); set CtlName to NumRight and Caption to "".

11. Below the word Score, place a label (seven characters by one character); set CtlName to Score and Caption to "".

12. Execute the **Code** command of the **View** menu to switch back to the Programming Environment. Select the module level code window of the form and change it to

```
CONST NumProbs = 5
DIM SHARED Probs(2, NumProbs) AS SINGLE
DIM SHARED Answer(NumProbs) AS SINGLE
DIM SHARED GotIt(NumProbs) AS INTEGER
CONST True = -1
CONST False = 0
CONST LtRed = 12
CONST White = 7      'actually light gray
CONST Black = 0
```

I added some arrays and defined six constants in the module-level code. NumProbs is the number of problems on the form. I could use the numeral 5 in the program, but using the variable name makes the code more readable. Using the variable also makes it simpler to expand the program to more problems. True and False are given their default values here so I can use the words rather than the numbers. LtRed is defined as the color attribute for light red. I also defined White (which actually looks light gray) and Black.

13. Press the Code button on the Project window and select the Form_Load event. Change it to read as follows:

```
SUB Form_Load ()
REM Initialize the random number generator
RANDOMIZE
REM Define the end-of-line character
eol$ = CHR$(13) + CHR$(10)
REM Fill the probs array with 2 sets of 5 values
REM between 0 and 100
FOR I = 1 TO 2
  FOR J = 1 TO NumProbs
    Probs(I, J) = INT(RND(1) * 100)
  NEXT J
  NEXT I
REM Insert the random numbers into the labels
REM and calculate the answers
FOR J = 1 TO NumProbs
  Label1(J).Caption = FORMAT$(Probs(1, J), " 00")
  + eol$ + FORMAT$(Probs(2, J), "+00")
  Answer(J) = Probs(1, J) + Probs(2, J)        'added line
NEXT J
END SUB
```

Here I added one line (marked 'added line) near the end of the procedure to calculate the answers for each of the displayed problems.

14. Execute the Event Procedures command on the Edit menu. Select the Text1 object and the KeyPress event and type the following:

```
SUB Text1_KeyPress (Index AS INTEGER, KeyAscii AS INTEGER)
REM Test for a return, if not, go on
IF KeyAscii <> 13 THEN GOTO SkipIt      'line 3

REM Block one
REM test for right or wrong answer when CR is pressed
IF Text1(Index).text = "" THEN          'line 7
  REM No value typed, do nothing
  GOTO SkipIt
ELSEIF Val(Text1(Index).text) = Answer(Index) THEN
  REM solution correct
  GotIt(Index) = True
ELSE                                    'line 13
  REM solution wrong
  GotIt(Index) = False
END IF
```

```
REM Block 2
REM When the last problem is done, score the test.
IF Index = NumProbs THEN                    'line 20
  REM Calculate scores
  NRight = 0
  NWrong = 0
  FOR I = 1 TO NumProbs
    IF GotIt(I) = True THEN
      NRight = NRight + 1
      Text1(I).ForeColor = Black
      Text1(I).BackColor = White
    ELSE
      NWrong = NWrong + 1
      Text1(I).ForeColor = LtRed
      Text1(I).BackColor = Black
    END IF
  NEXT I
  NumRight.Caption = STR$(NRight)      'line 35
  NumWrong.Caption = STR$(NWrong)
  Score.Caption = FORMAT$(NRight / NumProbs, "##%")
ELSE
  Text1(Index + 1).SetFocus            'line 39
END IF

SkipIt:
ENDSUB
```

The Text1_Keypress event automatically is passed two values: Index
and KeyAscii. Index is the value of the Index property of the control in the
control array that had the event. KeyAscii is the ASCII code of the key that
was pressed. The user types the answer in a text box and presses Enter.
When Enter is pressed, the code checks the answer and moves the focus to
the next problem. When the last problem is done, the program counts the
right and wrong answers, calculates the score, and displays the results.

The *focus* in Visual Basic refers to the control or form that currently
is active. The control or form currently with the focus receives any events
generated by the keyboard or mouse. If a command button is active,
pressing Enter activates that command button; if a text box has the focus,
anything you type appears in that text box. To move the focus to a different
object on a form, press the Tab key. To move the focus to the menu bar,

press the Alt key and then use the arrow keys to move from menu item to menu item. Press Esc to move back to the form. To move the focus with code, use the SetFocus method. The syntax of SetFocus is

object.SetFocus

where *object* is the name of the form or control you want to receive the focus.

Line 3 tests the value of KeyAscii to see whether Enter (ASCII code 13) was pressed. If not, the code jumps to SkipIt and returns control to the text box. If Return was pressed, the procedure executes block one.

Block one is a block IF statement that checks for three different situations:

- First, in line 7, it checks for no value in the text box. This occurs if the user presses Enter without typing anything. If that happens, the GOTO statement in line 10 jumps to SkipIt, ignoring the improper Return.

- Next, it compares what the user typed with the value in the array Answers() to see whether the user got the answer right. If so, the array GotIt() is set to True for that problem.

- Lastly, if the user has answered wrong, the code jumps to line 13, which changes GotIt() to False.

Block two of the code now checks whether this is the last problem. If not, the focus moves to the next problem in line 39.

The code starting in line 22 counts the number of correct and incorrect answers by first zeroing the counters NRight and NWrong. The code then loops over each problem and, using another block IF statement, adds one to either NRight or NWrong. If the answer was correct, it sets the ForeColor and BackColor properties of the text box to Black and White, which amounts to no change in the colors. If the answer is wrong, the colors are changed to light red on black to make it easy to spot wrong answers.

Starting in line 35, the code inserts the number of right and wrong answers in the labels at the bottom of the form and calculates the percentage score. The FORMAT$() function and the percent field specifier are used to calculate and convert the fraction to text. The percent field specifier automatically multiplies the value it is converting by 100.

Save the project, run it, and try to answer a few problems. Your results should look like Figure 5.5 (with different numbers, of course). I purposely answered the second problem incorrectly to demonstrate what happens when the user misses a question.

```
┌─■│───────────────Math3───────────│▼││▲├┐
│   81        09        22        36        02   │
│  +74       +67       +04       +15       +88   │
│  L         L         L         L         L     │
│                                                │
│   155      ▕23 ▏      26        51        10    │
│                                                │
│  Wrong     Right     Score                     │
│                                                │
│   1         4        80%                        │
│                                                │
└────────────────────────────────────────────┘
```

Figure 5.5. *Running version 3 of the self-paced learning program.*

Although this is a simple, five-problem math test, you easily could include more problems by increasing the sizes of the arrays and adding more labels to the form.

> For a challenge, try changing the logic so the user gets more than one try per problem. Also, you could make the program tell the user whether the answer is correct as soon as it's typed. There are many variations, depending on what you want to do. A structure like this can be adapted to other forms of self-paced teaching, such as multiple-choice problems.

What You Have Learned

This chapter explained how to define and use numeric data types. In addition, you controlled program flow with loops and logical branches. You have learned

● About the different numeric types

● About the capabilities of integers, floating-point numbers, and currency type numbers

● How to define numeric variables

- How to create formulas using numeric variables
- About array variables
- About control arrays
- About logical formulas
- How to control program flow with loops and logical variables
- How to create a self-paced learning program

Using Controls

Everything placed on a form is a control. Even the label and text boxes are
controls because they not only display text, they also initiate actions when
they are changed or clicked. This chapter investigates the more traditional
controls: buttons, check boxes, and scroll bars. More complex controls
(such as menus) are discussed in later chapters.

In This Chapter

This chapter shows you the use of

● Command buttons

● Option buttons

● Check boxes

● Scroll bars

Using a Command Button to Initiate an Action

A command button is a standard push button, which you push or click to make something happen. You also can double-click a button or press a key while a button has the focus to initiate an action. You create a command button in the same manner as any other control: select the command button tool from the Toolbox window and draw the button on a form.

The Advanced Annuity Calculator

Creating an annuity calculator, with buttons to select the calculation to perform, is a good exercise in using command buttons. I realize that almost every book on programming calculates annuities as an example—and I'm going to do it, too. Although annuities are calculated using well-known but nasty little formulas, they are immensely useful in many home and business situations.

An annuity calculator enables you to deal with accounts that have periodic deposits or withdrawals and that grow or deplete at a specific interest rate. You can calculate what you owe the bank every month when you finance a house or car. Annuities also tell you how fast an investment grows in an interest-bearing account, or how much money you must put into an account now to have some specific amount later.

The advanced annuity calculator has five text boxes and five command buttons to calculate the interest rate, payment, number of periods, present value, and future value. It uses cash-flow conventions to determine the sign of the dollar values—that is, cash received is positive and cash paid out is negative. Whether a transaction is paid in or out depends on your point of view. If you're the bank, a car payment is positive; if you're the car buyer, the payment is negative. Be sure to pick your point of reference before using the calculator.

To calculate one of these five values, you must solve one of two equations for that value. The first (Equation 6.1) is used for all calculations in which IRate, the interest rate, is nonzero. The second (Equation 6.2) is used whenever IRate is zero.

$$PVal\ (1+IRate\ )^{NPer} +Pmt \left(\frac{(1+IRate\ )^{NPer} -1}{IRate} \right)+FVal\ =0$$

Equation 6.1. *Used if* IRate *is not equal to zero.*

$$PVal\ +Pmt\ *NPer +FVal\ =0$$

Equation 6.2. *Used if* IRate *is equal to zero.*

Here, IRate is the fractional interest rate per period (the fraction, not the percent), NPer is the number of payment periods, Pmt is the periodic payment, PVal is the present value—that is, the amount of money in the account now—and FVal is the future value, or the amount of money in the account at some future time. If you're dealing with a savings account in a bank, the payment rate probably is zero, the present value is your initial deposit, and the future value is what you will have after several years. If you're calculating a car loan, the present value is what you owe—and you want the future value to be zero, indicating a paid-off loan.

To create this calculator, you need five sets of formulas: solutions of the two annuity equations (6.1 and 6.2) for each of the values. The results of solving these two equations are one pair of equations for each value except the rate, and a *transcendental equation* for the rate. A transcendental equation is one for which an analytical solution does not exist. To solve it, use the iterative numerical method known as *successive approximations,* explained in a moment.

First, draw the user interface for the problem. The interface has five text boxes for inputting or outputting numerical results, and five command buttons to determine which value to calculate. Follow these initial steps:

1. Start a new project. Execute the **New Project** command of the **File** menu, then execute the New Form command on the File menu and use ANUT.FRM for the filename. Execute the Save Project command on the File menu and use ANUT.MAK as the project filename.

2. Select the form and adjust its size to 43 by 14 characters. Set its Caption property to **Advanced Annuity Calculator**.

3. Draw five text boxes on the form, as shown in Figure 6.1. The top three are 13 by 3 characters; the bottom two are 19 by 3 char-acters.

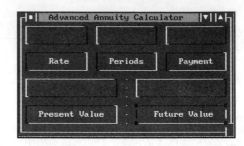

Figure 6.1. Layout of the form in the advanced annuity calculator.

4. Set the Text properties of all the text boxes to blank. Selecting the text boxes from left to right, top to bottom, set the CtrlName properties to **Rate**, **Per**, **Pay**, **PV**, and **FV**.

5. Below the five text boxes, draw five command buttons the same size as the text boxes.

6. Set the Caption properties of the five command buttons, left to right, to **Rate**, **Periods**, **Payment**, **Present Value**, and **Future Value**. Set the CtrlName properties, left to right, to **RateButton**, **PerButton**, **PayButton**, **PVButton**, and **FVButton**.

Now that the interface is drawn, define some global variables so they can be passed between procedures on the form. Here, five variables are defined to hold the numeric results. IRate is the interest rate, defined as a single-precision floating-point number. NPer is the number of periods, defined as an integer. Pmt, FVal, and PVal are the payment, present value, and future value, defined as double-precision, floating-point numbers. Double precision is needed here so that large numbers, like the mortgaged amount on a home, can be calculated accurately. The CURRENCY type does not work here; it appears that the intermediate values calculated in some of the formulas cause numeric overflow errors.

7. Execute the **C**ode command of the **V**iew menu to return to the Programming Environment. Open the form's top level (declarations) section and type

```
DIM SHARED IRate AS SINGLE, NPer AS INTEGER, Pmt AS DOUBLE
DIM SHARED FVal AS DOUBLE, PVal AS DOUBLE
```

Whenever a number is typed into one of the text boxes, you want to convert it to a number, and store it in the appropriate variable. Do this using the Change event procedures for each of the text boxes. The Change event occurs whenever the contents of a text box change.

8. Using the Event Procedures command of the Edit menu, create the following Change procedures for all five of the text boxes:

```
SUB Rate_Change ()
IRate = VAL(Rate.Text)
END SUB


SUB PV_Change ()
PVal = VAL(PV.Text)
END SUB


SUB Per_Change ()
NPer = VAL(Per.Text)
END SUB


SUB Pay_Change ()
Pmt = VAL(Pay.Text)
END SUB


SUB FV_Change ()
FVal = VAL(FV.Text)
END SUB
```

Now, if you solve the annuity equations for the number of periods, you get the following two equations (Equation 6.3 and Equation 6.4). These equations are to be calculated whenever the PerButton command button is pressed.

$$NPer = \frac{\text{Log}\left(\dfrac{Pmt - FVal * IRate}{Pmt + PVal * IRate}\right)}{\text{Log}(1 + IRate)}$$

Equation 6.3. *Used if* IRate *is not equal to zero.*

$$NPer = \frac{-(FVal + PVal)}{Pmt}$$

Equation 6.4. *Used if* IRate *is equal to zero.*

145

9. Execute the Event Procedures command of the Edit menu, select the `PerButton_Click` procedure, and type

```
SUB PerButton_Click ()
IF IRate <> 0 THEN
  NPer = LOG((Pmt - FVal * IRate) / (Pmt + PVal * IRate))
    / LOG(1 + IRate)
ELSE
  NPer = -(FVal + PVal) / Pmt
END IF
Per.Text = STR$(NPer)
END SUB
```

This procedure uses a block `IF` statement to select the equation to calculate, according to whether `IRate` is zero or not. If `IRate` isn't zero, the formula in line 3 is calculated; otherwise, the formula in line 5 is calculated. After the value of `NPer` is calculated, it's converted to text in line 7 and stored in the `Text` property of the `Per` text box. The Payment, Present Value, and Future Value buttons that follow are treated in the same way.

The formulas for the payment are shown in Equation 6.5 and Equation 6.6.

$$Pmt = \frac{IRate \; (PVal \; (1+IRate)^{NPer} + FVal \;)}{1 - (1+IRate)^{NPer}}$$

Equation 6.5. *Used if* `IRate` *is not equal to zero.*

$$Pmt = \frac{-(FVal + PVal \;)}{NPer}$$

Equation 6.6. *Used if* `IRate` *is equal to zero.*

10. Execute the Event Procedures command of the Edit menu, select the `PayButton_Click` procedure, and type

```
SUB PayButton_Click ()
IF IRate <> 0 THEN
  Pmt = IRate * (PVal * (1 + IRate) ^ NPer + FVal)
    / (1 - (1 + IRate) ^ NPer)
ELSE
  Pmt = -(FVal + PVal) / NPer
```

```
END IF
Pay.Text = FORMAT$(Pmt, "####.00")
END SUB
```

This is largely the same as in the PerButton_Click procedure, except that the conversion of the number Pmt into a string of text is accomplished with a FORMAT$() function. You could use dollar signs or commas in the formatting strings to make the numbers more readable, but the VAL() function won't be able to read them correctly if you do. This is because the VAL() function stops converting characters into numbers when it reaches a nonnumeric character—such as a dollar sign or comma.

Replace the VAL() function in these procedures with code that can convert a numeric text string containing dollar signs and commas into a numeric value, then use dollar signs and commas in the FORMAT$() function. Hint: Use the string functions to remove the dollar signs and commas, then use the VAL() function to convert the string into a number.

The PVButton, and the FVButton procedures are handled in the same manner as the PayButton. The equations for the present value and future value are shown in Equations 6.7, 6.8, 6.9, and 6.10.

$$PVal = \frac{-FVal - Pmt\left(\dfrac{(1+IRate)^{NPer}-1}{IRate}\right)}{(1+IRate)^{NPer}}$$

Equation 6.7. Used if IRate *is not equal to zero.*

$$PVal = -FVal - * NPer$$

Equation 6.8. Used if IRate *is equal to zero.*

$$FVal = -PVal(1+IRate)^{NPer} - Pmt\left(\frac{(1+IRate)^{NPer}-1}{IRate}\right)$$

Equation 6.9. Used if IRate *is not equal to zero.*

$$FVal = -PVal - Pmt * NPer$$

Equation 6.10. *Used if* IRate *is equal to zero.*

11. Execute the Event Procedures command of the Edit menu, select the PVButton_Click procedure, and type

```
SUB PVButton_Click ()
IF IRate <> 0 THEN
  PVal = -(FVal + Pmt * ((1 + IRate) ^ NPer - 1)
    / IRate) / ((1 + IRate) ^ NPer)
ELSE
  PVal = -FVal - Pmt * NPer
END IF
PV.Text = FORMAT$(PVal, "######.00")
END SUB
```

12. Execute the Event Procedures command of the Edit menu, select the FVButton_Click procedure, and type

```
SUB FVButton_Click ()
IF IRate <> 0 THEN
  FVal = -PVal * ((1 + IRate) ^ NPer)
    - Pmt * ((1 + IRate) ^ NPer - 1) / IRate
ELSE
  FVal = -PVal - Pmt * NPer
END IF
FV.Text = FORMAT$(FVal, "######.00")
END SUB
```

When you try to solve the annuity equations for the interest rate, you can't get an analytic solution. To solve this equation numerically, use a method known as *successive approximations*. A "method of successive approximations" might sound exotic and complicated, but it actually is quite simple. You guess a solution (the approximation), insert it in the right side of the equation, and use the result to make a second guess that's closer to the solution than the first guess. You do this over and over, getting closer and closer to the solution (*convergence*). You stop calculating when the solution is sufficiently accurate.

The equation is first solved so that IRate is on the left side of the equals sign and a function of IRate is on the right. Because there's more than one way to do this, the results may *diverge* (grow further apart) as you iterate if you choose the wrong approach. The simplest way to determine whether you have solved the equation correctly is to try it and see whether it converges to a solution. If it doesn't, try solving the equation a different way. Equation 6.11 is one such solution. Equation 6.12 is an analytic solution for the case where `Pmt` is zero.

$$IRate = \frac{Pmt\ (1 - (1 + IRate\ )^{NPer})}{PVal\ (1 + IRate\ )^{NPer} + FVal}$$

Equation 6.11. *Used if* `Pmt` *is not equal to zero.*

$$IRate = -1 + \left(-\frac{FVal}{PVal}\right)^{\frac{1}{NPer}}$$

Equation 6.12. *Used if* `Pmt` *is not equal to zero.*

In the next procedure, you solve for the interest rate using the method of successive approximations. First, guess a value of `IRate`, insert it in the right side of the equation, and calculate the result. Because this result should equal `IRate`, use it as the new approximation to the solution of the equation. Insert this new approximation on the right side of the equation again to produce yet another approximation to `IRate`. Continue this iteration until the solution converges—that is, until the value of `IRate` inserted into the equation equals the value calculated by inserting it. Actually, you could iterate forever without getting identical values, so continue iterating the equations until they differ by some small amount (tolerance, 0.001 in this case).

13. Execute the Event Procedures command of the Edit menu. Select the `RateButton_Click()` procedure and type

```
SUB RateButton_Click ()
DIM Denom AS DOUBLE
IF Pmt <> 0 THEN
  REM Give IRate an initial guess
  IRate = .5
  IRateOld = 0
  counter = 0
  REM Use the method of successive approximations
  REM to solve for the value of IRate
  REM Test for convergence and loop again if IRate isn't
  REM converged.
```

```
            DO WHILE Abs((IRate - IRateOld) / IRate) > .001    'line 12
              counter = counter + 1
              REM Quit if it didn't converge after 200 iterations
                IF counter > 200 THEN
↰                 MSGBOX "Problem didn't converge
                      after 200 iterations", 0
                  EXIT DO
                END IF
                IRateOld = IRate       'line 19
                Denom = PVal * (1 + IRateOld) ^ NPer + FVal
                IF Denom = 0 THEN
                  REM Go here if Denom is zero.
                  IRate = 0
↰                 MSGBOX "The interest rate is undefined
                      (divide by zero)", 0
                  EXIT DO
                ELSE
                  REM Use this equation if Pmt and Denom are not 0
                  IRate = Pmt * (1 - (1 + IRateOld) ^ NPer) / Denom
                END IF
              LOOP
            ELSE
              REM Use this equation if Pmt is 0.
              IRate = -1 + (-FVal / PVal) ^ (1 / NPer)       'line 32
            END IF
            Rate.Text = FORMAT$(IRate, "0.0000 ")
            END SUB
```

In this procedure, the first statement defines Denom, a double-precision, floating-point variable. Next, a block IF statement tests to check whether Pmt is zero. If it is, the alternate formula in line 33 is used to calculate the rate. If Pmt is not zero, the next four lines select the initial guess for IRate and also initialize the variables IRateOld and Counter. IRateOld holds the value inserted in the formula, and IRate holds the new value calculated from the formula. Counter counts the number of times the loop is iterated, so you can cancel the calculation if it isn't converging.

Line 12 starts a Do loop, which then ends with the Loop statement in line 30. The loop terminates when IRateOld and the calculated value IRate differ by only a tenth of a percent. The next six lines increment Counter and test whether it is greater than the 200-iteration limit. If the calculation reaches 200 iterations, it probably isn't going to converge, so the procedure displays a Message box informing you of that fact.

In line 19, IRateOld is set equal to the previously calculated value of IRate. In line 20, the denominator of the function is calculated. In line 21, a block IF statement tests whether the value of the denominator is zero. If it's not zero, the new value of IRate is calculated in line 28. If it's zero, and you used it anyway, the program crashes with a divide-by-zero error. Testing the denominator prevents this problem; the program shows a Message box if the denominator is zero.

14. Save the project with the Save Project command of the File menu.

15. Run the program, and type **0.01** (1 percent) in the rate box, **36** in the Periods box, **10000** in the Present Value box, and **0** in the Future Value box. This represents a loan, typical of one for a new car ($10,000 for three years at 12 percent a year).

16. Press the Payment button to calculate the payment of $–322.14. Your advanced annuity calculator now should look like Figure 6.2.

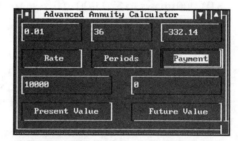

Figure 6.2. The advanced annuity calculator after calculating the payment required on a three-year, $10,000 loan at 12 percent per year.

Notice the $10,000 is positive, because you receive it from the bank, and the payment of $–322.14 is negative because you pay it to the bank. Note also that because you have not tested for every possible invalid value—such as a negative interest rate, or both PVal and FVal as zero—this program still can crash. If that happens, just rerun the program with different values, or insert more protection (IF statements) in the RateButton procedure to check for invalid data.

151

See whether you can make this program uncrashable by testing the inputs for inconsistent or out-of-range data before calculating a value. Each command button has its own set of invalid values. Look at the denominators of the fractions in the formulas to see what combinations of values make them zero. These sets of values are invalid, and should not be allowed in the input. Check also for large values that cause overflow errors. In the Rate calculation, there are input values that cause the equations to not converge. You may need to watch for those values and solve the problem differently if they are encountered.

To calculate any other quantity, insert values in the boxes for all but the one you want calculated, then press the button to calculate that value. For example, you can find out what interest rate you must have so that $10,000 grows to $20,000 in five years. Type **60** in the Periods box (five years * 12 months/year), **0** in the Payment box, **10000** in the Present Value box (positive because the bank is receiving the money), **-20000** in the Future Value box (negative because the bank is giving you back the money in the future), and press the Rate button. The program now looks like Figure 6.3, with the value 0.0116 in the rate box, which represents 13.92 percent per year (0.0116 * 12 months * 100 percent).

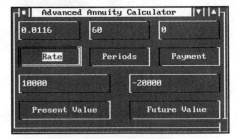

Figure 6.3. The advanced annuity calculator after calculating the interest rate necessary for $10,000 to increase to $20,000 in five years.

Using Option Buttons to Select an Option

Option buttons are used in groups, which you define by placing the option buttons on a form, frame, or picture window. All the option buttons placed directly on a single form, frame, or picture window constitute one group. Option buttons often are called *radio buttons* because they operate much like the station-changing buttons on a car radio. Only one option button in a group can be pressed at any one time, and pressing one button releases the previously pressed button.

To add option buttons to an application, first draw a frame or picture window with the frame or picture window tools, then draw the option buttons within the frame or picture window. Additionally, if you have only one group, you can draw them directly on a form. Option buttons have the property Value, which is True (–1) if the button is pressed or False (0) if it is released.

The Self-Paced Learning Program (Version 4)

To demonstrate the use of option buttons, add some to the self-paced learning program developed in Chapter 5, "Using Numbers and Control Structures." Version 3 of the program creates an addition test. This new version gives you the choice of addition, subtraction, multiplication, or division, which you select with a group of four option buttons.

1. Rename the project: execute the New Project command of the File menu, then execute the Add File command of the File menu and select MATH3.FRM. Execute the Save File As command of the File menu and use the new filename MATH4.FRM. Execute the Save Project command of the File menu and use MATH4.MAK as the project filename.

2. Using the Frame tool, draw a frame (17 by 4 characters) to the right of the Score text box as shown in Figure 6.4.

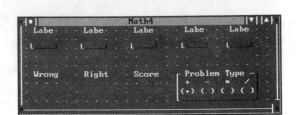

Figure 6.4. *Layout for version 4 of the self-paced learning program.*

3. Draw four option buttons (three characters by one character) left to right, along the bottom of the frame.

4. Draw four labels (three characters by one character) above the four option buttons.

5. Select each label and set the Caption properties to +, -, *, and /. Include a space before each math symbol.

6. Select the first option button on the left and set the Value property to **True**.

7. Select the frame and set the Caption property to **Problem Type**.

This completes the changes to the user interface. Now change the Form_Load procedure to check the option buttons when it sets up the problems. You also must add Click procedures to the option buttons to run the Form_Load procedure whenever one of the buttons is pressed.

8. Select the Form_Load procedure and change it to the following. The changes are in the last block.

```
SUB Form_Load ()
REM Initialize the random number generator
Randomize
REM Define the end-of-line character
eol$ = CHR$(13) + CHR$(10)
REM Fill the probs array with 2 sets of 5 values
REM between 0 and 100
FOR I = 1 TO 2
  FOR J = 1 TO NumProbs
    Probs(I, J) = INT(RND(1) * 100)
  NEXT J
NEXT I
REM Insert the random numbers into the labels
REM and calculate the answers
```

```
FOR J = 1 TO NumProbs
  IF Option1.Value = True THEN      'line 16
    Label1(J).Caption = FORMAT$(Probs(1, J), " 00")
      + eol$ + FORMAT$(Probs(2, J), "+00")
    Answer(J) = Probs(1, J) + Probs(2, J)
  ELSEIF Option2.Value = True THEN
    Label1(J).Caption = FORMAT$(Probs(1, J), " 00")
      + eol$ + FORMAT$(Probs(2, J), "-00")
    Answer(J) = Probs(1, J) - Probs(2, J)
  ELSEIF Option3.Value = True THEN
    Label1(J).Caption = FORMAT$(Probs(1, J), " 00")
      + eol$ + FORMAT$(Probs(2, J), "*00")
    Answer(J) = Probs(1, J) * Probs(2, J)
  ELSEIF Option4.Value = True THEN
    Label1(J).Caption = FORMAT$(Probs(1, J), " 00")
      + eol$ + FORMAT$(Probs(2, J), "\/00")
    Answer(J) = Probs(1, J) / Probs(2, J)
  END IF
  Text1(J).Text = ""         'line 29
  Text1(J).BackColor = White
  Text1(J).ForeColor = Black
NEXT J
NumRight.Caption = ""
NumWrong.Caption = ""
Score.Caption = ""
END SUB
```

The changes start in line 16, with a block IF statement. Each block of the block IF statement checks the Value property of one of the option buttons to find the one that is pressed. The contents of each block are nearly the same; the first line (line 17, for example) inserts the numbers in the label along with the symbol for the type of operation (+, -, *, /). Each block inserts a different symbol. The second statement in each block (line 18, for example) calculates the correct answer for the problem by using the operator selected with the option button.

The second FORMAT$() function in line 26 must have a division operator (/), but a slash used in a formatting string is a date-separation operator. To insert a formatting operator as a literal symbol rather than the operator, precede it with a backslash (\). The pair of characters, \/, produces a single / in the printed string.

Line 29 removes any old answers left from a previous test, and lines 30 and 31 reset the BackColor and ForeColor properties that were previously set for wrong answers, and lines 31, 32, and 33 remove any old scores. You also must move the focus back to the first text box, but this isn't the place to do it. The first time the Form_Load routine is called, the form has not been loaded yet, so there is no text box to which to move the focus. The routine would fail if you tried to move the focus to it. The next step takes care of that problem.

9. Select the Option1_Click procedure and type

```
SUB Option1_Click ()
Form_Load
Text1(1).SetFocus
END SUB
```

Here I introduce a new piece of the BASIC language, *procedure calling.* Up to now, the system has called all the procedures. When you click a control, the system calls the Click procedure for that control; if a text box is changed, the system calls the Changed procedure for that box. Not only can the system call a procedure, but any procedure can call any other procedure in its scope. To call a procedure, simply type its name in your code. When the called procedure completes, execution returns to the procedure that called it and begins at the statement after the calling statement.

The rules of scope for procedures are the same as they are for variables. Any procedure on a form is accessible by any other procedure on the same form, and any procedure in a module is available to any procedure in the application. Chapter 8, "Writing Custom Procedures," discusses procedures in more detail.

In the Option1_Click procedure, the second line calls the Form_Load procedure and runs it. When the Form_Load procedure is complete, control returns to the third line, which moves the focus to the first text box. The other three Option procedures work the same way. Because these procedures are all the same, you could also implement these procedures with a single procedure attached to a control array of option buttons.

10. Select the Option2_Click procedure and type

```
SUB Option2_Click ()
Form_Load
Text1(1).SetFocus
END SUB
```

11. Select the `Option3_Click` procedure and type

```
SUB Option3_Click ()
Form_Load
Text1(1).SetFocus
END SUB
```

12. Select the `Option4_Click` procedure and type

```
SUB Option4_Click ()
Form_Load
Text1(1).SetFocus
END SUB
```

13. Save the project, then run it.

You now can change the test type by pressing one of the option buttons. Notice how pressing one button releases whichever one was previously pressed.

> The subtraction test can have large numbers subtracted from small ones with a negative result. Add code to reverse the top and bottom numbers in the subtraction test when that is the case. Negative numbers are too advanced for most young children.

Using a Check Box to Set an Option

Unlike option buttons, check boxes are independent of each other, and more than one can be checked at the same time. Otherwise, they behave much like option buttons. When a check box is checked, its `Value` property is 1; if it's unchecked, the value is zero. The `Value` property also can be 2 if the check box is grayed (disabled). You draw check boxes the same way you draw option buttons, except that check boxes do not have to be on a frame because they are independent of each other. You can, however, put them on a frame if you want to visually group them.

The Envelope Addresser (Version 3)

Chapter 4, "Using Strings," introduced the envelope addresser, a simple program that prints addresses on envelopes. To demonstrate check boxes, add the following options to the envelope addresser:

- Optional return address

- Optional mailing date

- Optional stamp box

Follow these steps to add the options to version 1 of the envelope addresser:

1. Rename the project: execute the **New Project** command of the **File** menu, then execute the **Add** File command of the **File** menu and select ADDR11.FRM. Execute the Save File **As** command of the **File** menu and use the new filename ADDR31.FRM. Execute the **Add** File command again, select ADDR12.FRM, and save it as ADDR32.FRM. Execute the Save Project command on the **File** menu and use ADDR3.MAK as the project filename.

2. Switch to the Forms Designer, select the AddrBox form, and enlarge it to 12 by 11 characters.

3. Using the check box tool, draw three check boxes on the form as shown in Figure 6.5.

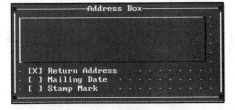

Figure 6.5. *Setup of the AddrBox form for version 3 of the envelope addresser.*

4. Change the Caption properties of the three check boxes to

```
Check1.Caption = Return Address
Check2.Caption = Mailing Date
Check3.Caption = Stamp Mark
```

Because most people want a return address, give the Check1 check box a default value of checked; leave the others unchecked.

5. Select the first check box and change its Value property to **1 - Checked**.

6. Select the AddrFrm form and add three labels as shown in Figure 6.6. Label2 is 36 characters by 5 characters, Label3 is 14 characters by 1 character, and Label4 is 7 characters by 3 characters. Set the properties of Label4 to

```
Caption = Stamp
BorderStyle = 1 - Single Line
```

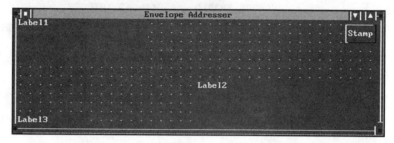

Figure 6.6. *Setup of the AddrFrm form for version 3 of the Envelope Addresser.*

This completes the changes to the interface. Now adjust the code so it reacts to changes in the check boxes. First, make the check boxes set the value of a variable whenever the user clicks on a check box.

7. Select the AddrBox form, execute the Event Procedures command of the **File** menu, select the Check1_Click procedure, and type

```
SUB Check1_Click ()
RetAddr = Check1.Value
END SUB
```

8. Select the Check2_Click procedure and type

```
SUB Check2_Click ()
ShowDate = Check2.Value
END SUB
```

9. Select the Check3_Click procedure and type

```
SUB Check3_Click ()
ShowStamp = Check3.Value
END SUB
```

159

To enable both forms to share variables, you must include duplicate COMMON SHARED statements in the module-level declarations in both forms. The simplest way to ensure that they're identical is to create an include file (.BI) and include it at the module level in both forms.

10. Execute the New **M**odule command of the **F**ile menu. Select the include file (.BI) and use the filename ADDR3.BI. In the window for ADDR3.BI, type the following code, which defines the variables that contain the values of the options, and defines the constants True, False, Checked, and Unchecked:

```
COMMON SHARED TheLine AS STRING
COMMON SHARED RetAddr AS INTEGER
COMMON SHARED ShowDate AS INTEGER
COMMON SHARED ShowStamp AS INTEGER
COMMON SHARED CONST True = -1, False = 0
COMMON SHARED CONST Checked = 1, Unchecked = 0
```

11. Execute the **S**ave File command of the **F**ile menu to save ADDR3.BI.

12. Open the declarations section of the AddrBox form and change it to

```
'$INCLUDE: 'ADDR3.BI'
```

13. Open the declarations section of the AddrFrm form and change it to

```
'$INCLUDE: 'ADDR3.BI'
DIM SHARED eol$
```

Now any declarations and definitions placed in the ADDR3.BI file automatically are included in the declarations sections of both forms. In the original version of the envelope addresser, the Form_Load procedure printed the return address on the form. The code that prints the return address has to be moved to the Form_Click procedure so you can use logical statements to decide to print the return address or not.

14. Cut the three lines that define the return address from the Form_Load procedure (saving them for the Form_Click procedure) by using the Cut command of the **E**dit menu. Add the default values of the check boxes to the Form_Load procedure, and insert the current date in the caption of Label3. The procedure now should read

```
SUB Form_Load ()
eol$ = CHR$(13) + CHR$(10)
RetAddr = Checked
ShowDate = Unchecked
ShowStamp = Unchecked
Label3.Caption = Date$
END SUB
```

15. Open the Form_Click procedure and paste in the text from the
    Form_Load procedure using the **Paste** command of the **Edit** menu.
    Change the Form_Click procedure until it appears as follows:

```
SUB Form_Click ()
IF ShowDate = Checked THEN
  Label3.Visible = True
ELSE
  Label3.Visible = False
END IF
IF ShowStamp = Checked THEN
  Label4.Visible = True
ELSE
  Label4.Visible = False
END IF
IF RetAddr = Checked THEN
  Label1.Caption = "William J. Orvis" + eol$
  Label1.Caption = Label1.Caption + "123 Some St." + eol$
  Label1.Caption = Label1.Caption + "Anywhere, CA  91234"
ELSE
  Label1.Caption = ""
END IF
Label2.Caption = TheLine            'line 19
AddrFrm.PrintForm
AddrBox.Show
END SUB
```

Notice there are three independent block IF statements. They're independent because each check box is independent of the others. The first
block IF statement, lines 2 through 6, checks whether the Mailing Date
check box is checked and changes the Visible property of Label3 to True
or False. The second block, lines 7 through 11, does the same for the
Visible property of Label4. The third IF block, lines 12 through 18,
checks the value of the Return Address check box and, if it's True, inserts
the return address into the Caption property of the Label1 box. If it isn't

161

True, it blanks the Caption property. In line 19, the value of the address is placed in the Caption property of the second label box, and in line 20 the form is printed. Line 21 redisplays Form1 so you can print a second envelope.

16. Save the project and run the program. Type the address for the envelope in the text box; select the options you want and then click the AddrFrm form to print the envelope.

Using Scroll Bars to Set a Value

The last controls discussed in this chapter are scroll bars, which are used to select a numeric value in some range. Because their use as a means of controlling windows is more familiar, you might not have thought of scroll bars as a way to set a value. However, a scroll bar returns a number that indicates the relative location of the *thumb* (the white square that slides along the scroll bar). When you move the thumb up and down (or left and right) the number stored in the Value property of the scroll bar changes accordingly.

It's up to the attached program to convert changes in that number to movement of a window. Also, there is no reason that a scroll bar can control only windows. You can use a scroll bar in any program where an integer has to be selected from a range. You can also use a scroll bar as a gauge, where the program's changing of the Value property makes the thumb move along some scale. The following two properties control the range of the number returned in the Value property:

Min   The minimum value of the scroll bar, when the thumb is at the left of a horizontal scroll bar or at the top of a vertical one

Max   The maximum value of the scroll bar, when the thumb is at the bottom or right

If a program changes the Value property, it causes the thumb to move, and moving the thumb with the mouse changes Value. Thus, a scroll bar can be used either as an indicator or an input device.

The Self-Paced Learning Program (Version 5)

The self-paced learning program currently uses numbers between 0 and 100 to create the math problems. My son has been complaining that the numbers in the multiplication test are too big for him, so I added a pair of horizontal scroll bars to the program to set the maximum range for the first (top) and second (bottom) numbers. This way, he can start with small numbers and, as he grows more proficient, he can increase the size of the numbers.

The following steps create version 5 of the self-paced learning program from version 4. The steps make the upper limits of the numbers used in the math test adjustable with two horizontal scroll bars:

1. Rename the project: execute the New Project command of the File menu, then execute the Add File command of the File menu and select MATH4.FRM. Execute the Save File **As** command of the File menu and use the new filename MATH5.FRM. Execute the Save Project command of the File menu and use MATH5.MAK as the project filename.

2. Switch to the Forms Designer and select Form1. Increase its size to 52 characters by 15 characters and change its `Caption` to **Math5**.

3. Add two horizontal scroll bars (31 characters by 1 character) as shown in Figure 6.7.

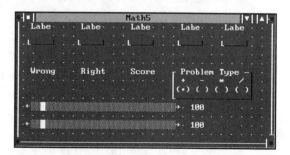

Figure 6.7. *Setup for version 5 of the self-paced learning program.*

4. Add two labels (ten characters by one character), as shown in the figure. Change the `CtlName` property of the upper label to `TopRange` and change the lower label to `BottomRange`.

5. Select the scroll bars and set their properties.

```
Max = 1000
Min = 0
Value = 100
LargeChange = 10
```

The LargeChange property controls how large a change you get when you click the gray area of a scroll bar above or below the thumb. Setting the Value property sets the initial, or default, position of the thumb.

6. Select the two new labels and set both Caption properties to 100.

7. Execute the Event Procedures command and select the HScroll1_Change procedure and type

```
SUB HScroll1_Change ()
TopRange.Caption = STR$(HScroll1.Value)
END SUB
```

8. Select the HScroll2_Change procedure and type

```
SUB HScroll2_Change ()
BottomRange.Caption = STR$(HScroll2.Value)
END SUB
```

This routine and the one in step 7 make the values shown in the two labels follow any movement of the thumb.

9. Select the Form_Load procedure and change it as follows (the changes are in lines 7 through 10):

```
SUB Form_Load ()
REM Initialize the random number generator
RANDOMIZE
REM Define the end-of-line character
eol$ = CHR$(13) + CHR$(10)
REM Fill the probs array with 2 sets of 5 values
FOR J = 1 TO NumProbs      'line 7
  Probs(1, J) = INT(RND(1) * HScroll1.Value)
  Probs(2, J) = INT(RND(1) * HScroll2.Value)
NEXT J              'line 10
REM Insert the random numbers into the labels and
REM calculate the answers
```

```
FOR J = 1 TO NumProbs
  IF Option1.Value = True THEN
    Label1(J).Caption = FORMAT$(Probs(1, J), " 00")
      + eol$ + FORMAT$(Probs(2, J), "+00")
    Answer(J) = Probs(1, J) + Probs(2, J)
  ELSEIF Option2.Value = True THEN
    Label1(J).Caption = FORMAT$(Probs(1, J), " 00")
      + eol$ + FORMAT$(Probs(2, J), "-00")
    Answer(J) = Probs(1, J) - Probs(2, J)
  ELSEIF Option3.Value = True THEN
    Label1(J).Caption = FORMAT$(Probs(1, J), " 00")
      + eol$ + FORMAT$(Probs(2, J), "*00")
    Answer(J) = Probs(1, J) * Probs(2, J)
  ELSEIF Option4.Value = True THEN
    Label1(J).Caption = FORMAT$(Probs(1, J), " 00")
      + eol$ + FORMAT$(Probs(2, J), "\/00")
    Answer(J) = Probs(1, J) / Probs(2, J)
  END IF
  Text1(J).Text = ""
  Text1(J).BackColor = White
  Text1(J).ForeColor = Black
NEXT J
NumRight.Caption = ""
NumWrong.Caption = ""
Score.Caption = ""
END SUB
```

The only changes in this routine are in lines 7 through 10, where the multipliers of the RND() functions are changed to the values from the two scroll bars. This version differs from version 4 of this program in that the outer loop is replaced with two equations, one for the upper values and one for the lower values.

10. Save the project, then run it. Change the lower scroll bar until the value reads 10; then press the multiplication option button. A test similar to Figure 6.8 appears. See also Plate 4 on the inside back cover of this book.

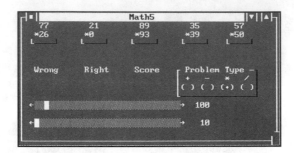

Figure 6.8. A multiplication test with numbers between 0 and 100 for the upper values and numbers between 0 and 10 for the lower values.

What You Have Learned

This chapter examined the more traditional controls: command buttons, option buttons, check boxes, and scroll bars. In this chapter you

- Learned that command buttons initiate actions, option buttons select one of a set of options, check boxes enable individual options, and scroll bars input integer values

- Created an advanced annuity calculator, two versions of a self-paced learning program, and a version of the envelope addresser

- Studied more complicated logical statements, remote procedures, and the method of successive approximations for solving transcendental equations

Creating Custom Menus

Instead of pressing buttons and checking boxes, you can control programs conveniently by using pull-down menus. When you select a menu command, it executes a procedure that can set options or perform complex calculations.

In This Chapter

You attach menus to forms by using the Menu Design window. Procedures then are written and attached to the commands on the menu. This chapter shows you how to

- Construct menus with the Menu Design window
- Attach procedures to menus
- Create the standard File and Edit menus

● Access the clipboard with the Edit menu

● Implement the Undo command

Using the Menu Design Window

In contrast to controls you draw on a form, menus are created in a Menu Design window, as shown in Figure 7.1. The top half of the window sets the properties of the currently selected menu item. The bottom half lists all the menus and menu items on a form. A menu item is any of the menu names or commands that show on a menu. The buttons along the center of the window insert and move menu items.

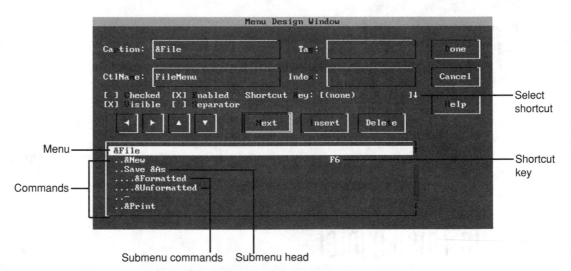

***Figure 7.1.** The Menu Design window.*

The items listed on the left side of the bottom of the window in Figure 7.1 are the menu names that appear in a form's menu bar. In this figure, **File** and **Edit** (not visible off the bottom of the list) are the two menus defined for this form. Menu commands and submenu headings are indented below the menu names. Here, **New**, **Print**, and **Exit** are menu commands under the **File** menu, and **Undo**, **Cut**, **Copy**, and **Paste** (remember, everything below **Print** is scrolled off the bottom of the window) are menu commands under the **Edit** menu. Submenu headings have additional menu items indented below them. When a submenu heading is selected, the submenu drops to the left or right of the submenu heading. Save **As** is a submenu heading under the **File** menu with **Formatted** and **Unformatted** as the submenu commands. Figure 7.2 shows the resulting menus defined in the Menu Design window in Figure 7.1, including the Save **As** submenu.

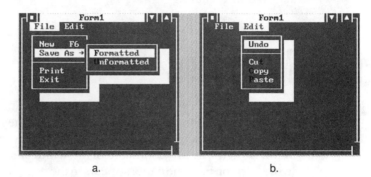

Figure 7.2. *The File menu with (a) the Save As submenu open and (b) the Edit menu open.*

Although a Visual Basic program can have five levels of submenus, try to avoid going beyond one or two. Too many levels can make your program confusing—see Figure 7.3, for example.

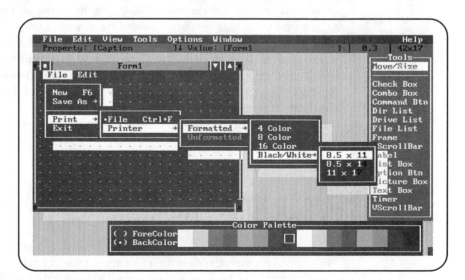

Figure 7.3. *Multiple levels of submenus can be confusing.*

A separator bar also can appear on a menu to separate the menu visually into two or more parts. For example, in Figure 7.2 there's a separator bar on the Edit menu between the Undo and Cut commands. You create a separator bar by typing a hyphen as the Caption of a menu item. Separator bars also must have control names, even though they cannot be selected or executed.

Editing Menu Items

To create a menu in the Forms Designer, open the form to which you want to attach a menu and then open the Menu Design window by executing the **Menu Design Window** command of the **Window** menu. Type a menu name in the Caption box; the name appears in the bottom window. Type a control name, which must be a legal variable name, in the CtlName box. You must supply a control name for each menu item (including separator bars, as mentioned earlier), even if you do not intend to attach code to the menu item.

Click the Next button and type another caption in the Caption box and another control name in the CtlName box. If you're entering a menu command or submenu name, click the right arrow to indent the name. Continue typing captions and control names until you've inserted all the menu items for all your menus in the window. To edit a menu item, select it and change the names in the Caption and CtlName boxes. To move a menu item up or down in the list, use the up and down arrows on the window. Change the indentation level with the left and right arrows on the window. The Delete button deletes the selected menu item, and the Insert button inserts a new item at the selection point by moving all those below it down one line.

Setting Menu Item Properties

Three main properties of menu items are set with check boxes in the Menu Design window: **Checked**, **Enabled**, and **Visible**. You can set these properties at design time, and adjust them at runtime.

The **Checked** check box places a *check mark* (a black dot) to the left of the item's name—see the File command of the **File** menu's Print submenu in Figure 7.3—and sets the command's Checked property to True. The Checked property most often is used to show whether the option accessed by the menu item is enabled. You can write code so that selecting a menu item sets the check mark and enables the option, and selecting it again removes the check mark and disables the option. You do this by changing the value of the Checked property. You cannot check a menu name or submenu head.

The Enabled property determines whether a menu item is executable. Disabled menu items are grayed on the menu, and cannot be selected; the Unformatted command in **Figure 7.3** is an example. You should disable menu items for commands and options that currently are unavailable.

If you disable a menu name, the whole menu is disabled.

The Visible property provides another way to control access to menu items. When the visible box is not checked or the Visible property is False, the menu item and all its submenus disappear from the menu bar. By having several menus, some visible and others not, you can make different menus (or different versions of the same menu) available at different times during the execution of your program.

Making a menu name invisible makes the whole menu invisible.

Two more properties of menu items can be set only at design time: shortcut (hot) keys and access (accelerator) keys. Shortcut keys are command or function keys that access a menu command directly from the keyboard without pulling down the menu. You create shortcut keys by selecting them from the Accelerator box of the Menu Design window. As a reminder, the selected key or key combination appears on the menu to the right of the command name. For example, in part A of **Figure 7.2**, if you pressed F6, the **New** command of the **File** menu would be executed. In **Figure 7.3**, if you pressed Ctrl-F, you would execute the File command of the **File** menu's **Print** submenu.

Access keys enable you to select menus and menu items without using the mouse. The access key for any menu item is bright white in the item's name on the screen. In this book, access keys are indicated with boldface type. When a program is running, activate the menu bar by pressing the Alt key, then pull down a menu by pressing its access key. When a menu is open, select menu items with the up and down arrow keys, or by pressing the access key for the item you want.

The access key for a menu item is selected when you type the `Caption` property. When you place an ampersand (&) before the letter you want to use, the letter appears bright white in the menu (see the **Formatted** menu item in Figures 7.1 and 7.2). You don't have to use the first letter in a menu item's name as the access key, although it's a good idea for frequently used items. You can place the ampersand anywhere in the menu item's name to cause the letter following the ampersand to become the access key.

> Be careful which letters you select for access keys, because if two menus or two items on the same menu have the same key, only the first item is selectable.

Attaching Code to a Menu

You attach code to a menu command in the same way you attach code to the other controls. Use the Event Procedures command of the **E**dit menu, and select the control name of the menu command and the `Click` event.

Creating the Standard Menus

Most modern applications contain at least two menus: the **F**ile menu and the **E**dit menu. The **F**ile menu starts and stops the application and opens, closes, and prints documents. The **E**dit menu contains the standard editing commands, **U**ndo, **C**ut, **C**opy, and **P**aste.

If you plan to open and close files, or you want to edit your application, it's important to make the commands operate in the standard way so other users do not have to learn new methods. For example, you might have invented the world's best method for editing text, but if your application doesn't have a working Edit menu with the standard Cut, Copy, and Paste commands, your frustrated users will think unkind things about you. If, however, they can use your code without having to learn anything new, they might not notice—but they won't be calling you to complain, either.

The clipboard is a special area in memory for storing text. If you plan to edit text in your application, you should have an Edit menu with the appropriate code attached to the commands on that menu to transfer text between the clipboard and the text being edited. When you cut or copy data in an application, a copy of the current selection is placed on the clipboard. When you paste data, the contents of the clipboard either are inserted at the insertion point or replace the current selection. Under the Windows operating system, the clipboard is a convenient way to share small amounts of data, because the clipboard is available to all running applications.

Creating the File Menu

A standard File menu contains the New, Open, Close, Save, Save As, Print, and Exit commands, or some similar set with the same functions. One or more of these commands might be missing in a particular program, or there might be additional commands. The File menu in Visual Basic is a good example; it contains commands for opening, saving, and deleting forms and projects, creating new forms and projects, printing, and ending the program.

The Envelope Addresser (Version 4)

The envelope addresser program currently is designed to print an envelope when you click the form. The only way to end the program is to execute Ctrl-Break in Visual Basic. Thus, the program needs an Exit command to make ending the program more convenient. This example also shows you how to add a Print Options submenu, which contains the options originally set on Form1. You no longer need Form1, so you will delete it and type the address directly on the AddrFrm form.

1. Rename the project: execute the New Project command of the File menu, then execute the Add File command of the File menu and select ADDR32.FRM. Execute the Save File As command of the File menu and use the new filename ADDR42.FRM. Execute the Add File command again, select the include file ADDR3.BI, and save it as ADDR4.BI. Execute the Save Project command of the File menu and use ADDR4.MAK as the project filename.

You cannot type on a label. To type the address directly on AddrFrm, you need a text box on AddrFrm. Also, you should include an outline around the text box so you can see where you're typing, but one that goes away when the form is printed—you don't want it to be printed on the envelope. The Outline property of a text box can be set at design time; however, it cannot be changed at runtime. To solve this problem, draw two text boxes, a visible one with an outline and an invisible one without. When you type in the visible, outlined box, the code duplicates the text in the invisible, unoutlined box. Because the Visible property can be changed at runtime, use it to make the outlined text box invisible and the unoutlined box visible when it's time to print the envelope.

2. Select Label2 on AddrFrm and delete it.

3. Draw a text box 36 characters by 5 characters where Label2 used to be. Change its properties as follows:

```
CtlName = PrintBox
Text = ""
BorderStyle = 0 - None
MultiLine = True
```

4. On top of the first text box, draw a second text box exactly the same size. Change the text box properties to

```
CtlName = EditBox
Caption = ""
BorderStyle = 1 - Fixed Single
MultiLine = True
```

Now attach the menu to AddrFrm. It has a New command to clear the form, a Print command to print it, a Print Options menu that enables you to change any of the options, and an Exit command to end the program.

5. Open the Menu Design window, and type the table of values given in Table 7.1 and shown in Figure 7.4. Use the arrow button to indent the menus and press Done when you are finished.

Table 7.1. Menu definitions for version 4 of the envelope addresser.

Caption	Control Name	Number of Indents
&File	FileMenu	0
&New	NewCmd	1
-	SepBar1	1
&Print	PrintCmd	1
Print &Options	OptionMenu	1
&Return Address	RetAddrCmd	2
Show &Date	ShowDateCmd	2
&Stamp Location	ShowStampCmd	2
-	SepBar2	1
E&xit	ExitCmd	1

This completes the interface. Now change the code. Much of the code can be copied from the old version of the program (or retyped) into the new one. First, change the global definitions in the ADDR4.BI file. Actually, you no longer need to define TheLine in a COMMON statement, because you no longer are passing it from one form to another. It also could be defined in a DIM SHARED statement. However, as it's already here, leave it alone.

6. Switch to the Programming Environment, open the ADDR4.BI include file, and change it to read

```
COMMON SHARED TheLine AS STRING
CONST True = -1, False = 0
```

7. Open the module level code window of ADDR42.FRM and change it to the following (if the Visual Basic system has inserted a '$FORM statement, be sure to remove it):

```
'$INCLUDE: 'ADDR4.BI'
DIM EOL$
```

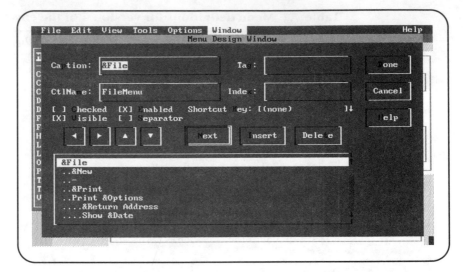

Figure *7.4. The Menu Design window for version 4 of the envelope addresser.*

8. Open the Form_Load procedure and change it to the following (pieces of this were copied from the old Form_Click procedure):

```
SUB Form_Load ()
eol$ = CHR$(13) + CHR$(10)
REM set initial values
RetAddrCmd.Checked = True
ShowDateCmd.Checked = False
ShowDateCmd.Checked = False
Label3.Caption = DATE$
Label3.Visible = False
Label4.Visible = False
REM Insert return address
Label1.Caption = "William J. Orvis" + eol$
Label1.Caption = Label1.Caption + "123 Some St." + eol$
Label1.Caption = Label1.Caption + "Anywhere, CA  91234"
PrintBox.Visible = True
EditBox.Text = ""
END SUB
```

Line 2 of this procedure defines the eol$ (end-of-line) character, then lines 3 through 6 set the initial values of the options. Lines 7 to the end perform the initial options, such as inserting the return address, hiding the date and stamp location, and hiding PrintBox.

9. The next procedure is executed whenever the **Return Address** menu command is executed. The procedure toggles the return address option on or off each time the menu command is executed. Much of this also can be copied from the Form_Load procedure.

Open the RetAddrCmd_Click procedure and type

```
SUB RetAddrCmd_Click ()
REM Reverse the check mark
RetAddrCmd.Checked = NOT RetAddrCmd.Checked
IF RetAddrCmd.Checked = True THEN
  Label1.Caption = "William J. Orvis" + eol$
  Label1.Caption = Label1.Caption + "123 Some St." + eol$
  Label1.Caption = Label1.Caption + "Anywhere, CA  91234"
ELSE
  Label1.Caption = ""
END IF
END SUB
```

Line 3 uses the NOT operator to change the Checked property of the **Return Address** command. The NOT operator changes True to False or False to True. Lines 4 through the end of this procedure are a block IF statement that checks the state of the check mark and, if it is True, inserts the return address in the Label1 label. If it's False, it blanks the contents of the label.

10. The next procedure performs a similar function for the **Show Date** command.

Open the ShowDateCmd_Click procedure and type

```
SUB ShowDateCmd_Click ()
REM Reverse the check mark
ShowDateCmd.Checked = NOT ShowDateCmd.Checked
IF ShowDateCmd.Checked = True THEN
  Label3.Visible = True
ELSE
  Label3.Visible= False
END IF
END SUB
```

Again, line 3 switches the state of the check on the Show **Date** menu command, and the block IF statement changes the Visible property of the Label3 label.

11. The next procedure does exactly the same thing for the **Stamp Location** menu command: it first switches the state of the check mark, then changes the property.

    Open the ShowStampCmd_Click procedure and type

    ```
    SUB ShowStampCmd_Click ()
    REM Reverse the check mark
    ShowStampCmd.Checked = NOT ShowStampCmd.Checked
    IF ShowStampCmd.Checked = True THEN
      Label4.Visible = True
    ELSE
      Label4.Visible = False
    END IF
    END SUB
    ```

12. The EditBox_Change procedure makes sure that whenever EditBox is changed, the invisible PrintBox also is changed. This way, when the form is printed, PrintBox contains the correct text.

    Open the EditBox_Change procedure and type

    ```
    SUB EditBox_Change ()
    PrintBox.Text = EditBox.Text
    END SUB
    ```

13. Open the PrintCmd_Click procedure and type

    ```
    SUB PrintCmd_Click ()
    REM switch between the edit box with the border and
    REM the edit box without the border for printing
    EditBox.Visible = False
    PrintBox.Visible = True
    Form2.PrintForm
    REM Switch back to the edit box
    PrintBox.Visible = False
    EditBox.Visible = True
    END SUB
    ```

    As shown previously, the **Print** menu command executes the PrintCmd procedure. It first makes EditBox invisible and PrintBox visible to eliminate the bounding box surrounding the address. The bounding box makes it easier to type the address, but you don't want it to be printed on the envelope. Next the procedure prints the form by using the `PrintForm` method, and then turns the bounding box back on.

14. The next two procedures are relatively simple. The **New** menu command calls the `Form_Load` procedure again to reset everything as it was at the beginning, and the **Exit** menu command executes the `END` statement to end the program.

    Open the `NewCmd_Click` procedure and type

    ```
    SUB NewCmd_Click ()
    Form_Load
    END SUB
    ```

15. Open the `ExitCmd_Click` procedure and type

    ```
    SUB ExitCmd_Click ()
    END
    END SUB
    ```

    In the event that someone double-clicks the close box on the form instead of ending the program with the **Exit** command, make the `Form_UnLoad` procedure call the `ExitCmd_Click` procedure.

16. Open the `Form_UnLoad` procedure and type

    ```
    SUB Form_UnLoad (Cancel AS INTEGER)
    ExitCmd_Click
    END SUB
    ```

17. Delete the `Form_Click` procedure by pressing the Code button on the Project window, selecting `Form_Click`, and pressing **Delete**. You no longer need this procedure because you've moved all its functions to other procedures.

18. Save the project and run it. The form should look like Figure 7.5.

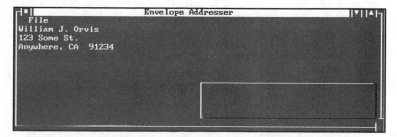

Figure 7.5. *Startup of version 4 of the envelope addresser.*

19. Type an address in the EditBox, and select any options from the Print Options submenu as shown in Figure 7.6.

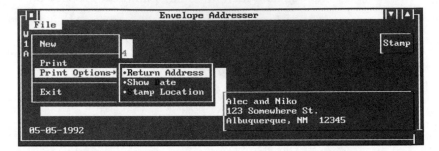

Figure 7.6. *Changing options in version 4 of the envelope addresser.*

20. Print an envelope by selecting the **Print** command of the **File** menu. To print another envelope, either edit the old address or clear the form with the **New** command and type a new address. Then print again.

Creating the Edit Menu

The next standard menu is the **Edit** menu, used to transfer text and graphics between the clipboard and a running application. The standard **Edit** menu commands are Undo, Cut, Copy, and Paste. Like the File menu, the Edit menu can have more or fewer commands, depending on the application.

Of all the commands, the Undo command is the most difficult to program. Undo returns the program to the state it had just before the last command executed or the last editing performed. Thus, any procedure that makes a change you want to be able to undo must save the original state, and signal the Undo command that something can be undone. Unfortunately, I cannot give you much help here because what you do or don't want to undo depends on your particular application.

Take editing, for example. Because you don't want Undo just to undo the last character typed, you must select certain events to mark the beginning of a piece of editing that can be undone. Standard editing actions include deleting one or more characters or executing a menu command.

The **Cut**, **Copy**, and **Paste** commands transfer data between the application and the clipboard. In a Windows application, the clipboard is a part of the system and all Windows applications have access to material placed on it. In DOS, the clipboard is available only within a single application. To make the clipboard available to multiple applications under DOS, write the contents of the clipboard to a specific disk file after performing a **Cut** or **Copy** command, and read that file into the clipboard before performing a **Paste** command. A good choice for the clipboard file name and location is C:\CLIPBRD.TXT. You transfer text between a program and the clipboard by using the CLIPBOARD object and the GETTEXT and SETTEXT methods.

The GETTEXT and SETTEXT methods transfer text between the clipboard and a Visual Basic program. The GETTEXT method works like a function and returns any text stored on the clipboard. SETTEXT does just the opposite and places text on the clipboard, replacing any text already there. The syntax of these methods are

```
Clipboard.GetText()
```

```
Clipboard.SetText String$
```

where *String$* is a string containing the text to be placed on the clipboard.

Three text box properties are needed to perform the **Cut**, **Copy**, and **Paste** functions correctly: SelLength, SelStart, and SelText. The SelLength property is a LONG integer that contains the number of characters selected in the text box. The SelStart property also is a LONG integer that contains the location of the first selected character, or the insertion point if no characters are selected. The SelText property is a string that contains the selected text. The SelText property has a unique characteristic: if you change it, the selected text in the text box is replaced with the changed text. Thus you can implement the **Cut**, **Copy**, and **Paste** commands simply by copying or changing the contents of the SelText property.

This characteristic of the SelText property makes it very easy to implement the **Cut**, **Copy**, and **Paste** commands. To create the **Copy** command to duplicate selected text, simply copy the contents of SelText to the clipboard by using the SETTEXT method. To create the **Cut** command, first copy the contents of SelText to the clipboard, then set SelText equal to the null string. To create the **Paste** command, equate SelText to the GETTEXT method, which replaces the currently selected text with the contents of the clipboard.

The Envelope Addresser Program (Version 5)

In this version of the envelope addresser application, you add an edit menu so that you can use the standard editing commands to edit the text in the edit box. Additionally, this version implements the Undo command of the Edit menu. To implement the Undo command, you have to decide what is "undoable." In this version, any Cut or Paste command is undoable, as is any sequence of one or more Backspace or Del keystrokes.

1. Rename the project: execute the New Project command of the File menu, then execute the Add File command of the File menu and select ADDR42.FRM. Execute the Save File As command of the File menu and use the new filename ADDR52.FRM. Execute Add File again, select the include file ADDR4.BI and save it as ADDR5.BI. Execute the Save Project command of the File menu and use ADDR5.MAK as the project filename.

2. Add the Edit menu to AddrFrm. Switch to the Forms Designer, open AddrFrm, open the Menu Design window, and add the following menu by using the values shown in Table 7.2. Don't remove the File menu in the process, but add this new menu definition after the definition of the File menu, as shown in Figure 7.7.

Table 7.2. Menu definitions for version 5 of the envelope addresser program.

Caption	Control Name	Number of Indents
&Edit	EditMenu	0
&Undo	UndoCmd	1
–	SepBar3	1
Cu&t	CutCmd	1
&Copy	CopyCmd	1
&Paste	PasteCmd	1

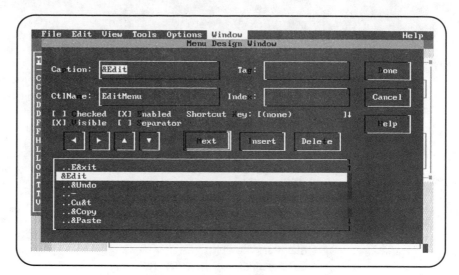

Figure 7.7. *The Menu Design window showing the added Edit menu.*

The Undo procedure has to watch for the Backspace and Delete keystrokes to determine when to start saving editing changes. To make the code more intuitive, make global constant definitions of the key codes for those two keys.

Key codes are numeric codes for the different keys on the keyboard (see Appendix C, "Key Code Chart"). You can either type them into your program or copy them from the file CONSTANT.TXT, where they are stored as constants. To copy them into a program, open the CONSTANT.BI file by executing the Add File command of the File menu. Next, scroll through the Code window until you find the definitions you want, then use the Copy command of the Edit menu to copy them onto the clipboard. Select the form or module where you want to use them, open its Code window, and paste the definitions by using the Paste command of the Edit menu. After you have pasted all the definitions you need, remove the CONSTANT.TXT file from the project by executing the Remove File command of the File menu. Alternatively, you can include the whole CONSTANT.BI file by using the $INCLUDE metacommand as you did with the global constants and definitions in ADDR5.BI.

3. Switch to the Programming Environment, open ADDR5.BI with the Add File command of the File menu, add the key definitions for Backspace and Delete to the file so it reads as follows. Save the file by executing the Save File command of the File menu.

```
COMMON SHARED TheLine AS STRING
CONST True = -1, False = 0
CONST KEY_BACK = &H8, KEY_DELETE = &H2E
```

4. In the declarations section of AddrFrm, add the definitions of three variables to store the state of the system for the Undo command. The section should now read as follows:

```
'$INCLUDE: 'ADDR5.BI'
DIM EOL$
DIM UndoText AS STRING, UndoLength AS LONG, UndoStart AS LONG
```

5. Open the Form_Load procedure and add three statements at the end to initialize the Undo variables. The procedure should now read as follows:

```
SUB Form_Load ()
eol$ = CHR$(13) + CHR$(10)
REM set initial values
RetAddrCmd.Checked = True
ShowDateCmd.Checked = False
ShowStampCmd.Checked = False
Label3.Caption = DATE$
Label3.Visible = False
Label4.Visible = False
REM Insert return address
Label1.Caption = "William J. Orvis" + eol$
Label1.Caption = Label1.Caption + "123 Some St." + eol$
Label1.Caption = Label1.Caption + "Anywhere, CA   91234"
EditBox.Text = ""
PrintBox.Visible = False
UndoText = ""
UndoStart = 0
UndoLength = 0
END SUB
```

The CopyCmd_Click procedure implements the **Copy** command. In that procedure, the selected text in EditBox is copied to the clipboard. You access the selected text with the SelText property and pass the text to the clipboard by using the SETTEXT method.

6. Execute the Event Procedures command of the Edit menu, create the `CopyCmd_Click` procedure, and type

```
SUB CopyCmd_Click ()
Clipboard.SetText EditBox.SelText
END SUB
```

The next three procedures save the state of the system for the Undo command. In the `CutCmd_Click` and the `PasteCmd_Click` procedures, the contents of `EditBox` are saved before the command is executed. The `SelStart` and `SelLength` properties also are saved; this way, the cursor position and the selection size can be restored. The third procedure, `EditBox_KeyDown`, intercepts keypresses being sent to `EditBox`, and saves the contents of `EditBox` whenever one or more Backspace or Del keys is pressed.

The `CutCmd_Click` procedure implements the Cut command. After the data is saved for the Undo command, the selected data in `EditBox` is copied to the clipboard, as in the `CopyCmd_Click` procedure. You then delete the selected text in line 9 by equating `SelText` to a null string.

7. Create the `CutCmd_Click` procedure and type

```
SUB CutCmd_Click ()
REM Save state for undo
UndoText = EditBox.Text
UndoStart = EditBox.SelStart
UndoLength = EditBox.SelLength
REM Cut the selected text out of the Text box
REM and put it on the Clipboard
Clipboard.SetText EditBox.SelText
EditBox.SelText = ""
END SUB
```

The `PasteCmd_Click` procedure implements the **Paste** command. Lines 2 through 5 save the data for the Undo command. Line 8 then replaces the selected text with the contents of the clipboard.

8. Create the `PasteCmd_Click` procedure and type

```
SUB PasteCmd_Click ()
REM Save state for undo                          line 2
UndoText = EditBox.Text
UndoStart = EditBox.SelStart
```

185

```
UndoLength = EditBox.SelLength
REM Replace the selected text with the contents
REM of the Clipboard
EditBox.SelText = Clipboard.GetText()        line 8
END SUB
```

9. Open the EditBox_KeyDown procedure and type

```
SUB EditBox_KeyDown (KeyCode AS INTEGER, Shift AS INTEGER)
STATIC Flag AS INTEGER
IF KeyCode = KEY_BACK OR KeyCode = KEY_DELETE THEN
   IF Flag = False THEN
     Flag = True
     UndoText = EditBox.Text
     UndoStart = EditBox.SelStart
     UndoLength = EditBox.SelLength
   END IF
ELSE
   Flag = False
END IF
END SUB
```

The EditBox_KeyDown procedure watches for KeyDown events directed at EditBox. This procedure captures those events before they are sent to EditBox. The key pressed is stored in the variable KeyCode, and Shift contains the state of the Ctrl, Shift, and Alt keys. The value of KeyCode and Shift must not be changed if you want the typed characters to reach EditBox eventually. The second statement defines the variable Flag as a STATIC variable. Normally, all the local variables in the EditBox_KeyDown procedure disappear as soon as the procedure ends. In this case, you want the variable Flag to stay around. Flag initially is False, but is set to True the first time Backspace or Del is pressed. Note that the initial value of all numeric values is 0, and all strings are the null string.

The next statement tests whether the key pressed is Backspace or Del. If it isn't either of these, the block IF statement sets Flag to False and ends. If a Backspace or Del key is pressed, the IF statement starting in line 4 is executed, testing the value of Flag. If Flag is False, this is the first Backspace or Del pressed, and it is time to save the contents of EditBox and to set Flag to True. If Flag is True, several consecutive Backspace or Del keys have been pressed, and the program doesn't have to do anything.

10. Create the `UndoCmd_Click` code window and type

```
SUB UndoCmd_Click ()
REM Restore the state
EditBox.Text = UndoText
EditBox.SelStart = UndoStart
EditBox.SelLength = UndoLength
END SUB
```

This procedure actually performs the Undo command and restores the contents of `EditBox`, the location of the cursor, and the characters selected.

11. Save the project and run it. Try typing some text in `EditBox`, then select, **C**ut, and **P**aste the text to a different place. Try the Undo command.

> Add a menu command to select one of two or three return addresses. Add another menu command to open a dialog box so you can input the return address. Add a menu to select one of several frequently used, built-in addresses and place the address in the text box.

When you execute the **C**ut command, the selected text should disappear, and the cursor should be located at the point where the text was removed. When the **P**aste command is executed, the selected text is replaced by the contents of the clipboard. If no text is selected, the clipboard contents are inserted at the insertion point. The cursor should be located at the end of the pasted text. The **C**opy command should make no apparent change to the text or the location of the insertion point. After a **C**ut or **P**aste command, the Undo command should return `EditBox` to the same state as before the **C**ut or **P**aste command, including the location of the cursor and the text selected. After you type some changes, Undo returns `EditBox` to its state just before the last **C**ut or **P**aste command was executed, or to the state just before the last Backspace or Del was pressed.

What You Have Learned

A common way of controlling windowed programs is with menus, and this chapter has investigated how you create and use them. Rather than pressing buttons and checking boxes to set options and execute commands, use menus. You create menus by using the Menu Design window, which attaches them to the top form. Procedures are attached to menu commands in the same way as other controls: by inserting code in the Code window for that command. Specifically, you learned to

- Construct menus with the Menu Design window

- Set the Checked, Enabled, and Visible properties

- Attach shortcut and access keys to menu items

- Attach procedures to menu commands

- Create the standard **F**ile and **E**dit menus

- Access the clipboard by using the C**u**t, **C**opy, and **P**aste commands

- Implement the **U**ndo command in the envelope addresser program

Writing Custom Procedures

Up to this point, the code in this book has been written in procedures that are attached to controls and forms. These procedures actually are event procedures because they're executed when some specific event—such as being clicked—occurs to a control or the form. In a couple of instances, you also executed an event procedure directly by placing its name in another procedure. Now it's time to look at the creation and use of procedures.

In This Chapter

This chapter investigates FUNCTION and SUB procedures, two types of procedures that differ only slightly from the event procedures used so far in this book. Specifically, this chapter teaches you how to

● Create and use SUB procedures

● Create and use user-defined functions

- Pass arguments to procedures

- Use list boxes

In this chapter you also create the automatic check register program, a program that records checks and deposits and automatically maintains the account balance.

What Are Procedures?

A *procedure* is a self-contained block of code that performs a specific task. The more specific the task, the easier the procedure is to write and maintain. Procedures enable you to group a block of statements together, give them a name, and use the name to execute the specified code. Procedures are the building blocks of a computer program.

When writing a program in Visual Basic, you naturally break it into procedures as you attach code to the different controls and forms. These event procedures break a program into tasks that are performed when each event occurs. Although Visual Basic creates these procedures automatically, any other procedures must be created by you, the programmer.

You might wonder, "Why bother with procedures?" You know what you want your code to do, so why separate it with artificial barriers? In the early days of computing, that's exactly the philosophy programmers followed. Memory was expensive, so programmers spent much of their time writing the most compact code possible. This compact code became known as "spaghetti code" because, unfortunately, the point of execution would jump all over the place with apparently random intent. Maintaining this code was only barely possible if you were the original programmer, and modifying it usually was impossible. It generally was faster to write a new program than to try to decipher someone else's program. Procedures were available, but were used only to reuse common blocks of code.

As restrictions on memory usage rapidly diminished, program design focused more on maintainability than on size. Modern programming practice encourages the use of procedures not only to reuse blocks of code, but to organize a program by its functions. Procedure use has increasingly modularized code, making modern code more readable and much easier to maintain or modify.

Procedures isolate not only the code associated with a task, but the data. All variables used in a single procedure, and not defined at a higher level (that is, in the declarations section of a form or module), are available only in that procedure. A variable of the same name in another procedure is unaffected by changes in the first variable. These variables are known as *local variables* because they are local to the procedure.

Communication with a procedure is conducted through global variables defined at a higher level in COMMON SHARED and DIM SHARED statements. Communication is also conducted through the procedure's arguments.

Creating SUB Procedures

All event procedures attached to controls are SUB procedures. A SUB procedure or subroutine begins with the keyword SUB and the procedure name, followed by an optional argument list in parentheses. Procedures that deal only with global variables do not have an argument list, but still must have the parentheses.

The argument list consists of the names of the local variables that receive the values sent to the SUB procedure by the calling routine, plus any needed type declarations (for example, AS INTEGER). All SUB procedures end with an END SUB statement. The syntax of the SUB statement, which is the heading of the SUB procedure, is

```
[STATIC] SUB subname ([arguments])
END SUB
```

where *subname* is the name of the SUB procedure and *arguments* is the argument list. The STATIC option makes all the variables defined in the SUB procedure persist from one call of the SUB procedure to the next. For example, a subroutine to calculate the sum of two numbers and return the value in a third could be written as follows:

```
SUB AddEmUp (NumOne AS SINGLE, NumTwo AS SINGLE,
    TheSum AS SINGLE)
TheSum = NumOne + NumTwo
END SUB
```

This procedure is so simple you probably would never write it yourself, but it does demonstrate all the parts of a SUB procedure. The first line

declares the procedure name and arguments, with each argument getting an explicit type declaration. The second line adds the first two arguments together and stores that value in the third, which is passed back to the calling routine in the argument list. You also could pass the value back in one of the first two arguments.

To execute or call a procedure from some other procedure, type the name of the procedure you want to call at the place you want it called. Follow the procedure name with the arguments you want sent to it. In contrast to the argument list in the heading of the SUB procedure, the argument list in the calling statement is not enclosed by parentheses. However, each argument in the calling statement corresponds, one for one, with the arguments in the procedure heading. If an argument is passing a value back to the calling procedure, a variable must be used to receive it; otherwise, you could use constant values. For example, to call the AddEmUp procedure from the Form_Click procedure, type

```
SUB Form_Click ()
A = 185
B = 723
AddEmUp A, B, C
Form1.PRINT A, B, C
AddEmUp 5, 7, ANumber
Form1.PRINT ANumber
END SUB
```

The first line defines the Form_Click event procedure. The second and third lines load the variables A and B with the values 185 and 723. The fourth line calls the procedure AddEmUp with A, B, and C as the arguments. Note that there are no parentheses around the arguments, as there are in the definition of AddEmUp. The fifth line prints the values of the three arguments after control returns from AddEmUp. The sixth line calls the procedure again, this time with constant values, rather than variables, as two of the arguments. The third argument still must be a variable because it receives the result of the SUB procedure's calculation. When this procedure is run, it produces this text on the form:

```
185             723             908
12
```

To write a procedure on a form in Visual Basic, execute the New **Sub** or New **Function** command of the **Edit** menu. Alternatively, type the first line of the procedure. As soon as you press Enter, Visual Basic creates a template for the new procedure, including the END SUB statement. To find the procedure, press the Code button on the Project window and select the procedure from the list. Do the same to create a SUB procedure in a module.

User-Defined Functions

In addition to SUB procedures, you also can create FUNCTION procedures. A FUNCTION procedure is similar to such built-in functions as SIN() or MID$(). A FUNCTION procedure, like a SUB procedure, can modify its arguments and execute BASIC statements. In addition, it returns a value stored in the function's name. The syntax of a function statement is

```
[STATIC] FUNCTION funcname ([arguments]) [AS type]
END FUNCTION
```

Here, *funcname* is the name of the function, and *arguments* is a comma-separated list of the names of the local variables that receive the values of the arguments from the calling procedure. Because a FUNCTION procedure returns a value in the function name, that name must have a type like any other variable. To set the type of the function name, either declare it globally with a COMMON or DIM statement, use a type-declaration suffix on the name, or include the AS type clause in the function statement. The STATIC option causes the variables to persist from one calling of the function to the next.

Before the end of the FUNCTION procedure, an assignment statement must assign a value to a variable with the same name as the function, to be returned by it when the END FUNCTION statement is reached. For example, the following function returns the sum of its two arguments:

```
FUNCTION AddEmUpFunc (VarOne AS SINGLE,
    VarTwo AS SINGLE) AS SINGLE
AddEmUpFunc = VarOne + VarTwo
END FUNCTION
```

Again, this function is overly simple, but it demonstrates the syntax of the FUNCTION statement. A function need not be this simple; it can contain many statements, including calls to other FUNCTION and SUB procedures. The first line of the example defines the function name, its data type, and the types of the arguments it expects. The second line calculates the sum of the two arguments and assigns that value to the function name. The third line ends the procedure.

The calling syntax of a FUNCTION procedure is somewhat different from that of a SUB procedure due to the value returned. A FUNCTION procedure is called in exactly the same way as any of the built-in functions. For example, this function might be called, in lines 4 and 6 of the Form_Click procedure, as

```
SUB Form_Click ()
A = 185
B = 723
C = AddEmUpFunc(A, B)
Form1.PRINT A, B, C
Form1.PRINT AddEmUpFunc(5, 7)
END SUB
```

This procedure gives exactly the same results as the one that used the AddEmUp SUB procedure. (I would be upset if it didn't.) Note that only two arguments are passed to the function, and the third is returned as the function name. The value assigned to C could just as easily have been returned as an argument as in the SUB procedure example. Note in the sixth line that the value returned by the function isn't assigned to a variable, but is passed directly to the PRINT method as one of its arguments.

Passing Arguments to Procedures

There are two ways to pass an argument to a SUB or FUNCTION procedure: as an address or as a value. The default is to pass arguments to a procedure by address. An address is the location of the variable in memory. By passing the address as an argument, the procedure that was called operates on the same variable as the procedure that called it, even though the calling procedure might have a different name for that variable from that in the called procedure.

If you don't want the procedure you are calling to have access to the original variable, pass the variable as a value, using the BYVAL keyword in front of the variable name when it is declared in the first line of the procedure. An alternative approach is to enclose the argument with parentheses in the calling statement. When a variable is passed as a value, the original variable is copied, and the copy is passed to the procedure. Because the procedure no longer is operating on the original variable, any changes it makes to the copy are not reflected in the original.

Formulas used as arguments of procedures always have their result passed as values, even though the default is by address. The values of properties cannot be passed by address. They must be either passed by value or assigned to another variable first, then passed to the procedure.

> Be careful of passing array variables by value: to do so, you must duplicate the whole array.

This example demonstrates calling by value and by address:

```
SUB Form_Click ()
A = 1
B = 2
C = 3
D = 4
PassTest A, B
Form1.PRINT A, B
PassTest (C), D
Form1.PRINT C, D
END SUB

SUB PassTest (One AS SINGLE, BYVAL Two AS SINGLE)
Form1.PRINT One, Two
One = 10
Two = 20
END SUB
```

When this program is run and the form clicked, the following values are printed:

```
1          2
10         2
3          4
3          4
```

Lines 2 through 5 of the Form_Click procedure initialize the four variables A, B, C, and D, as 1, 2, 3, and 4. In line 6, the PassTest Sub procedure is called, and is passed A and B as arguments. In the PassTest procedure, the first line specifies that the second argument is passed by value and the first is by address. The second line then prints the two variables One and Two, which have been passed the values 1 and 2. In

lines 3 and 4, the PassTest procedure changes the values of the arguments to 10 and 20, and then ends in line 5.

The current values of A and B are printed in line 7 of the Form_Click procedure. Because the first argument is passed by address, the new value of 10 is passed back from the variable One in the PassTest procedure to the variable A in the Form_Click procedure. The second argument is passed by value, so the new value of 20 for variable Two is not passed back to the variable B.

In line 8, the variables C and D are passed to the PassTest procedure. As before, the value of the second variable, D, is passed by value and is unchanged by the procedure. This time, however, the parentheses around C pass the first argument by value as well, so neither variable is changed outside the PassTest procedure.

Displaying and Selecting with Lists

Two new controls are list boxes and combo boxes. A list box holds a list of strings from which the user can choose. A combo box combines a list box with a text box, so users also can type a value not on the list in the list box.

There are three types of combo boxes, selected with the Style property. Figure 8.1 shows a list box and the three types of combo boxes.

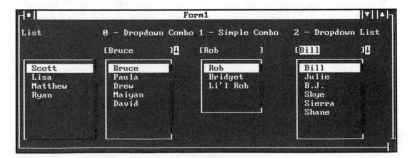

Figure 8.1. A list box and three types of combo boxes.

A list box contains a list of values, from which the user can select only one. A combo box combines a list box and a text box, and offers more options. A style 0 combo box is a drop-down combo box, with a text box at the top and a list box that drops down when the small down arrow on the right is pressed. If a list item is selected in the list part of the combo box, that list item is placed in the text part of the combo box, where it can be edited. Style 1 is a simple combo box, which also has a text box at the top and a list box below it. The only difference between a style 0 and style 1 combo box is that the list does not drop down in the style 1 combo box, but is permanently displayed. A style 2 combo box is a drop-down list box, which actually is a list box rather than a combo box because the box at the top only displays the currently selected item, and cannot be edited.

Use list and drop-down list boxes when you have a specific list of values for users to choose from, and don't want users to be able to type their own values. Use the simple and drop-down combo boxes when you have a list of possible values for users to select, but also want to enable users to type their own values. The drop-down versions of these boxes also save space on a form.

Although all these boxes respond to the Click event when an item is selected, it's better to let the user select an item, then use a button to signify acceptance of that item. This is especially true if the action performed is irreversible, such as the deletion of a file. You could then add a DoubleClick event on the list or combo box that also executes the button's event procedure. That way, a user can either click an item in the list and press the button to accept it, or double-click the list item. These actions have the same effect.

Combo and list boxes have some special properties and methods. The important methods are ADDITEM, which adds an item to a list, and REMOVEITEM, which removes an item from a list. Table 8.1 lists these properties.

Table 8.1. Special properties of combo and list boxes.

Property	Meaning
List	An array of strings, containing all the items in the list
ListCount	The number of items in a list
ListIndex	The index of the currently selected item
Sorted	An indicator of whether the list is sorted or displayed as input

All the text box properties, such as `SelLength`, `SelStart`, `SelText`, and `Text`, also apply to the text box part of the combo boxes. You cannot insert values in the list part of these boxes at design time, but must insert them at runtime using the `ADDITEM` method. The syntax of the `ADDITEM` method is

```
[form.] control.ADDITEM item$ [,index%]
```

where *form* is the name of the form to which the control is attached, *control* is the control name of the list or combo box, and `item$` is a string to insert into the list. (The *form* variable defaults to the form containing the statement if the variable is omitted.) The optional *index%* argument controls where the item is inserted in the list. If *index%* is omitted, the new item is inserted at the bottom of the list unless the `Sorted` property is True, in which case the item is inserted into its alphabetical location.

As you might expect, the `REMOVEITEM` method performs the opposite function of the `ADDITEM` method. The syntax is

```
[form.]control.REMOVEITEM index%
```

Items in a list are indexed from the top, starting with index number 0. The second item is index number 1, the third is 2, and so on. The `ListCount` property contains the number of items currently in the list, and the `ListIndex` property contains the index number of the currently selected item. To see the contents of the currently selected item, use the `List` property with `ListIndex` as the argument, in the following manner:

```
item$ = [form.] control.List([form.]control.ListIndex)
```

As you can see, the `List` property is an array of strings, and you are selecting the current one by using the `ListIndex` property. The `Text` property also contains the currently selected item when the item is selected, but can be changed afterward by the user.

The Automated Check Register Program

The automated check register program is a check register stored in the computer. It automatically inserts the next check number and date, has a combo box containing several common entries for the description field, and automatically maintains the account balance. The register is stored in a list box, and selecting an item in that list brings it into the text boxes for editing.

With some modification, you could use this program as a general purpose journal, which forms the beginning of an accounting system.

You begin creating the program by drawing the user interface:

1. Start a new project by executing the New Project command and then the New Form command of the File menu. Use CKREG1.FRM as the form's filename. Execute the Save Project command of the File menu and use CKREG.MAK as the project filename.

2. Adjust the size of the form to 78 characters by 14 characters, and set the following properties:

   ```
   Caption = Check Register
   ControlBox = False
   MaxButton = False
   BorderStyle = 3 - Fixed Double
   ```

3. Draw five labels on the form, as shown in Figure 8.2, and type the properties as shown in the following table.

	Label1	*Label2*	*Label3*	*Label4*	*Label5*
Caption	Number	Date	Description	Amount	Balance
Height	1	1	1	1	1
Width	7	8	19	10	8
Top	1	1	1	1	1
Left	2	9	21	47	61

Figure 8.2. *Layout of the form for the automated check register program.*

Draw a row of labels, text, and combo boxes to use as input boxes for an entry into the check register, as shown in Figure 8.2. The three text boxes are for the check number, the date, and the amount of the check or deposit, all of which are editable quantities. The combo box is for the description of the transaction, and has a list of standard transactions, plus an editable box to insert a transaction not on the list. The label box is for the balance, which cannot be edited because it depends on the previous balance and the current entry.

4. Draw a text box on the form to hold the check number, and set its properties as follows:

```
CtlName = CkNumBox
Height = 1
Width = 7
Top = 2
Left = 1
```

5. Draw another text box on the form to hold the date, and set its properties as follows:

```
CtlName = DateBox
Height = 1
Width = 12
Top = 2
Left = 8
```

6. Draw a third text box on the form to hold the amount, and set its properties as follows:

```
CtlName = AmountBox
Height = 1
Width = 13
Top = 2
Left = 46
```

7. Draw a Label on the form to hold the balance, and set its properties as follows:

```
CtlName = BalanceBox
Height = 1
Width = 12
Top = 2
Left = 61
BorderStyle = 0 - none
```

8. Draw a combo box on the form to hold the description of the transaction, and set its properties as follows:

```
CtlName = DescBox
Height = 1
Width = 26
Top = 2
Left = 20
Style = 0 - Dropdown Combo
```

9. Draw a list box on the form and type its properties, as follows:

```
CtlName = Register
Height = 5
Width = 75
Top = 6
Left = 0
```

Next, attach two option buttons to select whether the current entry is a payment or deposit, then three command buttons to control insertion and deletion of new records. (Your screen should look like Figure 8.2.) The New button sets up the entry boxes for a new entry, setting the current date, check number, and balance. The Insert button inserts the data currently in the text boxes into the check record, either at the end for a new entry or to replace an entry selected for corrections. The Delete button deletes the selected entry from the check record.

Note the ampersand (&) in the Caption properties of the controls for these buttons. That character marks the following letter in their names as an access key for the controls, just as it did for the menu commands in Chapter 7, "Creating Custom Menus." You can select a control with an access key by simultaneously pressing Alt and the access key. Note also that the Insert button has the Default property set to True. Only one control on a form can have its Default property set, and that control is clicked if the Enter key is pressed (assuming the focus is not on another command button).

10. Draw an option button on the form and set its properties as follows:

```
CtlName = Debit
Caption = P&ayment
Height = 1
Width = 12
Top = 4
Left = 2
Value = True
```

11. Draw a second option button on the form and set its properties as follows:

```
CtlName = Credit
Caption = D&eposit
Height = 1
Width = 13
Top = 4
Left = 16
Value = False
```

12. Draw a command button on the form and set its properties as follows:

```
CtlName = NewCmd
Caption = &New
Height = 3
Width = 10
Top = 3
Left = 32
```

13. Draw a second command button on the form and set its properties as follows:

```
CtlName = InsertCmd
Caption = &Insert
Height = 3
Width = 105
Top = 3
Left = 48
Default = True
```

14. Draw a third command button on the form and set its properties as follows:

```
CtlName = DeleteCmd
Caption = &Delete
Height = 3
Width = 10
Top = 3
Left = 64
```

15. Change the tab order of the controls so that pressing the Tab key moves the focus to the object that you most likely will want to

access next. Select the NewCmd command button and change its TabIndex property to 0. Select the rest of the controls on the form, in order, and set the TabIndex property according to Table 8.2.

Table 8.2. TabIndex values for the check register program.

CtlName	TabIndex
NewCmd	0
Register	1
DescBox	2
AmountBox	3
Debit	4
Credit	5
InsertCmd	6
CkNumBox	7
DateBox	8
DeleteCmd	9

16. Open the menu design window and create a File menu according to Table 8.3.

Table 8.3. The File menu setup for the check register program.

Caption	Control Name	Number of Indents
&File	FileMenu	0
&Print	PrintCmd	1
-	SepBar1	1
E&xit	ExitCmd	1

This completes the visual interface, which now should look like Figure 8.2.

The next step is to add code to these controls. First, define the constants True and False, then declare some variables at the form level to hold the check number (CkNum) and current balance (Balance). NewFlag is a flag that indicates whether this is a new record being inserted into the check record, or an old record being edited. InitialBalance is the starting balance for the program.

17. Open the declarations section of the form, and type the following. Note that Visual Basic automatically inserts several declarations here, so don't be alarmed when you see them.

```
CONST True = -1, False = 0
DIM SHARED CkNum AS INTEGER, Balance AS DOUBLE,
     NewFlag AS INTEGER
DIM SHARED InitialBalance AS DOUBLE
```

The Form_Load procedure initializes the variables and sets up the program. The procedure inserts the initial balance into the register, as if it were a deposit. I chose a starting number of 1000 for the checks in line 3 and an initial balance of $980 in line 4. Lines 6 through 14 load values in the DescBox list box. Because you cannot load a list box at design time, the running code must load it. Lines 16 through 21 load the initial values in the text boxes, then the routine Box2List is called in line 22. The Box2List routine takes the data from all the text boxes, stores it in a string, and returns that string to the argument Entry$. In line 23, the ADDITEM method inserts Entry$ into the Register list box.

You don't want users to insert data or change the entry type until they have either initialized a new record with the New button or selected a list item from the Register list box for editing, so the rest of this procedure disables the Insert and Delete buttons and the Deposit and Payment option buttons. After you press New or select a record, the buttons are enabled again.

18. Create the Form_Load procedure and type the following:

```
SUB Form_Load ()
InitialBalance = 980      'Set the initial values
CkNum = 1000
Balance = InitialBalance
'Insert some items in the Description list
DescBox.ADDITEM "Shane's Candy"
DescBox.ADDITEM "Travis Bank and Trust"
DescBox.ADDITEM "Jennie's Sewing Shop"
DescBox.ADDITEM "Today Computers"
```

```
DescBox.ADDITEM "Nicole's Day-care"
DescBox.ADDITEM "Adam's Consulting"
DescBox.ADDITEM "Orvis Cattle Co."
DescBox.ADDITEM "Pay"
DescBox.ADDITEM "Royalty Payment"
'Insert the initial balance in the register    line 15
    as a deposit
CkNumBox.Text = ""
DateBox.Text = "01-01-1992"
DescBox.Text = "Starting Balance"
Credit.Value = True
AmountBox.Text = "      980.00"
BalanceBox.Caption = "      980.00"
Box2List Entry$     'Store the data in the string Entry
Register.ADDITEM Entry$      'Store the new item in the
  Register
'Disable the Insert and Delete Buttons
InsertCmd.Enabled = False
DeleteCmd.Enabled = False
'Disable the Payment/Deposit options
Debit.Enabled = False
Credit.Enabled = False
END SUB
```

The New command button sets up the text boxes for a new entry. First, lines 2 and 3 enable the Debit and Credit option buttons. Lines 5 through 11 enter the default values for a check into the text boxes. Line 13 sets NewFlag to indicate that this is a new entry. A new record has now been initialized: enable the Insert command button in line 14 so the record can be stored, then disable the Delete button. The most logical thing for the user to do next is to select the description, so move the focus to the Description list in line 16.

19. Create the NewCmd_Click procedure and type the following:

```
SUB NewCmd_Click ()
Debit.Enabled = True
Credit.Enabled = True
'Set default values for a new check
Debit.Value = True
CkNumBox.Text = STR$(CkNum)
DateBox.Text = DATE$
DescBox.Text = ""
```

```
AmountBox.Text = ""
Balance = GetBalance(Register.ListCount - 1)
BalanceBox.Caption = FORMAT$(Balance, "0.00")
'Set the new flag and enable the Insert command
NewFlag = True
InsertCmd.Enabled = True
DeleteCmd.Enabled = False
DescBox.SetFocus
END SUB
```

After pressing the New button, you might want to insert a deposit rather than a check. Clicking the Deposit button executes the Credit_Click procedure, which changes the entry to a deposit, and deletes the check number. Clicking the Payment button executes the Debit_click procedure, changes the entry back to a check record, and inserts the check number back into the CkNumBox text box. Both procedures end by calling the AmountBox_Change procedure to update the balance.

20. Create the Credit_Click and Debit_Click procedures and type the following:

```
SUB Credit_Click ()
CkNumBox.Text = ""
AmountBox_Change
END SUB

SUB Debit_Click ()
CkNumBox.Text = STR$(CkNum)
AmountBox_Change
END SUB
```

After you complete filling the text boxes for a record, you press the Insert button. The procedure attached to this button first calls the Box2List procedure to copy the data from the text boxes and return it in the string Entry$. In line 3, a block IF statement breaks the routine into two different parts: one for a new record and one for a changed record. If the record is a new one, the procedure adds it to the Register list box by using the ADDITEM method in line 4. Then, if the entry was for a check (Debit.Value = True), the procedure adds one to the variable CkNum to advance the check number, and updates the current balance. The procedure then disables the Insert and Delete buttons so you can't insert or delete a record until you either press New or select a record to edit in the Register list box.

If the entry was for a changed record rather than for a new one, the block of code starting in line 14 is executed. Instead of using the ADDITEM method to add a new entry, this statement uses the List property of the Register list box to replace the existing entry with the edited one in the string Entry$.

The List property is an array of strings containing the items in the list, and the ListIndex property contains the currently selected one. Because an entry has been changed, the current balance in the replaced entry and all those following it might not be correct, so line 15 calls the FixBalance procedure to recalculate the balance for all the entries in the Register text box. Then the Register_Click procedure is called to read the corrected data back into the text boxes. The last few lines of the routine disable the option buttons and move the focus to the New command button.

21. Create the InsertCmd_Click procedure and type the following:

```
SUB InsertCmd_Click ()
Box2List Entry$    'copy the data into the string Entry
IF NewFlag = True THEN
  Register.ADDITEM Entry$
  If Debit.Value = True THEN
    CkNum = CkNum + 1
  END IF
  Balance = GetBalance(Register.ListCount - 1)
  REM If you wanted to print checks from this program
  REM you would call a check printing routine here.
  InsertCmd.Enabled = False
  DeleteCmd.Enabled = False
ELSE
  Register.List(Register.ListIndex) = Entry$
  FixBalance      'Recalculate the Balance field
  Register_Click
END IF
Debit.Enabled = False
Credit.Enabled = False
NewCmd.SETFOCUS
END SUB
```

The Register_Click procedure is executed whenever an item in the Register list box is clicked. The procedure first sets the flag NewFlag to False, indicating this is an old record rather than a new one. Then, in lines 4 and 5, Register_Click extracts the selected record into the string variable

Entry$ and calls the List2Box SUB procedure to put the values in the text boxes. In line 6, Register_Click uses the GetBalance FUNCTION procedure to get the current balance from the record just before the selected one (Register.ListIndex - 1). Finally, Register_Click enables the Insert and Delete buttons.

22. Create the Register_Click procedure and type the following:

```
SUB Register_Click ()
NewFlag = False
'Get the entry from the Register and put it in the text boxes
Entry$ = Register.Text
List2Box Entry$
Balance = GetBalance(Register.ListIndex - 1)
'Turn on the Insert and Delete commands
InsertCmd.Enabled = True
DeleteCmd.Enabled = True
END SUB
```

The DeleteCmd_Click procedure is executed when the Delete button is pressed. This procedure first checks whether the selected list item is not the first list item that contains the starting balance. If it isn't, the procedure deletes the selected item with the REMOVEITEM method. Because removing an item makes the current balance incorrect, the procedure calls the FixBalance SUB procedure to recalculate it. Finally, DeleteCmd_Click disables the Delete and Insert buttons.

23. Open the DeleteCmd_Click procedure and type the following:

```
SUB DeleteCmd_Click ()
IF Register.ListIndex > 0 THEN
  Register.REMOVEITEM Register.ListIndex
  FixBalance
END IF
DeleteCmd.Enabled = False
InsertCmd.Enabled = False
END SUB
```

The PrintCmd_Click procedure is executed whenever the **Print** command is selected from the **File** menu. The procedure starts a FOR/NEXT loop counting over the number of items in the list box (0 to ListCount-1.). The integer variable I%, which is the loop counter for the FOR/NEXT loop, selects the list item in line 30. This procedure then uses the PRINT method to print the list item. At the end, PrintCmd_Click executes the ENDDOC method to tell the printer it is done, and to begin printing.

24. Create the `PrintCmd_Click` procedure and type the following:

```
SUB PrintCmd_Click ()
FOR I% = 0 TO Register.ListCount - 1
  PRINTER.PRINT Register.List(I%)
NEXT I%
PRINTER.ENDDOC
END SUB
```

25. Create the `ExitCmd_Click` procedure and type

```
SUB ExitCmd_Click ()
END
END SUB
```

The `ExitCmd_Click` procedure is executed when the Exit command is selected from the File menu. The procedure simply executes an END statement to end the program. If the Control menu were enabled, you would need a `Form_Unload` procedure that also ends the program when someone double-clicks the Control menu button or selects Close from the control menu. However, I have disabled the form's control menu, making it impossible to close the form, except by using the **Exit** command.

The `AmountBox_Change` procedure is executed whenever you type a number into the Amount text box. The procedure checks the option buttons to see whether the value in the Amount text box is a deposit or a payment, and recalculates the value in the `BalanceBox` label accordingly. As a result, the value in the `BalanceBox` changes dynamically as you type a deposit or withdrawal.

26. Create the `AmountBox_Change` procedure and type the following:

```
SUB AmountBox_Change ()
IF Debit.Value = True THEN
  BalanceBox.Caption = FORMAT$(Balance
    - VAL(AmountBox.Text), "0.00")
ELSE
  BalanceBox.Caption = FORMAT$(Balance
    + VAL(AmountBox.Text), "0.00")
END IF
END SUB
```

This completes the event procedures; now we consider the user-defined procedures. As you type these procedures, be sure to select the correct type—FUNCTION or SUB—otherwise, the program does not work. The first user-defined procedure is `Box2List`, which copies the data from

the text boxes and returns it in a string variable that can be stored in the list box. The data is stored in the string variable as indicated in Table 8.4.

Table 8.4. Breakdown of the variable TheString$.

Contents	Starting Character	Length
Check number	1	6
Date	8	10
Description	19	25
Debit or credit	45	1
Amount	47	12
Balance	60	12

The Box2List procedure first initializes the value of TheString$ as a string of 71 spaces. In line 3, the MID$ statement is used to insert the check number into the first six character positions. Line 4 puts the date in ten character positions starting at position number 8. Line 5 inserts the description in 25 characters, starting at position number 19. Lines 6 through 10 insert a D or C at character position 45, depending on whether this is a payment or deposit. Next are two dollar amounts. Although all the items so far have been left-justified into the string locations, dollar amounts look better if they are right-justified. To right-justify the variables, create a temporary variable, Temp$, containing 12 blanks. Use the RSET method to right-justify the dollar amounts into the temporary variable, then insert the temporary variable into TheString$. Lines 11 through 13 insert the amount of the debit or credit starting at position 47, and lines 14 through 16 insert the balance starting in position 60.

27. Execute the New **S**ub command of the **F**ile menu, name the new procedure Box2List, and type the following:

```
SUB Box2List (TheString$)
TheString$= SPACE$(71)
MID$(TheString$, 1, 6) = CkNumBox.Text
MID$(TheString$, 8, 10) = DateBox.Text
MID$(TheString$, 19, 25) = DescBox.Text
IF Debit.Value = True THEN
  MID$(TheString$, 45) = "D"
```

```
ELSE
  MID$(TheString$, 45) = "C"
END IF
Temp$ = SPACE$(12)
RSET Temp$ = FORMAT$(VAL(AmountBox.Text), "0.00")
MID$(TheString$, 47, 12) = Temp$
Temp$ = SPACE$(12)
RSET Temp$ = BalanceBox.Caption
MID$(TheString$, 60, 12) = Temp$
END SUB
```

The List2Box SUB procedure reverses the process of the Box2List procedure. The List2Box procedure is passed TheString$, and uses the MID$() function to extract the six substrings listed in Table 8.1. The procedure then places those substrings in the appropriate label or text box.

28. Execute the New **S**ub command on the **E**dit menu, name the new procedure List2Box, and type the following:

```
SUB List2Box (TheString$)
CkNumBox.Text = MID$(TheString$, 1, 6)
DateBox.Text = MID$(TheString$, 8, 10)
DescBox.Text = MID$(TheString$, 19, 25)
IF MID$(TheString$, 45, 1) = "D" THEN
  Debit.Value = True
ELSE
  Credit.Value = True
END IF
Debit.Enabled = False
Credit.Enabled = False
AmountBox.Text = LTRIM$(MID$(TheString$, 47, 12))
BalanceBox.Caption = LTRIM$(MID$(TheString$, 60, 12))
END SUB
```

The FixBalance SUB procedure loops over all the list items in the Register list box, and calculates and updates the running balance in each item. The procedure calculates the balance for an item in line 5 by adding the previous balance returned by the GetBalance() FUNCTION procedure to the current debit or credit returned by the GetChange() FUNCTION procedure. The FixBalance procedure then updates the balance in the current item with the PutBalance SUB procedure.

29. Execute the New **Sub** command of the **File** menu, name the new procedure FixBalance, and type

```
SUB FixBalance ()
REM Fix the balance column after an adjustment
IF Register.ListCount > 0 THEN
  FOR I% = 0 TO Register.ListCount - 1
    Balance = GetBalance(I% - 1) + GetChange(i%)
    PutBalance I%, Balance
  NEXT I%
END IF
END SUB
```

The GetChange() procedure returns the debit or credit amount from the item number contained in its argument. Because this procedure returns a single value, make GetChange() a FUNCTION procedure. This procedure first checks whether the argument index is valid, then uses it to select a list item in the Register list box. The item is stored in Entry$. GetChange() extracts the amount from Entry$ in line 6 and stores it in a temporary, double-precision variable, Temp#. The procedure then tests whether this is a debit or credit, and returns a positive or negative value accordingly in GetChange.

30. Execute the New **Function** command of the **File** menu, name the new procedure GetChange(), and type the following:

```
FUNCTION GetChange (index AS INTEGER) AS DOUBLE
IF index < 0 THEN
  GetChange = 0
ELSE
  Entry$ = Register.List(index)
  Temp# = VAL(MID$(Entry$, 47, 12))
  IF MID$(Entry$, 45, 1) = "D" THEN
    GetChange = -Temp#
  ELSE
    GetChange = Temp#
  END IF
END IF
END FUNCTION
```

The GetBalance() and PutBalance() procedures either get or change the balance in the list item selected with index. GetBalance is a FUNCTION procedure because it returns a single value, and you want to use it the way you use a function. GetBalance() first checks for an out-of-range index, and extracts the list item into the string Entry$. Then GetBalance() extracts the numeric value of the balance and returns it in GetBalance. PutBalance() does just the opposite; it also checks the index, and extracts the list item into Entry$ in line 3. PutBalance() then replaces the value in the list item with the new value in lines 4 through 6. Finally, PutBalance() stores the list item back into the list in line 7.

31. Execute the New Function command of the File menu, name the new procedure GetBalance(), and type the following:

```
FUNCTION GetBalance (index AS INTEGER) AS DOUBLE
IF index < 0 THEN
  GetBalance = InitialBalance
ELSE
  Entry$ = Register.List(index)
  GetBalance = VAL(MID$(Entry$, 60, 12))
END IF
END FUNCTION
```

32. Execute the New Sub command of the File menu, name the new procedure PutBalance, and type the following:

```
SUB PutBalance (index AS INTEGER, bal AS DOUBLE)
IF index > 0 THEN
  Entry$ = Register.List(index)
  Temp$ = SPACE$(14)
  RSET Temp$ = FORMAT$(bal, "0.00")
  MID$(Entry$, 62) = Temp$
  Register.List(index) = Entry$
END IF
END SUB
```

33. Save the project and run it. Click the New button, then click the down arrow on the right side of the drop-down combo box. Your screen should look like Figure 8.3.

34. Select Shane's Candy as the description, type **50** as the amount, and press Enter or click the Insert button. The check register should now look like Figure 8.4.

35. Type several more entries, both payments and deposits. The check register should look something like Figure 8.5.

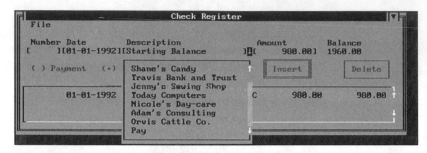

Figure 8.3. *The automated check register program with the description list pulled down.*

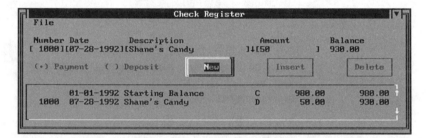

Figure 8.4. *The automated check register program with the first entry inserted.*

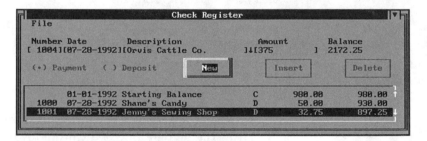

Figure 8.5. *The automated check register program with several entries.*

36. Select an entry from the Register list box, and note how it's extracted into the text boxes at the top of the form, as shown in Figure 8.6, and in Plate 2 on the inside front cover of this book. Try changing the amount, clicking Insert to make the change and update the balance. Try deleting an entry by selecting it and pressing the Delete button. Try printing with the Print command of the File menu.

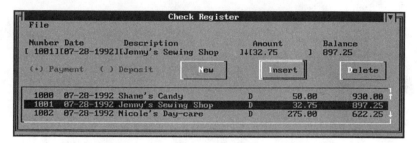

Figure 8.6. *The automated check register program with a list item selected.*

This check register program lacks a command to insert new records within the record rather than at the end. However, that would be a relatively easy command to add. Just follow the logic of the Insert command, but insert the record using an index with the ADDITEM method.

Because you have already typed all the names and numbers, you could add a command to read the Register list box and to print your checks for you. You would have to tell the routine which check to start with, and to skip any deposits. In addition, you could create a similar command that reads deposits and prints deposit slips.

Right now, the program also lacks a way to save all the entries after they have been entered, so don't spend a week typing all your checks into this program—you'll be upset when you exit the program and everything disappears. Saving the lists is covered in Chapter 9, "Using Sequential Files."

What You Have Learned

This chapter examined how to create procedures to modularize a program and reuse code. There are two types of procedures: SUB procedures and FUNCTION procedures. They are quite similar: both types of procedures accept values as arguments, do calculations, execute methods, and return values in the arguments. In addition, a FUNCTION procedure also returns a value stored in the function's name. The chapter also looked at list and combo boxes for inputting and storing lists of data. You have explored the details of

- SUB procedures

- FUNCTION procedures

- Arguments passed to procedures as values or addresses

- List and combo boxes

- An automated check register program

Using Sequential Files

Until now, you have saved programs in disk files with the save commands of Visual Basic's File menu, but you haven't saved the data within your programs. Saving data is essential; in the last chapter, for example, the check register program you developed is useless if you can't save the data in the Register list box. So now it's time to look at the different ways to use disk files to save and retrieve data.

In This Chapter

There are three types of disk files in Visual Basic: sequential, random access, and binary. Binary disk files are used for advanced applications that require access to the raw bytes of a data file, and are beyond the scope of this book. Random access files are discussed in Chapter 10, "Using Random Access Files." This chapter discusses

- Creating and opening sequential files
- Reading and writing data to sequential files
- Creating file-access dialog boxes
- Using the common dialog toolkit

Storing Data in Disk Files

The three types of data files used in Visual Basic are random access, binary, and sequential.

Random access files, as the name implies, are not accessed in linear fashion. They are accessed in fixed-length blocks, known as records, in any order. Random access files are discussed in Chapter 10, "Using Random Access Files."

Binary files actually are similar to random access files, except that binary files are read and written byte-by-byte rather than record-by-record, and no special significance is placed on the value of any byte (such as the carriage return line-feed pair). Binary files are beyond the scope of this book, so I won't discuss them any further.

Sequential files are text files, read or written sequentially (from the beginning to the end) as a linear sequence of variable-length lines of text, with a line-feed carriage return at the end of each line. They are text files that can be listed on the screen or printer with the DOS TYPE or PRINT commands, or can be opened with any word processor. Numbers are stored as a sequence of digits, much as you would type them on the screen. Because they are linear, they can be read or written, but not simultaneously. That is, you cannot be reading part of a file at the same time you're writing another part, although you can be reading two different parts at the same time.

Opening and Closing Sequential Files

Sequential files and, in fact, all files, are created or opened with the OPEN statement. The syntax of the OPEN statement is

↪ **OPEN** *name$* [**FOR** *mode*] [**ACCESS** *access*] [*lock*]
     AS [**#**]*filenumber%* [**LEN** = *rlen%*]

Here, *name$* is a string variable, or a quoted string containing the name of the file to open, and the path, if it isn't in the default directory. The path is the disk name and list of directories you must traverse to reach a file. For example, if the absolute path to the file FILE.TXT is

D:\DIR1\DIR2\DIR3\FILE.TXT

where D is the disk letter, DIR1, DIR2, and DIR3 are the directories you must traverse, and FILE.TXT is the filename and extension of the file. In this case, the file FILE.TXT is in directory DIR3, which is in directory DIR2, which is in directory DIR1, which is in the root directory of disk D. A path also can be relative to the current default directory. For example, if DIR2 is the current default directory, then the path

DIR3\FILE.TXT

points to the same file. The default directory is changed by several commands and programs, so you can't always depend on it to be a specific directory. In any program, it's much safer to use absolute paths because they always point to a specific file.

The *mode* of the file is either APPEND, BINARY, INPUT, OUTPUT, or RANDOM. The *access* argument controls the file-access type, and is either READ, WRITE, or READ WRITE. The *lock* argument has the value LOCK READ or LOCK WRITE, and controls access to a file by other processes. The *filenumber%* is a unique number that identifies the open file to all the other file-access commands. The *rlen%* argument is the record length, in bytes, to use with random access files.

For sequential files, the acceptable modes are INPUT, OUTPUT, or APPEND. When a file is opened FOR INPUT, the file already must exist, and you can only read data from it. When a file is opened FOR OUTPUT, it is opened if it exists or created if it does not exist, and you can only write data to it. When an existing file is opened FOR OUTPUT, writing starts at the first record, overwriting any old data in the file. The APPEND mode is a variation of OUTPUT. When the file is opened, writing starts at the end, preserving the old data.

The *access* and *lock* arguments apply to networked environments, where multiple users may have access to the same file. The *access* argument tells the system what access you want for the file, in case someone else already has it open. If that level of access is available, then you will be allowed to open the file. The *lock* argument tells the system what access you

are willing to allow others if you are the first to open the file. If you don't use the *lock* argument, then no one else will have access to the file. If you LOCK WRITE the file, then other programs can open and read it, but cannot change it. You do not need these arguments in a single-user situation.

You must include the *filenumber* argument with every OPEN statement, and use the argument with every command that accesses the file. Because you might have more than one file open at any one time, this number uniquely identifies each open file. Usually, the first file you open is file number 1, the second is 2, and so forth. If you close a file, you can reuse its file number. If you know how many files you have open, you can assign a constant for the file number. However, if you don't know how many files your program will have open, such as if you are creating a word processor that may have multiple files open simultaneously, use the FREEFILE function to give you the next available file number. For example:

```
InputFileNum% = FREEFILE
OPEN "MYFILE.TXT" FOR INPUT AS # InputFileNum%
```

This opens the file named MYFILE.TXT as a sequential file for reading only. The file number is selected with the FREEFILE function, so use the variable InputFileNum% whenever the file is accessed. If this is the only file accessed by a program, you could simply use the file number 1 to open the file and, as the following example shows, use the file number 1 with every file-access command.

```
OPEN "MYFILE.TXT" FOR INPUT AS #1
```

When you're done with a file, close it with the CLOSE statement. The CLOSE statement empties all Visual Basic's file buffers and gives the information to the system for writing to the disk. The CLOSE statement also releases the file numbers for reuse with other files. The syntax is

CLOSE [[**#**]*filenumber%*] [**,**[**#**]*filenumber%*]...

where *filenumber%* is the file number used when the file was opened. To close all open files, use the CLOSE statement without the file numbers.

File systems don't write bytes to open disk files as you send them; rather, file systems collect the bytes in file buffers. A file buffer is simply a place in memory where the information is stored until it is written to disk. When a buffer is full, the information is written to disk all at once. This is why you must close files before removing a disk. If you don't do so, the file might not be there in its entirety.

Writing Sequential Files

You write data to sequential files by using the PRINT # and WRITE # statements in much the same way that you use the PRINT and WRITE statements to print data on the screen or to the printer. The difference is in the inclusion of a *filenumber*, which directs the system to print the data to a disk file. All the formatting conventions discussed previously apply here as well. The format of the PRINT # statement is

PRINT # *filenumber%, expressionlist* [{;¦,}]

where *filenumber%* is the file number used when the file was opened, and *expressionlist* is a comma- or semicolon-separated list of expressions to be printed. Expressions that evaluate to strings are printed as is; expressions that evaluate to numbers are converted to strings before being sent to the file. If expressions are separated by commas, the point of printing moves to the next tab stop (one every 14 spaces) before printing the next item. If the expressions are separated by semicolons, the next item is printed immediately following the last. Normally a carriage-return line-feed pair is inserted at the end of every PRINT # statement, unless it ends in a semicolon or comma. For example, the fragment

```
A = 5.3
PRINT #1, "The length = ";A
```

would print the following:

```
The length = 5.3
```

in file number 1.

The second way to send data to a disk file is with the WRITE # statement. The WRITE # statement works much the same as the PRINT # statement, except that commas are inserted between printed expressions and strings are surrounded by quotation marks. Data written with a WRITE # statement is easier to read back into a program than that written with PRINT #. Thus, the PRINT # statement is used mostly for creating files that are to be read by people, while WRITE # is used for data that is going to be read by a computer program. For example, the fragment

```
A1 = 5.355
B1 = 4.788
PRINT #1, "The values, are: ", A1, B1, " units"
WRITE #1, "The values, are: ", A1, B1, " units"
```

221

would produce the following text in disk file number 1:

```
The values, are:          5.355          4.788          units
"The values, are: ",5.355,4.788," units"
```

Reading Sequential Files

After you have written data to a sequential file, you might want to read it back into a program. Actually, Visual Basic can read any text file as a sequential file. To read a sequential file, use the INPUT # and LINE INPUT # statements and the INPUT$() function.

The INPUT # Statement

The INPUT # statement reads data from a disk file into its arguments. The syntax is

INPUT # *filenumber%, expressionlist*

where *filenumber%* is the number that opened the file, and *expressionlist* is a list of Visual Basic variables that receive data read from the file.

When a file is read, leading spaces are ignored. For a number, the first nonblank character is assumed to be the start of the number and the first blank, comma, or the end-of-line character terminates it. For a string, the first nonblank character starts the string and a comma or the end of the line terminates it. If the string is quoted, everything between the quotation marks is included in the string, including commas. Thus, data written with the WRITE # statement is more accurately read than data written with PRINT #. For example, reading the disk file you previously created (with the PRINT # and WRITE # statements) with the code fragment

```
INPUT #1, A$, B, C, D$
INPUT #1, E$, F, G, H$
```

would store the following data in these variables:

```
A$ = "The values"
B = 0
C = 5.355
D$ = "4.788          units"
E$ = "The values, are: "
F = 5.355
G = 4.788
H$ = " units"
```

Note that the first INPUT # statement stopped reading the string into A$ at the first comma, so that the first numeric input, B, sees text rather than a number and gets a value of zero. Then the second numeric input, C, reads the first number, and the remaining number and string end up in D$. If you look at the contents of E$, F, G, and H$, you will see that they contain the same values as were written to the disk file with the WRITE # statement, which is why I indicated that WRITE # is better for files that are going to be read by another program.

The LINE INPUT # Statement

The LINE INPUT # statement inputs one line of text into a single string variable. It reads everything in a line up to a carriage return, including leading spaces, trailing spaces, commas, and quotation marks. The syntax is

LINE INPUT # *filenumber%, string$*

where *filenumber%* is the file number used in the OPEN statement, and *string$* is a string variable. For example, if you redo the previous example with LINE INPUT # statements, as follows:

```
LINE INPUT #1, A$
LINE INPUT #1, B$
```

the variables contain exactly what is in the file:

```
A$ = The values, are:         5.355       4.788        units
B$ = "The values, are: ",5.355,4.788," units"
```

The LINE INPUT # statement typically is used to input text files for a word processor or similar program, or in a program where you are going to use the string functions, such as MID$(), to extract portions of a line.

9

The INPUT$() Function

The last input method for sequential files is the INPUT$() function. The INPUT$() function is used to input every byte in a file, including line terminators. The INPUT # and LINE INPUT # statements skip carriage returns and line feeds, but the INPUT$() function reads every byte in a file and returns them in a string. The syntax is

INPUT$(*numbytes%*,[*#*]*filenumber%*)

where *numbytes%* is the number of bytes to read from the file and return, and *filenumber%* is the file number used in the OPEN statement. For example (using the same input file as in the preceding example), in

```
A$ = INPUT$(5,#1)
B$ = INPUT$(6,#1)
```

the string variables, A$ and B$, contain

```
A$ = The v
B$ = alues,
```

The EOF() Function

An auxiliary function used with sequential files, the EOF() function returns True if you have reached the end-of-file character. If you attempt to read past the end of the file, your program generates an error. If you don't know where the end-of-file is, use the EOF() function to test a file before reading from it. The syntax of the function is

Flag% = **EOF**(*filenumber%*)

where *filenumber%* is the file number used in the OPEN statement. In the following example, EOF(1) is tested, and if it is False (0), then it is okay to input another record:

```
False = 0
IF EOF(1) = False THEN INPUT#1, A$
```

Creating File-Access Dialog Boxes

Most modern programs that access files selected by the user do so with a file-access dialog box. A file-access dialog box is a form that lets you select the drive, directory (folder), and file from a list, instead of typing a filename. You create a file-access dialog box by using three special list controls: the drive, directory, and file list boxes.

A drive list box contains a drop-down list of all the drives on your machine. Selecting a drive from the list puts the drive letter in the list's Path property.

A directory list box contains a list of the directories on the current drive. Selecting a directory from the list places the path to that directory in the box's Path property.

A file list box displays a list of the files in the directory in its Path property. Clicking a file places the file's name in the box's FileName property.

An Open Dialog Box

Combining these three list boxes and some code on a form creates a file-access dialog box. The three list boxes aren't connected in any way, so changing the drive in the drive list box doesn't change the directory list box. You need some simple pieces of code to connect the three box types.

Changing the drive in the drive list box creates a Click event on that box and changes the Path property. In the Click event procedure for the drive list box, change the Path property of the directory list box to equal the new Path in the drive list box. Clicking a directory in the directory list box also creates a Click event and changes the Path property. In the Click event procedure of the directory list box, insert a formula to change the Path property of the file list box to that in the directory list box. Add a button to combine the FileName and Path properties, and you have an Open dialog box. Add a text box to insert a new filename, and you have a Save dialog box.

9

The Check Register Program (Version 2)

This new version of the check register program actually is a continuation of the example started in Chapter 8, "Writing Custom Procedures," because without a save capability, the check register program isn't much use. In this chapter you add **Open**, **Save**, and Save **As** commands to the File menu, and attach two new forms containing an Open dialog box and a Save As dialog box. The rest of the program remains largely unchanged.

1. Open the check register program and display Form1 in the Forms Designer.

2. Open the Menu Design window, and add **Open**, **Save**, and Save **As** commands to the File menu as indicated in Table 9.1.

Table 9.1. The Menu Design window for the check register program, version 2.

Caption	Control Name	Number of Indents
&File	FileMenu	0
&Open	OpenCmd	1
&Save	SaveCmd	1
Save &As	SaveAsCmd	1
-	SepBar2	1
&Print	PrintCmd	1
-	SepBar1	1
E&xit	ExitCmd	1

The following three procedures are attached to the three new commands on the File menu. Their only function is to pass control to the file-access dialog boxes. Note the constant AsModal following the SHOW method in each procedure. The constant is defined as the number 1 in the declarations section and makes the Dialog boxes modal. When a form is modal, you can't select any other forms until you close the modal form. Also, any code following the SHOW method that displayed a modal form isn't executed until the form is hidden or unloaded. If a form isn't modal, you can move to other forms by clicking them.

The `SaveCmd_Click` procedure tests the global variable `FileName` to see whether `FileName` is blank. If it's not blank, a file already is attached to this program, so the procedure calls the `SaveIt` SUB procedure to save the contents of the Register list box. If `FileName` is blank, the data hasn't been saved yet, and the procedure calls the `SaveDialog` form to attach a file.

3. Switch to the Programming Environment, create the `OpenCmd_Click` procedure, and type

```
SUB OpenCmd_Click ()
OpenDialog.SHOW AsModal
END SUB
```

4. Create the `SaveCmd_Click` procedure and type

```
SUB SaveCmd_Click ()
IF FileName <> "" THEN
  SaveIt
ELSE
  SaveDialog.SHOW AsModal
END IF
END SUB
```

5. Create the `SaveAsCmd_Click` procedure and type

```
SUB SaveAsCmd_Click ()
SaveDialog.SHOW AsModal
END SUB
```

The next steps move all the declarations and definitions in the declarations section into an include file (.BI) and then include that file in the declarations section of all the forms.

6. Open the declarations section of Form1 and cut everything but the automatically inserted DECLARE statements. Execute the New **Module** command of the File menu, select **Include File**, and use the name CKREGG.BI. Execute the **P**aste command to paste the declarations from Form1. Add the definition for the `FileName` variable and `AsModal` constant. Add $FORM metacommands for the three forms as well, to enable each form to access the others. It should now read as follows:

```
CONST True = -1, False = 0, AsModal = 1
COMMON SHARED CkNum AS INTEGER, Balance AS DOUBLE
COMMON SHARED NewFlag AS INTEGER
COMMON SHARED InitialBalance AS DOUBLE
COMMON SHARED FileName AS STRING
```

```
'$FORM Form1
'$FORM OpenDialog
'$FORM SaveDialog
```

7. Save the include file with the Save File command of the File menu.

8. Open the declarations section of Form1 again and add the following $INCLUDE metacommand. This should be the only statement that you have placed in the declarations section, though Visual Basic may have automatically inserted declarations for procedures defined or used in the form.

```
'$INCLUDE: 'CKREGG.BI'
```

9. Add a new form to this project by using the New Form command of the File menu. Save it as CKREG2.FRM. Set its properties as follows:

```
Caption = Open
Height = 11
Width = 47
ControlBox = False
FormName = OpenDialog
MaxButton = False
MinButton = False
```

10. Draw a file list box on the form with the following properties:

```
Top = 1
Left = 1
Height = 8
Width = 16
Pattern = *.*
```

The Pattern property controls what files are listed in the box. Using *.* (wildcard) lists all the files in the directory.

Because the Pattern property controls which files are visible in the file list box, you might want to allow the user to change that property. The simplest way to do this is to add a text box and have its Change procedure set the Pattern property of the file list box. You also can select a standard pattern with a set of option buttons, or select from a menu. A third option is to have a text box display the currently selected file in the file list box and, if you type something that isn't a filename, use it to set the pattern property.

11. Draw a directory list box on the form with these properties:

```
Top = 3
Left = 18
Height = 6
Width = 16
```

12. Draw a drive list box on the form with these properties:

```
Top = 1
Left = 18
Width = 16
```

13. Draw a command button on the form with these properties:

```
Caption = OK
CtlName = OKCmd
Top = 0
Left = 35
Height = 3
Width = 10
Default = True
```

14. Draw another command button on the form with these properties.
    (The form now should look like Figure 9.1.)

```
Caption = Cancel
CtlName = CancelCmd
Top = 3
Left = 35
Height = 3
Width = 10
```

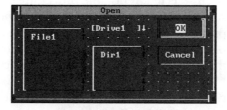

Figure 9.1. *Layout of the Open dialog box.*

15. Switch to the Programming Environment, create the `Drive1_Change` procedure, and type the following:

```
SUB Drive1_Change ()
Dir1.Path = Drive1.Drive
END SUB
```

This links the directory shown in the directory list to changes in the drive from the drive list.

16. Create the `Dir1_Change` procedure and type the following:

```
SUB Dir1_Change ()
File1.Path = Dir1.Path
END SUB
```

This links the file list to the directory selected in the directory list.

17. Create the `OKCmd_Click` procedure and type

```
SUB OKCmd_Click ()
IF File1.FileName = "" THEN
  MSGBOX "Please select a file first."
  EXIT SUB
END IF
FileName = File1.Path + "\" + File1.FileName    'line 6
ClearIt
ReadIt
OpenDialog.HIDE
END SUB
```

When the OK button is clicked, the `OKCmd_Click` procedure first checks the `FileName` property of the file list box to see whether a file has been selected. If not, the procedure displays a message box asking you to select a filename first, then executes the `EXIT SUB` statement to exit this `SUB` procedure. If a filename has been selected, line 6 combines the `Path` property with a backslash and the filename to produce a complete path to the selected file. Next the `ClearIt` procedure is called to clear the contents of the Register list box on Form1. Then the `ReadIt` procedure is called to read the contents of the selected file into the Register list box. Line 9 then hides the Open dialog box, passing control back to Form1.

18. Create the `CancelCmd_Click` procedure and type the following:

```
SUB CancelCmd_Click ()
OpenDialog.HIDE
END SUB
```

This command changes nothing, and returns control to Form1.

19. Create the `File1_DblClick` procedure and type the following:

```
SUB File1_DblClick ()
OKCmd_Click
END SUB
```

This procedure makes double-clicking a filename in the File list box the same as clicking the file and pressing the OK button. This completes the Open dialog box. Next, create the Save As dialog box, which is nearly identical to the Open dialog box, but adds a text box for the new filename.

A Save As Dialog Box

To create the Save As dialog box, follow these steps:

1. Execute the New Form command of the File menu and name it REG3.FRM. Change its properties to

```
Caption = Save As
Height = 11
Width = 48
ControlBox = False
FormName = SaveDialog
MaxButton = False
MinButton = False
```

2. Draw a file list box on the form with these properties:

```
Top = 3
Left = 1
Height = 6
Width = 16
Pattern = *.*
```

3. Draw a directory list box on the form with these properties:

```
Top = 3
Left = 18
Height = 6
Width = 16
```

4. Draw a drive list box on the form with these properties:

```
Top = 1
Left =
Width = 16
```

5. Draw a command button on the form with these properties:

```
Caption = OK
CtlName = OKCmd
Top = 0
Left = 35
Height = 3
Width = 10
Default = True
```

6. Draw another command button on the form with these properties:

```
Caption = Cancel
CtlName = CancelCmd
Top = 3
Left = 35
Height = 3
Width = 10
```

7. Draw a text box with these properties:

```
CtlName = FiName
Top = 0
Left =1
Height = 3
Width = 16
Text = ""
```

Your form now should look like Figure 9.2.

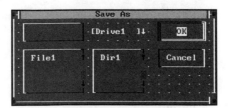

Figure 9.2. *Layout of the Save As dialog box.*

As with the Open dialog, much of the code in the Save As dialog is the same. Keep in mind that the names of the controls on both of these dialog boxes are the same, but because they are on two different forms, the names are local to those forms.

8. Switch to the Programming Environment, create the `Drive1_Change` procedure, and type the following:

```
SUB Drive1_Change ()
Dir1.Path = Drive1.Drive
END SUB
```

This action links the directory shown in the directory list to changes in the drive from the drive list.

9. Create the `Dir1_Change` procedure and type the following:

```
SUB Dir1_Change ()
File1.Path = Dir1.Path
END SUB
```

This links the file list to the directory selected in the directory list.

10. Create the `CancelCmd_Click` procedure and type the following:

```
SUB CancelCmd_Click ()
SaveDialog.HIDE
END SUB
```

This command changes nothing, and returns control to Form1.

11. Create the `OKCmd_Click` procedure and type

```
SUB OKCmd_Click ()
DIM thePath  AS STRING
'Test for no filename    line 3
IF FiName.Text = "" THEN
  MSGBOX "Type a filename first"
  EXIT SUB
END IF
'Test for path      line 8
IF INSTR(FiName.Text, "\") <> 0
   OR INSTR(FiName.Text, ":") <> 0 THEN
  MSGBOX "Filename only, no path"
  EXIT SUB
END IF
'Test for missing extension add .CKR if missing      line 13
```

233

```
FiName.Text = LTRIM$(RTRIM$(FiName.Text))
IF INSTR(FiName.Text, ".") = 0 THEN
  FiName.Text = LEFT$(FiName.Text,8) + ".CKR"
END IF
thePath = Dir1.Path + "\" + FiName.Text
'Check for existing file    line 19
IF DIR$(thePath) <> "" THEN
  Action = MSGBOX("File exists, overwrite?", 257)
  IF Action = 2 THEN EXIT SUB
END IF
'Open the file and save the check register data    line 24
FileName = thePath
File1.REFRESH
SaveIt
SaveDialog.HIDE
END SUB
```

This `OKCmd_Click` procedure is a little more complex than that in the Open dialog procedure, but only because it has to verify the filename before using it. The block of code from line 3 to line 7 checks whether you have typed a filename in the text box. If you haven't, it displays a message box asking you to do so first, then exits the procedure with an `EXIT SUB` statement. Lines 8 through 12 check whether you have typed a path in the text box as well as the filename by checking for the \ or : characters. Because you're going to create the path, you don't want users to type their own. A more complex Save As dialog could let users type their own paths.

Lines 13 through 18 of the procedure check whether the user has typed an extension on the filename by looking for the period. If not, the code block adds the .CKR extension in line 16. The `LTRIM$()` and `RTRIM$()` functions remove any blanks from the left and right sides of the filename. The `LEFT$()` function in line 16 extracts up to eight characters from the left side of the filename, ensuring that the name part of the filename is no more than eight characters long. Line 18 creates the complete path to the file by combining the directory path from the `Path` property of the directory box with a backslash and the filename from the text box.

Lines 19 through 23 of the procedure check for an existing file by using the `DIR$()` function. The `DIR$()` function returns the name of the file if it exists; otherwise, it returns an empty string. If the file already exists, a message box is displayed with an OK and a Cancel button (the 257 argument of the `MSGBOX` statement; see Chapter 15, "Command Reference," for a list of codes). If the user presses Cancel, the message box returns a value of 2, and the `EXIT SUB` statement is called to exit the procedure without overwriting the file. If the point of execution reaches line 24, the file can be created or opened, so pass the path to the global variable `FileName` and call the `SaveIt` `SUB` procedure to save the file.

> Change the `OKCmd` procedure so users can type a complete path rather than a filename. If the user types a path without a filename, make the procedure change the `Path` properties of the file list box, the directory list box, and the `Drive` property of the drive list box, then exit. If the path includes a filename, change the `Path` properties and open the file. If a pattern is typed rather than a filename, change the `Pattern` property of the file list box to that pattern.

12. Create the `File1_Click` procedure and type the following:

```
SUB File1_Click ()
FiName.Text = File1.FileName
END SUB
```

This step puts a selected filename in the text box if the user clicks it in the file list box.

13. Create the `File1_DblClick` procedure and type the following:

```
SUB File1_DblClick ()
OKCmd_Click
END SUB
```

This procedure makes double-clicking a filename in the file list box the same as clicking the file and pressing the OK button. This completes the Save As dialog box. Now create a code module for the `SaveIt`, `ClearIt`, and `ReadIt` `SUB` procedures.

14. Execute the **New Module** command of the **File** menu, select **Module**, and save the module as CKREGM.BAS.

15. Execute the **New Sub** command of the **File** menu, name the new procedure `SaveIt`, and type

```
SUB SaveIt ()
DIM I AS INTEGER
'Open the file and save the contents of Register
OPEN FileName FOR OUTPUT AS #1          'line 4
WRITE #1, Form1.Register.ListCount, CkNum, Balance,
   InitialBalance
```

235

```
FOR I = 0 TO Form1.Register.ListCount - 1          'line 6
  PRINT #1, Form1.Register.List(I)
NEXT I
CLOSE #1
END SUB
```

This procedure saves the contents of the Register list box in the file specified by the global variable FileName. Line 4 opens the file for sequential output. Line 5 writes the number of items in the list, and the value of the variables CkNum, Balance, and InitialBalance. These three values also are needed to restart the program from a data file. Note how the Register object on Form1 is accessed from this module by prefacing the object name with the form name. Unfortunately, you can't do this for user-defined variables, only for Visual Basic objects. User-defined variables have to be passed with COMMON SHARED statements.

Note also that I have used the WRITE # statement to ensure that I can extract the values correctly later. Lines 6 through 8 loop through all the items in the list box, and print each item to the disk file. I use the PRINT statement here because I am writing complete lines to the file, not individual values, though WRITE # would work as well. Line 9 closes the file.

16. Execute the New Sub command of the File menu, name the new procedure ClearIt, and type

```
SUB ClearIt ()
'Clear the contents of Register
WHILE Form1.Register.ListCount > 0
Form1.Register.REMOVEITEM 0
WEND
END SUB
```

This procedure simply clears the contents of the Register list box on Form1. Note again how I have added the form name to the list box name so I can access the object in Form1 from this module. The procedure works with a WHILE/WEND loop that checks the number of items in the Register list box by using the ListCount property. As long as there still is at least one item in the list, the loop executes the REMOVEITEM method on the first item (item number 0). This WHILE/WEND loop continues until there are no more items in the list box.

17. Execute the New **Sub** command of the **File** menu, name the new procedure ReadIt, and type

```
SUB ReadIt ()
DIM NumEntries AS INTEGER, aLine AS STRING
'Open the file and read into Register
OPEN FileName FOR INPUT AS #1
INPUT #1, NumEntries, CkNum, Balance, InitialBalance
FOR i = 1 TO NumEntries
LINE INPUT #1, aLine
Form1.Register.ADDITEM aLine
NEXT i
CLOSE #1
END SUB
```

This procedure complements the SaveIt SUB procedure. It first opens the file that has its name in the global variable FileName for sequential input. You can use the same file number here (file number 1) as you used in the SaveIt procedure because you close the file when you end that procedure. If that file were still open, you would have to use a different file number.

After opening the file, the procedure reads the number of entries into NumEntries, then reads the three values saved with the WRITE # statement back into the same variables by using the INPUT # statement. Using the NumEntries number, you know exactly how many lines of data to read, so you won't need to use the EOF() function each time to check for the end of the file. In this case, loop over the number of entries you previously wrote to the file. Because you wrote complete lines of text to the file, you can read them back with the LINE INPUT # statement. The LINE INPUT # statement loads each line into the variable aLine, and then the next statement inserts that line into the Register list box on Form1 with the ADDITEM method. Finally, the procedure closes the file.

18. Save the project; it's done. Run the program and insert a few values, then execute the **Save** command of the **File** menu. Note that it brings up the Save **As** dialog box, as shown in Figure 9.3, because you have not saved this data yet. Select a disk and directory by clicking the list boxes, type a filename (**REG1**), and press OK. The data is saved.

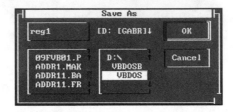

Figure 9.3. *The Save As dialog box.*

19. Change the data by adding a few more items, then execute **S**ave again. This time the program doesn't bring up the Save **As** dialog box because it already knows where to store the data.

20. Change the data again, then execute the **O**pen command. The Open dialog box, shown in Figure 9.4, appears. Select the old file and click OK. The old data is read, replacing the data currently in the Register list box.

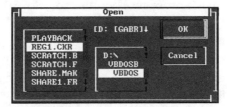

Figure 9.4. *The Open dialog box.*

You now have an operating check register program to keep track of your bank account. This program demonstrates linear record keeping, or *journaling*, which attaches each new entry to the end of the file of data. This is just one possible type. A ledger, for example, requires randomly accessed files, which are discussed in Chapter 10, "Using Random Access Files."

The Common Dialog Toolkit

Now that you have gone to all the work of creating your own **O**pen and Save **As** dialog boxes, I must mention that Microsoft has included a set of commonly used forms with Visual Basic. The forms are part of the common dialog toolkit described in Appendix E, "Visual Basic Toolkit Libraries." Note that the dialog boxes don't actually open and save files, they just return the filename and path. Your code must actually perform the operation.

To use these dialog boxes in an application, use the **Add** File command of the **File** menu to attach the CMNDLG.BAS code module and the CMNDLGF.FRM form module to a project. You also can attach the common dialog toolkit to a program by starting Visual Basic with the /L CMNDLG.QLB switch to load the library, and then including the file CMNDLG.BI in any form or code module that you want to display the dialog boxes. The file CMNDLG.LIB is also available for compiling the programs. The following is the syntax of the procedures that display the dialog boxes:

↪ **FileOpen** *filename$, path$, pattern$, title$, forecolor%,*
backcolor%, flags%, cancel%.

↪ **FileSave** *filename$, path$, pattern$, title$, forecolor%,*
backcolor%, flags%, cancel%

Here, *filename$* is a variable that will contain the selected file name, and *path$* will contain the file's path. When you call the procedure and place a string containing a pattern in *pattern$*, this pattern is used to select which files are displayed in the file list box. For example, use **.** for all files, or **.TXT* for all files with a .TXT extension. The *forecolor%* and *backcolor%* arguments set the foreground and background colors of the form.

Place a title for the dialog box in *title$*, and a file type selector in *flags%*. The file type selector is a number you create by adding the values listed in Table 9.2 for the file type options you want for the file list box. The default is the opposite of the options listed in the table, thus a selector value of 0 will list most commonly accessed files. The *cancel%* argument returns True (–1) if the user presses the Cancel button on the form, or False (0) if he presses OK. For more information, see the comments in the CMNDLG.BAS file.

Table 9.2. File type selectors for the common dialog toolkit.

Selector	Option
1	Skip archive files
2	Show hidden files
4	Skip normal files
8	Skip read-only files
16	Show system files

For example, the file open dialog box listing the .CKR check register files could be called with the following statement. The dialog has a gray background with black lettering and lists all normal files.

```
FileOpen FileName$, Path$, "*.CKR", "Open", 0, 7, 0, Cancel%
```

What You Have Learned

Three types of disk files are available in Visual Basic, and this chapter investigated the most common: sequential access files. Random access files are discussed in Chapter 10, "Using Random Access Files." The third type, binary files, is used primarily with advanced applications and is beyond the scope of this book. To access files within an application, you created Open and Save As dialog boxes and attached them to the check register program. In this chapter, you learned about

- Using the OPEN statement to open or create sequential files

- Writing sequential files with the WRITE # and PRINT # statements

- Reading sequential files with INPUT #, LINE INPUT #, and INPUT$()

- Creating file-access dialog boxes using drive, directory, and file list boxes

- Using the common dialog toolkit

Using Random Access Files

The second-most useful file type in Visual Basic is the random access file. A random access file differs from a sequential access file in that the individual records are read and written in any order, rather than only from the beginning to the end. The primary use of random access files is for database-type programs, such as a general ledger or inventory manager.

In This Chapter

Random access files are opened and closed in much the same manner as sequential files. However, the record length of a random access file is fixed, and the record length of a sequential file is variable. This fixed record length is necessary so that individual records can be located and accessed asynchronously. To implement the storing of values in fixed-length records, use a record-type variable composed of one or more standard type values, such as integers and strings. In this chapter, you will learn to

● Create user-defined record-type variables

● Create and open random access files

● Read and write records in random access files

● Create a datebook database program

Storing Data in Random Access Disk Files

Random access files, as the name implies, are not accessed in a linear fashion. They are accessed in fixed-length blocks, known as *records*, in any order. Random access files outwardly are text files, but you may not be able to read any of the numbers stored in them. Numbers are stored as binary data rather than character data. This procedure saves a considerable amount of memory, because a five-digit integer takes at least five bytes to be stored as text, and only two bytes to be stored as a binary integer.

Record lengths in random access files are fixed, and the default length is 128 bytes. Although record lengths of any size (up to 32,767 bytes) are allowed, sizes that are powers of two are more efficient. The record length is specified when you open the file.

Your computer actually reads data from a disk in fixed-length pieces called *sectors,* with each holding 512 bytes of data. If a record is 512 bytes long, or some number that is evenly divisible into 512 (a power of 2, as is 1, 2, 4, 8, 16, 32, 64, 128, and 256), then no record crosses a sector boundary. If a record does cross a sector boundary, then the computer must read two sectors from the disk rather than just one to get the whole record.

For example, if your record length is 500 bytes (a nice, round number), the first record is stored in the first 500 bytes of sector one. The second record crosses the boundary between sectors one and two with 12 bytes (512–500) stored at the end of the first sector and 488 bytes (500–12) stored at the beginning of the second. The third record again crosses a record boundary, using the last 24 bytes (512–488) of the second sector and the first 476 bytes (500–24) of the third, and so on. Each record but the first requires that two sectors be read from the disk to load one record.

On the other hand, if the record were just 12 bytes longer (512 bytes), it would fit a sector exactly, and every record would be completely contained within a single sector. If you can't use the extra bytes, you are still wasting only about two and a half percent of your disk space in exchange for cutting the access time in half.

The trade-off is file space versus file-access time. What you do depends on your application. If you have huge data files that aren't often accessed, you might want to sacrifice speed for reduced size. On the other hand, if your application spends too much time accessing the files, you might want to sacrifice some file space for increased speed.

Defining Record-Type Variables

In addition to the built-in variable types such as INTEGER and STRING, you can define your own variable types as combinations of existing types. Then, a single variable name passes the whole contents of a record rather than just a single value. To create a record-type variable, you must first define the variable type with a TYPE statement. The TYPE statement defines which of the built-in or user-defined variable types make up the record, and in what order. The syntax of the TYPE statement is

```
TYPE newtypename
  elementname AS typename
  elementname AS typename
  .
  .
  .
END TYPE
```

Here, *newtypename* is the name you're giving to the type definition, *elementname* is the name you're giving to the element that is going to be a part of this type,

and *typename* is the type of variable *elementname* is. The *typename* variable can be any of the built-in types—INTEGER, LONG, SINGLE, DOUBLE, CURRENCY, or STRING—or some previously defined type.

For example, the following TYPE definition defines the variable type DayType, which consists of three elements. The first is theDate, which is a double-precision floating point number for storing a date. The second is an integer named Flags, and the third is a fixed-length string named Msg. Strings normally are variable length and might be so in a general, user-defined type; but because the record length in a random access file is fixed, the length of any strings that make up the record variable also must be fixed. You create fixed-length STRING variables by adding an asterisk (*) and the string length following the STRING keyword:

```
TYPE DayType
  theDate AS DOUBLE
  Flags AS INTEGER
  Msg AS STRING * 118
END TYPE
```

If you add up the number of bytes needed to store this new variable, you find that they add up to 128 bytes exactly—eight bytes for the DOUBLE, two for the INTEGER, and 118 for the STRING. A length of 128 bytes is exactly half of the 512 byte sector length, so this record has one of the efficient lengths for random access file records. The length of a record-type variable must always be less than or equal to the record length defined with the OPEN statement.

To use a variable with a user-defined type, define it in exactly the same way as you define the type of any other variable: by using DIM and COMMON statements. For example:

```
DIM aLine AS STRING, Today AS DayType
COMMON SHARED theMonth(1 TO 31) AS DayType
```

The first line defines aLine as a string variable and Today as the new variable type DayType. The second line defines an array named Month of 31 DayType variables.

To access the parts of a user-defined variable type, combine the variable name with the element name, separated with a dot. For example:

```
Today.Flags = 2
Month(5).Msg = "Some interesting message"
Today.theDay = Now
```

The first line stores the number 2 in the Flags element (the integer) of Today, the second inserts a string in the Msg element of the fifth element of Month, and the third line uses the function Now to insert today's date and time into the theDay element of Today.

Opening a Random Access File

To open a random access file, use the OPEN statement (defined in Chapter 9, "Using Sequential Files") with a mode of RANDOM, and include a record length. For example:

```
OPEN "MYFILE.DBK" FOR RANDOM AS #1 LEN = 128
```

This opens the file MYFLE.DBK in the default directory as a random access file, with a file number of 1 and a record length of 128 bytes. The default record length for random access files is 128 bytes, so the length argument could have been omitted. However, it is better to specify the record length, so that when you are reading the program, you immediately know what it is.

When you are done with this file, close it in the same way as a sequential file, using a CLOSE # statement:

```
CLOSE #1
```

Reading and Writing Random Records

Now that you have the file open, you have to be able to read and write records. Records from a random access file are read with the GET # statement. The GET # statement syntax is

```
GET [#] filenumber%,[recordnumber&],recordvariable
```

Here, *filenumber%* is the file number used in the OPEN statement, *recordnumber&* is the number of the record you want to read, and *recordvariable* is the name of the record-type variable that receives the data. If you omit the record number, you get the next record in the file after the last one you read or wrote. For example:

```
GET #1,225,Today
```

This reads record number 225 from file number 1 and stores it in the DayType record variable Today. After you read a record into a record variable, you access the contents of that record by accessing the elements of the record variable.

Records are written in the same manner as they are read: by using the PUT # statement. The syntax and arguments are identical to those for the GET # statement, but the contents of the record variable are stored in a record on disk instead of retrieved.

PUT [**#**] *filenumber%,*[*recordnumber&*]*,recordvariable*

An example is

```
PUT #1, 12, Month(3)
```

which stores the third element of the array of record variables, Month(), in record 12 of file number 1. If that record doesn't yet exist, the file automatically is extended to include it.

The Datebook Program

The datebook program is a year-long electronic calendar of important dates and notes. When it starts, it automatically checks a week ahead and beeps if any of the dates are marked important. It then displays the current month with important dates marked in color. Clicking a date pops up a second window that shows the note attached to that date. In that window, you can create or edit the note and save it in the database file. The program consists of two forms: one contains a monthly calendar showing the important dates with attached notes, and the other shows the note attached to a selected date.

The monthly calendar form is made with 37 labels arranged in five rows of seven, plus one row of two. This structure holds any month. Also on the form are two arrows, used to move forward or backward one month. The File menu contains commands to create a new yearly database or to open a database other than the current year. A Month menu contains all the month names to rapidly move to a different month in the current year.

1. Start a new project: execute the New Project command of the File menu, then execute the New Form command of the File menu and use DBOOK1.FRM for the filename. Execute the Save Project command of the File menu and use DBOOK.MAK as the project filename.

2. Switch to the Forms Designer, and change the properties of the
   form to the following. This holds a calendar for one month, as
   shown in Figure 10.1.

```
Caption = Date Book
BorderStyle = 3 - Fixed Double
MaxButton = False
Height = 33
Width = 47
```

Setting the BorderStyle to 3 and MaxButton to False makes it impossible for other users to change the size of the form, which would spoil your user-interface.

Figure 10.1. *Layout for Form1 of the datebook program.*

3. Draw a label at the top to hold the name of the current month,
   and set its properties to

```
Caption = Month
CtlName = MonthBox
Top = 0
Left = 12
Height = 1
Width = 20
Alignment = 2 - Center
```

The next step is to create two arrow buttons to move the calendar forward or backward one month. Because there is no control that looks like an arrow, create one using a label and some symbols.

4. Draw a label on the upper left, with the following attributes:

```
CtlName = LeftArrow
Caption = <==
Top = 1
Left = 2
Height = 1
Width = 4
```

5. Draw a second label on the upper right, with the following attributes:

```
CtlName = RightArrow
Caption = ==>
Top = 0
Left = 39
Height = 1
Width = 4
```

6. Draw seven labels across the form containing the first letter of the days of the week, according to Table 10.1.

Now, create a control array of labels to form the calendar. Each label is both a date square on the calendar and a button that accesses the note attached to that date. Create the array by drawing the first box, then use the Copy and Paste commands of the Edit menu to create the rest.

Table 10.1. Properties for the datebook program's label boxes.

Caption	Left	Top	Height	Width
S	3	1	1	3
M	9	1	1	3
T	15	1	1	3
W	21	1	1	3
T	27	1	1	3
F	33	1	1	3
S	39	1	1	3

7. Draw a label with the following properties:

```
Caption = Day
CtlName = DayButton
Top = 2
Left = 1
Height = 3
Width = 6
BorderStype = 1 - Fixed Single
```

8. Select the label and execute the **Copy** command, then execute the **Paste** command. A dialog box appears asking you whether you want to create a control array. Click Yes.

9. Select the newly pasted label and drag it to the right of the first one. Continue pasting and dragging until you have five rows of seven boxes and one row of two boxes, as shown in Figure 10.1.

There are two menus on this application. The first menu is the standard **File** menu with **New**, **Open**, and **Exit** commands. The second is a **Month** menu with all the months of the year on it. The **Month** menu moves you quickly to any month in the current year.

10. Open the Menu Design window and create a **File** and a **Month** menu according to Table 10.2. The **Month** menu is a control array containing all the months of the year.

Table 10.2. The Menu Design window for the datebook program.

Caption	Control Name	Number of Indents	Index
&File	FileMenu	0	
&New	NewCmd	1	
&Open	OpenCmd	1	
-	SepBar1	1	
&Exit	ExitCmd	1	
&Month	MonthMenu	0	
&Jan	MonthCmd	1	1
&Feb	MonthCmd	1	2
Ma&r	MonthCmd	1	3

continues

Table 10.2. continued

Caption	Control Name	Number of Indents	Index
&Apr	MonthCmd	1	4
Ma&y	MonthCmd	1	5
J&un	MonthCmd	1	6
Ju&l	MonthCmd	1	7
Au&g	MonthCmd	1	8
&Sep	MonthCmd	1	9
&Oct	MonthCmd	1	10
&Nov	MonthCmd	1	11
&Dec	MonthCmd	1	12

11. Save the form.

This completes the design for the first form, which contains the calendar. Now, create a second form to use for reading and writing the notes being attached to the dates on the calendar.

12. Add this second form to the project with the New **Form** command of the **File** menu. Name it DBOOK2.FRM and set its properties as follows:

```
Caption = Reminder
BorderStyle = 3 - Fixed double
ControlBox = False
MaxButton = False
MinButton = False
Height = 11
Width = 44
```

13. Draw a text box on the form as shown in Figure 10.2—this is where you type the notes. Set its properties as follows:

```
CtlName = Message
Top = 3
Left = 1
Height = 6
Width = 29
Text = " "
```

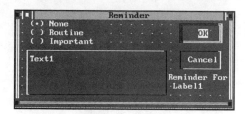

Figure 10.2. Layout for Form2 of the datebook program.

Next, create a control array of three option buttons for setting the importance of a note. The array has three option buttons, marked **None**, **Routine**, and **Important**. The **None** button clears the current note. The **Routine** button colors the date light blue (cyan) on the calendar, and the **Important** button colors the date red.

14. Create a control array of the following three option buttons. You can either create the first button and Copy and Paste it to create the others, or draw three option buttons and give them all the same CtlName. See Table 10.3 for the appropriate values for each button. These three buttons are used to indicate whether the attached note is routine or important.

Table 10.3. Values for the option buttons.

Caption	Index	Value	Top	Left	Height	Width
&None	0	True	0	2	1	15
&Routine	1	False	1	2	1	15
&Important	2	False	2	2	1	15

There are two command buttons on this form. The first is the OK button, which attaches the note to the calendar and saves it in the disk file. The second is the Cancel button, which discards any changes and returns you to the calendar.

15. Draw an OK command button with these properties:

```
Caption = OK
CtlName = OKCmd
Top = 0
Left = 32
```

```
Height = 3
Width = 9
Default = True
```

16. Draw a Cancel command button with these properties:

```
Caption = Cancel
CtlName = CancelCmd
Top = 3
Left = 32
Height = 3
Width = 9
Default = False
```

17. Draw a label below the Cancel button, with these properties:

```
Caption = Reminder for
Top = 6
Left = 30
Height = 1
Width = 12
```

18. Draw a label to hold the date, with these properties:

```
CtlName = DateBox
Top = 7
Left = 31
Height = 1
Width = 10
```

19. Save the form.

This completes the second form. Now attach code to the project. First, create an include file to contain the definitions for True, False, and asModal, and a list of color definitions copied from the file CONSTANT.BI included with Visual Basic. The program uses only BLACK, WHITE, YELLOW, CYAN, and RED; the others are included for completeness.

Next is the definition for the DayType type. This definition must come before any attempt to use it. After the DayType type definition are the definitions of some global variables.

- `FileName` is a string variable that contains the name of the currently open file.

- `theYear` is an integer containing the current year as a number.

- `theMonth` contains the current month as a number.

- `EOL` holds the end-of-line characters: carriage return and line feed.

- The variable `ChangeDate` is a record variable of type `DayType`.

- `Months()` is an array of 12 strings, each string containing the name of a month.

- `thisMonth()` is an array that holds the serial date numbers for each day in the current month.

- `OldBackColor` and `OldForeColor` are integer variables to hold the values of the background and text colors.

Note that the two arrays `Months()` and `thisMonth()` must first be defined in a `DIM` statement before they are included in the `COMMON` statement. `COMMON` can be used only to share variables and define types. You cannot use it to reserve space for array-type variables.

Serial date numbers are used in Visual Basic to store dates and times:

- The date is stored in the integer part of the number as the integer number of days since December 30, 1899 (12/30/1899). Negative values describe dates back to January 1, 1753 (1/1/1753).

- The time is stored in the fractional part of the number as a fraction of a whole day; for example, 0.5 is noon.

- The functions `DAY()`, `WEEKDAY()`, `MONTH()`, and `YEAR()` convert serial date numbers into integers representing the day of the month, day of the week, month of the year, and year.

- The function `DATEVALUE()` converts a text representation of a date into a serial date number. The function `DATESERIAL(year,month,day)` converts the three integers *year*, *month*, and *day* into a serial date number.

20. Switch to the Programming Environment, execute the New Module command of the File menu, select Include File (.BI), and use the filename DBOOKG.BI. You can copy all of the color constants from the file CONSTANT.BI included with Visual Basic. When you finish, the file should be as follows:

```
CONST True = -1, False = 0, asModal = 1

CONST BLACK = 0          'Colors from the file
CONST BLUE = 1           'CONSTANT.BI
CONST GREEN = 2
CONST CYAN = 3
CONST RED = 4
CONST MAGENTA = 5
CONST BROWN = 6
CONST WHITE = 7
CONST GRAY = 8
CONST BRIGHT_BLUE = 9
CONST BRIGHT_GREEN = 10
CONST BRIGHT_CYAN = 11
CONST BRIGHT_RED = 12
CONST PINK = 13
CONST YELLOW = 14
CONST BRIGHT_WHITE = 15


TYPE DayType              'Type declaration for the
'    TheDate AS DOUBLE     'record DayType, 128 bytes
    Flags AS INTEGER      'long
    Msg AS STRING * 118
END TYPE


COMMON SHARED FileName AS STRING   'The disk filename and path
COMMON SHARED theYear AS INTEGER   'The current year
COMMON SHARED theMonth AS INTEGER 'The current month
COMMON SHARED EOL AS STRING        'End-of-Line character
COMMON SHARED ChangeDate AS DayType   'Serial date
                                      'being changed
DIM Months(1 TO 12) AS STRING      'Dimension array for COMMON
COMMON SHARED Months() AS STRING   'Text names of the months
DIM thisMonth(36) AS DOUBLE        'Dimension array for COMMON
```

```
COMMON SHARED thisMonth() AS DOUBLE      'Array to hold
                                         'datenumbers
COMMON SHARED OldBackColor AS INTEGER    'Store old background
                                         'color
COMMON SHARED OldForeColor AS INTEGER 'Store old text color
' $FORM Form1
' $FORM Form2
```

21. Save the include file.

The Form_Load procedure sets up the problem. The first 15 lines define the EOL variable and fill the Months() array with the text of the 12 month names. Line 16 is a call to the ClearMonth procedure, which initializes the 36 labels on the calendar. Line 18 creates a filename from the current year by using the NOW function to get the current serial date number and the YEAR() function to extract the current year. The year (in four digits) then is combined with the .DBK file extension to form the filename. In line 19, the DIR$() function checks whether the file exists. If the file doesn't exist, the procedure exits; otherwise, the file is opened as a random access file with file number 1 in line 20. In line 21, the GET # statement extracts the first record. The actual year stored in the file is extracted from the TheDate item of the aDay record variable in line 22, and the file is closed in line 23. This ensures that there actually is a file for the desired year.

In line 24, the NOW function is used again with the MONTH() function to get the current month and store it in theMonth. In line 25, the FillMonth procedure is executed to insert the days and notes in the currently open year and month. In line 27, the LookAhead procedure is called with an argument of seven days. This procedure scans ahead the number of days specified, beeps, and prints a message if any day has the Important button set. The last line before the END SUB statement loads and then hides Form2. This gets Form2 into memory so its controls can be accessed before it is displayed.

22. For Form1, create the Form_Load procedure, and type

```
SUB Form_Load ()
DIM aDay AS DayType
EOL = CHR$(13) + CHR$(10)       'End-of-line character
Months(1) = "January"        'Fill Months array
Months(2) = "February"
Months(3) = "March"
```

```
Months(4) = "April"
Months(5) = "May"
Months(6) = "June"
Months(7) = "July"
Months(8) = "August"
Months(9) = "September"
Months(10) = "October"
Months(11) = "November"
Months(12) = "December"
ClearMonth
'If a file for the current year exists, get it    line 17
FileName = FORMAT$(YEAR(NOW), "0000") + ".DBK"
IF DIR$(FileName) = "" THEN EXIT SUB
OPEN FileName FOR RANDOM AS #1 LEN = 128
GET #1, 1, aDay
theYear = YEAR(aDay.TheDate)
CLOSE #1
theMonth = MONTH(NOW)
FillMonth
'Look ahead one week for important days'
LookAhead (7)
Form2.HIDE
END SUB
```

The New command in the following step creates a new year's data file. Lines 4 through 11 use an input box so you can enter a year, and then test the value returned. If the value is a blank, the procedure exits. Otherwise, the procedure stores the value in the variable theYear. Lines 11 through 18 convert the date into a filename, as before, and test whether a file already exists. If it does, the procedure sends you a message asking whether it's all right to overwrite the old file. If you do not want to overwrite it, press the Cancel button and the procedure then exits. Otherwise, the procedure opens or creates the file. In lines 19 through 22, the record variable is filled with blank data except for the first field, which contains the date of the record.

In lines 23 through 29, the file is opened and the blank data is written to it. This initializes the file by deleting any existing data in the file that could be mistaken for a message. The only thing that changes is the date, which is updated with each pass through the loop. Finally, the procedure checks whether this is the current year. If it is, the procedure switches to the current month. If not, it starts with January. FillMonth is called at the end to draw the current month.

23. Create the NewCmd_Click procedure, and type

```
SUB NewCmd_Click ()
DIM aDay AS DayType, I AS INTEGER, aYear AS STRING
DIM aMsg AS STRING, Action AS INTEGER
'Get a year from the user. Exit if blank.
theYear = 0
IF theYear < 1753 OR theYear > 2078 THEN
  aYear = INPUTBOX$("Type the year")
  IF aYear = "" THEN EXIT SUB
  theYear = VAL(aYear)
END IF
'Make a filename with the year and check for an    line 11
'existing file. Ask if it is OK to overwrite it.
FileName = FORMAT$(theYear, "0000") + ".DBK"
IF DIR$(FileName) <> "" THEN
  aMsg = "File already exists" + EOL + "Overwrite it?"
  Action = MSGBOX(aMsg, 257)
  IF Action = 2 THEN EXIT SUB   'If Cancel is pressed, exit
END IF
'load the record variable    line 19
aDay.TheDate = DATESERIAL(theYear, 1, 1) - 1
aDay.Flags = 0
aDay.Msg = SPACE$(118)
'Open the file and fill with data. line 23
OPEN FileName FOR RANDOM AS #1 LEN = 128
FOR I = 1 TO 366
  aDay.TheDate = aDay.TheDate + 1
  PUT #1, I, aDay
NEXT I
CLOSE #1
'If the new file is this year, display the current month
IF theYear = YEAR(NOW) THEN
  theMonth = MONTH(NOW)
ELSE
  theMonth = 1
END IF
FillMonth
END SUB
```

257

The **O**pen command procedure created in the next step works much the same way as the **N**ew command, but can be used only when the file already exists. The procedure first uses an input box to ask you for the year in line 10. When the year is validated, it uses the DIR$() function in line 17 to check whether the file exists. If the file doesn't exist, a message box is displayed in line 18, asking you to use the **N**ew command instead.

If the file does exist, it's opened as a random access file in line 24. The first record is read in line 25. The current year then is extracted from the first record. In lines 28 through 34, the program determines whether it is the current year, and displays the current month if it is.

24. Create the OpenCmd_Click procedure, and type

```
SUB OpenCmd_Click ()
DIM aDay As DayType, aYear AS STRING
DIM OldFileName AS STRING, OldYear AS INTEGER
'Save the old year in case the user changes his mind
OldYear = theYear
OldFileName = FileName
'Get a year from the user. Exit if it is a blank.
theYear = 0
IF theYear < 1753 OR theYear > 2078 THEN
  aYear = INPUTBOX$("Type the year")
  IF aYear = "" THEN EXIT SUB
  theYear = VAL(aYear)
END IF
'Make and validate a filename. Restore the old    line 14
'one and exit if it doesn't exist.
FileName = FORMAT$(theYear, "0000") + ".DBK"
IF DIR$(FileName) = "" THEN   'Check for existing file
  MSGBOX "File doesn't exist, use New"
  FileName = OldFileName
  theYear = OldYear
  EXIT SUB
END IF
'Open the file and get the correct year    line 23
OPEN FileName FOR RANDOM AS #1 LEN = 128
GET #1, 1, aDay
theYear = YEAR(aDay.TheDate)
CLOSE #1
'If it's this year, display the current month    line 28
IF theYear = YEAR(NOW) THEN
  theMonth = MONTH(NOW)
```

```
ELSE
  theMonth = 1
END IF
FillMonth
END SUB
```

The next few procedures set the right- and left-arrow labels so they work like real buttons; the buttons turn black when pressed with the mouse and white when released. To do this, use the MouseDown and MouseUp events rather than the Click event to activate the code. The MouseDown procedure is passed information about the state of the mouse, but changing the background color to black requires only the information that the mouse was pressed over the label. In the MouseUp procedure, turn the background color back to white (or whatever color it was). For the left arrow, subtract 1 from theMonth and for the right arrow, add 1. In both cases, make the value in theMonth wrap at 0 and 12 months so that pressing the left arrow in January causes a move to December, and pressing the right arrow in December moves to January. Finally, call the FillMonth procedure to draw the new month's calendar page.

25. Create the LeftArrow_MouseDown procedure, and type

```
SUB LeftArrow_MouseDown (Button AS INTEGER, Shift AS INTEGER,
  X AS SINGLE, Y AS SINGLE)
LeftArrow.BackColor = BLACK
END SUB
```

26. Create the LeftArrow_MouseUp procedure, and type

```
SUB LeftArrow_MouseUp (Button AS INTEGER, Shift AS INTEGER,
  X AS SINGLE, Y AS SINGLE)
LeftArrow.BackColor = WHITE
theMonth = theMonth - 1
IF theMonth = 0 THEN theMonth = 12
FillMonth
END SUB
```

27. Create the RightArrow_MouseDown procedure, and type

```
SUB RightArrow_MouseDown (Button AS INTEGER,
  Shift AS INTEGER, X AS SINGLE, Y AS SINGLE)
RightArrow.BackColor = BLACK
END SUB
```

10

28. Create the `RightArrow_MouseUp` procedure, and type

```
SUB RightArrow_MouseUp (Button AS INTEGER,
    Shift AS INTEGER, X AS SINGLE, Y AS SINGLE)
RightArrow.BackColor = WHITE
theMonth = theMonth + 1
IF theMonth = 13 THEN theMonth = 1
FillMonth
END SUB
```

The following `MonthCmd_Click` procedure is executed whenever one of the months is selected on the **Month** menu. The value of `Index` is equal to 1 for January, 2 for February, and so forth, so insert the value of `Index` into the variable `theMonth` and call `FillMonth` to draw the new month.

29. Create the `MonthCmd_Click` procedure, and type

```
SUB MonthCmd_Click (Index AS INTEGER)
theMonth = Index
FillMonth
END SUB
```

30. Create the `ExitCmd_Click` procedure, and type

```
SUB ExitCmd_Click ()
END
END SUB
```

Because someone may close the form by double clicking on the button on the upper-left corner, or by selecting close from the Control menu, create the following Form_Unload procedure to end the program if that happens. If you close the last form of a compiled program, the program will still be running in memory, but you will have no way to access it to make it stop.

31. Create the Form_Unload procedure, and type

```
SUB Form_Unload (cancel AS INTEGER)
ExitCmd_Click
END SUB
```

The labels that form the calendar also are buttons that open the appropriate note. They are handled in the following procedure in much the same way as the left-arrow and right-arrow buttons. The `DayButton_MouseDown` procedure changes the background color to black and the text color to white. The `DayButton_MouseUp` procedure reverses that step to make the button seem as if it were pressed. Line 5 calculates the record number containing the data for this date by subtracting the serial date number for January 1 of the current year from the selected date stored in the array thisMonth(), and adding 1. This gives the correct record number, because the records are stored in the file as sequential days starting with January 1. The program then reads the record and inserts the data into the controls on Form2. The form then is made visible as a modal form.

32. Create the DayButton_MouseDown procedure, and type

```
SUB DayButton_MouseDown (Index AS INTEGER, Button AS INTEGER,
   Shift AS INTEGER, X AS SINGLE, Y AS SINGLE)
OldBackColor = DayButton(Index).BackColor
OldForeColor = DayButton(Index).ForeColor
DayButton(Index).BackColor = BLACK
DayButton(Index).ForeColor = WHITE
END SUB
```

33. Create the DayButton_MouseUp procedure, and type

```
SUB DayButton_MouseUp (Index AS INTEGER, Button AS INTEGER,
   Shift AS INTEGER, X AS SINGLE, Y AS SINGLE)
DayButton(Index).BackColor = OldBackColor
DayButton(Index).ForeColor = OldForeColor
OPEN FileName FOR RANDOM AS #1 LEN = 128
RecNo = thisMonth(Index) - DateSerial(theYear, 1, 1) + 1
GET #1, RecNo, ChangeDate
CLOSE #1
Form2.DateBox.Caption =
   FORMAT$(ChangeDate.TheDate, "mm-dd-yyyy")
Form2.Message.Text = ChangeDate.Msg
Form2.FlagOpt(ChangeDate.Flags).Value = True
Form2.SHOW asModal
END SUB
```

34. Save the form.

When Form2 appears, any existing data for the selected date is displayed on the form for you to edit or delete. Whenever any changes are made to the large text box on Form2, the Message_Change procedure is executed. It simply stores the changed message in the Msg item of the ChangeDate record variable. It then checks the option buttons, and automatically clicks the Routine button, (FlagOpt(1)), if the message previously was empty.

35. Select Form2, create the `Message_Change` procedure and type

```
SUB Message_Change ()
ChangeDate.Msg = Message.Text
IF FlagOpt(0).Value = True AND Message.Text <> ""
   THEN FlagOpt(1).Value = True
END SUB
```

The following `FlagOpt_Click` procedure is called whenever one of the option buttons is pressed. When it is executed, it first stores the current state of the option buttons in the `Flags` item of the `ChangeDate` record variable. Next, it checks whether the None option button (the one with Index = 0) was pressed and, if so, clears the contents of the Message text box. Finally, it moves the focus to the Message text box. The `IF` statement is needed here to prevent this code from trying to move the focus while the form is hidden. Because the `DayButton` procedure makes changes to the values on this form before it makes the form visible, an error would be generated if this code attempted to set the focus while the form was hidden.

36. Create the `FlagOpt_Click` procedure and type

```
SUB FlagOpt_Click (Index AS INTEGER)
ChangeDate.Flags = Index
IF Index = 0 THEN Message.Text = ""
IF Message.visible THEN Message.SETFOCUS
END SUB
```

After making any changes in a message, the user presses the OK button to save the changes. The procedure attached to the OK button opens the data file, calculates the record number, and stores the edited record in the file. It then hides Form2 and calls the `FillMonth` procedure to redraw the month on Form1.

37. Create the `OKCmd_Click` procedure, and type

```
SUB OKCmd_Click ()
OPEN FileName FOR RANDOM AS #1 LEN = 128
RecNo = ChangeDate.TheDate - DATESERIAL(theYear, 1, 1) + 1
PUT #1, RecNo, ChangeDate
CLOSE #1
Form2.HIDE
FillMonth
END SUB
```

The procedure attached to the Cancel button simply hides Form2 without making any changes to the data file.

38. Create the `CancelCmd_Click` procedure and type

```
SUB CancelCmd_Click ()
Form2.Hide
END SUB
```

39. Save the project.

Several procedures stored on a code module do the real work of this program. The `ClearMonth` procedure loops over all the labels on Form1, deletes their captions, disables them, and resets the default background and foreground colors.

40. Add a new module by using the New Module command of the File menu and name the new module DBOOKM.BAS. Execute the New Sub command of the Edit menu, create the `ClearMonth` procedure, and type the following:

```
SUB ClearMonth ()
DIM I AS INTEGER
FOR I = 0 TO 36
Form1.DayButton(I).Caption = ""
Form1.DayButton(I).Enabled = False
Form1.DayButton(I).BackColor = WHITE
Form1.DayButton(I).ForeColor = BLACK
NEXT I
END SUB
```

The following `FillMonth` procedure inserts the data for the current month into the calendar. It first clears the calendar by using the `ClearMonth` procedure in line 5. In line 6, it inserts the name of the current month and the year into `MonthBox` at the top of the form. In lines 7, 8, and 9, it loops over all the months in the Month menu and unchecks them. It's easier here just to uncheck every item on the menu rather than trying to figure out which item is checked and then unchecking it. In line 10, the procedure checks the current month on the Month menu.

The next block of code inserts the data into the calendar. In line 11, the serial date number of the first day of the month is placed in the variable `StartDate`. Next, the data file is opened, and the record number containing the data for the first of the month is calculated. The record is read, the day,

10

which should be 1, is extracted from the serial date number in line 15, and the day of the week is extracted in line 16. The day of the week is used to determine which of the DayButton labels on Form1 holds the dates for this month.

In line 18, a loop starts that continues until the serial date number advances to the next month; it thus cycles over all the days in the current month. In line 19, the current date is inserted in the Caption property of the DayButton procedure. In line 20, the label is enabled and, in line 21, the current serial date number is stored in the array theMonth(). Lines 22 through 24 check whether the day is today; if it is, it's marked with an asterisk (*) inserted before the date, and colored yellow.

Lines 26 through 31 check the state of the option buttons to see whether this date has a note attached, and if so, whether the note is important. If a note is attached, the background color is changed to light blue (cyan). If the note is important, the background color is changed to red and the text is changed to white. Finally, this procedure increments the index for the next day, reads the next record, and extracts the day. This loop continues until the day is in the next month.

41. Create the FillMonth Sub procedure:

```
SUB FillMonth ()
DIM StartDate AS DOUBLE, aDay AS DayType
DIM theDay AS INTEGER, RecNo AS INTEGER
DIM Index AS INTEGER, I AS INTEGER, FirstIndex AS INTEGER
ClearMonth
Form1.MonthBox.Caption = Months(theMonth) + STR$(theYear)
FOR I = 1 TO 12
  Form1.MonthCmd(I).Checked = False
NEXT I
Form1.MonthCmd(theMonth).Checked = True
StartDate = DATESERIAL(theYear, theMonth, 1)     'line 11
OPEN FileName FOR RANDOM AS #1 LEN = 128
RecNo = StartDate - DATESERIAL(theYear, 1, 1) + 1
GET #1, RecNo, aDay
theDay = DAY(aDay.TheDate)
FirstIndex = WEEKDAY(StartDate) - 1     'line 16
Index = FirstIndex
```

```
      WHILE theMonth = MONTH(StartDate + Index - FirstIndex)
        Form1.DayButton(Index).Caption = STR$(theDay)
        Form1.DayButton(Index).Enabled = True
        thisMonth(Index) = aDay.TheDate
        IF aDay.TheDate = FIX(NOW) THEN
          Form1.DayButton(Index).Caption =
            "*" + Form1.DayButton(Index).Caption
          Form1.DayButton(Index).BackColor = YELLOW
        END IF
        IF aDay.Flags = 1 THEN        'line 26
          Form1.DayButton(Index).BackColor = CYAN
        ELSEIF aDay.Flags = 2 Then
          Form1.DayButton(Index).BackColor = RED
          Form1.DayButton(Index).ForeColor = WHITE
        END IF
        Index = Index + 1
        RecNo = RecNo + 1
        GET #1, RecNo, aDay
        theDay = DAY(aDay.TheDate)
      WEND
      CLOSE #1
    END SUB
```

The LookAhead procedure is executed by the Form_Load procedure of
Form1. It checks Days days ahead of the current day, beeps, and displays a
message box if it finds one with the Important option set. In line 6, the
variable StartDate is set to the serial date number for today. The FIX()
function removes any fraction of a day returned by the NOW function. Lines
10 through 14 loop over the number of days ahead, extract the records for
each of those days, and check the state of the option buttons. In line 12, if
a date is found that has the Important option set (aDay.Flags = 2), then
FoundIt is set to True and the program beeps. In line 19, if FoundIt was set
to True, it will display a message box that tells you there are important
messages.

42. Create the LOOKAHEAD SUB procedure:

```
SUB LookAhead (Days AS INTEGER)
'Look ahead Days for messages and beep if important
DIM StartDate AS DOUBLE, aDay AS DayType
DIM RecNo AS INTEGER, FoundIt AS INTEGER
DIM I AS INTEGER
StartDate = FIX(NOW)
```

10

```
OPEN FileName FOR RANDOM AS #1 LEN = 128
RecNo = StartDate - DATESERIAL(theYear, 1, 1) + 1
FoundIt = False
FOR I = 1 TO Days       'line 10
  GET #1, RecNo, aDay
  IF aDay.Flags = 2 THEN
    FoundIt = True
    Beep
  END IF
  RecNo = RecNo + 1
NEXT I
CLOSE #1
IF FoundIt THEN MSGBOX "You have important dates this week"
END SUB
```

43. Save the modules, then save the project.

44. Run the program. The first time there is no data file, so execute the New command and give it the current year. When the program finishes creating the new data file, the calendar window looks like Figure 10.3, with the current month visible and the current day marked with an asterisk and a yellow background.

***Figure 10.3.** The datebook program—startup at the current month.*

45. Click a date and the Reminder window opens, as shown in Figure 10.4. In the Reminder window, click the **I**mportant option button and type a note.

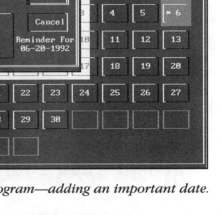

Figure 10.4. *The datebook program—adding an important date.*

Click OK to add the note and return to the calendar window. After adding a few routine or important dates, the calendar window should look like Figure 10.5.

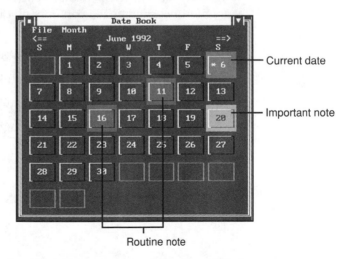

Figure 10.5. *The datebook program with notes added to some important dates.*

This completes the datebook program; use it for all your important dates.

 Try some of the other options, such as clicking the arrow buttons or using the **Month** menu to change the month. You could compile the program and place it in your AUTOEXEC.BAT file, so you see your current calendar every time you start up your computer. One reader suggested expanding the Reminder form and using this program for a daily diary.

What You Have Learned

This chapter discussed the use of random access files. A random access disk file is one in which the individual records are read or written independently of all the other records in the file. All records are defined to be the same length when the file is opened. A record-type variable defined with the TYPE statement determines the contents of a record. Specifically, this chapter discussed

- Using TYPE to create user-defined variables
- Using OPEN to open or create a random access disk file
- Reading and writing records with GET # and PUT #
- Creating a datebook database program to store important events

Using Color and Sound

Before you can draw graphics with Visual Basic, you have to prepare the drawing environment. The forms must be hidden, the graphics mode set, and the palettes and colors defined. Then you can use the methods and statements discussed in Chapter 12, "Drawing with Visual Basic," to paint pretty colors on the screen. In addition to colors, you can create sounds with Visual Basic, from irritating chirps to mediocre music (well, not everything's perfect).

In This Chapter

This chapter shows you how to prepare the drawing environment for drawing graphics on the screen. Statements exist to control the colors displayed, the palettes used, and even the patterns painted on the screen.

Another set of statements creates sounds from the built-in speaker. In this chapter, you will learn to

● Draw on forms and picture boxes

● Set the screen graphics mode

● Set the scale used for drawing on the screen

● Set the colors used for drawing

● Control sounds from the internal speaker

Graphics in Visual Basic for MS-DOS

The most significant departure from Visual Basic for Windows is the way Visual Basic for MS-DOS does graphics. In Visual Basic for Windows, all graphics take place on a form or picture box. In Visual Basic for MS-DOS, the forms all are created in text mode, so whenever any forms are present, you can create only text-type graphics. However, note that the whole interface to Visual Basic for MS-DOS is created with text-type graphics.

Older BASIC environments, such as GW-BASIC, BASICA, and QuickBASIC, do not have forms and windows, and draw their graphics directly on the screen. This is how Visual Basic for MS-DOS draws its graphics-mode graphics. To draw real graphics-mode graphics with Visual Basic for MS-DOS, you must remove all forms from the screen, set the screen mode and colors, and then draw your graphics.

Graphics on Forms

As previously mentioned, the only graphics that you can place on a form or picture box are text-mode graphics created using the graphics characters. The graphics characters consist of the ASCII characters from 128 through 255, plus a few characters between 0 and 32. To see what these characters are, let's create a short application that prints them all on a picture box. These characters and codes also are listed in Appendix B, "ASCII\ANSI Code Chart."

The ASCII Characters Program

The following application prints all of the ASCII characters on a form, including all the graphics characters. It also gives you an opportunity to experiment with the AutoRedraw property. By turning AutoRedraw on, you can cover and uncover the form, and the printed characters on the form are restored.

1. Start a new project: execute the New Project command of the File menu, then execute the New Form command of the File menu and use ASCIICH.FRM for the filename. Execute the Save Project command of the File menu and use ASCIICH.MAK as the project filename.

2. Switch to the Forms Designer, select the form, and change its properties to the following:

   ```
   FormName = Form1
   Caption = ASCII Characters
   Height = 20
   Width = 67
   ```

3. Open the Menu Design window and create a File menu as indicated in Table 11.1.

Table 11.1. The Menu Design window for the ASCII characters program.

Caption	Control Name	Number of Indents
&File	FileMenu	0
&0-127	C0127Cmd	1
&128-255	C128255Cmd	1
-	SepBar1	1
&Other Form	OtherCmd	1
&AutoRedraw On	AutoOnCmd	1
Auto&Redraw Off	AutoOffCmd	1
&Cls	ClsCmd	1

continues

Table 11.1. continued

Caption	Control Name	Number of Indents
BackColor &White	WhiteCmd	1
BackColor &Red	RedCmd	1
ForeColor Blac&k	BlackCmd	1
ForeColor Blu&e	BlueCmd	1
–	SepBar2	1
E&xit	ExitCmd	1

4. The form now should look like Figure 11.1. Save the form.

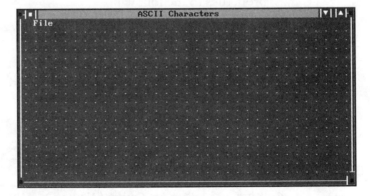

Figure 11.1. *Layout for Form1 of the ASCII characters program.*

Create a second, smaller form to use to cover and uncover the first form for experimenting with the AutoRedraw property.

5. Execute the New Form command of the File menu and give it the filename ASCIICH2.FRM.

6. Select the new form and set its properties to the following:

```
FormName = Form2
Caption = Overlay Form
Height = 8
Width = 43
```

7. Draw a command button on the form and set its Caption property to Ok.

8. The form now should look like Figure 11.2. Save the form.

Figure 11.2. Layout for Form2 of the ASCII characters program.

9. Switch to the Programming Environment, select the declarations section of Form1, and type

```
'$FORM Form2
CONST Black = 0
CONST Blue = 1
CONST Red = 4
CONST White = 7
CONST True = -1, False = 0
```

10. Create the C0127Cmd_Click procedure and type

```
SUB C0127Cmd_Click ()
CLS
FOR I = 1 TO 16
  FOR J = 0 TO 127 STEP 16
  K = I + J - 1
  IF K = 9 THEN
    PRINT FORMAT$(K, "000"); "-Tab ";
  ELSEIF K = 10 THEN
    PRINT FORMAT$(K, "000"); "- LF ";
  ELSEIF K = 13 THEN
    PRINT FORMAT$(K, "000"); "- CR ";
  ELSE
    PRINT FORMAT$(K, "000"); "- "; CHR$(K); "  ";
  END IF
  NEXT J
  PRINT
NEXT I
END SUB
```

273

This procedure first clears the form with the CLS method. The rest of the procedure scans through the numbers from 0 to 127, and prints the number and the character associated with that number. The two nested For/Next loops make the output occur in a 16-by-16 table. The block IF statement watches for character numbers 9, 10, and 13 (Tab, line feed, and carriage return), and inserts TAB, LF, and CR for them. If you didn't do this, you would execute the function instead of displaying the value on the screen. The next procedure does the same for characters 128 through 255.

11. Create the C128255Cmd_Click procedure and type

```
SUB C128255Cmd_Click ()
CLS
FOR I = 1 TO 16
FOR J = 128 TO 255 STEP 16
PRINT FORMAT$(I + J - 1, "000"); "- "; CHR$(I + J - 1); "  ";
NEXT J
PRINT
NEXT I
END SUB
```

12. Create the ExitCmd_Click procedure and type

```
SUB ExitCmd_Click ()
END
END SUB
```

The following commands are for experimenting with the AutoRedraw property. They display Form2 and turn AutoRedraw on and off.

13. Create the OtherCmd_Click procedure to display Form2, and type

```
SUB OtherCmd_Click ()
Form2.SHOW
END SUB
```

14. Create the AutoOffCmd_Click procedure, and type

```
SUB AutoOffCmd_Click ()
Form1.AutoRedraw = False
END SUB
```

15. Create the AutoOnCmd_Click procedure, and type

```
SUB AutoOnCmd_Click ()
Form1.AutoRedraw = True
END SUB
```

16. Create the `ClsCmd_Click` procedure, and type

```
SUB ClsCmd_Click ()
CLS
END SUB
```

17. Create the `WhiteCmd_Click` procedure, and type

```
SUB WhiteCmd_Click ()
BackColor = White
END SUB
```

18. Create the `RedCmd_Click` procedure, and type

```
SUB RedCmd_Click ()
Backcolor = Red
END SUB
```

19. Create the `BlackCmd_Click` procedure, and type

```
SUB BlackCmd_Click ()
ForeColor = Black
END SUB
```

20. Create the `BlueCmd_Click` procedure, and type

```
SUB BlueCmd_Click ()
Forecolor = Blue
END SUB
```

21. Select Form2, create the Command1_Click procedure, and type

```
SUB Command1_Click ()
Form2.HIDE
END SUB
```

22. Save the project and run it. Execute the **0-127** command of the File menu and your form should look like Figure 11.3, showing all the ASCII characters between 0 and 127.

23. Execute the **128-255** command of the File menu and the form should look like Figure 11.4, showing the ASCII graphics characters between 128 and 255.

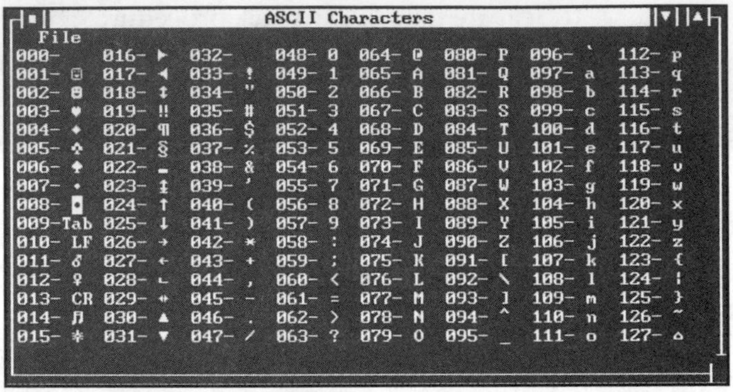

Figure 11.3. *The ASCII characters and codes from 0 to 127.*

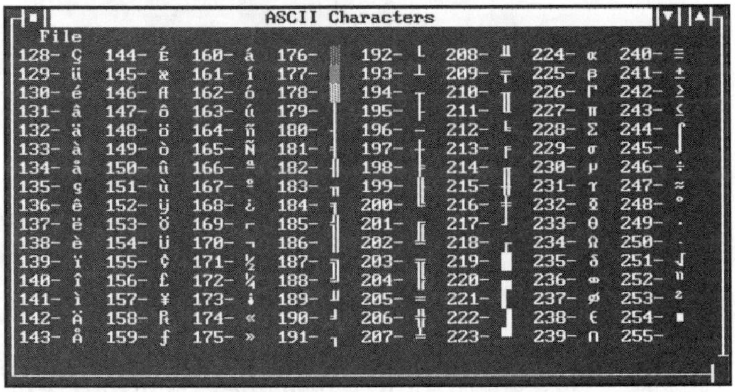

Figure 11.4. *The ASCII characters and codes from 128 through 255.*

Using these characters, you can create some simple designs on a form or picture box. Graphics drawn on a form or picture box are modified by the property settings of the form or picture box on which you draw. Forms and picture boxes have special properties, shown in Table 11.2, for controlling how and where drawing occurs on them. These properties control redrawing and set the default colors used for foreground and background, and the initial drawing location.

Table 11.2. Graphics properties of forms and picture boxes.

Property	Description
AutoRedraw	Sets the object to remember what was drawn on it
BackColor	Sets the background color

Property	Description
CurrentX	Sets the current horizontal location
CurrentY	Sets the current vertical location
ForeColor	Sets the foreground color
ScaleHeight	Sets the height of the drawing area in the scale units
ScaleWidth	Sets the width of the drawing area in scale units

Controlling Redrawing of Graphics

Whenever another window covers and then uncovers a form, the covering window erases the form's contents and you have to redraw them if you want to see them. Text boxes, labels, list boxes, and combo boxes all contain the text drawn on them, so they automatically redraw themselves. File list boxes, Directory list boxes, and Drive list boxes also contain the text they display, and redraw themselves. Forms and picture boxes with text or graphics characters printed on them at runtime do not contain those images, and thus do not automatically redraw themselves. Visual Basic or your program must handle the redrawing of these objects.

> Although the File, Directory, and Drive list boxes automatically redraw themselves, their contents aren't updated unless you change a directory. If you have added a file to a directory, or added a new subdirectory with your program, execute the REFRESH method for that box to cause it to update its contents.

There are two ways to redraw a window: let the system do it, or do it yourself. The AutoRedraw property controls who does the redrawing when a window is uncovered. If AutoRedraw is set to True, the system stores a copy of everything printed on a form or picture box on the persistent image in memory. The *persistent image* is a place in memory where the image of everything drawn on a form or picture box is stored. If part of a form or picture window is uncovered, or needs to be redrawn for any reason, the image on the uncovered part is redrawn by copying the image from the persistent image.

Use the other commands on the File menu in the ASCII characters program to experiment with the AutoRedraw property. Print something on the form, turn AutoRedraw on or off, and then use Form2 to cover or uncover Form1. For example, in Figure 11.5, the form in the background would have been cleared when the small form in the foreground was placed in front of it. With AutoRedraw set to True, the contents of the form are retained.

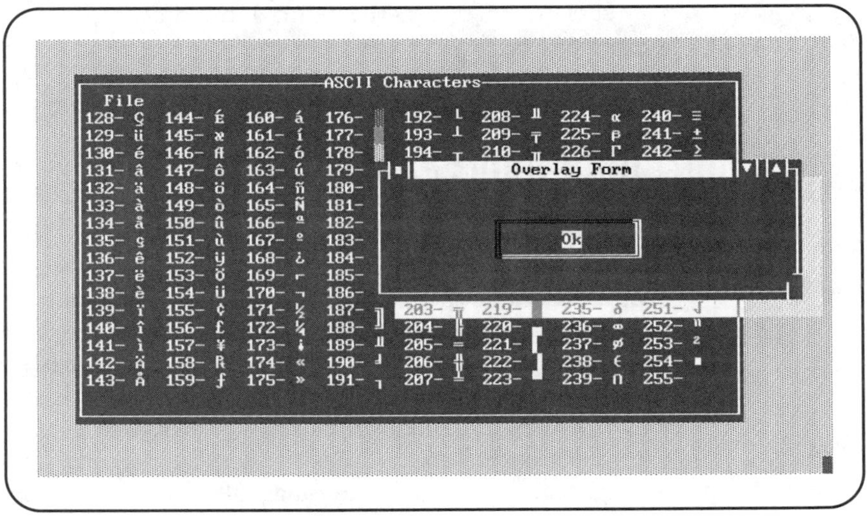

Figure 11.5. *Covering a form with AutoRedraw set to True.*

If AutoRedraw is set to False, uncovering a form or picture box causes a Paint event for that object. If you want to redraw the object, you must place code in the Paint event procedure.

Although it's certainly more convenient to let the system redraw uncovered objects, especially if the image is difficult to reconstruct, there are some caveats to using the AutoRedraw property.

1. Saving the image on each form and picture box uses additional memory. If you have only one graphic in an application, it isn't a problem. If you have many forms and picture boxes that

contain graphics, it could become a problem. This caveat is more important in Visual Basic for Windows, where graphic images are stored rather than character graphics.

2. When AutoRedraw is True, drawing and printing is done on the persistent image in memory. When your drawing procedure finishes and your program is in the idle loop, the persistent image is copied to the screen. (A program is in the *idle loop* when it's waiting for you to do something, such as press a button.) If you have a procedure that takes a long time to run, you won't see anything on the screen until it finishes.

3. You can override the problem described in number 2 by executing the REFRESH method for the object whenever you want the persistent image copied to the screen. However, this slows down your program significantly by causing your whole drawing to be drawn multiple times; once on the persistent image and again on the screen every time you execute REFRESH.

4. If you change AutoRedraw from True to False at runtime, everything in the persistent image becomes the background of the form or picture box, and is not erased with the CLS method. If you later change AutoRedraw back to True, the image in the persistent bitmap replaces everything drawn since you changed AutoRedraw to False when the image is refreshed. The image isn't immediately refreshed, but waits until you make a change and enter the idle loop, or until you execute the REFRESH method.

5. You must set AutoRedraw to True if you want to print graphics drawn on a form or picture box by using the PRINTFORM method.

6. If you change the BackColor property, the persistent image is changed to that color no matter what the state of AutoRedraw.

Setting the Scale

The default scale used in a form or picture box is character widths and heights, and cannot be changed. Because you're operating in character mode, you have no choice but to measure things in character widths and

heights. The scale is measured down and right from the upper-left corner of the drawing area (just below the title bar of a form). The location of the drawing point is stored in the CurrentX and CurrentY properties of the object being drawn on. The drawing point is where the next printed character will appear.

Setting Screen Colors

The ForeColor and BackColor properties control the default colors used for foreground and background objects. Foreground objects are the black parts of text and graphics characters. The background is the blank area of a form or picture box. You can experiment with changing the background and foreground colors with the ASCII Characters program to see what changes.

You set the colors at design time by using the Color Palette window, or at runtime by using either the defined colors from the CONSTANT.BI file (included with Visual Basic) or with the RGB() and QBCOLOR() functions. You already have set some of the colors by using both the Color Palette window and color constants. Now let's look at the numbers themselves. A color is stored as a color attribute, which is a number from 0 to 15 (see Table 11.3). This is significantly different from the way Visual Basic for Windows handles colors. Windows colors have a much wider range than the MS-DOS colors. However, if you use the definitions in CONSTANT.BI or the RGB() and QBCOLOR() functions to get your color attribute, your program will work in both environments. The numbers will be different, but they will represent the same colors.

Table 11.3. Color attributes for the standard colors.

Color	Attribute
BLACK	0
BLUE	1

Color	Attribute
GREEN	2
CYAN	3
RED	4
MAGENTA	5
BROWN	6
WHITE	7
GRAY	8
BRIGHT_BLUE	9
BRIGHT_GREEN	10
BRIGHT_CYAN	11
BRIGHT_RED	12
PINK	13
YELLOW	14
BRIGHT_WHITE	15

You can access or set the system default colors by using the ControlPanel property of the SCREEN object. The ControlPanel property operates like an array of values, with each element of the array controlling a different screen attribute. The syntax is

`SCREEN.ControlPanel(element) = value`

where *element* is the array element containing the system property you want to change (see Table 11.4) and *value* is the value to which you want to change it. In all cases, you should use the identifier from the CONSTANT.BI file rather than the numeric value of the array element. This is both for readability and for compatibility with Visual Basic for Windows.

Table 11.4 The system default properties from CONSTANT.BI.

Identifier	*Element*	*Description/Value Range*
ACCESSKEY_FORECOLOR	0	Access key foreground color (0–15)
ACTIVE_BORDER_BACKCOLOR	1	Active border background color (0–15)
ACTIVE_BORDER_FORECOLOR	2	Active border foreground color(0–15)
ACTIVE_WINDOW_SHADOW	3	Active window shadow effect (Boolean)
COMBUTTON_FORECOLOR	4	Command button foreground color (0–15)
DESKTOP_BACKCOLOR	5	Desktop background color (0–15)
DESKTOP_FORECOLOR	6	Desktop foreground color (0–15)
DESKTOP_PATTERN	7	Desktop fill pattern (ASCII 0–255)
DISABLED_ITEM_FORECOLOR	8	Disabled menu/dialog item foreground color (0-15)
MENU_BACKCOLOR	9	Menu, background color (0–15)
MENU_FORECOLOR	10	Menu, foreground color (0–15)
MENU_SELECTED_BACKCOLOR	11	Menu, background color of a selected item (0–15)
MENU_SELECTED_FORECOLOR	12	Menu, foreground color of a selected item (0–15)
SCROLLBAR_BACKCOLOR	13	Scroll bar background color (0–15)
SCROLLBAR_FORECOLOR	14	Scroll bar foreground color (0–15)

Identifier	Element	Description/Value Range
THREE_D	15	Three-dimensional effect for controls with border (Boolean)
TITLEBAR_BACKCOLOR	16	Title bar background color (0–15)
TITLEBAR_FORECOLOR	17	Title bar foreground color (0–15)

The `RGB()` function is an alternate way of creating colors without using the constant values from CONSTANT.BI. The `RGB()` function takes three integer arguments, one each for the red, green, and blue intensities, and returns the color attribute that most closely resembles that color. The syntax is

```
RGB(red%,green%,blue%)
```

where *red%*, *green%*, and *blue%* are integer values in the range 0 to 255. For example:

```
Color = RGB(255,0,0)
```

would give the variable `Color` the value 12, which, as indicated in Table 11.3, is bright red.

A second function, `QBCOLOR()`, sets the color value for the 16 standard QuickBASIC colors, which are the same as the 16 standard Visual Basic for MS-DOS colors. In Visual Basic for MS-DOS, this function is basically a do-nothing, because it simply passes the input through to the output. However, if you have defined all your colors with this function, your program (the color part anyway) will work without change in both the MS-DOS and Windows versions of Visual Basic.

Graphics on the Screen

True graphics-mode graphics can be created only in full-screen mode in Visual Basic for MS-DOS. This is different from Visual Basic for Windows, where all graphics must occur on a form. The methods used are consistent with earlier versions of BASIC, and similar to the methods used in Visual Basic for Windows.

Clearing the Screen

To do full-screen graphics, you must first clear all forms from the screen. You can do this individually with the HIDE method by using the following syntax:

```
form.HIDE
```

where *form* is the form you want to hide. You also can set the Visible property of the form to False, which is what the HIDE method does. Alternatively, you can hide all visible forms by using HIDE with the Screen object with the following syntax:

```
Screen.HIDE
```

When you're finished creating graphics, use the SHOW method to make the forms visible again. The syntax is the same as that of the HIDE method. Using Screen.SHOW makes all forms hidden with Screen.HIDE visible again.

Setting the Graphics Mode

The graphics mode is set with the SCREEN statement after all forms have been hidden. The syntax of the SCREEN statement is as follows:

```
SCREEN mode
```

where *mode* is the screen mode to set. There are several different screen modes; which ones that are available on your machine depends on the monitor and graphics adapter you have. Table 11.5 shows the modes, graphics resolutions, number of color attributes, and the number of colors that can be assigned to the attributes. See Chapter 15, "Command Reference," for a complete description of the SCREEN statement, including which modes are available for which types of graphics adapters.

When you are done displaying graphics and want to redisplay the forms, you must first switch back to text mode (SCREEN 0) before using the SHOW method to redisplay the forms. Forms cannot be displayed in any of the graphics modes.

Table 11.5. The graphics screen modes.

Mode	Resolution	Attribute	Color
0	Text mode	2	16
1	320 x 200 color	4	16
2	640 x 200 b/w	2	16
3	720 x 348 b/w	1	1
4	640 x 400 color	1	16
7	320 x 200 color	16	16
8	640 x 200 color	16	16
9	640 x 350 color	$4^1, 16^2$	64
10	640 x 350 b/w	4	9
11	640 x 480 color	2	256
12	640 x 480 color	16	256
13	320 x 200 color	256	256

[1] *64K EGA memory*
[2] *128K EGA memory*

Setting the Color

The color that the drawing commands use is set in one of two ways:

- Using the COLOR statement to set the foreground and background colors.

- Using a color attribute in a drawing command to override the foreground color set with the COLOR statement.

The COLOR statement uses the following syntax to set the foreground and background color for the screen:

```
COLOR [forecolor][,backcolor][,bordercolor]
```

or

```
COLOR [backcolor][,palette]    'screen mode 1 only
```

Here, *forecolor* is the foreground color, *backcolor* is the background color, and *bordercolor* is the color of the border of the screen. The border color is not available on all monitors. All these colors are set with color attributes such as those in Table 11.3. The second syntax is only for screen mode 1. In screen mode 1, there are three fixed palettes of colors selected with the palette argument. If you omit the palette argument, you get the default palette; otherwise, if palette is an even number, you get the even palette, or if it is odd, you get the odd palette. See Chapter 15, "Command Reference," for a complete description of the COLOR statement.

The Screen Colors Program

To look at some of these colors, create the screen colors program. This program clears the screen and cycles through the 16 possible color attributes.

1. Start a new project: execute the New Project command of the File menu, then execute the New Form command of the File menu and use COLOR1.FRM for the filename. Execute the Save Project command of the File menu and use COLOR1.MAK as the project filename.

2. Select the form, reduce its size, and draw a command button on it, as shown in Figure 11.6. The actual size and placement aren't important.

Figure 11.6. Form layout for the screen colors program.

3. Switch to the Programming Environment. Create the Command1_Click procedure and type:

```
SUB Command1_Click ()
Screen.HIDE                'hide all forms
SCREEN 8                   'switch to graphics mode
FOR J = 1 TO 2             'cycle through the colors 2 times
FOR I = 0 TO 16            'cycle through 16 colors
theColor = QBCOLOR(I)      'use for compatibility with VB Win
COLOR , theColor           'set the background color
SLEEP (1)                  'pause 1 second
NEXT I
NEXT J
SCREEN 0                   'switch back to text mode
Screen.SHOW                'redisplay the form
END SUB
```

This procedure first hides all displayed forms, and then switches to screen mode 8. This assumes you have an EGA or VGA adapter and a color monitor. If you have a CGA adapter, you can use screen mode 1 only. Next, the procedure uses two nested FOR/NEXT loops to cycle through the 16 colors twice. If you have a CGA adapter, you can cycle through only the four available attributes rather than 16. Finally, the procedure switches back to text mode, redisplays the forms, and ends, leaving the form on the screen again.

4. Save the project and run it. The form with the command button appears on the screen. Pressing the button causes the screen to clear and cycle twice through the 16 standard colors.

287

Setting the Scale

When creating graphics in full-screen mode, you can set the part of the screen where graphics appear, and set the scale used when drawing there. The *viewport* is a rectangle on the screen where graphics can be drawn. The default viewport is the whole screen, and drawing can occur anywhere there. To restrict drawing to a specific rectangle, use the VIEW statement to define a new viewport. The syntax of the VIEW statement is

VIEW[SCREEN][(x1,y1)-(x2,y2) [,[background][,[border]]]]

Here, SCREEN is a keyword indicating that the coordinates are relative to the whole screen and not an existing viewport. The coordinates x1, y1, x2, and y2 identify the upper-left corner and the lower-right corner of the viewport. *background* is the color to use for the background of the viewport. *border* is the line color to use to draw a box around it. Both colors default to the current background color.

The default scale on the screen is pixels. The current screen mode determines the number of pixels per inch—see Table 11.5. The origin of the coordinate system is the upper-left corner of the screen, with the horizontal coordinate increasing to the right and the vertical coordinate increasing down.

This isn't a familiar coordinate system for most people. However, you can change the system by using the WINDOW statement. The syntax of the WINDOW statement is as follows:

WINDOW [[SCREEN] (x1!,y1!)-(x2!,y2!)]

where SCREEN is a keyword that indicates that the coordinate system reads down and to the right, the same as the screen. If you omit SCREEN, the coordinates read up and to the right. You define the coordinate system to use in the current viewport with the (x1!,y1!)-(x2!,y2!) arguments. The values x1! and y1! fix the values of the x,y coordinates of the upper-left corner, and x2!,y2! fix the coordinates of the lower-right corner. If you omit these arguments, the coordinate system reverts to the default screen coordinates (pixels).

Chapter 12, "Drawing with Visual Basic," features examples showing the usage of these statements.

Using Sound

There are three statements for producing sound with Visual Basic: BEEP, SOUND, and PLAY. The simplest is the BEEP statement, which plays a simple system beep when executed. The SOUND statement has more control than BEEP, and the PLAY statement generates music. The BEEP statement is the only sound-oriented statement compatible with Visual Basic for Windows.

Using the BEEP Statement

The BEEP statement produces a simple system beep. It is most useful as a signal to users that something has happened that demands their attention, such as the completion of a long-running process. It's also useful in debugging to signal when a program has reached a specific point. The statement's syntax is

BEEP

Using the SOUND Statement

The SOUND statement offers much more control than the BEEP statement. SOUND can control the duration and *pitch* (frequency) of the emitted sound. Its syntax is

SOUND *frequency, duration*

where *frequency* is the frequency of the sound in *hertz* (cycles/second). The range is 37 to 32,767 Hz, but most people can't hear sounds above 13,000 Hz. *duration* is the duration of the sound in clock ticks. The range is 0 to 65,535, and there are 18.2 ticks per second. The value 0 turns off a tone, as does executing a PLAY statement.

Using the PLAY Statement

The PLAY statement is designed for playing music. The argument is a string containing the musical notes, which are placed in the music buffer for the system to play. Music can be played in the background, allowing other processing to continue while the music is playing. The PLAY statement can be coupled with a PLAY event trap (see the ON PLAY statement in Chapter 15, "Command Reference") to refill the music buffer whenever it's getting low on notes to play. The syntax of the statement is

PLAY *music-macro$*

where *music-macro$* is a string containing music macro commands. See PLAY in Chapter 15 for a discussion of the music macro string, and the flag example in Chapter 12, "Drawing with Visual Basic."

What You Have Learned

This chapter discussed the Visual Basic methods that prepare a form or the screen to be drawn on. Specifically discussed were the properties and methods that set the colors to draw with and the screen modes for drawing on the screen. Drawing on a form can be done only with graphics characters. True graphics-mode drawing requires that all forms are hidden. In this chapter, you learned about

- Controlling the redrawing with the AutoRedraw property
- Drawing on forms with graphics characters
- Setting the foreground and background colors with constants, and the RGB() and QBCOLOR() functions
- Preparing the screen for full-screen graphics
- Setting the viewport and coordinate system for full-screen graphics
- Playing sounds and music

Drawing with Visual Basic

Although Visual Basic does not have an extensive set of drawing tools, it does have a line-and-rectangle tool, a circle tool, and a point-plotting tool. Using these simple tools, and the capability to set the screen colors, you can draw many useful figures. All the drawing statements apply to drawing on the screen, with no forms showing, as this is the only graphics environment available to Visual Basic for DOS. Note that these statements match similar methods used for drawing on forms in Visual Basic for Windows.

In This Chapter

This chapter shows you how to create graphic images with Visual Basic. Visual Basic for DOS has three statements, compatible with Visual Basic for Windows, for drawing on the screen: LINE, CIRCLE, and PSET. The LINE method draws lines and rectangles, the CIRCLE method draws circles, and the PSET method sets the color of a single point.

In this chapter, you will learn to

● Draw circles and pie sections

● Draw lines and rectangles

● Set the color of a point on the screen

● Play music

Compatibility of the Examples

The examples in this chapter assume that you have an EGA, VGA, or compatible monitor and a graphics card that can display screen mode 8. If you have a CGA or Hercules-compatible monitor, you must change the SCREEN, COLOR, and VIEW statements to allow for the differences in color and resolution properties of your system. Hercules-compatible monitors require that you load the MSHERC.COM terminate-and-stay-resident (TSR) program before the Hercules screen modes can be set. See the descriptions of these commands in Chapter 15, "Command Reference," for a list of the available properties. If you don't have a graphics card in your system, you may as well skip this chapter—you won't be able to do any of the examples.

Making Circles and Pie Slices

The CIRCLE method is used to draw circles, filled circles, arcs, pie slices, and filled pie slices on forms, picture boxes, and the PRINTER object. The syntax of the CIRCLE method is

```
[object.]CIRCLE[STEP](xc!,yc!),radius![,[color&]
[,[startang!][,[endang!][,aspect!]]]]
```

where *object* is the object to be drawn on, *(xc!,yc!)* is the location of the center of the circle, *radius!* is the radius of the circle, *color&* is the color to use to draw the outline of the circle or arc, *startang!* and *endang!* are the starting and ending angles (in radians) of the pie slice, and *aspect!* is the aspect ratio of the object. If you use the STEP argument, the coordinates of the center of the circle are treated as relative to the current drawing location. If the *startang!* and *endang!* arguments are positive, they mark the end points of an arc. If they're negative, they still mark the end points of an arc, but a line also is drawn from the center of the circle to the end of the arc, creating a pie slice.

Be careful with the *aspect!* argument: it may not behave the way you think it does. The *aspect ratio* is the height divided by the width of the ellipse, measured in the screen coordinates (pixels) even if a user system of coordinates has been established with the WINDOW statement. Because the number of pixels in the horizontal direction is not equal to the number of pixels in the vertical direction, an aspect of 1 is not a circle.

The default value of *aspect!* gives a circle in whatever monitor and screen mode currently is in operation. This default value can be calculated from the following:

```
(4/3)*(Ypixels/Xpixels)
```

where *Ypixels* and *Xpixels* are the vertical and horizontal screen resolution in the current screen mode. The 4/3 applies to a standard monitor, which has a width-to-height ratio of 4 to 3. For screen mode 8 (640 by 200), the value is

```
0.416 = (4/3)*(200/640)
```

Other things to consider are the starting and ending angles, which are calculated so that the angles are correct for the default aspect ratio (a circle). For an ellipse, either the x or y coordinate of the end of the arc is stretched by the aspect ratio. Thus, as the aspect ratio increases, the visual representation of the angle also increases. Imagine drawing a pie slice on a piece of rubber, and then stretching that rubber in one direction. That's how Visual Basic applies the aspect ratio to the circle.

The Drawing Test Program

The drawing test program is a simple program used to experiment with the drawing tools. The tool is chosen with a button on a form. The drawing then takes place on the full screen.

1. Start a new project: execute the New Project command of the File menu, then execute the New Form command of the File menu and use FLAG1.FRM for the filename. Execute the Save Project

command of the File menu and use FLAG.MAK as the project filename. The reason for these names will be apparent in a moment.

2. Select Form1, and set its properties as follows:

```
Caption = Drawing
Height = 17
Width = 65
```

3. Draw the Exit command button on the form as shown in Figure 12.1, with the following properties:

```
CtlName = ExitCmd
Caption = Exit
Height = 3
Width = 13
Top = 12
Left = 48
```

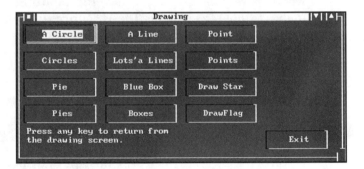

Figure 12.1. *Layout of the drawing program.*

4. Draw a command button on the form, with the following properties. For now, don't worry about the other buttons on the form.

```
CtlName = CircleCmd
Caption = A Circle
Height = 3
Width = 15
Top = 0
Left = 0
```

5. Save the form, switch to the Programming Environment, create the ExitCmd_Click procedure, and type

```
SUB ExitCmd_Click ()
END
END SUB
```

6. Open the declarations section of the form and type the following. The first block of color definitions is copied from the CONSTANT.BI file included with Visual Basic. The rest of the definitions are used later in this example.

```
CONST BLACK = 0
CONST BLUE = 1
CONST GREEN = 2
CONST CYAN = 3
CONST RED = 4
CONST MAGENTA = 5
CONST BROWN = 6
CONST WHITE= 7
CONST GRAY = 8
CONST BRIGHT_BLUE = 9
CONST BRIGHT_GREEN = 10
CONST BRIGHT_CYAN = 11
CONST BRIGHT_RED = 12
CONST PINK = 13
CONST YELLOW = 14
CONST BRIGHT_WHITE = 15
CONST True = -1, False = 0
TYPE FlagType
  Xmin AS SINGLE
  Xmax AS SINGLE
  Ymin AS SINGLE
  Ymax AS SINGLE
  Stripe AS SINGLE
  Rbox AS SINGLE
END TYPE
```

Note that Visual Basic inserts DECLARE statements here as you add SUB procedures to this form. Don't remove them; your program needs them to identify which names are procedures and which are variable names. If you run a program and obtain an error in a statement containing a procedure call, and that error indicates that something is wrong with a variable or assignment statement, then check whether that procedure has been declared. Visual Basic may think that the procedure name is a variable

name, and is trying to make an assignment statement out of the procedure name and its arguments. To fix this, manually insert a declaration for the procedure at the module level of the form. See Chapter 15, "Command Reference," for a complete description of the DECLARE statement. This applies only to procedures you write yourself, not to event procedures.

7. Create the CircleCmd_Click procedure, and type

```
SUB CircleCmd_Click ()
'Draw a Blue Circle
DIM theHeight AS SINGLE, theWidth AS SINGLE
'Prepare the screen
Screen.HIDE
SCREEN 8
theHeight = 10000
theWidth = 12000
WINDOW (0, theHeight)-(theWidth, 0)
COLOR Blue, White
'Draw the circle
CIRCLE (theWidth/2,theHeight/2),theHeight/10, Red'
'Fill the circle
PAINT (theWidth/2,theHeight/2),Blue,Red'
WaitForKey                          'Pause for a keystroke
SCREEN 0
Screen.SHOW
END SUB
```

This procedure first prepares the screen, as described in the last chapter. It then initializes the theHeight and theWidth variables, which are going to be the limits for the user defined y- and x-scale for the screen. The WINDOW statement then applies these limits to the screen. After this statement is executed, the screen's origin is in the lower-left corner; the scale ranges from 0 to 12,000 horizontally and from 0 to 10,000 vertically. Next, the CIRCLE statement is executed. This draws a red circle in the center of the screen. The radius of the circle is one-tenth of the height of the screen. The PAINT statement then fills the circle with blue color out to the first red pixels it finds. The partial syntax of the PAINT statement follows; see Chapter 15, "Command Reference," for the complete syntax.

PAINT [**STEP**](*x!*,*y!*)[,[*color%*]][,*bordercolor&*]]

Here, STEP indicates that the x,y coordinates are specified in relation to the current position of the graphic cursor, and not the current origin on the screen. The two values x!,y! are the x,y coordinates of any point within the region to be filled. This point must not be on the line surrounding the region, but can be anywhere within the region. color% is the fill color to use to fill the region, and bordercolor& is the stopping color for the fill: the fill stops when it reaches a border of this color.

Next, the program pauses for you to admire your work. It does this by calling the WaitForKey procedure (which you will soon create). When that procedure returns, the SCREEN statement is called to change back to text mode, and the form is redisplayed with the SHOW method.

You can print on the screen only from a code module, not from a form. Because the WaitForKey procedure writes "Press any key to continue" at the bottom of the screen, the procedure must be placed in a code module.

8. Open the declarations section and copy everything there. Execute the New Module command of the File menu and create a code module named FLAG.BAS. Paste the declarations, and add the $FORM metacommand as shown in the following. The $FORM metacommand gives procedures in this module access to the properties and controls in the listed form.

```
CONST BLACK = 0
CONST BLUE = 1
CONST GREEN = 2
CONST CYAN = 3
CONST RED = 4
CONST MAGENTA = 5
CONST BROWN = 6
CONST WHITE = 7
CONST GRAY = 8
CONST BRIGHT_BLUE = 9
CONST BRIGHT_GREEN = 10
CONST BRIGHT_CYAN = 11
CONST BRIGHT_RED = 12
CONST PINK = 13
CONST YELLOW = 14
CONST BRIGHT_WHITE = 15
CONST True = -1, False = 0
TYPE FlagType
   Xmin AS SINGLE
   Xmax AS SINGLE
   Ymin AS SINGLE
   Ymax AS SINGLE
```

297

```
      Stripe AS SINGLE
      Rbox AS SINGLE
   END TYPE
   '$FORM Flag1
```

9. Create a new SUB procedure named WaitForKey, with the New **Sub** command on the **Edit** menu, and type

```
SUB WaitForKey ()
WIDTH 80
LOCATE 25, 5
PRINT "Press any key to continue";
WHILE INKEY$ = "":WEND
END SUB
```

This procedure sets the character size with the WIDTH statement, and moves the text cursor to the bottom of the screen (line 25, character 5) with the LOCATE statement. It then prints "Press any key to continue" along the bottom of the screen and pauses for you to press a key. The semicolon at the end of the PRINT statement prevents the PRINT statement from automatically inserting a carriage return there, which would scroll the screen up one line and ruin the graphics.

The pause for you to press a key is implemented with a WHILE/WEND loop and an INKEY$ function. The WHILE/WEND loop actually consists of two statements, but they are both placed on the same line, separated by a colon. The loop would work the same if the colon were replaced with a carriage return. The INKEY$ function checks the keyboard for a pressed key. If no key has been pressed, it returns null; otherwise it returns the key pressed. The loop then continues running until you press a key and INKEY$ doesn't return null.

10. Save the project, run it, and click the A Circle button; the screen should look like Figure 12.2. Press any key to continue, then press the Exit button to end the program.

Now, this isn't terribly exciting, even though it's a pretty blue circle with a bright red rim. Draw a few more circles to make things more interesting.

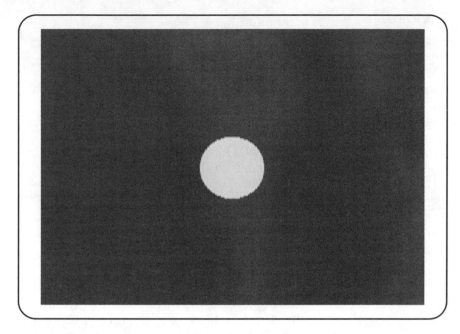

Figure 12.2. *Result of pressing the A Circle button.*

11. Switch to the Forms Designer and add another command button below the first. Set its properties to

```
Caption = Circles
CtlName = CirclesCmd
Height = 3
Width = 15
Top = 0
Left = 3
```

12. Switch back to the Programming Environment, create the CirclesCmd_Click procedure, and type the following. (You can copy much of this from the previous procedure.)

```
SUB CirclesCmd_Click ()
'Draw 100 Circles
DIM theColor AS INTEGER, I AS INTEGER
DIM theHeight AS SINGLE, theWidth AS SINGLE
'Prepare the screen
```

```
Screen.HIDE
SCREEN 8
theHeight = 10000
theWidth = 12000
WINDOW (0, theHeight)-(theWidth, 0)
COLOR Blue, White
FOR I = 1 TO 100                     'line 12
  XC = RND(1) * theWidth
  YC = RND(1) * theHeight
  Radius = RND(1) * theHeight / 2
  theColor = QBCOLOR(RND(1) * 15)
  CIRCLE (XC, YC), Radius, theColor
  PAINT (XC, YC), theColor, theColor
NEXT I
WaitForKey        'Pause for a keystroke
SCREEN 0
Screen.SHOW
END SUB
```

The first few lines of this procedure are the same as in the `CircleCmd_Click` procedure, where the drawing environment is set up. In line 12, a `FOR/NEXT` loop starts that iterates the enclosed block of statements 100 times, which draws 100 circles on the screen. Just drawing 100 circles won't be interesting, so use random numbers to set the arguments of the `CIRCLE` method. Lines 13 and 14 calculate a random location for the center of the circle. Because the random number function `RND(1)` always returns a number between 0 and 1, scale it with `theWidth` and `theHeight`. This ensures that the center always is on the screen.

In line 15, the radius of the circle is calculated and scaled to be a maximum of one-half the height of the screen (that just seems like a nice size to make it). In line 16, the `QBCOLOR()` function and the `RND()` function are used to randomly select one of the 16 standard colors. (The `QBCOLOR()` function isn't really needed here, but is included to make this code compatible with Visual Basic for Windows.) Finally, in line 17 the `CIRCLE` method is called to draw the circle, and in line 18, `PAINT` is called to fill the circle.

13. Save the program and run it. Press the Circles button and see what happens. You should see something like Figure 12.3. (Kind of pretty, don't you think?) Press any key to continue, then press the Exit button to end the program.

Figure 12.3. *Execution of the Circles procedure.*

The CIRCLES method can do more than simply create circles. It creates ellipses if you make the aspect! argument to a value different from the default value. The method also creates arcs and filled pie slices if you use the startang! and endang! arguments. If startang! and endang! are positive, the method draws an arc. If they're negative, the method draws a filled pie slice.

14. Switch to the Forms Designer and draw a command button. Set its properties to

```
Caption = Pie
CtlName = PieCmd
Height = 3
Width = 15
Top = 6
Left = 0
```

15. Switch to the Programming Environment and create the PieCmd_Click procedure. Type the following. (You can copy most of it from the previous procedure to save yourself some typing.)

```
SUB PieCmd_Click ()
'Draw a Red Pie Slice
DIM theHeight AS SINGLE, theWidth AS SINGLE
'Prepare the screen
Screen.HIDE
SCREEN 8
theHeight = 10000
theWidth = 12000
WINDOW (0, theHeight)-(theWidth, 0)
COLOR Blue, White
CIRCLE (theWidth / 2, theHeight / 2), theHeight / 10,
   Blue, -1, -2, 1        'Draw the Pie
PAINT (theWidth / 2, theHeight / 2 + theHeight / 20),
   Red, Blue       'Fill the circle
WaitForKey                    'Pause for a keystroke
SCREEN 0
Screen.SHOW
END SUB
```

This procedure works like the `Circle` procedure, with the addition of -1 and -2 for the starting and ending angles. The angles are measured in radians, starting from the positive x axis (that is, 3 o'clock is 0 and 12 noon is $^{\pi}/_2$ radians). Thus, the arc is drawn from one radian ($1 * ^{180}/_\pi = 57.3$ degrees) to two radians (114.6 degrees). The two values are negative, so lines also are drawn from the center of the circle to each end of the arc. The `PAINT` statement fills the arc with red.

16. Save the project and run it. It should look like Figure 12.4.
Press any key to continue, then press the Exit button to end
the program.

Not terribly exciting, is it? But if random circles were interesting, how about random pies?

17. Switch to the Forms Designer, draw a command button, and set its
properties to

```
Caption = Pies
CtlName = PiesCmd
Height = 3
Width = 15
Top = 9
Left = 0
```

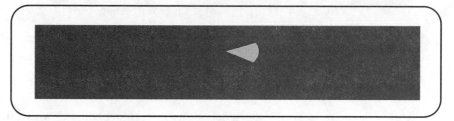

Figure 12.4. Execution of the Pie procedure.

18. Switch to the Programming Environment, create the `PiesCmd_Click` procedure, and type the following. You can copy most of this from the `CirclesCmd_Click` procedure and save yourself some typing.

```
SUB PiesCmd_Click ()
'Draw 100 Pies
DIM theColor AS Integer, I AS Integer
DIM theHeight AS Single, theWidth AS Single
'Prepare the screen
Screen.HIDE
SCREEN 8
theHeight = 10000
theWidth = 12000
WINDOW (0, theHeight)-(theWidth, 0)
COLOR Blue, White
RANDOMIZE
CAspect = (4 / 3) * (200 / 640)    'the aspect ratio
                                   'to give a circle

FOR I = 1 TO 100
  XC = RND(1) * theWidth
  YC = RND(1) * theHeight
  Radius = RND(1) * theHeight / 3
  theColor = QBCOLOR(RND(1) * 15)
  PieStart = RND(1) * 6
  PieEnd = RND(1) * 6
  Aspect = RND(1) * .8 + .2
  CIRCLE (XC, YC), Radius, theColor,
          -PieStart, -PieEnd, Aspect
  theAngle = (PieEnd + PieStart) / 2
  IF PieStart > PieEnd THEN theAngle = theAngle + 3.14159
  xp = XC + (Radius * .5) * COS(theAngle)
  yp = YC + (Radius * .5) * SIN(theAngle) * aspect / CAspect
```

```
   PAINT (xp, yp), theColor, theColor
NEXT I
WaitForKey        'Pause for a keystroke
SCREEN 0
Screen.SHOW
END SUB
```

This is identical to the `Circle` procedure, with the addition of the `PieStart`, `PieEnd`, and `Aspect` variables. `PieStart` and `PieEnd` are given random values between 0 and 6 radians (6 is slightly less than 2π, the number of radians in a circle.) The variable `Aspect` is given a value between 0.2 and 1.0. Note that for screen mode 8, an aspect of 0.416 is a circle; values less than this are ellipses with the long horizontal axis, and values greater than this produce ellipses with a long vertical axis. Another difference is the calculation of the coordinates for the `PAINT` statement. The coordinates must locate a pixel inside the pie slice. The calculation finds the angle of the center of the pie slice and then moves one-tenth of the length of the radius in that direction.

19. Save the project, run it, and press the Pies button. Yeoww! The screen looks like a Pac-Man attack—see Figure 12.5. Note that occasionally the `PAINT` command fills the whole screen: this is a bug discussed in Chapter 13, "Debugging and Error Trapping." Press any key to continue, then press the Exit button to end the program.

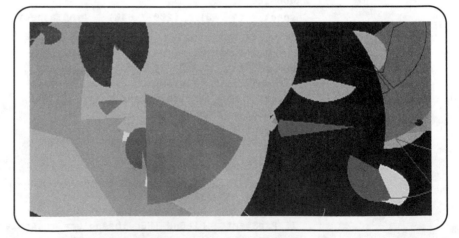

Figure 12.5. *Execution of the Pies procedure. (Look out, it's a Pac-Man attack!)*

Making Lines and Boxes

The LINE statement works much like the CIRCLE statement, except that it produces lines and filled rectangles rather than circles. The syntax of the LINE statement is

LINE[[**STEP**](*xst!*,*yst!*)]-[**STEP**](*xen!*,*yen!*)[,[*color&*],**B**[**F**]]]

Here, *xst!* and *yst!* are either the x,y coordinates to the start of a line or the upper-left corner of a box, and *xen!* and *yen!* are the x,y coordinates of the end of the line or the lower-right corner of a box. If you omit the starting point, drawing is from the current position of the graphic cursor (the last point drawn to). If STEP is used, the coordinates are considered to be relative to the previous point plotted. The B parameter specifies that this is a box rather than a line, and the F parameter specifies that if it's a box, it is to be filled with the same color as the bounding line specified with *color&*.

Let's create a procedure to use this statement to draw a line on the form:

1. Switch to the Forms Designer, draw a command button, and set its properties to

```
Caption = A Line
CtlName = LineCmd
Height = 3
Width = 15
Top = 0
Left = 16
```

2. Switch to the Programming Environment, create the LineCmd_Click procedure, and type the following. (You can copy most of it from the PieCmd_Click procedure and save yourself some typing.)

```
SUB LineCmd_Click ()
'Draw a Blue Line
DIM theHeight AS SINGLE, theWidth AS SINGLE
'Prepare the screen
Screen.HIDE
SCREEN 8
theHeight = 10000
theWidth = 12000
WINDOW (0, theHeight)-(theWidth, 0)
COLOR Blue, White
```

```
LINE (theWidth * .05, theHeight * .1)-(theWidth * .9,
    theHeight * .8), Blue          'draw a line
WaitForKey                         'Pause for a keystroke
SCREEN 0
Screen.SHOW
END SUB
```

Here, the first few lines are the same as those in previous procedures. The LINE statement draws a blue line from a point near the lower-left corner of the screen to a point near the upper-right corner by stating the coordinates as fractions of the height and width.

3. Save the project, run it, and press the A Line button. Your screen should look like Figure 12.6. Press any key to continue, then press the Exit button to end the program.

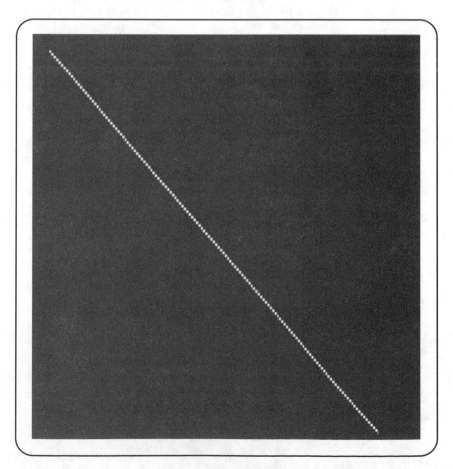

Figure 12.6. *Execution of the A Line procedure.*

Do the same here as for the circles and pies, and draw many lines on the screen using random numbers to set the starting and ending points and the colors.

4. Switch to the Forms Designer. Draw a command button and set its properties to

```
Caption = Lots o' Lines
CtlName = LinesCmd
Height = 3
Width = 15
Top = 3
Left = 16
```

5. Switch to the Programming Environment, create the LinesCmd_Click procedure, and type the following. (You can copy most of it from the CirclesCmd_Click procedure and save yourself some typing.)

```
SUB LinesCmd_Click ()
'Draw 100 Lines
DIM theColor AS INTEGER, I AS INTEGER
DIM theHeight AS SINGLE, theWidth AS SINGLE
DIM XL AS SINGLE, XR AS SINGLE
DIM YL AS SINGLE, YR AS SINGLE
'Prepare the screen
Screen.HIDE
SCREEN 8
theHeight = 10000
theWidth = 12000
WINDOW (0, theHeight)-(theWidth, 0)
RANDOMIZE
COLOR Blue, White
FOR I = 1 TO 100
  XL = RND(1) * theWidth
  YL = RND(1) * theHeight
  XR = RND(1) * theWidth
  YR = RND(1) * theHeight
  theColor = QBCOLOR(RND(1) * 15)
```

12

```
    LINE (XL, YL)-(XR, YR), theColor
NEXT I
WaitForKey        'Pause for a keystroke
SCREEN 0
Screen.SHOW
END SUB
```

Here, you generate four random numbers to specify the x,y coordinates of the start and end of a line and another random number for the color. These values then are used as arguments to the LINE statement, which draws a line.

6. Save the project, run it, and press the Lots o' Lines button. Your screen should look like Figure 12.7. Press any key to continue, then press the Exit button to end the program.

An interesting variation on the LinesCmd_Click procedure is one I call Spinners, shown on the inside front cover in Plate 3. As with all the examples, it uses the drawing test program as a base. First, two pairs of points are selected randomly. Next, the program calculates the point that is one-twentieth of the distance from one point to the next in each pair, and draws a line between them. The program then steps another one-twentieth of the distance and draws another line. This continues until it reaches the second point in each pair. Then, two new pairs of points are created with the second point from each of the original two pairs, plus two new random points, added to them. The program continues drawing lines and adding new points until it completes 20 pairs of points.

Another variation is to draw multisided geometric figures. Set up the program to calculate points on a circle, input the angle through which to move each step, and draw a line. Continue rotating and drawing lines until you come back to your starting point. If you set the angle to 120 degrees, you get a triangle. If you set it to 90 degrees, you get a square. If you set it to 88 degrees, the program draws around in a circle 44 times, creating something that looks like string art.

There are many other variations. Have fun with this program and see what you can come up with.

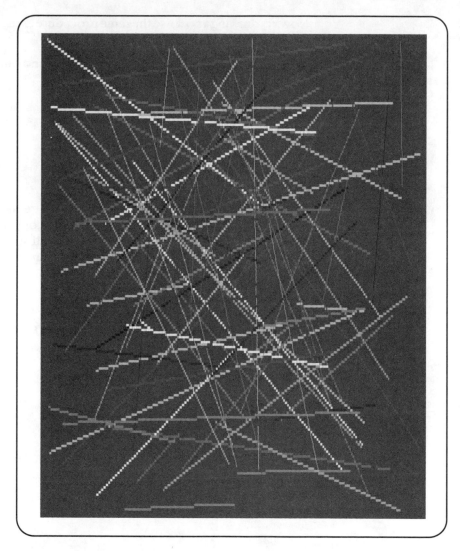

Figure 12.7. *Execution of the Lots o' Lines procedure.*

Now, try drawing a box. Use the same procedure as the `LineCmd_Click`, but add the `B` parameter.

7. Switch to the Forms Designer. Draw a command button and set its properties to

```
Caption = Blue Box
CtlName = BoxCmd
Height = 3
Width = 15
Top = 6
Left = 16
```

8. Switch to the Programming Environment, create the `BoxCmd_Click` procedure, and type the following. (You can copy most of it from the `LineCmd_Click` procedure and save yourself some typing. The only differences are the comment at the top and the `BF` added to the end of the `LINE` statement.)

```
SUB BoxCmd_Click ()
'Draw a Blue Box
DIM theHeight AS SINGLE, theWidth AS SINGLE
'Prepare the screen
Screen.HIDE
SCREEN 8
theHeight = 10000
theWidth = 12000
WINDOW (0, theHeight)-(theWidth, 0)
COLOR Blue, White
LINE (theWidth * .05, theHeight * .1)-(theWidth * .9,
    theHeight * .8), Blue, BF      'draw a line
WaitForKey                         'Pause for a keystroke
SCREEN 0
Screen.SHOW
END SUB
```

9. Save the project, run it, and click the Blue Box button. The window now should look like Figure 12.8. Press any key to continue, then press the Exit button to end the program.

Now, how about a bunch of boxes?

10. Switch to the Forms Designer. Draw a command button and set its properties to

```
Caption = Boxes
CtlName = BoxesCmd
Height = 3
Width = 15
Top = 9
Left = 16
```

Figure 12.8. Execution of the blue box program.

11. Open the BoxesCmd_Click procedure and type the following code.
    (You can copy most of it from the LinesCmd_Click procedure to
    save yourself some typing. Again, the change is in the comment at
    the top and the BF added to the LINE statement.)

```
SUB BoxesCmd_Click ()
'Draw 100 Boxes
DIM theColor AS INTEGER, I AS INTEGER
DIM theHeight AS SINGLE, theWidth AS SINGLE
DIM XL AS SINGLE, XR AS SINGLE
DIM YL AS SINGLE, YR AS SINGLE
'Prepare the screen
Screen.HIDE
SCREEN 8
theHeight = 10000
theWidth = 12000
WINDOW (0, theHeight)-(theWidth, 0)
RANDOMIZE
COLOR Blue, White
FOR I = 1 TO 100
  XL = RND(1) * theWidth
  YL = RND(1) * theHeight
  XR = RND(1) * theWidth
  YR = RND(1) * theHeight
  theColor = QBCOLOR(RND(1) * 15)
  LINE (XL, YL)-(XR, YR), theColor, BF
NEXT I
WaitForKey          'Pause for a keystroke
SCREEN 0
Screen.SHOW
END SUB
```

12. Save the project, run it, and click the Boxes button. Psychedelic!
    The window now should look like Figure 12.9. Press any key to
    continue, then press the Exit button to end the program.

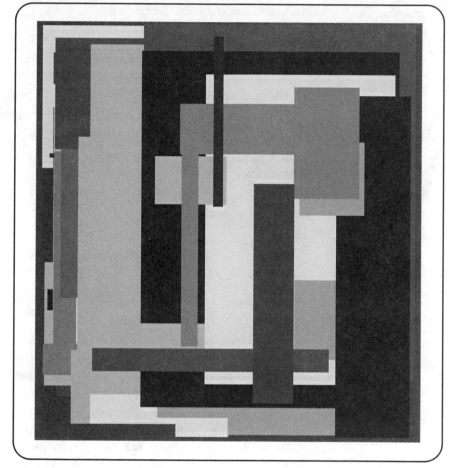

Figure 12.9. *Execution of the Boxes procedure.*

Drawing Points

Points on the screen are set individually with the PSET statement, and read with the POINT function. The syntax of the PSET statement is

PSET [**STEP**]*(x!,y!)*[*,color&*]

where *x!* and *y!* are the x,y coordinates of the point, and *color&* indicates the color you've chosen for the point. If you use STEP, the point is relative to the previous point. If you omit *color&*, the current foreground color is used.

The syntax of the POINT function is

```
POINT (x!,y!)
```

The definitions of the arguments are the same as for the PSET method, except that this method returns the color rather than setting it.

Let's try coloring a single point on the screen, and then draw a bunch of random colored points. Draw a circle around the single point to make it easy to find.

1. Switch to the Forms Designer. Draw a command button and set its properties to

```
Caption = Point
CtlName = PointCmd
Height = 3
Width = 15
Top = 0
Left = 32
```

2. Draw a second command button below it, and set its properties to

```
Caption = Points
CtlName = PointsCmd
Height = 380
Width = 1215
Top = 3120
Left = 2760
```

3. Switch to the Programming Environment, create the PointCmd_Click procedure, and type the following code. (Most of this can be copied from the CircleCmd_Click procedure.)

```
SUB PointCmd_Click ()
'Draw a Yellow point surrounded by a circle
DIM theHeight AS SINGLE, theWidth AS SINGLE
'Prepare the screen
Screen.HIDE
SCREEN 8
theHeight = 10000
theWidth = 12000
WINDOW (0, theHeight)-(theWidth, 0)
COLOR Blue, Black
CIRCLE (theWidth / 2, theHeight / 2), theHeight / 10, Red
PSET (theWidth / 2, theHeight / 2), Yellow
WaitForKey        'Pause for a keystroke
```

```
SCREEN 0
Screen.SHOW
END SUB
```

4. Save the project, run it, and click the Point button. A yellow dot is drawn at the center of the screen, with a red circle surrounding it to make it easier to find. The window now should look like Figure 12.10. Press any key to continue, then press the Exit button to end the program.

Figure 12.10. *Execution of the Point procedure.*

5. Create the `PointsCmd_Click` procedure and type the following code. (You can copy much of this from the `CirclesCmd_Click` procedure.)

```
SUB PointsCmd_Click ()
'Draw 2000 points
DIM theColor AS INTEGER, I  AS INTEGER
DIM theHeight AS SINGLE, theWidth AS SINGLE
'Prepare the screen
Screen.HIDE
SCREEN 8
theHeight = 10000
theWidth = 12000
WINDOW (0, theHeight)-(theWidth, 0)
COLOR Blue, Black
FOR I = 1 TO 2000
  XC = RND(1) * theWidth
  YC = RND(1) * theHeight
  theColor = QBCOLOR(RND(1) * 15)
  PSET (XC, YC), theColor
NEXT I
BEEP
WaitForKey        'Pause for a keystroke
SCREEN 0
Screen.SHOW
END SUB
```

6. Save the project, run it, and click the Points button. Two thousand multicolored points are drawn all over the screen. The window now should look like Figure 12.11. Press any key to continue, then press the Exit button to end the program.

The Draw Flag Program

Now that you know how to use the drawing statements, try something more interesting—drawing an American flag on the screen. The red and white stripes, a blue rectangle, and 50 white stars all can be drawn with the LINE statement, the first two with the B option and the stars without this option. First, let's just draw a star.

1. Switch to the Forms Designer. Draw a command button and set its properties to

```
Caption = Draw Star
CtlName = StarCmd
Height = 3
Width = 15
Top = 6
Left = 32
```

2. Switch to the Programming Environment, create the StarCmd_Click method, and type

```
SUB StarCmd_Click ()
'Draw a star
DIM theHeight AS SINGLE, theWidth AS SINGLE
DIM theFlag AS FlagType
DIM XC AS SINGLE, YC AS SINGLE, RLen AS SINGLE
'Prepare the screen
Screen.HIDE
SCREEN 8
theFlag.Xmin = 0        'bounding box
theFlag.Xmax = 44
theFlag.Ymin = 0
theFlag.Ymax = 26
theFlag.Stripe = 0      'stripe height
theFlag.Rbox = 44       'right side of star box
ScaleIt theFlag         'scale the screen
CLS
```

```
BlueRec theFlag          'draw a blue rectangle
XC = theFlag.Rbox / 2
YC = theFlag.Ymax / 2
RLen = theFlag.Ymax / 2
Star XC, YC, RLen         'draw a star
PAINT (XC, RLen), White   'fill the star
WaitForKey                'Pause for a keystroke
SCREEN 0
Screen.SHOW
END SUB
```

Figure 12.11. *Execution of the Points procedure.*

This procedure uses the FlagType record type, defined in the declarations section, to save space passing information to the SUB procedures. The FlagType type contains the bounding box of the rectangle to hold the flag, the width of a stripe, and the width of the blue rectangle. A *bounding box* is a rectangle that completely contains the flag. In this procedure, you want to draw a single star on a blue background, so set the stripe height to 0 and the width of the blue box to the width of the flag. After theFlag is loaded, the procedure calls the ScaleIt SUB procedure to scale the screen. Note that the procedure is passed only the name of the record-type variable theFlag rather than each of its components. The components still are passed, but in the record-type variable.

Next the procedure clears the screen, calls the BlueRec SUB procedure to draw the blue rectangle, and then calls the Star SUB procedure to draw a star. The arguments to the Star SUB procedure are the x,y location of the center of the star and the length of a side. Now create those three SUB procedures.

3. Switch to the FLAG.BAS module, create a new SUB procedure named ScaleIt by using the New Sub command of the Edit menu, and type

```
SUB ScaleIt (C AS FlagType)
VIEW (100, 50)-(500, 150)
WINDOW (C.Xmin, C.Ymax)-(C.Xmax, C.Ymin)
END SUB
```

This procedure uses the VIEW statement to select a rectangle in the center of the screen as the viewport for drawing. The arguments used here are the x,y coordinates of the upper-left and lower-right corners, in pixels. The allowed numbers depend on the current screen mode; the numbers in this example are for mode 8 (640 by 200 pixels). If your system does not support screen mode 8, you may have to change these numbers to make this program work. See the SCREEN and VIEW statements in Chapter 15, "Command Reference," for more information.

4. Create the BlueRec procedure, and type

```
SUB BlueRec (C AS FlagType)
'Draw a blue rectangle
LINE (C.Xmin, 6 * C.Stripe)-(C.Rbox, C.Ymax), Blue, BF
END SUB
```

This routine draws the blue rectangle in the upper-left corner of the flag. To do so, it uses the LINE method with the B and F options to draw a filled, blue rectangle.

5. Create the Star SUB procedure, and type

```
SUB Star (XC, YC, Slen AS Single)
'Draw a 5 pointed star, one point at a time
DIM Lmin AS SINGLE, Lmax AS SINGLE
Lmin = Slen * .25
Lmax = Slen * .75
PointAng = 1.26   'radians, 2*Pi/5, the angle between points
HPointAng = PointAng / 2 'the half angle of a point
RotAng = 1.57   'radians, rotate the star
FOR K = 1 TO 5
  'x,y location of the point
  Xpt = Lmax * COS(RotAng + (K - 1) * PointAng) + XC
  Ypt = Lmax * SIN(RotAng + (K - 1) * PointAng) + YC
  'x,y location of the right valley
  XptR = Lmin * COS(RotAng - HPointAng +
         (K - 1) * PointAng) + XC
  YptR = Lmin * SIN(RotAng - HPointAng +
         (K - 1) * PointAng) + YC
  'x,y location of the left valley
  XptL = Lmin * COS(RotAng + HPointAng +
         (K - 1) * PointAng) + XC
  YptL = Lmin * SIN(RotAng + HPointAng +
         (K - 1) * PointAng) + YC
  'Draw the two lines
  LINE (XptR, YptR)-(Xpt, Ypt), White
  LINE (Xpt, Ypt)-(XptL, YptL), White
NEXT K
END SUB
```

This procedure first defines Lmin and Lmax as one-quarter and three-quarters of the point length SLen. It then defines PointAng as 1.26 radians, which is the angle between two points on a five-pointed star; HPointAng, which is half PointAng; and RotAng, the angle through which you want to rotate the star before drawing it.

Using this data, the procedure starts a FOR/NEXT loop over the five points on a star. The block of code within the loop calculates the following three x,y locations on a star's point:

- Xpt,Ypt is the location of the tip of the point.

- XptR,YptR is the valley between two points to the right of the first point.

- XptL,YptL is the location of the valley to the left of the first point.

Finally, two lines are drawn on the object, one on each side of a point. The loop causes five points to be drawn on the Picture window, rotating each to align the valley points. Finally, a PAINT statement fills the star with white.

6. Save the procedure, run it, and press the Draw Star button. A star like the one in Figure 12.12 is drawn. Note how each point is made up of three lines. Press any key to continue, then press the Exit button to end the program.

Now, draw the flag.

7. Switch to the Forms Designer. Draw a command button and set its properties to

```
Caption = Draw Flag
CtlName = FlagCmd
Height = 3
Width = 15
Top = 9
Left = 32
```

8. Switch to the Programming Environment. Create the FlagCmd_Click procedure, and type

```
SUB FlagCmd_Click ()
'Draw an American flag
DIM theFlag AS FlagType
'Prepare the screen
Screen.HIDE
SCREEN 8
theFlag.Xmin = 0        'bounding box
theFlag.Xmax = 44
theFlag.Ymin = 0
theFlag.Ymax = 26
theFlag.Stripe = 2      'stripe height
theFlag.Rbox = 26       'right side of star box
ScaleIt theFlag         'scale the screen
CLS
DrawStripes theFlag     'draw the stripes
BlueRec theFlag         'draw a blue rectangle
DrawStars theFlag       'draw the stars
WaitForKey              'pause for a keystroke
SCREEN 0
Screen.SHOW
END SUB
```

Figure 12.12. Execution of the draw star program.

This time the theFlag record-type variable is loaded with values that create a flag. The width of the bounding box is 44 user-defined units, and the height is 26; each stripe is 2 units tall, and the blue box is 26 units wide. After the record-type variable is loaded, the ScaleIt procedure is called to scale the screen and CLS clears it. Next the DrawStripes SUB procedure draws the stripes, the BlueRec SUB procedure draws the blue rectangle and, finally, the DrawStars SUB procedure draws the stars.

9. Switch to the code module. Create the DrawStripes procedure, and type

```
SUB DrawStripes (C AS FlagType)
'Draw the stripes
DIM I AS Integer, theColor AS Integer
'Calculate the position of the stripes
'and alternate the colors between red and white.
theColor = White
FOR I = 1 TO 13
   IF theColor = White THEN theColor = Red
        ELSE theColor = White
   LINE (C.Xmin, (I - 1) * C.Stripe)-(C.Xmax, I * C.Stripe),
        theColor, BF
   NEXT I
END SUB
```

This procedure draws the 13 alternating red and white stripes. There actually are six long stripes and seven short stripes, but the procedure draws 13 long stripes. Then the procedure draws the blue rectangle over one corner. The procedure first defines the variable Color as white, and

creates a loop over the 13 stripes, starting at the bottom. The first statement in the FOR/NEXT loop causes the value of Color to alternate between red and white. The second uses the LINE command with the B and F options to draw a stripe.

10. Create the DrawStripes procedure, and type

```
SUB DrawStars (C AS FlagType)
DIM I AS Integer, J AS Integer
'Calculate the position of each star, then draw it.
DX = C.Rbox / 12
DY = 7 * C.Stripe / 10
'First the 5 rows of 6 stars
FOR I = 1 TO 5
  FOR J = 1 TO 6
    XC = -DX + J * 2 * DX
    YC = 6 * C.Stripe - DY + I * 2 * DY
    Star XC, YC, C.Stripe / 2
    PAINT (XC, YC), White
  NEXT J
NEXT I
'next the 4 rows of 5 stars
FOR I = 1 TO 4
  FOR J = 1 TO 5
    XC = J * 2 * DX
    YC = 6 * C.Stripe + I * 2 * DY
    Star XC, YC, C.Stripe / 2
    PAINT (XC, YC), White
  NEXT J
NEXT I
END SUB
```

This last procedure calculates the position of each star on the blue rectangle, and calls the Star SUB procedure to draw them. It does this by first calculating the positions of five rows of six stars, and then calculating the positions of the remaining four rows of five stars. In both cases, nested FOR/NEXT loops are used. The first loop selects the five rows, and the second selects the six stars along each row. DX and DY are the star-to-star spacings in the horizontal and vertical directions.

11. Save the project, run it, and click the Draw Flag button. The flag appears, as shown in Figure 12.13, and makes you want to stand up and cheer! Press any key to continue, then press the Exit button to end the program.

Now we need a little music to go along with the flag.

Figure 12.13. *Execution of the draw flag program.*

12. Select the FlagCmd_Click procedure and add one line to call the PlayIt procedure:

```
SUB FlagCmd_Click ()
'Draw an American flag
DIM theFlag AS FlagType
'Prepare the screen
Screen.HIDE
SCREEN 8
theFlag.Xmin = 0       'bounding box
theFlag.Xmax = 44
theFlag.Ymin = 0
theFlag.Ymax = 26
theFlag.Stripe = 2     'stripe height
theFlag.Rbox = 26      'right side of star box
ScaleIt theFlag        'scale the screen
CLS
```

```
DrawStripes theFlag    'draw the stripes
BlueRec theFlag        'draw a blue rectangle
DrawStars theFlag      'draw the stars
PlayIt
WaitForKey             'pause for a keystroke
SCREEN 0
Screen.SHOW
END SUB
```

13. Switch to the FLAG.BAS module, create the PlayIt procedure, and type

```
SUB PlayIt ()
PLAY "MB MS O4 C4 < A8 F A4 > C F2"
PLAY "A8 G8 F < A4 B > C2 C8 C8 A2 G8 F4 E2"
PLAY "D8 E8 F4 F4 C < A F"
PLAY ">A8 A8 A4 B-4 > C C2"
PLAY "< B-8 A8 G A B- B-2"
PLAY "B- A2 G8 F4 E2 D8 E8 F F C <A F"
END SUB
```

This procedure uses the PLAY statement and music macro strings to play the music. The letters A through F stand for notes. The left-angle bracket (<) moves the tune down an octave. The right-angle bracket (>) moves the tune up an octave. See Chapter 15, "Command Reference," for details.

14. Run the program and press the Draw Flag button again.

The Plot It Program

If you can tear yourself away from the circles and pies, you can put all this together and make something useful. The plot it program is a simple data plotter that demonstrates the principles of creating a grid and plotting data. The program itself consists of two forms: one for to control the program and another on which to input the data. It's not a sophisticated plotting program, but could easily be expanded or even incorporated into another program. There's also a Presentation Graphics toolbox in the Pro version of Visual Basic (See Appendix E, "Visual Basic Toolkit Libraries"), with procedures to draw many common charts on the screen.

1. Start a new project: execute the New Project command of the File menu, then execute the New Form command of the File menu and use PLOT1.FRM for the filename. Execute the Save Project command of the File menu and use PLOT.MAK as the project filename.

2. Select Form1, and set its properties to

```
Caption = Plot It
FormName = Form1
Height = 14
Width = 19
BorderStyle = 3 - Fixed Double
MaxButton = False
```

3. Draw a command button on the form, as shown in Figure 12.14, and set its properties to

```
Caption = Input Data
CtlName = InputCmd
Height = 3
Width = 13
Top = 1
Left = 2
```

4. Draw a command button on the form and set its properties to the following. Disable this button at the start, because you don't want to plot anything until some data has been inserted.

```
Caption = Plot It
CtlName = PlotItCmd
Enabled = False
Height = 3
Width = 13
Top = 4
Left = 2
```

5. Draw a command button on the form and set its properties to

```
Caption = Done
CtlName = DoneCmd
Height = 3
Width = 13
Top = 7
Left = 2
```

6. Switch to the Programming Environment, execute the New Module command of the File menu, select Include File, use PLOT.BI as the filename, and type

```
DIM xyData(500, 2) AS SINGLE
COMMON SHARED xyData() AS SINGLE        'x,y data
COMMON SHARED DataLen AS SINGLE         'length of filled array
COMMON SHARED Xmin AS SINGLE, Xmax AS SINGLE   'x axis limits
COMMON SHARED Ymin AS SINGLE, Ymax AS SINGLE   'y axis limits
CONST True = -1, False = 0
CONST asModal = 1
```

Figure 12.14. Layout of the plot it program.

The first line defines a large, two-dimensional array to hold the x,y data to be plotted. Because you cannot dimension an array in a COMMON statement, dimension it first in a DIM statement and then place it in COMMON. Next is DataLen, which contains the number of elements of xyData that have been filled with data. Xmin, Xmax, Ymin, and Ymax contain the upper and lower x,y limits for the plot. The last two lines define the constants True, False, and Modal.

7. Select Form1. Select the declarations section, and type

```
'$INCLUDE: 'PLOT.BI'
'$FORM InputDialog
DIM SHARED theheight AS SINGLE, theWidth AS SINGLE
CONST BLACK = 0
CONST BLUE = 1
CONST GREEN = 2
CONST CYAN = 3
CONST RED = 4
CONST MAGENTA = 5
CONST BROWN = 6
CONST WHITE = 7
```

```
CONST GRAY = 8
CONST BRIGHT_BLUE = 9
CONST BRIGHT_GREEN = 10
CONST BRIGHT_CYAN = 11
CONST BRIGHT_RED = 12
CONST PINK = 13
CONST YELLOW = 14
CONST BRIGHT_WHITE = 15
```

8. Create the `InputCmd_Click` procedure, and type

```
SUB InputCmd_Click ()
InputDialog.SHOW asModal
PlotItCmd.Enabled = True
END SUB
```

This procedure displays the second form as a modal form for inputting the data. When complete, this procedure enables the Plot It button.

9. Create the `PlotItCmd_Click` procedure, and type

```
SUB PlotItCmd_Click ()
'Prepare the screen
Screen.HIDE
SCREEN 8
COLOR WHITE, BLACK

'draw the plot
DrawAxes
PlotData
'pause when done
WaitForKey
SCREEN 0
Screen.SHOW
END SUB
```

This procedure prepares the screen for graphics, as in the last program. It then simply calls two other procedures to create the plot: DrawAxes to draw the axes and PlotData to plot the data.

10. Open the `DoneCmd_Click` procedure, and type

```
SUB DoneCmd_Click ()
END
END SUB
```

11. Create the DrawAxes SUB procedure, and type

```
SUB DrawAxes ()
DIM VTic AS SINGLE, HTic AS SINGLE
DIM ShapFac AS SINGLE
'The following two statements assume you are using SCREEN 8
'If you are using a different screen mode, you will have to
'change them to fit the mode's limits.
VIEW (100, 10)-(600, 180)
ShapeFac = ((600 - 100) / (180 - 10)) * (200 / 640) * (4 / 3)
VTic = .02 * (Ymax - Ymin)
HTic = .02 * (Xmax - Xmin) / ShapeFac
WINDOW (Xmin - HTic, Ymax + VTic)-(Xmax + HTic, Ymin - VTic)
LINE (Xmin - HTic, Ymin)-(Xmax + HTic, Ymin)        'line 12
LINE (Xmin, Ymin - VTic)-(Xmin, Ymax + VTic)
LINE (Xmax, Ymin - VTic)-(Xmax, Ymin + VTic)
LINE ((Xmin + Xmax) / 2, Ymin - VTic)-((Xmin + Xmax) /
      2, Ymin + VTic)
LINE (Xmin - HTic, Ymax)-(Xmin + HTic, Ymax)
LINE (Xmin - HTic, (Ymin + Ymax) / 2)-
      (Xmin + HTic, (Ymin + Ymax) / 2)
PrintLabels
END SUB
```

This procedure draws the axes on the screen. In line 7, it selects a viewport on the screen and then, in line 8, it calculates ShapeFac, a shape factor, from the width and height of the viewport and the shape of the screen. ShapeFac is used to adjust the length of horizontal lines so that they appear the same length as similar vertical lines even though the viewport, the screen, and pixels aren't square. Next, the routine defines VTic and HTic, the vertical and horizontal tick-mark lengths, as two percent of the height or width of the box, with HTic adjusted with ShapeFac.

Next the routine uses the WINDOW statement to set the scale of the viewport to that stored in Xmin, Xmax, Ymin, and Ymax. The minimum and maximum values are moved in from the edge of the viewport by the tick amount so there's room to draw the tick marks. In lines 12 through 17, the procedure uses the LINE method to draw the x,y axes, and tick marks at the ends and centers of each axis.

12. Create the PlotData SUB procedure, and type

```
SUB PlotData ()
DIM I AS INTEGER
```

```
PSET (xyData(1, 1), xyData(1, 2))
FOR I = 1 TO DataLen
  LINE -(xyData(I, 1), xyData(I, 2))
NEXT I
END SUB
```

The PlotData procedure plots the data on the existing grid. It first uses PSET to move the drawing point to the first x,y data point. The procedure then loops over all the data in the xyData array, using the LINE method with only one data point to draw lines from the current position to that given in the argument to the method.

Next, create the WaitForKey and PrintLabels procedures in a code module. The WaitForKey procedure is identical to that used in the last project.

13. Execute the New Module command of the File menu, create a code module named PLOT.BAS, and type

```
'$INCLUDE: 'PLOT.BI'
```

14. Using the New Sub command of the Edit menu, create a new SUB procedure named WaitForKey and type the following. (You could also open the FLAG.BAS module, copy it, and paste it here.)

```
SUB WaitForKey ()
WIDTH 80
LOCATE 25, 5
PRINT "Press any key to continue";
WHILE INKEY$ = "":WEND
END SUB
```

15. Using the New Sub command of the Edit menu, create a new SUB procedure named PrintLabels and type the following:

```
SUB PrintLabels ()
LOCATE 2, 8
PRINT Ymax;
LOCATE 22, 8
PRINT Ymin;
LOCATE 24, 13
PRINT Xmin;
LOCATE 24, 73
PRINT Xmax;
END SUB
```

This procedure must be in a code module to be able to print on the screen. It uses the LOCATE statement to position the print cursor on the screen, and PRINT statements to print the minimum and maximum values of the x,y axes. The semicolons at the end of each PRINT statement prevent scrolling on the screen.

This completes the plotting portion of the program. Now it's time to plot some data. In this demonstration, I create a simple dialog box for inputting the data. Depending on your application, you might have the data produced by a calculation, or read from a data file. To make the plotting portion work, you must fill the data array xyData(), put the number of data points in the DataLen variable, and set the plot limits in the Xmin, Xmax, Ymin, and Ymax variables.

16. Attach a new form to the project, store it in PLOT2.FRM, and set its properties to

```
Caption = Input Dialog
FormName = InputDialog
Height = 17
Width = 51
BorderStyle = 3 - Fixed Double
MinButton = False
MaxButton = False
```

17. Draw a text box on the form, as shown in Figure 12.15, and set its properties to

```
CtlName = DataBox
Height = 14
Width = 21
Top = 1
Left = 0
ScrollBars = 2 - Vertical
MultiLine = True
Text = ""
```

18. Draw four text boxes to hold the plot limits, and set their properties according to Table 12.1.

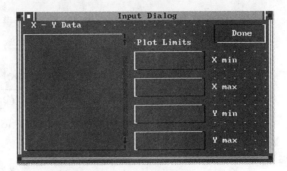

Figure 12.15. *Layout of the Input dialog box.*

Table 12.1. Properties for the four text boxes.

Control Name	Height	Width	Left	Top	Text
XminBox	3	15	22	3	" "
XmaxBox	3	15	22	6	" "
YminBox	3	15	22	9	" "
YmaxBox	3	15	22	12	" "

19. Draw a label on the form, and set its properties to

    ```
    Caption = X-Y Data
    Height = 1
    Width = 13
    Top = 8
    Left = 2
    ```

20. Draw another label on the form, and set its properties to

    ```
    Caption = Plot Limits
    Height = 1
    Width = 14
    Top = 2
    Left = 23
    ```

21. Draw four labels on the form, and set their properties according to Table 12.2.

Table 12.2. Properties for the four label boxes.

Caption	Height	Width	Left	Top
X min	1	9	38	4
X max	1	9	38	7
Y min	1	9	38	10
Y max	1	9	38	13

22. Draw a Done command button, and set its properties to

```
CtlName = DoneCmd
Caption = Done
Height = 3
Width = 11
Top = 0
Left = 38
```

23. Switch to the Programming Environment, and type the following line in the declarations section of the Input Dialog form:

```
'$INCLUDE: 'PLOT.BI'
```

The following four procedures copy the values of Xmin, Xmax, Ymin, and Ymax from the text boxes into the variables whenever the user types in one of the boxes.

24. Create the XminBox_Change procedure, and type

```
SUB XminBox_Change ()
Xmin = VAL(XminBox.Text)
END SUB
```

25. Create the XmaxBox_Change procedure, and type

```
SUB XmaxBox_Change ()
Xmax = VAL(XmaxBox.Text)
END SUB
```

26. Create the YminBox_Change procedure, and type

```
SUB YminBox_Change ()
Ymin = VAL(YminBox.Text)
END SUB
```

27. Create the YmaxBox_Change procedure, and type

```
SUB YmaxBox_Change ()
Ymax = VAL(YmaxBox.Text)
END SUB
```

28. Open the DoneCmd_Click procedure, and type

```
SUB DoneCmd_Click ()
DIM Start AS INTEGER, End1 AS INTEGER, End2 AS INTEGER
'Check limit boxes
IF (XmaxBox.Text = "" OR XminBox.Text = ""          'line 4
   OR YmaxBox.Text = "" OR YminBox.Text = "") THEN
   MSGBOX "Type plot limits first."
   EXIT SUB
END IF
'Load the data array
DataLen = 0
Start = 1
End1 = INSTR(Start, DataBox.Text, ",")
End2 = INSTR(End1 + 1, DataBox.Text, CHR$(13))
WHILE End1 <> 0 AND End2 <> 0
   DataLen = DataLen + 1
   xyData(DataLen, 1) = VAL(MID$(DataBox.Text,
   Start, End1 - Start))
   xyData(DataLen, 2) = VAL(MID$(DataBox.Text,
    End1 + 1, End2 - End1 - 1))
   Start = End2 + 1
   End1 = INSTR(Start, DataBox.Text, ",")
   End2 = INSTR(End1 + 1, DataBox.Text, CHR$(13))
WEND
InputDialog.HIDE
END SUB
```

This procedure must take the data out of the text box, convert it to numbers, and store those numbers in the data array. You must type x,y data into the text box, separating the x,y values with commas and pressing Enter after each y data value. In line 4, the procedure first checks the four plot-

limit boxes to ensure that the user has typed data in each one. If not, the procedure displays an error message and exits. If data is in all the boxes, the procedure begins looking for data in the DataBox text box.

Using the INSTR() function in line 11, this procedure locates the first comma in the Text property of DataBox and assigns the character number to End1. In line 12 it looks for the first carriage return (ASCII code 13) and assigns its location to End2. The x data should be between the beginning of the string and the comma, and the y data should be between the comma and the carriage return. In line 13, the procedure starts a WHILE/WEND loop that continues until the INSTR() functions find no more values. If a pair of values is found, the values are added to the data array.

Line 14 increments the value of DataLen. The MID$() function in line 15 extracts the substring containing the x value from the Text property of DataBox. The value lies between character positions Start and End1. The VAL() function immediately converts the extracted substring to a value, which is then stored in xyData. Line 16 does the same for the y value. In line 17, the starting position stored in Start is moved to one character beyond the carriage return. The procedure then looks for another comma and carriage return. This loop continues until it finds no more numbers. The procedure then hides itself, and returns to Form1 so you can plot the data.

29. Save the project and run it. Press the Input Data button and type some data, including the plot limits. The Input dialog box should look like Figure 12.16.

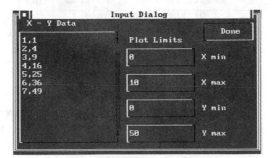

Figure 12.16. The Input dialog box for the plot it program.

30. Click Done on the Input dialog box, then press the Plot It button on Form1. The data is plotted on the screen, which now should look like Figure 12.17. Press any key to continue, then press Exit to end the program.

You can create many variations of this program, because it's still in a primitive form. It lacks labels for the axes and a title, which could be loaded in the Input dialog box. It also could calculate the plot limits automatically by examining the maximum and minimum values in the data. How you change it depends on what you want it to do.

Don't let the fact that this is a simple plot program lead you think that it has limited scope. As Figure 12.18 shows, you can use this program to create a three-dimensional wireframe plot. In fact, the plot form is identical to that developed to create Figure 12.17. You create the entire wireframe plot by manipulating the data. The data plotted is

$\text{Cos}(x\,\pi/2)\text{Cos}(y\,\pi/2)\text{Exp}(xy/10)$.

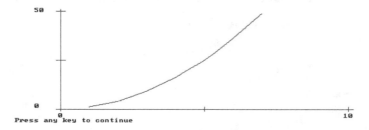

Figure 12.17. *Plotting data with the plot it program.*

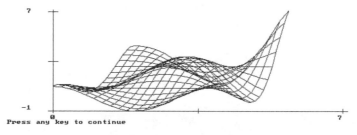

Figure 12.18. *A three-dimensional wireframe plot created with the plot it program.*

What You Have Learned

In this chapter you learned about the Visual Basic statements that draw on the screen. Unlike Visual Basic for Windows, which can only do graphics on forms or picture boxes, Visual Basic for DOS can draw only on the whole screen. You can also draw on the PRINTER object to produce printed graphics.

In detail, you have learned about

● Using the CIRCLE method to draw circles and pie sections

● Using the LINE method to draw lines and rectangles

● Using the PSET method to set the color of a point on the screen

● Using the POINT method to get the color of a point on the screen

● Playing music

13

Debugging and Error Trapping

You've just completed your latest and greatest application, which surely will bring the world rushing to your door—but when you run the application, it does something entirely unexpected. Say hello to a programming bug. There's no way to completely avoid these little monsters, so now you must learn what you can do about them. (Kicking the computer might make you feel better, but won't make the bugs go away. Actually, kicking the computer does make the bugs go away, but your program goes away too.)

In This Chapter

This chapter covers two related topics: debugging and error trapping. Although they sound similar, they are significantly different. *Debugging* is the process of eliminating known errors from a program. These errors include misspelled keywords, misplaced commas, and incorrect program logic. *Error trapping* is the process of handling unexpected events that

would normally cause a program to crash. Errors that you can trap include numeric overflow, divide-by-zero, and file-not-found errors. These types of errors are caused, for the most part, by unexpected values appearing in a formula or by the user typing an incorrect path or filename. In this chapter, you learn how to

- Debug applications
- Locate and fix syntax errors
- Locate and fix logical errors
- Use tools that find errors
- Use error trapping
- Handle trapped errors

The Art of Debugging

Debugging computer programs is more art than engineering, which often is disconcerting to new programmers who are becoming used to the rigid structure of a computer language. But there is no rigorous method for locating programming bugs. Successfully locating logical errors in complex programs demands all of a programmer's knowledge and experience. The more the programmer knows about the operation of the language, the problem being solved, and even the basic electronic operation of a computer, the more quickly he or she can locate the problem. Fixing a problem usually is trivial compared to finding it.

However, now that I've worried you somewhat, I must add that being able to locate and fix a problem in a huge mass of code is an extremely rewarding experience, with nearly immediate gratification. When a bug is fixed, the program immediately works—at least most of the time. In no other branch of engineering can you fix a problem and so quickly see the results.

Luckily, the complexity of your programs increases gradually with your experience and ability, so the increase in bugs you generate is gradual, too. Don't worry too much about the bugs in your programs; finding them is part of the fun.

The first step in debugging is having well-documented, modularized code. Keep code blocks and procedures reasonably small and as single-minded as possible. That is, make sure the function of each block or procedure is well-defined and well-known. Use remarks liberally, especially whenever you do something that isn't obvious. This adds to the work of creating code, but dramatically reduces the time needed to correct or change that code.

The second step in debugging is to realize that a computer is completely logical, and does *exactly* what you tell it to do. A program bug can make a computer seem to have a peculiar mind of its own, but realize it is actually doing what you told it to do, literally. With that in mind, read on and see how to discover bugs.

Syntax Errors

The most common bug is the syntax error. It's also the easiest to find. The Visual Basic interpreter finds most syntax errors for you. As soon as you type a line of code, the interpreter checks it for syntax errors, and finds most of the problems. Others show up as soon as you try to run your code. Thus, syntax errors come in two flavors: design-time and runtime.

Syntax errors are generated when you stray from the strict guidelines, or *grammar,* of the computer language. They involve misspelling key words, inserting the wrong number or type of arguments to a function, inserting the wrong punctuation in a programming statement, or using undeclared procedures.

Design-Time Syntax Errors

Design-time errors are revealed to you when you're typing your code. These errors involve the syntax of a single line of code, such as missed punctuation or misspelled key words. The design-time interpreter looks at each line you type as soon as you move the cursor out of that line. It then compares what you have typed with the syntax of the language. It cannot check the value or type of variables in a statement, only the number of variables and punctuation. If it can't make sense of what you've done, it tells you so.

You probably already have seen several of these errors as you typed the example programs in this book. Either that, or you are a splendid typist who never makes a mistake. I wish I had that ability, but my fingers don't always seem to do what my head is telling them to do, so I generate syntax errors frequently. Luckily, I know right away when I have made an error and can fix it.

Runtime Syntax Errors

The second type of syntax error is the runtime syntax error (although not all runtime errors are syntax errors). As soon as you run a code with the interpreter (or compile it with the compiler), the runtime syntax checker examines your program as a whole, checking the interrelationships of the different program lines. Runtime syntax errors occur when you use the wrong type of argument in a function, have incorrect block structures, or have undefined external procedures. Most Visual Basic functions and methods require specific variable types as arguments. If you give a function the wrong variable type, the runtime syntax checker stops the program, displays the offending program line, and displays a message about possible corrections to that line. This can be done only at runtime because the code that defines the variable types (in this case, the DIM and COMMON statements) is physically separated from the place the variable actually is used. For example:

```
DIM B AS INTEGER
A = VAL(B)
```

Here, the VAL() function expects B to be a STRING type variable. As the point of execution reaches the first statement, B is defined as an integer. When execution reaches the second statement, VAL() generates an error.

Another common runtime syntax error is misused block structures, such as a block IF statement missing its END IF statement or a FOR/NEXT loop missing its NEXT statement. Again, these errors cannot be determined at design time, but are revealed when you attempt to run the code and the syntax checker can check whether blocks are correctly set up. For example:

```
A = 3 * 5
Printer.PRING A
NEXT I
```

Here the NEXT I statement needs a matching FOR statement, so this code generates a runtime syntax error.

Runtime Errors

True runtime errors, as opposed to runtime syntax errors, are not caused by the syntax of a statement but by the values stored in the variables that are used in the statement. Arithmetic errors, such as overflow and divide-by-zero, are common. The hardware determines most of these errors and passes them back to Visual Basic, which stops the code and sends you a message. Arithmetic errors often result from a logical error in the program design, when the wrong values are inserted into a calculation. For example:

```
A = 3 * 0
B = 1/A
```

generates a divide-by-zero error because A is incorrectly set to zero.

Undeclared procedures cause a common error in Visual Basic. Every nonevent procedure must be defined before it is used. However, Visual Basic places all user-defined procedures at the end of the module, so it's possible for one procedure to call another before the other procedure has been defined. To take care of this problem, place DECLARE statements in the declarations section of a form or code module to declare the name of a procedure at the very beginning of a module. For the most part, Visual Basic takes care of this for you. Whenever you save a file, Visual Basic places DECLARE statements in the declarations section for all of the procedures in the file. You probably have seen these statements already.

You also must declare any external procedures that you use (for example, those in other modules). Visual Basic may or may not be able to do this for you. If a procedure name isn't defined, Visual Basic treats the procedure name as a variable name—which usually results in a syntax error. If you get a syntax error for a statement that calls another procedure, and the description of the error seems to be treating the procedure name as a variable, or the CALL statement as an assignment statement, then check whether the procedure has been declared. If the procedure being called is in another module, copy the declaration for it out of the declarations section of that other module and paste it into the declarations section of the calling module.

File-system errors occur when a requested file-related action cannot be completed; for example, when you open a file for input that does not exist, or print to a file that has not yet been opened. Again, these types of errors usually result from logical errors in a program's design. Table 13.1 contains a list of the Visual Basic runtime errors and error numbers.

13

The first two columns of Table 13.1 were generated with the following simple piece of code, which inserts the table into a text box. The ERROR$() function produces Visual Basic's error message for the given error number used as an argument. If there is no error defined for a number, it returns "Unprintable error." The IF statement skips all undefined error numbers.

```
SUB Command1_Click ()
CLS
dummy = DOEVENTS()
FOR I = 1 TO 1000
  IF ERROR$(I) <> "Unprintable error" THEN
    Text1.Text = Text1.Text + STR$(I) + "   " +
        ERROR$(I) + CHR$(13) + CHR$(10)
  END IF
NEXT I
END SUB
```

Table 13.1. Visual Basic runtime errors.

Code	Error	Description
1	NEXT without FOR	A NEXT statement was encountered without a corresponding FOR.
2	Syntax error	The current line includes a syntax error.
3	RETURN without GOSUB	A RETURN statement was encountered without a corresponding GOSUB.
4	Out of DATA	You are attempting to read beyond the end of the last DATA statement.
5	Illegal function call	This usually is caused by calling a function with invalid or out-of-range arguments (for example, SQR(-1)).

Code	Error	Description
6	Overflow	The result of a calculation is greater than the largest number that can be stored in the variable to receive that result.
7	Out of memory	Code and data storage have filled all available memory.
8	Label not defined	You are referencing a program label that does not exist in the current module.
9	Subscript out of range	The value of an array subscript is not within the range defined in the DIM statement.
10	Duplicate definition	You defined a variable with the same name as a variable that already exists.
11	Division by zero	A numeric calculation has a zero in the denominator.
12	Illegal in direct mode	You have attempted to execute a statement in the Immediate window, and the statement cannot be executed there.
13	Type mismatch	A string variable has been equated to a numeric variable, or a function argument is the wrong type.
14	Out of string space	All the strings in the modules or forms use more than 64K bytes of memory.
16	String formula too complex	A string expression is too complicated to evaluate; break it into smaller segments.

continues

Table 13.1. continued

Code	Error	Description
17	Cannot continue	A change was made in Break mode that prevents the code from being restarted.
18	Function not defined	You have referenced an undefined user function (define it with the DEF FN statement).
19	No RESUME	An ON ERROR statement is active and missing its RESUME statement.
20	RESUME without error	A RESUME statement was encountered without an active ON ERROR statement.
24	Device timeout	An accessed device has taken too long to respond.
25	Device fault	An accessed device has indicated a problem.
26	FOR without NEXT	A FOR loop is missing its NEXT statement.
27	Out of paper	The printer is out of paper.
29	WHILE without WEND	A WHILE loop is missing its WEND statement.
30	WEND without WHILE	A WEND statement has been encountered without first encountering a WHILE statement.
33	Duplicate label	There are two labels in this module with the same name.
35	Subprogram not defined	An undefined procedure was called.
37	Argument-count mismatch	The number of arguments given in a procedure call does not match the number needed by the procedure.

Code	Error	Description
38	Array not defined	You have used an array variable without first defining it.
40	Variable required	You are using a literal value where a variable is required.
50	FIELD overflow	You have declared a field larger than the file buffer.
51	Internal error	There is an internal Visual Basic error, probably a bug in Visual Basic.
52	Bad file name or number	A file number is being used for a file that hasn't been opened yet, or an invalid filename is being used.
53	File not found	You have tried to access a file that doesn't exist.
54	Bad file mode	You used GET # or PUT # with a sequential file, used INPUT # on a file opened for output only, or used PRINT # on files opened for input only.
55	File already open	You have attempted to use the OPEN statement to open a sequential file that already is open, or to use the KILL statement to delete an open file.
56	FIELD statement active	You are attempting to access a disk buffer that already is accessed with a FIELD variable.
57	Device I/O error	A device driver has issued an error.

continues

Table 13.1. continued

Code	Error	Description
58	File already exists	You used a NAME statement to change a filename to one that already exists.
59	Bad record length	A record variable is larger than the record length specified in the OPEN statement.
61	Disk full	A disk filled up while writing a file.
62	Input past end of file	An attempt has been made to read beyond the end-of-file marker on a file.
63	Bad record number	You specified a negative record number in a GET # or PUT # statement.
64	Bad file name	You specified a filename that does not follow DOS conventions.
67	Too many files	You have exceeded the number of files that can be open at any one time.
68	Device unavailable	A device, such as a printer, currently is off line.
69	Communication-buffer	The buffer on a serial port overflow has overflowed.
70	Permission denied	You tried to write to a locked or protected file.
71	Disk not ready	A floppy disk isn't inserted, or the door on a drive isn't closed.
72	Disk-media error	A disk drive reports that a requested sector is unreadable.

Code	Error	Description
73	Feature unavailable	You are attempting to access a feature, such as a Visual Basic for Windows feature, that is unavailable.
74	Rename across disks	A NAME statement attempted to move a file to a different drive.
75	Path/File access error	The attempted path/file combination does not exist; or, an attempt to write a write-protected file occurred.
76	Path not found	An attempted path does not exist.
80	Feature removed	A feature has been removed from this version.
81	Invalid name	A table or index name in an ISAM (Indexed Sequential Access Method, discussed in Chapter 14, "Advanced-Language Features") database is too long or contains invalid characters.
82	Table not found	You specified an ISAM database table name that does not exist.
83	Index not found	You specified an ISAM index that is not a part of a table.
84	Invalid column	You used an ISAM column name that does not exist.
85	No current record	You tried to access the current record in an ISAM database when none is current.

continues

13

Table 13.1. continued

Code	Error	Description
86	Duplicate value for unique index	You tried to create a unique ISAM index on a column that contains duplicate values.
87	Invalid operation on NULL index	You attempted an ISAM index operation on the null index.
88	Database needs repair	An ISAM database is inconsistent and needs to be repaired (use the ISAMREPR program).
89	Insufficient ISAM buffers	Not enough buffers are available for ISAM.
105	Unprintable error	This is an internally used temporary error number. Don't use this for a user-defined error number.
260	No Timer available	You tried to allocate more than 16 Timers.
271	Invalid screen mode	You tried to set the screen mode to a value that is not available on this system.
272	Invalid when forms are showing	A graphics or keyboard executed when forms are showing.
340	Control array element does not exist	A control-array index is out of range.
341	Invalid object array index	A control-array index is larger than 32,767 or less than 0.
342	Not enough room to allocate control array	Not enough memory exists to create a control array.

Code	Error	Description
343	Object not an array	You applied an index to an object that is not a control array.
344	Must specify index for object array	You accessed a control array without an index.
345	Reached limit: cannot create any more controls for this Form	You attempted to create more than 255 controls on a form.
360	Object already loaded	A control specified in a control array already is loaded.
361	Can't load or unload this object	You tried to load or unload a system object, such as a printer, or to unload a nonarray control.
362	Can't unload controls created at design time	You tried to unload a control at design time.
364	Object was unloaded	A form was unloaded by its own `Form_Load` procedure.
365	Unable to unload within this context	A form could not be unloaded.
380	Invalid property value	An invalid value was applied to a property.
381	Invalid property array index	An index applied to a property that accepts an index is less than 0 or greater than 32,767.
382	Property cannot be set at run time	You tried to change a property that only can be changed at design time.
383	Property is read-only	You tried to change a read-only property.

continues

13

349

Table 13.1. continued

Code	Error	Description
384	Property can't be modified when form is minimized or maximized	You tried to change Top, Left, Height, or Width with the form maximized or minimized.
385	Must specify index when using property array	You tried to access the Fonts or List property without using an array index.
386	Property not available at runtime	You tried to access CtlName or FormName at runtime.
387	Property can't be set on this control	You tried to check a top-level menu or make all submenus invisible.
400	Form already displayed; can't show modally	You tried to make a form modal that already was visible.
401	Can't show nonmodal form when modal form is displayed	You tried to show a nonmodal form while a modal form is visible.
402	Must close or hide topmost modal form first	You tried to hide or unload a modal form that has other modal forms above it. Modal forms must be unloaded from the top down.
410	Property can't be modified on MDI form	You tried to change a restricted property on a Multiple Document Interface form (see Chapter 14, "Advanced-Language Features").
420	Invalid object reference	You referenced an object on an unloaded form.

Code	Error	Description
421	Method not applicable for this object	You applied an inappropriate method to an object.
422	Property not found	You referenced a property that does not apply to the object in the reference.
423	Property or control not found	You referenced a property or control that is not part of the referenced form.
424	Object required	You used a property in a reference where an object should be.
425	Invalid object use	You tried to assign a value to a control or form rather than to a property.
430	No currently active control	You used `ActiveControl` when no control had the focus.
431	No currently active form	You used `ActiveForm` when no form was active.
480	Can't create `AutoRedraw` image	There's not enough memory to create the persistent bitmap.

Logical Errors

Logical errors occur when the computer is doing what you told it to do, but not what you wanted it to do. When you're lucky, the cause is obvious and you fix it. More often, these errors are hard to find because the cause

of the error can be far from the statement that produced the outward appearance of the error. For example, if you get a divide-by-zero error, the statement that made the divisor zero can be far from the statement in which the division operation occurred; or a logical error might not even generate an error message, but result in an incorrect value calculated and printed by a program. Here's where your experience and intuition come into play.

The Timer Program

This simple little program demonstrates a logical bug—see whether you can find it. The program uses the last control on the Toolbox window, the timer. The timer basically is an alarm clock that runs in the background and generates a `Timer` event whenever its time runs out. The timer's `Interval` property stores the amount of time, in milliseconds, to wait before generating a `Timer` event. Using the timer to generate one-second events, this program counts those events and displays the value of the counter in a label.

1. Start a new project: execute the New Project command of the File menu, then execute the New Form command of the File menu and use TIMER.FRM for the filename. Execute the Save Project command of the File menu and use TIMER.MAK as the project filename.

2. Select `Form1`, and set its properties to

   ```
   Caption = The Timer
   Height = 5
   Width = 51
   BorderStyle = 3 - fixed double
   ControlBox = False
   MaxButton = False
   MinButton = False
   ```

3. Draw a label on the form, as shown in Figure 13.1, with these properties:

   ```
   Height = 1
   Width = 25
   Top = 1
   Left = 10
   Caption = ""
   ```

Figure 13.1. Layout for the Timer program.

4. Draw a command button on the form, with these properties:

```
CtlName = OnCmd
Height = 3
Width = 10
Top = 8
Left = 37
Caption = On/Off
```

5. Draw a timer to the left of the label. The location isn't important because the timer is invisible in the running application. Set its properties to

```
Interval = 1000
Enabled = False
```

6. Switch to the Programming Environment, create the Timer1_Timer procedure, and type

```
SUB Timer1_Timer ()
DIM I AS INTEGER
I = I + 1
Label1.Caption = STR$(I)
END SUB
```

This procedure is executed whenever the Timer event occurs, which is once per second. When executed, it increments the value of I by 1 and inserts that number in the Caption property of the label; thus, the label counts seconds whenever the timer is running.

7. Create the OnCmd_Click procedure and type

```
SUB OnCmd_Click ()
Timer1.Enabled = NOT Timer1.Enabled
END SUB
```

This procedure turns the timer on and off by applying the NOT logical operator on the timer's Enabled property. The NOT operator changes True to False or False to True.

13

353

8. Save the project, run it, and click the On/Off button.

What happens? The timer doesn't count, but displays a 1 all the time. This isn't what you told the computer to do—or is it? In the next few sections, you learn how to track down the problem.

To locate a logical error, gather all the information you have about it: where it occurred, what the program was doing, what was the error, whatever information you have. Use this information to estimate the most probable cause of the error and then check that piece of code. If that doesn't work, try using some of the debugging tools (discussed in the next section) to get more information about the bug and what it's doing. Keep gathering information and looking at the code until you find out what's happening.

Debugging Tools

Not all of debugging is done through intuition and magic. There are some excellent tools built into Visual Basic that greatly reduce the amount of work involved in locating and fixing programming bugs. In fact, it's much easier to debug Visual Basic programs than programs in most other high-level languages, primarily because Visual Basic is an *interpreted language*. This means you can make changes and adjustments in the code and immediately run it to see the results. In fact, you can make adjustments while the code is running by pressing Ctrl-Break, making the change, then issuing the **C**ontinue command of the **R**un menu.

> The difference between a compiler and an interpreter is in the way they convert and execute code. An interpreter directly executes the text file containing the code you have written, and a compiler converts it into a file of machine-language codes first, then executes those machine-language codes. Machine-language codes are the numeric codes that the microprocessor in your computer executes. Interpreters still must convert the text version of a code into machine language, but they do it one line at a time. An interpreter reads a single line of code, converts it to machine language, executes it, then continues with the next line of code. A compiler converts the whole code into machine language first, then it executes the machine language.

The Visual Basic interpreter is actually intermediate between a true interpreter and a compiler. The Visual Basic interpreter converts a program into p-code, which is not machine language, but which is faster to interpret than the text representation of a code.

Breaking a Running Code

If a code is running, and you want to pause it for awhile so you can examine the values of the variables, you must break the code. I don't mean to smash it with a hammer—though I have been tempted a few times—but to make it stop executing; that is, to *break* its execution. There are three ways to break a running code:

- Pressing Ctrl-Break
- Encountering a STOP statement in a program
- Encountering a breakpoint inserted with the Toggle **B**reakpoint command (F9) of the **D**ebug menu

A fourth way is encountering a runtime error, which automatically breaks the code at the line where the error occurs.

When a program is in break mode, you can examine code in the code windows, display values in the Debug window, change the values of variables in the Immediate window, and even change code. When you're done, issue the **C**ontinue command of the **R**un menu. Your code starts up where it left off.

To break a code using Ctrl-Break, the code must first be running. This command is somewhat imprecise about its stopping point in the code because many statements can be executed between the time you decide to press Ctrl-Break and the time your finger actually presses the button. As soon as you press Ctrl-Break, the code immediately stops execution, opens a code window, and highlights the next line of code—the one it's about to execute. You see something similar when a code encounters a runtime error, but then you know the highlighted statement is the one causing the error.

13

The STOP statement and Toggle **B**reakpoint command cause a code to stop in a specific place. Use these when you think you know where a problem is and want to stop the execution at that spot. The STOP statement is like any other Visual Basic statement. You type it into your code and, when it is executed, the code stops. STOP differs from the END statement for interpreted code. When an END statement is encountered, the code is stopped and unloaded and all the variables are erased. You must restart the code from scratch if you use END. STOP, however, simply halts the code. Everything still is in memory and can be restarted from the stopping point. If you compile the code, though, the STOP statement behaves exactly the same way as an END statement.

To use the Toggle **B**reakpoint command, select the statement at which you want the code to stop and click the Toggle **B**reakpoint command. Your code behaves exactly as if you had inserted a STOP statement there. To remove a breakpoint, select the statement and press Toggle **B**reakpoint again, or click the Clear **A**ll Breakpoints command to remove all breakpoints. The biggest difference between STOP and a breakpoint is that STOP stays in a code like any other statement while a breakpoint disappears as soon as you end Visual Basic or load another program.

Examining and Changing Things

With your program in break mode, you can examine code and variables, and even change things. To change code while in Break mode, simply type the changes in the appropriate code window. You can change most statements without affecting the running code. A few things that you can't change are

- Variable definitions, such as those in DIM and COMMON statements

- Loop control statements, such as FOR/NEXT

- SUB and FUNCTION procedure calls

If you change these things, your code becomes inconsistent and must be restarted rather than continued. Visual Basic warns you when a change will force a restart.

To examine the values of variables, open the Debug window, select the variable in the Code window, and execute the Instant Watch command of the **D**ebug menu. A window such as the one shown in Figure 13.2

appears, showing the variable and its current value. If you click the Add Watch button, that variable is added to the Debug window. The Debug window continuously displays the variable's current value, as shown in Figure 13.3.

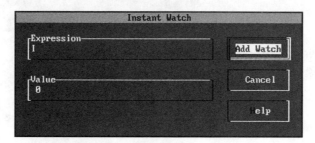

Figure 13.2. *The Instant Watch dialog box.*

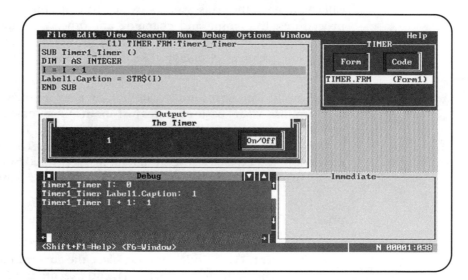

Figure 13.3. *The variable* I, *the contents of* Label1.Caption, *and the value of the expression* I + 1 *are watch variables in the Debug window.*

You also can use the Add Watch command to add watch variables or short expressions to the Debug window. When you execute the Add Watch command, the dialog box shown in Figure 13.4 appears. In this dialog box, type the variable or expression you want displayed. Be sure the code window is open for the procedure that contains the variable you want watched.

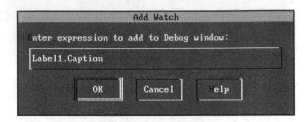

Figure 13.4. The Add Watch dialog box.

To change the value of a variable, type in the Immediate window an assignment statement equating the variable to its new value. For example, to reset the value of count, you could type **count=0** in the Immediate window. You can examine or change only those variables in the active call chain. The active call chain includes the procedure currently being executed and those procedures that called that procedure. To see the active call chain, open the Calls window, which contains the names of all active procedures. Examining and changing any other procedures makes no sense anyway: why, for example, would you want to examine a variable that hasn't even been defined yet? Its value has no meaning until it's in the active call chain.

You also can use the Immediate window to experiment with functions and formulas. Visual Basic executes just about any statement you type, and you can print the results by using the PRINT statement. The only restriction is that it can execute only a single line at a time. To get around this restriction, you can stack several statements, separated by colons, on one line to execute a short piece of code in the Immediate window.

Now let's use these tools to figure out what's wrong with the Timer program. (Bear with me if you've already figured it out.)

1. The problem probably is in the Timer1_Timer procedure, so open the Timer1_Timer Code window, place the cursor in the first executable statement (I = I + 1), and execute the Toggle **Breakpoint** command. The statement is highlighted, as shown in Figure 13.5, to indicate that it has a breakpoint set. I also have opened the Debug window, the Output window, and the Immediate window.

2. Run the program and click the On/Off button. The program stops at the breakpoint and displays the Code window—see Figure 13.6.

3. Select the I in the statement I = I + 1 and execute the Instant Watch command. The dialog box appears to show you the value of I. As you might expect, the value 0 is displayed the first time the Timer1_Timer procedure is executed.

Highlight indicating that a breakpoint is set

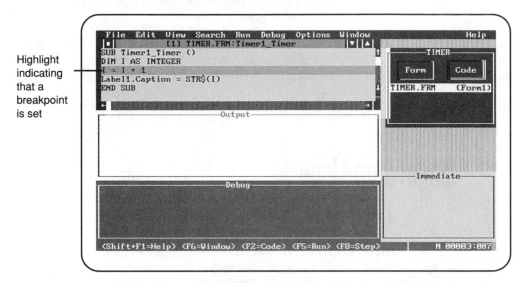

Figure 13.5. Setting a breakpoint.

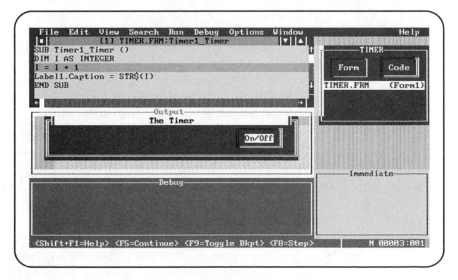

Figure 13.6. Stopping at a breakpoint.

4. Click the **A**dd Watch button to add I to the Debug window. Execute the **A**dd Watch command and add Text1.Text and I + 1 to the Debug window. The screen should look like Figure 13.3. I also have opened the Output window so I can see what's on the form as well. Another way to see the Output window when you're in break mode is to press F4.

5. Select the **C**ontinue command (F5) of the **R**un menu. The code runs for a moment and then hits the breakpoint again. Check the Debug window: I is still 0. Do this step several times; the value of I is zero every time.

Single Step Mode

Rather than pressing **C**ontinue to continue running a program after it has been in break mode, you can press Single step (F8) to execute one statement of the program and return to break mode. Use this command to step through a program, one step at a time, so you can watch the execution and examine the value of the variables at each step.

The Procedure step command (F10) works the same way as Single step, except when it reaches a call to another procedure. The Single step command moves to the called procedure and begins executing code there, one step at a time. The Procedure step command runs all the code in the called procedure and returns to break mode only when the called procedure returns to the procedure that called it. The Single step command thus moves you throughout your program, but the Procedure step command takes you step-by-step through a single procedure.

The History trace command (Shift-F8) works like the Single step command, except that it steps a program backward one statement. To use the History trace command, you must have enabled program history storage by executing the **H**istory On command of the **D**ebug menu before running the program. You can trace backward a maximum of 20 statements.

Also useful here are the Execute to cursor (F7) command and the Set Next Statement command of the **D**ebug menu. The Execute to cursor command causes execution to continue, and then to break again when it reaches the statement containing the cursor. The Set **N**ext Statement command changes the next statement to be executed. Use the command to reexecute a statement or block of statements after making a change, and to see the effect of that change.

6. Still in the `Timer1_Timer` Code window, press F8 (Single Step) and watch the execution point move to the next statement, as shown in Figure 13.7. The value of I is 1, as you would expect.

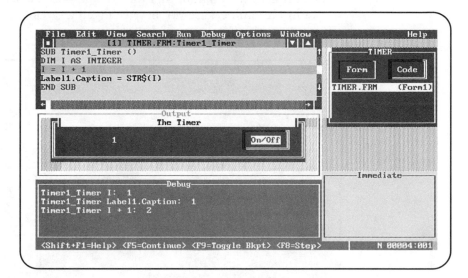

Figure 13.7. *Single stepping to the next statement and checking* I *again.*

7. Press F8 again, and the execution point moves to the END SUB statement. Press F8 a third time and the execution point exits the procedure to the system. None of the Step keys follow the execution into the system procedures, only those procedures you write yourself. In the system, the execution waits in the idle loop for an event to occur. In this case it waits for the next Timer event, reenters the Timer1_Timer procedure, and stops at the first executable statement (the I = I + 1 statement). Check the value of I, and it's 0 again. I is being incremented as it is supposed to, but it is reset to 0 each time the procedure is called.

The problem should be obvious by now: each time a procedure ends, all its local variables are lost and reset to 0 when the procedure is called again. The variable I is local to this procedure because it was defined in the DIM statement at the beginning of the procedure. To make this program work, you must make the value of I persist from one call of the procedure

to the next. One way to do that is to move the definition of I to the declarations area of the form. A simpler method that keeps I local is to change the DIM statement to a STATIC statement.

8. Select the Timer1_Timer procedure, select the DIM statement, and change the word DIM to STATIC. Click elsewhere in the procedure and Visual Basic displays a message advising you that you will have to restart the program after this change—see Figure 13.8. You must restart because you have changed a variable definition, making the running application inconsistent.

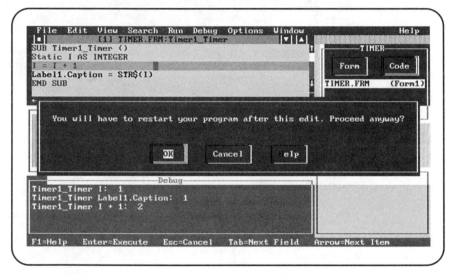

Figure 13.8. *Changing a* DIM *statement in break mode causes you to have to restart a program.*

9. Click OK, select the I = I + 1 statement, execute the Toggle Breakpoint command to turn off the breakpoint, run the program again, and click the On/Off button. It works! See Figure 13.9. Press Ctrl-Break to quit the program.

10. Execute the **M**ake Exe File command of the **F**ile menu to compile the program as TIMER.EXE.

11. Run the Timer program and click the On/Off button. You have a working Timer.

12. End the Timer program and continue. Oh, oh! Another logical error. There's no way to turn it off.

Figure 13.9. *The Timer program, working at last.*

The code does not include a **Quit** or **Exit** command, and you disabled the form's Control box in Step 2. If you're running under a shell program such as Dosshell, Windows, or DESQview, you can press the hot key to return to the shell and kill the program from there. Otherwise, the only way to end this program is to warmboot your computer (Ctrl-Alt-Del). To fix the Timer program, turn the Control box back on for the form.

One other type of watch that I have not mentioned yet is the *watchpoint.* A watchpoint is similar to a watch variable, except that it executes a break when a logical expression becomes True. You insert watchpoints the same way you insert a watch variable, but you type a ogical expression rather than the variable name. When the expression is True, your program stops.

Sounds

Often, when debugging a program, you don't want many details about a program's execution but want to know when it reaches a particular location in the code. In this situation, the BEEP statement is useful. Simply insert it at the point of interest, and your code beeps at you whenever it reaches that point. You can get more elaborate by inserting different beep codes at different points in your program to signal where you are.

Unfortunately, you can't string several beeps in a row. The sounds all run together and you get a buzz rather than a beep, so you can't tell how many beeps you have. To create multiple beeps in a code, you can insert a call to a simple Beeper procedure like this one:

```
SUB Beeper (NumBeeps AS INTEGER)
DIM I AS INTEGER, J AS INTEGER
FOR I = 1 TO NumBeeps
  BEEP
  FOR J = 1 TO 10000
  NEXT J
NEXT I
END SUB
```

Call this procedure from every location where you want to hear a marker. Follow the procedure name by the number of beeps you want to hear. That number is passed to the variable NumBeeps, which is used as the upper limit on a FOR/NEXT loop. The procedure executes a BEEP, then executes a second FOR/NEXT loop. Note that the NEXT statement in the second loop immediately follows the FOR statement, so this loop does nothing but waste some time to create a pause between beeps. You might have to adjust the upper limit of the second loop so you can discern the number of beeps. The value 10,000 seems to work well for my machine, but the number you use depends on your machine. Pick a number just large enough so you can hear the number of beeps.

An alternative for the second loop is a WHILE/WEND loop, like the following, which watches the value of the TIMER() function. The TIMER() function returns the number of seconds since midnight, so if you wait until its integer value changes, you get a one-second pause. I find this too long, though.

```
SUB Beeper (NumBeeps AS INTEGER)
DIM I AS INTEGER, J AS INTEGER
FOR I = 1 TO NumBeeps
BEEP
J = TIMER
WHILE J = INT(TIMER)
WEND
NEXT I
END SUB
```

For example, in the nonworking version of the Timer program, you could insert the first Beeper procedure with I as the argument. Then the program would beep the value of I to you each time it executes. Try it and see.

Debugging Code

A final method of tracing bugs is to insert debugging code. Debugging code usually consists of PRINT or assignment statements strategically placed in a code to print their location and the values of important variables.

If you have more than one debugging statement, be sure to include a short piece of text to identify the location of the statement doing the printing. In a large code, with many debugging statements, put a global

Debug flag in the declarations section and use it in an IF statement to control the execution of the debugging statements. For example:

```
IF DebugFlag THEN DebugFrm.PRINT "I am here",J
```

or

```
IF DebugFlag THEN DebugFrm.Text1.Text = DebugFrm.Text1.Text
   + "I am here " + STR$(J) + eol$
```

Here, the statements do nothing if the value of DebugFlag is False. If it's True, the first statement prints I am here, then the value of the variable J on the form named DebugFrm. The second statement adds the same message to the Text1 text box on the same form. This way you can leave the debugging statements in your code and they won't do much but slow it down a little. When you want to print the debugging values, either insert a statement at the beginning of your code that sets DebugFlag to True, or break the code, and type **DebugFlag = .1** in the Immediate window. When you click Continue, the debugging statements are activated.

The Role of Error Trapping

Debugging involves searching for the causes of an error. When you figure out the cause, you fix your code and—you hope—never have that error again. Some errors you can't control; for example, trying to open a file for input that doesn't exist. If the user of your code does this, an error message appears and the code stops in break mode. If you're running a compiled version of your code, it quits and is removed from memory. Generally, you would prefer that did not happen—just as you would be thoroughly upset if, right after you had typed your magnum opus, your word processor quit without letting you save anything just because you mistyped a filename. To handle problems like this, use error trapping.

Error trapping allows your program to take control when an error occurs. All the runtime errors listed in Table 13.1 are "trappable" by your program (meaning that they can be captured by your code and handled internally). When an error occurs, your error-trap code takes control, checks to see what the error is, fixes it if possible, and then returns you to the place at which the problem occurred. Each procedure can have its own specific error-handling procedure, or there can be a module-level error

13

handler. The error handler is enabled with the ON ERROR statement. If a runtime error occurs when the error handler is enabled, the block of code pointed to by the ON ERROR statement is executed.

How Visual Basic Traps Errors

When Visual Basic encounters a runtime error, it puts the error number from Table 13.1 in the function ERR and checks whether any error handler is available. If so, it executes the handler and lets it take care of the error. If the handler also generates an error, Visual Basic checks whether the procedure that called the procedure with the error has an error handler. If no error handler is available, or if none can handle the error, the code quits and displays an error message concerning the original error.

If you're running the program in interpreted mode, it displays the error message, then displays the offending statement. If you are running a compiled version of the code, it quits after displaying one of the error messages in Table 13.1.

Setting a Trap for Errors

To set up an error trap, insert an ON ERROR GOTO statement near the beginning of a procedure with the errors you want to trap. This statement must be placed before any statement that might cause a trappable error. The syntax of the statement is

```
ON [LOCAL] ERROR {GOTO label ¦ RESUME NEXT ¦ GOTO 0}
```

The LOCAL keyword indicates that the error handler is in the current procedure; if you omit that keyword, the error handler must be in the module-level code. Because only code modules can have executable code at the module level, you can have global-error handlers only in code modules, not in form modules. If you use the GOTO *label* clause (where *label* is a valid label within the same procedure), the block of code following that label is set as the current error-handling procedure. Control isn't passed to the error handler with the ON ERROR statement; the

ON ERROR statement marks only the first statement of the error handler. Control is passed to the error handler only when an error occurs. Although an error handler must be in the same procedure as the ON ERROR statement, it might immediately call some other procedure to handle the error. This way you can combine all similar error handling in a SUB or FUNCTION procedure, then pass control to that procedure from the different error handlers in a program.

If you use the RESUME NEXT clause, your code skips the statement that caused the error and continues running with the next one. This statement does not define an error handler. Be careful of this because skipping statements can make your code inconsistent. The main use for the RESUME NEXT clause is to save an error to handle later. If you're doing something that should not be stopped to handle an error, such as receiving data in a telecommunications program, use the RESUME NEXT statement. Only the last error encountered is returned by the ERR function, so if you encounter a second error before handling the first, the error number of the first error is lost.

The last clause, GOTO 0, disables error trapping in this routine. Use this clause to turn off error checking after the vulnerable statements have been executed.

To test an error trap, use the ERROR statement. The ERROR statement takes a single number as its argument, and that number is the code for the error you want to simulate. Whenever Visual Basic executes an ERROR statement, it simulates getting the error specified by that argument and either displays an error dialog box or executes your error-trapping code. The ERROR statement also is used to create your own errors. For example, in a File Open dialog box, if you already have an error handler for file-not-found errors, and that error handler warns the user and requests a new filename, you can use the existing mechanism to handle files with an incorrect file type by creating a user-defined error. Otherwise, you must write practically the same block of code to handle the file type errors as you do for file-not-found errors.

You can use any of the missing numbers from Table 13.1 as user-defined errors, but make sure that if you have a user-defined error, you also have an error trap enabled to handle it. Also, note that future versions of Visual Basic might use some of these unused error numbers.

Getting Information About an Error

After you have trapped an error, you must get information about it, such as what error occurred and where it occurred. When error checking is not enabled, Visual Basic displays a dialog box that informs you what error occurred and, if you are running in interpreted mode, then displays the error message.

After an error has occurred, the ERR function returns the error number (see Table 13.1). To get the text of an error message, call the ERROR$() function with the error number as its argument. The function returns the text description of the error. This is the same description you get when Visual Basic displays an error message.

Getting the location of the error is more difficult. In older versions of BASIC, each line in a program was consecutively numbered. If you number your lines, the number of the line closest to the line containing the error is returned by the ERL function. Because Visual Basic programs rarely use line numbers, this might not be very useful unless you specifically number the statements with which you expect to have problems.

The ERR and ERL functions are valid only in the procedure where the error occurs, and are reset to 0 whenever you execute a RESUME or ON ERROR statement. They also might be reset if you call some other procedure, so save the values they return at the beginning of your error handler if you plan to use them.

Creating an Error Handler

As mentioned previously, an error handler may reside in the same procedure as the ON ERROR statement that activated it, or at the module level. When you use a local error handler, you usually don't want it in a position where it can be executed during the normal operation of your procedure. A good place to put it is at the end of your procedure, separated from the rest of the procedure with an EXIT SUB or EXIT FUNCTION statement.

An error handler can contain whatever you choose; the only requirement is that it end with a RESUME statement. Commonly, error handlers first use the ERR function to see what the error is, and then use a block IF statement to decide what to do in each case. Rarely would you code an error handler for all of the possible errors listed in Table 13.1. Usually, you write code for the errors you expect and then, for the rest, write an ELSE clause that prints an error message and ends the program, or at least exits that procedure.

Every error handler must end with a RESUME, RESUME NEXT, or RESUME *label* statement. The RESUME statement returns the execution point to the statement that caused the problem, and tries to execute it again. This is the most common case: the handler corrects the problem and lets the program try again. The RESUME NEXT statement returns execution to the next statement after the one that caused the problem. In this case, the error handler must handle the work of the statement that caused the problem, then skip it. The RESUME *label* statement resumes execution at the statement following the label.

For example, a formula that contains a division operation runs the risk of having zero as the divisor. An important case is the integrand of the sine integral Si(x) shown in the following procedure fragment. The integrand is equal to the sine of x divided by x. At x equals zero, the integrand is zero divided by zero, which is one; however, Visual Basic gives a divide-by-zero error. To make this work correctly, trap the divide-by-zero error and replace the result with 1.

```
FUNCTION Si(x AS SINGLE) AS SINGLE
'function to calculate the sine integral
'statements to integrate sin(x)/x from x to infinity
.
.
.

Integrand = SIN(xint)/xint
.
.
.

END FUNCTION
```

Because the integral can pass through 0, xint can equal 0 and the routine crashes, even though Sin(0)/0 is equal to 1. To fix this, add an error handler to the procedure in this way:

```
FUNCTION Si(x AS SINGLE) AS SINGLE
'function to calculate the sine integral
'statements to integrate sin(x)/x from x to infinity
```

```
ON Local ERROR GOTO FixSin      'turn the error handler on
.
.
.
Integrand = SIN(xint)/xint
.
.
.
EXIT FUNCTION
FixSin:
IF ERR = 11 THEN
  INTEGRAND = 1
ELSE
  MSGBOX ERROR$(ERR)
  STOP
END IF
RESUME NEXT
END FUNCTION
```

Line 4 enables the error handler. If line 8 is executed and no error is encountered, the procedure continues normally. If an error is encountered, control passes to the block of code following the FixSin: label. The error handler first checks whether the error is the expected divide-by-zero (error number 11). If it is a divide-by-zero error, the procedure sets the value of Integrand to 1 and resumes with the statement after the one with the divide by 0 error. If it isn't a divide-by-zero error, this procedure sends the error message to the user and ends. You might want to move the ON ERROR statement down to a position just before the INTEGRAND statement and put an ON ERROR GOTO 0 statement after it. This assures that the INTEGRAND statement is the one with the problem, and not some other statement with a division error.

What You Have Learned

This chapter discussed debugging programs and trapping errors. Debugging is finding and removing errors from a program, and error trapping is writing code to correct situations when the error can't be avoided.

The types of errors involved in debugging are syntax errors and logical errors. Syntax errors occur because you have incorrectly applied the grammar of the Visual Basic language. Logical errors occur when your code does what you told it to do, but not what you wanted it to do.

Error trapping can trap only runtime errors, and is used to capture errors that normally would crash an application. After an error is captured, an error-handling routine determines what is to be done to correct the error.

This chapter specifically discussed the following topics:

- Syntax errors
- Runtime errors
- Logical errors
- Programs in break mode
- Sounds that mark sections of code
- Debugging code and the Immediate window
- Error trapping with the ON ERROR statement
- The ERR and ERL functions, which obtain information about an error
- The RESUME statement, which enables you to exit an error handler

14

Advanced-Language Features

The advanced features of Visual Basic are somewhat beyond the scope of an introductory book. However, they represent important capabilities that you eventually will want to include in your programs. These features include controlling the DOS file system, creating and using libraries, dragging and dropping controls, and creating database programs. As your understanding of Visual Basic programming increases, you eventually will want to use these capabilities, so I discuss them briefly here. You can discover the details, as you need them, in the Visual Basic reference manuals and in higher-level books on this subject. Note that some of these feature are available only in the Pro version of Visual Basic for MS-DOS.

In This Chapter

Visual Basic has several advanced features, including libraries, binary file access, and database management capabilities. This chapter discusses

- Creating libraries
- Accessing files in binary mode
- Dragging and dropping controls
- Managing the file system
- Making help files
- Accessing an ISAM database
- Creating a Multiple-Document Interface program
- Using special libraries
- Designing custom controls
- Using program overlays
- Programming with mixed languages

Creating and Using Libraries

Libraries provide a convenient way to group together routines that are common to several projects. They also are useful in that they provide compiled modules that you can use with interpreted programs in the Visual Basic programming environment. Two different types of libraries are used in the Visual Basic environment: Quick libraries and LIB libraries. There also are two different types of LIB libraries: runtime LIB libraries and stand-alone LIB libraries.

Quick libraries (.QLB) are a special form of library that can be used only with the programming environment. To use them, use the /L *libname* option when invoking Visual Basic. A special library is included with Visual Basic: VBDOS.QLB. VBDOS.QLB contains the routines for issuing system calls to the DOS system. You must load this library before you can use the functions contained within it. There are other libraries available for linking with a program that does not use forms, or does not use graphics or floating point calculations, or does not need fancy editing capabilities. By using these library files instead of the default libraries when creating an executable file, you will significantly reduce the size of that file.

To see what libraries are contained in a .QLB library, open the QLIBVIEW program in the Programming Environment. The program is a library browser for .QLB libraries, and is included with Visual Basic.

You can create your own libraries of procedures using the Programming Environment. You can also create them by running the compiler, linker, and library manager individually, but using the Programming Environment is much simpler. Something to remember when creating Quick libraries: a Quick library must be self-contained. That is, procedures in a Quick library can only call other procedures in the same Quick library—so be sure to include all needed procedures in the library.

To create a Quick library, start the Programming Environment, using the /L *libname* switch to include any existing Quick libraries in the new library you are creating. Use the Add File and Add Module commands to open all the procedures you want to include in your library. When you create your library, all procedures currently in the Programming Environment are included, including old libraries loaded with /L and all forms and modules shown in the Project window. Execute the Make Library command of the Run menu; you will see the dialog box shown in Figure 14.1. Insert the name for the library and any options you want, then click the Make Library button, or the Make Library and Exit button. Sit back and Visual Basic will automatically create your library.

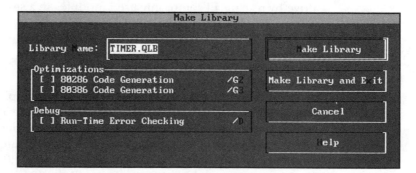

Figure 14.1. The Make Library dialog box.

As you create a Quick library file, you should also create an include file (.BI). The include file should contain DECLARE statements for all the procedures in the Quick library that you want to be callable by another program, while that program is being edited and run in the Programming Environment. The DECLARE statement has the following syntax:

```
DECLARE {FUNCTION|SUB} name [([arguments])]
```

Here, FUNCTION or SUB indicate whether this procedure returns a value; *name* is the literal name of the procedure, and *arguments* are the needed arguments and types for the procedure. All argument types must be declared in the statement so that, at runtime, Visual Basic can check the arguments being passed to the procedure. (See the complete description of DECLARE in Chapter 15, "Command Reference.") As you create procedures in the Programming Environment, Visual Basic automatically inserts correctly written DECLARE statements in the module-level section, so it's simplest to just copy them from there when you create your include file.

The LIB libraries are more general-purpose libraries of object modules that the LINK linker can use. Because the linker cannot use Quick libraries, you usually create libraries in pairs: a Quick library for programs being run in the Programming Environment, and a LIB library to use when compiling your programs into executable applications. When you create a Quick library using the Make Library command of the Programming Environment's **R**un menu, both types of libraries automatically are created.

The LIB libraries come in runtime versions as well as stand-alone versions. Runtime libraries do not have to be linked with a program that needs them at compile time, but are dynamically linked at runtime. The advantage of a runtime-linked library is the space you save on your disk drive by placing all commonly used modules in a single library instead of giving every program its own copy. The disadvantage is that if the library is not available with the program, the program cannot run. If a program is fully linked with a stand-alone library, everything it needs is self-contained, so no other files need be available.

You also can create libraries with other compilers, such as a C or FORTRAN compiler, and still be able to link them with the Programming Environment. You need to take some special considerations into account when linking such foreign libraries: the DECLARE statement must include some codes that indicate the library type because different programming languages pass variables differently, and Visual Basic must know how to pass those variables properly.

Binary Files

Binary data files actually are any data file type opened with the BINARY file type in the OPEN statement. When a file is opened AS BINARY, every byte of the file is accessible and changeable, as if it were a random-access file with one-byte-long records. Use this file type when you have to look at the raw bytes of a file. A virus checker would be one such program because it needs to search the contents of an executable file for a particular sequence of bytes. You can open any file AS BINARY, including executable (.EXE and .COM) files.

Use the GET and INPUT$ statements to read data from the binary file, and the PUT statement to store data. When using GET and PUT, the number of bytes read or written is equal to the number of bytes in the variables used as arguments to the statements.

Dragging and Dropping

If you want movable controls on a form rather than fixed ones, you have two options:

- Change the DragMode property of the control to

  1 - Automatic

- Use the DRAG method in the controls MouseDown event procedure

Whichever of these methods you use, when you place the mouse pointer on the control and press the mouse button, you can drag an outline of the control around the form. However, dragging a control does not actually move the control, only its outline. To move the control, use the MOVE method in the form's DragDrop event procedure. For example, to drag a picture box around on a form, follow these steps:

1. Draw a small picture box on a form. Set its DragMode property to

   1 - Automatic

2. Run the program, place the mouse pointer on the picture box, press the left mouse button, and drag an outline of the picture box around the screen.

377

When you release the mouse button to drop the picture box, the picture box jumps back to its original location, because you didn't move the picture box; you only dragged its outline around. To move the picture box itself, add a MOVE method to the form's DragDrop procedure.

3. End the program. Create the Form_DragDrop procedure and type the following:

```
SUB Form_DragDrop (Source AS CONTROL, X AS SINGLE,
   Y AS SINGLE)
Source.MOVE X, Y
END SUB
```

The DragDrop event occurs whenever a control is dragged over a form (or other control) and dropped. The Source argument contains the name of the control (the picture box) that was dragged over and dropped on the form. The X and Y arguments contain the location of the mouse pointer when the control was dropped.

The MOVE method is used here to move the control to the new coordinates. A difficulty here is that the upper-left corner of the control is moved to the x,y location supplied by the DragDrop procedure. The x,y location is not the upper-left corner of the outline being dragged around the form, but the location of the mouse pointer on that outline. (When you run this program, you'll see what I mean.)

4. Run the program, and then drag and drop the picture box around on the form. Note where the outline is, and where the picture box moves when you release the mouse button. End the program when you're done.

If you want the dragged control to align with the outline when it is moved, you must capture the x,y coordinates of the MouseDown event on the control and subtract that location from the x,y coordinates in the DragDrop procedure. The following steps do this:

5. Open the form's declarations section and type definitions for the variables to contain the x and y offsets as follows. Also, define two constants to be used later.

```
DIM Shared XOffset AS SINGLE
DIM Shared YOffset AS SINGLE
CONST StartDrag = 1
CONST Drop = 2
```

6. Create the `Picture1_MouseDown` procedure and type the following:

```
SUB Picture1_MouseDown (Button AS INTEGER,
  Shift AS INTEGER, X AS SINGLE, Y AS SINGLE)
XOffset = X
YOffset = Y
Picture1.DRAG StartDrag
END SUB
```

This procedure stores the location of the `MouseDown` event on `Picture1`, and manually initiates dragging with the `DRAG` method.

7. Select the `Form_DragDrop` procedure and change it to the following:

```
SUB Form_DragDrop (Source AS CONTROL, X AS SINGLE,
  Y AS SINGLE)
Source.Drag DROP
Source.MOVE X - XOffset, Y - YOffset
END SUB
```

This procedure ends manual dragging and moves the picture box. The procedure offsets that move by the location of the initial `MouseDown` event on the picture box.

8. Click the View Form button on the Project window, select the `Picture1` picture box and change its `DragMode` property to
`0 - Manual.`

9. Run the program and drag and drop the picture box. Again, note where the outline is and where the picture box moves when the mouse button is released. Now the picture box and the outline should align. End the program when you're done, and save it if you like.

This method works for all controls that have a `MouseDown` event, which includes list boxes, labels, file list boxes, and picture boxes. For all other controls, such as command buttons, manually insert the values of `XOffset` and `YOffset` that offset the move to the center of the control (the most obvious place to click a control before dragging it). See Chapter 15, "Command Reference," for more information on using these properties.

14

File System Management

File system control is not truly an advanced feature, but it is not widely used in BASIC anymore. The original BASICs were the operating systems for several early machines and, as such, had to be able to control the file system. Current BASICs are programming environments within the current operating system, so although they rarely have to move and copy files, the capability still exists from the earlier versions. The DOS file system is controlled from within a Visual Basic program with commands similar to the DOS system commands. The following statements and functions can be used in any Visual Basic program to control the file system; see the descriptions of the individual commands in Chapter 15, "Command Reference," for more information:

CHDIR	Change to a different default directory
CHDRIVE	Change the current drive
CURDIR$	Get the current directory path
DIR$	Return a list of files
KILL	Delete a file
MKDIR	Create a subdirectory
NAME AS	Change the name of a file or move it to a different directory
RMDIR	Delete a subdirectory

Making Online Help Files

Visual Basic includes a help toolkit so that you can add online help to your programs in a hypertext-like format. More than just a text file of instructions, a hypertext help file is a cross-referenced file of topics, with links to other topics in the same file. As you read a topic, you click a link and are immediately transported to the linked topic.

To make your own help file, use your word processor or Visual Basic to create a text file that contains all the text of your help file. Divide that file into topics, with the topic text preceded by the word .TOPIC: (including the period and colon) and the name of the topic. Within any topic, you can place a link to another topic by inserting the other topic's name surrounded by the symbols ▶ and ◀ (ASCII codes 16 and 17). Be sure to spell the name of the linked topic exactly as it is given in the definition of the topic. The following is a fragment of a help file with three topics, that includes a link from the first topic to the third:

```
.TOPIC:
Creating HELP files for Visual Basic
This is the text of the topic. It will be displayed
in a window when help is requested. To create a branch to
another topic, surround it with special arrow characters.
For example, a hyperlink to the third topic would be
done as follows,▶The third topic ◀. When the user clicks
between the arrows, the help topic displayed will change
to the topic whose name is between the arrows.
.TOPIC:
The name of the second topic
The text of the second topic. The help utility does not
word wrap, so you must explicitly insert returns in
the text, to keep the line lengths less than 60 characters.
.TOPIC:
The third topic
This is the text of the third topic.
```

Note that the word .TOPIC: must be on a line by itself, preceded with a period and followed by a colon. The line following the word is the name of the topic, with the text of the topic starting on the third line. A topic continues until another .TOPIC: or the end of the file is encountered. Don't forget to include the Index and the Table of Contents topics, with hypertext pointers to the rest of the topics in the file.

To use a help file in your program, you must include the files HELP.BAS, HELPF.FRM, and HELPUTIL.FRM in your application, or link your application with HELP.QLB in the programming environment and HELP.LIB in a compiled program. Insert the following statement at the module level of any module that calls functions from the Help Toolkit:

```
'$INCLUDE: 'HELP.BI'
```

To start up help, first initialize the help routines by calling the HelpRegister procedure, with the help filename as the argument. Next, call the HelpShowTopic routine followed by a valid topic name. The first time you call this routine, you will usually use the Table of Contents topic name to show the contents when the help dialog opens. When you are done, call the HelpClose procedure to close the help file.

All the details you need to know to create online help files are in the example help file included with the toolkit.

ISAM Database Programming

The Pro version of Visual Basic includes the tools and libraries to implement an *Indexed Sequential Access Method* (*ISAM*) database. ISAM is supplied as a set of callable procedures that set up the database files; add or delete records in those files; index the files; and perform the searching, sorting, and extracting needed to produce meaningful reports from the database information. Appendix E, "Visual Basic Toolkit Libraries," lists the functions available to manipulate an ISAM database file. A complete description of ISAM is beyond the scope of this book.

Multiple Document Interface Programming

The Pro version of Visual Basic includes the capability of creating *Multiple Document Interface* (*MDI*) programs. A standard Visual Basic program has only a single form active at any one time. If you select another form, the first form is deactivated. On the other hand, in an MDI program, a *main* form or *container* form always is active, and one of several child forms contained within it also is active. When a child form is minimized, its minimized window appears on the bottom of the container form (see Figure 14.2). Visual Basic is an MDI program. The container form covers the whole screen and has all the main menus, such as File, Edit, and so forth. On that container form are all the child forms, which are the Visual Basic windows such as the Code windows, the Toolbox window, and the Project window.

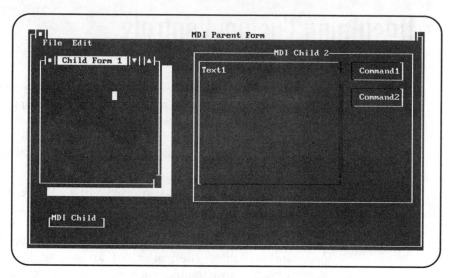

Figure 14.2. *A Multiple-Document Interface program layout.*

Creating an MDI application isn't much more complicated than creating a single form application. Create a single form to be the container form and set its FormType property to 1 - MDI. The form will expand to fill the screen, and can no longer be resized. Now, all new forms that you create are child forms of the MDI form. You can create menus on the MDI form, but you cannot attach any controls to it.

After this point, programming an MDI application is nearly the same as programming any other Visual Basic application. You attach controls to your forms, and write code for those controls. The only restriction is that the MDI form must be the startup form, and it must load all the child forms using the SHOW method.

Special Toolbox Libraries

Visual Basic contains several toolbox libraries for doing matrix and financial calculations, presentation graphics, and database management (ISAM, described previously). See Appendix E, "Visual Basic Toolkit Libraries," for a list of the contents of those libraries.

Designing Custom Controls

The Pro version of Visual Basic contains the libraries you need to produce custom controls. By creating a custom control, you expand the capabilities of Visual Basic beyond the set of controls included with the package. A custom control can be any object you want to design; for example, a button that stays down when you press it, or a plot window that graphs data passed to it.

A custom control consists of two parts: a header file describing the control for the environment, and a code block for controlling how the control behaves and how it responds to events and methods. The code block can be written in any language that can be linked with the linker, including Visual Basic. The header file is an assembly language file that must be assembled by an assembler such as Microsoft Macro Assembler (MASM). You can create the header file by hand or use the CUSTGEN.EXE utility included with Visual Basic Pro.

A custom control can receive all the same events as any other Visual Basic control, plus a custom event you can define for whatever you want. In the header file, you define which events your control will respond to, and which are to be passed to a user's program. Visual Basic automatically handles several of the events, such as CLS or DRAG. In addition, you define procedures that are called whenever one of the controls properties are read or changed. That way, you can implement any changes required by the change of the property. Visual Basic also automatically handles many standard properties, such as background color.

When a standard event occurs to your control, Visual Basic first checks whether your control handles that event. If your control does, it then looks in the header file for a procedure to handle the event. If no procedure is available to handle the event, Visual Basic passes the event to the user's program. When one of your procedures is passed an event, that event is not automatically passed to the user's program. If you want the user's program to receive the event after you are done with it, you must explicitly pass the event by using the INVOKEEVENT method.

Creating Overlays

The Pro version of Visual Basic can break a program into a main or root program and some number of overlays. An *overlay* is a block of code that is only read into memory when it is needed, and then swapped out when some other block is needed. To *swap out* is to copy a block of code in memory to a disk file and copy another block from a disk file into memory so the new block can run. Thus, with overlays, a program that is much larger than physical memory can be run. Visual Basic itself is an overlaid program.

When a program is run, the root program is read into memory and begins running. The root program stays in memory until the program completes. When a program branches to a procedure in one of the overlays, the overlay manager reads that overlay into memory and transfers control to the called procedure. When the procedure completes, the overlay stays in memory, in case it is needed again. If another overlay is needed, it is read into memory as well.

If there is not enough memory to read in an overlay, then some of the overlays already in memory are swapped out to make room for it. Later, if the swapped-out overlays are needed again, other overlays are swapped out and the needed overlays are swapped back in.

When an overlay needs to be swapped out, the overlay manager needs to find a place to put it. If possible, the overlay is stored in extended or expanded memory; otherwise, it is stored on disk. Retrieving an overlay from extended or expanded memory is much faster than retrieving it from disk, but all this is handled automatically.

Creating a program that uses overlays is relatively simple. First, outside of the Programming Environment, compile—but don't link—all the code modules with the BASIC compiler BC. Next, create a text file that has a .DEF file extension, and have the file list the names of all the object code files that are to be used as overlays. Finally, link the program, using the name of the .DEF file as the fifth filename argument to the linker program LINK (see Appendix F, "Program Command Lines and Options," for the complete command line for LINK).

The format of the .DEF files is as follows:

```
SEGMENTS
'modulename' CLASS 'BC_CODE' OVL:1
'modulename' CLASS 'BC_CODE' OVL:2
```

14

Here, the file must start with the word SEGMENTS. The next two lines define which code modules (segments) are to be used as overlays. *modulename* is the name of the file containing the code module or segment. Note that only code modules can be overlays, all form modules must be part of the main segment. Use a CLASS of BC_CODE for modules created with the BASIC compiler, or a CLASS of CODE for modules created with some other language such as C. The number following the word OVL: determines in which overlay to place the code module. More than one code module can be placed in a single overlay. However, there is a maximum size of 64K per overlay, and 4K is a good size for efficient operation.

As you might expect, the hard part is deciding which modules to place in an overlay. You must choose carefully, otherwise *thrashing* can occur. Thrashing occurs when two or more overlays are continually swapped in and out of memory, significantly degrading program operation. Try to group procedures and modules that are used together in the same overlay, so that the overlay can be loaded, used, and then swapped out. For example, in an accounting program, the code that produces an income statement would make a good overlay, and the spell checker of a word processor would make another. Put procedures used throughout a program in the main program so that they are always available.

Using Procedures from Other Languages

Visual Basic lets you link libraries created with other languages to a Visual Basic program. That way, a library of core procedures created with C, FORTRAN, or assembly language can be used with a Visual Basic front end. This provides an existing program a more responsive user interface. This also enables you to combine the relative strengths of two or more languages, such as Visual Basic's easily created user interface and C's simpler access to lower-level memory structures (such as the individual bits in a byte).

To use a procedure created in another language, a DECLARE statement must be inserted in a BASIC program module for each procedure in the library that the module uses. The DECLARE statement defines the procedure name, the arguments and argument types, and the program-calling conventions. In addition, the procedures must be in a library file compatible with Visual Basic. The .LIB type library files created by many library managers can be used with the Visual Basic linker.

The syntax of the DECLARE statement is as follows, for SUB and FUNCTION procedures:

```
DECLARE SUB procname [CDECL] [ALIAS procalias$][([arglist])]
```

```
DECLARE FUNCTION procname [CDECL] [ALIAS procalias$]
[([arglist])] [AS type]
```

Here, SUB indicates the procedure is a SUB procedure, which does not return a value, and FUNCTION indicates the procedure is a FUNCTION, which does return a value. The argument *procname* is the name the procedure is to have in the Visual Basic program. If the procedure stored in the library has a different name there from *procname*, that different name must be specified with the ALIAS *procalias$* clause. The keyword CDECL indicates the routine uses C-type arguments and calling sequence, and *arglist* is the argument list to be passed to the external procedure.

See Chapter 15, "Command Reference," for a complete description of the DECLARE statement.

What You Have Learned

This chapter points you to some of the advanced capabilities of Visual Basic. These features are somewhat beyond the scope of an introductory book, but I expect that you eventually will want to use them, if only to experiment with the capabilities of Visual Basic. To try them out, create some simple applications and experiment with the functions and methods. This chapter examined

- Using libraries
- Using binary file access

- Dragging and dropping controls
- Managing the file system
- Making help files
- Accessing an ISAM database
- Creating Multiple-Document Interface programs
- Designing custom controls
- Using overlays
- Programming with multiple languages
- Using special libraries

Congratulations. You have made it to the end of Part II. By now you should be able to use the essential capabilities of Visual Basic. Parts III ("Visual Basic Reference") and IV ("Appendixes") are reference sections, so—unless you read technical manuals for fun—you probably will find these sections most useful for explanations of the specific aspects of Visual Basic which you are using.

Part III

Visual Basic
References

Command Reference

This chapter of the reference section is an alphabetical list of Visual Basic functions, operators, statements, data types, methods, and metacommands. Chapter 16, "Properties," lists Visual Basic properties. Chapter 17, "Events," lists Visual Basic events, and Chapter 18, "Objects," lists the Visual Basic objects.

Each section in this chapter addresses a single language element. First is the element name preceded by an icon that indicates the element's type. There are six icons:

D Data type

F Function

$ Metacommand

M Method

O Operator

S Statement

Following the element name are up to seven subsections giving the element's **Purpose**, followed by the **Syntax**, the **Arguments**, a more complete **Description**, any values it **Returns**, usage under **For example**, and a list of similar or complementary functions under **See also**.

Purpose

The **Purpose** section is a brief statement of the function of the language element.

Syntax

As in Part II "Opening Up Visual Basic," syntax statements have a structured form to list all the options and arguments:

- The parts of the command that must be typed verbatim are shown in monospace bold type, such as `END`.

- Placeholders for variables are in *monospace italic* and, where appropriate, are suffixed with a variable type suffix character such as *$* or *%*.

- Optional arguments are enclosed in square brackets(`[ ]`).

- Mutually exclusive items are separated by vertical lines (`¦`) and enclosed in curly braces (`{}`). You can use only one item from a list of mutually exclusive items.

- Repeated clauses are followed by an ellipsis (`. . .`).

Example 1:

`END [{FUNCTION¦SELECT¦SUB¦TYPE}]`

In this example, the keyword `END` must be typed verbatim, so it is in bold. `END` is followed by an optional list of arguments; remember that options are shown within square brackets. If you choose to have an argument, you must select one of the four keywords shown—`FUNCTION`, `SELECT`, `SUB`, or `TYPE`— because they are surrounded by curly braces and separated by vertical bars.

Example 2:

MSGBOX(*msg$*[,*type%*[,*title$*]])

In this example, you must type the keyword MSGBOX verbatim, so it is shown in boldface type. The string argument *msg$* is a placeholder for a string constant or a string variable, as indicated by its italics and the $ suffix. The two other arguments are optional and so are shown in square brackets.

But is there an extra bracket around *title$*? When you see brackets within brackets, treat the arguments as a pair. In this case the second argument, *type%*, is optional and can be used alone; if you use the third argument, *title$*, you must include the second, *type%*.

Arguments

The **Arguments** section describes each of the arguments listed in the **Syntax** section. For variables, such as *type%*, you need not use the suffix characters when you use the functions; these characters merely indicate the type of variable the function or statement expects. For numeric values, any variable type can be used and it will be automatically converted to the type shown in the descriptions. In most cases, you can use either of the following for the argument:

- A variable containing the required value.

- A literal value for the argument. A *literal* is simply a number typed at the correct location in the argument list, or, if a string argument is required, a string of text between double quotation marks.

The suffix characters are

Type	*Suffix*
INTEGER	%
LONG	&
SINGLE	!
DOUBLE	#
CURRENCY	@
STRING	$

In cases that have many options, such as the OPEN statement, I have simplified the syntax statements by using placeholders for the options and including the option list in the **Arguments** section.

For functions and operators, the value returned by the function or the result of the operation is described in the **Returns** section.

 # ABS

Purpose	The ABS() function calculates and returns the absolute value of *number*.
Syntax	**ABS**(*number*)
Arguments	*number* is a number of any type, or a formula that evaluates to a number.
Description	The absolute value of a number is the value of the positive magnitude of the number.
Returns	The result is the absolute (positive) value of a number. The numeric type of the result is the same type as the argument.
For example	The following two assignment statements both assign the value 1 to the variables on the left:

```
A = ABS(-1)      'Assigns the value 1 to A
aVal = ABS(1)    'Assigns the value 1 to aVal
```

See also	SGN() function

 # ADDITEM

Purpose	The ADDITEM method adds a new entry to a list or combo box.
Syntax	[*form.*]*control*.**AddItem** *item$*[,*index%*]
Arguments	*form* is the name of the form containing the control.

control is the name of a list or combo box. If the name of the form isn't included, this argument defaults to the form containing this method.

item$ is the string item to add to the control's list.

index% is the location at which to insert the string item in the list or combo box's list of items. The first item is number 0, the second is 1, and so forth. If this argument is omitted and the list or combo boxes' Sorted property is False, the item is added at the end of the list. If this argument is omitted and Sorted is True, the item is listed alphabetically.

Description   The ADDITEM method adds new items to the List property in a list or combo box. You can load list and combo boxes with items only at runtime; you cannot load them at design time.

For example   The example code fragment adds the text A new item to the List3 list box on Form1. This code adds the new text to the end of the list unless the boxes' Sorted property is True, in which case it adds it at its alphabetical position in the list.

```
Form1.List3.ADDITEM "A new item"
```

See also   REMOVEITEM method
List property
ListCount property
ListIndex property
Sorted property

AND

Purpose   The AND operator combines two logical expressions or all the bits in two numeric values using the logical AND operation.

Syntax   *express1* **AND** *express2*

Arguments   *express1* and *express2* are logical expressions, numeric expressions, or numeric values.

Description   The AND operator combines two logical values according to the following truth table. If two numeric values are combined, the operator is applied bit-by-bit to the corresponding bits in the two values; that is, each bit in the result is equal to the logical AND of the corresponding bits in the two values.

A	B	A **and** B
True	True	True
True	False	False
False	True	False
False	False	False

Returns   The logical AND of the two expressions equals True (–1) or False (0) if *express1* and *express2* are logical expressions. If *express1* and *express2* are numeric expressions or values, the result is the bitwise logical AND of the same bits in each of the two expressions.

For example   The following IF statement causes a beep only if both A and B are True:

```
IF A AND B THEN BEEP
```

See also   EQV operator
IMP operator
NOT operator
OR operator
XOR operator

D ANY

Purpose   The data type ANY suppresses data type checking and matches any data type in a DECLARE statement.

Syntax   *variable* **AS ANY**

Arguments   *variable* is a variable name.

Description   The data type ANY is used in DECLARE statements to disable data-type error checking for values passed to an external library procedure.

For example   The following statement declares the name and arguments to a SUB procedure (DoItAgain) in an external library (MYLIB.LIB). The argument ArgA is not checked for type when a value is passed to the external procedure. The argument ArgB must be an INTEGER, and is checked for type before being passed to the external procedure.

```
DECLARE SUB DoItAgain Lib "MYLIB.LIB"
(ArgA AS ANY, ArgB AS INTEGER)
```

See also   DECLARE statement
TYPE statement
CONTROL data type
CURRENCY data type
DOUBLE data type
FORM data type
INTEGER data type
LONG data type
SINGLE data type
STRING data type

ASC

Purpose   The ASC() function returns the ASCII code of the first character of the string argument.

Syntax   **ASC(***astring$***)**

Arguments   *astring$* is a string of any length; only the first character is examined.

Description   The ASCII character set consists of 128 standard characters, plus a second set of 128 characters defined in the ANSI standard. Each character has a code between 0 and 255. The ASC() function returns the code for the first character in the argument. Use the CHR$() function to convert codes back to characters.

> The second 128 characters, which are the graphics characters, are different in DOS and Windows applications. See Appendix B, "ASCII/ANSI Code Chart."

Returns   The result is the ASCII code for the first character in the string argument.

For example   The following two assignment statements assign the variables A and B the ASCII codes for R and 7:

```
A = ASC("R")       'assigns A the code 82
B = ASC("7")       'assigns B the code 55
```

See also CHR$() function

 ATN

Purpose The ATN() function calculates and returns the first quadrant arctangent of number.

Syntax **ATN**(*number*)

Arguments *number* is a number of any numeric type, or a formula that evaluates to a number.

Description The arctangent of a number is the angle whose tangent is the number. The arctangent function is the inverse of the tangent function. This function returns an angle in the positive half space between $-\pi/2$ and $\pi/2$. The actual angle also could be in the negative half space, because

$$\text{Tan}(\theta) = \text{Tan}(\theta + \pi)$$

for any angle θ. To convert from degrees to radians, multiply by $\pi/180$. To calculate the arcsine and arccosine using the arctangent function, use the following:

```
arcsine(T) = ATN(T/SQRT(1 - T^2))
Pi = 3.141593
arccosine(T) = Pi/2 - ATN(T/SQRT(1 - T^2))
```

Returns The result is the arctangent of *number* expressed in radians. It is in the range $-\pi/2$ to $\pi/2$, where π is 3.141593.

For example The following two assignment statements assign the arctangent of 3.25 to the variable on the left, one in radians and one in degrees:

```
A = ATN(3.25)            'Assigns the arctangent
                         'in radians of 3.25 to A.
B = ATN(3.25)*180/3.141593 'Assigns the
                         'arctangent in degrees
                         'of 3.25 to B.
```

See also COS() function
SIN() function
TAN() function

 **BEEP**

Purpose	The BEEP statement causes a system beep.
Syntax	**BEEP**
Arguments	None
Description	The BEEP statement causes a system beep from the computer's speaker.
For example	The following SUB procedure emits NumBeeps beeps, each separated by a short pause determined by the second FOR/NEXT loop:

```
SUB Beeper (NumBeeps AS INTEGER)
DIM I AS INTEGER, J AS INTEGER
FOR I = 1 TO NumBeeps
 BEEP
 FOR J = 1 TO 10000        'Delay Loop
NEXT J                     'Delay Loop
NEXT I
END SUB
```

See also	None

 **BLOAD**

Purpose	The BLOAD statement loads a memory image from a disk file back into memory. This statement is not available in Visual Basic for Windows.
Syntax	**BLOAD** *filename$[,offset%]*
Arguments	*filename$* is a string containing the filename of the file containing the memory image, and an optional directory path if the file isn't in the current directory. The filename may contain the * and ? wildcard characters, where * matches any number of any characters and ? matches any single character. The path, including the disk letter, has the following syntax:

[drive:][[\]directory[\directory...\]]filename

where *drive* is the drive letter, *directory* is a directory name, and *filename* is the file to delete. Omit this argument to use the current drive. If the first

backslash is omitted, the path is assumed to start in the default directory of the specified drive. Use CHDIR and CHDRIVE to change the current directory.

offset% is the offset to the address in memory where loading is to begin, in the range 0 to 65,535 bytes. *offset%* is relative to the base address set with the DEF SEG statement.

Description   The BLOAD statement is used to load a memory image stored in a disk file back into memory. The memory image must have been saved with the BSAVE statement. Use the DEF SEG statement to set the base address in memory for loading.

For example   The following statement loads the memory image stored in the file MEMIMG.IMG into memory starting at byte address 16,322:

```
BLOAD MEMIMG.IMG, 16322
```

See also   BSAVE statement

 BSAVE

Purpose   The BSAVE statement saves a memory image into a disk file. This statement is not available in Visual Basic for Windows.

Syntax   **BSAVE** *filename$,offset%,length%*

Arguments   *filename$* is a string containing the filename of the file to contain the memory image, and an optional directory path if the file doesn't go in the current directory. The path, including the disk letter, has the following syntax:

```
[drive:][[\]directory[\directory...\]]filename
```

where *drive* is the drive letter, *directory* is a directory name, and *filename* is the file to delete. Omit this argument to use the current drive. If the first backslash is omitted, the path is assumed to start in the default directory of the specified drive. Use CHDIR and CHDRIVE to change the current directory.

offset% is the offset to the address in memory where saving is to begin, in the range 0 to 65,535 bytes. *offset%* is relative to the base address set with the DEF SEG statement.

length% is the number of bytes to save in the range 0 to 65,535.

Description   The BSAVE statement is used to save a memory image stored into a disk file. Later, you can restore the memory image to memory by using the BLOAD statement. Use the DEF SEG statement to set the base address in memory for loading.

For example   The following statement stores into the file MEMIMG.IMG an image of memory 1,024 bytes long starting at byte address 16,322:

```
BSAVE MEMIMG.IMG, 16322, 1024
```

See also   BLOAD statement

CALL

Purpose   The CALL statement passes control to a SUB procedure or external library procedure.

Syntax   **CALL** *routinename* [*(arglist)*]

or

routinename [*arglist*]

Arguments   *routinename* is the name of the SUB or library procedure to execute.

arglist is the argument list for the called procedure. This is a comma-delimited list of variables, formulas, or constants, as required by the called function. Preface arguments with the BYVAL keyword to pass the argument as a value rather than as an address. You cannot use BYVAL if the argument is an array.

Description   The CALL statement executes a SUB procedure or a procedure in an external library. The CALL keyword is not used in most Visual Basic programs, but is included for compatibility with other software. If you use the CALL keyword, place the argument list within parentheses. If you do not use the CALL keyword, the argument list must not be within parentheses. External procedures must first be declared with a DECLARE statement.

The arguments to the called procedure are passed by reference; that is, only the address of the argument is passed to the procedure, and not the value of the variable itself. If an argument in the argument list is a formula, Visual Basic creates a temporary variable for the result and passes the address of the variable. You can force a variable to be passed as a copy rather than as

15

401

the original variable by enclosing it in parentheses. This protects a variable passed to a called procedure. If the procedure changes the value of the variable, it actually changes the value of the copy and not that of the original variable.

Another way to protect a variable passed to a called procedure is to precede the variable name with the BYVAL keyword here, in the heading of the SUB procedure, or in the DECLARE statement for the external procedure. The BYVAL keyword causes the value of an argument to be passed rather than the actual argument itself.

For example   The Sumit procedure has three arguments. The following two statements both call the SumIt procedure with the same arguments. In both cases, only a copy of the variable B is passed, so the original value remains unchanged.

```
CALL SumIt(A, (B), C)
SumIt A, (B), C
```

See also   DECLARE statement
SUB statement

 # CALL ABSOLUTE

Purpose   The CALL ABSOLUTE statement passes control to a machine language procedure in memory. This statement is not available in Visual Basic for Windows.

Syntax   **CALL ABSOLUTE** ([*arglist*,] *offset%*)

Arguments   *arglist* is the argument list for the called procedure. This is a comma-delimited list of variables, formulas, or constants, as required by the called function.

offset% is the offset to the address in memory at which execution is to begin, in the range 0 to 65,535 in bytes. *offset%* is relative to the base address set with the DEF SEG statement.

Description   The CALL ABSOLUTE statement executes a machine language program in memory. To use this function, you must attach the library file VBDOS.QLB to Visual Basic, and include the file VBDOS.BI in your program. Use the */L libname* option when starting Visual Basic to attach the library. The library VBDOS.LIB must be available when you compile a program that uses this function. Set the base address in memory with the DEF SEG statement.

For example   If a machine language procedure has two arguments and starts at an offset of 512 bytes in the current segment, then the following statement will execute that procedure:

```
CALL ABSOLUTE ((A, B),512)
```

See also   CALL statement
DECLARE statement
DEF SEG statement

CALLS

Purpose   The CALLS statement passes control to a procedure written in a different language. This statement is not available in Visual Basic for Windows.

Syntax   **CALL**[**S**] *routinename* [(*arglist*)]

Arguments   *routinename* is the name of the procedure to execute.

arglist is the argument list for the called procedure. This is a comma-delimited list of variables, formulas, or constants, as required by the called function. Precede an argument with the BYVAL keyword to pass the argument as a value rather than as an address. Preface an argument with the SEG keyword to pass the value as a segmented (far) address. An array argument cannot use the BYVAL or SEG keywords.

Description   The CALLS statement executes a procedure written in a different, non-BASIC language.

The arguments to the called procedure are passed by reference; that is, only the address of the argument is passed to the procedure, and not the value of the variable itself. If an argument in the argument list is a formula, Visual Basic creates a temporary variable and passes the address of the variable. You can force a variable to be passed as a copy, rather than as the original variable, by enclosing it in parentheses. This protects a variable passed to a called procedure. If the procedure changes the value of the variable, it actually changes the value of the copy and not that of the original variable.

Another way to protect a variable passed to a called procedure is to precede the arguments with the BYVAL or SEG keywords. The BYVAL keyword forces the argument to be passed as an address. The SEG keyword forces the argument to be passed as a segmented (long) address. BYVAL or SEG cannot be used if the argument is an array.

15

For example   If an external procedure named DoIt has two arguments, and the first must be passed as a value rather than as an address. Then the following statement will execute that procedure:

```
CALLS DoIt BYVAL A, B
```

See also   CALL statement
DECLARE statement

 CCUR

Purpose   The CCUR() function converts a number of any numeric type to the CURRENCY type.

Syntax   **CCUR**(*number*)

Arguments   *number* is a number of any type, or a formula that evaluates to a number.

Description   The CCUR() function converts a number in any numeric type to the CURRENCY type. You do not need this function if you assign a number to a CURRENCY type variable, because Visual Basic automatically does the conversion in such cases. This function is useful to force a calculation to be done in CURRENCY type if the calculation contains other numeric types.

If every number used in a calculation is of the same numeric type, the entire calculation is done in that type. If a calculation contains different numeric types, Visual Basic converts everything to the most precise type before doing the calculation.

Returns   The result is *number* converted to the CURRENCY data type.

For example   The following SUB procedure contains a simple formula involving two different numeric types. Applying the CCUR() function to theRate forces it to the CURRENCY data type, so the entire formula now is in the CURRENCY data type.

Be careful when you do this to values with more than four characters to the right of the decimal: anything beyond four is rounded off.

```
FUNCTION SalesTax (theCash AS CURRENCY,
theRate AS SINGLE) AS CURRENCY
SalesTax = theCash * CCUR(theRate)
END FUNCTION
```

See also   CDBL function
CINT function
CLNG function
CSNG function

CDBL

Purpose   The CDBL() function converts a number of any numeric type to the DOUBLE type.

Syntax   **CDBL(***number***)**

Arguments   *number* is a number of any type, or a formula that evaluates to a number.

Description   The CDBL() function converts a number in any numeric type to the DOUBLE type. You do not need this function if you assign a number to a DOUBLE-type variable, because Visual Basic automatically does the conversion in such cases. This function is useful to force a calculation to be done in DOUBLE type if the calculation contains other numeric types.

If every number used in a calculation is of the same numeric type, the entire calculation is done in that type. If a calculation contains different numeric types, Visual Basic converts everything to the most precise type before doing the calculation.

Returns   The result is *number* converted to the DOUBLE data type.

For example   The following SUB procedure contains a simple formula involving two different numeric types. Applying the CDBL() function to Value2 forces it to the DOUBLE data type, so the entire formula now is in the DOUBLE data type.

```
FUNCTION MultiplyEm (value1 AS DOUBLE,
Value2 AS INTEGER) AS DOUBLE
MultiplyEm = Value1*CDBL(Value2)
END FUNCTION
```

See also   CCCUR function
CINT function
CLNG function
CSNG function

 CHAIN

Purpose   The CHAIN statement is used to pass control to another BASIC program. This statement is not available in Visual Basic for Windows.

Syntax   **CHAIN** *filename$*

Arguments   *filename$* is a string containing the name of the file to which to pass control, and an optional directory path if the file isn't in the current directory. The path, including the disk letter, has the following syntax:

[*drive:*][[\]*directory*[*directory...*\]]*filename*

where *drive* is the drive letter, *directory* is a directory name, and *filename* is the file to delete. Omit this argument to use the current drive. If you omit the first backslash, the path is assumed to start in the default directory of the specified drive. Use CHDIR and CHDRIVE to change the current directory.

Description   The CHAIN statement loads another BASIC program into memory and executes it. To pass variables to the chained program, store the variables in a COMMON statement.

For example   The following procedure passes control to the program MYNO2.BAS:

```
CHAIN " MYNO2.BAS
```

See also   CALL statement
COMMON statement
DECLARE statement

 CHDIR

Purpose   The CHDIR statement sets the default directory for a drive.

Syntax   **CHDIR** *path$*

Arguments *path$* is a string containing the directory path, including the disk letter, with the following syntax:

[*drive:*][\]*directory*[*directory*]...

where *drive* is the drive letter and *directory* is a directory name. Omit the drive argument to use the current drive. If you omit the first backslash, the path is assumed to start in the default directory of the specified drive. The string must be less than 128 bytes long.

Description Disk operations that do not specify a directory take place in the default directory on the current drive. The CHDIR statement changes the default directory on a disk drive. Most commands that manipulate the directory system or open or create files can take a complete path and directory as an argument. By using this command first, these commands need only specify the filename. If no disk drive is specified in the *path$* argument, the statement changes the default directory on the current drive. If a drive is specified in the *path$* argument, the default directory is changed on that drive.

Even if an alternate drive is specified, this statement does not change the current drive. Use the CHDRIVE statement to change the current drive.

For example The following statement changes the default directory on the C drive to \TOOLS\UTILITIES:

CHDIR "C:\TOOLS\UTILITIES"

The next statement changes the default directory relative to the old default directory:

CHDIR "PROGRAMS\C"

That is, if the current default directory is

C:\TOOLS\UTILITIES

this command would change it to

C:\TOOLS\UTILITIES\PROGRAMS\C

See also CHDRIVE statement
KILL statement
MKDIR statement
NAME statement
RMDIR statement
CURDIR$ function
DIR$ function

 CHDRIVE

Purpose   The CHDRIVE statement changes the current drive.

Syntax   **CHDRIVE** *drive$*

Arguments   *drive$* is a string containing the letter of the drive to make the current drive. The drive letter must be the first character in the string; any other characters in the string are ignored.

Description   The default directory on the current drive is where disk operations take place when the directory isn't explicitly defined. Each disk has a default directory set with the CHDIR statement, and the current disk is set with the CHDRIVE statement.

For example   The following statement changes the current drive to the A drive:

```
CHDRIVE "A"
```

The next statement changes the current drive to the C drive. The balance of the argument string is ignored.

```
CHDRIVE "C:\TOOLS"
```

See also   CHDIR statement
KILL statement
MKDIR statement
NAME statement
RMDIR statement
CURDIR$ function
DIR$ function

 CHR$

Purpose   The CHR$() function returns the character defined by the ASCII code.

Syntax   **CHR$**(*code*)

Arguments   *code* is an ASCII code. This must be an integer between 0 and 255.

Description   The ASCII character set consists of 128 standard characters, plus a second 128 characters defined in the ANSI standard. Each character has a code between 0 and 255. The CHR$() function returns the character defined by the ASCII code number used as its argument. Use the ASC() function to convert characters back to ASCII codes.

> The second 128 characters, which are the graphics characters, differ in DOS and Windows applications. See Appendix B "ASCII/ANSI Code Chart."

Returns   The result is a single character string containing the character defined by the ASCII code.

For example   The following procedure prints a table of ASCII codes and characters on the screen. It skips the first 32 characters (0 through 31), which are control characters such as Enter and Backspace.

```
SUB CodeTable
FOR I = 32 TO 255
   PRINT I, CHR$(I)
NEXT I
END SUB
```

See also   ASC() function

CINT

Purpose   The CINT() function converts a number of any numeric type to the INTEGER type by rounding.

Syntax   **CINT(**number**)**

Arguments   number is a number of any type, or a formula that evaluates to a number.

Description   The CINT() function converts a number in any numeric type to the INTEGER type. You don't need this function if you assign number to an INTEGER type variable, because Visual Basic automatically does the conversion in that case. This function is useful to force a calculation to be done in INTEGER type if the calculation contains other numeric types. If every number used in a calculation is of the same numeric type, the entire calculation is done in that type. If a calculation contains different numeric types, Visual Basic converts everything to the most precise type before doing the calculation.

CINT() is most useful for converting floating point numbers to integers by rounding rather than truncation, as is done by the INT and FIX functions.

Returns   The result is *number* converted to the INTEGER data type.

For example   The following table shows how CINTS(), INT(), and FIX() convert different values:

Value	CINT	INT	FIX
3.7	4	3	3
3.4	3	3	3
–3.7	–4	–4	–3
–3.4	–3	–4	–3

See also   CCUR function
CLNG function
CSNG function
FIX function
INT function

 CIRCLE

Purpose   The CIRCLE statement draws circles, ellipses, filled circles, filled ellipses, arcs, pie slices, and filled pie slices on the screen. In Visual Basic for Windows, this statement also can draw these graphics on forms, picture boxes, or the printer.

Syntax   **CIRCLE [STEP]**(*xc!,yc!*), *radius!*[,[*color%*]
[,[*startang!*][,[*endang!*][,*aspect!*]]]]

Arguments   STEP is a keyword that specifies that the coordinates specifying the center of the circle are relative to the current position specified by the CurrentX and CurrentY properties.

xc! and *yc!* are the *x, y* coordinates of the center of the circle. See the SCREEN statement for a discussion of drawing measurement units.

radius! is the radius of the circle.

color% is the color attribute number specifying the color to use for the circle's outline. Omit this value to use the current ForeColor. If the object is closed (a circle, ellipse, or pie slice) it is filled with the current ForeColor. See the RGB() function for more information on colors.

startang! and *endang!* are the starting and ending angles of an arc or pie slice, measured in radians. The 0 angle is at 3:00, and angles increase counterclockwise. If a negative value is used for an angle, its absolute value defines the end of the arc, and another line is drawn from the center of the circle to that end of the arc.

aspect! is the aspect ratio of the circle. If the argument is omitted, a circle is drawn. The value of this argument that produces a circle is equal to

(4/3)(screen height/screen width)

where the screen height and screen width are measured in pixels. If the aspect ratio is less than this value, an ellipse is drawn with the long axis horizontal. If the aspect ratio is greater than this value, an ellipse is drawn with the long axis vertical.

Description The CIRCLE method produces circles, filled circles, ellipses, filled ellipses, arcs, pie slices, and filled pie slices on the screen. Only completely closed figures are filled; these are circles, ellipses, and pie slices. To make a pie slice rather than an arc, use negative angles for the starting and ending angles of the arc. This forces the drawing of lines from the center of the circle to the ends of the arc. Circles can be drawn only if there are no forms visible on the screen.

The drawing is affected by the settings of all the drawing properties: CurrentX, CurrentY, Color, Screen, and ForeColor.

For example The following statements hide the existing form, set screen mode 7 (640 by 200 color graphics), and draw a circle on the screen. The center is 200 pixels from the left side of the screen and 150 down from the top, and the radius is 50 pixels. The circle is outlined and filled with red—3 is the color attribute for red.

```
HIDE
SCREEN 7
CIRCLE (200, 150), 50, 3
```

The following statement creates an elliptical, filled pie slice with an aspect ratio of 0.8 on the current form. The *x, y* location and the radius of the circle are the same as for the preceding statement. This time the object is outlined

in the current ForeColor because no color is specified. The arc ranges from one to two radians (57 to 114 degrees) and lines are drawn from the center to the ends of the slice.

```
CIRCLE (200, 150), 50, , -1, -2, .8
```

See also   COLOR statement
LINE statement
SCREEN statement
QBCOLOR( ) function
RGB( ) function
CurrentX property
CurrentY property
ForeColor property

 CLEAR

Purpose   The CLEAR method deletes the current contents of the CLIPBOARD.

Syntax   **CLIPBOARD.CLEAR**

Arguments   None

Description   The CLEAR method clears the contents of the CLIPBOARD.

For example   The following statement clears the contents of the clipboard:

CLIPBOARD.CLEAR

See also   CLEAR statement
SETDATA method
GETDATA method

 CLEAR

Purpose   The CLEAR statement reinitializes the environment. This statement is not available in Visual Basic for Windows.

Syntax   **CLEAR** [,*stacksize%*]

Arguments *stacksize%* is the amount of memory to allocate for the stack. All procedure return addresses and automatic (local) variables are stored on the stack.

Description The CLEAR statement resets the Visual Basic environment. It releases all file buffers, clears all variables, and initializes the stack. If the argument is given, CLEAR sets the amount of memory available for the stack. The stack is where all the arguments and return addresses for procedure calls are stored.

For example The following statement resets the environment and allocates 1024 bytes for the stack:

```
CLEAR ,1024
```

See also STACK statement
CLEAR method
STACK function

# CLNG

Purpose The CLNG() function converts a number of any numeric type to the LONG integer type by rounding.

Syntax **CLNG(***number***)**

Arguments *number* is a number of any type, or a formula that evaluates to a number.

Description The CLNG() function converts a number in any numeric type to the LONG integer type. This function is not needed if you assign *number* to a LONG type variable, because Visual Basic automatically does the conversion in that case. CLNG() is useful to force a calculation to be done in LONG type if the calculation contains other numeric types. If every number used in a calculation is of the same numeric type, then the entire calculation is done in that type. If a calculation contains different numeric types, Visual Basic converts everything to the most precise type before doing the calculation.

Returns The result is *number* converted to the LONG integer data type.

For example The following FUNCTION procedure contains a simple formula involving two different numeric types. Applying the CINT() function to Value2 forces it to the LONG data type, so the entire formula now is in the LONG data type.

```
FUNCTION MultiplyEm Value1 AS LONG,
Value2 AS DOUBLE) AS LONG
MultiplyEm = Value1*CINT(Value2)
END FUNCTION
```

See also   CCCUR function
                 CDBL function
                 CINT function
                 CSNG function
                 FIX function
                 INT function

 CLOSE

Purpose   The CLOSE statement closes open disk files.

Syntax   **CLOSE** [[#]*filenum*][,[#]*filenum*]...

Arguments   *filenum* is the file number used when the file was opened with the OPEN
                statement. Omitting the # symbol has no effect. Omit all file numbers to
                close all open files.

Description The CLOSE statement closes one or more open disk files, and releases the file
                number for reuse. The file numbers assigned to each disk file to be closed
                are listed in the arguments. If no arguments are used, all open disk files are
                closed.

For example The first example closes file numbers 1 and 2:

                CLOSE #1, #2

                The second example closes only file number 1:

                CLOSE 1

                The third example closes all open files:

                CLOSE

See also   OPEN statement

 CLS

Purpose	The CLS method clears text from a form or picture box.
Syntax	[*object.*]**CLS**
Arguments	*object* is the name of the object to clear: a form or picture box. Omit this argument to clear the form containing this statement.
Description	The CLS method clears text drawn on a form or picture box at runtime. Printing that occurs at runtime is not affected if AutoRedraw was True when the printing occurred and was set to False before CLS was executed. The values of the CurrentX and CurrentY properties are set to 0.
For example	The following statement clears the contents of the Picture1 picture box:
	`Picture1.CLS`
See also	CLS Statement AutoRedraw property

 CLS

Purpose	The CLS statement clears all or part of the screen. This statement is not available in Visual Basic for Windows.
Syntax	**CLS** [*code%*]
Arguments	*code%* is a numeric code specifying what parts of the screen to clear. If you omit the code, this statement clears the graphics viewport (set with the VIEW statement), if it exists. If there is no graphics viewport, this statement clears the text viewport (set with the VIEW PRINT statement). If no viewports are defined, CLS clears the whole screen. The codes cause this statement to clear specific areas.

Code	Clears
0	Whole screen
1	Graphics viewport or whole screen
2	Text viewport or whole screen

15

Description   The CLS statement clears all or part of the screen when in graphics mode. It can clear the whole screen, the graphics viewport, or the text viewport. The graphics viewport is defined with the VIEW statement and the text viewport is set with the VIEW PRINT statement.

For example   The following statement clears the graphics viewport:

```
CLS 1
```

See also   VIEW statement
VIEW PRINT statement
CLS method

 COLOR

Purpose   The COLOR statement sets the color of text printed on the screen when forms are not showing. This statement is not available in Visual Basic for Windows.

Syntax   For screen mode 0 (text only):
COLOR [*foreground&*][,[*background&*][,*border&*]]

For screen mode 1:
COLOR [*background&*][,*palette%*]

For screen modes 4, 12, and 13:
COLOR [*foreground&*]

For screen modes 7, 8, 9, and 10:
COLOR [*foreground&*][,*background&*]

Arguments   *foreground&* is the color attribute for foreground objects such as text.

background& is the color attribute for the screen background.

border& is the color attribute for the border of the screen.

palette& is the number 0 or 1, which specifies the color palette to use.

Description   The COLOR statement sets the foreground and background colors to use on the screen. The syntax and codes used depend on the currently invoked screen mode set with the SCREEN statement. See RGB for a discussion of colors.

For example   The following statements set the screen mode to 7, the text color to bright white (15) and the background color to blue (1):

```
SCREEN 7
COLOR 15, 1
```

See also   PALETTE statement
SCREEN statement
RGB function
QBCOLOR function

 **COM**

Purpose   The COM statement enables or disables trapping of serial communication port events.

Syntax   `COM(port&) {ON|OFF|STOP}`

Arguments   *port&* is the number of the serial port to watch (1 for COM1 or 2 for COM2).

ON enables trapping.

OFF disables trapping and ignores any communication events.

STOP disables trapping but saves any communication events that occur while trapping is disabled.

Description   The COM statement enables or disables event trapping for communication events. Set the procedure to execute when a communication event occurs with the ON COM() statement. Set communication parameters with the OPEN COM statement.

For example   The following statement enables event trapping for communication port 1 (COM1):

```
COM(1) ON
```

See also   ON COM() statement
OPEN COM() statement

 **COMMAND$**

Purpose	The COMMAND$ function returns the command-line arguments used to launch Visual Basic or a Visual Basic application.
Syntax	**COMMAND$**
Arguments	None
Description	The COMMAND$ function returns everything after the /CMD option in the command line used to launch Visual Basic, or everything after the program name in the command line used to launch a Visual Basic application. Command lines are set in the File Manager for applications launched from Windows, and are typed at the command line for applications launched from DOS. You can change the contents of the command line when running in interpreted mode by executing the **M**odify COMMAND$ command of the **R**un menu.
Returns	The result is a string containing the command-line arguments.
For example	The following assignment statement assigns the contents of the command line to the string theLine$:

```
theLine$ = COMMAND$
```

See also	None

 **COMMON**

Purpose	The COMMON statement defines global storage for variables shared between modules. This statement is not available in Visual Basic for Windows.
Syntax	**COMMON** [**SHARED**] [*/blockname/*] *var, var,...*
Arguments	SHARED indicates that the variables are available to all procedures within the module containing the COMMON statement.
	blockname is the name of a named, common block. Only procedures with the same-named COMMON statement can share the variables.
	var is one of the variables to share.

Description The COMMON statement allows variables to be shared among procedures within a module or among other modules. The COMMON statements in each of the modules that are to share the variables must be identical. Insert the COMMON statements with the $INCLUDE metacommand to ensure that they are the same. Named COMMON statements are used to restrict which procedures can share a variable.

For example If you place the following statement in the header of each of an application's modules, the variables theKey and theDate will be shared with all the modules in that application:

```
COMMON SHARED theKey, theDate
```

See also CONST statement
DIM statement

 CONST

Purpose The CONST statement defines constants for use in Visual Basic programs.

Syntax **CONST** *name* = *value*,[*name* = *value*]...

Arguments *name* is the name of the constant value, which must be a legal Visual Basic variable name.

value is the value to give the constant. This value is usually only literals, but it can include other constants and simple arithmetic (+, -, *, /) or logical (=, <, >, <>, <=, >=) operators.

Description The CONST statement defines constants for use in a program's code. Constants enable you to use words such as True and False instead of –1 and 0, thus making code much more readable. The words are much easier to understand than the raw numeric codes they stand for. Once defined, a constant cannot be redefined within a program.

For example The following statement defines the constants True and False:

```
CONST True = -1, False = 0
```

See also COMMON statement
DIM statement

15

D CONTROL

Purpose   The data type CONTROL matches any control name passed to a SUB or FUNCTION procedure.

Syntax   *variable* **AS CONTROL**

Arguments   *variable* is a variable name.

Description   The data type CONTROL is used in SUB and FUNCTION procedure headings to declare a variable as type CONTROL so that you can pass a control name to a procedure. You can then use the variable as a control name. To see what kind of a control has been passed to a procedure, use the following expression in an IF statement:

```
TypeOf object IS objecttype
```

For example   The following procedure defines Pic as a CONTROL type and then uses an IF statement to check whether Pic is a picture box. If it is, the procedure sets the background color to red and the foreground color to blue (the constants Red and Blue were defined elsewhere.)

```
SUB ColorIt (Pic AS CONTROL)
IF TypeOf Pic IS PictureBox THEN
  Pic.BackColor = Red
  Pic.ForeColor = Blue
END IF
END SUB
```

See also   DECLARE statement
IF statement
TYPE statement
ANY data type
CURRENCY date type
DOUBLE date type
FORM date type
INTEGER data type
LONG date type
SINGLE data type
STRING data type

COS

Purpose The COS() function calculates and returns the cosine of an angle, in radians.

Syntax **COS(***angle***)**

Arguments *angle* is an angle in radians expressed as a number, or a formula that evaluates to a number of any numeric type.

Description The COS() function calculates the cosine of an angle expressed in radians. Use the following to calculate the cosine of an angle expressed in degrees:

```
Pi = 3.141592654
theCosine = Cos(dAngle*Pi/180))
```

where dAngle is measured in degrees.

Returns The result is the cosine of *angle*, a number between –1 and +1.

For example The following two assignment statements calculate the cosine of two angles, one in radians and one in degrees:

```
A = COS(3.25)          'Assigns the cosine of 3.25
                       'radians to A = -0.99413.
Pi = 3.141592654
B = COS(27.8*Pi/180)   'Assigns the cosine of 27.8
                       'degrees to B = 0.88458.
```

See also ATN() function
SIN() function
TAN() function

CSNG

Purpose The CSNG() function converts a number of any numeric type to the SINGLE-precision, floating-point type.

Syntax **CSNG(***number***)**

Arguments *number* is a number of any type, or a formula that evaluates to a number.

Description   The CSNG() function converts a number in any numeric type to the SINGLE type. Numbers are rounded, if necessary, during the conversion. You don't need this function if you assign *number* to a SINGLE-type variable because in that case Visual Basic automatically does the conversion. You can use this function to force a calculation to be done in SINGLE type if the calculation contains other numeric types. If every number used in a calculation is of the same numeric type, the entire calculation is done in that type. If a calculation contains different numeric types, Visual Basic converts everything to the most precise type before doing the calculation.

Returns   The result is *number* converted to the SINGLE data type.

For example   The following SUB procedure contains a simple formula involving two different numeric types. Applying the CSNG() function to Value2 forces it to the SINGLE data type, so the entire formula now is in the SINGLE data type.

```
FUNCTION MultiplyEm (Value1 AS SINGLE,
Value2 AS DOUBLE)AS INTEGER
MultiplyEm = Value1*CSNG(Value2)
END FUNCTION
```

See also   CCCUR function
CDBL function
CINT function
CLNG function
INT function
FIX function

F CSRLIN

Purpose   The CSRLIN function returns the row the cursor is in. This statement is not available in Visual Basic for Windows.

Syntax   **CSRLIN**

Arguments   None

Description   The CSRLIN function is used to determine which line the cursor is in on the screen. Use the POS function to get the column location or the LOCATE statement to move the cursor to a specific position. This function is available only if no forms are visible.

Returns The result is the row number of the row that contains the cursor. The first row on the screen is number 1 at the top of the screen. Row numbers increase as you move down the screen.

For example The following two assignment statements get the row and column that contain the cursor:

```
xLoc = POS      'the column number
yLoc = CSRLIN   'the row number
```

See also LOCATE statement
POS function

CURDIR$

Purpose The CURDIR$ function returns the default directory on the specified drive.

Syntax **CURDIR$**[(*drive$*)]

Arguments *drive$* is a string containing the letter of the drive to examine. The drive letter must be the first character in the string; any other characters in the string are ignored. Omit this argument to use the current drive.

Description The default directory on the current drive is where disk operations occur when the directory isn't explicitly defined. Each disk has a default directory set with the CHDIR statement. The current disk is set with the CHDRIVE statement. Use the CURDIR$ function to get the current default path for a drive.

Returns The result is a string containing the directory path, including the disk letter, with the following syntax:

drive:*directory**directory*

where *drive* is the drive letter and *directory* is a directory name.

For example If the current directory on the C drive is \TOOLS\UTILITIES, thePath$ contains C:\TOOLS\UTILITIES:

```
thePath$ = CURDIR$("c")
```

See also   CHDIR statement
CHDRIVE statement
KILL statement
MKDIR statement
NAME statement
RMDIR statement
DIR$ function

 CURRENCY

Purpose   The data type CURRENCY matches or defines currency type variables.

Syntax   *variable* **AS CURRENCY**

Arguments   *variable* is a variable name.

Description   The data type CURRENCY is used in SUB and FUNCTION procedure headings to declare a variable as CURRENCY type so that Visual Basic can check values passed to the procedure. The data type CURRENCY also is used in a DIM, COMMON, or STATIC statement to define a variable as CURRENCY type. The CURRENCY data type is an 8-byte, fixed-point number, with 15 digits to the left of the decimal and 4 digits to the right, which ranges from −922,337,203,685,477.5808 to 922,337,203,685,477.5807. The CURRENCY type is optimized for calculations in which numeric accuracy is important, such as in money transactions.

For example   The following FUNCTION procedure defines theCash as CURRENCY type in the function heading so that Visual Basic can check the type of values passed to it. The procedure then calculates and returns the amount of sales tax as a CURRENCY-type value.

```
FUNCTION SalesTax (theCash AS CURRENCY,
theRate AS SINGLE) AS CURRENCY
SalesTax = theCash * CCUR(theRate)
END FUNCTION
```

See also   COMMON statement
DIM statement
STATIC statement
TYPE statement
ANY data type

CONTROL data type
DOUBLE data type
FORM data type
INTEGER data type
LONG data type
SINGLE data type
STRING data type

CVI, CVL, CVS, CVD, CVC, CVSMBF, and CVDMBF

Purpose The CVI, CVL, CVS, CVD, CVC, CVSMBF, and CVDMBF functions convert string representations of numbers stored in a random access file with a FIELD statement back into numbers. These functions are not available in Visual Basic for Windows.

Syntax

CVI(*number$*)	'Integer
CVL(*number$*)	'Long
CVS(*number$*)	'Single
CVD(*number$*)	'Double
CVC(*number$*)	'Currency
CVSMBF(*number$*)	'Single MBF
CVDMBF(*number$*)	'Double MBF

Arguments *number$* is a string representation of a number of the indicated type.

Description The CV*xx* functions are used with the FIELD statement and the MK*x*$ functions to store numbers in a random access file. The FIELD statement can store strings only in a random access file, so the MK*x*$ functions convert numbers into string-like values. The CV*x* functions convert the string-like values back into numbers. Note that these string-like values are not string representations of a number, but the binary values with a string header to make the system think they're strings. These functions are somewhat out of date; newer programs use the TYPE statement instead to define fields in a random-access file.

MBF is a Microsoft Binary Format numeric string.

15

Returns   The result is a number of the indicated type.

For example   The following assignment statement converts a string-like number (A$) from a random access file into a usable number:

```
aVal - CVS(A$)
```

See also   FIELD statement
OPEN statement
MKX() functions

 DATA

Purpose   The DATA statement defines a set of data values within a program. This statement is not available in Visual Basic for Windows.

Syntax   DATA *value1, value2,...*

Arguments   *value1* and *value2* are comma-delimited lists of numeric or string constants. You must enclose strings in double quotation marks.

Description   The DATA statement defines an internal set of values, which are read into variables using the READ statement. Use the RESTORE statement to set a particular DATA statement as the next one to be read.

For example   The following statements define some values with a DATA statement, use RESTORE to set that DATA statement as the next one to be read, and then read the values into some variables with a READ statement:

```
label1: DATA 27.5, 34, "gold", 0.234
        RESTORE label1
        READ aVal, aNum, Z$, theFrac
```

See also   READ statement
RESTORE statement

# DATE$

Purpose	The DATE$ function gets and returns the current date from the system clock.
Syntax	**DATE$**
Arguments	None
Description	The DATE$ function gets the system date in a string. Use the DATE$ statement to set the date. To get the current date as a date number, use the NOW function or apply the DATEVALUE() function to the string returned by DATE$.
Returns	The result is a string containing the system date in the format:

mm-dd-yyyy

where *mm* is the month, *dd* is the day, and *yyyy* is the year.

For example   The following assignment statement assigns the current date to the string variable A$:

```
A$ = DATE$      'Assign the current date to A$
```

See also
DATE$ statement
TIME$ statement
DATESERIAL() function
DATEVALUE() function
DAY() function
HOUR() function
MINUTE() function
MONTH() function
NOW function
SECOND() function
TIME$ function
TIMER function
TIMESERIAL() function
TIMEVALUE() function
WEEKDAY() function
YEAR() function

S DATE$

Purpose The DATE$ statement sets the system clock.

Syntax **DATE$** = *datestring$*

Arguments *datestring$* is a string containing the date to which to set the clock, in one of the following formats:

mm-dd-yyyy
mm-dd-yy
mm/dd/yy
mm/dd/yyyy

where *mm* is the month, *dd* is the day, and *yy* or *yyyy* is the year. The year must be between 1980 and 2099.

Description The DATE$ statement sets the date in the system clock. Depending on your system, you also may have to run a setup program to change the date permanently.

For example The following statement sets the system date to January 1, 1992:

DATE$ = "1/1/1992"

You also could use

DATE$ = "01/01/1992"

See also TIME$ statement
DATE$ function
DATESERIAL() function
DATEVALUE() function
DAY() function
HOUR() function
MINUTE() function
MONTH() function
NOW function
SECOND() function
TIME$ function
TIMER function
TIMESERIAL() function
TIMEVALUE() function
WEEKDAY() function
YEAR() function

☐F☐ DATESERIAL

Purpose The DATESERIAL function calculates a serial date number from the month, day and year.

Syntax **DATESERIAL(**`year%,month%,day%`**)**

Arguments `year%` is the year as a numeric value between 1753 and 2078, or a formula that evaluates to a number in that range. The last two digits of the date can be used for dates after 1900.

`month%` is the month as a number from 1 to 12, or a formula that evaluates to a number in that range.

`day%` is the day as a number from 1 to 31, or a formula that evaluates to a number in that range.

Description The DATESERIAL() function converts numeric expressions representing the month, day, and year to a serial date number.

The month, day, and year are integer values depicting the date. The serial date number is a double-precision, floating point number—rather than INTEGER or LONG—because it also stores the time to the right of the decimal. Using serial date numbers, you quickly can figure out the number of days between two events by simply subtracting the serial date numbers. Serial date numbers containing the time can be added to serial date numbers containing the date to store both the date and time in the same number.

Returns The result is the serial date number. A serial date number is a double-precision number containing the date, represented as the number of days since December 30, 1899. Negative serial date numbers represent dates from January 1, 1753, to December 30, 1899. Times are represented as fractions of a day. Years after 1900 are represented by the same serial date numbers used in several popular spreadsheet programs.

For example The following statement stores the serial date number (31853.0) for March 17, 1987, in the variable `theDate`:

```
theDate = DATESERIAL(1987,3,17)   'the date
                                  'number for
                                  '3/17/87
```

15

See also

DATE$ statement
TIME$ statement
DATE$ function
DATEVALUE() function
DAY() function
HOUR() function
MINUTE() function
MONTH() function
NOW function
SECOND() function
TIME$ function
TIMER function
TIMESERIAL() function
TIMEVALUE() function
WEEKDAY() function
YEAR() function

 DATEVALUE

Purpose   The DATEVALUE function calculates a serial date number from a string containing a date.

Syntax   **DATEVALUE(***date$***)**

Arguments   *date$* is a string containing the date to which to set the clock, in one of the following formats:

mm-dd-yyyy
mm-dd-yy
mm/dd/yy
mm/dd/yyyy

where *mm* is the month, *dd* is the day, and *yy* or *yyyy* is the year. It also can recognize the month as a word or abbreviation, as in the following examples:

March 18, 1990
Dec. 21, 1982
24-July-1985
16-Nov-1988

Description   The DATEVALUE() function converts a string containing the date to a serial date number.

The serial date number is a double-precision, floating-point number that stores the date to the left of the decimal and the time to the right. Using serial date numbers, you quickly can figure out the number of days between two events by simply subtracting the serial date numbers. Serial date numbers containing the time can be added to serial date numbers containing the date to store both the date and time in the same number.

Returns   The result is the serial date number. A serial date number is a double-precision number containing the date represented as the number of days since December 30, 1899. Negative serial date numbers represent dates from January 1, 1753, to December 30, 1899. Times are represented as fractions of a day. Years after 1900 are represented by the same serial date numbers used in several popular spreadsheet programs.

For example   The following statement stores the serial date number (31853.0) for March 17, 1987, in the variable theDate:

```
theDate = DATEVALUE("March 17, 1987")   'the date
                                        'number for
                                        '3/17/87
```

See also   DATE$ statement
TIME$ statement
DATE$ function
DATESERIAL() function
DAY() function
HOUR() function
MINUTE() function
NOW function
SECOND() function
TIME$ function
TIMER function
TIMESERIAL() function
TIMEVALUE() function
WEEKDAY() function
YEAR() function

 DAY

Purpose   The DAY function calculates the day of the month from a serial date number.

Syntax   **DAY(***serialdate#***)**

Arguments   *serialdate#* is a serial date number. A serial date number is a double-precision number containing the date, represented as the number of days since December 30, 1899. Negative serial date numbers represent dates from January 1, 1753 to December 30, 1899. Times are represented as fractions of a day. Years after 1900 are represented by the same serial date numbers used in several popular spreadsheet programs.

Description   The DAY() function takes a serial date number and returns the day of the month represented by that number.

Use the MONTH() and YEAR() functions to extract the month and year. To extract the time, use the HOUR(), MINUTE(), and SECOND() functions.

Returns   The result is the day of the month as an integer from 1 to 31.

For example   The following statement extracts the day of the month from the serial date number for March 17, 1987:

```
theDay = DAY(318530)      'Extracts the day (17)
                         'from the date number
```

See also   DATE$ statement
TIME$ statement
DATE$ function
DATESERIAL() function
DATEVALUE() function
HOUR() function
MINUTE() function
MONTH() function
NOW function
SECOND() function
TIME$ function
TIMER function
TIMESERIAL() function
TIMEVALUE() function
WEEKDAY() function
YEAR() function

DECLARE (Visual Basic Procedures)

Purpose This version of the DECLARE statement defines the interface to all Visual Basic procedures defined in a program.

Syntax **DECLARE {FUNCTION¦SUB}** *procname* [**(**[*arglist*]**)**]

Arguments SUB indicates the procedure is a SUB procedure and does not return a value.

FUNCTION indicates the procedure is a FUNCTION and does return a value.

procname is the name the procedure is to have in the program as literal text, not a quoted string or variable.

arglist is the argument list to be passed to the external procedure. This argument list has the following syntax:

↳ [**BYVAL**] *arg*[**()**][**AS** *type*][**,**[**BYVAL**]*arg*[**()**]
[**AS** *type*]]...

BYVAL indicates the following argument is to be passed as a value rather than as an address that points to the variable containing the value. Numbers are passed as the type indicated in the statement. Strings are passed as an address to a null-terminated string.

arg is a variable name. Only the type has meaning here. Follow array variables with empty parentheses.

type is one of the following Visual Basic types: ANY, CONTROL, CURRENCY, FORM, INTEGER, LONG, SINGLE, DOUBLE, or STRING. Use the AS *type* clause or a type suffix symbol, but not both, to declare the type of the variable. (See the beginning of this chapter for information on suffix symbols.) The ANY type is not allowed as the type of a function.

Description The DECLARE statement defines the interface to an internal Visual Basic procedure. Visual Basic normally creates these statements automatically.

For example The following declares the interface to the procedure InvertRect. It has two arguments: hdc, which is passed by value, and a user defined type, lpRect, passed by address.

```
DECLARE FUNCTION InvertRect (BYVAL hdc,lpRect AS RECT)
```

See also DECLARE (non-BASIC procedures) statement
CALL statement
FUNCTION statement
SUB statement

15

 # DECLARE (Non-BASIC Procedures)

Purpose   The DECLARE statement for non-BASIC procedures defines the interface to a procedure in an external library. The Visual Basic for Windows version of this statement is significantly different.

Syntax ⤸   **DECLARE SUB** *procname* [**CDECL**] [**ALIAS** *procalias$*]
[([*arglist*])]

⤸ **DECLARE FUNCTION** *procname* [**CDECL**] [**ALIAS**
procalias$] [([*arglist*])] [**AS** *type*]

Arguments   SUB indicates the procedure is a SUB procedure and does not return a value.

FUNCTION indicates the procedure is a FUNCTION and does return a value.

procname is the name the procedure is to have in the program as literal text, not a quoted string or variable.

CDECL indicates that the routine uses C-type arguments and calling sequence.

procalias$ is the name of the procedure in the external library, if the name differs from *procname*. Use this argument to change the name of a procedure if it conflicts with a name in Visual Basic.

arglist is the argument list to be passed to the external procedure. This argument list has the following syntax:

⤸ [**BYVAL¦SEG**] *arg*[**()**][**AS** *type*][**,**[**BYVAL¦SEG**]
arg[**()**][**AS** *type*]]...

BYVAL indicates that the following argument is to be passed as a value rather than as an address that points to the variable containing the value. Numbers are passed as the type indicated in the statement. Strings are passed as an address to a null-terminated string.

SEG indicates the following argument is to be passed as a segmented address (a far address).

arg is a variable name. Only the type has meaning here. Follow array variables with empty parentheses.

type is one of the following Visual Basic types: ANY, CONTROL, CURRENCY, FORM, INTEGER, LONG, SINGLE, DOUBLE, or STRING. Use the AS *type* clause or a variable suffix symbol, but not both, to declare the type of the variable. (See the beginning of this chapter for information on suffix symbols.) The ANY type is not allowed as the type of a function.

Description The DECLARE statement defines the interface to an external procedure so that a Visual Basic program can call that procedure in the same manner as any internally defined procedure (a normal, user-defined procedure in a program). The Quick library (QuickLib, or .QLB) file containing the procedure must be attached to Visual Basic. Use the /L *libname* option when starting Visual Basic to attach the library. The Lib version of the library (.LIB) must be available to compile a program using this procedure.

For example The following declares the interface to the library function InvertRect. It has two arguments: hdc, which is passed by value, and a user defined type, lpRect, passed by address.

```
DECLARE FUNCTION InvertRect
BYVAL hdc,lpRect AS RECT)
```

See also DECLARE (BASIC procedures) statement
CALL statement
FUNCTION statement
SUB statement

DEF FN

Purpose The DEF FN statement defines an internal function. This statement is not available in Visual Basic for Windows.

Syntax **DEF FN***procname* [(*params*)] = *expression*

or

DEF FN*name*[(*params*)]
    [*block of statements*]
FN*name* = *expression*
    [*block of statements*]
[**EXIT DEF**]
    [*block of statements*]
END DEF

Arguments   *procname* is the argument list for the function in the following syntax:

> [**BYVAL**] *arg*[()][**AS** *type*][,[**BYVAL**]*arg*[()]
> [**AS** *type*]]...

BYVAL indicates the following argument is to be passed as a value, rather than as an address that points to the variable containing the value. Numbers are passed as the type indicated in the statement. Strings are passed as an address to a null-terminated string.

arg is a variable name. Only the type has meaning here. Follow array variables with empty parentheses.

type is one of the following Visual Basic types: ANY, CONTROL, CURRENCY, FORM, INTEGER, LONG, SINGLE, DOUBLE, or STRING. Use the AS *type* clause or a variable suffix symbol, but not both, to declare the type of the variable. (See the beginning of this chapter for information on suffix symbols.) The ANY type is not allowed as the type of a function.

expression is a numerical or string formula.

Description   The DEF FN statement declares an internal function. This is largely for compatibility with older versions of BASIC, as a FUNCTION procedure is a much more portable way to declare a function.

For example   The following DEF FN statement defines a function named AddEmUp, which returns the sum of its arguments:

```
DEF FNAddEmUp(A,B)
FNAddEmUp = A + B
END DEF
```

See also   FUNCTION statement
SUB statement

 DEF SEG

Purpose   The DEF SEG statement sets the current segment base address. This statement is not available in Visual Basic for Windows.

Syntax   **DEF SEG** [[=] *base-addr%*]

Arguments   *base-addr%* is the base or starting address of the current segment in memory. The value is equal to the absolute memory address divided by 16.

Description   The DEF SEG statement defines the starting address of the current segment in memory. This provides the base address for the BSAVE, BLOAD, CALL ABSOLUTE, PEEK, and POKE statements, which use an offset from this value.

For example   The following statements set the segment address, load a memory image, and then execute that image, passing it the contents of the variable aValue. The offset from the beginning of the current segment is 10 bytes.

```
DEF SEG 4090
BLOAD "MYPROC.BIN",10
CALL ABSOLUTE (aValue,10)
```

See also   BLOAD statement
BSAVE statement
CALL ABSOLUTE statement
PEEK statement
POKE statement

S DEFtype

Purpose   The six DEF*type* statements declare default types for variables beginning with specific letters.

Syntax   **DEFCUR** *range*[,*range*]...   'Currency type
DEFINT *range*[,*range*]...   'Integer type
DEFLNG *range*[,*range*]...   'Long type
DEFSNG *range*[,*range*]...   'Single type
DEFDBL *range*[,*range*]...   'Double type
DEFSTR *range*[,*range*]...   'String type

Arguments   *range* is a single letter, or a range of letters. Ranges of letters are separated by a hyphen. The statements are not case-sensitive, so A-D is the same as a-d. The range A-Z is special in that it defines all variables as the specified type, including the extended characters with ASCII codes beyond 128 (see CHR$()).

Description   The DEF*type* statements define the default variable types for all variables beginning with a specific letter. Other forms of character typing (such as the character type suffix symbols), DIM statements, and COMMON statements override any definitions made by these statements. Each DEF*type* statement defines the letters or ranges of letters in its arguments as a specific type.

Use these in the declarations section of a form or module. The DEF*type* statements do not follow the rules of scope, but apply only to the module or form in which they are used.

For example The following statement defines all variables beginning with A, C, R, S, T, W, X, Y, or Z as the INTEGER data type:

```
DEFINT A,C,R-T,W-Z
```

The next statement defines all variables beginning with B, D, G, H, I, or J as the DOUBLE data type:

```
DEFDBL b,d,g-j
```

See also COMMON statement
DIM statement
STATIC statement

 DIM

Purpose The DIM statement defines variables and declares their type in forms and modules.

Syntax
```
DIM [SHARED] variable [([subscripts])]
[AS type][,variable [([subscripts])]
[AS type]]...
```

Arguments SHARED makes the declared variables accessible to other procedures in a module.

variable is a variable name. Array names are followed by parentheses and the subscript range.

subscripts can be up to 60 subscripts. Omit subscripts to define a dynamic array whose subscripts and size are defined later in a program with a REDIM statement. The syntax of the subscript ranges is

```
[lower% TO]upper%[,[lower% TO]upper%]...
```

lower% is the lower limit for the array subscripts. If this argument is omitted, 0 is assumed unless the OPTION BASE statement has been executed. (See the OPTION BASE statement for more information.)

upper% is the upper limit for array subscripts.

type is one of the following Visual Basic types: CONTROL, CURRENCY, FORM, INTEGER, LONG, SINGLE, DOUBLE, STRING, STRING*length*, or any user type defined with the TYPE statement. *length* is the length of a fixed-length string. Use the AS *type* clause or a variable suffix symbol, but not both, to declare the type of the variable. (See the beginning of this chapter for information on suffix symbols.)

Description   The DIM statement declares the type of variables and sets the dimensions of array-type variables. When defined, all arrays are initialized to 0. Use DIM SHARED at the module level to define variables available to the entire form or module. Alternatively, use DIM at the procedure level to define variables available only in a procedure. Use the COMMON statement to define global variables.

There are two types of arrays in Visual Basic: static and dynamic. *Static* arrays are defined with a fixed number of elements and thus have a fixed length. They can be redimensioned, but the new total size in bytes must be the same or less than the old size.

A *dynamic* array is defined initially at the global or module level with no dimensions. The size and dimensions are determined later, at the procedure level, with a REDIM statement. Memory is allocated for the array when the dimensions are added. Use the ERASE statement to deallocate the memory of dynamic arrays.

For example   The following statement defines the variable myFile as a string variable, then defines anArray as a two-dimensional array of integers. The first dimension of the array ranges from 3 to 6 and the second ranges from 0 to 10, giving a total of 44 elements in the array.

```
DIM myFile AS STRING, anArray(3 TO 6,10) AS INTEGER
```

See also   COMMON statement
CONST statement
ERASE statement
OPTION BASE statement
REDIM statement
STATIC statement
$DYNAMIC metacommand
$STATIC metacommand

15

 DIR$

Purpose	The DIR$ function returns a matched filename.
Syntax	**DIR$**[(*filespec$*)]
Arguments	*filespec$* is a string containing a filename, or a path and filename. A path specifies the location of a file in the directory system and has the following syntax:

[*drive*:][\]*directory*[*directory*]

where *drive* is the drive letter and *directory* is a directory name. Omit this argument to use the current drive. If you omit the first backslash, the path is assumed to start in the default directory of the specified drive. The filename in the file specification may contain the wildcard characters * and ?, where * matches any number of any characters and ? matches any single character. The *filespec$* argument must be specified the first time DIR$ is called. After the first time, if this argument is omitted, the name of the next file that matches the previous *filespec$* is returned.

Description The DIR$() function returns the filename of any file that matches the *filespec$* argument. To match multiple files in the same directory, omit the *filespec$* argument after the first call; the function returns the next matching file with each call. If no files match, the function returns the null string. DIR$() is particularly useful for testing for the existence of a file before trying to open it with the OPEN statement, because trying to use the OPEN statement with a nonexistent file for input causes an error.

Returns The result is a string containing the filename that matched the *filespec%* argument.

For example The following code fragment tests for the existence of a file before trying to open it. If the file doesn't exist, the fragment displays a message box instead of trying to open the file.

```
IF DIR$(FileName$) <> "" THEN
   OPEN FileName$ FOR INPUT AS #1
ELSE
   SGBOX "The File doesn't exist"
END IF
```

440

See also   CHDIR statement
CHDRIVE statement
KILL statement
MKDIR statement
NAME statement
RMDIR statement
DIR$ function

S DO/LOOP

Purpose   The DO/LOOP statement iterates a block of statements until a condition is true.

Syntax   **DO** [{**WHILE¦UNTIL**}] *condition*]
   [*statements*]
   [**EXIT DO**]
   [*statements*]
LOOP

or

DO
   [*statements*]
   [**EXIT DO**]
   [*statements*]
LOOP [{**WHILE¦UNTIL**} *condition*]

Arguments   WHILE is a keyword that indicates to iterate the loop while the condition is True.

UNTIL is a keyword that indicates to iterate the loop until the condition becomes True.

condition is a logical expression or value.

EXIT DO is a statement that causes immediate termination of the innermost loop and continuation of the program after the LOOP statement.

statements is a block of executable statements to be iterated.

15

Description   The DO/LOOP statement iterates a block of code until a condition changes. If you use the WHILE keyword, the block of statements is executed as long as the condition is True. If you use the UNTIL keyword, the block of statements is iterated until the condition becomes True. Use the EXIT DO statement to exit a loop prematurely.

For example   The following code fragment calculates the factorial of A by multiplying A times factorial, then reducing A by one. As long as A is greater than 1, the loop continues.

```
factorial = 1
DO WHILE A>1
   factorial = A*factorial
   A = A - 1
LOOP
```

See also   FOR/NEXT statement
WHILE/WEND statement

DOEVENTS

Purpose   The DOEVENTS function passes control to the system so that Visual Basic can process system events.

Syntax   **DOEVENTS()**

Arguments   None

Description   The DOEVENTS function passes control back to the Visual Basic system so that Visual Basic can process system events, such as updating windows and handling user input. Visual Basic does this automatically when it waits for an event to occur, such as a button being pressed. If you have a section of code that runs for a long time, you may want to pass control back to the system occasionally.

Be careful of passing control back during a Click event handler. You might get a second click on the object during the system update period, which would start a second copy of the procedure before the first one is done with what it was doing.

Returns   The result is the number of forms that Visual Basic has loaded.

For example   The following assignment statement executes the DOEVENTS function and stores the value returned in the variable A:

```
A = DOEVENTS()
```

See also   None

D DOUBLE

Purpose   The data type DOUBLE matches or defines double-precision, floating-point variables.

Syntax   *variable* **AS DOUBLE**

Arguments   *variable* is a variable name.

Description   The data type DOUBLE is used in SUB and FUNCTION procedure headings to declare a variable as a double-precision, floating-point type so that Visual Basic can check values passed to the procedure. DOUBLE also is used in DIM, GLOBAL, or STATIC statements to define a variable as double-precision, floating-point type. The DOUBLE data type is an 8-byte, floating point number that ranges from $-1.797693134862315 \times 10^{308}$ to $-4.94066 \times 10^{-324}$ for negative numbers and 4.94066×10^{-324} to $1.797693134862315 \times 10^{308}$ for positive numbers. You can also define the DOUBLE data type by appending the # character to the variable name. Double-precision constants are written with a D between the mantissa and the exponent (for example, $1.23456789 \times 10^{56} = 1.23456789D56$).

For example   The following procedure defines ANumber as a double-precision type in the function heading so that Visual Basic can check the type of values passed to it. The procedure then scales the value by dividing by 10,000.

```
SUB ScaleIt (ANumber AS DOUBLE)
ANumber = ANumber/10000#
END SUB
```

See also   COMMON statement
DIM statement
STATIC statement
TYPE statement

15

443

ANY data type
CONTROL data type
CURRENCY data type
FORM data type
INTEGER data type
LONG data type
SINGLE data type
STRING data type

 DRAG

Purpose   The DRAG method controls the dragging of controls on a form.

Syntax   `[form.][control.]DRAG [action%]`

Arguments   *control* is the name of a control on a form. If the control is on another form, include the name of the form as well. If the name of the form isn't included, this argument defaults to the control on the form containing the method.

action% is one of the following codes indicating the action to take concerning the dragging of a control:

0   Cancel the drag operation.

1   Begin the drag operation.

2   End the drag operation and drop the control.

Description   The DRAG method controls the dragging of controls. You need this method only when the control's DragMode property is set to manual. You normally execute a DRAG 1 when you get a MouseDown event in the control, then do a DRAG 2 when you get a MouseUp event in the control. The mouse determines where an outline of a control is dragged, but you must move the control with the MOVE method if you want the control to move and stay there. When you drag a control and then execute a DRAG 2 method for it, the object you're over gets a DragDrop event.

For example   The following three procedures manually drag a label across a form, then move the label to the new position when the mouse button is released. The label's DragMode property is set to 1 - manual:

↪ SUB Label1_MouseDown (Button AS INTEGER, Shift AS
INTEGER, X AS SINGLE, Y AS SINGLE)
Label1.DRAG 1
END SUB

↪ SUB Label1_MouseUp (Button AS INTEGER, Shift AS
INTEGER, X AS SINGLE, Y AS SINGLE)
Label1.DRAG 2
END SUB

↪ SUB Form_DragDrop (Source AS CONTROL, X AS SINGLE,
Y AS SINGLE)
Source.MOVE X, Y
END SUB

See also   MOVE method
DragOver event

S DRAW

Purpose   The DRAW statement executes commands stored in a Graphics Macro Language (GML) string. This statement is not available in Visual Basic for Windows.

Syntax   **DRAW** *gmlstring$*

Arguments   *gmlstring$* is a string containing GML commands. The following GML commands are allowed:

U*pixels* draws *pixels* upward.

D*pixels* draws *pixels* downward.

L*pixels* draws *pixels* left.

R*pixels* draws *pixels* right.

E*pixels* draws diagonally up and to the right.

F*pixels* draws diagonally down and to the right.

G*pixels* draws *pixels* down and to the left.

H*pixels* draws up and to the left.

15

445

M*x-pixels, y-pixels* draws a line from the current point to the point *x-pixels, y-pixels*.

M± *x-pixels,*± *y-pixels* draws a line relative to the current position.

B makes all the following drawing commands move the cursor without drawing.

N makes the following drawing command move the cursor back to the starting point after drawing.

A*angle* sets the drawing angle for future drawing (rotates the coordinate system). *angle* is one of the following values:

0	0 degrees
1	90 degrees
2	180 degrees
3	270 degrees

Figures rotated by 90 or 270 degrees are scaled by four-thirds so their shape won't change when they're rotated.

TA*degrees* is the relative rotation of the graphics-drawing coordinate system. *degrees* is the angle of rotation in a counterclockwise direction and ranges from –360 to +360.

C*color* sets the color for future drawing (see the COLOR statement).

S*scale-factor* sets the scale factor for future drawing commands. The value ranges from 1 to 255, and is equal to four times the number of pixels to move when drawing. The default is 4.

X*gmlstring$* executes the GML commands stored in the string variable *gmlstring$* and then returns.

P*fill-color,outline-color* paints a region with *fill-color*. The region must be bounded with *outline-color*. Both arguments are color attributes (see the COLOR statement).

Description The DRAW statement provides a way to execute a drawing program. Images are stored as codes in GML strings, which the DRAW statement plays back and draws on the screen. Arguments must be either integer numbers or a variable name preceded with an equal sign and followed with a semicolon. Codes are separated with semicolons, but the semicolons are required only when the code would be ambiguous. This command can be executed only if no forms are visible.

For example   The following statements create a GML string and draw it with the DRAW statement. The codes draw a red rectangle filled with blue.

```
z$ = "C4;BM200,100;U50;R100;D50;L100;P1,4"
DRAW z$
```

See also   CIRCLE statement
COLOR statement
LINE statement
SCREEN statement

 $DYNAMIC

Purpose   The $DYNAMIC metacommand specifies that all arrays declared in following DIM statements are to be dynamic. This statement is not available in Visual Basic for Windows.

Syntax   {REM¦'} **$DYNAMIC**

Arguments   REM and ' indicate that the line is a remark statement. Metacommands are compiler directives, and must be inserted as remark statements.

Description   The $DYNAMIC metacommand is a compiler directive specifying that all arrays defined in following DIM statements are dynamic arrays. Array storage is allocated at runtime instead of statically allocated at compile time. To change to static allocation, see the $STATIC metacommand. You can reallocate dynamic arrays at runtime to reuse the memory they occupied.

For example   The following statements have array A() declared as a static array, while array B() is dynamic:

```
DIM A(50)
REM $Dynamic
DIM B(75)
```

See also $STATIC metacommand

15

 END

Purpose	The END statement closes all files and ends a program.
Syntax	`END`
Arguments	None
Description	When executed, the END statement closes all open files and ends a program. To cause an interpreted program to pause, use the STOP statement rather than END. STOP is the same as END in a compiled program.
For example	The following procedure is attached to the Exit command of a **File** menu. When **Exit** is executed, this procedure is called to end the program.

```
SUB ExitCmd_Click ()
END
END SUB
```

See also	STOP statement

 ENDDOC

Purpose	The ENDDOC method tells the Printer object to start printing a document.
Syntax	`PRINTER.ENDDOC`
Arguments	None
Description	The ENDDOC method applies only to the PRINTER object. When printing a document, executing ENDDOC terminates the printing.
For example	The following procedure prints the string Something on the printer and then releases the page for printing:

```
SUB PrintSomething
PRINTER.PRINT "Something"
PRINTER.ENDDOC
END SUB
```

See also	NEWPAGE method

 ENVIRON

Purpose   The ENVIRON statement adds or changes a DOS environment variable. This statement is not available in Visual Basic for Windows.

Syntax   **ENVIRON** *environ-string$*

Arguments   *environ-string$* is a string containing the environment variable to add or change.

Description   DOS contains a table of strings, known as the *environment*. Several different DOS commands write into this table, including PATH and SET. Most entries consist of a variable name, an equal sign, and a string of information. Applications also can leave messages in this table for later applications.

For example   The following procedure changes the contents of the DOS Path variable:

```
ENVIRON "PATH=C;\;F:\VBDOS"
```

See also   ENVIRON$() function

 ENVIRON$

Purpose   The ENVIRON$() function reads a DOS environment variable from the operating system.

Syntax   **ENVIRON$({** *name$¦number%* **})**

Arguments   *name$* is a string containing the name of the environment variable to return.

number% is the number of the environment variable to return, counting from the top of the table.

Description   DOS contains a table of strings, known as the *environment*. Several different DOS commands write into this table, including PATH and SET. Most entries consist of a variable name, an equals sign, and a string of information. Applications also can leave messages in this table for later applications. The function is case-sensitive, so the string in *name$* must be all uppercase.

449

Returns The resulting string contains the requested environment variable. The ENVIRON$() function returns the contents of one entry in this string table. If you call the function with a number as the argument, it returns that string from the table, including the variable name and the equal sign. If you call the function with the variable name, it returns only the string to the right of the equal sign.

For example The following statement prints the contents of the PATH variable on the current form:

```
PRINT ENVIRON$("PATH")
```

See also ENVIRON statement

 EOF

Purpose The EOF() function returns True if the next item to be read from a disk file is the end-of-file mark.

Syntax EOF(*filenumber%*)

Arguments *filenumber%* is the file number used when the file was opened.

Description An attempt to read beyond the end-of-file mark of a disk file generates an error. To prevent this, execute the EOF() function before each read operation.

Returns The resulting value is True (–1) or False (0), depending on whether the end-of-file has been read.

For example The following code fragment reads a file until it reads the end-of-file mark:

```
DO UNTIL EOF(1)
  LINE INPUT #1,A$
  Printer.PRINT A$
LOOP
```

See also None

O EQV

Purpose The EQV operator combines two logical expressions, or all the bits in two numeric values, using the logical equivalence operation.

Syntax *express1* **EQV** *express2*

Arguments *express1* and *express2* are logical expressions, numeric expressions, or numeric values.

Description The EQV operator combines two logical values according to the following truth table. If two numeric values are combined, the operator is applied bit-by-bit to the corresponding bits in the two values. That is, each bit in the result is equal to the logical equivalence of the corresponding bits in the two values.

A	B	A EQV B
True	True	True
True	False	False
False	True	False
False	False	True

Returns The logical EQV of the two expressions equals True (–1) or False (0) if *express1* and *express2* are logical expressions. If *express1* and *express2* are numeric expressions, the result is the bitwise logical EQV of the same bits in each of the two expressions.

For example The following IF statement causes a beep if both A and B are True, or if both A and B are False:

```
IF A EQV B THEN BEEP
```

See also AND operator
IMP operator
NOT operator
OR operator
XOR operator

15

451

S ERASE

Purpose   The ERASE statement zeroes static arrays and deallocates dynamic arrays.

Syntax   **ERASE** *array* [*,array*]...

Arguments   *array* is an array variable to erase.

Description   The ERASE statement performs two different functions, depending on the array type. There are two types of arrays in Visual Basic: static and dynamic. *Static* arrays are defined with a fixed number of elements and thus have a fixed length. They can be redimensioned, but the new total size in bytes must be the same or less than the old size. ERASE zeroes all the elements of a static array.

A *dynamic* array initially is defined with no elements. The size is determined later, with a REDIM statement. Memory is allocated for the array when the dimensions are added. ERASE deallocates the memory of dynamic arrays and returns it to the system. When a dynamic array is erased, you must give it dimensions again before you can use it.

For example   The following statement defines anArray as an 11-element array:

```
DIM anArray(10)
```

The next three statements fill each element with the number 0.

```
FOR I = 0 TO 10
  anArray(i) = 0
NEXT I
```

The last line performs exactly the same function as the preceding three lines using the ERASE statement:

```
ERASE anArray
```

See also   CONST statement
DIM statement
GLOBAL statement
OPTION BASE statement
REDIM statement
STATIC statement
$DYNAMIC metacommand
$STATIC metacommand

ERDEV, ERDEV$

Purpose   The ERDEV and ERDEV$ functions return the name and error from the last device experiencing a critical error. These functions are not available in Visual Basic for Windows.

Syntax   **ERDEV**
ERDEV$

Arguments   None

Description   The ERDEV function returns the error code for the last device experiencing a critical error. The function returns a two-byte number, with the DOS error number in the lower byte and the device header information in the upper byte. To extract the upper or lower byte, mask the returned value by using a logical AND to combine it with &HFF00 (upper) or &H00FF (lower).

The ERDEV$ function returns a string containing the name of the device that experienced the error.

Returns   ERDEV returns the error number. ERDEV$ returns the name of the device experiencing the error.

For example   The following two statements extract the error number and the device:

```
errnum = ERDEV AND &H00FF 'get the error number
Dev Name = ERDEV$   'Assign the value 1 to aVal
```

See also   ERL function
ERR function

ERL

Purpose   The ERL function returns the line number of the line that generated the last error (or, if not all lines are numbered, the line number of the closest numbered line, if any, before the line that generated the last error).

Syntax   **ERL**

Arguments   None

Description The ERL function, along with the ERR function, usually is used in an error trap created with the ON ERROR GOTO statement. They both are zeroed by the RESUME statement, a SUB or FUNCTION call within an error handler, or another ON ERROR statement, so save the values if you want to use them. Because most modern programs do not have line numbers, this statement isn't very useful. If you need to know which line in your code is having an error, number the lines in that part of the code and use the ERL function in your error procedure.

Returns The result is the line number. If all lines are numbered, this result is the number of the line that had the last error. If not all lines are numbered, it is the closest numbered line before the statement with the error. The function returns 0 if there are no line numbers in a procedure.

For example The following statement goes in an error trap using ERR, the ERROR$ function, and ERL to print the text description of the last error and the line number of the line that generated the error:

```
MSGBOX ERROR$(ERR) + " At line number:" + STR$(ERL)
```

See also ERR statement
ERROR statement
ON ERROR GOTO statement
ERDEV function
ERDEV$ function
ERR function
ERROR$() function

 ERR

Purpose The ERR function returns the error number of the last error.

Syntax **ERR**

Arguments None

Description The ERR function, along with the ERL function, usually is used in an error trap created with the ON ERROR GOTO statement. Both functions are zeroed by the RESUME statement, a SUB or FUNCTION call, or another ON ERROR statement, so save the values if you want to use them. Use the ERROR$() function to get the text of the error from the error number.

Returns The result is the error number of the last error. Table 13.1 lists the errors and error numbers.

For example The following statement goes in an error trap to print the description of the error by using ERR and the ERROR$ function, and to print the line number by using ERL:

```
MSGBOX ERROR$(ERR) + " At line number:" + STR$(ERL)
```

See also ERR statement
ERROR statement
ON ERROR GOTO statement
ERDEV function
ERDEV$ function
ERL function
ERROR$() function

ERR

Purpose The ERR statement sets the value of ERR.

Syntax **ERR** = *value%*

Arguments *value%* is the error number to which to set ERR in the range 0 to 32,767. Table 13.1 lists Visual Basic's error numbers.

Description The ERR function, along with the ERL function, usually is used in an error trap created with the ON ERROR GOTO statement. Both functions are zeroed by the RESUME statement, a SUB or FUNCTION call, or another ON ERROR statement, so save the values if you want to use them. Use the ERR statement to set a Visual Basic or user-defined error type to communicate error information between procedures. Setting ERR does not cause an error condition; use the ERROR statement to initiate a user-defined error or to simulate a BASIC error.

A possible use for a user-defined error code is to reuse an existing error handler for a user-defined error or condition, such as "parameter out of range."

For example The following statement sets ERR to 36, one of Visual Basic's unused error codes:

```
ERR = 36
```

See also ERROR statement
ON ERROR GOTO statement
ERDEV function
ERDEV$ function
ERL function
ERR function
ERROR$() function

 ERROR

Purpose The ERROR statement initiates an error condition in Visual Basic.

Syntax **ERROR** *errornumber%*

Arguments *errornumber%* is an error number—either one of Visual Basic error numbers from Table 13.1, or one of the unused codes as a user-defined error.

Description The ERROR statement either simulates a Visual Basic error condition or initiates a user-defined error condition. If an error trap is in place, the error trap is called when this statement is executed. If an error trap is not active, Visual Basic displays an error message and ends the program.

A possible use for a user-defined error code is to reuse an existing error handler for a user-defined error or condition, such as "parameter out of range."

For example The following statement simulates an overflow error (error code 6):

```
ERROR 6
```

See also ERR statement
ON ERROR GOTO statement
ERDEV function
ERDEV$ function
ERL function
ERR function
ERROR$() function

ERROR$

Purpose	The ERROR$() function returns the text description of an error number.
Syntax	**ERROR$(***errornumber%***)**
Arguments	*errornumber%* is an error number of any type, or a formula that evaluates to a number.
Description	The ERROR$() function gets a text description of an error condition. If the description is to contain a filename, a hole marked by two single quotation marks is left for the filename.
Returns	The result is a string describing the error number.
For example	The following procedure prints a table of all the Visual Basic error codes and their descriptions:

```
SUB Form_Click ()
FOR I = 1 TO 1000
  IF ERROR$(I) <> "User-defined error" THEN
    PRINTER.PRINT I, ERROR$(I)
  END IF
NEXT I
END SUB
```

See also	ERR statement
	ERROR statement
	ON ERROR GOTO statement
	ERDEV function
	ERDEV$ function
	ERL function
	ERR function

15

EVENT

Purpose	The EVENT statement globally enables or disables event trapping. This statement is not available in Visual Basic for Windows.
Syntax	**EVENT {On¦Off}**

Arguments On and Off are switches to enable or disable event trapping.

Description The EVENT statement globally enables or disables all event trapping. Individual types of trappable events are enabled or disabled with the COM, KEY, PEN, PLAY, STRIG, TIMER, and UEVENT statements. To compile code with event traps, the /W or /V switch must be used with the BC.EXE compiler.

Disabling event trapping speeds up compiled code because the code does not need to check whether the events have occurred. The EVENT statement only applies to the indicated event types. Form- and control-type events are not affected by this statement.

For example The following statements enable a 10-second timer event:

```
EVENT ON                       'Turn on event trapping
ON TIMER(10) GOSUB DoTimer     'Define the trap
TIMER ON                       'Enable the timer trap
WHILE TRUE                     'Wait for the event to
WEND                           'occur
END

DoTimer:                       'Jump here to handle the
PRINT "Got timer event"        'event
RETURN
```

See also COM statement
KEY statement
OFF statement
ON statement
PEN statement
PLAY statement
STRIG statement
TIMER statement
UEVENT statement

F EXP

Purpose The EXP() function calculates and returns the exponential of a number.

Syntax **EXP(**_number_**)**

Arguments _number_ is a number of any type, or a formula that evaluates to a number.

Description   The EXP() function calculates the exponential of a number. The exponential is the number **e** (2.71828...), the base of the natural logarithms, raised to the power *number*.

Returns   The result is the numeric value of **e** raised to the power *number*.

For example   The following two assignment statements calculate the exponential of 1, which returns the value of **e** (2.71828...), and the exponential of 4.7 (109.947):

```
A = EXP(1)      'Assigns the value of e to A
B = EXP(4.7)    'Assigns the exponential of 4.7 to B
```

See also   LOG() function

 FIELD

Purpose   The FIELD statement defines the contents of a record buffer. This statement is not available in Visual Basic for Windows.

Syntax   **FIELD** [#]*filenum%,* *len%* **AS** *variable$* [*,len%* **AS** *variable$*]...

Arguments   *filenum%* is the file number used by the OPEN statement to open the file.

len% is the length of a field, in characters.

variable$ is a string variable whose contents are to be stored in the field.

Description   The FIELD statement defines the contents of a random access file buffer. Note that this is an old statement, included for compatibility with older versions of BASIC. Use the TYPE statement for new programs.

When a random-access file is opened, the length of its file buffer is specified in bytes in the OPEN statement. The FIELD statement partitions that buffer into pieces, with each piece containing the contents of a single variable. Only string-type variables may be stored in a file buffer partitioned with a FIELD statement, so use the MKI$, MKL$, MKS$, MKD$, MKC$, MKSMBF$, and MKDMBF$ functions to convert numeric values into string-like values so they can be stored with a FIELD statement. Use the CVI, CVS, CVD, CVC, CVSMBF, and CVDMBF functions to convert the string-like variables back into numbers.

The FIELD statement specifies where the different variables are stored in the buffer. After that, whenever the variables are referenced, the specified contents of the buffer are accessed instead.

The number of bytes needed for each variable is determined by the type of that variable. The following table lists the lengths:

INTEGER	Two bytes
LONG	Four bytes
SINGLE	Four bytes
DOUBLE	Eight bytes
CURRENCY	Eight bytes
STRING	One byte per character

For example The following statements open a disk file for random access with six-byte records. The FIELD statement defines the first two bytes as the two-byte string A$ and the next four bytes as the four-byte string B$. Next, two variables are loaded: an integer and a single-precision, floating-point number. The MKI$ and MKS$ functions convert the numbers into string-like variables, which are stored in A$ and B$. Because the field statement has defined A$ and B$ as parts of the file buffer, the values stored in A$ and B$ are stored in the buffer as well. The PUT statement stores the buffer in the disk file.

```
OPEN "myfile.dat" FOR RANDOM AS #1 LEN = 6
FIELD #1, A$ As 2, B$ AS 4
anInteger% = 78
aSingle! = 32.7874
LSET A$ = MKI$(anInteger%)
LSET B$ = MKS$(aSingle!)
PUT #1,1
```

See also OPEN statement
MKC$ function
MKD$ function
MKI$ function
MKL$ function
MKS$ function
MKDMBF$ function
MKSMBF$ function

 FILEATTR

Purpose   The FILEATTR function returns information about an open file.

Syntax   `FILEATTR(`*filenumber%*`, `*attribute%*`)`

Arguments   *filenumber%* is the file number used in the OPEN statement when the file was opened.

attribute% is a code (1 or 2) indicating the attribute to return.

Description   The FILEATTR function returns either the mode of an open file or the operating system's handle for the file. The handle is an address of an address that points to a block of memory containing a file's buffers and other file information.

Returns   The resulting numeric value is the file mode if *attribute%* is 1, or the operating system's handle to the file if *attribute%* is 2. The modes returned are

1   Input
2   Output
4   Random
8   Append
32   Binary

See the OPEN statement for a description of the modes.

For example   The following statement stores the mode of file number 1 in the variable A.

`A = FILEATTR(1,1)`

See also   OPEN statement

 FILES

Purpose   The FILES statement lists all the files in a directory. This statement is not available in Visual Basic for Windows.

Syntax   `FILES [`*path$*`]`

Arguments   *path$* is a string containing a path to the directory to be listed. A path specifies the location of a directory in the directory system and has the following syntax:

[*drive:*][\]*directory*[*directory*]

where *drive* is the drive letter and *directory* is a directory name. Omit this argument to use the current drive. If you omit the first backslash, the path is assumed to start in the default directory of the specified drive. The filename in the file specification may contain the wildcard characters * and ?. The wildcard * matches any number of any characters, and ? matches any single character.

Description   The FILES statement lists all the files in a directory. Use this in the Immediate window to see what files are in the default directory.

For example   The following statement lists the files in the current directory:

FILES

The next statement lists the files in the myfiles directory on the C drive:

FILES "c:\myfiles"

See also   CHDIR statement
KILL statement
MKDIR statement
NAME AS statement
RMDIR statement

 FIX

Purpose   The FIX() function converts a number of any numeric type to an integer by truncating the fractional part.

Syntax   FIX(*number*)

Arguments   *number* is a number of any type, or a formula that evaluates to a number.

Description   The FIX() function converts a number in any numeric type to an integer by truncating the fractional part. Use this function to extract the whole number from a fractional number without rounding.

Returns The result is *number* converted to an integer.

For example The following table shows how CINT(), INT(), and FIX() convert different values:

Value	CINT	INT	FIX
3.7	4	3	3
3.4	3	3	3
–3.7	–4	–4	–3
–3.4	–3	–4	–3

See also CCCUR function
CDBL function
CLNG function
CSNG function
INT function

 # $FORM

Purpose The $FORM metacommand enables access to the properties of external forms. This statement is not available in Visual Basic for Windows.

Syntax {REM¦'} **$FORM** *formname*

Arguments REM and ' specify that the line is a remark. A metacommand is a compiler directive and must be placed in a remark statement.

formname is the literal name of the external form to whose properties you want access.

Description The $FORM metacommand enables access to the properties of other forms. Normally, you can access the properties of a form only within that form. This metacommand enables you to access the properties of another form. This metacommand must be in the declarations section of the form.

For example The following statements in Form1 access the properties of Form2:

```
REM $FORM Form2          'In the declarations section of
CONST False = 0          'Form1
                         'In some procedure in Form1
Form2.Visible = False    'Make Form2 invisible
```

See also $DYNAMIC metacommand
$FORM metacommand
$INCLUDE metacommand
$STATIC metacommand

FOR/NEXT

Purpose The FOR/NEXT statement iterates a block of statements a specified number of times.

Syntax **FOR** *counter* = *start* **TO** *end* [**STEP** *increment*]
   [*statements*]
   [**EXIT FOR**]
   [*statements*]
NEXT[*counter*,[*counter*]...]

Arguments *counter* is a variable to store the number of iterations of the loop.

start is the starting value of *counter*.

end is the ending value of *counter*.

increment is the amount to increment *counter* each time the loop iterates. If you omit this argument, 1 is assumed. This value may be negative if *end* is less than *start*, in which case the loop counts down rather than up.

EXIT FOR is a statement that causes immediate termination of the innermost loop and continuation of the program after the NEXT statement.

statements is a block of executable statements to be iterated.

Description The FOR/NEXT statement iterates a block of code a specified number of times, counted with a counter. Each time the loop iterates, the counter is incremented either by 1 or by the STEP value, if specified, and then compared to the ending value. If the counter is greater than the ending value, the loop terminates and execution continues with the statement after the NEXT statement. FOR/NEXT loops can be nested, and a single NEXT statement can terminate several loops by including the counters of each variable with the NEXT keyword. Use the EXIT FOR statement to exit a loop prematurely.

For example   The following code fragment calculates the factorial of A by looping A times with a FOR/NEXT loop and multiplying the counter, B, times factorial.

```
factorial = 1
FOR B = 1 TO A
   factorial = B*factorial
NEXT B
```

See also   DO/LOOP statement
WHILE/WEND statement

 FORM

Purpose   The data type FORM matches any form name passed to a SUB or FUNCTION procedure.

Syntax   *variable* **AS FORM**

Arguments   *variable* is a variable name.

Description   The data type FORM is used in SUB and FUNCTION procedure headings to declare a variable as type FORM so that a form name can be passed to a procedure. The variable then can be used as a form name.

For example   The following procedure defines aForm as a FORM type and adds the item Program One to the List1 list box on that form:

```
SUB AddProgram (aForm AS FORM)
aForm.List1.AddItem "Program One"
END SUB
```

See also   DECLARE statement
IF statement
TYPE statement
ANY data type
CONTROL data type

15

CURRENCY data type
DOUBLE data type
INTEGER data type
LONG data type
SINGLE data type
STRING data type

FORMAT$

Purpose The FORMAT$ function converts numbers into formatted text.

Syntax **FORMAT$(**`number`[`,theformat$`]**)**

Arguments `number` is a number of any type, or a formula that evaluates to a number.

`theformat$` is a string containing the formatting commands. If you omit this argument, the FORMAT$ function formats numbers in the same manner as the STR$() function. The formatting string has up to three sections delimited by semicolons. The format is

`"section1[;section2[;section3]]"`

If you include only `section1`, it applies to all numbers. If you have only two sections, `section1` applies to positive values and zeroes, and `section2` applies to negative values. If you include all three sections, `section1` applies to positive values, `section2` to negative values, and `section3` to zeroes.

Description The FORMAT$() function uses a specific format to convert numbers to text.

Create a formatting string with symbols placed wherever you want numbers in the resulting string. The following are the symbols usable in the FORMAT$ function:

\# A nonrequired digit. This is a placeholder for a digit. If a number has more digits to the left of the decimal than there are formatting characters, the extra digits are printed anyway. If there are less digits to the left of the decimal than there are formatting characters, the formatting characters are ignored. If there are more digits to the right of the decimal than there are formatting characters, the number is rounded to the number of formatting characters. Essentially, you're placing a formatting character everywhere you want a character to appear in the converted number.

0   A required digit. This is placeholder for a digit, and is the same as the # placeholder except that leading and trailing zeroes are included. If the converted number does not have a digit in this position, a zero is inserted. For example, numbers formatted with "0.00" always have a leading zero if there are no characters to the left of the decimal, and always have two characters to the right of the decimal.

.   A placeholder for the decimal point. Place this in the string of placeholders where you want the decimal point to appear.

%   A placeholder for a percent sign. This character multiplies by 100 the number being formatted.

,   A placeholder for a comma to separate thousands. Placing two commas adjacent to each other causes FORMAT$ to omit the three digits that would have appeared between them. Placing a comma immediately to the left of the decimal causes FORMAT$ to omit the first three characters to the left of the decimal.

E+, E-, e+, e-   Converts the number in scientific format (a number times a power of 10, the exponent) by following the number with an E or e and then the power of 10. If you follow the E with a minus sign, negative exponents will have a minus sign. If you follow the E with a plus sign, positive exponents will have plus signs and negative numbers will have minus signs.

:   The time separator for converting a serial date number into a time. Insert a colon between hours and minutes and between minutes and seconds.

( )   Surrounding a number, these symbols cause negative numbers to be surrounded by parentheses.

$ Inserted as a literal character.

+, -   Inserted where they appear in the formatting string.

\   Displays the following character as a literal.

" "   Any characters enclosed in double quotation marks are

	inserted as literal characters. To insert a double quotation mark, use the CHR$(34) function.
/	Separator for converting a serial date number into a printed date. Use this character to separate the day from the month and the month from the year.
d	Displays the day without a leading 0.
dd	Displays the day with a leading 0.
ddd	Displays the abbreviated name of a day of the week (for example, Mon, Tue).
dddd	Displays the full text of the day of the week (for example, Monday).
ddddd	Displays a complete date in the format mm/dd/yy.
m	Displays the month without a leading 0.
mm	Displays the month with a leading 0.
mmm	Displays the abbreviation for the month.
mmmm	Displays the full text of the month's name.
yy	Displays the year as a two-digit number.
yyyy	Displays the day as a complete year.
h	Displays the hour.
hh	Displays the hour with a leading 0.
m	Displays the minutes.
mm	Displays the minutes with a leading 0.
s	Displays the seconds.
ss	Displays the seconds with a leading zero.
tttt	Displays a complete time in the format hh:mm:ss (a.m.).
AM/PM	Converts a time to a 12-hour clock; uses A.M. and P.M.
am/pm	Converts a time to a 12-hour clock; uses a.m. and p.m.
A/P	Converts a time to a 12-hour clock; uses A and P to specify morning and afternoon.

a/p	Converts time to a 12-hour clock; uses a and p to specify morning and afternoon.

Returns The resulting string contains the number formatted according to the designated format.

For example Using the FORMAT$() function and formatting strings often is confusing. The best way to set up a formatting string is to experiment with it in the Immediate window. Open the Immediate window and start typing PRINT statements into it, trying different variations of the FORMAT$() function. The following table lists the different values and variations of the formatting string:

n	FORMAT$(n,"0.00")	FORMAT$(n,"#.##")
.023	0.02	.02
38	38.00	38.
27.999	28.00	28.

n	FORMAT$(n,"0.000")	FORMAT$("#.###")
27.999	27.999	27.999

n	FORMAT$(n,"$0.00;($0.00)")	
15.35	$15.35	
−15.35	($15.35)	

n	FORMAT$(n,"mm/dd/yy")	FORMAT$(n,"hh:mm:ss")
34359.6	01-25-94	14:24:00

n	FORMAT$(n,"dd mmm yyyy")	FORMAT$(n,"mmmm yyyy")
34359.6	25 Jan 1994	January 1994

n	FORMAT$(n,"mm/dd/yy hh:mmAM/PM")
34459.6	05-05-94 02:24PM

n	FORMAT$(n,"+0.000E+00")	FORMAT$(n,"0.000E-00")
34459.6.	3.446E+04	3.446E04

n	FORMAT$(n,"#,###,###.0")	FORMAT$(n,"#,###,.")
1000000	1,000,000.0	3.446E04

See also HEX$() function
OCT$() function
STR$() function

FRE

Purpose The FRE() function returns the amount of available memory. This statement is not available in Visual Basic for Windows.

Syntax **FRE**(*number* | *string$*)

Arguments *number* is a numeric code that determines the block of memory to examine. Using any other number causes an illegal function call error message. The codes are

-1   Bytes of free far memory

-2   Bytes of free stack space

-3   KBytes of free expanded memory

string$ is a string variable or a literal string. If a string variable is used, the function returns the number of bytes available in the segment where the variable is stored. If a literal string is used, it returns the number of bytes of string space available.

Description The FRE() function examines memory and returns the amount of memory available in the memory segment indicated by the code. For string-type variables, the FRE() function also initiates "garbage collection"; that is, the collection of all free string space into a single, contiguous block.

Returns The result is the amount of memory available in the indicated area. FRE(-3) returns the error "Feature Unavailable" if there is no expanded memory available.

For example The following assignment statement assigns the amount of string memory to the variable StrMem:

```
StrMem = FRE("hello")     'get free string memory
```

See also CLEAR statement
ERASE statement

 FREEFILE

Purpose The FREEFILE function gets a valid file number for use with an OPEN statement.

Syntax FREEFILE

Arguments None

Description When opening and closing many files, you can become confused about which files are open and what file numbers they're using. Because you cannot have more than one file open with the same file number, use this function to supply an available file number.

Returns The result is the next available file number.

For example The following assignment statement assigns the first available file number to the variable FileNum%:

```
FileNum% = FREEFILE
```

See also OPEN statement

 FUNCTION

Purpose The FUNCTION statement declares the interface to a function procedure.

Syntax [**STATIC**] **FUNCTION** *procname* [(*arglist*)][**AS** *type*]
[*statements*]
[*procname* = *expression*]
[**EXIT FUNCTION**]
[*statements*]
[*procname* = *expression*]
END FUNCTION

Arguments STATIC indicates the variables of the procedure do not go away when the procedure exits.

procname is the name the procedure is to have in the program.

arglist is the argument list to be passed to the procedure. The argument list can have the following syntax:

[BYVAL] *arg*[**()**][**AS** *type*][**,**[**BYVAL**]*arg*[**()**][**AS** *type*]]...

BYVAL indicates the following argument is to be passed as a value rather than as an address that points to the variable containing the value. Numbers are passed as the type indicated in the statement. Strings are passed as an address to a null-terminated string.

arg is a variable name. Follow array variables with empty parentheses.

type is one of the following Visual Basic types: CONTROL, CURRENCY, FORM, INTEGER, LONG, SINGLE, DOUBLE, STRING, or a user-defined type. Use the AS *type* clause or a variable suffix symbol, but not both, to declare the type of a variable or function. (See the beginning of this chapter for information on suffix symbols.)

EXIT FUNCTION is a statement that exits the function before reaching the end.

statements is some or no statements.

procname = *expression* Before exiting, you must assign a value to the function's name if you want the function to return a value.

Description   The FUNCTION statement defines the interface to an internal function procedure so that a Visual Basic program can call it. The interface contains the arguments and types, and the type of the value returned by the function. Internal functions must have parentheses even if they have no arguments. To use an internal function without parentheses, define it in a DECLARE statement.

Returns   The result is whatever the function is programmed to return.

For example   The following function calculates and returns the factorial of the number N. Because N is changed in the function and you don't want it changed in the calling procedure, it is passed the function by value (BYVAL) so that only the local copy is changed.

```
FUNCTION Factorial (BYVAL N AS INTEGER) AS LONG
Factorial = 1
WHILE N>0
  Factorial = Factorial * N
  N = N - 1
WEND
END FUNCTION
```

See also   CALL statement
DECLARE statement
SUB statement

GET (File I/O)

Purpose   The GET statement reads a record from a random access or binary disk file.

Syntax   `GET [#]filenumber%[,recnum&][,recvariable]`

Arguments   *filenumber%* is the file number used when the file was opened with the OPEN statement.

recnum& is the number of the record to get in a random access file. If you omit this argument, the next record in the file is returned. File records are consecutively numbered with the first record as record number 1. If the file is opened as binary, *recnum&* is the byte number at which to start reading.

recvariable is a variable to hold the contents of the record whose length is less than or equal to the length of a record defined when the file is opened. This is usually a user-defined variable, defined with the TYPE statement. If you omit this variable, the record contents must have been defined with the FIELD statement.

Description   The GET statement reads a record's worth of data from a random access or binary disk file into a record variable. The record variable can be any type of variable as long as its total length is less than the length of a record. For random access files, the length of a record is defined with the LEN *reclen* clause of the OPEN statement. In most cases, you define a record-type variable with the TYPE statement and use that variable to access the disk file. The default length is 128 bytes. You also can use the FIELD statement, although that is archaic. For binary files, the record length is as many bytes as can fit into the record variable.

For example   The following statements first define the record variable DayType in the module header. They then define the variable aDay as type DayType, open a disk file whose name is stored in the variable FileName, and read the first 128-byte record into aDay.

15

In the module header:

```
TYPE DayType           'Type declaration for the
TheDate AS DOUBLE      'record DayType, 128 bytes
Flags AS INTEGER       'long
MSG AS STRING * 118
END TYPE
```

In a procedure:

```
DIM aDay AS DayType
OPEN FileName FOR RANDOM AS #1 LEN = 128
GET #1, 1, aDay
```

See also   OPEN statement
PUT statement

GET (Graphics)

Purpose   The GET statement puts a copy of a graphics image into an variable. This statement is not available in Visual Basic for Windows.

Syntax   GET [**STEP**](*x1!*,*y1!*)-[**STEP**](*x2!*,*y2!*),
array[(*index%*)]

Arguments   STEP is a keyword that indicates that the following coordinate is relative to the current graphics position.

x1! and *y1!* are the *x, y* coordinates of the upper-left corner of the image to be captured.

x2! and *y2!* are the *x, y* coordinates of the lower-right corner of the image to be captured.

array is the name of the array in which to store the image. The array can be of any type, but must have a length that is sufficient to hold the image.

index% is the position in the array at which to start storing the image.

Description   The graphics version of the GET statement is used to transfer graphics on the screen into an array variable. The image is specified as a rectangle, with the upper-left and lower-right corners. The units used are pixels, and the number of pixels in the vertical and horizontal direction depend on the current graphics mode set with the SCREEN statement. The origin of the coordinate system used depends on the current graphics window set with the VIEW statement. The default is pixels counted down and to the right from the upper-left corner of the screen.

The array can be of any type; it must just be large enough to hold the image. The contents of the array elements will be meaningless to you if you attempt to access them, and may even cause errors. To figure the minimum size for an array, in bytes, use the following formula:

`4+INT((width*bits+7)/8)*planes*height`

width and *height* are the width and height of the image in pixels.

bits is the number of bits per pixel, which depends on the current screen mode (see the following table).

planes is the number of graphics planes, which depends on the current screen mode (see the following table).

Screen Mode	Colors	bits	planes
1 (320 x 200)	4	2	1
2 (640 x 200)	1	1	1
3 (Hercules)	1	1	1
4 (Hercules)	1	1	1
7 (320 x 200)	16	1	4
8 (640 x 200)	16	1	4
9 (640 x 350)	$4^1 16^2$	1	$2^2 4^1$
10 (640 x 350)	4	1	2
11 (640 x 480)	2	1	1
12 (640 x 480)	16	1	4
13 (320 x 200)	256	8	1

[1] >64K EGA memory

[2] 64K EGA memory

For example   The following statement copies the image in the rectangle with an upper-left corner that is 10 pixels right and 25 pixels down from the upper-left corner of the screen, and whose lower-right corner is 100 pixels right and 200 pixels down from the upper-left corner of the screen into the array variable A:

```
GET (10,25)-(100,200), A
```

If this is in screen mode 10, A must be at least

```
16,896 = 4+INT((91*1+7)/8)*2*176
```

bytes long. If A is an integer array, it must contain at least 8448 (= 16,896/2) elements.

See also   CIRCLE statement
LINE statement
PUT statement
SCREEN statement

 GETTEXT

Purpose   The GETTEXT method retrieves a text string from the CLIPBOARD object.

Syntax   **CLIPBOARD.GETTEXT()**

Arguments   None

Description   The GETTEXT method gets a text string from the CLIPBOARD object. Use GETTEXT as you would use a function.

Returns   The result is a text string from the CLIPBOARD object, or the null string ("") if the clipboard is empty.

For example   The following assignment statement retrieves any text on the clipboard and stores it in the Text property of the Text1 text box:

```
Text1.Text = CLIPBOARD.GETTEXT()
```

See also   SETTEXT method

S GOSUB/RETURN

Purpose   The GOSUB statement transfers control to a subroutine within a procedure. A RETURN statement transfers it back.

Syntax   **GOSUB** {*line* ¦ *label*}
RETURN

Arguments   *line* is a line number to which to branch if the program lines are numbered.

label is a label to which to branch.

Description   The GOSUB statement works with the RETURN statement to implement a subroutine call within a procedure. When a program branches to a subroutine, execution begins there and continues until a RETURN statement is reached. When the RETURN statement is reached, the program branches back to the statement immediately following the GOSUB statement. Both the GOSUB statement and the subroutine it calls must be within the same procedure.

Subroutines have the same uses as SUB procedures; that is, they allow the reuse of blocks of code. However, there are no local variables in subroutines, as there are in SUB procedures. The GOSUB statement is available largely for compatibility with older versions of BASIC, because the newer SUB procedures are far superior to subroutine calls.

For example   The following, do-nothing procedure demonstrates calling a subroutine within a procedure:

```
SUB someprocedure ()
some lines of code
branch to the subroutine
GOSUB SubA
SubA returns here
more statements
EXIT SUB
SubA:
the subroutine's statements
RETURN
END SUB
```

15

477

See also   FUNCTION statement
GOTO statement
IF statement
ON/GOSUB statement
ON/GOTO statement
SELECT statement
SUB statement

 GOTO

Purpose   The GOTO statement transfers control to a different location within a procedure.

Syntax   **GOTO** {*line*|*label*}

Arguments   *line* is a line number to which to branch if the program lines are numbered.

label is a label to which to branch.

Description   The GOTO statement causes an unconditional branch to another location in a procedure. That location is marked either by a line number (if the lines are numbered) or a label. Both the GOTO statement and the label to which it branches must be in the same procedure.

Most well-structured code rarely needs GOTO statements. Block IF, SELECT CASE, FOR/NEXT, DO/LOOP, and WHILE/WEND structures should cover most applications, so avoid using GOTO if possible. When you must use a GOTO statement, make sure that the location to which it branches is nearby; if not, document both ends of the branch with remarks.

For example   The following, do-nothing procedure demonstrates branching within a procedure. As you can see, it can become confusing.

```
SUB someprocedure ()
some lines of code
branch to somewhere else
GOTO somewhere
label2:
more statements
GOTO done
somewhere:
```

```
some statements
GOTO label2
done:
END SUB
```

See Also FUNCTION statement
GOSUB/RETURN statement
IF statement
ON/GOSUB statement
ON/GOTO statement
SELECT statement
SUB statement

 HEX$

Purpose The HEX$() function converts a number into a string of hexadecimal characters.

Syntax **HEX$**(*number*)

Arguments *number* is a number of any type, or a formula that evaluates to a number.

Description The HEX$ function converts numbers into a string of hexadecimal numbers, just as the STR$() function converts numbers into a string of decimal numbers. Hexadecimal numbers are base 16, and use the characters 0 through 9 and A through F to represent the numbers 0 through 15. Thus &H0A in hexadecimal is 10 in decimal. The &H, which designates this as a hexadecimal string, is not returned by this function. Floating-point numbers are rounded to an integer before conversion to a hexadecimal string.

Returns The result is the number converted into hexadecimal number.

For example The following is a list of the results of several HEX$() statements:

Value	HEX$()
135	87
135.2	87
135.7	88
255	FF

Value	HEX$( )
256	100
257	101
15	F
16	10
17	11
9	9
10	A
11	B
252	FC
253	FD
254	FE
5533	FFFD
65534	FFFE
65535	FFFF
65536	10000

See also   FORMAT$( ) function
OCT$( ) function
STR$( ) function

 HIDE

Purpose   The HIDE method hides a form without unloading it from memory.

Syntax   [{*form*.|**SCREEN.**}]**HIDE**

Arguments   *form* is the name of a form to hide. If you omit this argument, the form on which this command resides is assumed.

SCREEN is the SCREEN object, and hides all visible forms on the screen.

Description   The HIDE method hides a form, without unloading it, by setting the form's Visible property to False. Because the form isn't unloaded, the running program can access all the controls on the form, and the properties can be read or changed. If the form isn't loaded when the command is executed, it is loaded first and then hidden. Applying HIDE to the SCREEN object is useful when preparing to do graphics procedures, because you must hide all forms before switching to graphics mode.

For example   The Cancel command button on a file open dialog is an obvious use for the HIDE method. The following example hides the file open dialog box and returns control to the main form without changing any of the variables:

```
SUB CancelCmd_Click ()
OpenDialog.HIDE
END SUB
```

See also   LOAD statement
UNLOAD statement
SHOW method
VISIBLE property

 # HOUR

Purpose   The HOUR function calculates the hour of the day from a serial date number.

Syntax   **HOUR(**serialdate#**)**

Arguments   serialdate# is a serial date number. A serial date number is a double-precision number containing the date, represented as the number of days since December 30, 1899. Negative serial date numbers represent dates from January 1, 1753, to December 30, 1899. Times are represented as fractions of a day. Years after 1900 are represented by the same serial date numbers used in several popular spreadsheet programs.

Description   The HOUR() function takes a serial date number and returns the hour of the day represented by that number.

Use the DAY(), MONTH(), and YEAR() functions to extract the day, month, and year. To extract the time, use the MINUTE() and SECOND() functions.

Returns   The result is the hour of the day as an integer from 1 to 24.

For example The following statement extracts the hour (12) from a serial date number for noon on March 17, 1987:

```
theHour = HOUR(31853.5)    'Extracts the hour (12)
                           'from the date number
```

See also DATE$ statement
TIME$ statement
DATE$ function
DATESERIAL function
DATEVALUE function
DAY function
MINUTE function
MONTH function
NOW function
SECOND function
TIME$ function
TIMER function
TIMESERIAL function
TIMEVALUE function
WEEKDAY function
YEAR function

S IF

Purpose The IF statement makes a decision based on a condition and executes different code depending on that decision.

Syntax IF *condition* THEN *tstatements* [**ELSE** *fstatements*]

or

```
IF condition1 THEN
   [statements]
[ELSEIF condition2 THEN
   statements]
[ELSE
   statements]
END IF
```

Arguments   *condition*, *condition1*, and *condition2* are logical formulas that result in a value of True (–1) or False (0). It also may be a TYPEOF clause to test the type of an object. The TYPEOF clause has the following syntax:

TYPEOF *object* IS *type*

where *object* is a variable containing a reference to an object and *type* is the type of control from the following list:

```
CheckBox              Label
ComboBox              ListBox
CommandButton         Menu
DirListBox            OptionButton
DriveList Box         PictureBox
FileListBox           TextBox
Frame                 Timer
HScrollBar            VScrollBar
```

statements is any number of statements to execute.

tstatements is statements to execute when the condition is True.

fstatements is statements to execute when the condition is False.

ELSEIF is a clause to test for another condition.

ELSE is a clause to receive all other instances that don't invoke the IF or ELSEIF clauses.

Description   The simple IF statement executes the *tstatements* if *condition* is True and *fstatements* if *condition* is False. The block IF statement executes the first block of statements if *condition1* is True. If not, it tests *condition2* and executes the second block of statements if *condition2* is True. There can be as many ELSEIF statements as you need, and they are evaluated in order. If none of the IF or ELSEIF clauses is True, then the ELSE clause is executed.

For example   The following procedure uses the block IF statement either to save the file or to create and save it with the save dialog. SaveIt is another procedure written to save the file.

```
SUB SaveCmd_Click ()
IF FileName <> "" THEN
   SaveIt
ELSE
   SaveDialog.SHOW 1
END IF
END SUB
```

15

See also   GOTO statement
SELECT statement

 IMP

Purpose   The IMP operator combines two logical expressions or all the bits in two numeric values by using the logical implies operation.

Syntax   *express1* **IMP** *express2*

Arguments   *express1* and *express2* are logical expressions, numeric expressions, or numeric values.

Description   The IMP operator combines two logical values according to the following truth table. If two numeric values are being combined, the operator is applied bit-by-bit to the corresponding bits in the two values. That is, each bit in the result is equal to the logical implies of the corresponding bits in the two values being combined.

A	B	A IMP B
True	True	True
True	False	False
False	True	True
False	False	True

Returns   The logical implies of the two expressions equals True (–1) or False (0) if *express1* and *express2* are logical expressions. If *express1* and *express2* are numeric values or expressions that result in numeric values, the result is the bitwise logical implies of the same bits in each of the two values.

For example   The following IF statement does not cause a beep if A is False and B is True:

```
IF A IMP B THEN BEEP
```

See also   AND operator
EQV operator
NOT operator
OR operator
XOR operator

$ $INCLUDE

Purpose   The $INCLUDE metacommand inserts the contents of another file at the indicated point. This statement is not available in Visual Basic for Windows.

Syntax   {REM|'} **$INCLUDE:** *'filename'*

Arguments   REM and ' identify the line as a remark statement. Metacommands are compiler directives, and must be inserted in code as remark statements.

filename is a literal string containing the filename and an optional directory path if the file isn't in the current directory. The path, including the disk letter, has the following syntax:

[*drive*:][[\]*directory*[*directory*...\]]*filename*

where *drive* is the drive letter, *directory* is a directory name, and *filename* is the file to delete. Omit this argument to use the current drive. If you omit the first backslash, the path is assumed to start in the default directory of the specified drive. Use CHDIR and CHDRIVE to change the current directory.

Description   The $INCLUDE metacommand inserts the contents of other files at the designated place. This is useful for inserting library header files (.BI files) at the module level of forms or modules to define the functions in a library so you can use them. It is also useful for inserting the same global declarations in more than one module, which ensures that you've declared everything the same way each time. $INCLUDE is also useful for inserting a file of definitions such as CONSTANT.BI, which is included with Visual Basic.

For example   The following statements, placed in the declarations section of a module, insert the definitions in the files CONSTANT.BI and VBDOS.BI:

```
REM $INCLUDE CONSTANT.BI
REM $INCLUDE VBDOS.BI
```

See also   None

15

 INKEY$

Purpose The INKEY$ function checks the keyboard to see whether a key has been pressed, and returns that key if it has. This function is unavailable if any forms are showing. This statement is not available in Visual Basic for Windows.

Syntax INKEY$

Arguments None

Description The INKEY$ function, available when no forms are showing, returns the key pressed at the keyboard.

Returns The result is the key pressed if a key has been pressed, or the null string (" ") if none have been pressed. For some special keys, such as the function keys, the command returns two bytes, a zero byte, and the key's scan code. (See Appendix D, "Scan Code Chart.")

For example The following code fragment pauses a procedure until the Enter key is pressed:

```
WHILE INKEY$ <> CHR$(13)
WEND
```

See also INPUT statement
LINE INPUT statement
INPUT$ function

  INP

Purpose The INP() function reads a byte from an I/O port. This statement is not available in Visual Basic for Windows.

Syntax INP(*portnum%*)

Arguments *portnum%* is a valid machine port number in the range 0 to 65,535. You'll need a technical manual for your machine to get a list of the valid machine port numbers.

Description The INP() function along with the OUT() statement gives you direct control of a machine's hardware I/O ports.

Returns	The result is a single byte from the port.
For example	The following assignment statement gets one byte from port 2:

```
a = INP(2)
```

See also	OUT statement
	WAIT statement

 # INPUT

Purpose	The INPUT statement gets a line of data from the keyboard. This function is unavailable if any forms are showing. This statement is not available in Visual Basic for Windows.
Syntax	**INPUT** [;][*prompt$*{;│,}] *arglist*
Arguments	; (the first semicolon) causes the cursor to stay on the same line after the user presses Enter.
	prompt$ is a prompt string.
	; (the second semicolon) causes a question mark to appear after the prompt.
	, does not print a question mark.
	arglist is a list of one or more variable names to receive the data typed at the keyboard.
Description	The INPUT statement gets a line of data from the keyboard. The argument list must match the data being typed at the keyboard. See the INPUT # statement for a description of how the typed input is parsed into the arguments. To input a complete line of data, use the LINE INPUT statement.
For example	The following statement prints a prompt, then inputs an integer and a string from the keyboard:

```
INPUT "Input a number and a name:", num%, A$
```

See also	INPUT # statement
	LINE INPUT statement
	PRINT statement
	WRITE statement

15

S INPUT

Purpose   The INPUT # statement reads data from a sequential file.

Syntax   `INPUT # filenumber%,arglist`

Arguments   `filenumber%` is the file number used when the file was opened with the OPEN statement.

`arglist` is a list of variables to receive the data from the file.

Description   The INPUT # statement reads data from a sequential data file into its arguments. Leading spaces are ignored when reading a file. For a number, the first nonblank character is assumed to be the start of the number, and either the first blank, the first comma, or the end of the line terminates it. For a string, the first nonblank character starts the string and a comma or the end of the line terminates it. If the string is quoted, everything between the quotation marks is included in the string, including commas. Thus, data written with the WRITE # statement is more accurately read than data written with PRINT #.

For example   A disk file written with the following statements

```
A1 = 5.355
B1 = 4.788
PRINT #1, "Values, are: ", A1, B1, " units"
WRITE #1, "Values, are: ", A1, B1, " units"
```

produces

```
Values, are: 5.355          4.788           units
"Values, are: ",5.355,4.788," units"
```

Reading those values with the following INPUT # statements

```
INPUT #1, A$, B, C, D$
INPUT #1, E$, F, G, H$
```

stores the following data in these variables:

```
A$ = "Values"
B = 0
C = 5.355
D$ = "4.788          units"
E$ = "Values, are: "
```

```
F = 5.355
G = 4.788
H$ = " units"
```

Note how the first INPUT # statement stopped reading the string into A$ at the first comma, so that the first numeric input, B, sees text rather than a number and gets a value of zero. The second numeric input, C, then reads the first number, and the remaining number and string end up in D$.

See also   GET statement
LINE INPUT # statement
OPEN statement
PRINT # statement
PUT statement
WRITE # statement
INPUT$ function

 INPUT$

Purpose   The INPUT$() function reads a string of characters from a disk file.

Syntax   **INPUT$(**num% [#]filenumber%**)**

Arguments   num% is the number of characters to read from the file.

filenumber% is the file number used when the file was opened with the OPEN statement.

Description   The INPUT$() function reads a specified number of characters from a disk file. Unlike the INPUT # statement, no characters are ignored by this function. It reads the disk file byte-by-byte, including carriage returns, line feeds, and other control characters. Use this function when you need access to every byte of a file. Also, to get every character sent to a particular serial port, use this function when the device opened with the OPEN statement is that serial port.

Returns   The resulting string contains num% characters read from the disk file.

For example   If a disk file opened with file number 1 contains the following data:

```
Values, are: 5.355          4.788          units
"Values, are: ",5.355,4.788," units"
```

15

489

reading those values with the following INPUT$() function:

```
A$ = INPUT$(65, #1)
```

would store the following data in A$:

```
A =
Values, are: 5.355        4.788          units
"Values, are: "
```

Note that A$ contains not only the text, but also the carriage return and line feed at the end of the line, both of which count towards the 65 characters read.

See also   GET statement
INPUT # statement
LINE INPUT # statement
OPEN statement
PRINT # statement
PUT statement
WRITE # statement

 INPUTBOX$

Purpose   The INPUTBOX$() function displays a dialog box and waits for user input.

Syntax   **INPUTBOX$(***prompt$*[, *title$*[, *default$*[,*x%, y%*]]]**)**

Arguments   *prompt$* is a prompt string of up to 255 characters. The string automatically wraps the words to fit in the dialog box.

title$ is a string to use as the title of the dialog box. Only 40 characters can be displayed in the title. Characters after 40 are truncated. If you omit this argument, nothing is placed in the title of the box.

default$ is a string to place in the input box. The user can accept or change the string. The string has no maximum length, although only 39 characters are visible at any one time. If you omit this argument, the input box is empty.

x% and *y%* determine the *x, y* position of the upper-left corner of the box, measured down from the top of the screen and right from the left side of the screen. If you omit these arguments, the box appears in the upper-middle part of the screen.

Description The INPUTBOX$() function gets small amounts of data from the user. The function displays a dialog box with an instruction area, an input area, an OK button, and a Cancel button. The instructions and response are not limited in length, although only 39 characters of the response can be seen at any one time. You can insert a default response by including the default argument.

Returns If the user pressed OK or Return, the resulting string contains the contents of the input box. If the user pressed Cancel, the result is a null string (" ").

For example The following statement creates a simple dialog box and places the text typed by the user in the string variable A$:

```
A$ = INPUTBOX$("Type the number below and press OK")
```

See also MSGBOX statement
MSGBOX function

 # INSTR

Purpose The INSTR() function locates a substring within a string.

Syntax INSTR([*start&,*]*searched$,find$*)

Arguments *start&* is the character position at which to start searching in *searched$*; the character position is a number of any type, or a formula that evaluates to a number. If you omit this argument, it is assumed to be 1 (the first character position).

searched$ is the string to search.

find$ is the substring for which to search.

Description The INSTR() function locates a substring within another, longer string. Only the first occurrence of a substring is located. Use the *start&* argument to locate other occurrences of the substring.

Returns The resulting numeric value is the character position of the first character of the first occurrence of the *find$* string in the *searched$* string. The first character of the string is character number 1. If the substring isn't found, this function returns 0. If the *find$* string is empty, this function returns *start&*.

For example The following lists the results from various searches within a string:

```
A$ = "This is the string, to be "
A$ = A$ + "searched for a substring"
```

INSTR	Result
INSTR(A$,"string")	13
INSTR(14,A$,"string")	45
INSTR(A$,",")	19
INSTR(20,A$,",")	0

See also LEN function

INT

Purpose The INT() function converts a number of any numeric type to the largest integer less than or equal to the number.

Syntax **INT(** *number* **)**

Arguments *number* is a number of any type, or a formula that evaluates to a number.

Description The INT() function converts a number of any numeric type to the largest integer that is less than or equal to the number. This function is not needed if you assign number to an INTEGER type variable, because Visual Basic automatically does the conversion in such cases. This function is useful for forcing a calculation to be done in INTEGER type if the calculation contains other numeric types. If every number used in a calculation is of the same numeric type, the entire calculation is done in that type. If a calculation contains different numeric types, Visual Basic converts everything to the most precise type before doing the calculation.

Returns The result is the largest integer less than or equal to *number*.

For example The following table shows how CINT(), INT(), and FIX() convert different values:

Value	CINT()	INT()	FIX()
3.7	4	3	3
3.4	3	3	3
−3.7	−4	−4	−3
−3.4	−3	−4	−3

See also CCCUR function
CDBL() function
CLNG function
CSNG function
FIX function

D INTEGER

Purpose The data type INTEGER matches or defines two-byte integer variables.

Syntax *variable* **AS INTEGER**

Arguments *variable* is a variable name.

Description The data type INTEGER is used in SUB and FUNCTION procedure headings to declare a variable as a two-byte integer so that Visual Basic can check values passed to the procedure. It also is used in DIM, COMMON, or STATIC statements to define a variable as a two-byte integer. The INTEGER data type is a two-byte integer number that ranges from 32,768 to –32,767. You can also define the INTEGER data by appending the % character to the variable name.

For example The following procedure defines ANumber and I as INTEGER data types, and AddEmUp as an INTEGER type function. The function adds up and returns all the integers from 1 to ANumber.

```
FUNCTION AddEmUp (ANumber AS INTEGER) AS INTEGER
DIM I AS INTEGER
AddEmUp = 0
FOR I = 1 TO ANumber
  AddEmUp = AddEmUp + I
NEXT I
END FUNCTION
```

15

See also   COMMON statement
DIM statement
STATIC statement
TYPE statement
ANY data type
CONTROL data type
CURRENCY data type
DOUBLE data type
FORM data type
LONG data type
SINGLE data type
STRING data type

INTERRUPT, INTERRUPTX

Purpose   The INTERRUPT() and INTERRUPTX() statements make DOS system calls from within an executing application. These statements are not available in Visual Basic for Windows.

Syntax   **CALL INTERRUPT**✕ (*intrpt-num%, inregs, outregs*)

Arguments   *intrpt-num%* is the MS-DOS interrupt number, with a range of 0 through 255.

inregs is a variable of type RegType (or RegTypeX, if INTERRUPTX is used). This variable contains the values of the registers before the interrupt is called. To use the current values of the DS and ES registers, set them equal to –1. The following are the TYPE definitions of the RegType and RegTypeX variable types.

```
TYPE RegType              TYPE RegTypeX
   AX AS INTEGER             AX AS INTEGER
   BX AS INTEGER             BX AS INTEGER
   CX AS INTEGER             CX AS INTEGER
   DX AS INTEGER             DX AS INTEGER
   BP AS INTEGER             BP AS INTEGER
   SI AS INTEGER             SI AS INTEGER
   DI AS INTEGER             DI AS INTEGER
   Flags AS INTEGER          Flags AS INTEGER
END TYPE                     DS AS INTEGER
                             ES AS INTEGER
                          END TYPE
```

outregs is a variable of type RegType (or RegTypeX, if INTERRUPTX is used). The variable contains the values of the registers after the interrupt is called.

Description The INTERRUPT() and InterruptX() routines allow a program to call MS-DOS service routines directly. The only difference between these routines is that InterruptX() also includes the ES and DS registers. You will need a DOS technical manual to get the interrupt numbers and the register contents required to make these calls. To use these functions, you must attach the library file VBDOS.QLB to Visual Basic and include the file VBDOS.BI in the declarations section of the module that will contain the functions. Use the /L *libname* option when starting Visual Basic. The library VBDOS.LIB must be available to compile a program that uses this function.

For example The following statement performs the same function—printing the screen—as pressing the PrtSc key:

```
DIM InReg AS RegType, OutReg AS RegType
CALL INTERRUPT(&H05,InReg,OutReg)
```

See also IOCTL() function

IOCTL

Purpose The IOCTL statement sends a control string to a device driver. This statement is not available in Visual Basic for Windows.

Syntax **IOCTL** [#] *filenum, ctlstr$*

Arguments *filenum* is the file number used when the device driver was opened with the OPEN statement.

ctlstr$ is a control string to send to the device driver.

Description The IOCTL statement sends control strings to device drivers. You must first open a path to the driver by using the OPEN statement. Use the IOCTL$ function to receive messages from the device driver. You must refer to the technical manual for the driver to which you want to send messages, and learn what kind of commands the driver responds to and what values it returns.

For example The following statements open a path to a device driver named XLDR, send it the command string `"rpt"`, and then wait for a returned string:

```
OPEN "C:\XLDR" FOR OUTPUT AS #1
IOCTL #1, "rpt"
A$ = IOCTL$(1)
```

See also OUT statement
INP() function
IOCTL$ function

 **IOCTL$**

Purpose The IOCTL$() function gets a message from an open device driver. This statement is not available in Visual Basic for Windows.

Syntax **IOCTL$(**filenum**)**

Arguments filenum is the file number used when a path to the driver was opened with the OPEN statement.

Description The IOCTL$() function is used with the IOCTL statement to send and receive messages from a device driver. You must refer to the technical manual for the driver to which you want to send messages, and learn what kind of commands the driver responds to and what values it returns.

Returns The result is the message from the device driver.

For example The following statements open a path to a device driver named XLDR, send it the command string `"rpt"`, and then wait for a returned string:

```
OPEN "C:\XLDR" FOR OUTPUT AS #1
IOCTL #1, "rpt"
A$ = IOCTL$(1)
```

See also IOCTL statement
OUT statement
INP() function

S KEY (Assign Function Keys)

Purpose   The KEY statement assigns command strings to the function keys. This statement is not available in Visual Basic for Windows.

Syntax   `KEY {key%, string$|LIST|ON|OFF}`

Arguments   `key%` is the function-key number from the following table:

key%	*Function Key*
1 to 10	F1 to F10
15 to 25	User-defined key combination
30	F11
31	F12

`string$` is a string of up to 15 characters to assign to the key.

LIST prints a list of the key assignments on the screen. No forms can be showing for this to work.

ON and OFF turn the display of the function key line on or off. No forms can be showing if the function key line at the bottom of the screen is to be visible.

Description   The KEY statement defines or displays the string assignments of the function keys. You can use these while programming to insert often-used commands. INKEY$, INPUT, and INPUT$ read the strings attached to the keys as if the user typed the strings, so you can use function keys to simulate or speed user input. Use the CHR$() function to add control characters (such as Enter) to the key string. You can define the function keys by using the Immediate window.

In addition, key numbers 15 through 25 are available for user-defined keys. These define special key combinations, such as Alt-Tab, as a single key so it can be trapped with the KEY() ON trap. For the key string, combine the modifier code and the scan codes into a single string. Appendix D, "Scan Code Chart," lists the scan codes. The following are the modifier codes:

15

497

Code	Keys
0	No modification
1, 2, 3	Left Shift
4	Ctrl
8	Alt
32	Num Lock
64	Caps Lock
128	Extended characters (those on an extended keyboard, such as Del and Ins)

For example
The following statement defines Key 1 (F1) as "run" followed by Enter:

```
KEY 1,"run"+CHR$(13)
```

The following statements define Alt-A as special-character 15, set up a subroutine to execute if the key combination is pressed, and turn on key trapping. When RETURN is reached at the end of the trap handler, execution returns to the statement following the one executed when the trap was triggered.

```
KEY 15, CHR$(8)+CHR$(30)    'define Alt-A as key 15
ON KEY(15) GOSUB DoKey      'define trap handler
KEY(15) ON                  'enable trap
other statements
DoKey:                      'start of the trap handler
statements to handle the key trap
RETURN                      'return to the executing code
```

See also
KEY() ON statement
ON KEY() GOSUB statement
INKEY$ function

S KEY() ON (Key Trapping)

Purpose   The KEY() ON statement activates key trapping. This statement is not available in Visual Basic for Windows.

Syntax   KEY(*keynum*){ON|OFF|STOP}

Arguments   *keynum* is the key number from the following table:

keynum	*Key*
0	All keys
1 to 10	F1 through F10
11	Up arrow
12	Left arrow
13	Right arrow
14	Down arrow
15 to 25	Special keys defined with the KEY statement
30	F11
31	F12

ON enables key trapping.

OFF disables key trapping of the specified key. Any trappable events that occur are lost.

STOP pauses key trapping. Trappable events are saved until key trapping is turned back on.

Description   The KEY()ON statement is used with the KEY statement and the ON KEY() GOSUB statement to implement key trapping. Whenever key trapping is enabled, the keyboard is watched for the key or key combination specified with the KEY statement. If the key or keys are pressed, execution jumps to the subroutine procedure specified in the ON KEY()GOSUB statement.

15

For example The following statements define Alt-A as special character 15, set up a subroutine to execute if the key combination is pressed, and turn on key trapping. When the RETURN is reached at the end of the trap handler, execution returns to the statement after the one that was executed when the trap was triggered.

```
KEY 15, CHR$(8)+CHR$(30) 'define Alt-A as key 15
ON KEY(15) GOSUB DoKey     'define trap handler
KEY(15) ON                 'enable trap
other statements
DoKey:                     'start of the trap handler
statements to handle the key trap
RETURN                     'return to the executing code
```

See also KEY statement
ON KEY() GOSUB statement
INKEY$ function

KILL

Purpose The KILL statement deletes a disk file.

Syntax **KILL** *filename$*

Arguments *filename$* is a string containing the filename, and an optional directory path if the file isn't in the current directory. The filename can contain the * and ? wildcard characters, where * matches any number of any characters and ? matches any single character. The path, including the disk letter, has the following syntax:

[*drive*:][[\]*directory*[*directory*...\]]*filename*

where *drive* is the drive letter, *directory* is a directory name, and *filename* is the file to delete. Omit this argument to use the current drive. If you omit the first backslash, the path is assumed to start in the default directory of the specified drive. Use CHDIR and CHDRIVE to change the current directory.

Description The KILL statement deletes any file. It does not delete directories; use RMDIR to do that. The filename may contain wildcard characters to select multiple files for deletion.

For example   The following statement deletes the file MYFILE.DOC in the current directory:

```
KILL "myfile.doc"
```

The next statement deletes all executable files (.EXE files) in the APPS directory on disk c:

```
KILL "c:\apps\*.exe"
```

See also   CHDIR statement
CHDRIVE statement
MKDIR statement
NAME statement
RMDIR statement
CURDIR$ function
DIR$ function

LBOUND

Purpose   The LBOUND function returns the smallest allowed array subscript.

Syntax   **LBOUND**(*array*[,*dimension%*])

Arguments   *array* is an array-type variable.

dimension% is for multidimensional arrays. This number specifies the dimension to examine. The first dimension is number 1.

Description   The LBOUND function works with the UBOUND function to examine the lower and upper index values of an array's dimensions.

Returns   The resulting numeric value is the lowest allowed subscript for the array dimension.

For example   The following code line is from the general procedure of a form, and defines the array variable anArray. The table shows the results of the operation of LBOUND and UBOUND for different arguments:

```
DIM anArray(4 TO 23,-6 TO 5,8) AS INTEGER
```

15

Function	Result
LBOUND(anArray,1)	4
UBOUND(anArray,1)	23
LBOUND(anArray,2)	-6
UBOUND(anArray,2)	5
LBOUND(anArray,3)	0
UBOUND(anArray,3)	8

See also   DIM statement
COMMON statement
STATIC statement
UBOUND function

LCASE$

Purpose   The LCASE$() function converts all the characters in a string to lowercase.

Syntax   **LCASE$(**_string$_**)**

Arguments   _string$_ is a string, or a formula that results in a string, to be converted.

Description   The LCASE$() function converts all the characters in a string to lowercase. This is useful when you want to compare two strings and the case of the characters in unimportant.

Returns   The result is the contents of _string$_ with each character converted to lowercase.

For example   The following lines demonstrate the use of LCASE$ and UCASE$:

```
A$ = "This Is a StRinG to ConVeRt"
```

Function	Result
LCASE$(A$)	this is a string to convert
UCASE$(A$)	THIS IS A STRING TO CONVERT

See also   UCASE$() function

 **LEFT$**

Purpose	The LEFT$() function extracts a substring from the left side of a string.
Syntax	**LEFT$(***string$,numchar&***)**
Arguments	*string$* is a string, or a formula that results in a string.
	numchar& is the number of characters to extract from the string.
Description	The LEFT$() function extracts a substring from the left side of a string. Use it with the RIGHT$() and MID$() functions to extract different substrings.
Returns	The resulting string contains the leftmost *numchar&* characters from *string$*.
For example	The following is from the Immediate window and compares the LEFT$(), RIGHT$(), and MID$() functions:

A$ = "This is a string to examine"

Function	*Result*
LEFT$(A$,6)	This i
RIGHT$(A$,5)	amine
MID$(A$,9,5)	a str

See also   MID$ statement
MID$ function
RIGHT$ function

 15

 **LEN**

Purpose	The LEN() function returns the number of characters in a string or the number of bytes in a variable.

Syntax   `LEN(`*variable*`)`

Arguments   *variable* is a string, a formula that results in a string, or a variable name.

Description   The `LEN()` function returns the number of characters in a string, or the number of bytes necessary to store a variable. This function works for all variable types, including user-defined record variables defined with the `TYPE` statement.

Returns   The result is the number of characters in a string or the number of bytes in a variable.

For example   The following `TYPE` definition statements and `DIM` statement are from the declarations section of a module. The remaining lines are typed in the Immediate window, followed by what is displayed on the screen. These demonstrate the use of `LEN` to get the length of a user-defined type and a string.

```
TYPE DayType          'TYPE declaration for the
  TheDate AS DOUBLE   'record DayType, 128 bytes
  Flags AS INTEGER    'long
  MSG AS STRING * 118
END TYPE
DIM SHARED ChangeDate AS DayType   'Serial date
                                   'being changed


Immediate: PRINT LEN(ChangeDate)
On Screen: 128
Immediate: A$ = "A string to examine"
Immediate: PRINT LEN(A$)
On Screen: 19
```

See also   `INSTR` function

 **LET**

Purpose   The `LET` statement is an assignment statement.

Syntax   `[LET]` *variable* `=` *formula*

Arguments   *variable* is a variable name to receive the value generated by *formula*. For numeric types, if the type of value generated by *formula* is different from that of *variable*, LET converts the number by rounding and truncating the type of *variable*.

formula is a formula or constant value to assign to *variable*.

Description   The assignment statement assigns values to variables. The LET keyword is not needed, and is available only for compatibility with older versions of BASIC.

For example   The following are assignment statements:

```
A = 1
LET B = 3
aVal = 3 * A + B
aString$ = "This is a string"
aString2$ = LEFT$(aString$,9) + " dumb" +
    RIGHT$(aString$,7)
```

See also   LSET statement
RSET statement

 # LINE

Purpose   The LINE statement draws lines, rectangles, and filled rectangles on the screen. This statement is not available in Visual Basic for Windows.

Syntax   LINE [[**STEP**](*x1!*,*y1!*)]-[**STEP**](*x2!*,*y2!*)[,[*color&*]
,**B**[**F**]]][,*style%*]

Arguments   STEP is a keyword that specifies that the coordinates following it are relative to the current position of the graphics cursor.

x1!, *y1!*, *x2!*, and *y2!* are the x, y coordinates of the ends of a line, or the upper-left and lower-right corners of a rectangle. The coordinates are measured in the current coordinate system, determined by the screen mode set with the SCREEN statement. If you omit the first pair of coordinates, they are assumed to be the current position specified by the CurrentX and CurrentY properties.

color& is the color attribute specifying the color to use for the line or the rectangle's outline. Omit this argument to use the current ForeColor. See the RGB() function for more information on colors.

15

B is an option indicating that a box is to be drawn. If you omit this option, a line is drawn.

F is an option indicating that the box is to be filled with the color specified by the *color&* argument or, if you omit *color&*, with the current ForeColor.

style% is an integer whose bits determine which pixels are on and which are off when a line is drawn. For example, the hexadecimal number &HF0F0 has the binary pattern 11110000 11110000, which draws a dashed line with dashes and spaces of equal length.

Description   The LINE method draws lines, boxes, and filled boxes on the screen. No forms can be visible when this statement is used.

For example   The following statement draws a filled rectangle on the screen:

```
LINE (200, 100)-(300,150), 1, BF
```

The next statement draws a line from the current graphics cursor location to the indicated location:

```
LINE -(200, 100)
```

See also   CIRCLE statement
COLOR statement
SCREEN statement
QBCOLOR function
RGB function

LINE INPUT

Purpose   The LINE INPUT statement reads a complete line of data from the keyboard whenever no forms are showing. This statement is not available in Visual Basic for Windows.

Syntax   `LINE INPUT` [;][*prompt$*{;|,}] *string$*

Arguments   ; (the first semicolon only) causes the cursor to stay on the same line after the user presses Enter.

prompt$ is a prompt string.

; (the second semicolon only) causes a question mark to appear after the prompt.

, does not print a question mark.

string$ is a string variable to receive the contents of the line read from the keyboard.

Description The LINE INPUT statement reads a line of data from the keyboard into a string variable. When reading, all the characters in the line are placed into the string, including any leading spaces and up to, but not including, the carriage return/line feed at the end of the line.

For example The following statement gets a line of text from the keyboard and puts it in the variable A$:

```
LINE INPUT A$
```

See also GET statement
INPUT statement
INPUT # statement
LINE INPUT # statement
OPEN statement
PRINT statement
PRINT # statement
PUT statement
WRITE statement
WRITE # statement
INPUT$ function

S LINE INPUT

Purpose The LINE INPUT # statement reads complete lines of data from a sequential file.

Syntax `LINE INPUT #filenumber%,string$`

Arguments *filenumber%* is the file number used when the file was opened with the OPEN statement.

string$ is a string variable to receive the contents of the line read from the file.

Description The LINE INPUT # statement reads a line of data from a sequential data file into a string variable. When reading a file, the statement places all the characters in the line into the string, including any leading spaces and up to, but not including, the carriage return/line feed at the end of the line.

For example A disk file written with the following statements:

```
A1 = 5.355
B1 = 4.788
PRINT #1, "The values, are: ", A1, B1, " units"
WRITE #1, "The values, are: ", A1, B1, " units"
```

produces

```
Values, are: 5.355          4.788              units
"Values, are: ",5.355,4.788," units"
```

Reading those values with the following INPUT # statements:

```
LINE INPUT #1, A$
LINE INPUT #1, E$
```

stores the following data in these variables:

```
A$ = Values, are: 5.355          4.788              units
E$ = "Values, are: ",5.355,4.788," units"
```

See also   GET statement
INPUT statement
INPUT # statement
LINE INPUT statement
OPEN statement
PRINT statement
PRINT # statement
PUT statement
WRITE statement
WRITE # statement
INPUT$ function

S LOAD

Purpose   The LOAD statement loads a form or control array element into memory.

Syntax   **LOAD** *object*

Arguments   *object* is the name of a form or control array element to load. The form's Visible property determines whether or not the form is visible after it is loaded.

Description   The LOAD statement loads a form or control array element into memory at runtime. Whether a form is visible or not depends on its Visible property. Use the HIDE method to load a form but not display it. Use the SHOW method to load a form and display it. You also can use the LOAD method to add elements to a control array. The first element of the control array must be on the form already, but subsequent elements can be loaded and attached to the form at runtime.

For example   The following statement loads element number 2 of an Option button control array. Element number 0 must already be on the form.

```
LOAD OPTION1(2)
```

See also   UNLOAD statement
HIDE method
SHOW method
VISIBLE property

 LOC

Purpose   The LOC() function returns the current record or byte position in an open file.

Syntax   **LOC(**_filenumber%_**)**

Arguments   *filenumber%* is the file number used when the file was opened with the OPEN statement.

Description   The LOC() function returns the current record or byte position in a file being read or written by Visual Basic.

Returns   The result is the current location in an open disk file. If the file was opened as a random access file, the number of the last record accessed is returned. For a sequential file, the result is the byte location of the last byte accessed in the file, divided by 128. For binary files, the result is the byte location of the last byte accessed.

For example The following statement assigns the current location in file number 1 to the variable theLocation:

```
theLocation = LOC(1)
```

See also OPEN statement
EOF function
LOF function

 **LOCATE**

Purpose The LOCATE statement moves the text cursor to a specific position on the screen. This statement is not available in Visual Basic for Windows.

Syntax LOCATE [*row*%] [,[*column*%] [,[*cursor*%]
[,*start*% [,*stop*%]]]]

Arguments *row*% is the row in which to insert the cursor, counting down from the top of the screen.

column% is the column in which to insert the cursor, counting from the left.

cursor% is a flag indicating whether the cursor is visible or not:

0   Invisible

1   Visible

start% and *stop*% are numbers between 1 and 31 specifying the vertical size of the cursor in scan lines. The top of a character is at 0 and the bottom is between 7 and 9. If *start*% is greater than *stop*%, a two-part cursor is created.

Description The LOCATE statement moves the text cursor to a specific position on the screen. No forms can be visible when this statement executes. Use the CurrentX and CurrentY properties to move the cursor in a form or picture box.

For example The following statement moves the text cursor to the third row down from the top and the tenth character position from the left:

```
LOCATE 3, 10
```

See also CSRLIN function
POS function

S LOCK/UNLOCK

Purpose   For networked files, the LOCK and UNLOCK statements control access to an open file.

Syntax   LOCK [#]*filenumber*%[,*startrec&* [**TO** *endrec&*]]
UNLOCK [#]*filenumber*%[,*startrec&* [**TO** *endrec&*]]

Arguments   *filenumber*% is the file number used when the file was opened with the OPEN statement.

startrec& is the first record number of a file to lock, or the single record to lock if *endrec*% is omitted. For binary mode files, this number is measured in bytes from the beginning of the file. The first record is number 1. This argument is ignored in a sequential access file. If you omit this argument, the entire file is locked or unlocked.

endrec& is the ending record of a range of records to lock.

Description   Networked files can be accessed by more than one application at the same time. To prevent two applications from trying to change the same record at the same time, the LOCK statement reserves the indicated records for the use of one application only. The UNLOCK statement then releases the records again. The SHARE.EXE program must have been run in DOS versions 3.1 and later to enable locking. You cannot lock earlier versions of DOS. When locking and unlocking a block of records, the arguments of LOCK and UNLOCK must match exactly. You cannot lock individual records in a file opened in sequential mode; the entire file must be locked.

> Be sure to unlock all locked records before closing a file, or unpredictable results may occur.

15

For example   The following lines first lock and then unlock records 27 through 95 of file number 1:

```
LOCK #1,27 To 95
'other statements that change these records
UNLOCK #1, 27 To 95
```

See also   OPEN statement

 LOF

Purpose	The LOF() function returns the length of an open file.
Syntax	**LOF(** *filenumber%* **)**
Arguments	*filenumber%* is the file number used when the file was opened with the OPEN statement.
Description	The LOF() function returns the length of the file in bytes. If it's a random access file, divide by the length of a record to get the number of records in the file.
Returns	The result is the length of the file, in bytes.
For example	The following statement assigns the length of file number 1 to the variable theLength:

```
theLength = LOF(1)
```

See also	EOF function
	LOC function
	OPEN statement

 LOG

Purpose	The LOG() function calculates and returns the natural logarithm of a number.
Syntax	**LOG(** *number* **)**
Arguments	*number* is a number of any type, or a formula that evaluates to a number.
Description	The LOG() function calculates the natural logarithm of a number. The base of natural logarithms is the number **e** (2.71828...). To get the common (base 10) logarithm of a number, use the following construction:

```
LOG10 = LOG(number)/LOG(10)
```

Returns	The resulting numeric value is the natural logarithm of *number*.

For example   The following three assignment statements calculate the log of 10 (2.30259), the log of 4.7 (1.54756), and the common logarithm of 4.7 (0.672098):

```
A = LOG(10)
B = LOG(4.7)
C = LOG(4.7)/LOG(10)
```

See also   EXP() function

 # LONG

Purpose   The data type LONG matches or defines four-byte integer variables.

Syntax   *variable* **AS LONG**

Arguments   *variable* is a variable name.

Description   The data type LONG is used in SUB and FUNCTION procedure headings to declare a variable as a four-byte integer so that Visual Basic can check values passed to the procedure. It also is used in a DIM, COMMON, or STATIC statement to define a variable as a four-byte integer. The LONG data type is a four-byte integer number that ranges from –2,147,483,648 to 2,147,483,647. You can also define the LONG data type by appending the & character to the variable name.

For example   The following procedure defines ANumber and I as LONG integers, and AddEmUp as a LONG integer function. The function adds up and returns all the integers from 1 to ANumber.

```
FUNCTION AddEmUp (ANumber AS LONG) AS LONG
DIM I AS LONG
AddEmUp = 0
FOR I = 1 TO ANumber
  AddEmUp = AddEmUp + I
NEXT I
END FUNCTION
```

See also   COMMON statement
DIM statement
STATIC statement
TYPE statement
ANY data type

513

CONTROL data type
CURRENCY data type
DOUBLE data type
FORM data type
INTEGER data type
SINGLE data type
STRING data type

LPOS

Purpose   The LPOS() function returns the character position in the current line being printed on the printer. This statement is not available in Visual Basic for Windows.

Syntax   **LPOS(*code*)**

Arguments   *code* is a code number indicating the printer port to examine:

0	LPT1
1	LPT2
2	LPT3
3	LPT4

Description   The LPOS() function keeps track of the character position in the current line. This number is in error if the printer issues its own line feed.

Returns   The result is the number of characters sent to the printer since the last carriage return.

For example   The following statement assigns the number of characters printed in the current line on LPT1 to the variable nchars:

```
nchars = LPOS(0)
```

See also   LPRINT statement

S LPRINT

Purpose The LPRINT statement prints on the printer connected to the LPT1: printer port. This statement is not available in Visual Basic for Windows.

Syntax LPRINT [**USING** *format$*;] *arglist* [{;|,}]

Arguments *format$* is a format string to control the printing of the values in *arglist*. See the FORMAT$ function for an explanation of formatting strings.

arglist is a comma- or semicolon-separated list of values or variables to be printed. If you use the USING clause, its formatting string controls where values are printed. If you do not use the USING clause, commas between values cause each value to skip to the next tab stop (every 14 spaces). If you use semicolons, each value is printed immediately after the last, with no inserted spaces.

; (the second semicolon only) or , suppresses the carriage return at the end of the line.

Description The LPRINT statement prints values and text strings on a printer connected to the LPT1: printer port. If you use the USING clause, you can format the values as they are printed. You also can print on the printer by using the OPEN statement with LPT1: as the device name, and then use PRINT # statements. Do not use LPRINT when you have an open connection to LPT1: created with the OPEN statement.

For example The following statements print formatted numbers on the printer. Both blocks of statements have the same effect.

```
OPEN "LPT1:" FOR OUTPUT AS # 1
aVal = 32.85
PRINT # 1 USING "   ###0.0";aVal
CLOSE #1

LPRINT USING "   ###0.0";aVal
```

See also OPEN statement
PRINT # statement
PRINT USING statement
FORMAT$ function

 LSET

Purpose	The LSET statement left-justifies strings and copies record variables.
Syntax	**LSET** *fixedstring$* = *string$* **LSET** *recvar1* = *recvar2*
Arguments	*fixedstring$* is a fixed-length string.
	string$ is a string or a formula that results in a string to be left-justified in the fixed-length string.
	recvar1 and *recvar2* are user-defined record variables.
Description	The LSET statement left-justifies a string in a fixed-length string or copies user-defined record variables. When you left-justify a string into a fixed-length string, only as much of the left side of the string as fits in the fixed-length string is copied. If the string is shorter than the fixed-length string, the remainder of the right side of the fixed-length string is filled with blanks. Use RSET to right-justify strings.

> When you copy record-type variables of different types, interesting results may occur because the record variable is filled in the same manner as strings. That is, bytes from one variable are copied one-for-one into the target variable without regard for the type of number that occupies those bytes. Do this at your own risk.

For example	The following lines define a fixed-length string and left-justify the word Welcome:

```
DIM anFString AS STRING *10
LSET anFString = "Welcome"
```

The variable anFString now contains "Welcome   ".

See also	FIELD statement LET statement RSET statement

 **LTRIM$**

Purpose	The LTRIM$ function removes leading blanks from the left side of a string.
Syntax	**LTRIM$(**string$**)**
Arguments	string$ is a string or a formula that results in a string.
Description	The LTRIM$() function removes leading spaces from strings. Use the RTRIM$() function to remove trailing spaces.
Returns	The result is the argument string with the blanks removed from the left side.
For example	The following line trims the blanks from the left side of a string and stores it in A$:

```
A$ = LTRIM$("     234.45      ")
```

A$ now contains the string "234.45   ".

See also	RTRIM function

 **MID$**

Purpose	The MID$() function extracts a substring from within a string.
Syntax	**MID$(**string$,start&[,numchar&]**)**
Arguments	string$ is a string, or a formula that results in a string.
	start& is the number of the first character in the string to extract. The first character in the string is number 1.
	numchar& is the number of characters to extract from the string. If you omit this argument, the right side of the string is extracted.
Description	The MID$() function extracts a substring from within another string. Use it with the LEFT$() and RIGHT$() functions to extract different substrings.
Returns	The resulting string contains numchar& characters from string$ starting at character number start&.

15

For example The following is from the Immediate window and compares the LEFT$(), RIGHT$(), and MID$() functions:

```
A$ = "This is a string to examine"
```

Function	Result
LEFT$(A$,6)	This i
RIGHT$(A$,5)	amine
MID$(A$,9,5)	a str

See also MID$ statement
LEFT$ function
RIGHT$ function

 MID$

Purpose The MID$ statement replaces a substring within a string.

Syntax **MID$(**_string$_,_start&_[,_numchar&_]**)** = _substring$_

Arguments _string$_ is a string to have its substring replaced.

start& is the number of the first character to replace. The first character in the string is number 1.

numchar& is the number of characters to replace. Omit this argument to use all of _substring$_.

substring$_ is a string or formula that results in a string to replace the substring in _string$.

Description The MID$ statement replaces a substring within a string. The replacement is done character-by-character, so the resulting string does not change length. You cannot insert a longer or shorter substring within a string with this function.

For example When the following statements are typed in the Immediate window:

```
A$ = "This is a string to examine"
MID$(A$,11,6) = "  dog "
```

```
PRINT A$
```

this appears on the screen:

```
"This is a  dog  to examine"
```

To replace a substring in *string$* with a longer or shorter *substring$*, use something like the following:

```
A$ = LEFT$(string$,start& - 1) + substring$ +
MID$(string$, start& + numchar& - 1)
```

See also LEFT$ function
MID$ function
RIGHT$ function

F MINUTE

Purpose The MINUTE function extracts the minute of the hour from a serial date number.

Syntax **MINUTE(***serialdate#***)**

Arguments *serialdate#* is a serial date number. A serial date number is a double-precision number containing the date represented as the number of days since December 30, 1899. Negative serial date numbers represent dates from January 1, 1753, to December 30, 1899. Times are represented as fractions of a day. Years after 1900 are represented by the same serial date numbers used in several popular spreadsheet programs.

Description The MINUTE() function takes a serial date number and returns the minute of the hour represented by that number. Use the HOUR() and SECOND() functions to extract the hour and second. To extract the date, use the DAY(), MONTH(), and YEAR() functions.

Returns The result is the minute of the hour as an integer from 1 to 60.

For example The following statement extracts the MINUTE (0) from a serial date number for noon on March 17, 1987:

```
theMinute = MINUTE(31853.5)  'Extracts the minute
                      '(0) from the date number
```

519

See also   DATE$ statement
TIME$ statement
DATE$ function
DATESERIAL function
DATEVALUE function
DAY function
HOUR function
MONTH function
NOW function
SECOND function
TIME$ function
TIMER function
TIMESERIAL function
TIMEVALUE function
WEEKDAY function
YEAR function

MKC$, MKD$, MKI$, MKL$, MKS$, MKDMBF$, and MKSMBF$

Purpose   The MKC$, MKI$, MKL$, MKS$, MKD$, MKSMBF$, and MKDMBF$ functions convert binary numbers into string-like values that you can store in string fields defined with the FIELD statement. These statements are not available in Visual Basic for Windows.

Syntax   **MKI$**(*number%*)   '2-byte INTEGER
MKL$(*number&*)   '4-byte LONG
MKS$(*number!*)   '4-byte SINGLE
MKD$(*number#*)   '8-byte DOUBLE
MKC$(*number@*)   '8-byte CURRENCY
MKSMBF$(*number!*)   '4-byte SINGLE to MBF
MKDMBF$(*number#*)   '8-byte DOUBLE to MBF

Arguments   *number%*, *number&*, *number!*, *number#*, and *number@* are numbers of any type, or formulas that evaluate to numbers. They are converted into numbers of the indicated type by rounding or by extending the number of digits.

Description The MKI$, MKL$, MKS$, MKD$, MKC$, MKSMBF$, and MKDMBF$ functions are used with the FIELD statement to store binary numbers in random access files. Because you can store strings only in fields defined with the FIELD statement, these functions make a binary number look like a fixed-length string so it can be stored in these fields. The converted number occupies the same number of bytes as the original number. Convert the numbers back to binary with the CVI, CVL, CVS, CVD, CVC, CVSMBF, and CVDMBF functions.

The MKSMBF$ and MKDMBF$ functions store the values as Microsoft Binary Format values.

All these functions are available primarily for compatibility with older versions of BASIC. In any new program, use the TYPE statement instead.

Returns The result is a value that looks like a string to the system, but actually is a binary number.

For example The following statements open a disk file for random access with six-byte records. The FIELD statement defines the first two bytes as the two-byte string A$ and the next four bytes as the four-byte string B$. Next, two variables—an integer and a single-precision, floating-point number—are loaded. The MKI$ and MKS$ functions are used to convert the numbers into string-like variables, which are stored in A$ and B$. Because the FIELD statement has defined A$ and B$ as parts of the file buffer, the values stored in A$ and B$ are stored in the buffer as well. The PUT statement stores the buffer in the disk file.

```
OPEN "myfile.dat" FOR RANDOM AS #1 LEN = 6
FIELD #1, A$ AS 2, B$ AS 4
anInteger% = 78
aSingle! = 32.7874
LSET A$ = MKI$(anInteger%)
LSET B$ = MKS$(aSingle!)
PUT #1,1
```

See also FIELD statement
CVC function
CVD function
CVI function
CVL function
CVS function
CVDMBF function
CVSMBF function

15

 MKDIR

Purpose	The MKDIR statement creates a new directory in the file system.
Syntax	**MKDIR** *path$*
Arguments	*path$* is a string containing the new directory path, including the disk letter, with the following syntax:

[*drive:*][\]*directory*[*directory*]

where *drive* is the drive letter and *directory* is a directory name. To use the current drive, omit *drive*. If you omit the first backslash, the path is assumed to start in the default directory of the specified drive. The string must be less than 128 bytes long.

Description The MKDIR statement creates a new directory in the file system in the same manner as the DOS command of the same name. To use the current drive, omit the disk drive specification in the *path$* argument. If you omit the first backslash, the path is assumed to be relative to the default directory on either the current drive (if no drive is specified) or on the specified drive.

> Using this function, you can create directories with blanks embedded in their names, and these directories cannot be accessed with the MS-DOS file system commands.

For example The first statement creates the UTIL directory in the TOOLS directory on the C drive. The second statement creates the C directory in the PROGRAMS directory, which is in the current default directory. That is, if the current directory was D:\APPS, the PROGRAMS directory must be in the APPS directory and the new C directory is created in the PROGRAMS directory.

```
MKDIR "C:\TOOLS\UTIL"
MKDIR "PROGRAMS\C"
```

See also CHDIR statement
CHDRIVE statement
KILL statement
NAME statement

`RMDIR` statement
`CURDIR$` function
`DIR$` function

ⓞ MOD

Purpose The `MOD` operator performs modulus arithmetic on two integers.

Syntax *express1* **MOD** *express2*

Arguments *express1* and *express2* are integer values, or expressions that result in integer values.

Description The `MOD` operator combines two integer expressions by using modulo arithmetic. For two integer values, modulo arithmetic returns the remainder from an integer division. That is, `6 MOD 4` is 2, the remainder of the integer division of 6 by 4. `INTEGER` division is performed with the `\` operator. The modulus operator is useful for things such as determining the actual angle from angles larger than 360 degrees, or figuring feet and inches from inches.

Returns The resulting integer value is equal to *express1* modulo *express2*, which is the remainder of the integer division of *express1* by *express2*.

For example The following table lists the results from several `MOD` operations:

Operation	*Result*
`6\4`	1
`6 MOD 4`	2
`370 MOD 360`	10
`1300 MOD 360`	220
`STR$(75\12)+ " feet "`	6 feet
`STR$(75 MOD 12)" inches"`	3 inches

See also None

 MONTH

Purpose	The MONTH function calculates the month of the year from a serial date number.
Syntax	`MONTH(`*serialdate#*`)`
Arguments	*serialdate#* is a serial date number. A serial date number is a double-precision number containing the date represented as the number of days since December 30, 1899. Negative serial date numbers represent dates from January 1, 1753, to December 30, 1899. Times are represented as fractions of a day. Years after 1900 are represented by the same serial date numbers used in several popular spreadsheet programs.
Description	The MONTH() function takes a serial date number and returns the month of the year represented by that number. Use the DAY(), WEEKDAY(), and YEAR() functions to extract the day, weekday, and year. Use the HOUR(), MINUTE(), and SECOND() functions to extract the time.
Returns	The result is the month of the year as an integer from 1 to 31.
For example	The following statement extracts the month of the year from the serial date number for March 17, 1987:

```
theMonth = MONTH(31853)    'Extracts the month (3)
                           'from the date number
```

See also	DATE$ statement
	TIME$ statement
	DATE$ function
	DATESERIAL function
	DATEVALUE function
	DAY function
	HOUR function
	MINUTE function
	NOW function
	SECOND function
	TIME$ function
	TIMER function
	TIMESERIAL function
	TIMEVALUE function
	WEEKDAY function
	YEAR function

 MOVE

Purpose	The MOVE method moves or resizes a form or control at runtime.
Syntax	[*object.*]**MOVE** *left!*[,*top!*[,*width!*[,*height!*]]]
Arguments	*object* is the object to move; any form or control other than timers and menus.

left! is the distance from the left edge of the drawing area to the left edge of the object.

top! is the distance from the top of the drawing area to the top of the object.

width! is the width of the object.

height! is the height of the object.

Description   The MOVE method moves or scales an object while a program is running. The drawing area is the screen, form, or frame on which the object lies. Forms lie on the screen, so the measure is from the top-left corner of the screen. Controls that lie on a form measure from the top-left corner of the form, excluding the title bar. Controls on a frame measure from the top-left corner of the frame.

The coordinate system used to indicate where to move is in character widths (horizontal) and character heights (vertical).

For example   The following moves the Command1 command button to the location 5 characters down and 40 characters left of the upper-left corner of the form:

```
Command1.MOVE 5,40
```

See also   SCALE method
Height property
Left property
ScaleHeight property
ScaleLength property
ScaleRight property
ScaleWidth property
Top property
Width property

15

 MSGBOX

Purpose	The MSGBOX() function displays a dialog box containing a message and waits for the user to press a button.
Syntax	**MSGBOX**(*message$*[, *type%*[, *title$*]])
Arguments	*message$* is a string message up to 255 characters long. The string automatically word-wraps to fit in the dialog box.

title$ is a string to use as the title of the dialog box. If you omit this argument, "Microsoft Visual Basic" is used.

type% is a code number that determines the type of dialog box to display and the number and type of buttons. Add the codes together to come up with the code for the box you want. The codes are

Button(s)		*Icon*	
Code	Result	Code	Result
0	OK	16	Critical Message
1	OK and Cancel	32	Warning Query
2	Abort, Retry, and Ignore	48	Warning Message
3	Yes, No, and Cancel	64	Information
4	Yes and No		Message
5	Retry and Cancel		
0	First button		
256	Second button		
512	Third button		

Description   The MSGBOX() function sends a message to the user, or asks a question that the user can answer by pressing some buttons. The number and type of buttons, the icon, and the default button are determined by a type code. Create the type code by adding the codes in the preceding table. Add to the code for the buttons you want, the code for the icon, and the code for the default button. The default button is the one selected when you press Enter. The Esc key always selects the Cancel button.

Returns   The resulting numeric code determines which button the user pressed. The codes are

1	OK	5	Ignore
2	Cancel	6	Yes
3	Abort	7	No
4	Retry		

For example   The following statement creates a simple message box with OK and Cancel buttons and the Critical Message icon. The OK button is active. The code consists of 1 + 16 + 0 = 17 for the options listed. A receives a 1 or 2, depending on which button was pressed.

```
A = MSGBOX$("Kiss the Cook!",17)
```

See also   MSGBOX statement
INPUTBOX$ function

S MSGBOX

Purpose The MSGBOX statement displays a dialog box containing a message and waits for the user to press a button.

Syntax **MSGBOX** *message$*[, *type%*[, *title$*]]

Arguments *message$* is a string message up to 255 characters long. The string automatically word-wraps to fit in the dialog box.

title$ is a string to use as the title of the dialog box. If you omit this argument, "Microsoft Visual Basic" is used.

type% is a code number that determines the type of dialog box to display, and the number and type of buttons. Add the codes together to come up with the code for the box you want. Because this box does not return a value, the codes for multiple buttons serve no purpose. The codes are

| Button(s) | | Icon | |
Code	Result	Code	Result
0	OK	16	Critical Message
1	OK and Cancel	32	Warning Query
2	Abort, Retry, and Ignore	48	Warning Message
3	Yes, No, and Cancel	64	Information Message
4	Yes and No		
5	Retry and Cancel		

The Default Button	
Code	Result
0	First button
256	Second button
512	Third button

Description The MSGBOX statement is nearly identical to the MSGBOX() function, except that it does not return a value. MSGBOX sends a message to the user. The number and type of buttons, the icon, and the default button are determined by a type code, although any of the combinations with more than one button serve no purpose because the box does not return a value. Create the type code by adding the codes in the preceding table. Add to the code for the buttons you want, the code for the icon, and the code for the default button. The default button is the one selected when you press Enter. The Esc key always selects the Cancel button.

For example The following statement creates a simple message box with the OK button and the Critical Message icon. The OK button is active. The code consists of 0 + 16 + 0 = 16 for the options listed.

```
MSGBOX$("Kiss the Cook!",16)
```

See also INPUTBOX$ function
MSGBOX function

 # NAME

Purpose The NAME statement moves and changes the name of a disk file.

Syntax `NAME oldfile$ AS newfile$`

Arguments `oldfile$` is the old filename, in a string, and an optional directory path if the file isn't in the current directory. The filename may contain the * and ? wildcard characters, where * matches any number of any characters and ? matches any single character. The path, including the disk letter has the following syntax:

```
[drive:][[\]directory[\directory...\]]filename
```

where *drive* is the drive letter, *directory* is a directory name, and *filename* is the name of the file. Omit the *drive* argument to use the current drive. If you omit the first backslash, the path is assumed to start in the default directory of the specified drive. Use CHDIR and CHDRIVE to change the current directory.

newfile$ is the new filename in a string and an optional path.

Description The NAME statement moves and renames files. If only the filenames are different, NAME changes the name. If the directory paths are different, NAME moves the file to the new directory and, optionally, changes the name.

For example The following changes the name of MYFILE.DOC to YOURFILE.DOC in the default directory:

```
NAME "myfile.doc" AS "yourfile.doc"
```

See also CHDIR statement
CHDRIVE statement
KILL statement
MKDIR statement
RMDIR statement
CURDIR$ function
DIR$ function

NEWPAGE

Purpose The NEWPAGE method advances the page on the printer.

Syntax PRINTER.NEWPAGE

Arguments None

Description The NEWPAGE method advances the page on the printer. The printer automatically advances a page when text is printed beyond the bottom, and also when the ENDDOC method is executed. NEWPAGE advances an unfilled page within a document.

For example   The following line advances the page on the printer:

PRINTER.NEWPAGE

See also   ENDDOC method
Page property

 NOT

Purpose   The NOT operator reverses the logical value of a logical expression, or each of the bits in a numeric value.

Syntax   **NOT** *express1*

Arguments   *express1* is a logical expression, numeric expression, or numeric value.

Description   The NOT operator converts a logical value according to the following truth table. If it's applied to a numeric value, the operator is applied bit-by-bit to each bit in the value; that is, each bit in the result is equal to the logical NOT of the corresponding bit in the value.

A	NOT A
True	False
False	True

Returns   The logical NOT of an expression equals True (–1) or False (0) if *express1* is a logical expression. If *express1* is a numeric expression, the result is the bitwise logical inverse of the bits in the argument.

For example   The following IF statement causes a beep only if A is False:

IF NOT A THEN BEEP

See also   AND operator
EQV operator
IMP operator
OR operator
XOR operator

15

NOW

Purpose	The NOW function gets and returns the current date and time from the system clock as a serial date number.
Syntax	NOW
Arguments	None
Description	The NOW function gets the current date and time as a serial date number. To find the difference in days, subtract the later serial date number from the earlier one. Use the DATE$ or TIME$ functions to get the current date or time as a string.
Returns	The result is the serial date number for the current date and time. A serial date number is a double-precision number containing the date represented as the number of days since December 30, 1899. Negative serial date numbers represent dates from January 1, 1753, to December 30, 1899. Times are represented as fractions of a day. Years after 1900 are represented by the same serial date numbers used in several popular spreadsheet programs.
For example	The following assignment statement assigns the current date and time to the double-precision variable A#:

```
A# = NOW      'Assign the current date to A#
```

See also	DATE$ statement
	TIME$ statement
	DATE$ function
	DATESERIAL function
	DATEVALUE function
	DAY function
	HOUR function
	MINUTE function
	MONTH function
	SECOND function
	TIME$ function
	TIMER function
	TIMESERIAL function
	TIMEVALUE function
	WEEKDAY function
	YEAR function

 OCT$

Purpose	The OCT$() function converts a number into a string of octal characters.
Syntax	**OCT$(** *number* **)**
Arguments	*number* is a number of any type, or a formula that evaluates to a number.
Description	The OCT$() function converts numbers into octal numbers in a string, just as the STR$() function converts numbers into decimal numbers in a string. Octal numbers are base 8, and use the characters 0 through 7. Thus, &O12 in octal is 10 in decimal. The &O, which designates that this as an octal string, is not returned by this function. Floating-point numbers are rounded to an integer before conversion to an octal string.
Returns	The resulting string is the number converted into an octal number.
For example	The following lists the results from several OCT$ functions:

OCT$ *Function*	*Result*
OCT$(135)	207
OCT$(135.2)	207
OCT$(135.7)	210
OCT$(6)	6
OCT$(7)	7
OCT$(8)	10
OCT$(9)	11
OCT$(10)	12
OCT$(11)	13
OCT$(63)	77
OCT$(64)	100
OCT$(65)	101
OCT$(511)	777
OCT$(512)	1000

15

533

OCT$ *Function*	*Result*
OCT$(513)	1001
OCT$(65534)	177776
OCT$(65535)	177777
OCT$(65536)	200000

See also   FORMAT$ function
HEX$ function
STR$ function

 # ON ERROR/RESUME

Purpose   The ON ERROR/RESUME statements enable and return from an error-handling routine.

Syntax   `ON [LOCAL] ERROR {GOTO line|RESUME NEXT|GOTO 0}`
`RESUME {[0]|NEXT|line}`

Arguments   LOCAL indicates that the error handler is local to this procedure. Local error handers are disabled when the procedure exits. They also apply to procedures that are called by the procedure with the local error handler, unless the called procedures have a local error handlers of their own.

GOTO *line* enables the error-handling routine that starts at *line*, where *line* is a line number or label. The line must be in the same procedure as the ON ERROR statement.

RESUME NEXT, when used with the ON ERROR statement, ignores any errors and resumes processing at the next statement after the error.

> Be careful with this argument; use it in time-critical applications to temporarily store an error for handling a short time later. For example, in a communications program, if you stop to handle a transmission error, you might miss part of a transmission, so store the error and handle it when the transmission ends.

GOTO 0 disables the error handler.

0 resumes execution at the statement that caused the error after you correct the problem in the error handler.

NEXT resumes execution at the statement after the one that caused the error.

line resumes execution at *line*, where *line* is a line number or a label.

Description The ON ERROR/RESUME statement traps all the runtime errors listed in Table 13.1 and sends control to the error handler at the indicated line when an error occurs. The error handler then handles the error if it can, or sends a message and quits the application if it cannot. The ERR function returns the error number of the last error and, if the lines are numbered, the ERL function returns the line number at which the error occurred. The ERROR$() function returns the text of the error message. The error handler must end with a RESUME statement. An error handler defined at the module level applies to all procedures in the module.

For example The following procedure contains an outline of a function to calculate the sine integral, and an error handler to trap the possible divide-by-zero error (error number 11). At xint = 0, SIN(xint) also is 0, but the quotient is 1 even though Visual Basic gives a divide-by-zero error. If the error isn't a divide-by-zero error, the error handler displays a message box containing the error message and then ends the application.

```
FUNCTION Si(x AS SINGLE) AS SINGLE
'function to calculate the sine integral
'statements to integrate sin(x)/x from x to infinity
ON ERROR GOTO FixSin     'turn the error handler on
.
.
.
Integrand = SIN(xint)/xint
.
.
.EXIT FUNCTION
FixSin:
IF ERR = 11 THEN  'Error 11 is divide by 0
  Integrand = 1
ELSE
  MSGBOX ERROR$(ERR)
  STOP
END IF
RESUME NEXT
     END FUNCTION
```

15

See also ERL function
ERR function
ERROR$( ) function

 ON event GOSUB

Purpose The ON *event* GOSUB statement defines the event handler for the specified event. This statement is not available in Visual Basic for Windows.

Syntax **ON** *event* **GOSUB** *line*

Arguments *event* is the name of a trappable event:

COM(*portnum%*)	Serial port
KEY(*keynum%*)	Keyboard trap
PEN	Light pen
PLAY(*notesleft%*)	Background music
STRIG(*trigger%*)	Joystick trigger
TIMER(*time%*)	Timer trap
UEVENT	User-defined event

where

portnum% is the serial port number, such as 1 for COM1:.

keynum% is the key number of the key to trap. See the KEY statement for a list.

notesleft% is the number of notes left in the music buffer that will cause a trap. As notes are played, they are removed from the music buffer. When the number of notes left in the music buffer reaches this number, the trap is executed.

trigger% is a code indicating the joystick trigger that will cause this trap to occur:

	Joystick A		Joystick B	
Code	Trigger		Code	Trigger
0	Trigger 1		2	Trigger 1
4	Trigger 2		6	Trigger 2

time% is the time in seconds to wait before causing a trap.

line is a line number or label to jump to if the indicated trap occurs.

Description The ON *event* GOSUB statement defines the event-handling routine for the indicated event trap. Error trapping is not enabled until an *event* ON statement, such as KEY() ON, is executed. This statement does not cause an immediate jump to the event handler; normal code continues to execute until the event occurs, at which time the subroutine branch to the event handler is executed. A RETURN statement at the end of the event handler returns to the next statement after the statement that was executing when the event occurred.

For example The following statements define Alt-A as special character 15, set up a subroutine to execute if the key combination is pressed, and turn on key trapping. When the RETURN is reached at the end of the trap handler, execution returns to the statement following the one that was executed when the trap was triggered.

```
KEY 15, CHR$(8)+CHR$(30)   'define Alt-A as key 15
ON KEY(15) GOSUB DoKey     'define trap handler
KEY(15) ON                 'enable trap
other statements
DoKey:                     'start of the trap handler
statements to handle the key trap
RETURN                     'return to the executing code
```

See also COM() ON statement
KEY() ON statement
ON ERROR statement
PEN ON statement
PLAY() ON statement
STRIG() ON statement
TIMER() ON statement
UEVENT ON statement

Purpose	The ON...GOSUB statement is a computed branch to one of several subroutines.
Syntax	**ON** *number* **GOSUB** *label*[,*label*[,*label*]]...
Arguments	*number* is a number of any type, or a formula that evaluates to a number between 0 and 255.
	label is a line number or a label of a subroutine.
Description	The ON...GOSUB statement causes a branch to one of several subroutines in the same procedure. This procedure is largely for compatibility with older versions of BASIC. SUB procedures and the SELECT CASE statement are much more powerful than ON...GOSUB.

The subroutine is selected according to the value of the *number* argument. The value of *number* is rounded to an integer that identifies the label to be selected: if *number* rounds to 1, the program branches to the subroutine that starts at the first label; if *number* rounds to 2, the program branches to the subroutine that starts at the second label; and so forth. If *number* rounds to 0 or to a value larger than the number of labels in the list, control drops through to the next statement after the ON...GOSUB statement. If *number* is negative or greater than 255, an error results. Subroutines end with a RETURN statement. When subroutines end control passes to the line after the ON...GOSUB statement. See GOSUB for a discussion of subroutines.

For example The following, do-nothing procedure demonstrates the ON...GOSUB statement. If A equals 1, the statement branches to the label lab1 and does something. The RETURN statement at the end of that subroutine returns control to the statement after the ON...GOSUB statement. If A equals 2, the statement branches to lab2. If A equals 3, the statement branches to lab3. The subroutines are placed after the EXIT PROCEDURE statement so they are not executed accidently during the procedure's normal operation

```
ON A GOSUB lab1,lab2,lab3
other statements
EXIT PROCEDURE          lab1:
'do something
RETURN
lab2:
'do something different
```

```
RETURN
lab3:
'do a third thing
RETURN
END PROCEDURE
```

See also GOSUB/RETURN statement
GOTO statement
ON   GOTO statement
SELECT CASE statement

ON...GOTO

Purpose The ON...GOTO statement is a computed branch to one of several labels.

Syntax ON *number* **GOTO** *label*[,*label*[,*label*]]...

Arguments *number* is a number of any type, or a formula that evaluates to a number between 0 and 255.

label is a line number or a label.

Description The ON...GOTO statement causes a branch to one of several statements in the same procedure. This procedure is largely for compatibility with older versions of BASIC. SUB procedures and the SELECT CASE statement are much more powerful than ON...GOTO. The statement is selected according to the value of the *number* argument. The value of *number* is rounded to an integer that identifies the label to be selected: if *number* rounds to 1, control branches to the first label; if *number* rounds to 2, it branches to the second label; and so forth. If *number* rounds to 0 or to a value larger than the number of labels in the list, control drops through to the next statement after the ON...GOTO statement. If *number* is negative or greater than 255, an error results.

For example The following, do-nothing procedure demonstrates the ON...GOTO statement. If A equals 1, the statement branches to label lab1. If A equals 2, the statement branches to lab2. If A equals 3, the statement branches to lab3. When each of the blocks of code that were branched to is complete, you need a GOTO statement to skip over the intervening blocks of code. A SELECT CASE statement would be much simpler solution here.

15

```
ON A GOSUB lab1,lab2,lab3
other statements
lab1:
'do something
OTO DONE
lab2:
'do something different
GOTO DONE
lab3:
'do a third thing
done:
END PROCEDURE
```

See also   GOSUB/RETURN statement
GOTO statement
ON...GOSUB statement
SELECT CASE statement

 OPEN

Purpose   The OPEN statement establishes a connection to a disk file or other device driver.

Syntax   **OPEN** *filename$* [**FOR** *mode*] [**ACCESS** *access*] [*lock*]
AS [**#**]*filenum%* [**LEN** = *rlen%*]

or

OPEN *mode*,[**#**]*filenum%*,*filename$*,[*rlen%*]

Arguments   *filename$* is a string containing the filename and an optional directory path if the file isn't in the current directory, or the name of a standard DOS device. The path, including the disk letter, has the following syntax:

[*drive*:][[\]*directory*[*directory*...\]]*filename*

where *drive* is the drive letter, *directory* is a directory name, and *filename* is the file to name. Omit the *drive* argument to use the current drive. If you omit the first backslash, the path is assumed to start in the default directory of the specified drive. Use CHDIR and CHDRIVE to change the current directory.

In addition to opening a communication path to a disk file, you can open a path to a device driver by using its name and path in place of the filename, or you can use any of the following DOS device drivers, within quotation marks, in place of the filename. See the OPEN COM statement for more information on COM1, COM2, and COM3.

KYBD:	Keyboard (input)
SCRN:	Screen (output)
LPT1:	Parallel printer port 1 (output)
LPT2:	Parallel printer port 2 (output)
LPT3:	Parallel printer port 3 (output)
COM1:	Serial port 1 (input/output)
COM2:	Serial port 2 (input/output)
CONS:	Console, screen, and keyboard (I/O)
PIPE:	Pipe (output)

mode is the mode of the file: APPEND, BINARY, INPUT, OUTPUT, or RANDOM. In the second syntax, use A, B, I, O, or R to make the same choices. For sequential files, the allowed modes are INPUT, OUTPUT, or APPEND. When you open a file FOR INPUT, the file must already exist and you can only read data from it. When you open a file FOR OUTPUT, it is opened if it exists, or created if it does not, and you can only write data to it. When you open an existing file FOR OUTPUT, writing starts at the first record, overwriting any old data in the file. The APPEND mode is a variation of OUTPUT in which, when the file is opened, writing starts at the end, preserving the old data. RANDOM creates a random access file in which each record can be read or written in any order. BINARY files are similar to RANDOM files, but they access the file byte-by-byte rather than record-by-record.

access controls the file access type and is either READ, WRITE, or READ WRITE. The *access* argument applies to networked environments, in which multiple users can have access to the same file. The *access* argument controls what access you want for the file in case someone else already has it open.

lock has the value SHARED, LOCK READ, LOCK WRITE, or LOCK READ WRITE and controls access to a file by other processes. The *lock* argument applies only to networked environments. *lock* controls what access to the file you allow others if you are the first to open it. SHARED allows everyone access. LOCK

READ prevents anyone from reading it. LOCK WRITE prevents anyone from writing to it. LOCK READ WRITE prevents anyone from reading or writing to the file. The *lock* argument applies to the whole file. Use the LOCK statement to lock individual records rather than the entire file.

filenum% is a unique number that identifies the open file to all the other file-access commands. You must include the *filenum* argument with every OPEN statement, and use the argument with every command that accesses the file. Because you may have more than one file open at any one time, this number uniquely identifies that file. Usually, the first file you open is file number 1, the second is 2, and so forth. If you close a file, you can reuse its file number. If you know how many files you have open, you can assign a constant for the file number. However, if you have a situation in which you don't know how many files you have open—such as a word processor having multiple files open at the same time—use the FREEFILE function to give you the next available file number.

rlen% is the record length, in bytes, to use with random access files. The default record length is 128 bytes.

Description The OPEN statement creates an access path between an application and a disk file or other device driver. The access path is identified with the file number, which is assigned to the file with the OPEN statement. After the file number is defined, all statements that access the file use that file number to identify it as the file they want to access.

There are three types of disk files: sequential access, random access, and binary. Sequential access files are standard text files. Everything written to them is readable with a word processor or printable with the DOS TYPE command. They get their name from the fact that they are sequentially read or written to, in order from the beginning to the end. Random access files also are text files, but have fixed-length records set with the LEN option on the OPEN statement. Any record can be read or written in any order without disturbing the rest of the file. Binary files can read or write randomly any single byte in the file.

When you are done with any file, close it with the CLOSE statement. The CLOSE statement also releases the file number for reuse by another file.

For example The following lines demonstrate opening and then closing the file MYFILE.DBK as a random access file, with file number 1 and a record length of 128 bytes. The record length isn't really needed here because 128 is the default length, but including it makes what you're doing more clear.

```
OPEN "MYFILE.DBK" FOR RANDOM AS #1 LEN = 128
'some statements
CLOSE #1
```

See also   CLOSE statement
FIELD statement
GET statement
INPUT statement
INPUT$ function
LINE INPUT statement
OPEN COM statement
PUT statement
PRINT # statement
PRINT # USING statement
WRITE # statement

S OPEN COM

Purpose   The OPEN COM statement establishes a connection to a serial port and sets its communication parameters. This statement is not available in Visual Basic for Windows.

Syntax   **OPEN** "**COM**$port$:[$baud$-$rate$][,[$parity$][,[$data$-$bits$]
    [,[$stop$-$bits$]]]][,**RS**][,**CS**[n]][,**DS**[n]]
    [,**CD**[n]][,**OP**[n]][,**TB**[n]][,**RB**[n]]
    [{**ASC**|**BIN**}][,**LF**][,**PE**]" [**For** $mode$]
    AS [**#**]$filenum$% [**LEN** ***=** $rlen$%]

Arguments $port$ is the number (1 or 2) of the serial port (COM1 or COM2).

$baud$-$rate$ is the baud rate, or speed, of the serial port. The default is 300. The following is a list of the allowed values:

75	110	150	300	600
1200	1800	2400	4800	9600

$parity$ adds another bit to each byte to detect any transmission errors. The default is even. The following lists the allowed values:

S	Space
M	Mark
O	Odd
E	Even
N	None

data-bits is an integer specifying the number of data bits transmitted for each character. The allowed values are 4, 5, 6, 7, and 8. The default is 7.

stop-bits is an integer specifying the number of stop bits transmitted after each character to mark the end of the character. The allowed values are 1 and 2. The default is 1, except at 75 and 110 baud, where the default is 2.

RS, when specified, ignores RTS (request to send) signal.

CS[*n*], DS[*n*], CD[*n*], and OP[*n*] set the timeout for the signals CTS (clear to send), DSR (data set ready), CD (carrier detect), and for the total time to open the port. *n* is the number of milliseconds for a program to wait for a signal before generating a timeout error. The defaults are CS1000, DS1000, CD0, and OP10000, respectively.

ASC and BIN control character translation. ASC causes the data to be treated as text: tabs are expanded into spaces, a return is forced at the end of each line, and a Ctrl-Z is forced at the end of a transmission. BIN, the default, does no character translation.

TB[*n*] and RB[*n*] set the number of bytes in the transmission and receive buffers. *n* is the number of bytes. The defaults are TB128 and RB128, respectively.

LF specifies to send a line feed with every carriage return. The default is to send a carriage return only.

PE, when used, enables parity checking. The eighth bit of each byte is used to tell whether the byte was corrupted in transmission. The parity (EVEN, ODD, SPACE, and MARK) determines how the other bits are combined to create the parity bit.

mode is either INPUT, OUTPUT, or RANDOM. The default is RANDOM.

filenumber% is a unique number that identifies the open communication path for all other commands that want to use it. You can use the FREEFILE function to give you the next available file number.

rlen% is the buffer size for the communication buffer. The default is 128 bytes.

Description The OPEN COM statement creates an access path between an application and a serial port. The access path is identified with the file number, which is assigned to the port by this statement. Once the file number is assigned, all statements that access the port use the file number to identify it. In addition, you can set many of the communication parameters.

When you're done, close the connection by using the CLOSE statement.

For example The following line opens the COM1 serial port to 2400 baud speed, 8 data bits, 1 stop bit, no parity, and 2 second timeouts:

```
OPEN "COM1:2400,8,1,N,CS2000,DS2000" AS #1
```

See also CLOSE statement
FIELD statement
GET statement
INPUT statement
INPUT$ function
LINE INPUT statement
OPEN statement
PUT statement
PRINT # statement
PRINT # USING statement
WRITE # statement

OPTION BASE

Purpose The OPTION BASE statement changes the default lower limit for array variables.

Syntax OPTION BASE *number*%

Arguments *number*% is the number 0 or 1, which becomes the default lower limit for arrays.

Description When an array variable is defined with the DIM, COMMON, or STATIC statement and the lower limit isn't explicitly given in the definition, the default value is 0. The OPTION BASE statement can change that default to 1.

For example   The following changes the default lower limit to 1:

OPTION BASE 1

See also   COMMON statement
DIM statement
STATIC statement

S OPTION EXPLICIT

Purpose   The OPTION EXPLICIT statement forces all variables to be defined explicitly before they are used.

Syntax   **OPTION EXPLICIT**

Arguments   None

Description   Normally, most variables are defined when they are first used and do not need to be declared explicitly in a DIM, STATIC, or COMMON statement. If you should mistype a variable name, the mistyped variable becomes a new variable, causing a logical error in a program. The OPTION EXPLICIT statement prevents errors of this type by forcing all variables to be explicitly defined in a DIM, COMMON, or SHARED statement prior to use.

For example   The following statement, placed in the declarations section of a module, forces all variables in all procedures in that module to be declared explicitly:

OPTION EXPLICIT

See also   COMMON statement
DIM statement
STATIC statement

O OR

Purpose   The OR operator combines two logical expressions, or all the bits in two numeric values, by using the logical OR operation.

| | Syntax | *express1* **OR** *express2* |

Arguments   *express1* and *express2* are logical expressions, numeric expressions, or numeric values.

Description   The OR operator combines two logical values according to the following truth table. If two numeric values are combined, the operator is applied bit-by-bit to the corresponding bits in the two values. That is, each bit in the result is equal to the logical OR of the corresponding bits in the two values.

A	B	A OR B
True	True	True
True	False	True
False	True	True
False	False	False

Returns   The logical OR of the two expression equals True (–1) or False (0) if *express1* and *express2* are logical expressions. If *express1* and *express2* are numeric expressions, the result is the bitwise logical OR of the same bits in each of the two expressions.

For example   The following IF statement causes a beep when either A or B is True:

```
IF A OR B THEN BEEP
```

See also   AND operator
EQV operator
IMP operator
NOT operator
XOR operator

 **OUT**

Purpose   The OUT statement sends a byte to an I/O port. This statement is not available in Visual Basic for Windows.

Syntax   **OUT** *portnum%,data%*

Arguments   *portnum%* is a valid machine port number in the range 0 to 65,535. You will need a technical manual for your machine to get a list of the valid machine port numbers.

data% is the numeric value of the byte to send to the indicated machine port.

Description   The OUT statement, along with the INP() function, gives you direct control of a machine's hardware I/O ports.

For example   The following statement sends a byte of data to port 2:

```
OUT 2,theData
```

See also   WAIT statement
INP() function

 PAINT

Purpose   The PAINT statement fills a region with a color or pattern. This statement is not available in Visual Basic for Windows.

Syntax   PAINT [**STEP**](*x!,y!*)[,[{*color%*|*tile$*}]
[,[*bordercolor&*][,*background$*]]]

Arguments   STEP indicates that the x,y coordinates are specified in relation to the current position of the graphic cursor, and not the upper-left corner of the screen.

x! and *y!* specify the x,y location of any point within the region to be filled. This point must not be on the line surrounding the region.

color% is the fill color to use to fill the region.

tile$ is a string containing a fill pattern to use to fill the region. Using the contents of the string, a mask is generated; this mask is 8 bits wide by up to 64 bits tall. Each byte in the string creates one 8-bit row in the mask. The mask is then replicated all over the area to be filled. The bits in this mask determine the color of each area of the screen. The result depends on the current screen mode. In mode 2 (monochrome) each 1 bit in the screen causes one pixel to be white. In screen mode 1 (2 bits per pixel) each pair of bits controls one pixel.

bordercolor& is the stopping color for the fill. The fill stops when it reaches a border of this color.

background$ is a one-byte string that specifies the color to ignore when filling so you can fill a pattern over a colored area.

Description The PAINT statement fills a region on the screen with a color. The region must be completely surrounded with the *bordercolor&*, or the painting will "leak out" into the surrounding area.

For example The following statements draw two intersecting cyan (1) circles and fill their intersection with magenta (2):

```
SCREEN 1
CIRCLE (200,100) 50,1
CIRCLE (150,100,50,1
PAINT (175,100)2,1
```

See also CIRCLE statement
COLOR statement
LINE statement
SCREEN statement

S PALETTE

Purpose The PALETTE statement changes the color attached to a color attribute. This statement is not available in Visual Basic for Windows.

Syntax **PALETTE**[*attribute%,color%*]

Arguments *attribute%* is the integer number of the color attribute to change.

color% is the integer number of the color to attach to the color attribute.

Description Each screen mode has only a certain number of color attributes available that specify all the colors that may be on the screen at any one time. You cannot use the PALETTE statement with MPDA or CGA monitors. For example, in screen mode 9 with an EGA adapter and a color monitor, there are 16 attributes and a possible 64 colors. Thus, although there are 64 possible colors, only 16 different colors may show at any one time. The PALETTE statement changes the color bound to any one attribute. Use the PALETTE USING statement to change the colors bound to all the color attributes. Note that changing the color of an attribute immediately changes that color everywhere it appears on the screen.

For example   The following statement changes the default color of attribute 2 in screen mode 1 from light magenta (2) to red (4):

```
SCREEN 1
PALETTE 2, 4
```

See also   COLOR statement
PALETTE USING statement
SCREEN statement
QBCOLOR() function
RGB() function

S PALETTE USING

Purpose   The PALETTE USING statement changes the colors attached to several color attributes. This statement is not available in Visual Basic for Windows.

Syntax   PALETTE USING *color-array%*[(*index%*)]

Arguments   *color-array%* is an array of color numbers to apply to the attributes. Consecutive elements of the array are applied to consecutive attributes.

index% is an integer index to the first element of the array of color numbers to apply to the set of attributes. If you omit *index%*, the first element of the array is applied to the first attribute.

Description   Each screen mode has only a certain number of color attributes available that specify all the colors that may be on the screen at any one time. You cannot use the PALETTE USING statement with MPDA or CGA monitors. For example, in screen mode 9 with an EGA adapter and a color monitor, there are 16 attributes and a possible 64 colors. Thus, although there are 64 possible colors, only 16 different colors may show at any one time. The PALETTE USING statement changes the colors bound to all the attributes for a particular screen mode. To change a single attribute, use the PALETTE statement. Note that changing the color of an attribute immediately changes that color everywhere it appears on the screen.

For example   The following statements change the default colors in screen mode 1 to red (4), white (7), and blue (3):

```
SCREEN 1
theColors(1) = 4
theColors(2) = 7
theColors(3) = 3
PALETTE USING theColors(1)
```

See also   COLOR statement
PALETTE statement
SCREEN statement
QBCOLOR( ) function
RGB( ) function

 PCOPY

Purpose   The PCOPY statement copies the contents of one graphics page to another. This statement is not available in Visual Basic for Windows.

Syntax   **PCOPY** *source-page%*, *dest-page%*

Arguments   *source-page%* is the page number of the source page, in the range 0 to the number of pages supported by the graphics adapter in the current screen mode (see the SCREEN statement).

dest-page% is the page number of the destination page, in the range 0 to the number of pages supported by the graphics adapter in the current screen mode.

Description   The PCOPY statement copies one graphics page to another. This primarily is used for animation, to eliminate flicker as images change. Drawing is done to an offscreen page, then copied to the visible page.

For example   The EGA graphics adapter with 256K of memory has eight graphics pages in screen mode 7, numbered 0 through 6. The following statement copies the contents of page 4 to page 0:

```
PCOPY 4, 0
```

See also   CIRCLE statement
COLOR statement
DRAW statement
LINE statement
SCREEN statement
QBCOLOR( ) function
RGB( ) function

15

551

 **PEEK**

Purpose	The PEEK function is used to directly read the contents of a byte in memory. This statement is not available in Visual Basic for Windows.
Syntax	**PEEK(**`offset%`**)**
Arguments	`offset%` is the offset from the beginning of the current segment to the byte to be extracted. The range is 0 to 65,535. The current segment is set with the DEF SEG statement.
Description	The PEAK() function is used to read the contents of a single location in memory. Use POKE to change those contents and CALL to execute a program stored there.
Returns	The result is the contents of a byte in memory.
For example	The following statement reads the contents of a memory location that is offset by 50 bytes from the beginning of the current segment, and stores it in the variable A:

```
A = PEEK(50)
```

See also	DEF SEG statement
	POKE statement

 PEN

Purpose	The PEN() function gets the state of the light pen.
Syntax	**PEN(**`code`**)**
Arguments	`code` is a code number indicating what to return:

0 returns True (–1) if the pen has been used since the last time this statement was called or False (0) if it has not.

1 returns the x-coordinate of the last pen down event. A *pen down* event occurs when the pen is touched to the screen.

2 returns the y-coordinate of the last pen down event.

3 returns the current state of the pen: 1 if down or 2 if not.

4 returns the last known y-coordinate.

5 returns the last known y-coordinate.

6 returns the row number of the last pen down event.

7 returns the column number of the last pen down event.

8 returns the last known row.

9 returns the last known column.

Description The PEN() function reads the state of the pen. The mouse must be disabled for this to work. The PEN ON statement must have been enabled prior to an attempt to use it.

Returns The result is the value of the parameter indicated by the code.

For example The following statements turn on a pen-event trap and then handle it:

```
PEN ON          'turn on pen event trapping
PEN(3)          'see whether the pen is up or down.
```

See also ON PEN statement
PEN ON statement
PEN() function

PEN ON

Purpose The PEN ON statement activates or deactivates trapping light-pen events. This statement is not available in Visual Basic for Windows.

Syntax PEN {ON|OFF|STOP}

Arguments ON turns on event trapping of the light-pen event.

OFF turns off light-pen trapping.

STOP pauses trapping light-pen events, and saves any light-pen events until a PEN ON statement is executed.

Description The PEN ON statement activates trapping of light-pen events. The mouse must be disabled to use this statement, because it emulates a light pen. The event trap must have previously been defined with an ON PEN statement.

15

For example The following statements enable a light-pen event-trap procedure:

```
ON PEN GOSUB doPen   'define the pen event trap
PEN ON               'turn on pen event trapping
'do something while waiting for a trap
doPen:               'label at the start of the trap
PEN STOP             'turn off the trap while
                     'handling this event
'handle the event
PEN ON               'turn the trap back on
RETURN
```

See also ON PEN statement
PEN() function

 PLAY

Purpose The PLAY statement plays a music macro string.

Syntax **PLAY** *music-macro$*

Arguments *music-macro$* is a string containing music macro commands, with the same format as the DRAW statement. Macro commands that are unambiguous can be run together. Ambiguous commands, such as those that contain a filename, are separated with a semicolon. The music macro commands are as follows:

A to G play the indicated note in the current octave.

and + make the note preceding it sharp.

- makes the note preceding this flat.

L*n* sets the length of the following notes, where L1 is a whole note, L2 is a half note, and so on. The value of *n* can range from 1 to 64.

MF plays the following notes in the foreground.

MB plays the following notes in the background. Up to 32 notes can be saved in the music queue to play in the background.

MN (Music-Normal) plays notes for 7/8 of the time set with L*n*, with a 1/8 of the time pause between notes.

ML (Music-Legato) play notes continuously, with no pauses between notes.

MS (Music-Staccato) plays notes for 3/4 of the time set with L*n*, with a 1/4 of the time pause between notes.

N*n* indicates to play note number *n*, where *n* ranges from 0 to 84 (seven octaves). A value of 0 is a pause.

O*n* sets the current octave to *n*, where *n* ranges from 0 to 6. Middle C is in octave 3; the default octave is 4.

P*n* indicates to pause for *n* periods, where *n* ranges from 1 to 64.

T*n* sets the tempo by specifying the number of quarter notes per minute. The value of *n* ranges from 32 to 255. The default is 120.

. (a period following a note) increases the length of that note by three halves. Multiple periods continue to increase the length by three halves each time.

X*music-string$* indicates to play another music macro string and return here when it is complete, much like calling a subroutine. *music-string$* is a pointer to another music macro string in memory (see the Description section).

> indicates to move all the following notes up one octave.

< indicates to move all the following notes down one octave.

Description The PLAY statement plays a music macro string. A music macro string is much like a program for playing music. The music macro string consists of a series of music commands, which you can separate with spaces. To use the X command, you need the address of a music macro string in memory. Use the VARPTR$() function to supply that address, as shown in the example. In the same manner, you can insert the value of a variable for one to the numeric values with the VARPTR() function.

For example The following statements play a patriotic song:

```
Music$ = "MB MS O4 C4 <A8 F A4 >C F2" 'spaces
                                       'optional
PLAY Music$
Music$ = "A8 G8 F <A4 B >C2 C8 C8 A2 G8 F4 E2"
PLAY Music$
Music$ = ">A8 A8 A4 B-4 >C C2"
Music1$ = "<B-8 A8 G A B- B-2"
PLAY "D8 E8 F4 F4 C <A F X" + VARPTR$(Music$)
PLAY "X" + VARPTR$(Music1$)
PLAY "B- A2 G8 F4 E2 D8 E8 F F C <A F"
```

See also   ON PLAY statement
PLAY() function

 **PLAY**

Purpose   The PLAY() function returns the number of notes left in the music queue. This statement is not available in Visual Basic for Windows.

Syntax   **PLAY(***dummy***)**

Arguments   *dummy* is a dummy number; any numeric value will do.

Description   The PLAY() function returns the number of notes left to play in the music queue. The music queue can hold a maximum of 32 notes. When playing music in the background, use this function to see how many notes you can add to the queue to fill it up. You also can use the ON PLAY event trap to trap to a subroutine whenever the contents of the music queue gets low.

Returns   The result is the number of notes left in the music queue.

For example   The following assignment statement adds some more notes to the music queue if the queue has less than 15 notes left:

```
IF PLAY(0) < 10 THEN
  PLAY "MB MS O4 C4 <A8 F A4 >C F2"
END IF
```

See also   ON PLAY statement
PLAY statement

 **PMAP**

Purpose   The PMAP() function translates between user and screen coordinates. This statement is not available in Visual Basic for Windows.

Syntax   **PMAP(***value***,***mapping***)**

Arguments   *value* is the coordinate value to be converted as a number of any type, or a formula that evaluates to a number.

mapping is a code specifying what coordinate and what transformation to perform—user coordinates to screen coordinates or screen coordinates to user coordinates:

Code	Conversion
0	x-coordinate, user to screen
1	y-coordinate, user to screen
2	x-coordinate, screen to user
3	y-coordinate, screen to user

Description The PMAP() function converts between user and screen coordinates. The default coordinate system is screen coordinates, with the origin in the upper-left corner and positions measured down and to the right in pixels. The number of pixels per inch depends on the current screen setting. Use the WINDOW and VIEW statements to define a user system of coordinates.

Returns The result is the converted value specified by the code.

For example The following two assignment statements convert a location in user units to a location in screen units:

```
XScreen = PMAP(XUser,0)
YScreen = PMAP(YUser,1)
```

See also SCREEN statement
VIEW statement
WINDOW statement

 POINT

Purpose The POINT function returns the color of a point on the screen, or the x,y location of the graphics cursor. This statement is not available in Visual Basic for Windows.

Syntax `POINT({x!,y!|code})`

Arguments *x!* and *y!* are the x,y coordinates of the point to examine in user coordinates, if they are defined, or in screen coordinates if not.

code is a code number indicating what data to return about the current location of the graphics cursor:

Code	Returns
0	x-coordinate, in screen coordinates
1	y-coordinate, in screen coordinates
2	x-coordinate, in user coordinates
3	y-coordinate, in user coordinates

Description   The POINT function returns the color of a point on the screen, or the current location of the graphics cursor. The location of the graphics cursor is the last point drawn or moved to on the screen. The default coordinate system is screen coordinates, with the origin in the upper-left corner and positions measured down and to the right in pixels. The number of pixels per inch depends on the current screen setting. Use the WINDOW and VIEW statements to define a user system of coordinates. If no user system of coordinates has been defined, codes 2 and 3 return the position in screen coordinates. For this function to work, no forms can be visible. See the RGB function for a discussion of colors.

Returns   The result is the color of the selected point, or its location. If the x,y coordinates are outside of the screen, the function returns –1.

For example   The following gets the location and color of the current location of the graphics cursor:

```
xLoc = POINT(2)
yLoc = POINT(3)
theColor& = POINT(xLoc,yLoc)
```

See also   CIRCLE statement
LINE statement
PRINT statement
PSET statement
SCREEN statement
QBCOLOR function
RGB function

 POKE

Purpose	The POKE statement is used to directly change the contents of a byte in memory. This statement is not available in Visual Basic for Windows.
Syntax	POKE *offset%*, *value%*
Arguments	*offset%* is the offset from the beginning of the current segment to the byte to be extracted. The range is 0 to 65,535. The current segment is set with the DEF SEG statement.
	value% is the value to which to change the byte in memory, in the range 0 to 255.
Description	The POKE statement changes the contents of a single location in memory. Use PEEK to read those contents and CALL to execute a program stored at that location.
For example	The following statement changes the contents of byte 50 in the current segment to 129:

POKE 50,129

See also	CALL statement
	DEF SEG statement
	PEEK statement

 POS

Purpose	The POS() function returns the current position in a line of the text cursor. This statement is not available in Visual Basic for Windows.
Syntax	POS(*dummy*)
Arguments	*dummy* is a dummy argument. Any number will do.
Description	The POS() function returns the location in a line of the text cursor. The location is measured in characters from the right. Us CSRLIN() to get the line containing the cursor, or the LOCATE function to move it to a specific position.

Returns   The result is the current position of the text cursor in a line.

For example   The following two assignment statement get the x,y location of the text cursor:

```
xLoc = POS(1)
yLoc = CSRLIN(1)
```

See also   LOCATE statement
SCREEN statement
CSRLIN() function
POINT() function

S PRESET and PSET

Purpose   The PRESET and PSET statements draw a point on the screen. This statement is not available in Visual Basic for Windows.

Syntax   {**PRESET**|**PSET**} [**STEP**] (*x!*, *y!*)[,*color*]

Arguments   STEP indicates that the x,y coordinates are specified in relation to the current position of the graphics cursor and not the upper-left corner of the screen.

x! and *y!* specify the x,y location of the point to be drawn.

color% is the color attribute to use to color the point. The colors available depend on the current screen mode.

Description   The PRESET and PSET statements color a pixel on the screen. No forms can be visible when these functions are used.

For example   The following statements get the location of the current graphics cursor and color it with color attribute 2:

```
xLoc = POINT(2)
yLoc = POINT(3)
PSET (xLoc,yLoc),2
```

See also   LOCATE statement
POINT function

 PRINT

Purpose   The PRINT statement prints data on the screen. This statement is not available in Visual Basic for Windows.

Syntax   **PRINT** [**USING** *format$*;]*arglist*[{;|,}]

Arguments   *format$* is a format string to control the printing of the values in *arglist*. See the FORMAT$ function for an explanation of formatting strings.

arglist is a list of variables and expressions to print. Numeric variables are converted automatically to strings. Commas between arguments print the next argument at the next tab stop (there's a tab stop every 14 characters).

; (a semicolon between arguments) prints the next argument immediately after the last one, with no added spaces between them. Normally, a carriage return/line feed is placed in the file after the arglist is printed. A semicolon at the end of the line leaves the insertion point at the right side of the last character printed.

, (a comma placed at the end of the line) moves the insertion point to the next tab field.

Description   The PRINT statement prints data to the screen. No forms can be visible when you use this statement.

For example   The following statement prints a formatted number on the screen:

```
PRINT USING "   ###0.0";aVal
```

See also   GET statement
INPUT # statement
LINE INPUT # statement
LPRINT statement
OPEN statement
PRINT # statement
PUT statement
WRITE # statement
PRINT method
FORMAT$ function
INPUT$ function

15

 PRINT

Purpose   The PRINT method writes data on a form, a picture box, or the PRINTER object.

Syntax   [*object*.]**PRINT** *arglist*[{;|,}]

Arguments   *object* is the name of the object to draw on, a form, a picture box, or the keyword PRINTER. Omit this argument to use the form containing this statement.

arglist is a list of variables and expressions to print. Numeric variables are converted automatically to strings. Commas between arguments print the next argument at the next tab stop (one every 14 characters).

; (a semicolon between arguments) prints the next argument immediately after the last one, with no added spaces between them. Normally, a carriage return/line feed is printed after *arglist* is printed. A semicolon at the end of the line leaves the insertion point at the right side of the last character printed.

, (a comma is placed at the end of the line) moves the insertion point to the next tab field.

Description   The PRINT method prints text and numbers on a form, a picture box, or the PRINTER object. Printing starts at the position indicated by the CurrentX and CurrentY properties.

For example   The following statements

```
A1 = 5.355
B1 = 4.788
Picture1.PRINT, "Values, are: ", A1, B1, " units"
```

produce

```
Values, are: 5.355        4.788           units
```

on the Picture1 picture box.

See also   GET statement
INPUT # statement
LINE INPUT # statement
LPRINT statement
OPEN statement

PRINT statement
PUT statement
WRITE # statement
PRINT method
INPUT$ function

 PRINT #

Purpose	The PRINT # statement prints data to a disk file.
Syntax	**PRINT** #*filenumber*%,[**USING** *format$*;]*arglist*[{;|,}]
Arguments	*filenumber*% is the file number used when the file was opened with the OPEN statement.

format$ is a format string to control the printing of the values in *arglist*. See the FORMAT$ function for an explanation of formatting strings.

arglist is a list of variables and expressions to print. Numeric variables are converted automatically to strings. Commas between arguments print the next argument at the next tab stop (there's a tab stop every 14 characters).

; (a semicolon between arguments) prints the next argument immediately after the last one, with no added spaces between them. Normally, a carriage return/line feed is placed in the file after the *arglist* is printed. A semicolon at the end of the line leaves the insertion point at the right side of the last character printed.

, (a comma placed at the end of the line) moves the insertion point to the next tab field.

Description	The PRINT # statement prints data in a disk file in exactly the same manner as the PRINT method prints to the screen. This statement is primarily used to create files that are displayed with the DOS TYPE command or by a word processor. If you plan to read the data back into a BASIC program, consider the WRITE # statement instead.
For example	A disk file written with the following statements

```
A1 = 5.355
B1 = 4.788
PRINT #1, "Values, are: ", A1, B1, " units"
WRITE #1, "Values, are: ", A1, B1, " units"
```

15

produces the following:

```
Values, are: 5.355          4.788          units
"Values, are: ",5.355,4.788," units"
```

Reading those values with the following INPUT # statements

```
INPUT #1, A$, B, C, D$
INPUT #1, E$, F, G, H$
```

stores the following data in these variables:

```
A$ = "The values"
B = 0
C = 5.355
D$ = "4.788          units"
E$ = "Thevalues, are: "
F = 5.355
G = 4.788
H$ = " units"
```

Note that the first INPUT # statement stopped reading the string into A$ at the first comma so that the first numeric input, B, sees text rather than a number and gets a value of zero. The second numeric input, C, then reads the first number, and the remaining number and string end up in D$.

See also   GET statement
INPUT # statement
LINE INPUT # statement
OPEN statement
PRINT statement
PUT statement
WRITE # statement
PRINT method
FORMAT$ function
INPUT$ function

PRINTFORM

Purpose   The PRINTFORM method sends a copy of a the form to the printer.

Syntax   [*form.*]**PRINTFORM**

Arguments   *form* is the name of a form. If you omit this argument, the form that contains this statement is assumed.

Description   The PRINTFORM method sends a character-by-character image of a form to the printer. The following special graphics characters are translated as shown before printing:

* ┘,┚, └, ┗, ┌,		
┏,┌,┐	(corners)	+
↓	(on combo box)	v
|■|	(close box)	¦ - ¦
—,=	(horizontal lines)	-
|, ||	(vertical lines)	¦
|▲|	(maximize button)	¦ ^ ¦
| - |	(minimize button)	¦ v ¦
·	(option button)	*
┚	(resize button)	+
|▲|	(restore button)	¦ + ¦
■	(scroll bar)	#
↓	(scroll down)	v
←	(scroll left)	<
→	(scroll right)	>
▌	(scroll up)	^
■	(shadow)	Not printed

For example   The following statement prints the InputDialog form:

InputDialog.PRINTFORM

See also   PRINT method
AutoRedraw property
PrintTarget property

S PUT (File I/O)

Purpose   The PUT statement stores a record in a random access or binary disk file.

Syntax   `PUT [#]filenumber%[,recnum&],recvariable`

Arguments   `filenumber%` is the file number used when the file was opened with the OPEN statement.

`recnum&` is the number of the record to store in a random access file. Omit this argument to use the next record in the file. File records are consecutively numbered, with the first record as record number 1. If the file is opened as binary, `recnum&` is the byte number at which to start writing.

`recvariable` is any variable whose length is less than or equal to the length of a record defined when the file is opened. This usually is a user-defined variable defined with the TYPE statement.

Description   The PUT statement writes a records worth of data to a random access or binary disk file. The record variable may be any type of variable, as long as its total length is less than the length of a record. For random access files, the length of a record is defined with the LEN = `reclen` clause of the OPEN statement. In most cases, you define a record type variable with the TYPE statement and use that to access the disk file. In addition, you can use the FIELD statement to break the disk file buffer into fields. The default length is 128 bytes. For binary files, the record length is as many bytes as can fit into the record variable.

For example   The following statements first define the record variable DayType in the module's declaration section. They then define the variable aDay as type DayType, open a disk file whose name is stored in the variable FileName, load aDay with data, and write it to the first record in the file.

In the declarations section:

```
TYPE DayType          'Type declaration for the
  TheDate AS DOUBLE 'record DayType, 128 bytes
  Flags AS INTEGER  'long
  MSG AS STRING * 118
END TYPE
```

In a procedure:

```
DIM aDay AS DayType
OPEN FileName FOR RANDOM AS #1 LEN = 128
```

```
aDay.TheDate = NOW
aDay.Flags = 1
aDay.Msg = ""
PUT #1, 1, aDay
```

See also   GET statement
                OPEN statement

S PUT (Graphics)

Purpose   The PUT statement transfers a graphics image from an array variable to the screen. This statement is not available in Visual Basic for Windows.

Syntax   **PUT** [**STEP**]$(x!,y!)$, $array$[$(index\%)$]$,method$

Arguments   STEP specifies that the coordinates are relative to the current graphics cursor position.

$x!$ and $y!$ specify the x,y coordinates of the upper-left corner of the image to be captured.

$array$ is the name of the array in which the image is stored. The array can be of any type, but must have a length that is sufficient to hold the image.

$index\%$ is the position in the array at which to start extracting the image.

$method$ is the method to use to combine the image with what is already on the screen. The allowed keywords are as follows:

PSET replaces what is on the screen with the image.

PRESET replaces what is on the screen with the inverse of the image; that is, black changes to white, and white to black.

AND combines the background and the image by using the logical AND operation. The effect is that the image only replaces the parts of the background that already have an image.

OR combines the background and the image with a logical OR operation. The effect is to add the image and the background together.

XOR combines the background and the image using the logical exclusive OR operation. The result is that the images are inverted where they overlap.

15

Description The graphics version of the PUT statement transfers a graphics image from an array variable to the screen. There can be no forms showing when you use this statement. PUT is the inverse of the graphics GET statement.

For example The following statement copies the image stored in A to a rectangle on the screen that has an upper-left corner that is 10 pixels right and 25 pixels down from the upper-left corner of the screen:

```
PUT (10,25), A, PSET
```

See also CIRCLE statement
GET statement
LINE statement
SCREEN statement

 # QBCOLOR

Purpose The QBCOLOR() function returns the color attribute for the standard QuickBASIC colors.

Syntax **QBCOLOR**(*colorcode%*)

Arguments *colorcode%* is a code number ranging from 0 to 15, representing one of the following 16 standard colors:

Code	Color	Code	Color
0	Black	8	Gray
1	Blue	9	Light blue
2	Green	10	Light green
3	Cyan	11	Light cyan
4	Red	12	Light red
5	Magenta	13	Light magenta
6	Yellow or brown	14	Light yellow
7	White	15	Bright white

Description　This function is only for compatibility with Visual Basic for Windows, where it converts color attributes to RGB color numbers. Here, it just returns the same number it was given. See the RGB() function for a discussion of colors.

Returns　The result is the same color attribute that was used as an argument.

For example　The following assignment statement assigns the color number for light red to the variable theColor:

```
theColor = QBCOLOR(12)
```

See also　HEX$ function
RGB() function

 # RANDOMIZE

Purpose　The RANDOMIZE statement initializes the seed of the random-number generator.

Syntax　**RANDOMIZE** [*number%*]

Arguments　*number%* is a number of any type, or a formula that evaluates to a number. Omit *number%* to use the current value of the TIMER() function.

Description　Random numbers in computer programs aren't truly random, but are pseudo-random numbers generated by a function whose output distribution is reasonably random. Consequently, every time you run a Visual Basic program, you get the same sequence of random numbers from the RND() function. There are cases where this is desirable (debugging, for example), but usually you want a different set of numbers every time you run a code.

Random-number generators have a seed value that initializes the function that generates the random numbers, and the RANDOMIZE statement sets that value. If you don't use the RANDOMIZE statement, or always use the same seed value when you run a program, you'll get the same sequence of random numbers every time.

A convenient way to get around that is to omit the *number%* argument on the RANDOMIZE statement, because doing so forces RANDOMIZE to use the value of the TIMER() function. The TIMER() function returns the number of seconds since midnight, so it's highly unlikely that you would get the same sequence of numbers with each run.

15

Use the RANDOMIZE function once near the beginning of your program, before you use any of the RND() functions. In most cases, it is unnecessary to run RANDOMIZE more than once in any program.

For example The following lines initialize the random-number generator and then generate two random numbers: val1, between 0 and 10, and val2, between 5 and 10.

```
RANDOMIZE
val1 = RND * 10
val2 = RND *5 + 5
```

See also RND function
TIMER function

READ

Purpose The READ statement reads data from internal DATA statements into program variables. This statement is not available in Visual Basic for Windows.

Syntax **READ** *varlist*

Arguments *varlist* is a list of variables to receive the data.

Description The READ statement reads data from internal DATA statements into program variables. Use the RESTORE statement to start reading at a particular data statement.

For example The following statements define some values with a DATA statement, use RESTORE to set that DATA statement as the next one to be read, and then read the values into some variables with a READ statement:

```
label1: DATA 27.5, 34, "gold", 0.234
        RESTORE label1
        READ aVal, aNum, Z$, theFrac
```

See also DATA statement
RESTORE statement

S REDIM

Purpose The REDIM statement declares the elements of dynamic arrays, or reallocates static arrays, at the procedure level.

Syntax
```
REDIM [PRESERVED][SHARED] variable(subscripts)
[AS type][,variable (subscripts)
[AS type]]...
```

Arguments PRESERVED specifies that the existing data in the array is to be preserved when the upper limit of an array is changed.

SHARED makes the variables available to all procedures in a module.

variable is a variable name. Array names are followed by parentheses and the subscript range. There can be up to 60 subscripts for static arrays or eight for dynamic arrays. The syntax of the subscript ranges is

```
[lower% TO]upper%[,[lower% TO]upper%]...
```

lower% is the lower limit for the array subscripts. If you omit this argument, 0 is assumed unless the OPTION BASE statement has been executed. (See the OPTION BASE statement.)

upper% is the upper limit for array subscripts.

type is one of the following Visual Basic types: CONTROL, CURRENCY, FORM, INTEGER, LONG, SINGLE, DOUBLE, STRING, STRING*length, or any user type defined with the TYPE statement. *length* is the length of a fixed-length string. Use the AS *type* clause or a variable suffix symbol, but not both, to declare the type of the variable. (See the beginning of this chapter for information on variable suffix symbols.) You cannot change the type of a static array.

Description The REDIM statement changes the number of elements in each dimension of a static array, or sets the number of elements in a dynamic array. When defined, all arrays are initialized to 0. REDIM is used only at the procedure level.

There are two types of arrays in Visual Basic: static and dynamic. Static arrays are defined with a fixed number of elements and thus have a fixed length. You can redimension static arrays, but the new total size in bytes must be the same or less than the old size. You can change only the number of elements in each dimension; you cannot change the number of dimensions or the numeric type of the array.

A dynamic array initially is defined at the module level with no dimensions. The size and dimensions are determined later at the procedure level with a REDIM statement. Memory is allocated for the array when the dimensions are added. Use the ERASE statement to deallocate the memory of dynamic arrays.

For example   Assume anArray was defined in the declarations section of a module as

```
DIM anArray(10,3) AS INTEGER
```

The following statement redefines anArray with the first dimension of the array ranging from 3 to 6 and the second from 0 to 10. Note that this has the same number of dimensions and total number of elements as the original array; they simply are arranged differently.

```
REDIM anArray(3 To 6,10) AS INTEGER
```

See also   COMMON statement
CONST statement
DIM statement
ERASE statement
OPTION BASE statement
STATIC statement

REFRESH

Purpose   The REFRESH method updates the contents of a control after changes.

Syntax   [*object.*]**REFRESH**

Arguments   *object* is the name of the object to refresh; the object is either a form or a control. Omit this argument to use the form containing the statement.

Description   Most Visual Basic objects are refreshed whenever a program is waiting for an event to occur. Use the REFRESH method, however, if you're making changes to a control and want to refresh its contents without exiting a procedure. The DOEVENTS() function also refreshes controls but, additionally, takes care of any events waiting to be handled. REFRESH updates the objects without handling any other pending events. REFRESH also updates the list of filenames in a file list box after adding or deleting any.

> Using REFRESH or DOEVENTS() significantly slows down a drawing program.

For example   The following statement refreshes a picture box named BlackBoard:

```
BlackBoard.REFRESH
```

See also   DOEVENTS function

 REM

Purpose   The REM statement sets the balance of the line as a remark.

Syntax   **REM** *anything*

or

[*statement*]   '*anything*

Arguments   *anything*, as the name indicates, can be anything. The running program ignores this argument.

statement is any programming line.

Description   The REM, or remark, statement documents the operation of a program. A running program ignores any line that begins with the REM keyword, or any text that follows a single quotation mark ('). You can add any text you want in a remark: explain what you're doing, define variables, and so forth.

Use remarks liberally in a program. They make it much easier to understand and debug your program. They quickly pay for the time spent typing them by reducing the time required to modify or debug a program. Although a running program ignores remarks, you can branch to them by using GOTO or GOSUB statements if your program lines are numbered.

For example   The following three lines contain remarks. The first two are all remarks. The last one has an executable statement at the beginning of a line and a remark at the end.

```
REM This is a remark, anything can go here.
'This is also a remark,
aVal = ABS(1)   'but not the beginning of this line.
```

See also   None

573

 REMOVEITEM

Purpose The REMOVEITEM method removes an entry from a list or combo box.

Syntax `control.`**`REMOVEITEM`** `index%`

Arguments `control` is the name of a list or combo box. if the control is on another form, include the name of the form with the name of the control as follows: `form.control`. If you don't include the name, this argument defaults to the control on the form containing the method.

`index%` is the number of the item in the list or combo box to remove. The first item is number 0, the second is 1, and so forth. Use the `ListCount` property to determine the largest number `index%` can be. The last item in the list is number `ListCount - 1`.

Description The REMOVEITEM method removes items from the list in a list or combo box.

For Example The following code fragment repeatedly removes the first item of the `List1` list box on `Form2` until the list is empty:

```
WHILE Form2.List1.ListCount >0
  Form2.List1.REMOVEITEM 0
WEND
```

See also ADDITEM method
List property
ListCount property
ListIndex property

 RESET

Purpose The RESET statement flushes all file buffers and then closes all disk files.

Syntax **`RESET`**

Arguments None

Description The RESET statement empties all file buffers and closes all files. When a program writes to a disk file, it doesn't really write to the disk but to a buffer in memory. When the buffer is full, the buffer is written to disk as a block.

The primary use of RESET is to ensure that any buffers linked to files on removable media are written to disk, even if they aren't full. The media then can be safely removed. Otherwise, a file on a removed disk may be incomplete. Ending an executable program or the Visual Basic program has the same effect. Ending an interpreted program running within Visual Basic may not close the files completely until you end Visual Basic.

If your program does not open any disk files, there is no reason to execute RESET.

For example   The following procedure is for an Exit command that ends a program. Before executing the END statement, it executes RESET to ensure that all disk files have been closed and the file buffers have been flushed to the files:

```
SUB ExitCmd_Click ()
'End the program
RESET
END
END SUB
```

See also   DOEVENTS function

S RESTORE

Purpose   The RESTORE statement sets the first DATA statement to be read with the READ statement. This statement is not available in Visual Basic for Windows.

Syntax   **RESTORE** [{*line*|*label*}]

Arguments   *line* is the line number of the DATA statement to set as the first to be read.

label is the label of the DATA statement to be set as the first one to be read. If you do not specify a line or label, the first DATA statement in the module is specified.

Description   The RESTORE statement specifies which data statement is to be read first with the READ statement.

For example   The following statements define some values with a DATA statement, use RESTORE to set that DATA statement as the next one to be read, and then read the values into some variables with a READ statement:

```
label1: DATA 27.5, 34, "gold", 0.234
        RESTORE label1
        READ aVal, aNum, Z$, theFrac
```

See also   DATA statement
                READ statement

 RGB

Purpose   The RGB() function creates a color attribute from three color intensities.

Syntax   **RGB(**_red%_,_green%_,_blue%_**)**

Arguments   _red%_ is the intensity of red as an integer ranging from 0 (black) to 255 (bright red).

green% is the intensity of green as an integer ranging from 0 (black) to 255 (bright green).

blue% is the intensity of blue as an integer ranging from 0 (black) to 255 (bright blue).

Description   The RGB() function is available for compatibility with Visual Basic for Windows. RGB converts three color intensities (red, green, and blue) into one of the 16 color attributes that most closely resembles the Visual Basic color number.

A Visual Basic for Windows color number is a single LONG integer. Within that integer are four one-byte codes. The rightmost three bytes contain the color in RGB format. The rightmost byte contains the intensity of red. The second byte from the right contains the intensity of green. The third byte from the right contains the intensity of blue. Each byte holds a value that ranges from 0 to 255, where 0 is no color, or black, and 255 is the brightest.

The simplest way to represent these values is as hexadecimal numbers (see the HEX$() function), where each byte is represented by a pair of hexadecimal digits. The following are some standard colors and their associated color numbers:

Color	Hexadecimal Value
Black	&H000000
Red	&H0000FF
Green	&H00FF00
Yellow	&H00FFFF
Blue	&HFF0000
Magenta	&HFF00FF
Cyan	&HFFFF00
White	&HFFFFFF

Visual Basic for DOS uses the standard 16 BASIC color attributes. The number of attributes available and the number of colors that you can assign to those attributes are determined by the adapter card and monitor in a system, and the screen mode set with the SCREEN statement. (See the SCREEN statement for a list of what colors and attributes are available for the different screen modes.) In most cases, the standard attributes and colors are as follows:

Attribute	Color
0	Black
1	Blue
2	Green
3	Cyan
4	Red
5	Magenta
6	Brown
7	White
8	Gray
9	Light blue
10	Light green

continues

Attribute	Color
11	Light cyan
12	Light red
13	Light magenta
14	Yellow
15	Intense white

Returns The result is an integer containing the color attribute that most closely resembles the RGB color generated in Visual Basic for Windows.

For example The following assignment statement assigns the color attribute for light red to the variable theColor:

```
theColor = RGB(255,0,0)
```

See also COLOR statement
PALETTE statement
SCREEN statement
HEX$ function
QBCOLOR function

RIGHT$

Purpose The RIGHT$() function extracts a substring from the right side of a string.

Syntax **RIGHT$(***string$***,***numchar&***)**

Arguments *string$* is a string, or a formula that results in a string.

numchar& is the number of characters to extract from the string.

Description The RIGHT$() function extracts a substring from the right side of a string. Use this function with the LEFT$() and the MID$() functions to extract different substrings.

Returns The resulting string contains the rightmost *numchar&* characters from *string$*.

For example   The following is from the Immediate window and compares the LEFT$(),
RIGHT$(), and MID$() functions:

```
A$ = "This is a string to examine"
```

Function	*Result*
LEFT$(A$,6)	This i
RIGHT$(A$,5)	amine
MID$(A$,9,5)	a str

See also   LEFT$() function
MID$() function

RMDIR

Purpose   The RMDIR statement removes a subdirectory from the file system.

Syntax   **RMDIR** *path$*

Arguments   *path$* is a string containing the path to the directory to be removed,
including the disk letter, with the following syntax:

[*drive*:][\]*directory*[*directory*]

where *drive* is the drive letter and *directory* is a directory name. Omit the
drive argument to use the current drive. If you omit the first backslash, the
path is assumed to start in the default directory of the specified drive. The
string must be less than 128 characters long.

Description   The RMDIR statement deletes a directory in the file system in the same
manner as the DOS command of the same name. The directory to delete
must be empty or an error results. If you do not specify a disk drive in the
path$ argument, RMDIR uses the current drive. If you omit the first backslash,
the path is assumed to be relative to the default directory on either the
current drive (if no drive is specified) or on the specified drive.

For example   The following statement deletes the UTILITIES directory in the TOOLS
directory on the C drive:

```
RMDIR "C:\TOOLS\UTILITIES"
```

The next statement deletes the C directory within the PROGRAMS directory within the current default directory; that is, if the current directory is D:\APPS, the command deletes the D:\APPS\PROGRAMS\C directory.

```
RMDIR "PROGRAMS\C"
```

The following code fragment uses the DIR$( ) function to see whether the directory in the Path$ variable is empty before trying to delete it:

```
IF DIR$(thePath$) = "" THEN
RMDIR thePath$
ELSE
  MSGBOX "The directory isn't empty"
END IF
```

See also   HDIR statement
CHDRIVE statement
KILL statement
MKDIR statement
NAME statement
CURDIR$ function
DIR$ function

RND

Purpose   The RND( ) function returns a random number between 0 and 1.

Syntax   **RND**[(*number#*)]

Arguments   *number#* is a number of any type, or a formula that evaluates to a number. If *number#* is a negative number, RND( ) returns the same number every time. If *number#* is 0, it returns the previous number again. If *number#* is positive or omitted, the next random number in the sequence is returned.

Description   Random numbers in computer programs aren't truly random, but are pseudo-random numbers generated by a function whose output distribution is reasonably random. Consequently, every time you run a Visual Basic program, you get the same sequence of random numbers from the RND( ) function. There are cases where this is desirable (debugging, for example), but usually you want a different set of numbers every time you run a code.

Random-number generators have a seed value that initializes the function that generates the random numbers, and the RANDOMIZE statement sets that value. The RND() function returns the next number in the random-number sequence, or, if the argument is negative or 0, a specific random number.

Returns The result is a random number between 0 and 1. To get a random number with a different range, multiply RND by the width of the range and add the value of the lower limit.

For example The following lines initialize the random-number generator and then generate two random numbers: val1, between 0 and 10, and val2, between 5 and 10:

```
RANDOMIZE
val1 = RND * 10
val2 = RND *5 + 5
```

See also RANDOMIZE function
TIMER function

 # RSET

Purpose The RSET statement right-justifies strings.

Syntax **RSET** *fixedstring$* = *string$*

Arguments *fixedstring$* is a fixed-length string.

string$ is a string to be right-justified in the fixed-length string, or a formula that results in a string to be right-justified in the fixed-length string.

Description The RSET statement right-justifies a string in a fixed-length string. When you right-justify a string into a fixed-length string, only as much of the right side of the string as will fit in the fixed-length string is copied. If the string is shorter than the fixed-length string, the remainder of the left side of the fixed-length string is filled with blanks. To left-justify strings, use LSET.

For example The following lines define a fixed-length string and right-justify the word "Welcome" into it:

```
DIM anFString AS STRING *10
RSET anFString = "Welcome"
```

The variable anFString now contains Welcome.

581

See also   LET statement

                LSET statement

 **RTRIM\$**

Purpose	The RTRIM\$() function removes trailing blanks from the right side of a string.
Syntax	**RTRIM\$(**string\$**)**
Arguments	string\$ is a string, or a formula that results in a string.
Description	The RTRIM\$ function removes trailing spaces from strings. To remove leading spaces, use the LTRIM\$() function.
Returns	The result is the argument string with the blanks removed from the right side.
For example	The following line trims the blanks from the right side of a string and stores it in A\$:

```
A$ = RTRIM$("      234.45      ")
```

A\$ now contains the string "   234.45".

See also   LTRIM function

 **RUN**

Purpose	The RUN statement runs a BASIC program in memory, or starts another application. This statement is not available in Visual Basic for Windows.
Syntax	**RUN** [{line|filename\$}]
Arguments	line is the line number of a line at the module level of a non-form module.

filename\$ is a string containing the filename of a BASIC program (.BAS) or an executable file (.EXE or .COM), and an optional directory path if the file isn't in the current directory. The path, including the disk letter, has the following syntax:

```
[drive:][[\]directory[\directory...\]]filename
```

where *drive* is the drive letter, *directory* is a directory name, and *filename* is the filename. Omit the *drive* argument to use the current drive. If you omit the first backslash, the path is assumed to start in the default directory of the specified drive. You can change the current directory and the current drive by using CHDIR and CHDRIVE.

Description   The RUN statement runs a BASIC program starting at a specific line number, or executes an external program. When you're in the Visual Basic programming environment, the RUN command must reference a line number or a numeric label—alphanumeric labels are not allowed here—in the current module. Encountering a RUN command in a code is the same as ending the program and then starting it up again from scratch. All files are closed and all variables are initialized. To run another program with variables intact, use the CHAIN statement.

A compiled code can not execute an external BASIC program, but must reference an executable file.

For example   The following statement loads and runs the program BEAR.BAS:

```
RUN "BEAR.BAS"
```

See also   CHAIN statement

SADD

Purpose   The SADD() function returns the address of a string variable in memory. This statement is not available in Visual Basic for Windows.

Syntax   **SADD(***string-variable***)**

Arguments   *string-variable* is a string variable for which you want to get the address in memory.

Description   The SADD() function gets the address in memory of a string variable. You use this function primarily when calling external procedures, written in other languages, that need access to that string.

Don't change the length of a string passed to an external procedure in this manner. Visual Basic can move strings, so get this address just before you need it. To get the segment address, use the SSEG() function.

Returns   The result is the integer (two-byte) number of bytes between the start of the current data segment, set with DEF SEG, and the start of the string.

For example   The following assignment statement gets the address of a string:

```
offset% = SADD(aString$)
```

See also   CALL statement
DEF SEG statement
SSEG() function
SSEGADD() function

SCREEN

Purpose   The SCREEN statement sets the current screen mode. This statement is not available in Visual Basic for Windows.

Syntax   SCREEN [*mode*][,[*color-switch*]
[,[*active-page*][,*visual-page*]

Arguments   *mode* is the screen mode to invoke, as given in the following table. Not all modes can be invoked for all combinations of monitor card and monitor.

Mode	Resolution	Attribute	Colors	Pages
0	Text mode	2	16	1
1	320 × 200 Color	4	16	1
2	640 × 200 B/W	2	16	1
3	720 × 348 B/W	1	1	2
4	640 × 400 Color	1	16	1
7	320 × 200 Color	16	16	$2^1, 4^2, 8^3$

8	640 × 200 Color	16	16	1^1, 2^2, 4^3
9	640 × 350 Color	4^1, 16^2	64	2
10	640 × 350 B/W	4	9	2
11	640 × 480 Color	2	256	1
12	640 × 480 Color	16	256	1
13	320 5 200 Color	256	256	1

[1] *64K EGA memory*

[2] *128K EGA memory*

[3] *256K EGA memory*

Screen Mode 0 (Text Only):
Adapters: MDPA, CGA, Hercules, Olivetti, EGA, VGA, or MCGA
Text format: 40 × 25, 40 × 43, 40 × 50, 80 × 25, 80 × 43 (EGA or VGA),
80 × 50 (VGA)
16 colors/2 attributes
16 colors/16 attributes (CGA or EGA)
64 colors/16 attributes (EGA or VGA)
Set background, border, and text colors.
Add 16 to text color to get blinking text.

Screen Mode 1 (320 × 200 Graphics):
Adapters: CGA, EGA, VGA, or MCGA
Text format: 40 × 25
8 background colors
3 palettes of 3 foreground colors set with the Color statement (CGA)
16 colors/4 attributes (EGA, VGA, or MCGA)

Screen Mode 2 (640 × 200 Graphics):
Adapters: CGA, EGA, VGA, or MCGA
Text format: 80 × 25
2 colors: black and white (CGA)
16 colors/2 attributes (EGA or VGA)

Screen Mode 3 (720 × 348 Graphics):
Adapters: Hercules, Olivetti, or AT&T, monochrome monitor
Text format: 80 × 25
2 screen pages
Load MSHERC.COM

15

Screen Mode 4 (640 × 400 Graphics):
Adapters: Hercules, Olivetti, or AT&T
Text format: 80 × 25
16 colors/1 attribute
Background is black
Load MSHERC.COM

Screen Mode 7 (320 × 200 Graphics):
Adapters: EGA or VGA
Text format: 40 × 25
2 pages (64K adapter memory)
4 pages (128K adapter memory)
8 pages (256K adapter memory)
16 colors/16 attributes

Screen Mode 8 (640 × 200 Graphics):
Adapters: EGA or VGA
Text format: 80 × 25
1 page (64K adapter memory)
2 pages (128K adapter memory)
4 pages (256K adapter memory)
16 colors/16 attributes

Screen Mode 9 (640 × 350 Graphics):
Adapters: EGA or VGA
Text format: 80 × 25, 80 × 43
1 page (64K adapter memory)
1 page (128K adapter memory)
2 pages (256K adapter memory)
16 colors/4 attributes (64K adapter memory)
64 colors/16 attributes (>64K adapter memory)

Screen Mode 10 (640 × 350 Graphics):
Adapters: EGA or VGA, monochrome monitor
Text format: 80 × 25, 80 × 43
1 page (128K adapter memory)
2 pages (256K adapter memory)
9 shades of gray/4 attributes

Screen Mode 11 (640 × 480 Graphics):
Adapters: VGA or MCGA
Text format: 80 × 30, 80 × 60
256K colors/2 attributes

Screen Mode 12 (640 × 480 Graphics):
Adapters: VGA
Text format: 80 × 30, 80 × 60
256K colors/16 attributes

Screen Mode 13 (320 × 200 Graphics):
Adapters: VGA or MCGA
Text format: 40 × 25
256K colors/256 attributes

color-switch is a code to enable and disable color in modes that allow color:

Mode 0 (text):

0	color
1	black/white

Modes >0:

0	Black/white
1	Color

active-page and *visual-page* are for monitor-and-adapter combinations with more than one page of video memory. These two numbers determine which is the active page (the one being drawn on) and which is the visual page (the one that can be seen). These enable drawing on one page while the other is being viewed, and therefore are used for smooth animation.

Description The SCREEN statement sets the current screen mode for all following graphics and drawing commands. This statement can be used only when no forms are showing. Execute this statement before doing any drawing, to set the available colors and the screen resolution. Use the WINDOW and VIEWPORT statements to set the drawing area and define a coordinate system. Use the PALETTE statement to change the color associated with a color attribute.

The standard colors are   as follows:

Attribute	*Color*
0	Black
1	Blue
2	Green
3	Cyan
4	Red

continues

Attribute	Color
5	Magenta
6	Brown
7	White
8	Gray
9	Light blue
10	Light green
11	Light cyan
12	Light red
13	Light magenta
14	Yellow
15	Intense white

The three palettes used in mode 1 are as follows:

Default palette:

Attribute	Color
0	Black
1	Light cyan
2	Light magenta
3	Intense white

Even palette set with `Color ,,0`:

Attribute	Color
0	Black
1	Green
2	Red
3	Brown

Odd palette set with Color ,,1:

Attribute	Color
0	Black
1	Cyan
2	Magenta
3	White

For example The following statement sets screen mode 2 (640 by 200 monochrome graphics):

```
SCREEN 2
```

See also COLOR statement
PALETTE statement
QBCOLOR() function
RGB() function

SCREEN

Purpose The SCREEN function returns the character or color at a particular location on the screen.

Syntax SCREEN(row%,column%[,flag%])

Arguments row% is the row containing the character to examine.

column% is the column containing the character to examine.

flag% is a code indicating what to return concerning the character at the intersection of row% and column%. The codes are as follows,

Code Returns
0   The ASCII code of the character (default)
1   The foreground color

Description The SCREEN() function returns the ASCII code or the foreground color of a particular character on the screen. See Appendix B "ASCII/ANSI Code Chart" for a list of ASCII codes and characters.

Returns The result is the ASCII code or color code of a character on the screen.

For example The following statement gets the color of the character on the third row down from the top and the 15th column from the left of the screen:

```
theColor = SCREEN(3,15,1)
```

See also LOCATE statement
POS function
CSRLIN function
POINT function

 SECOND

Purpose The SECOND function calculates the second of the minute from a serial-date number.

Syntax `SECOND(serialdate#)`

Arguments `serialdate#` is a serial-date number. A serial-date number is a double-precision number containing the date represented as the number of days since December 30, 1899. Negative serial-date numbers represent dates from January 1, 1753 to December 30, 1899. Times are represented as fractions of a day. Years after 1900 are represented by the same serial-date numbers used in several popular spreadsheet programs.

Description The SECOND() function takes a serial-date number and returns the second of the minute represented by that number. To extract the day, month, and year, use the DAY(), MONTH(), and YEAR() functions. To extract the time, use the MINUTE(), and HOUR() functions.

Returns The result is the second of the minute as an integer from 1 to 59.

For example The following statement extracts the second (0) from a serial-date number for noon on March 17, 1987:

```
theSecond = SECOND(31853.5)
```

See also DATE$ statement
TIME$ statement
DATE$ function
DATESERIAL function
DATEVALUE function
DAY function

MINUTE function
MONTH function
NOW function
TIME$ function
TIMER function
TIMESERIAL function
TIMEVALUE function
WEEKDAY function
YEAR function

 SEEK

Purpose   The SEEK() function returns the current read/write location in a disk file.

Syntax   **SEEK(**`filenumber%`**)**

Arguments   `filenumber%` is the file number assigned to a file when it was opened with the OPEN statement.

Description   The SEEK() function gets the number of the next record or byte in a file following the last one accessed. The first byte or record in a file is number 1, the second is number 2, and so forth. This complements the LOC() function, which returns the last record or byte accessed. To set the position in a file, use the SEEK statement.

Returns   The result is the current position in the open file. For random-access files, this is the number of the record following the last one accessed. For sequential files, this is the number of the next byte to be read or written. For binary files, this is the number of the byte following the last one accessed.

For example   The following line stores the current read/write position for file number 1 in the variable A&:

```
A& = SEEK(1)
```

See also   OPEN statement
SEEK statement
EOF function
LOC function
LOF function

 SEEK

Purpose	The SEEK statement sets the current read/write position in a disk file.
Syntax	**SEEK** [#]*filenumber%*, *location&*
Arguments	*filenumber%* is the file number assigned to a file when it was opened with the OPEN statement.
	location& is the location at which the next read or write operation is to occur. This must be a LONG integer greater than 0. For random-access files, this is the record number. For sequential-access and binary files, this is the byte number. Both bytes and records number the first record as 1, the second as 2, and so forth.
Description	The SEEK statement sets the current position in a file for read and write operations. This is largely for sequential-access and binary files, because the record number used with GET and PUT statements overrides the settings of this statement.
For example	The following statement moves the current position in file number 1 to the 25th byte if it is a sequential or binary file, or the 25th record if it is a random-access file:

```
SEEK #1, 25
```

See also	GET statement
	OPEN statement
	PUT statement
	EOF function
	LOC function
	LOF function
	SEEK function

 SELECT CASE

Purpose	The SELECT CASE statement selects one of a group of blocks of code to execute according to the value of an expression.

Syntax   `SELECT CASE` *expression*
          [`CASE` {*val1*|*val1* `TO` *val2*|`IS` *oper val3*}
↳   [,{*val1*|*val1* `TO` *val2*|`IS` *oper val3*}]...
          [*block1*]]
          [`CASE` {*val1*|*val1* `TO` *val2*|`IS` *oper val3*}
↳   [,{*val1*|*val1* `TO` *val2*|`IS` *oper val3*}]...
          [*block2*]]
          [`CASE ELSE`]
          [*blockelse*]
          `END SELECT`

Arguments   *expression* is any text or numeric expression.

CASE is a CASE statement. If the value of *expression* matches one of the values or ranges that follow the CASE keyword, the block of code following that CASE statement is executed. There can be as many CASE statements as are needed.

val1, *val2*, and *val3* are string or numeric values to compare to the value of *expression* to select which code block to execute. If only a single value is used, it must match *expression* exactly to select a block. If the TO clause is used, the expression must be within the specified range. If the IS clause is used, the expression must fit the relationship given by the *oper* operator.

oper is a logical operator ($>$, $<$, $>=$, $<=$, $=$, or $<>$.)

block1, *block2*, and *blockelse* are blocks of code to execute if *expression* matches a CASE statement. Only the first block whose CASE statement matches *expression* is executed.

CASE ELSE is a statement that specifies that the block of code that follows it be executed if none of the other CASE statements match.

Description   The SELECT CASE statement is a powerful way to select among several blocks of code by using the value of an expression as a selector. Only one of the blocks of code within the SELECT CASE statement is executed. When the SELECT CASE statement is encountered, the value of *expression* is calculated and compared to the values and ranges on the first CASE statement. If a match is found, the block of code following that statement is executed and then execution jumps to the statement following the END SELECT statement. If a match isn't found, the next CASE statement is checked. This continues until a match is found or, if no match is found, the code block after the CASE ELSE statement is executed. If there is no match and no CASE ELSE statement, execution continues after the END SELECT statement.

593

The comparisons done in the CASE statements must match exactly. If *expression* is text, it must match both character and case. If a range is given, the ASCII codes of the characters determine the extent of the range (see CHR$() and Appendix B, "ASCII/ANSI Code Chart").

For example   The following code block prints text strings to the screen according to the value of the variable Action. If Action equals 5, the first CASE statement is activated and

```
Action = 5
```

is printed. Note that the second CASE statement won't be activated even though Action is in its range. If Action is in the range 2 to 6, but not equal to 5, the second CASE statement is activated and

```
2 < Action < 6 but not 5
```

is printed. If Action is 9 or greater than 10, the third CASE statement is activated and

```
Action = 9, or is greater than 10
```

is printed. If Action does not fit any of these ranges, the last CASE statement is activated, and

```
Action did not fit anything
```

is printed.

```
SELECT CASE Action
  Case 5
    SCREEN.PRINT "Action = 5"
  CASE 2 TO 6
    SCREEN.PRINT " 2 < Action < 6 but not 5"
  CASE IS > 10, 9
    SCREEN.PRINT "Action = 9, or is greater than 10"
  CASE ELSE
    SCREEN.PRINT "Action did not fit anything"
END SELECT
```

See also   IF...THEN statement
ON...GOSUB statement
ON...GOTO statement

SETFOCUS

Purpose The SETFOCUS method moves the focus to the specified control.

Syntax *object*.**SETFOCUS**

Arguments *object* is the name of the object to which to move the focus. The object must be available to receive the focus.

Description The SETFOCUS method moves the focus to the specified object.

For example The following moves the focus to the Command1 command button:

```
Command1.SETFOCUS
```

See also ActiveControl property

SETMEM

Purpose The SETMEM() function changes the size of the far memory heap and returns its size. This statement is not available in Visual Basic for Windows.

Syntax **SETMEM**(*bytes-change*)

Arguments *bytes-change* is the number of bytes by which to increase or decrease the far heap.

Description The far heap is an area of memory in which many of Visual Basic's data values, such as strings, are stored. The SETMEM() function can change the amount of memory in this far heap. Use this function to deallocate some of the far heap to allow another language's heap manager to allocate the memory. The first time you use SETMEM(), you cannot increase the size of the far heap because the far heap is initialized at the maximum size.

Returns The result depends on the argument. If the argument is less than or greater than 0, SETMEM() returns the maximum size for the heap. If the argument is 0, the function returns the current size of the heap.

For example The following assignment statement reduces the far heap by 1,024 bytes:

```
a = SETMEM(-1024)
```

See also FRE() function

15

 **SETTEXT**

Purpose	The SETTEXT method puts a text string onto the CLIPBOARD object.
Syntax	**CLIPBOARD.SETTEXT** *text$*
Arguments	*text$* is the text string to put on the CLIPBOARD object.
Description	The SETTEXT method puts a text string onto the CLIPBOARD object.
For example	The following statement puts the contents of the Text property of the Text1 text box onto the clipboard:

```
CLIPBOARD.SETTEXT Text1.Text
```

See also	GETTEXT method

 **SETUEVENT**

Purpose	The SETUEVENT statement signals that a user-defined event has occurred. This statement is not available in Visual Basic for Windows.
Syntax	**SETUEVENT**
Arguments	None
Description	The SETUEVENT statement signals to a program that a user-defined event has occurred. SETUEVENT is loaded with any compiled program and when any library is loaded into the programming environment with the /L switch. To be used, an event trap must have been defined with the ON UEVENT GOSUB statement and enabled with the UEVENT ON statement. The SETUEVENT statement is the only way to activate a UEVENT event trap.
For example	The following procedure defines and enables a user event trap and then activates it:

```
ON UEVENT GOSUB DoEvent    'define the trap
UEVENT ON                  'enable the trap
some statements
IF some-user-condition THEN
  SETUEVENT                'activate the trap
```

```
END IF
some statements
DoEvent:                        'start of the trap handler
handle the event
RETURN                          'continue after handling
                                 'the trap
```

See also   ON UEVENT statement
UEVENT ON statement

 **SGN**

Purpose   The SGN() function returns the sign of a number.

Syntax   **SGN(***number***)**

Arguments   *number* is a number of any type, or a formula that evaluates to a number.

Description   The SGN() function gets the sign of a numeric value.

Returns   The result is the sign of *number*. If *number* is greater than 0, it returns 1. If *number* is less than 0, it returns –1. If number equals 0, it returns 0.

For example   The following lines assign –1 to A, 0 to B, and 1 to C:

```
A = SGN(-376)
B = SGN(0)
C = SGN(476.98)
```

See also   ABS function

 **SHARED**

Purpose   The SHARED statement defines variables in SUB and FUNCTION procedures, and shares those variables with the module-level code that contains the procedures. This statement is not available in Visual Basic for Windows.

Syntax **SHARED** *variable*[([*subscripts*])][**AS** *type*]
[,*variable*[([*subscripts*])][**AS** *type*]]...

Arguments
variable is a variable name. Array names are followed by parentheses and the subscript range. There can be up to 60 subscripts. Omit subscripts to define a dynamic array whose subscripts and size are defined later in a program with a REDIM statement. The syntax of the subscript ranges is

[*lower%* **TO**]*upper%*[,[*lower%* **TO**]*upper%*]...

lower% is the lower limit for the array subscripts. If you omit this argument, 0 is assumed unless the OPTION BASE statement has been executed. (See the OPTION BASE statement for more information.)

upper% is the upper limit for array subscripts.

type is one of the following Visual Basic types: CONTROL, CURRENCY, FORM, INTEGER, LONG, SINGLE, DOUBLE, STRING, STRING*length*, or any user type defined with the TYPE statement. *length* is the length of a fixed-length string. Use the AS *type* clause or a variable suffix symbol, but not both, to declare the type of the variable. (See the beginning of this chapter for information on suffix symbols.)

Description
The SHARED statement—like the DIM and COMMON statements—declares the type of variables and sets the dimensions of array-type variables. In addition, it shares those variables with any module level code in the same form or module. The SHARED statement can be used only in a SUB or FUNCTION procedure.

When defined, all arrays are initialized to 0. Use DIM SHARED at the form or module level to define variables available to the entire form or module. Alternatively, use DIM at the procedure level to define variables available only in a procedure. Use the COMMON statement to define global variables.

For example
The following statement defines the variable myFile as a string variable, then defines anArray as a two-dimensional array of integers. The first dimension of the array ranges from 3 to 6 and the second ranges from 0 to 10, giving a total of 44 elements in the array. These variables now are available in the procedure that contains the SHARED statement and in the module-level code of the module that contains the procedure.

```
SHARED myFile AS STRING, anArray(3 To 6,10)
AS INTEGER
```

See also
COMMON statement
CONST statement
DIM statement

ERASE statement
OPTION BASE statement
REDIM statement
STATIC statement
$DYNAMIC metacommand
$STATIC metacommand

 SHELL

Purpose	The SHELL statement suspends Visual Basic and launches another application. This statement is not available in Visual Basic for Windows.
Syntax	**SHELL** *program$*
Arguments	*program$* is a string containing the program name, including the path if the program isn't in the current directory, and any command-line switches. If you omit *program$*, another command-line interpreter (COMMAND.COM) is launched.
Description	The SHELL statement is used to launch another application. When that application completes, Visual Basic resumes with the statement after the SHELL statement.
For example	The following lines run the Timer program developed in Part II, "Opening Up Visual Basic":

```
SHELL "Timer.exe"
```

See also	None

 SHOW

Purpose	The SHOW method makes a form visible.
Syntax	[{*form.*|**SCREEN.**}]**SHOW** [*modal%*]
Arguments	*form* is the name of a form to show. If you omit this argument, the form on which this command resides is assumed.

SCREEN if used, makes visible all forms hidden with the SCREEN.HIDE statement.

modal% determines whether a form is modal or modeless. If the *modal%* argument is 1, the form is modal, and no other form in the program can be made active until this form is hidden or unloaded. If this argument is 0, the form is modeless and you can cover the form simply by clicking the other window.

Description   The SHOW method displays a form. If the form has not yet been loaded, the SHOW method loads it. (To load a form so that you can access its properties, yet leave it unseen, use the HIDE method.) A form that has been made visible with this method can be modal or modeless. Modal forms must be handled and closed before any other forms in a program can be accessed. Making a form modal prevents any other form in the program from being made active, although other programs can be made active. The code after the line containing the SHOW method is not executed until the modal form is closed or hidden.

Use modal forms for dialog boxes whose questions must be answered before a program can continue. You can send nonmodal forms to the background by simply clicking some other form.

For example   The **Save** command of the **File** menu is an obvious place to use the SHOW method. This procedure checks whether the variable FileName contains a filename. If it does, the procedure calls the SaveIt procedure to save the file; otherwise, the procedure calls the SaveDialog dialog box to get a filename. Nothing else can be done until the Save Dialog dialog box is closed.

```
SUB SaveCmd_Click ()
IF FileName <> "" THEN
  SaveIt
ELSE
  SaveDialog.Show 1
END IF
END SUB
```

See also   HIDE method
LOAD method
UNLOAD method
Visible property

 SIN

Purpose	The SIN() function calculates and returns the sine of an angle in radians.
Syntax	**SIN(***angle***)**
Arguments	*angle* is an angle in radians as a number, or as a formula that evaluates to a number of any numeric type.
Description	The SIN() function calculates the sine of an angle, expressed in radians. To calculate the sine of an angle expressed in degrees, use the following:

```
Pi = 3.141592654
theSine = SIN(dangle*Pi/180))
```

where *dangle* is measured in degrees.

Returns	The result is the sine of *angle*, a number between –1 and 1.
For example	The following two assignment statements calculate the sine of two angles, one in radians and one in degrees:

```
A = SIN(3.25)      'Assigns the sine of 3.25 radians
                   'to A = -0.108195.
Pi = 3.141592654
B = SIN(27.8*Pi/180)   'Assigns the sine of 27.8
                       'degrees to B = 0.466387.
```

See also	ATN function COS function TAN function

 SINGLE

Purpose	The data type SINGLE matches or defines single-precision, floating-point variables.
Syntax	*variable* **AS SINGLE**
Arguments	*variable* is a variable name.

Description   The data type SINGLE is used in SUB and FUNCTION procedure headings to declare a variable as a single-precision, floating-point type so that Visual Basic can check values passed to the procedure. It also is used in a DIM, COMMON, SHARED, or STATIC statement to define a variable as single-precision, floating-point. The SINGLE data type is a four-byte, floating-point number that ranges from -3.402823×10^{38} to -1.401298×10^{-45} for negative numbers and 1.401298×10^{-45} to 3.402823×10^{38} for positive numbers. You can also define the SINGLE data type by appending the ! character to the variable name. SINGLE precision constants are written with an E between the mantissa and the exponent (that is, $1.234\times10^{56} = 1.234E56$).

For example   The following procedure defines ANumber as a SINGLE precision type in the function heading so that Visual Basic can check the type of values passed to it. The function then scales the value by dividing by 10,000.

```
SUB ScaleIt (ANumber AS DOUBLE)
ANumber = ANumber/10000!
END SUB
```

See also   COMMON statement
DIM statement
SHARED statement
STATIC statement
TYPE statement
ANY data type
CONTROL data type
CURRENCY data type
FORM data type
INTEGER data type
LONG data type
DOUBLE data type
STRING data type

 SLEEP

Purpose   The SLEEP statement suspends program operation for a specified number of seconds, or until a key is pressed. This statement is not available in Visual Basic for Windows.

Syntax	**SLEEP** [*seconds%*]
Arguments	*seconds%* is the integer number of seconds to pause. If *seconds%* is 0 or omitted, Visual Basic pauses until a key is pressed or an active event is trapped.
Description	The SLEEP statement suspends a program for the specified number of seconds or, if the argument is 0 or omitted, until a key is pressed or an event trap is triggered. Event traps, such as COM or ERROR, must be defined and enabled to interrupt the SLEEP statement.
For example	The following statement causes a program to pause for 30 seconds:
	SLEEP 30
See also	ON *event* statements *event* ON statements WAIT statement

SOUND

Purpose	The SOUND statement plays tones through the speaker. This statement is not available in Visual Basic for Windows.
Syntax	**SOUND** *frequency, duration*
Arguments	*frequency* is the frequency of the sound in hertz (cycles per second). The range is 37 to 32,767, but sounds above approximately 13,000 Hz can't be heard by most people.
	duration is the duration of the sound in clock ticks. The range is 0 to 65,535, and there are 18.2 ticks per second. The value 0 turns off a tone, as does executing a PLAY statement.
Description	The SOUND statement plays tones through the computer's speakers.
For example	The following statement produces a 1 kHz tone for 2 seconds:
	SOUND 1000,36
See also	BEEP statement ON PLAY statement PLAY statement

 SPACE$

Purpose	The SPACE$() function returns a string of spaces.
Syntax	**SPACE$(***number***)**
Arguments	*number* is a number of any type, or a formula that evaluates to a number.
Description	The SPACE$() function generates a string of spaces. It often is used to space printed text, or to initialize a string variable.
Returns	The result is a string of *number* spaces.
For example	The following statement fills A$ with 10 spaces:

```
A$ = SPACE$(10)
```

See also	SPC function
	STRING$ function

 SPC

Purpose	The SPC function skips a specified number of spaces in a PRINT # statement or PRINT method.
Syntax	**SPC(***number%***)**
Arguments	*number%* is a number of any type, or a formula that evaluates to a number.
Description	The SPC() function is usable only in a PRINT statement or method. It causes the print position to move right the indicated number of spaces.
For example	The following statements are from the Immediate window followed by the output on the screen:

```
PRINT SPC(5);"h";SPC(5); "h"
     h      h
PRINT SPC(10);"H"
          H
```

See also	SPACE$ function
	TAB function

 SQR

Purpose	The SQR() function calculates the square root of a number.
Syntax	**SQR**(*number*)
Arguments	*number* is a number of any type, or a formula that evaluates to a number greater than or equal to 0. Negative values of *number* cause an error.
Description	The SQR() function calculates the square root of a number.
Returns	The result is the square root of *number*.
For example	The following line stores the square root of 16 (4) in A:

```
A = SQR(16)
```

See also	None

 SSEG

Purpose	The SSEG() function returns the segment address of a string variable in memory. This statement is not available in Visual Basic for Windows.
Syntax	**SSEG**(*string-variable*)
Arguments	*string-variable* is a string variable for which you want to get the segment address in memory.
Description	The SSEG() function is used to get the segment address in memory of a string variable. This primarily is used when calling external procedures, written in other languages, that need access to that string.

Don't change the length of a string passed to an external procedure in this manner. Visual Basic can move strings in memory, so get this address just before you need it. To get the offset from the segment address, use the SADD() function, or SSEGADD() to get both.

605

Returns   The result is a two-byte segment address of the current data segment set with DEF SEG.

For example   The following assignment statement gets the segment address of a string:

```
segaddr% = SSEG(aString$)
```

See also   CALL statement
DEF SEG statement
SADD() function
SSEGADD() function

 **SSEGADD**

Purpose   The SSEGADD() function returns the segment and offset address of a string variable in memory. This statement is not available in Visual Basic for Windows.

Syntax   **SSEGADD(** *string-variable* **)**

Arguments   *string-variable* is a string variable for which you want to get the address in memory.

Description   The SSEGADD() function gets the segment address and the offset in that segment of a string variable. You use this function primarily when calling external procedures, written in other languages, that need access to a string.

 Don't change the length of a string passed to an external procedure in this manner. Visual Basic can move strings in memory, so get this address just before you need it. To get the segment address or the offset alone, use the SSEG() and SADD() functions.

Returns   The result is a four-byte value containing the segment address in the first two bytes and the offset in the second two bytes. The segment is the current data segment set with DEF SEG, and the offset is to the start of the string in that segment.

For example   The following assignment statement gets the far address of a string:

```
faraddress% = SSEGADD(aString$)
```

See also   CALL statement
DEF SEG statement
SADD() function
SSEG() function

 **STACK**

Purpose   The STACK function returns the maximum memory that can be allocated for the stack. This statement is not available in Visual Basic for Windows.

Syntax   **STACK**

Arguments   None

Description   The STACK function determines the maximum amount of memory available for the program stack. The stack is where local variables and procedure return addresses are stored.

Returns   The result is the maximum number of bytes that you can allocate for the stack.

For example   The following assignment statement stores the maximum stack size in A:

```
A = STACK
```

See also   STACK statement

 **STACK**

Purpose   The STACK statement sets the size of the stack. This statement is not available in Visual Basic for Windows.

Syntax   **STACK** *size&*

Arguments *size&* is a long integer specifying the size of the stack in bytes. The minimum value is 325 bytes; anything less than that defaults to 325. The default is 3K bytes.

Description The STACK statement sets the size of the stack. The stack is where a procedure's local variables and return addresses are stored. The STACK statement is allowed only at the module level. You can get the maximum value by using the STACK function.

For example The following statement uses the STACK statement and the STACK function to allocate the maximum possible memory for the stack:

```
STACK STACK
```

See also STACK function

$STATIC

Purpose The $STATIC metacommand specifies that all arrays specified in following DIM statements are statically allocated. This statement is not available in Visual Basic for Windows.

Syntax [REM|'] $STATIC

Arguments REM and ' indicate that the lines are remarks; metacommands are compiler directives, and must be inserted as remarks in the BASIC program.

Description The $STATIC metacommand specifies that all array variables specified in DIM statements that follow this command are to be allocated statically at compile time. Use the $DYNAMIC metacommand to allocate arrays dynamically at runtime. You can reinitialize and redimension statically allocated arrays by using the REDIM statement. The ERASE statement zeroes them out, but does not release the memory. With dynamically allocated arrays, the ERASE statement frees the memory for other uses.

For example The following statements allocate the array A(2500) as a static array and B(1000) as a dynamic array:

```
REM $STATIC
DIM A$(2500) AS SINGLE
REM $DYNAMIC
DIM B(1000) AS SINGLE
```

See also   COMMON statement
           DIM statement
           ERASE statement
           REDIM statement
           SHARED statement
           STATIC statement
           $DYNAMIC metacommand

 STATIC

Purpose   The STATIC statement defines variables, declares their type at the procedure level, and makes their values persist from one call of the procedure to the next.

Syntax   **STATIC** *variable*[([*subscripts*])][**AS** *type*]
          [,*variable*[([*subscripts*])][**AS** *type*]]...

Arguments   *variable* is a variable name. Array names are followed by parentheses and the subscript range. There can be up to 60 subscripts, with the following syntax:

[*lower%* **TO**]*upper%*[,[*lower%* **TO**]*upper%*]...

lower% is the lower limit for the array subscripts. If you omit *lower%*, 0 is assumed unless the OPTION BASE statement has been executed. (See the OPTION BASE statemcnt.)

upper% is the upper limit for array subscripts.

type is one of the following Visual Basic types: CONTROL, CURRENCY, FORM, INTEGER, LONG, SINGLE, DOUBLE, STRING, STRING*length*, or any user type defined with the TYPE statement. *length* is the length of a fixed-length string. Use the AS *type* clause or a variable suffix symbol, but not both, to declare the type of the variable. (See the beginning of this chapter for information on variable suffix symbols.)

Description   The STATIC statement is used at the procedure level to declare the type of variables and to set the dimensions of array-type variables. Using STATIC at the procedure level is nearly identical to using DIM, except that the variables persist from one call of the procedure to another. Variables defined with DIM are redefined and zeroed each time the procedure is called. Use DIM to define variables at the form or module level.

15

If the entire procedure is declared STATIC with the SUB or FUNCTION statement, you can use either STATIC or DIM to define variables, because everything is static.

For example The following statement defines the variable myFile as a string variable, then defines anArray as a two-dimensional array of integers. The first dimension of the array ranges from 3 to 6 and the second ranges from 0 to 10, giving a total of 44 elements in the array.

```
STATIC myFile AS STRING, anArray(3 TO 6,10)
AS INTEGER
```

See also COMMON statement
CONST statement
DIM statement
ERASE statement
FUNCTION statement
OPTION BASE statement
REDIM statement
SUB statement
$STATIC metacommand

STICK

Purpose The STICK() function gets the position of the joysticks. This statement is not available in Visual Basic for Windows.

Syntax STICK(*code*)

Arguments *code* is a numeric code indicating which coordinate to return:

0	Save the coordinates and return the x-coordinate of joystick A
1	Return the y-coordinate of joystick A
2	Return the x-coordinate of joystick B
3	Return the y-coordinate of joystick B

Description   The STICK( ) function returns the position of the joysticks. You must use code 0 first, because that code not only returns the x-coordinate of joystick A, it also stores the values of the other coordinates for retrieval with the STICK( ) function.

Returns   The result is the position of the indicated joystick. The range is 0 to ± 200.

For example   The following statements get the x- and y-coordinates of joystick B:

```
Dummy = STICK(0)      'read coordinates
xval = STICK(2)
yval = STICK(3)
```

See also   ON STRIG statement
STRIG ON statement
STRIG( ) function

 # STOP

Purpose   The STOP statement pauses a program running in the Visual Basic environment, or ends a compiled program.

Syntax   **STOP** [*errorlevel%*]

Arguments   *errorlevel%* is the error level to return to the DOS operating system for use with batch files and non-Visual Basic programs.

Description   The STOP statement primarily is for debugging purposes. STOP pauses the operation of a code so that its variables can be examined. Use the Continue command of the **Run** menu to continue running the program. In a compiled application, STOP behaves the same as the END statement: the program is ended, files are closed, and control is returned to the operating system with an *errorlevel* value. Breakpoints set with the Toggle Breakpoint command of the **Debug** menu have the same effect as STOP, except that they go away when the file is closed.

For example   In the following procedure, the STOP statement stops execution at that point every time the FOR/NEXT loop is iterated. When execution is stopped, you can examine the values of the variables by using PRINT statements in the Immediate window. Restart the program by using the Continue command.

```
SUB DrawStripes (C AS FlagType, Pic AS CONTROL)
'Draw stripes
```

15

```
DIM I AS INTEGER, Color AS INTEGER
'Calculate the position of the stripes, and
'alternate the colors between RED and WHITE.
Color = WHITE
FOR I = 1 TO 13
IF Color = WHITE THEN Color = RED ELSE Color = WHITE
  Pic.Line (C.Xmin, (I - 1) * C.Stripe)-(C.Xmax, I
  * C.Stripe), Color, BF
  STOP
NEXT I
END SUB
```

See also   END statement

SYSTEM statement

 **STR$**

Purpose   The STR$() function converts a number into a string of decimal characters.

Syntax   **STR$(**number**)**

Arguments   *number* is a number of any type, or a formula that evaluates to a number.

Description   The STR$() function converts a number into a string of text. The string returned preserves the accuracy of the original number in the most compact form. To convert a number using a specific format, use the FORMAT$() function.

Returns   The resulting string is the number converted into a decimal number. The conversion displays all significant digits in the most compact format.

For example   The following lists the results of various STR$(0) commands:

STR$()	*Result*
STR$(135)	135
STR$(135.4)	135.4
STR$(135.7)	135.7
STR$(12345678901234567890)	1.23456789012346D+19

STR$(0.12345678901234567890)	.123456789012346
STR$(123456789000000)	123456789000000
STR$(0.00000000001)	.00000000001
STR$(12345678900000000)	1.23456789D+16
STR$(0.000000000000000001)	1D-18

See also   FORMAT$ function
HEX$ function
OCT$ function

STRIG

Purpose   The STRIG() function gets the state of the joystick triggers. This statement is not available in Visual Basic for Windows.

Syntax   **STRIG(*code*)**

Arguments*   *code* is a code number indicating what to return:

Code	Return
0	Returns −1 if trigger A1 has been pressed since the last STRIG(0) call; otherwise, returns 0.
1	Returns −1 if trigger A1 currently is down, or 0 if it is not.
2	Returns −1 if trigger B1 has been pressed since the last STRIG(2) call; otherwise, returns 0.
3	Returns −1 if trigger B1 currently is down, or 0 if it is not.
4	Returns −1 if trigger A2 has been pressed since the last STRIG(4) call; otherwise, returns 0.
5	Returns −1 if trigger A2 is currently down, or 0 if it is not.

continues

6	Returns –1 if trigger B2 has been pressed since the last STRIG(6) call; otherwise, returns 0.
7	Returns –1 if trigger B2 is currently down, or 0 if it is not.

Description The STRIG() function reads the state of the joystick triggers.

Returns The result is 0 or –1, depending on the state of the triggers and the code.

For example The following statement reads the state of trigger A1:

```
stateA1 = STRIG(1)  'see if trigger A1 is pressed
```

See also ON STRIG statement
STRIG() ON statement

 STRIG() ON

Purpose The STRIG() ON statement activates or deactivates trapping joystick-trigger events. This statement is not available in Visual Basic for Windows.

Syntax STRIG(*code*) {ON|OFF|STOP}

Arguments *code* is a code indicating which trigger trap to enable:

Code	Trigger Trap
0	Joystick A, Trigger 1
2	Joystick B, Trigger 1
4	Joystick A, Trigger 2
6	Joystick B, Trigger 2

ON turns on event trapping.

OFF turns off event trapping.

STOP pauses trapping joystick-trigger events, and saves any events until a STRIG() ON statement is executed.

Description The STRIG() ON statement activates trapping of joystick-trigger events. The event trap must previously have been defined with an ON STRIG statement. A STRIG() STOP is executed automatically when an ON STRIG() event trap is called, and a STRIG() ON is called when the trap returns.

For example The following statements enable a joystick-trigger, event-trap procedure:

```
ON STRIG(0) GOSUB doEvent  'define the event trap
STRIG(0) ON                'turn on event trapping
'do something while waiting for a trap
doEvent:             'label at the start of the trap
                     'STRIG() STOP is automatically
                     'called here.
'handle the event
                     'STRIG() ON is automatically
                     'called before the RETURN.
RETURN
```

See also ON STRIG() statement
STRIG() function

StringAddress

Purpose The StringAddress() function returns the address of a Visual Basic string to a non-Visual Basic procedure.

Syntax **StringAddress(**_string-descriptor%_**)**

Arguments _string-descriptor%_ is the address of a string descriptor of a Visual Basic string.

Description The StringAddress() function is used by non-Visual Basic procedures to get the address of a Visual Basic string.

Returns The result is the address of a Visual Basic string.

For example The following assignment statement gets the address of a Visual Basic string. The variable theAddr contains the address of a string descriptor.

```
A = StringAddress(theAddr)
```

See also StringAssign statement
StringLength function
StringRelease function

 StringAssign

Purpose	The StringAssign statement copies a Visual Basic string to a non-Visual Basic procedure or a string in a non-Visual Basic procedure to Visual Basic.
Syntax	**StringAssign(***source&,slen%,dest&,dlen%***)**
Arguments	*source&*, for the source string, is the address of a fixed-length string or the address of a string descriptor for a variable-length string.
	slen%, for the source string, is the length of a fixed-length string or 0 for a variable-length string.
	dest&, for the destination location, is the address of a fixed-length string or the address of a string descriptor for a variable-length string.
	dlen%, for the destination location, is the length of a fixed-length string or 0 for a variable-length string.
Description	The StringAssign statement is used by non-Visual Basic procedures to move Visual Basic and non-Visual Basic strings in memory.
For example	The following assignment statement moves a 10-character, fixed-length string from Visual Basic to an external fixed-length string. The variable theAddr contains the address of the fixed-length string and theDest contains the address where it is to be moved.

```
StringAssign(theAddr,10,theDest,10)
```

See also	StringAddress function
	StringLength function
	StringRelease function

StringLength

Purpose	The StringLength() function returns the length of a Visual Basic variable-length string to a non-Visual Basic procedure.
Syntax	**StringLength(***string-descriptor%***)**

616

Arguments   *string-descriptor*% is the address of a string descriptor of a Visual Basic variable-length string.

Description   The StringLength() function is used by non-Visual Basic procedures to get the length of a Visual Basic string.

Returns   The result is the length of a Visual Basic string.

For example   The following assignment statement gets the length of a Visual Basic string. The variable theAddr contains the address of a string descriptor.

```
A = StringLength(theAddr)
```

See also   StringAssign statement
StringAddress function
StringRelease function

StringRelease

Purpose   The StringRelease statement allows a non-Visual Basic procedure to deallocate a Visual Basic variable-length string.

Syntax   **StringRelease(***string-descriptor*%**)**

Arguments   *string-descriptor*% is the address of a string descriptor of a Visual Basic variable-length string.

Description   The StringRelease statement is used by non-Visual Basic procedures to deallocate a Visual Basic string and release the memory for other uses.

For example   The following assignment statement deallocates a Visual Basic string. The variable theAddr contains the address of a string descriptor.

```
StringRelease(theAddr)
```

See also   StringAssign statement
StringAddress function
StringLength function

15

617

 **STRING$**

Purpose	The STRING$() function returns a string of characters.
Syntax	**STRING$(**number&,{code%\|string$}**)**
Arguments	number& is a number of any type, or a formula that evaluates to a number. This is the number of copies of the character to make.
	code% is the ASCII code (see CHR$()) of the character to be repeated.
	string$ is a string. The first character in the string is used as the character to be repeated.
Description	The STRING$() function produces a string containing a character repeated number& times. For a string of spaces, use the SPACE$() function.
Returns	The resulting string contains number& copies of the character whose ASCII code is code%, or which is the first character in string$.
For example	The following assignment statements set A$ to ggggg and B$ to 10 carriage returns. Note that only the g in ghi is repeated.

```
A$ = STRING$(5,"ghi")
B$ = STRING$(10,13)
```

See also	SPACE$ function

 **STRING**

Purpose	The data type STRING matches or defines string variables.
Syntax	variable **AS STRING** [*len]
Arguments	variable is a variable name.
	*len is the integer length of a fixed-length string.
Description	The data type STRING is used in SUB and FUNCTION procedure headings to declare a variable as a string type so that Visual Basic can check values passed to the procedure. STRING also is used in a DIM, GLOBAL, or STATIC statement to define a variable as a string. The STRING data type normally has

a variable length and uses one byte per character. Fixed-length strings primarily are used in user-defined variable types used with random-access disk files. You also can define the STRING data type by appending the $ character to the variable name. You define STRING constants by surrounding them with double quotation marks.

For example   The following FUNCTION procedure defines tstString as a STRING variable, then uses a WHILE/WEND loop and the INSTR() function to count and return the number of commas in tstString:

```
FUNCTION NCommas (tstString AS STRING) AS INTEGER
DIM counter AS INTEGER, start AS INTEGER
counter = start = 1
      WHIL INSTR(start, tstString, ",")>0
         start = INSTR(start, tstString, ",") + 1
         co
nter = counter + 1
WEND
NCommas = counter
END FUNCTION
```

See also   COMMON statement
DIM statement
STATIC statement
TYPE statement
ANY data type
CONTROL data type
CURRENCY data type
DOUBLE data type
FORM data type
INTEGER data type
LONG data type
SINGLE data type

15

 SUB

Purpose   The SUB statement declares the interface to a SUB procedure.

Syntax   [**STATIC**] **SUB** *procname* [(*arglist*)]
[*statements*]

```
[EXIT SUB]
[statements]
END SUB
```

Arguments   STATIC indicates that the variables of the procedure do not go away when the procedure exits.

procname is the name the procedure has in the program.

arglist is the argument list passed to the procedure. The argument list can have the following syntax:

```
[ByVal] arg[()][AS type][,[ByVal]arg[()][AS type]]
```

ByVal indicates the following argument is passed as a value rather than as an address that points to the variable containing the value. Numbers are passed as the type indicated in the statement. Strings are passed as an address to a null-terminated string.

arg is a variable name; only the type has meaning here. Follow array variables with empty parentheses.

type is one of the following Visual Basic types: CONTROL, CURRENCY, FORM, INTEGER, LONG, SINGLE, DOUBLE, STRING, or a user-defined type. Use the AS *type* clause or a variable suffix symbol, but not both, to declare the type of the variable. (See the beginning of this chapter for information on variable suffix symbols.) You cannot change the type of a static array.

EXIT SUB is a statement to terminate the procedure before reaching the end.

statements is some or no statements.

Description   The SUB statement defines the interface to a SUB procedure so that a Visual Basic program can call the procedure. The interface contains the names of the arguments and their types. The interface also can declare the procedure as STATIC, which makes all local variables persist from one execution to the next.

For example   The following SUB procedure calculates and returns the factorial of the number N in the variable theFact. Because N is changed in the function and you don't want it changed in the calling procedure, the value ByVal passes N to this procedure so that only the local copy is changed.

```
SUB Factorial (ByVal N AS INTEGER, theFact AS LONG)
theFact = 1
WHILE N>0
  theFact = theFact * N
  N = N - 1
```

```
WEND
END SUB
```

SUB procedures also can be called recursively, with a procedure even calling itself. Each time the procedure is called, it gets a new set of local variables so the variable's values won't conflict with each other. You cannot do this if the procedure uses global variables or is declared STATIC. The following procedure also calculates the factorial by recursively calling itself to calculate the factorial of N-1 until N equals 1.

```
SUB Factorial (N AS INTEGER, theFact AS LONG)
IF N <= 1 THEN
theFact = 1
EXIT SUB
END IF
Factorial N - 1, theFact
  theFact = theFact * N
END SUB
```

See also   CALL statement
DECLARE statement
FUNCTION statement

SWAP

Purpose   The SWAP statement exchanges the values of two variables. This statement is not available in Visual Basic for Windows.

Syntax   **SWAP** *var1*, *var2*

Arguments   *var1* and *var2* are two variables of the same type.

Description   The SWAP statement exchanges the values of two variables. Both variables must be of the same type.

For example   The following statement exchanges the values of two integers:

```
SWAP Number1%, Number2%
```

See also   LET statement

15

 SYSTEM

Purpose	The SYSTEM statement ends a program, closes all files, and returns control to the operating system.
Syntax	**SYSTEM** [*errorlevel%*]
Arguments	*errorlevel%* is an error level to return to the DOS operating system for use with batch files and non-Visual Basic programs.
Description	The SYSTEM statement behaves the same as the END statement: the program is ended, files are closed, and control is returned to the operating system with an *errorlevel* value.
For example	The following statement ends execution and returns an *errorlevel* of 2:

SYSTEM 2

See also	END statement STOP statement

 TAB

Purpose	The TAB function skips to a specified column number in a PRINT # statement or PRINT method.
Syntax	**TAB(***column%***)**
Arguments	*column%* is the column number (character position) to which to skip. If you already are past that column, the insertion point moves down one line and then skips to the column. If *column%* is greater than the width of a line in a file set with the WIDTH statement, TAB moves to the *column%* MOD *width* column, where *width* is the width of a line. The width of a column equals the width of a character.
Description	You can use the TAB() function only in a PRINT statement or method. It causes the print position to move to the indicated column.
For example	The following statements were typed in the Immediate window and are followed by the results that are printed on the screen. This is a useful way to test the operation of functions and methods.

```
PRINT TAB(10);"H";Tab(10);"H"
         H
         H
PRINT "This contains more than 12 characters";
TAB(12);"More text"
This contains more than 12 characters
            More text
```

See also SPACE$ function
SPC function

TAN

Purpose The TAN() function calculates and returns the tangent of an angle in radians.

Syntax `TAN(angle)`

Arguments *angle* is an angle in radians as a number or a formula that evaluates to a number of any numeric type.

Description The TAN() function calculates the tangent of an angle expressed in radians. Note that the tangent has poles at $\pm\pi/2$, $\pm 3\pi/2$, and so on. The TAN() function generates an overflow error at those values. To calculate the tangent of an angle expressed in degrees, use the following:

```
Pi = 3.141592654
theTangent = TAN(dangle*Pi/180))
```

where *dangle* is measured in degrees.

For example The following two assignment statements calculate the tangent of two angles, one in radians and one in degrees:

```
A = TAN(3.25)
'Assigns the tangent of 3.25 radians to A = 0.108834
Pi = 3.141592654
B = TAN(27.8*Pi/180)
'Assigns the tangent of 27.8 degrees to B = 0.527240
```

Returns The result is the tangent of *angle*, a number between $-\infty$ and $+\infty$.

See also ATN function
COS function
SIN function

 **TEXTHEIGHT**

Purpose	The TEXTHEIGHT method returns the height some text will occupy.
Syntax	[*object.*]**TEXTHEIGHT**(*string$*)
Arguments	*object* is the name of the object on which to print: a form, a picture box, or the keyword PRINTER. Omit this argument to use the form containing the statement.
	string$ is a string of text.
Description	You use this method as you would use a function. The TEXTHEIGHT method uses the current values of the Font property of the object to determine how much vertical space is needed to print the text.
Returns	The result is the height used by the text in *string$* if it were printed on the indicated object.
For example	The following line determines how much vertical space is required to print the string "This is a short string" on Form1, and stores the space in A:

```
A = Form1.TEXTHEIGHT("This is a short string")
```

See also	FontName property
	FontSize property
	ScaleHeight property
	ScaleMode property

 TEXTWIDTH

Purpose	The TEXTWIDTH method returns the width some text will occupy.
Syntax	[*object.*]**TEXTWIDTH**(*string$*)
Arguments	*object* is the name of the object on which to print: a form, a picture box, or the keyword PRINTER. Omit this argument to use the form containing the statement.
	string$ is a string of text.

Description You use this method as you would use a function. The TEXTWIDTH method uses the current values of the Font property of the object to determine how much horizontal space is needed to print the text.

Returns The result is the width used by the text in *string$* if it were printed on the indicated object.

For example The following line determines how much horizontal space is required to print the string "This is a short string" on Form1 and stores it in A:

```
A = Form1.TEXTWIDTH("This is a short string")
```

See also FontName property
FontSize property
ScaleMode property
ScaleWidth property

TIME$

Purpose The TIME$ function gets and returns the current time from the system clock.

Syntax **TIME$**

Arguments None

Description The TIME$ function gets the system time in a string. Use the TIME$ statement to set the time. Use the NOW function to get the current time as a serial-date number.

Returns The result is an eight-character string containing the system date in the format

hh:mm:ss

where *hh* is the hour, *mm* is the minute, and *ss* is the second.

For example The following assignment statement assigns the current time to the string variable A$:

```
A$ = TIME$      'Assign the current time to A$
```

See also DATE$ statement
TIME$ statement
DATE$ function

15

DATESERIAL function
DATEVALUE function
DAY function
HOUR function
MINUTE function
MONTH function
NOW function
SECOND function
TIMER function
TIMESERIAL function
TIMEVALUE function
WEEKDAY function
YEAR function

 **TIME$**

Purpose   The TIME$ statement sets the system time.

Syntax   **TIME$** = *timestring$*

Arguments   *timestring$* is a string containing the time to which to set the clock in one of the following formats:

hh
hh:mm
hh:mm:ss

where *hh* is the hour, *mm* is the minute, and *ss* is the second.

Use a 24-hour clock for times after noon.

Description   The TIME$ statement sets the time in the system clock. Depending on your system, you may also have to run a setup program to make the date change permanent.

For example   The following statement sets the system time to 1:27 p.m.:

TIME$ = "13:27"

See also   DATE$ statement
DATE$ function
DATESERIAL function

DATEVALUE function
DAY function
HOUR function
MINUTE function
MONTH function
NOW function
SECOND function
TIME$ function
TIMER function
TIMESERIAL function
TIMEVALUE function
WEEKDAY function
YEAR function

TIMER

Purpose   The TIMER function returns the number of seconds since midnight.

Syntax   `TIMER`

Arguments   None

Description   The TIMER function returns the number of seconds since midnight as a single-precision number. Use TIMER to time operations. TIMER also initializes the random-number generator with the RANDOMIZE statement.

Returns   The resulting SINGLE numeric value is the number of seconds since midnight.

For example   The following lists results printed on the screen from using the TIMER functions in the Immediate window:

```
PRINT TIMER
 60847.71
PRINT TIMER
 60852.82
FOR I = 1 TO 10:PRINT TIMER:NEXT I
 60911.48
 60911.60
 60911.76
 60911.98
 60912.14
```

15

```
                   60912.37
                   60912.58
                   60912.75
                   60912.96
                   60913.19
```

See also   RANDOMIZE statement
              TIMER event
              TIMER control

S TIMER ON

Purpose   The TIMER ON statement activates or deactivates trapping timer events. This statement is not available in Visual Basic for Windows.

Syntax   `TIMER {ON|OFF|STOP}`

Arguments   ON turns on event trapping.

OFF turns off event trapping.

STOP pauses trapping timer events, and saves any events until a TIMER ON statement is executed.

Description   The TIMER ON statement activates trapping of timer events. The event trap must previously have been defined with an ON TIMER() statement, and the number of seconds to wait set there. A TIMER STOP automatically is executed when an ON TIMER() event trap is called, and a TIMER ON statement is called when the trap returns.

For example   The following statements enable a timer event trap procedure, and set it to activate every 10 seconds:

```
ON TIMER(10) GOSUB doEvent  'define the event trap
TIMER ON                'turn on event trapping
'do something while waiting for a trap
doEvent:                'label at the start of the trap
                        'TIMER STOP is automatically
                        'called here.
'handle the event
                        'TIMER ON is automatically
                        'called before the RETURN.
RETURN
```

See also   ON TIMER() statement
TIMER function

 TIMESERIAL

Purpose   The TIMESERIAL function calculates a serial-date number from the hour, minute, and second.

Syntax   **TIMESERIAL(**_hour%,minute%,second%_**)**

Arguments   _hour%_ is the hour as a numeric value between 0 and 23, or a formula that results in a number in that range.

minute% is the minute as a number from 0 to 59, or a formula that results in a number in that range.

second% is the second as a number from 0 to 59, or a formula that results in a number in that range.

Description   The TIMESERIAL() function converts numeric expressions representing the hour, minute, and second to a serial-date number. The hour, minute, and second are integer values depicting the time. The serial-date number is a double-precision, floating-point number that stores the time to the right of the decimal and the date to the left. Serial-date numbers containing the time may be added to serial-date numbers containing the date to store both the date and time in the same number.

Returns   The result is the serial-date number. A serial-date number is a double-precision number containing the date represented as the number of days since December 30, 1899. Negative serial-date numbers represent dates from January 1, 1753, to December 30, 1899. Times are represented as fractions of a day. Years after 1900 are represented by the same serial-date numbers used in several popular spreadsheet programs.

For example   The following statement stores the serial-date number (0.5) for 12:00 noon in the variable theTime:

```
theTime = TIMESERIAL(12,0,0)
'the date number for noon
```

See also   DATE$ statement
TIME$ statement

DATE$ function
DATESERIAL function
DATEVALUE function
DAY function
HOUR function
MINUTE function
MONTH function
NOW function
SECOND function
TIME$ function
TIMER function
TIMEVALUE function
WEEKDAY function
YEAR function

TIMEVALUE

Purpose   The TIMEVALUE function calculates a serial-date number from a string containing a time.

Syntax   **TIMEVALUE(*time$*)**

Arguments   *time$* is a string containing the time to which to set the clock, in one of the following formats:

hh:mm:ss
hh:mm
hh:mm:ssxm
hh:mmxm

where *hh* is the hour between 0 and 23, *mm* is the minute between 0 and 59, *ss* is the second between 0 and 59, and *xm* can be PM, AM, p.m., or a.m. If you don't use the a.m. and p.m., you must use a 24-hour clock.

Description   The TIMEVALUE() function converts a string containing the time to a serial-date number. The serial-date number is a double-precision, floating-point number that stores the date to the left of the decimal and the time to the right. Serial-date numbers containing the time may be added to serial-date numbers containing the date to store both the date and time in the same number.

Returns The result is the serial-date number. A serial-date number is a double-precision number containing the date represented as the number of days since December 30, 1899. Negative serial-date numbers represent dates from January 1, 1753, to December 30, 1899. Times are represented as fractions of a day. Years after 1900 are represented by the same serial-date numbers used in several popular spreadsheet programs.

For example The following statement stores the serial-date number (31853.0) for 1:24 p.m. in the variable theTime:

```
theTime = TIMEVALUE("1:24PM")
'the date number for 1:24 PM
```

See also DATE$ statement
TIME$ statement
DATE$ function
DATESERIAL function
DATEVALUE function
DAY function
HOUR function
MINUTE function
NOW function
SECOND function
TIME$ function
TIMER function
TIMESERIAL function
WEEKDAY function
YEAR function

 **TRON, TROFF**

Purpose The TRON and TROFF statements activate or deactivate tracing of a program's execution. This statement is not available in Visual Basic for Windows.

Syntax TRON
TROFF

Arguments None

Description The TRON and TROFF statements turn tracing on or off. When tracing is on, each BASIC statement is highlighted when it is activated. Tracing also can be turned on and off on the **Debug** menu.

For example The following procedure brackets some problem code with a TRON/TROFF statement so the execution can be followed:

```
TRON
theVal = SIN(theAngle)/theAngle
theval2 = TAN(theAngle)
TROFF
```

See also STOP statement

TYPE

Purpose The TYPE statement is used in the module-declarations section to combine several variable types into a user-defined type.

Syntax
```
TYPE newtypename
elementname AS typename
[elementname AS typename

   .

   .

   .]
END TYPE
```

Arguments *newtypename* is the name for the new type definition.

elementname is the name for the element that is going to be a part of this new type.

typename is the type of variable that *elementname* is. *typename* can be any of the built-in types: INTEGER, LONG, SINGLE, DOUBLE, CURRENCY, or STRING, or some other user-defined type.

Description In addition to built-in variable types, such as INTEGER and STRING, you can define your own variable types by combining built-in types. You use record-type variables like any other variable, and pass them to FUNCTION or SUB procedures by using a single name to pass the entire contents of the record.

To create a record-type variable, you first must define the record type with a TYPE statement, then define a variable with that type. The TYPE statement defines which variables make up the record, and in what order.

Once a type is defined, you must define a variable as that type by using a DIM, COMMON, or STATIC statement. This record variable now has all the parts defined in the TYPE statement. To access the contents of a record variable, type the record variable name followed by a dot, and then the *elementname*.

For example   The following TYPE definition would be in the module header, and defines the variable type DayType, which consists of three elements. The first is theDate, which is a DOUBLE-precision, floating-point number for storing a date. The second is an INTEGER named Flags. The third is a fixed-length STRING named Msg.

```
TYPE DayType
  theDate AS DOUBLE
  Flags AS INTEGER
  Msg AS STRING * 118
END TYPE
```

The next statements define variables with the new type. The first line defines aLine as a string variable and Today as the new variable type DayType. The second line defines an array named Month of 31 DayType variables.

```
DIM aLine AS STRING, Today AS DayType
COMMON theMonth(1 TO 31) AS DayType
```

Finally, in a procedure, the elements of the user-defined type are accessed by combining the variable name and the element names of the type. The first line stores a 2 in the Flags element of Today (the INTEGER). The second inserts a string in the Msg element of the fifth element of Month. The third line uses the function NOW to insert today's date and time into the theDay element of Today.

```
Today.Flags = 2
Month(5).Msg = "Some interesting message"
Today.theDay = NOW
```

See also   COMMON statement
DIM statement
LSET statement
STATIC statement

 UBOUND

Purpose	The UBOUND function returns the largest allowed array subscript.
Syntax	**UBOUND(**array[**,**dimension%]**)**
Arguments	array is an array-type variable.
	dimension%, for multidimensional arrays, is a number specifying the dimension to examine. The first dimension is number 1.
Description	The UBOUND() function works with the LBOUND() function to examine the upper and lower index values for an array's dimensions.
Returns	The resulting numeric value is the largest allowed subscript available for the array dimension.
For example	The first line is from the general procedure of a form, and defines the array variable anArray:

```
DIM anArray(4 TO 23,-6 TO 5,8) AS INTEGER
```

The following lines list the results of various LBOUND and UBOUND functions:

Function	Result
LBOUND(anArray,1)	4
UBOUND(anArray,1)	23
LBOUND(anArray,2)	6
UBOUND(anArray,2)	5
LBOUND(anArray,3)	0
UBOUND(anArray,3)	8

See also	COMMON statement
	DIM statement
	STATIC statement
	LBOUND function

 UCASE$

Purpose	The UCASE$() function converts all the characters in a string to uppercase.
Syntax	**UCASE$(***string$***)**
Arguments	*string$* is a string, or a formula that results in a string, to be converted.
Description	The UCASE$() function converts all the characters in a string to uppercase. This is useful when you want to compare two strings and the case of the characters is unimportant.
Returns	The resulting string is all uppercase.
For example	The following lines are typed in the Immediate window, and are followed by what is printed on the screen:

```
A$ = "This Is a StRinG to ConVeRt"
PRINT LCASE$(A$)
this is a string to convert
PRINT UCASE$(A$)
THIS IS A STRING TO CONVERT
```

See also	LCASE$ function

UEVENT ON

Purpose	The UEVENT ON statement activates or deactivates trapping user events. This statement is not available in Visual Basic for Windows.
Syntax	**UEVENT {ON|OFF|STOP}**
Arguments	ON turns on event trapping.
	OFF turns off event trapping.
	STOP pauses trapping user events, and saves any events until a UEVENT ON statement is executed.
Description	The UEVENT ON statement activates trapping of user-defined events. The event trap must have been defined previously with an ON UEVENT statement. A user-defined event is triggered with a SETUEVENT statement. When the

15

UEVENT event trap is triggered, a UEVENT STOP automatically is executed to prevent overlapping events. At the end of the event trap, a UEVENT ON automatically is executed to continue trapping user-defined events.

For example The following statements enable a user event trap procedure, then trigger it:

```
ON UEVENT GOSUB doEvent  'define the event trap
UEVENT ON                'turn on event trapping
'do something
IF something THEN SETUEVENT 'test something
                              'and trigger the event
doEvent:            'label at the start of the trap
                    'UEvent Stop is automatically
                    'inserted here.
'handle the event
                    'UEvent On is automatically
                    'inserted here.
RETURN
```

See also ON UEVENT statement
SETUEVENT function

 UNLOAD

Purpose The UNLOAD statement unloads a form, or control array element from memory.

Syntax **UNLOAD** *object*

Arguments *object* is the name of a form or control array element to unload.

Description The UNLOAD statement unloads a form or control array element from memory. To simply hide the form without unloading it, use the HIDE method. You can also use the UNLOAD method to remove elements from a control array. Only elements attached to a control array at runtime with the LOAD statement can be unloaded.

For example The following statement unloads element number 2 of an option button-control array:

```
UNLOAD Option1(2)
```

See also   LOAD statement
HIDE method
SHOW method
Visible property

 VAL

Purpose   The VAL() function converts a number in a text string into a value.

Syntax   **VAL(***string$***)**

Arguments   *string$* is a string containing a number in the leftmost character positions. VAL() ignores any leading blanks, tabs, and line feeds when looking for a number. The function continues reading numbers until it encounters a character that it cannot interpret as a number, such as a comma, a letter other than D or E, or a carriage return. VAL() does not recognize dollar signs, percent signs, or commas as a part of a number.

Description   The VAL() function converts a number in a string to a value. This is the inverse of the STR$() and FORMAT$() functions. If the numbers to be converted contain formatted characters, such as dollar signs and commas, you must remove them first by using the INSTR() function to locate them and the MID$() function to extract them.

Returns   The result is the numeric value of the number in *string$*.

For example   The following lists the results from applying VAL to various strings:

Function	*Result*
VAL(" -1234.56 ")	−1234.56
VAL(" 1.23E22,")	1.23D+22
VAL(" $123.34")	0
VAL(" -1,234,567.99")	−1
VAL(" abc 123.45")	0

See also   FORMAT$ function
STR$ function

 # VARPTR, VARPTR$, and VARSEG

Purpose   The VARPTR(), VARPTR$(), and VARSEG() functions return the address of a variable in memory. This statement is not available in Visual Basic for Windows.

Syntax   **VARPTR(***variable***)**
VARPTR$(*variable***)**
VARSEG(*variable***)**

Arguments   *variable* is any legal variable name. If the variable does not exist in memory, it is created.

Description   The VARPTR(), VARPTR$(), and VARSEG() statements get the location of a variable in memory. VARPTR() returns the offset of the variable in the current segment, VARSEG() returns the segment address for the variable, and VARPTR$() returns a string version of the address.

Returns   For VARPTR(), the result is the byte offset in memory of the variable.

For VARPTR$(), the result is a three-byte string. The first byte contains the variable type as a number, the second byte contains the offset, and the third contains the segment address.

For VARSEG(), the result is the address of the segment containing the variable.

For example   The following two assignment statements assign the value of the segment address and the offset to segAddr, and offset. The third statement assigns the whole address as a string.

```
segAddr = VARSEG(aValue)
offset = segAddr(aValue)
aString$ = VARPTR$(aValue)
```

See also   None

 VIEW

Purpose   The VIEW statement defines a viewport on the screen for drawing graphics. This statement is not available in Visual Basic for Windows.

Syntax   ⤷ VIEW[**SCREEN**][(*x1,y1*)-**i**(*x2,y2*) [,[*background*] [,[*border*]]]]

Arguments   SCREEN is a keyword indicating that the coordinates are relative to the screen, and not to an existing viewport.

x1,y1 and *x2,y2* are the coordinates of the upper-left corner and the lower-right corner of the graphics viewport rectangle.

background is a background fill color.

border is the line color.

Description   The VIEW statement defines the graphics window on the screen. When BASIC is initialized, the graphics window is the whole screen with the origin in the upper-left corner. Use the VIEW statement to restrict the window to a smaller rectangle. The origin also moves to the upper-left corner of the new graphics window. Any drawing outside of that rectangle is clipped. If VIEW is executed without any variables, it resets the viewport to the whole screen. The screen must be in one of the graphics modes set with the SCREEN statement before VIEW can be used to define a viewport. Use the WINDOW statement to change the coordinate system used in the graphics window.

For example   The following statements create a graphics viewport on the screen and leave the colors alone:

```
SCREEN 1                'Turn on graphics mode 1
VIEW SCREEN (250,100)-(300,180)
```

See also   SCREEN statement
WINDOW statement

15

 VIEW PRINT

Purpose   The VIEW PRINT statement redefines the scrollable portion of the screen. This statement is not available in Visual Basic for Windows.

Syntax   **VIEW PRINT** [*upper-line* **TO** *lower-line*]

Arguments   *upper-line* and *lower-line* are the line numbers of the upper and lower scrollable lines on the window. The top line on the screen is line number 1, and the others count down from the top. The bottom line is line number 25, and normally is not included in a scrollable window.

Description   The VIEW PRINT statement defines the active scrollable section of the window. Printed lines scroll down to this line and then the whole screen begins to scroll. Executing VIEW PRINT without any arguments resets the default values of 1 through 24.

For example   The following statement defines lines 1 to 10 as the scrolling part of the window:

```
VIEW PRINT 1 TO 10
```

See also   SENDKEYS statement

 WAIT

Purpose   The WAIT statement pauses execution of a program until a specific byte pattern appears on a machine port. This statement is not available in Visual Basic for Windows.

Syntax   **WAIT** *port*, *and-mask*[,*xor-mask*]

Arguments   *port* is the number of a machine port in your machine. You will need a DOS technical manual to get a list of valid machine port numbers.

and-mask and *xor-mask* are an AND mask and an OR mask to apply to any data coming from the port. The program starts with the *xor-mask*, then applies the *and-mask*. If the result is 0, the statement waits for another byte; otherwise, it continues with the next statement.

Description   The WAIT statement pauses a program and waits for a specific byte to appear on the port. The byte to wait for is defined with two masks, which are logically applied to the incoming byte stream.

For example   The following statements are waiting for port 3 to send a byte greater than 31:

```
andMask = 96
WAIT 3, andMask
```

See also   OUT statement
INP() function

 WEEKDAY()

Purpose   The WEEKDAY() function calculates the day of the week from a serial-date number.

Syntax   **WEEKDAY(** *serialdate#* **)**

Arguments   *serialdate#* is a serial-date number. A serial-date number is a double-precision number containing the date represented as the number of days since December 30, 1899. Negative serial-date numbers represent dates from January 1, 1753 to December 30, 1899. Times are represented as fractions of a day. Years after 1900 are represented by the same serial-date numbers used in several popular spreadsheet programs.

Description   The WEEKDAY() function takes a serial-date number and returns the day of the week represented by that number. WEEKDAY() uses 1 for Sunday and 7 for Saturday. Use the DAY(), MONTH(), and YEAR() functions to extract the day, month, and year. To extract the time, use the HOUR(), MINUTE(), and SECOND() functions.

Returns   The result is the day of the week, with Sunday as number 1 and Saturday as number 7.

For example   The following statement extracts the day of the week (3, which is Tuesday) from the serial-date number for March 17, 1987:

```
theWeek = WEEKDAY(31853)
'Extracts the weekday (3) from the date number
```

See also DATE$ statement
TIME$ statement
DATE$ function
DATESERIAL function
DATEVALUE function
DAY function
HOUR function
MINUTE function
MONTH function
NOW function
SECOND function
TIME$ function
TIMER function
TIMESERIAL function
TIMEVALUE function
YEAR function

WHILE/WEND

Purpose The WHILE/WEND statement iterates a block of statements until a condition is False.

Syntax **WHILE** *condition*
statements
WEND

Arguments *condition* is a logical expression or value.

statements is a block of executable statements to be iterated.

Description The WHILE/WEND statement iterates a block of code until a condition changes to False.

For example The following code fragment calculates the factorial of A by multiplying A times factorial, and then reducing A by 1. As long as A is greater than 1, the loop continues.

```
factorial = 1
```

```
WHILE A>1
  factorial = A*factorial
  A = A - 1
WEND
```

See also   FOR/NEXT statement
          DO/LOOP statement

S WIDTH

Purpose   The WIDTH statement assigns a line width to the printer, or the screen. This statement is not available in Visual Basic for Windows.

Syntax   **WIDTH** [*width%*][, *height%*]   'for the screen
        WIDTH LPRINT *width%*   'for the printer

Arguments   *width%* is the width, in characters, of a line on the printer or the screen. Printing beyond this width causes a carriage return and line feed, and printing continues on the next line down. The argument for the printer must be an integer in the range 0 to 255. A width of 0 or 255 indicates infinite width. For the screen, this must be 40 or 80.

height% is the number of lines to print on the screen. Depending on your printer adapter, this can have the values 25, 30, 43, 50, or 60.

LPRINT indicates that this width applies to the printer.

Description   The WIDTH statement specifies a width for output sent to the printer or the screen. After every *width%* characters, a carriage return and a line feed are inserted in the output and the printing continues on the next line down. Use a width of 0 or 255 to not check the width of printed text and force the printer to handle the carriage returns.

For example   The following line sets the width to 80 characters:

```
WIDTH LPRINT 80
```

See also   OPEN statement
          PRINT statement
          WIDTH # statement
          WIDTH property

15

 WIDTH #

Purpose	The WIDTH # statement assigns a line width to a disk file.
Syntax	**WIDTH** {#*filenumber*%|*device$*}, *width*%
Arguments	*filenumber*% is the file number assigned to the file when it was opened with the OPEN statement.

device$ is a string containing one of the following valid device names:

Name	Device
COM1:	Serial port 1
COM2:	Serial port 2
LPT1:	Parallel port 1
LPT2:	Parallel port 2
LPT3:	Parallel port 3
SCRN:	The screen

width% is the width, in characters, of a line in a disk file. Printing beyond this width causes a carriage return and line feed, and printing continues on the next line down. This argument must be an integer in the range 0 to 255. A width of 0 or 255 indicates infinite width.

Description	The WIDTH # statement specifies a width for a disk file or other device. Use a width of 0 or 255 to not check the width of printed text. This statement is useful when creating print files, when the program does not keep track of how many characters are printed on each line.
For example	The following line sets the width of file number 1 to 80 characters:

```
WIDTH #1, 80
```

See also	OPEN statement
	PRINT statement
	WIDTH statement
	Width property

S WINDOW

Purpose The WINDOW statement defines a user system of coordinates for the screen.

Syntax WINDOW [[SCREEN] (x1!,y1!)-(x2!,y2!)]

Arguments SCREEN indicates that the coordinate system reads down and to the right the same as the screen. If you omit SCREEN, the coordinates read up and to the right.

x1!, y1!, x2!, and y2! are the coordinates to fix the upper-left and lower-right corners the graphics window. If you omit these coordinates, the coordinate system reverts to screen coordinates (pixels).

Description The WINDOW statement sets the coordinate system to use on the graphics window. When the system is initialized, the graphics window consists of the whole screen. The coordinate system is in pixels, with the origin in the upper-left corner, and increases down and to the right. The current screen mode set with the SCREEN statement determines the number of pixels along each side of the screen. You can restrict the graphics window to a smaller window on the screen by using the VIEW statement. The WINDOW statement enables you to apply a standard user coordinate system to the current graphics window by specifying the values in the upper-left and lower-right corners. The new coordinate system increases up and to the right unless you use the SCREEN option.

For example The following statements set screen mode 1 (320 by 200), set the graphics window to the lower-right corner, and set a coordinate system with the origin in the lower-right corner with x and y axes that range from 0 to 100:

```
SCREEN 1
VIEW (160,100)-(319,199)
WINDOW (0,100)-(100,0)
```

See also CIRCLE statement
DRAW statement
LINE statement
SCREEN statement
VIEW statement

15

S WRITE

Purpose The WRITE # statement prints delimited data to a disk file.

Syntax **WRITE** #*filenumber%*,*arglist*

Arguments *filenumber%* is the file number used when the file was opened with the OPEN statement.

arglist is a list of variables and expressions to print. Numeric variables automatically are converted to strings before being printed. Arguments are separated by commas, and printed strings are surrounded by quotation marks.

Description The WRITE # statement prints data in a disk file and delimits that data so that it can read accurately with the INPUT # statement. Each argument is separated by a comma, and string arguments are surrounded by quotation marks. If you're creating a file to be read by a word processor or to be printed with the DOS TYPE command, consider using the PRINT # statement instead.

For example A disk file written with the following statements

```
A1 = 5.355
B1 = 4.788
PRINT #1, "Values, are: ", A1, B1, " units"
WRITE #1, "Values, are: ", A1, B1, " units"
```

would produce:

```
Values, are: 5.355          4.788          units
"Values, are: ",5.355,4.788," units"
```

Reading those values with the following INPUT # statements

```
INPUT #1, A$, B, C, D$
INPUT #1, E$, F, G, H$
```

would store the following data in these variables:

```
A$ = "Values"
B = 0
C = 5.355
D$ = "4.788          units"
E$ = "Values, are: "
```

```
F = 5.355
G = 4.788
H$ = " units"
```

Note that the first INPUT # statement stops reading the string into A$ at the first comma so that the first numeric input, B, sees text rather than a number and gets a value of 0. The second numeric input, C, then reads the first number, and the remaining number and string ends up in D$.

See also   GET statement
INPUT # statement
LINE INPUT # statement
OPEN statement
PRINT # statement
PUT statement
INPUT$ function

 XOR

Purpose   The XOR operator combines two logical expressions or all the bits in two numeric values by using the logical exclusive OR operation.

Syntax   *express1* **XOR** *express2*

Arguments   *express1* and *express2* are logical expressions, numeric expressions, or numeric values.

Description   The XOR operator combines two logical values according to the following truth table. If two numeric values are combined, the operator is applied bit-by-bit to the corresponding bits in the two values; that is, each bit in the result is equal to the logical exclusive OR of the corresponding bits in the two values being combined.

A	B	A XOR B
True	True	False
True	False	True
False	True	True
False	False	False

Returns The logical exclusive OR of the two expressions equals True (–1) or False (0) if *express1* and *express2* are logical expressions. If *express1* and *express2* are values or numeric expressions that evaluate to values, the result is the bitwise logical exclusive OR of the same bits in each of the two values.

For example The following IF statement causes a beep when A or B are True, but not both:

```
IF A XOR B THEN BEEP
```

See also AND operator
EQV operator
IMP operator
NOT operator
OR operator

 YEAR

Purpose The YEAR function extracts the year from a serial-date number.

Syntax **YEAR(***serialdate#***)**

Arguments *serialdate#* is a serial-date number. A serial-date number is a double-precision number containing the date represented as the number of days since December 30, 1899. Negative serial-date numbers represent dates from January 1, 1753 to December 30, 1899. Times are represented as fractions of a day. Years after 1900 are represented by the same serial-date numbers used in several popular spreadsheet programs.

Description The YEAR() function takes a serial-date number and returns the year represented by that number. Use the DAY(), MONTH(), and YEAR() functions to extract the day, month, and year. To extract the time, use the HOUR(), MINUTE(), and SECOND() functions.

Returns The result is the year as a number from 1753 to 2078.

For example The following statement extracts the year from the serial-date number for March 17, 1987:

```
theYear = YEAR(31853)
'Extracts the year (1987) from the date number
```

See also   DATE$ statement
TIME$ statement
DATE$ function
DATESERIAL function
DATEVALUE function
DAY function
HOUR function
MINUTE function
MONTH function
NOW function
SECOND function
TIME$ function
TIMER function
TIMESERIAL function
TIMEVALUE function
WEEKDAY function

15

Properties

This section deals with the properties of objects. Properties are those attributes of an object that control what the object looks like and how it reacts to different events. For each property in this section, the following items are listed:

Purpose   A brief description of what the property contains, plus any caveats or special requirements for the property.

Objects   Which controls have that property.

Type   What type of variable the property expects. If the type is listed as BOOLEAN, it actually is an INTEGER, with two allowed values: –1 for True and 0 for False.

Available   Design Time—can the value of this property be changed at design time?

Runtime Read—can the value of this property be determined at runtime?

Runtime Write—can the value of this property be changed at runtime?

See also   A listing of related and complementary properties and functions.

Accessing Properties

You set properties available at design time by selecting the object, selecting the property in the Properties list box, and setting its value in the Settings box. Properties available at runtime are accessed by name. To get the value of a property at runtime, use a statement with the following syntax. Optional elements are in brackets ([ ]). Placeholders for variables, objects, and property names are in *monospace italics*. Characters shown just as you should use them in the syntax appear in **bold monospace**. For example:

```
variable = [form.][control[(index)].]property
```

- *variable* is some variable with the correct type to receive the value of the property.

- *form* is the name of the form the control is on; if you omit this name, the current form is assumed.

- *control* is the name of the control that has the property being accessed; if you omit this name, the current form is assumed to have the *property*.

- *index* is the index number for the particular control in a control array.

- *property* is the name of the property. If *property* is a numeric type, *variable* can be of any type, and the value of *property* is forced to that type by truncation and rounding. Note that you can lose data if the type of *variable* is less precise than the type of *property*. If *property* is a STRING type, *variable* must be of type STRING, or an error results.

To set a property at runtime, just reverse the previous assignment statement:

```
[form.][control[(index)].]property = variable
```

The arguments are the same as for reading the property, except that *variable* can be an expression that evaluates to a value the property expects.

You can access all properties in this manner, and generally use them like any other variable.

ActiveControl

Purpose	The ActiveControl property of the SCREEN object contains a reference to the control that currently has the focus. ActiveControl is used to access the properties of that control at runtime. For example, to access the CtlName property of the active control, use the following:

```
SCREEN.ActiveControl.CtlName
```

Objects	Screen
Type	CONTROL
Available	Design Time: No
	Runtime Read: Yes
	Runtime Write: No
See also	ActiveForm property

ActiveForm

Purpose	The ActiveForm property of the SCREEN object contains a reference to the currently active form. Use ActiveForm to access the properties of the active form at runtime. The properties are accessed in a manner similar to that used in the following example to get the CtlName property:

```
SCREEN.ActiveForm.FormName
```

Objects	Screen
Type	Form
Available	Design Time: No
	Runtime Read: Yes
	Runtime Write: No
See also	ActiveControl property

Alignment

Purpose The Alignment property controls the alignment of the text in a label.

Objects Label

Type INTEGER code:

    0   Left-justify (the default)

    1   Right-justify

    2   Center

Available Design Time: Yes

    Runtime Read: Yes

    Runtime Write: Yes

See also None

Archive

Purpose The Archive, Hidden, Normal, ReadOnly, and System properties apply to a file list box and control the display of files with these attributes.

Objects File list box

Type BOOLEAN:

    True (–1)   Display files with this attribute (default for Archive, Normal, and ReadOnly).

    False (0)   Don't display files with this attribute (default for Hidden and System).

Available Design Time: Yes

    Runtime Read: Yes

    Runtime Write: Yes

See also   Hidden property
Normal property
Pattern property
ReadOnly property
System property

Attached

Purpose   The Attached property indicates whether a scroll bar is attached to a form or not. This property is not available in Visual Basic for Windows.

Objects   Scrollbar

Type   BOOLEAN:

True (–1)   The scroll bar is attached to the form.

False (0)   The scroll bar is not attached to the form.

Available   Design Time: Yes

Runtime Read: Yes

Runtime Write: Yes

See also   LargeChange property
Max property
Min property
SmallChange property

AutoRedraw

Purpose   The AutoRedraw property controls whether drawing performed on a form or picture box is stored on the persistent bitmap. If AutoRedraw is enabled, the system takes care of redrawing the object if it's covered by another window and then uncovered. This applies only to graphics drawn on the object and text printed on the object at runtime, not to anything drawn at design time. AutoRedraw must be True for the PrintForm to work.

Objects Form, picture box

Type BOOLEAN:

  True (–1) Enables the system to redraw the object.

  False (0) Disables redrawing by the system. The application must decide whether it wants to redraw the window when it receives a Paint event.

Available Design Time: Yes

  Runtime Read: Yes

  Runtime Write: Yes

See also PRINTFORM method
Paint event

AutoSize

Purpose The AutoSize property controls whether a control is sized automatically to fit its contents.

Objects Label, picture box

Type BOOLEAN:

  True (–1) Automatically resize the control to fit the contents.

  False (0) Don't change the size of the control (the default).

Available Design Time: Yes

  Runtime Read: Yes

  Runtime Write: Yes

See also None

BackColor

Purpose The BackColor property controls the background color of an object. Setting the background color of a control erases all text printed on the control. It does not erase the text associated with the control.

Objects	Check box, combo box, command button, directory list box, drive list box, form, frame, label, list box, option button, picture box, scroll bars, textbox
Type	INTEGER, containing a color attribute (see the RGB() function).
Available	Design Time: Yes
	Runtime Read: Yes
	Runtime Write: Yes
See also	RGB() function
	ForeColor property

BorderStyle

Purpose The BorderStyle property sets an object's border type. Borders are thick or thin, and are resizeable or fixed. You can change the shape of a resizeable object at runtime by dragging its borders. You cannot change the size of a fixed object.

Objects Form, label, picture box, text box

Type INTEGER code for a form:

0 None.

1 *Fixed single.* A thin, single-line border that cannot be resized by dragging. The Control box, Minimize button, and Maximize button are optional controls for this border.

2 *Sizable* (the default). A thin, single-line border that can be resized by dragging. The Control box, Minimize button, and Maximize button are optional controls for this border.

3 *Fixed double.* A two-line border that cannot be resized by dragging. The Control box is an optional control for this border, but the Minimize and Maximize buttons are not available.

4 *Sizable double.* A two-line border that can be resized by dragging. The Control box, Minimize button, and Maximize button are optional controls for this border.

5   *Fixed solid.* A thick-line border that cannot be resized by
dragging. The Control box is an optional control for this border,
but the Minimize button and Maximize button are not available.

6   *Sizable solid.* A thick-line border that can be resized by dragging. The Control box, Minimize button, and Maximize button
are optional controls for this border.

INTEGER code for a label:

0   None.

1   Fixed single.

2   Fixed double.

INTEGER code for a control:

0   None.

1   Fixed single (default for picture box and text box).

Available   Design time: Yes

Runtime Read: Yes

Runtime Write: No

See also   ControlBox property
Maxbutton property
Minbutton property

Cancel

Purpose   The Cancel property controls whether a command button is the Cancel
button. If it is, pressing Esc automatically clicks it. It also is the default
button on the form, if no other button has been designated go with the
Default property. You press the default button by pressing the Enter key.
Only one command button on a form can be the Cancel button.

Objects   Command button

Type   BOOLEAN:

True (–1)	The command button is the Cancel button. Pressing Esc is equivalent to pressing the Cancel button. Pressing Enter is equivalent to pressing the Cancel button if no other button has the Default property set.
False (0)	The command button is not the Cancel button (the default).

Available Design Time: Yes

Runtime Read: Yes

Runtime Write: Yes

See also Default property

Caption

Purpose The Caption property contains the title of an object or the contents of a label. The Caption is the text displayed in the title bar of a form, in a label, on the front of a button, or on the labels of option buttons and check boxes. This text differs from the control name in the CtlName property, although both have the same default strings.

To set an access key for a control, place an ampersand (&) immediately before the letter you want to press to move the focus to that control. The letter appears underlined when displayed.

Because labels cannot receive the focus, giving them an access key causes the focus to move to the next control after the label in the tab order set with the TabIndex property. To give access keys to controls that don't have a Caption, such as text and picture boxes, place a label with an access key just before the control.

Objects Form, check box, command button, frame, label, menu, option button

Type STRING

Available Design Time: Yes

Runtime Read: Yes

Runtime Write: Yes

See also AutoSize property
CtlName property
TabIndex property

Checked

Purpose	The Checked property controls whether a menu item is checked.
Objects	Menu
Type	BOOLEAN:

True (–1)	The menu item is checked.
False (0)	The menu item is not checked (the default).

Available	Design Time: Yes
	Runtime Read: Yes
	Runtime Write: Yes
See also	Enabled property

ControlBox

Purpose	The ControlBox property controls whether a form has a control box in the upper-left corner. A control box has a menu that contains the commands **M**ove, **Mi**nimize, **Ma**ximize, **C**lose, **R**estore, and **S**ize. Other commands automatically disable different entries in the control box's menu.
Objects	Form
Type	BOOLEAN:

True (–1)	The form has a control box (the default).
False (0)	The form does not have a control box.

Available	Design Time: Yes
	Runtime Read: Yes
	Runtime Write: No
See also	BorderStyle property
	Maxbutton property
	Minbutton property

ControlPanel

Purpose The `ControlPanel` property operates like an array of values that set numerous screen properties, such as color and desktop pattern. Each element of the property array contains the value for one of the screen properties. The property is set in the following manner:

    SCREEN.ControlPanel(property) = value

where `property` is the property you want to set and `value` is its setting. The number to use for `value` depends on the property being set. This property is not available in Visual Basic for Windows.

Objects Screen

Type `INTEGER` array. The following properties are settable with the `ControlPanel` property. Their definitions are in the file CONSTANTS.BI, included with the Visual Basic package. You can use either the number or the definition from the file.

Element	Property
0	ACCESSKEY_FORECOLOR
1	ACTIVE_BORDER_BACKCOLOR
2	ACTIVE_BORDER_FORECOLOR
3	ACTIVE_WINDOW_SHADOW
4	COMBUTTON_FORECOLOR
5	DESKTOP_BACKCOLOR
6	DESKTOP_FORECOLOR
7	DESKTOP_PATTERN
8	DISABLED_ITEM_FORECOLOR
9	MENU_BACKCOLOR
10	MENU_FORECOLOR
11	MENU_SELECTED_BACKCOLOR
12	MENU_SELECTED_FORECOLOR
13	SCROLLBAR_BACKCOLOR

Element	Property
14	SCROLLBAR_FORECOLOR
15	THREE_D
16	TITLEBAR_BACKCOLOR
17	TITLEBAR_FORECOLOR

Available   Design Time: No

Runtime Read: Yes

Runtime Write: No

See also   SCREEN statement

CtlName

Purpose   The CtlName property sets the name by which the object is known in the code windows. The control name must be a valid Visual Basic identifier (a variable name). The CtlName has to be less than 40 characters long, start with an alphabetic character, and contain alphabetic and numeric characters and the underscore (_). In a control array, all the controls have the same CtlName.

Objects   Check box, combo box, command button, directory list box, drive list box, file list box, frame, horizontal scroll bar, label, list box, menu item, option button, picture box, timer, vertical scroll bar

Type   STRING

Available   Design Time: Yes

Runtime Read: Yes

Runtime Write: No

See also   FormName property

CurrentX

Purpose	The last thing printed on a form determines the CurrentX and CurrentY properties. These properties identify the location on an object at which the next character will be printed. CurrentX returns the horizontal co-ordinate, or text-column number, of the point. CLS and NEWPAGE reset CurrentX and CurrentY to the origin (usually the upper-left corner of the object).
Objects	Form, picture box
Type	SINGLE; the x-coordinate of the current print location measured in charac-ter widths from the left side of the object.
Available	Design Time: No
	Runtime Read: Yes
	Runtime Write: Yes
See also	CurrentY property

CurrentY

Purpose	The last thing printed on a form determines the CurrentX and CurrentY properties. They identify the location on an object at which the next character will be printed. CurrentY controls the vertical coordinate, or row number, of the point. CLS and NEWPAGE reset CurrentX and CurrentY to the origin (usually the upper-left corner of the object). Drawing or printing on the screen moves CurrentY.
Objects	Form, picture box
Type	SINGLE; the y-coordinate of the current print location measured in charac-ter heights down from the top of the object.
Available	Design Time: No
	Runtime Read: Yes
	Runtime Write: Yes
See also	CurrentX property

Default

Purpose   The Default property controls which command button is the default. The default command button gets pressed any time you press Enter instead of using the mouse. Only one button on a form can be the default button, and setting a default button disables that property in all the other command buttons.

Objects   Command button

Type   BOOLEAN:

True (–1)	Make this command button the default button.
False (0)	Do not make this command button the default button (this value is the default).

Available   Design Time: Yes

Runtime Read: Yes

Runtime Write: Yes

See also   Cancel property

DragMode

Purpose   The DragMode property controls automatic or manual dragging of the control. Use the DRAG method to drag a control manually and the MOVE method to make the move.

Objects   Check box, combo box, command button, directory list box, drive list box, file list box, frame, horizontal scroll bar, label, list box, option button, picture box, text box, vertical scroll bar

Type   INTEGER code:

0	Manual dragging; use the DRAG method (the default).
1	Automatic dragging; press the mouse over the object to drag it. The object does not respond to Click events.

Available   Design Time: Yes

Runtime Read: Yes

Runtime Write: Yes

See also   None

Drive

Purpose   The Drive property sets or returns the drive selected in a Drive list box. Setting the Drive property also regenerates the Drive list box.

Objects   Drive list box

Type   STRING; only the first character is significant when setting the Drive property, and is assumed to be the drive letter.

Available   Design Time: No

Runtime Read: Yes

Runtime Write: Yes

See also   FileName property
Path property
Pattern property

Enabled

Purpose   The Enabled property determines whether a control can respond to user input.

Objects   Check box, combo box, command button, directory list box, drive list box, file list box, frame, horizontal scroll bar, label, list box, menu, option button, picture box, text box, timer, vertical scroll bar

Type   BOOLEAN:

True (−1)   The object can respond to events; the timer is counting.

False (0)   The object does not respond to events; the timer is not counting.

Available   Design Time: Yes

Runtime Read: Yes

Runtime Write: Yes

See also   `Checked` property

FileName

Purpose   The `FileName` property sets or returns the selected filename in a file list box. In addition, you can include a path when setting it to change the directory or disk.

Objects   File list box

Type   `STRING`, containing the filename. You can include a path and drive letter when setting this property, and you can use wildcard characters in the filename. Including the path and drive letter in this property changes the `Path` and `Drive` properties as well. Including wildcard characters in the filename changes the `Pattern` property. The wildcard characters are *, which matches any number of characters, and ?, which matches any single character. The syntax of a path is

```
[drive:][[\][directory][\directory]...\]filename
```

Available   Design Time: No

Runtime Read: Yes

Runtime Write: Yes

See also   `Drive` property
`Path` property
`Pattern` property

ForeColor

Purpose   The `ForeColor` property controls the foreground color of an object. The foreground color is the color used for text and graphics characters drawn on an object.

Objects	Check box, combo box, directory list box, drive list box, form, frame, label, list box, option button, picture box, printer, text box
Type	INTEGER, containing a color attribute (see the RGB() function).
Available	Design Time: Yes
	Runtime Read: Yes
	Runtime Write: Yes
See also	RGB() function
	BackColor property

FormName

Purpose	The FormName property sets the name by which the form is known in the code windows. The form name must be a valid Visual Basic identifier. A valid identifier consists of alphabetic and numeric characters and the underscore (_) and is less than 40 characters long. The first character must be alphabetic.
Objects	Form
Type	STRING
Available	Design Time: Yes
	Runtime Read: Yes
	Runtime Write: No
See also	CtlName property

FormType

Purpose	The FormType property sets the type of a form. Forms can be either normal or a Multiple Document Interface (MDI) parent form. An MDI program has one MDI parent form that fills the whole screen. All other forms are child forms of the MDI form. An MDI parent form cannot have any controls

attached, but can have menus that you can access without moving the focus from a selected child form. Only one form in an application can be an MDI form, and it is also the startup form. This is only available in the Professional edition of Visual Basic.

Objects   Form

Type   INTEGER code:

0   Normal form

1   MDI parent form, only one allowed per program

Available   Design time: Yes

Runtime Read: Yes

Runtime Write: No

See also   None

Height

Purpose   The Height property sets or returns the height of a form or control, or returns the length of a sheet of paper for the printer, or the height of the screen. The unit of measure is the character height. As a control or form is resized, the value of this property changes.

Objects   Check box, combo box, command button, directory list box, drive list box, file list box, form, frame, horizontal scroll bar, label, list box, option button, picture box, printer, screen, text box, vertical scroll bar

Type   SINGLE

Available   Design Time:
Yes: Controls
No: Screen, printer

Runtime Read: Yes

Runtime Write:
Yes: Controls
No: Screen, printer

See also   Width property

Hidden

Purpose The `Archive`, `Hidden`, `Normal`, `ReadOnly`, and `System` properties apply to a file list box and control the display of files with these attributes.

Objects File list box

Type BOOLEAN:

True (-1)	Display files with this attribute (default for `Archive`, `Normal`, and `ReadOnly`).
False (0)	Don't display files with this attribute (default for `Hidden` and `System`).

Available Design Time: Yes

Runtime Read: Yes

Runtime Write: Yes

See also `Archive` property
`Normal` property
`Pattern` property
`ReadOnly` property
`System` property

Index

Purpose The `Index` property identifies an element in a control array. You create a control array at design time by making several objects' `CtlNames` the same. In run mode, you can add extra elements to the control array by using the `LOAD` statement.

Objects Check box, combo box, command button, directory list box, drive list box, file list box, form, frame, horizontal scroll bar, label, list box, menu, option button, picture box, text box, timer, vertical scroll bar

Type INTEGER

Available	Design Time: Yes
	Runtime Read: Yes
	Runtime Write: No
See also	LOAD statement
	UNLOAD statement

Interval

Purpose   The Interval property sets or returns the amount of time a timer has to wait before issuing a Timer event. Only 16 timers are available. If a timer is unavailable, an error results. The timer issues a Timer event whenever the amount of time set by the Interval property has passed. The timing is turned on and off with the Enabled property.

Objects   Timer

Type   LONG, a time in milliseconds

Available   Design Time: Yes

Runtime Read: Yes

Runtime Write: Yes

See also   Timer event

LargeChange

Purpose   The LargeChange property of a scroll bar controls how much the scroll bar's value changes whenever the gray area above or below the thumb is clicked. (A thumb is a white triangle that moves up and down on a scroll bar.)

Objects   Horizontal scroll bar, vertical scroll bar

Type   INTEGER

Available   Design Time: Yes

Runtime Read: Yes

Runtime Write: Yes

See also Max property
Min property
SmallChange property

Left

Purpose The Left property sets or returns the horizontal position of an object. This position is the distance between the left edge of an object and the left edge of the object that contains it. The unit of measure is the character width. As a control or form is moved, the value of this property changes.

Objects Check box, combo box, command button, directory list box, drive list box, file list box, form, frame, horizontal scroll bar, label, list box, option button, picture box, text box, vertical scroll bar

Type SINGLE, a distance in character widths.

Available Design Time: Yes

Runtime Read: Yes

Runtime Write: Yes

See also Height property
Top property
Width property

List

Purpose The List() property is a string array that contains the contents of list boxes with one list item in each element of the array. Lists can be set or read only at runtime. New items are added to the list with the ADDITEM method and removed with the REMOVEITEM method. After you add an item to a list, you can read or change that item by reading or changing its element of the list array. The drive, directory, and file list boxes are read only at runtime; the system writes them.

Objects Combo box, directory list box, drive list box, file list box, list box

Type   STRING array, with one list item in each element of the array. The first item is in element 0 of the array. The ListCount property contains the number of elements in the array.

Available   Design Time: No

Runtime Read: Yes

Runtime Write: Yes (combo and list boxes only)

See also   ADDITEM method
REMOVEITEM method
ListCount property
ListIndex property

ListCount

Purpose   The ListCount property contains the number of elements in a list. To add or remove items, use the ADDITEM and REMOVEITEM methods.

Objects   Combo box, directory list box, drive list box, file list box, list box

Type   INTEGER

Available   Design Time: No

Runtime Read: Yes

Runtime Write: No

See also   ADDITEM method
REMOVEITEM method
List property
ListIndex property

ListIndex

Purpose   The ListIndex property contains the item number of the currently selected item in a list. The first item in a list is number 0. Use the element number from ListIndex to select the array element in the List property to get the text of the currently selected item. Change the value of `ListIndex` to change the selected item in a list box. For combo boxes, the item selected with `ListIndex` might not be the same as the `Text` property because the user can edit the `Text` property.

Objects   Combo box, directory list box, drive list box, file list box, list box

Type   `INTEGER`; equals −1 if no item is selected. The first item in the list is item number 0.

Available   Design Time: No

           Runtime Read: Yes

           Runtime Write: Yes

See also   `ADDITEM` method
           `REMOVEITEM` method
           `List` property
           `ListCount` property

Max

Purpose   The `Max` property controls the value of a scroll bar when the thumb is all the way right for a horizontal scroll bar, or all the way down for a vertical scroll bar. Use `Max` with the `Min` property to define the complete range of scroll bar movement. Note that `Max` can be less than `Min`, which reverses the sense of a scroll bar.

Objects   Horizontal scroll bar, vertical scroll bar

Type   `INTEGER`; the maximum value of a scroll bar.

Available   Design Time: Yes

           Runtime Read: Yes

           Runtime Write: Yes

See also   `LargeChange` property
           `Min` property
           `SmallChange` property

Maxbutton

Purpose The `Maxbutton` property controls whether there is a Maximize button on the upper-right corner of a form. The Maximize button enables you to enlarge the form to full screen. The `BorderStyle` property of the form determines whether a Maximize button is allowed.

Objects Form

Type BOOLEAN:

True (–1)   Include a Maximize button (the default).

False (0)   Do not include a Maximize button.

Available Design Time: Yes

Runtime Read: Yes

Runtime Write: No

See also `BorderStyle` property
`ControlBox` property
`Minbutton` property

Min

Purpose The `Min` property controls the value of a scroll bar when the thumb is all the way left for a horizontal scroll bar, or all the way up for a vertical scroll bar. Use `Min` with the `Max` property to define the complete range of scroll bar movement. Note that `Max` can be less than `Min`, which reverses the sense of a scroll bar.

Objects Horizontal scroll bar, vertical scroll bar

Type INTEGER; the minimum value of a scroll bar.

Available Design Time: Yes

Runtime Read: Yes

Runtime Write: Yes

See also   LargeChange property
Max property
SmallChange property

Minbutton

Purpose   The Minbutton property controls whether there is a Minimize button on the upper-right corner of a form. The Minimize button enables a form to be collapsed to an icon. The BorderStyle property of the form determines whether a Minimize button is allowed.

Objects   Form

Type   BOOLEAN:

True (–1)   Include a Minimize button (the default).

False (0)   Do not include a Minimize button.

Available   Design Time: Yes

Runtime Read: Yes

Runtime Write: No

See also   BorderStyle property
ControlBox property
Minbutton property

MousePointer

Purpose   The MousePointer property controls the icon displayed as the mouse pointer when it's over an object.

Objects   Check box, combo box, command button, directory list box, drive list box, file list box, form, frame, horizontal scroll bar, label, list box, option button, picture box, screen, text box, vertical scroll bar

Type INTEGER code:

0 Shape determined by the control (the default)

1 Arrow arrow

2 Cross

3 I-beam

4 Icon: a small square within a square

5 Size: two crossed double arrows

6 Size NE SW: double arrow diagonal from lower left to upper right

7 Size NS: double arrow pointing up and down

8 Size NW SE: double arrow, diagonal from lower right to upper left

9 Size WE: double arrow pointing left and right

10 Up arrow

11 Wait: hourglass

12 No drop: a square with a slashed circle

Available Design Time: Yes

Runtime Read: Yes

Runtime Write: Yes

See also None

MultiLine

Purpose The MultiLine property enables a text box to contain more than one line. If you're typing in a text box on a form with no default button (a button with its Default property set to True), pressing Enter moves down a line if the MultiLine property is True. If there is a default button, pressing Enter presses the button instead, so use Ctrl-Enter to move down a line.

Objects Text box

Type   BOOLEAN:

  True (–1)   Allow multiple lines of text.

  False (0)   Allow single lines of text even if the string contains a
                 carriage return (the default).

Available   Design Time: Yes

         Runtime Read: Yes

         Runtime Write: No

See also   Default property

Normal

Purpose   The Archive, Hidden, Normal, ReadOnly, and System properties apply to a file
        list box. They control the display of files with these attributes.

Objects   File list box

Type   BOOLEAN:

  True (–1)   Display files with this attribute (default for Archive,
                 Normal, and ReadOnly).

  False (0)   Don't display files with this attribute (default for Hidden
                 and System).

Available   Design Time: Yes

         Runtime Read: Yes

         Runtime Write: Yes

See also   Archive property
        Hidden property
        Pattern property
        ReadOnly property
        System property

Parent

Purpose The Parent property contains the name of the form on which this control lies. Use this property with methods and other properties as you would use the form name. To get the form name, examine the FormName property with Parent as the form as follows:

```
Parent.FormName
```

Objects Check box, combo box, command button, directory list box, drive list box, file list box, frame, horizontal scroll bar, label, list box, option button, picture box, text box, timer, vertical scroll bar

Type Form

Available Design Time: No

Runtime Read: Yes

Runtime Write: No

See also ActiveControl property
ActiveForm property

Path

Purpose The Path property controls the current path in a directory or file list box. The Path contains the complete, absolute path to the directory displayed in the directory and file list boxes. Changing the Path property changes the directory the boxes display. In the file list box, Path does not contain the filename; use the FileName property to get it. To create a complete path to a file, combine the Path property with a backslash and the FileName property. The syntax of a path is

```
[drive:][[\][directory][\directory]...]
```

Objects Directory list box, file list box

Type STRING, containing the path to the displayed directory

Available Design Time: No

Runtime Read: Yes

Runtime Write: Yes

See also Drive property
FileName property
Pattern property

Pattern

16

Purpose The Pattern property controls the files displayed in a file list box. The Archive, Hidden, Normal, ReadOnly, and System properties control the type of file displayed, and the Pattern property controls the names of displayed files. Use the * and ? wildcard characters to select a set of files to display.

Objects File list box

Type STRING, containing a DOS-type pattern to match to filenames. Use the wildcard character * to match any number of characters, and ? to match any single character. The default is *.* (all files).

Available Design Time: Yes

Runtime Read: Yes

Runtime Write: Yes

See also Archive property
Hidden property
Normal property
Path property
ReadOnly property
System property

PrintTarget

Purpose The PrintTarget property of the PRINTER object indicates where data sent to the printer is to go.

Objects Printer

Type STRING containing the printer port (LPT1, LPT2, or LPT3) or a filename. If a filename is used, the printed output goes to the file rather than to the printer.

Available Design Time: Yes

     Runtime Read: Yes

     Runtime Write: Yes

See also LPRINT statement
     PRINTFORM method

ReadOnly

Purpose The Archive, Hidden, Normal, ReadOnly, and System properties apply to a file list box. They control the display of files with these attributes.

Objects File list box

Type BOOLEAN:

   True (–1)   Display files with this attribute (the default for Archive, Normal, and ReadOnly).

   False (0)   Don't display files with this attribute (the default for Hidden and System).

Available Design Time: Yes

     Runtime Read: Yes

     Runtime Write: Yes

See also Archive property
     Hidden property
     Normal property
     Pattern property
     System property

ScaleHeight

Purpose The ScaleHeight property with the ScaleWidth property returns the interior height and width of an object.

Objects Form, picture box, printer

Type	INTEGER; the interior height of the object, in character heights. This is the usable height and does not include borders or the menu bar.
Available	Design Time: Yes (read only)
	Runtime Read: Yes
	Runtime Write: No
See also	ScaleWidth property

ScaleWidth

Purpose	The ScaleHeight property with the ScaleWidth property returns the interior height and width of an object.
Objects	Form, picture box, printer
Type	INTEGER; the interior width of the object, in character widths. This is the usable width and does not include borders.
Available	Design Time: Yes (read only)
	Runtime Read: Yes
	Runtime Write: No
See also	ScaleHeight property

Scrollbars

Purpose	The Scrollbars property enables scroll bars on a multiline text box. The MultiLine property also must be True.
Objects	Text box
Type	INTEGER code:

0	None (the default)
1	Horizontal scroll bars
2	Vertical scroll bars
3	Both

Available	Design Time: Yes
	Runtime Read: Yes
	Runtime Write: No
See also	MultiLine property

SelLength

Purpose The SelLength property contains the number of selected characters in a text or combo box. SelLength works with the SelStart and SelText properties to facilitate text editing in those boxes. When the user selects text in a text box, or in the edit box portion of a combo box, SelStart contains the character position of the first character selected, SelLength contains the number of characters selected, and SelText contains the actual text. Setting the value of SelLength or SelStart causes the indicated text to be selected in the box. Equating SelText to a string replaces the selected text with the string. Note that the length of the string and the length of the selected text do not have to be the same, which is useful for implementing cut and paste operations.

If you change any of these properties, change SelText first because changing it resets SelLength to 0. Change SelStart next because it also changes SelLength to 0. Finally, change SelLength.

Objects Combo box, text box

Type INTEGER; the length of the selected text, in characters.

Available Design Time: No

Runtime Read: Yes

Runtime Write: Yes

See also SelStart property
SelText property
Text property

SelStart

Purpose The SelStart property contains the number of the first selected character in a text or combo box. SelStart works with the SelLength and SelText properties to facilitate text editing in those boxes. When the user selects text in a text box, or in the edit box portion of a combo box, SelStart contains the character position of the first character selected, SelLength contains the number of characters selected, and SelText contains the actual text. Setting the value of SelLength or SelStart causes the indicated text to be selected in the box. Equating SelText to a string replaces the selected text with the string. Note that the length of the string and the length of the selected text do not have to be the same, which is useful for implementing cut and paste operations.

If you change any of these properties, change SelText first because changing it resets SelLength to 0. Change SelStart next because it also changes SelLength to 0. Finally, change SelLength.

Objects Combo box, text box

Type Long; the character number of the first selected character or, if no characters are selected, the location of the insertion point. The first character is character number 0, and the beginning of the string to the left of the first character is location number 0.

Available Design Time: No

Runtime Read: Yes

Runtime Write: Yes

See also SelLength property
SelText property
Text property

SelText

Purpose The SelText property contains the selected characters in a text or combo box. It works with the SelLength and SelStart properties to facilitate text editing in those boxes. When the user selects text in a text box, or in the edit box portion of a combo box, SelStart contains the character position of the first character selected, SelLength contains the number of

characters selected, and SelText contains the actual text. Setting the value of SelLength or SelStart causes the indicated text to be selected in the box. Equating SelText to a string replaces the selected text with the string. Note that the length of the string and the length of the selected text do not have to be the same, which is useful for implementing cut and paste operations.

If you change any of these properties, change SelText first because changing it resets SelLength to 0. Change SelStart next because it also changes SelLength to 0. Finally, change SelLength.

Objects	Combo box, text box
Type	STRING; the selected text.
Available	Design Time: No
	Runtime Read: Yes
	Runtime Write: Yes
See also	SelLength property
	SelStart property
	Text property

SmallChange

Purpose	The SmallChange property of a scroll bar controls how much the scroll bar's value changes whenever scroll arrows are clicked.
Objects	Horizontal scroll bar, vertical scroll bar
Type	INTEGER; the amount to change the Value property when the scroll arrows are clicked.
Available	Design Time: Yes
	Runtime Read: Yes
	Runtime Write: Yes
See also	LargeChange property
	Max property
	Min property

Sorted

Purpose The Sorted property controls whether items in a list or combo box are sorted in alphabetical order. When new items are added to the list with the ADDITEM method, they automatically are inserted at the correct alphabetical location. If you specify a location with the ADDITEM method, strange results can occur. Note that the ListIndex property for an item might change after the ADDITEM method has been executed, because Visual Basic might need to adjust the list to insert the new item at its correct location.

Objects Combo box, list box

Type BOOLEAN:

True (–1)   Sort the items alphabetically.

False (0)   Don't sort the items; place new items at the end (the default).

Available Design Time: Yes

Runtime Read: Yes

Runtime Write: No

See also ADDITEM method
REMOVEITEM method
List property
ListCount property
ListIndex property

Style

Purpose The Style property controls the type of combo box displayed. If you want a user to be able to select from a list or to type an entry, use styles 0 or 1. Style 0 saves room on the form by hiding the list until it's needed. Use style 2 when you want the user to be able to select from a list but not to edit the entry.

Objects Combo box

Type	INTEGER code:

0   Drop-down combo box. This box has an editable text box and a drop-down list.

1   Simple combo box. This box has an editable text box and a list box.

2   Drop-down list box. This box has a drop-down list only. You cannot edit the entry.

Available   Design Time: Yes

Runtime Read: Yes

Runtime Write: No

See also   SelLength property
SelStart property
SelText property

System

Purpose   The Archive, Hidden, Normal, ReadOnly, and System properties apply to a file list box. They control the display of files with these attributes.

Objects   File list box

Type   BOOLEAN:

True (–1)   Display files with this attribute (the default for Archive, Normal, and ReadOnly).

False (0)   Don't display files with this attribute (the default for Hidden and System).

Available   Design Time: Yes

Runtime Read: Yes

Runtime Write: Yes

See also   Archive property
Hidden property
Normal property
ReadOnly property

TabIndex

Purpose   The `TabIndex` property indicates a control's location in the tab order. All controls on a form are in the tab order, and pressing the Tab key moves to the next control in the tab order. The initial tab order is the same order in which you drew the controls on the form. Use the `TabIndex` property to read or change the tab order. When you change a control's `TabIndex` property, the `TabIndex` of all the other controls on the form are adjusted to account for the change.

Disabled controls, labels, and frames are in the tab order but cannot receive the focus, so if you tab to one of them, the focus moves to the next control in the tab order. Use this feature to give an access key to a text box by placing a label with an access key just before the text box in the tab order. When the access key for the label is pressed, the focus cannot move to the label, so it moves to the next control, the text box. You can do the same for any control that does not have a `Caption` property to use for specifying an access key.

Objects   Check box, combo box, command button, directory list box, drive list box, file list box, frame, horizontal scroll bar, label, list box, option button, picture box, text box, vertical scroll bar

Type   `INTEGER`; the location of the control in the tab order. Valid numbers range from 0 to one less than the number of controls on the form.

Available   Design Time: Yes

Runtime Read: Yes

Runtime Write: Yes

See also   `TabStop` property

TabStop

Purpose   The `TabStop` property controls whether a tab stops at a control. All controls on a form are in the tab order, and pressing the Tab key moves to the next control in the tab order. The initial tab order is the same order in which you drew the controls on the form. Use the `TabIndex` property to read or change the tab order. Use the `TabStop` property to skip a control when tabbing.

Objects	Check box, combo box, command button, directory list box, drive list box, file list box, horizontal scroll bar, list box, option button, text box, vertical scroll bar
Type	BOOLEAN:

True (–1)	The tab stops at this control (the default).
False (0)	The tab does not stop at this control.

Available	Design Time: Yes
	Runtime Read: Yes
	Runtime Write: Yes

See also	TabIndex property

Tag

Purpose	The Tag property is a user-definable string property attached to a control. It usually is used for identification, but use it for whatever you want. It's useful for identifying a control that is passed to a procedure. You also can use it to share information that is carried along with the control's name, such as a previous location or a value to use with an Undo procedure.
Objects	Check box, combo box, command button, directory list box, drive list box, file list box, form, frame, horizontal scroll bar, label, list box, menu, option button, picture box, text box, timer, vertical scroll bar
Type	STRING; anything goes.
Available	Design Time: Yes
	Runtime Read: Yes
	Runtime Write: Yes
See also	None

Text

Purpose   The Text property contains the contents of a text box, the text box part of a combo box, or the selected item in a list or drop-down list box.

Objects   Combo box, list box, text box

Type   STRING; whatever is in the text box.

Available   Design Time: Yes

              Runtime Read: Yes

              Runtime Write: Yes, except for list and drop-down list combo boxes

See also   List property
ListCount property
ListIndex property
SelLength property
SelStart property
SelText property

Top

Purpose   The Top property sets or returns the vertical position of an object. It is the distance from the top edge of an object to the top edge of the object that contains it. The scale used is character heights. As a control or form is moved, the value of this property changes.

Objects   Check box, combo box, command button, directory list box, drive list box, file list box, form, frame, horizontal scroll bar, label, list box, option button, picture box, text box, vertical scroll bar

Type   INTEGER; the vertical position of an object

Available   Design Time: Yes

              Runtime Read: Yes

              Runtime Write: Yes

See also   Height property
Left property
Width property

Value

Purpose   The Value property contains the current state of a control.

Objects   Check box, command button, horizontal scroll bar, option button, vertical scroll bar

Type   INTEGER code (check box):

0   Off (the default)

1   On

2   Grayed

BOOLEA (command button, option button):

True (–1)   The button is pressed. Only one option button in a group can be pressed at any time.

False (0)   The button is not pressed (the default).

INTEGER (scroll bar); the current location of the thumb as a value between the limiting values stored in the Min and Max properties for the scroll bar.

Available   Design Time: Yes for all but the command button

Runtime Read: Yes

Runtime Write: Yes

See also   Text property

Visible

Purpose   The Visible property controls whether a control or form can be seen. The user cannot interact with an invisible control or form, but an invisible control or form can be accessed by code. The SHOW and HIDE methods set a form's Visible property.

Objects   Check box, combo box, command button, directory list box, drive list box, file list box, form, frame, horizontal scroll bar, label, list box, menu, option button, picture box, text box, vertical scroll bar

The timer always is invisible.

Type   BOOLEAN:

           True (–1)   The object is visible (the default).

           False (0)   The object is hidden.

Available   Design Time: Yes

           Runtime Read: Yes

           Runtime Write: Yes

See also   HIDE method
           SHOW method
           WindowState property

Width

Purpose   The Width property sets or returns the width of a form, a control, a sheet of paper for the PRINTER, or the SCREEN. The unit of measure is the character width. As a control or form is resized, the value of this property changes.

Objects   Check box, combo box, command button, directory list box, drive list box, file list box, form, frame, horizontal scroll bar, label, list box, option button, picture box, printer, screen, text box, vertical scroll bar

Type   SINGLE, a distance measured in character widths

Available   Design Time: Yes (Controls)
                             No (SCREEN, PRINTER)

           Runtime Read: Yes

           Runtime Write: Yes (Controls)
                             No (SCREEN, PRINTER)

See also   Height property
           Left property
           Top property

WindowState

Purpose   The WindowState property controls whether a form is normal, minimized, or maximized.

Objects   Form

Type   INTEGER code:

        0   Normal (the default)

        1   Minimized to an icon

        2   Maximized to full screen

Available   Design Time: Yes, but does not take effect until runtime

            Runtime Read: Yes

            Runtime Write: Yes

See also   Visible property

Events

Events are messages from Visual Basic objects indicating that something has happened to that object. When events are passed to a program, they trigger event procedures in that program. When any event occurs, such as when you press a key or click a button, the event is placed in an event queue, which is simply a first-in-first-out list. As soon as one event is processed, the next one is taken from the queue and processed. Some events trigger others and add them to the queue. For example, pressing a key causes a KeyDown event, followed by a KeyUp event, and then a KeyPress event. If you were typing into a text box, a Changed event would follow the KeyPress event, and so forth.

When a Form loads and is shown, the following events occur in order: Load, Resize, Paint, GotFocus.

When a key is pressed and the focus is in an editable item, the following events occur in order: KeyDown, KeyUp, KeyPress, Change. If the item with the focus is a command button, an option button, or a check box, and the key is the Enter or Spacebar, a Click event replaces the Change event.

When the mouse is clicked, the following events occur in order: MouseDown, MouseUp, Click.

This chapter lists all the events and the event procedure headers and describes the arguments in the following format:

Event Name

Purpose	A description of what causes this particular event to occur.
Procedure header	The header for the event procedure.
Arguments	Arguments of the event procedure.
Objects	Objects to which this event occurs.
See also	A listing of related events.

Change

Purpose	The Change event occurs when the contents of a control change.
Procedure header	SUB *object*_Change (Index AS INTEGER)
Arguments	*object* is the object that changed.
	Index, for a control array of the objects, is equal to the Index property of the changed object.
Objects	Combo box, directory list box, drive list box, horizontal scroll bar, label, picture box, text box, vertical scroll bar
See also	None

Click

Purpose The Click event occurs when an object is clicked with the mouse. It also occurs when you press Enter or Spacebar when a command button, an option button, or a check box is selected. Pressing Esc causes a Click event to a command button that has its Cancel property set to True. Pressing Enter causes a Click event to a command button that has its Default property set to True. You also can trigger a Click event with code by changing the Value property of a command button, an option button, or a check box to True.

Procedure header `SUB object_Click (Index AS INTEGER)`

Arguments *object* is the object that is clicked.

Index, for a control array of the objects, is equal to the Index property of the clicked object.

Objects Check box, combo box, command button, directory list box, file list box, form, label, list box, menu, option button, picture box

See also None

DblClick

Purpose The DblClick event occurs when an object is rapidly clicked twice with the mouse. It also occurs when you use code to change the Path property of a directory list box, or the FileName property of a file list box to a valid filename.

Procedure header `SUB object_DblClick (Index AS INTEGER)`

Arguments *object* is object that is double-clicked.

Index, for a control array of the objects, is equal to the Index property of the double-clicked object.

Objects Check box, combo box, command button, directory list box, file list box, form, label, list box, menu, option button, picture box

See also None

DragDrop

Purpose The DragDrop event occurs when a control is dragged over a form or control and then released. You can perform a drag event with a mouse or by using the DRAG method.

Procedure header
```
SUB object_DragDrop (Index AS INTEGER,
  Source AS CONTROL, X AS SINGLE,
  . Y AS SINGLE)
```

Arguments *object* is the object that was dropped on.

Index, for a control array of the objects, is equal to the Index property of the form or object that was dropped on.

Source is the control that was dragged and dropped.

X and Y specify the x,y position of the mouse pointer when the Source is dropped on the object.

Objects Check box, combo box, command button, directory list box, drive list box, file list box, form, frame, horizontal scroll bar, label, list box, option button, picture box, text box, vertical scroll bar

See also None

DragOver

Purpose The DragOver event occurs when a control is dragged over an object. Events occur every time the mouse pointer is moved while dragging an object.

Procedure header
```
SUB object_DragOver (Index AS INTEGER,
  Source AS CONTROL, X AS SINGLE,
  Y AS SINGLE, State AS INTEGER)
```

Arguments *object* is the object that is dragged over.

Index, for a control array of dragged-over objects, is equal to the Index property of the object that is dragged over.

Source is the control that is being dragged.

X and Y specify the x,y position of the mouse pointer when the event occurs.

State is a code indicating that the Source was

0   Entering the dragged-over object

1   Leaving the dragged-over object

2   Moving while over the dragged-over object

Objects   Check box, combo box, command button, directory list box, drive list box, file list box, frame, form, horizontal scroll bar, label, list box, option button, picture box, text box, vertical scroll bar

See also   None

DropDown

Purpose   The DropDown event occurs when the list of a drop-down list box is just about to drop down.

Procedure header   `SUB object_Dropdown (Index AS INTEGER)`

Arguments   *object* is the combo box CtlName.

Index, for a control array of the objects, is equal to the Index property of the combo box that is going to drop its list.

Objects   Combo box

See also   None

GotFocus

Purpose   The GotFocus event occurs when an object gets the focus. You can get the focus either by user action, such as pressing Tab or clicking with the mouse, or by code using the SETFOCUS method.

Procedure header   `SUB object_GotFocus (Index AS INTEGER)`

Arguments   *object* is the object that got the focus.

Index, for a control array of the objects, is equal to the Index property of the control that got the focus.

Objects Check box, combo box, command button, directory list box, drive list box, file list box, form, horizontal scroll bar, list box, option button, picture box, text box, vertical scroll bar

See also LostFocus event

KeyDown

Purpose The KeyDown event occurs when a control has the focus and a key is pressed. The KeyUp and KeyPress events occur when the key is released. The KeyUp and KeyDown events get key codes rather than characters from the system. In Visual Basic for MS-DOS, the key codes for the printable characters are the same as the ASCII character codes. Special codes exist for the nonprintable keys on the keyboard, such as the function keys. There also are codes that differentiate between the keypad and the equivalent key on the main keyboard. See Appendix B, "ASCII Code Chart," for a list of ASCII codes, and Appendix C, "Key Code Chart," for a list of key codes. The codes for the special keys also are available in the file CONSTANT.BI, included with Visual Basic.

Procedure header ⟶
```
SUB object_KeyDown ([Index AS INTEGER,]
KeyCode AS INTEGER, Shift AS INTEGER)
```

Arguments *object* is the object that has the focus when a key is pressed.

Index, for a control array of the objects, is equal to the Index property of the object that has the focus when the key is pressed.

KeyCode is the key's code number (see also Appendix B, "ASCII Code Chart," Appendix C, "Key Code Chart," and the file CONSTANT.BI, included with Visual Basic for a list of key codes).

Shift is a code indicating which of the modifier keys is held down when the key is pressed. The value of this code equals the sum of the following codes for the modifier keys held down:

1 Shift

2 Ctrl

4 Alt

Objects   Check box, combo box, command button, directory list box, drive list box, file list box, form, horizontal scroll bar, list box, option button, picture box, text box, vertical scroll bar

See also   KeyPress event
KeyUp event

KeyPress

Purpose   The KeyPress event occurs when an object has the focus and a key is pressed and released. Because the KeyPress event occurs before a keystroke is given to the control, you can filter the input here if necessary. If you change the value of KeyAscii, the changed value is given to the control.

Procedure header   ⤷
```
SUB object_KeyPress ([Index AS INTEGER,]
     KeyAscii AS INTEGER)
```

Arguments   *object* is the object that has the focus when the key is pressed.

Index, for a control array of the objects, is equal to the Index property of the object that has the focus when the key is pressed.

KeyAscii is the ASCII code of the key pressed (see Appendix B, "ASCII Code Chart"). Use CHR$() to convert the code to text.

Objects   Check box, combo box, command button, directory list box, drive list box, file list box, form, horizontal scroll bar, list box, option button, picture box, text box, vertical scroll bar

See also   KeyDown event
KeyUp event

KeyUp

Purpose   The KeyUp event occurs when a control has the focus and a pressed key is released. A KeyPress event follows. The KeyUp and KeyDown events get key codes rather than characters from the system. In Visual Basic for DOS, the key codes for the printable characters are the same as the ASCII character codes. Special codes exist for the nonprintable keys on the keyboard, such as the function keys. Codes also exist to differentiate between the keypad

and the equivalent key on the main keyboard. See Appendix B, "ASCII Code Chart," for a list of ASCII codes, and Appendix C, "Key Code Chart," for a list of key codes. The codes for the special keys also are available in the file CONSTANT.BI, included with Visual Basic.

Procedure header ⤷
```
SUB object_KeyUp (Index AS INTEGER,
KeyCode AS INTEGER, Shift AS INTEGER)
```

Arguments   `object` is the object that has the focus when a key is released.

`Index`, for a control array of the objects, is equal to the `Index` property of the object that has the focus when the key is released.

`KeyCode` is the key's code number (see Appendix B, "ASCII Code Chart," Appendix C, "Key Code Chart," and the file CONSTANT.TXT, included with Visual Basic, for a list of key codes).

`Shift` is a code indicating which of the modifier keys is held down when the key is pressed. The value of this code equals the sum of the following codes for the modifier keys held down:

1   Shift

2   Ctrl

4   Alt

Objects   Check box, combo box, command button, directory list box, drive list box, file list box, form, horizontal scroll bar, list box, option button, picture box, text box, vertical scroll bar

See also   KeyDown event
KeyPress event

Load

Purpose   The Load event occurs when a form is loaded. This is a good place to put startup code for a program.

Procedure header
```
SUB Form_Load ()
```

Arguments   None

Objects   Form

See also   Unload event

LostFocus

Purpose   The LostFocus event occurs when an object loses the focus. The focus can be lost either by user action, such as pressing Tab or clicking with the mouse, or with code that uses the SETFOCUS method.

Procedure header   `SUB object_LostFocus (Index AS INTEGER)`

Arguments   *object* is the object that lost the focus.

Index, for a control array of the objects, is equal to the Index property of the object that lost the focus.

Objects   Check box, combo box, command button, directory list box, drive list box, file list box, form, horizontal scroll bar, list box, option button, picture box, text box, vertical scroll bar

See also   GotFocus event

MouseDown

Purpose   The MouseDown event occurs when a mouse button is pressed and the mouse pointer is over an object. The MouseDown, MouseUp, and MouseMove events distinguish between the different buttons of the mouse and the state of the Shift, Ctrl, and Alt keys at the time. The Click event responds only to the left mouse button.

Procedure header
```
SUB object_MouseDown ([Index AS INTEGER,]
Button AS INTEGER, Shift AS INTEGER,
X AS SINGLE, Y AS SINGLE)
```

Arguments   *object* is the object on which the mouse pointer lies.

Index, for a control array of the objects, is equal to the Index property of the object under the mouse pointer.

Button is the mouse button pressed, specified with one of the following codes:

1   Left button

2   Right button

Shift is the state of the modifier keys when the button is pressed. The state is specified as one of the following codes:

1   Shift

2   Ctrl

4   Alt

If you hold down more than one key, the codes for the different keys are added together. For example, if both the Alt and Ctrl keys were pressed, Shift would equal 6.

X and Y specify the x,y location of the mouse pointer when the mouse button is pressed.

Objects   Directory list box, file list box, form, label, list box, picture box

See also   Click event
MouseMove event
MouseUp event

MouseMove

Purpose   The MouseMove event occurs when a mouse pointer is moved over an object. The MouseDown, MouseUp, and MouseMove events return the state of the mouse buttons, and the Shift, Ctrl, and Alt keys at the time of the event. The Click event responds only to the left mouse button.

Procedure header
```
SUB object_MouseMove ([Index AS INTEGER,]
Button AS INTEGER, Shift AS INTEGER,
X AS SINGLE, Y AS SINGLE)
```

Arguments   *object* is the object the mouse pointer is over.

Index, for a control array of the objects, is equal to the Index property of the object under the mouse pointer.

Button is the mouse button that is down when the event occurs. The button is specified with one of the following codes:

1   Left button

2   Right button

If you press more than one button, the codes are added together.

Shift is the state of the modifier keys when the event occurs. The state is specified as one of the following codes:

1   Shift

2   Ctrl

4   Alt

The codes for the different keys are added together if you hold down more than one key.

X and Y specify the x,y location of the mouse pointer when the event occurs.

Objects   Directory list box, file list box, form, label, list box, picture box

See also   Click event
MouseDown event
MouseUp event

MouseUp

Purpose   The MouseUp event occurs when you release a pressed mouse button while the mouse pointer is over an object. The MouseDown, MouseUp, and MouseMove events return the state of the mouse buttons and of the Shift, Ctrl, and Alt keys at the time of the event. The Click event responds only to the left mouse button.

Procedure header
```
SUB object_MouseUp ([Index AS INTEGER,]
Button AS INTEGER, Shift AS INTEGER,
X AS SINGLE, Y AS SINGLE)
```

Arguments   object is the object on which the mouse pointer lies.

Index, for a control array of the objects, is equal to the Index property of the object under the mouse pointer.

Button is the mouse button released, specified as a code:

1   Left button

2   Right button

Shift is the state of the modifier keys when the button is released. The state is specified with one of the following codes:

1 Shift

2 Ctrl

4 Alt

If you hold down more than one key, the codes for the different keys are added together.

X and Y is the x,y location of the mouse pointer when the mouse button is released.

Objects Directory list box, file list box, form, label, list box, picture box

See also Click event
MouseDown event
MouseMove event

Paint

Purpose The Paint event occurs when the contents of a form or picture box are uncovered and need to be redrawn. If AutoRedraw is set to True for the object, the system takes care of redrawing it. Redrawing applies only to text and graphics drawn on the objects at runtime. The REFRESH method also invokes a Paint event. Be careful with Paint event procedures; you can create a cascade of events. (Imagine what would happen if a REFRESH method were placed within a Paint event procedure.)

Procedure header SUB *object*_**Paint (Index AS INTEGER)**

Arguments *object* is the form or picture box that needs repainting.

Index, for a control array of the objects, is equal to the Index property of the object that needs redrawing.

Objects Form, picture box

See also None

PathChange

Purpose   The PathChange event occurs when you change the Path or FileName properties of a control.

Procedure header   SUB *object*_**PathChange (Index AS INTEGER)**

Arguments   *object* is the object whose Path or FileName properties changed.

Index, for a control array of the objects, is equal to the Index property of the object whose Path or FileName properties have changed.

Objects   Directory list box, file list box

See also   PatternChange event

PatternChange

Purpose   The PatternChange event occurs when the Pattern property of a file list box changes.

Procedure header   SUB *object*_**PatternChange (Index AS INTEGER)**

Arguments   *object* is the name of the file list box.

Index, for a control array of the objects, is equal to the Index property of the affected file list box.

Objects   File list box

See also   PathChange event

Resize

Purpose   The Resize event occurs when a form is first displayed or is resized.

Procedure header   SUB Form_Resize ()

Arguments	None
Objects	Form
See also	None

Timer

Purpose	The Timer event occurs when a timer's time interval expires. When you use a timer like an alarm clock, use this procedure to take action when the alarm goes off. The Timer event does not stop a timer; it continues to count down to the next Timer event.
Procedure header	`SUB object_Timer ([Index AS INTEGER])`
Arguments	*object* is the name of the timer. Index, for a control array of the objects, is equal to the Index property of the timer that had an event.
Objects	Timer
See also	None

Unload

Purpose	The Unload event occurs just before a form is unloaded. Use it to save values and clean up any loose ends before you remove the form from memory. When you remove a form from memory, any data stored in its variables is lost unless those variables are defined in a COMMON statement, or put somewhere by the Unload event procedure.
Procedure header	`SUB Form_Unload ()`
Arguments	None
Objects	Form
See also	Load event

18

Objects

The objects of Visual Basic consist primarily of controls and the form. These objects are the visual pieces that comprise an application. Other objects include the CLIPBOARD, PRINTER, and SCREEN objects. These last three objects are for interacting with the clipboard, controlling the printer, and receiving information about what is visible on the screen.

Part II, "Opening Up Visual Basic," covers the operation and use of the controls. This chapter briefly describes each object and the properties, events, and methods that apply to it in the following format:

Object Name

Purpose	Describes what the object is used for.
Properties	Lists the properties of the object.
Events	Lists the events that can happen to the object.
Methods	Lists the methods that affect this object.

Check Box

Purpose   The check box control sets nonexclusive options; therefore, you can check or uncheck any number of check boxes in a group. The check box is a square box followed by a label. When you check the check box, there's an X in the box. The check box is related to the option buttons used to select exclusive options. The state of the check box is given by the Value property, which can have the following values:

0   Unchecked

−1   Checked

2   Grayed (disabled)

Properties

BackColor	Caption	CtlName
DragMode	Enabled	ForeColor
Height	Index	Left
MousePointer	Parent	TabIndex
TabStop	Tag	Top
Value	Visible	Width

Events

Click	DragDrop	DragOver
GotFocus	KeyDown	KeyPress
KeyUp	LostFocus	

Methods

DRAG	MOVE	REFRESH
SETFOCUS		

CLIPBOARD

Purpose   The CLIPBOARD object temporarily stores text for later reuse. No visual control is associated with the CLIPBOARD object, and only methods apply to it.

Properties   None

Events   None

Methods

CLEAR	GETTEXT	SETTEXT

Combo Box

Purpose   The combo box is a combination of a list box and a text box. The combo box enables a user to select a value from a list, or to type a value. The `Style` property determines the appearance of the combo box. Variations include a text box above a list box, a text box above a drop-down list box, and a drop-down list box.

Properties

BackColor	CtlName	
DragMode	Enabled	ForeColor
Height	Index	Left
List	ListCount	ListIndex
MousePointer	Parent	SelLength
SelStart	SelText	Style
Sorted	TabIndex	TabStop
Tag	Text	Top
Visible	Width	

Events

Change	Click	DblClick
DragDrop	DragOver	DropDown
GotFocus	KeyDown	KeyPress
KeyUp	LostFocus	

Methods

ADDITEM	DRAG	MOVE
REFRESH	REMOVEITEM	SETFOCUS

Command Button

Purpose   The command button, along with the menus, is the primary method for initiating action in a program. The command button is a rectangle with rounded corners and a `Caption` across its face. Command buttons initiate events, rather than setting options as the option buttons and check boxes do.

Properties

BackColor	Cancel	Caption
CtlName	Default	DragMode
Enabled	Height	Index
Left	MousePointer	Parent

TabIndex	TabStop	Tag
Top	Value	Visible
Width		

Events

Click	DragDrop	DragOver
GotFocus	KeyDown	KeyPress
KeyUp	LostFocus	

Methods

DRAG	MOVE	REFRESH
SETFOCUS		

Directory List Box

Purpose   The directory list box is a special version of a list box that is linked to the DOS file system. It's designed to work with the file list box and the drive list box to make a complete disk file access system. The directory list box appears as a list of file folders for a disk specified in the Path property. When the user clicks a directory, it reveals its subdirectories, and the path to the selected directory appears in the Path property.

Properties

BackColor	CtlName	DragMode
Enabled	ForeColor	Height
Index	Left	List
ListCount	ListIndex	MousePointer
Parent	Path	TabIndex
TabStop	Tag	Top
Visible	Width	

Events

Change	Click	DragDrop
DragOver	GotFocus	KeyDown
KeyPress	KeyUp	LostFocus
MouseDown	MouseMove	MouseUp

Methods

DRAG	MOVE	REFRESH
SETFOCUS		

Drive List Box

Purpose   The drive list box is a special version of a list box that is linked to the DOS
file system. It is designed to work with the directory list box and the file list
box to make a complete disk file access system. The drive list box is a drop-
down list of the disk drive and its name. Clicking a disk puts its letter in the
Path property.

Properties

BackColor	CtlName	DragMode
Drive	Enabled	ForeColor
Height	Index	Left
List	ListCount	ListIndex
MousePointer	Parent	TabIndex
TabStop	Tag	Top
Visible	Width	

Events

Change	DragDrop	DragOver
GotFocus	KeyDown	KeyPress
KeyUp	LostFocus	

Methods

DRAG	MOVE	REFRESH
SETFOCUS		

File List Box

Purpose   The file list box is a special version of a list box that is linked to the DOS file
system. It is designed to work with the directory list box and the drive list
box to make a complete disk file access system. The file list box contains a
list of the files in the directory specified in its Path property. Clicking a file
puts its name in the FileName property.

Properties

Archive	BackColor	CtlName
DragMode	Enabled	FileName
ForeColor	Height	Hidden
Index	Left	List
ListCount	ListIndex	MousePointer
Normal	Parent	Path
Pattern	ReadOnly	System
TabIndex	TabStop	Tag
Top	Visible	Width

Events	Click	DblClick	DragDrop
	DragOver	GotFocus	KeyDown
	KeyPress	KeyUp	LostFocus
	MouseDown	MouseMove	MouseUp
	PathChange	PatternChange	

Methods	DRAG	MOVE	REFRESH
	SETFOCUS		

Form

Purpose The form object is the basis of all windowed Visual Basic applications. All the controls are attached to a form.

Properties	AutoRedraw	BackColor	BorderStyle
	Caption	ControlBox	CurrentX
	CurrentY	Enabled	ForeColor
	FormName	Height	Left
	MaxButton	MinButton	MousePointer
	ScaleHeight	ScaleWidth	Tag
	Top	Visible	Width
	WindowState		

Events	Click	DblClick	DragDrop
	DragOver	GotFocus	KeyDown
	KeyPress	KeyUp	Load
	LostFocus	MouseDown	MouseMove
	MouseUp	Paint	Resize
	Unload		

Methods	CIRCLE	CLS	HIDE
	LINE	MOVE	POINT
	PRINT	PRINTFORM	PSET
	REFRESH	SETFOCUS	SHOW
	TEXTHEIGHT	TEXTWIDTH	

Frame

Purpose   A frame is a control for grouping other controls. It's a square box with a caption at the top. Any controls placed on a frame move with the frame when you move it. Option buttons placed on a frame form a single option-button group, separate from any other option buttons on the form.

Properties

BackColor	Caption	CtlNam
DragMode	Enabled	ForeColor
Height	Index	Left
MousePointer	Parent	TabIndex
Tag	Top	Visible
Width		

Events   DragDrop   DragOver

Methods   DRAG   MOVE   REFRESH

Horizontal Scroll Bar

Purpose   A horizontal scroll bar can scan quickly through a long list of numbers or items. Visually, it is the same as any scroll bar at the side of a Windows window: a long, thin rectangle with a slider in the middle, known as the thumb. The thumb is dragged with the mouse to move quickly from one end of the scroll bar to the other. Clicking the gray area above or below the thumb moves the thumb in the direction and distance specified by the LargeChange property. Clicking the arrows at each end moves the thumb in that direction by one SmallChange amount.

Although a scroll bar usually is associated with movement within a window, it is actually a control that either displays or returns an integer value according to the location of the thumb. Programmers must create code that coordinates that value with a window or list. The position of the thumb is stored as a number in the Value property. The number is between the values of the Min and Max properties.

Properties

Attached	CtlName	DragMode
Enabled	Height	Index
LargeChange	Left	Max

18

Min	MousePointer	Parent
SmallChange	TabIndex	TabStop
Tag	Top	Value
Visible	Width	

Events	Change	DragDrop	DragOver
	GotFocus	KeyDown	KeyPress
	KeyUp	LostFocus	

Methods	DRAG	MOVE	REFRESH

Label

Purpose A label contains text you want the user to read but not change. A label is a rectangular box filled with the text stored in its Caption property.

Properties	Alignment	AutoSize	BackColor
	BorderStyle	Caption	CtlName
	DragMode	Enabled	ForeColor
	Height	Index	Left
	MousePointer	Parent	TabIndex
	Tag	Top	Visible
	Width		

Events	Change	Click	DblClick
	DragDrop	DragOver	MouseDown
	MouseMove	MouseUp	

Methods	DRAG	MOVE	REFRESH

List Box

Purpose A list box contains a list of selectable items. It's a rectangular window filled with lines of text; each line is a list item. If there are more items than can fit in the window, a scroll bar is displayed to enable you to scroll the list. You cannot load a list at design time, but a running program must fill it with data using the ADDITEM method.

Properties	BackColor	CtlName	DragMode
	Enabled	ForeColor	Height

	Index	Left	List
	ListCount	ListIndex	MousePointer
	Parent	Sorted	TabIndex
	TabStop	Tag	Text
	Top	Visible	Width
Events	Click	DblClick	DragDrop
	DragOver	GotFocus	KeyDown
	KeyPress	KeyUp	LostFocus
	MouseDown	MouseMove	MouseUp
Methods	ADDITEM	DRAG	MOVE
	REFRESH	REMOVEITEM	SETFOCUS

Menu

Purpose A menu is most closely related to command buttons because it is used to initiate events, though you also can use it to set options. A menu is a pull-down list of items attached to the top of a form. Each item is a separate command that initiates some piece of code. You can check items to indicate selected options, or gray them to indicate unavailability.

Properties	Caption	Checked	CtlName
	Enabled	Index	Parent
	Tag	Visible	
Events	Click		
Methods	None		

Option Button

Purpose Option buttons are used to set exclusive options, so you can press only one option button in a group. Option buttons are round circles with a label to their right. When you press an option button, a black dot appears in the center. Option buttons are related to check boxes, which set nonexclusive options. You can group option buttons by placing them on a frame.

Properties	BackColor	Caption	CtlName
	DragMode	Enabled	ForeColor

715

	Height	Index	Left
	MousePointer	Parent	TabIndex
	TabStop	Tag	Top
	Value	Visible	Width
Events	Click	DblClick	DragDrop
	DragOver	GotFocus	KeyDown
	KeyPress	KeyUp	LostFocus
Methods	DRAG	MOVE	REFRESH
	SETFOCUS		

Picture Box

Purpose A picture box displays text and graphics created with the extended characters.

Properties	AutoRedraw	AutoSize	BackColor
	BorderStyle	CtlName	CurrentX
	CurrentY	DragMode	Enabled
	ForeColor	Height	Index
	Left	MousePointer	Parent
	ScaleWidth	TabIndex	TabStop
	Tag	Top	Visible
	Width		
Events	Change	Click	DblClick
	DragDrop	DragOver	GotFocus
	KeyDown	KeyPress	KeyUp
	LostFocus	MouseDown	MouseMove
	MouseUp	Paint	
Methods	CIRCLE	CLS	DRAG
	LINE	MOVE	POINT
	PRINT	PSET	REFRESH
	SETFOCUS	TEXTHEIGHT	TEXTWIDTH

PRINTER

Purpose The PRINTER object communicates with the printer. Draw or print on the printer exactly as you would on a picture box or form. When you issue the NEWPAGE or ENDDOC methods, the page is printed. You also can use the PRINTFORM method to print a form as it appears on the screen.

Properties

CurrentX	CurrentY	ForeColor
Height	PrintTarget	ScaleHeight
ScaleWidth	Width	

Events None

Methods

CIRCLE	ENDDOC	LINE
NEWPAGE	PRINT	PSET
TEXTHEIGHT	TEXTWIDTH	

SCREEN

Purpose The SCREEN object accesses objects displayed on the screen.

Properties

ActiveControl	ActiveForm	ControlPanel()
Height	MousePointer	Width

Events None

Methods None

Text Box

Purpose A text box is used to receive text from the user. It is a rectangular box in which text can be typed, selected, and edited with the keyboard. The clipboard and the Cut, Copy, and Paste commands are not supported unless you add code.

Properties

BackColor	BorderStyle	CtlName
DragMode	Enabled	ForeColor
Height	Index	Left
MousePointer	MultiLine	Parent

18

ScrollBars	SelLength	SelStart
SelText	TabIndex	TabStop
Tag	Text	Top
Visible	Width	

Events	Change	DragDrop	DragOver
	GotFocus	KeyDown	KeyPress
	KeyUp	LostFocus	
Methods	DRAG	MOVE	REFRESH
	SETFOCUS		

Timer

Purpose   A timer is a control that works like an alarm clock. You set its Interval property for a specific number of milliseconds and it issues a Timer event whenever that time has passed. Note that a limited number of timers are available (16 total in Windows). A timer always is invisible on a form.

Properties	CtlName	Enabled	Index
	Interval	Parent	Tag

Events   Timer

Methods   None

Vertical Scroll Bar

Purpose   A vertical scroll bar enables you to scan quickly through a long list of numbers or items. Visually, it's the same as any scroll bar at the side of a Windows window: a long, thin rectangle with a slider in the middle, known as the thumb. You drag the thumb with the mouse to move quickly from one end of the scroll bar to the other. Clicking the gray area above or below the thumb moves the thumb in the direction and distance specified by the LargeChange property. Clicking the arrows at each end moves the thumb in that direction by one SmallChange amount.

Although a scroll bar usually is associated with movement within a window, it actually is a control that either displays or returns an integer value according to the location of the thumb. Programmers must create code that coordinates that value with a window or list. The INTEGER value is between the Min and Max properties.

Properties		
Attached	CtlName	DragMode
Enabled	Height	Index
LargeChange	Left	Max
Min	MousePointer	Parent
SmallChange	TabIndex	TabStop
Tag	Top	Value
Visible	Width	

Events		
Change	DragDrop	DragOver
GotFocus	KeyDown	KeyPress
KeyUp	LostFocus	

Methods		
DRAG	MOVE	REFRESH

Part IV

Appendixes

Installing Visual Basic

Installing Visual Basic is relatively simple, with most of the work done by the Setup program. Take care of the following few steps before doing the installation:

1. Check the hardware and software.

2. Write-protect the distribution disks.

3. Copy the distribution disks.

Checking Your Hardware

Visual Basic requires some specific hardware and software to run, so before you open your Visual Basic package, be sure you have the necessary equipment:

Hardware

- You must have at least an IBM XT or compatible computer to run Visual Basic for MS-DOS. This is the minimum machine; a 286 or later machine would be better.

- You need at least 640 kilobytes (640K) of memory, although two-to-four megabytes is much better.

- You need a hard disk with about 11 megabytes (11M) free for the complete Visual Basic Pro package. The standard version requires about 8M of disk space. You can get away with about 4.5M if you leave out the libraries, the examples, the tutorial, and the help files.

- You need a graphics monitor and card, such as the CGA, EGA, VGA, 8514, Hercules, or compatible, to do the graphics, though the Forms part of the program will work with a text-only system. You shouldn't use anything less than an EGA system if you want to take full advantage of Visual Basic's capabilities.

- You need a mouse. You may be able to get by without one, but don't try. It's much easier if you have a mouse, and they are relatively inexpensive.

Software

- You must have DOS 3.0 or later running on your system. DOS 5.0 or later is better, because you can put more of the drivers and system software in upper memory (between 640K and 1M), freeing up more memory for Visual Basic. The software created by Visual Basic should run on machines with DOS 2.2 or later.

- If you want to translate applications between Visual Basic for Windows and Visual Basic for MS-DOS, you need Microsoft Windows 3.0 or later, and Visual Basic for Windows 1.0 or later. Both of these softwares need more powerful hardware than that previously listed for Visual Basic for MS-DOS. You don't need this software if you are not planning to translate programs to or from the Windows environment.

Write-Protecting the Distribution Disks

As soon as you take the distribution disks out of the box, protect them. To protect them, put write-protect tabs on the 5 1/4-inch disks and slide open the write protect tabs on the 3 1/2-inch disks. This not only protects the disks from accidental erasure and unwanted changes, but also protects them from virus attacks.

Copying the Distribution Disks

The second step is to copy the distribution disks with the DOS `DISKCOPY` command. Both 5 1/4-inch and 3 1/2-inch disks come with Visual Basic, so copy the set you plan to use for installation.

There are two methods for copying the disks with DOS, depending on whether you have one or two disk drives of the same type. If you do have a second drive, use the following steps. If you don't have a second drive, use the steps in the next section. Note that to use the `DISKCOPY` command, either your DOS system directory must be in your current path or you must be in that directory. If you execute the `DISKCOPY` command and get an invalid command error, try moving to the DOS directory by using the `CD` (change directory) command, and then try executing `DISKCOPY` again. The following steps assume C:\DOS is where your system files are stored.

You can copy low-density (360K) 5 1/4-inch disks using a high-density 5 1/4-inch drive and a low-density 5 1/4-inch drive, but the source disks must be placed in the high-density drive and the destination disks must be in the low-density drive. A high-density 5 1/4-inch drive can format and write low-density disks; however, the disks may not be readable in other drives, and may not be reliable. This problem is caused by the read/write head on the high-density drive, which writes a thinner track than the heads on a low-density drive. The high-density drives need the thinner tracks to get more information on the same sized disk.

continues

725

continued

Low-density 5 1/4-inch disks should always be formatted and written in low-density drives, though they can be read in either high- or low-density drives. High-density disks can only be read, written, and formatted in high-density drives.

High-density 3 1/2-inch disk drives do not have this problem, because they automatically adjust themselves for the type of disk (high- or low-density) that is inserted in them.

To copy disks using the DISKCOPY command and two floppy-disk drives, use the following steps. The A drive is the source drive and the B drive is the destination drive. If your disk drives have different drive letters, insert your drive letters for the ones in the commands.

1. At the DOS prompt, type

   `C:\DOS>DISKCOPY A: B:`

2. When instructed to do so, put the locked distribution disk in drive A, the destination disk in drive B, and press Return. Note that the destination disk does not have to be blank or formatted.

3. Remove the disks when each copy is done.

4. You are asked whether you want to copy another disk. Type Y and press Enter, and copy the rest of the distribution disks. After copying the last disk, type N and press Enter to quit.

To copy disks by using the DISKCOPY command and a single floppy disk drive (A:), use the following steps. The A drive is assumed to be both the source and destination drive. If your single drive has a different drive letter, substitute your drive letter for the one used in the command.

1. At the DOS prompt, type

   `C:\DOS>DISKCOPY A: A:`

2. When instructed, insert the locked distribution disk in drive A and press Enter.

3. When instructed, remove the distribution disk, place the destination disk in drive A, and press Enter. Note that the destination disk does not have to be blank or formatted.

4. Exchange the disks when requested until the copy is complete.

5. You are asked whether you want to copy another disk. Type Y and press Enter, and copy the rest of the distribution disks. After copying the last disk, type N in answer to the question and press Enter to quit.

Installing with Setup

Now that you have a copy of your distribution set, you can run the Setup program to install Visual Basic. Follow these steps:

1. Insert Disk 1 of the distribution set in your A drive and type

   C:\>A:

   A:\>SETUP

2. A window appears, as shown in Figure A.1, giving you the option of installing Visual Basic, building libraries, or exiting. Select the Install option and press Return.

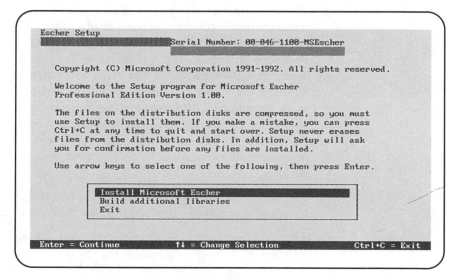

```
Escher Setup
                            Serial Number: 00-046-1100-MSEscher


  Copyright (C) Microsoft Corporation 1991-1992. All rights reserved.

  Welcome to the Setup program for Microsoft Escher
  Professional Edition Version 1.00.

  The files on the distribution disks are compressed, so you must
  use Setup to install them. If you make a mistake, you can press
  Ctrl+C at any time to quit and start over. Setup never erases
  files from the distribution disks. In addition, Setup will ask
  you for confirmation before any files are installed.

  Use arrow keys to select one of the following, then press Enter.


        ┌─────────────────────────────────────────┐
        │ Install Microsoft Escher                 │
        │ Build additional libraries               │
        │ Exit                                     │
        └─────────────────────────────────────────┘

  Enter = Continue        ↑↓ = Change Selection        Ctrl+C = Exit
```

Figure A.1. *Starting the installation.*

3. The next window, shown in Figure A.2, asks you to personalize your copy of Visual Basic. Type your name, or your company name, and press Return.

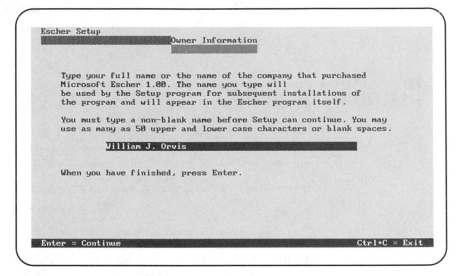

Figure A.2. Personalizing Visual Basic.

4. The next window, shown in Figure A.3, asks you to specify the math processor option you want to install with Visual Basic. The 80X87-emulator option lets each program test for a math coprocessor, and use it if it is available. If a coprocessor isn't available, it uses a software emulator to do math operations. The alternate math option ignores any math coprocessor and does all math operations with software. The alternate math option will be slightly faster than the emulator math option on machines that don't have a coprocessor. Most people will use the first option, because it offers the most flexibility. Make your choice and press Return.

5. The next window, shown in Figure A.4, lets you select the character set to use. Make your selection and press Return.

6. The next four windows—shown in Figures A.5, A.6, A.7, and A.8—let you select the directories for the executable files, the source files, the library files, and the help files. The default is to place

them all in the same directory. I prefer to place them in different directories, but the choice is yours. Change the suggested directories if you want to, and press Return after each one to continue.

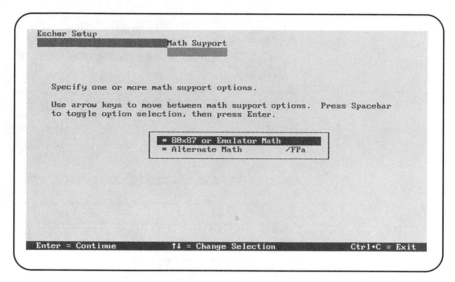

Figure A.3. *Selecting the math processor option.*

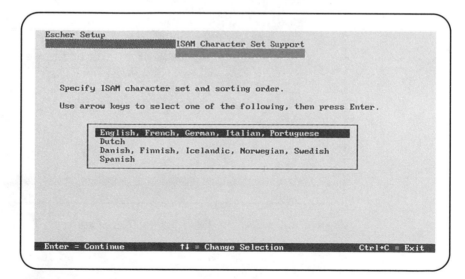

Figure A.4. *Selecting the character set.*

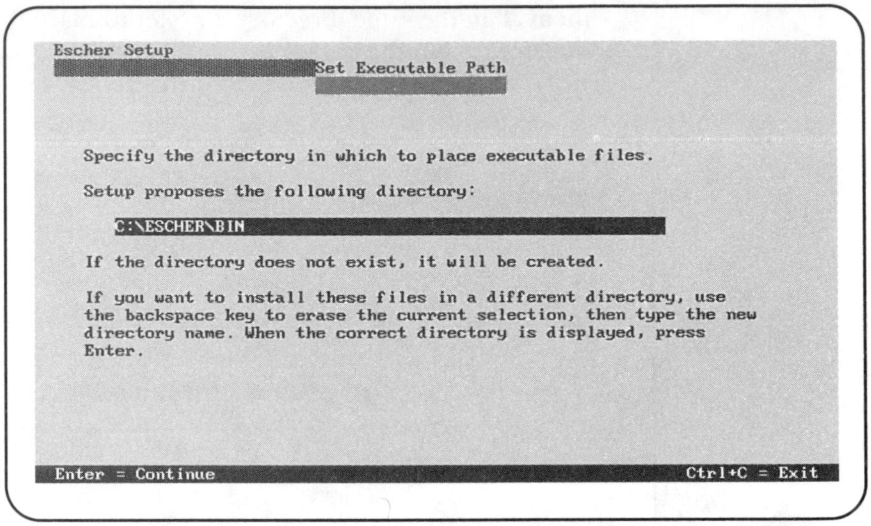

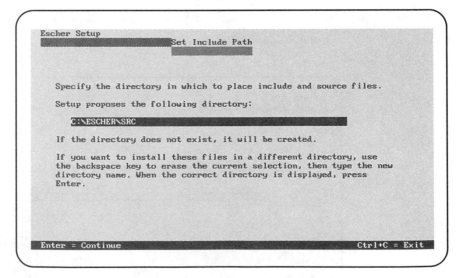

Figure A.5. *Selecting the directory for the executable files.*

Figure A.6. *Selecting the directory for the source files.*

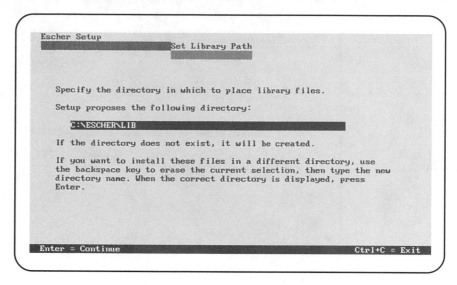

Figure A.7. *Selecting the directory for the library files.*

Figure A.8. *Selecting the directory for the help files.*

7. After you've made all your selections, the screen in Figure A.9 appears to let you check your selections and make changes if necessary. Press Return to continue, or use the arrow keys to move down to the item you want to change and press Return to change it.

731

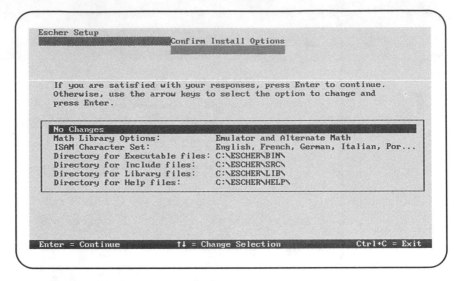

Figure A.9. *Checking your selections.*

8. Now you can sit back and relax while Setup does the installation. When Setup needs another disk, a screen like that shown in Figure A.10 appears. Insert the requested disk and press Return to continue.

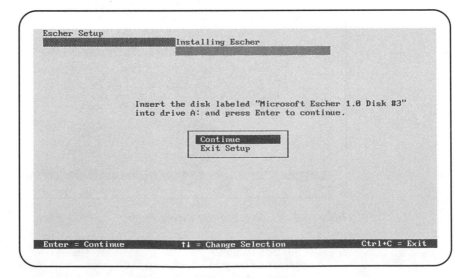

Figure A.10. *A request to change a disk.*

9. When the installation is complete, you will see the screen in Figure A.11, where you can either quit or run the tutorial.

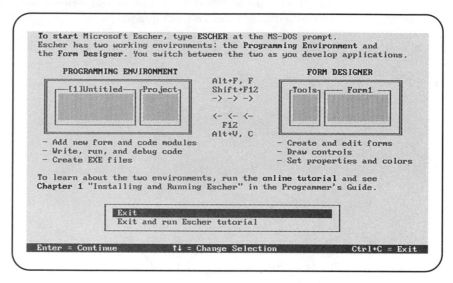

To start Microsoft Escher, type ESCHER at the MS-DOS prompt.
Escher has two working environments: the **Programming Environment** and
the **Form Designer**. You switch between the two as you develop applications.

PROGRAMMING ENVIRONMENT   FORM DESIGNER

```
┌─[1]Untitled─┐ ┌─Project─┐        Alt+F, F       ┌─Tools─┐ ┌─ Form1 ─┐
│             │ │         │        Shift+F12       │       │ │         │
│             │ │         │        -> -> ->        │       │ │         │
│             │ │         │                        │       │ │         │
│             │ │         │        <- <- <-        │       │ │         │
└─────────────┘ └─────────┘           F12          └───────┘ └─────────┘
                                    Alt+V, C
```

- Add new form and code modules   - Create and edit forms
- Write, run, and debug code   - Draw controls
- Create EXE files   - Set properties and colors

To learn about the two environments, run the **online tutorial** and see
Chapter 1 "Installing and Running Escher" in the Programmer's Guide.

```
┌──────────────────────────────────────────┐
│ Exit                                       │
│ Exit and run Escher tutorial               │
└──────────────────────────────────────────┘
```

Enter = Continue   ↑↓ = Change Selection   Ctrl+C = Exit

Figure A.11. The installation is complete.

Installation Problems

If you have problems with the setup program, try turning off any disk caching programs, such as SMARTDRV, and try again. You may also need to turn off any virus checkers. If SETUP still does not work, there is an alternate installer on disk 1. To use the alternate installer, copy the file ALTSETUP.BAT from disk 1 onto your hard disk. For example:

```
C:>COPY A:\ALTSETUP.BAT C:\
```

Now run ALTSETUP with three arguments: the number of disks in the installation set, the drive to be used to install from, and the drive to install to. For example, if there are eight disks in the installation set, and you are going to be placing them in drive A:, and want to install VBDOS on drive C:, use the following command line, and follow the instructions:

```
C:>ALTSETUP 8 A: C:
```

If this does not work, read the text file PACKING.TXT on disk 1 of the installation set for instructions on manually copying and decompressing the files. You can open it with most word processors, or type it to the screen with the DOS TYPE command.

ASCII/ANSI Code Chart

All character information in BASIC applications is stored as strings of codes. The most commonly used characters are the ASCII (American Standard Code for Information Interchange) codes, which comprise the first 128 codes in this table. Windows applications support most of the 256 character ANSI (American National Standards Institute) code set, of which the ASCII codes are a subset. However, in DOS, the second 128 characters (codes 128 through 255) follow the IBM character set. The following table contains the ANSI characters (Windows), the DOS characters, and their ASCII/ANSI codes in both hexadecimal and decimal format.

Windows Character	DOS Character	Hex Code	Decimal Code
none	nul	&H00	0
none	☺	&H01	1
none	☻	&H02	2
none	♥	&H03	3

continues

Windows Character	DOS Character	Hex Code	Decimal Code
none	◆	&H04	4
none	♣	&H05	5
none	♠	&H06	6
none	•	&H07	7
Backspace	▯	&H08	8
Tab	○	&H09	9
Line feed	▯	&H0A	10
none	♂	&H0B	11
none	♀	&H0C	12
Carriage return	♪	&H0D	13
none	♫	&H0E	14
none	¤	&H0F	15
none	▶	&H10	16
none	◀	&H11	17
none	↕	&H12	18
none	‼	&H13	19
none	¶	&H14	20
none	§	&H15	21
none	▬	&H16	22
none	↕	&H17	23
none	↑	&H18	24
none	↓	&H19	25
none	→	&H1A	26
none	←	&H1B	27
none	∟	&H1C	28
none	↔	&H1D	29
none	▲	&H1E	30

Windows Character	DOS Character	Hex Code	Decimal Code
none	▼	&H1F	31
Space		&H20	32
!	!	&H21	33
"	"	&H22	34
#	#	&H23	35
$	$	&H24	36
%	%	&H25	37
&	&	&H26	38
'	'	&H27	39
(	(	&H28	40
)	)	&H29	41
*	*	&H30	42
+	+	&H31	43
,	,	&H2A	44
-	'	&H2B	45
.	.	&H2C	46
/	/	&H2D	47
0	0	&H2E	48
1	1	&H2F	49
2	2	&H32	50
3	3	&H33	51
4	4	&H34	52
5	5	&H35	53
6	6	&H36	54
7	7	&H37	55
8	8	&H38	56

continues

B

Windows Character	DOS Character	Hex Code	Decimal Code
9	9	&H39	57
:	:	&H3A	58
;	;	&H3B	59
<	<	&H3C	60
=	=	&H3D	61
>	>	&H3E	62
?	?	&H3F	63
@	@	&H40	64
A	A	&H41	65
B	B	&H42	66
C	C	&H43	67
D	D	&H44	68
E	E	&H45	69
F	F	&H46	70
G	G	&H47	71
H	H	&H48	72
I	I	&H49	73
J	J	&H4A	74
K	K	&H4B	75
L	L	&H4C	76
M	M	&H4D	77
N	N	&H4E	78
O	O	&H4F	79
P	P	&H50	80
Q	Q	&H51	81
R	R	&H52	82
S	S	&H53	83

Windows Character	DOS Character	Hex Code	Decimal Code
T	T	&H54	84
U	U	&H55	85
V	V	&H56	86
W	W	&H57	87
X	X	&H58	88
Y	Y	&H59	89
Z	Z	&H5A	90
[	[	&H5B	91
\	\	&H5C	92
]	]	&H5D	93
^	^	&H5E	94
_	_	&H5F	95
`	`	&H60	96
a	a	&H61	97
b	b	&H62	98
c	c	&H63	99
d	d	&H64	100
e	e	&H65	101
f	f	&H66	102
g	g	&H67	103
h	h	&H68	104
i	i	&H69	105
j	j	&H6A	106
k	k	&H6B	107
l	l	&H6C	108
m	m	&H6D	109

continues

B

Windows Character	DOS Character	Hex Code	Decimal Code
n	n	&H6E	110
o	o	&H6F	111
p	p	&H70	112
q	q	&H71	113
r	r	&H72	114
s	s	&H73	115
t	t	&H74	116
u	u	&H75	117
v	v	&H76	118
w	w	&H77	119
x	x	&H78	120
y	y	&H79	121
z	z	&H7A	122
{	{	&H7B	123
|	|	&H7C	124
}	}	&H7D	125
~	~	&H7E	126
none	⌂	&H7F	127
none	Ç	&H80	128
none	ü	&H81	129
,	é	&H82	130
f	â	&H83	131
"	ä	&H84	132
…	à	&H85	133
†	å	&H86	134
‡	ç	&H87	135
^	ê	&H88	136

Windows Character	DOS Character	Hex Code	Decimal Code
‰	ë	&H89	137
Š	è	&H8A	138
‹	ï	&H8B	139
Œ	î	&H8C	140
none	ì	&H8D	141
none	Ä	&H8E	142
none	Å	&H8F	143
none	É	&H90	144
'	æ	&H91	145
'	Æ	&H92	146
"	ô	&H93	147
"	ö	&H94	148
•	ò	&H95	149
-	û	&H96	150
—	ù	&H97	151
~	ÿ	&H98	152
™	Ö	&H99	153
š	Ü	&H9A	154
›	¢	&H9B	155
œ	£	&H9C	156
none	¥	&H9D	157
none	û	&H9E	158
Ÿ	ƒ	&H9F	159
none	á	&HA0	160
¡	í	&HA1	161
¢	ó	&HA2	162

continues

B

Windows Character	DOS Character	Hex Code	Decimal Code
£	ú	&HA3	163
¤	ñ	&HA4	164
¥	Ñ	&HA5	165
⊥	a̱	&HA6	166
§	o̱	&HA7	167
¨	¿	&HA8	168
©	⌐	&HA9	169
a	¬	&HAA	170
«	½	&HAB	171
¬	¼	&HAC	172
—	¡	&HAD	173
®	«	&HAE	174
—	»	&HAF	175
°	▒	&HB0	176
±	▓	&HB1	177
2	█	&HB2	178
3	│	&HB3	179
´	┤	&HB4	180
µ	╡	&HB5	181
¶	╢	&HB6	182
•	╖	&HB7	183
,	╕	&HB8	184
1	╣	&HB9	185
°	║	&HBA	186
»	╗	&HBB	187
¼	╝	&HBC	188
½	╜	&HBD	189

Windows Character	DOS Character	Hex Code	Decimal Code
¾	⊣	&HBE	190
¿	⌐	&HBF	191
À	└	&HC0	192
Á	⊥	&HC1	193
Â	⊤	&HC2	194
Ã	├	&HC3	195
Ä	─	&HC4	196
Å	┼	&HC5	197
Æ	╞	&HC6	198
Ç	╟	&HC7	199
È	╚	&HC8	200
É	╔	&HC9	201
Ê	╩	&HCA	202
Ë	╦	&HCB	203
Ì	╠	&HCC	204
Í	═	&HCD	205
Î	╬	&HCE	206
Ï	╧	&HCF	207
Đ	╨	&HD0	208
Ñ	╤	&HD1	209
Ò	╥	&HD2	210
Ó	╙	&HD3	211
Ô	╘	&HD4	212
Õ	╒	&HD5	213
Ö	╓	&HD6	214
×	╫	&HD7	215

continues

743

Windows Character	DOS Character	Hex Code	Decimal Code
ø	┬	&HD8	216
Ù	┘	&HD9	217
Ú	┌	&HDA	218
Û	█	&HDB	219
Ü	▄	&HDC	220
Ý	▐	&HDD	221
▌	▌	&HDE	222
ß	▀	&HDF	223
à	α	&HE0	224
á	β	&HE1	225
â	Γ	&HE2	226
ã	π	&HE3	227
ä	Σ	&HE4	228
å	σ	&HE5	229
æ	μ	&HE6	230
ç	γ	&HE7	231
è	Φ	&HE8	232
é	ø	&HE9	233
ê	Ω	&HEA	234
ë	δ	&HEB	235
ì	∞	&HEC	236
í	ø	&HED	237
î	ε	&HEE	238
ï	η	&HEF	239
δ	≡	&HF0	240
ñ	±	&HF1	241
ò	≥	&HF2	242

Windows Character	DOS Character	Hex Code	Decimal Code
ó	≤	&HF3	243
ô	⌠	&HF4	244
õ	⌡	&HF5	245
ö	÷	&HF6	246
÷	≈	&HF7	247
ø	°	&HF8	248
ù	■	&HF9	249
ú	▪	&HFA	250
û	√	&HFB	251
ü	n	&HFC	252
ý	2	&HFD	253
p	▮	&HFE	254
ÿ	a	&HFF	255

B

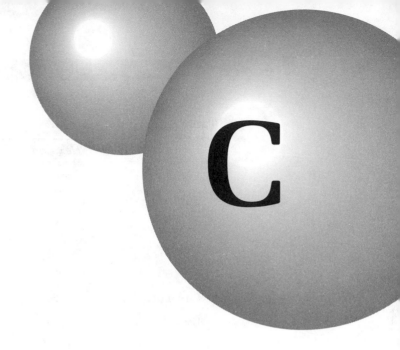

Key Code Chart

The `KeyUp` and `KeyDown` event procedures require the key codes listed in Table C.1. These key codes identify particular keys on the keyboard that are being pressed. The printable alphabetic characters are represented by their ASCII codes (see Appendix B, "ASCII/ANSII Code Chart"). This table lists the nonprintable characters in addition to codes that differentiate between the same keys on the keypad and the main keyboard. Not every keyboard supports all of these codes.

Table C.1. The key code chart.

Main Keyboard Keys

Key	Hex Code	Decimal Code
Cancel	&H3	3
Backspace	&H8	8
Tab	&H9	9
Clear	&HC	12

continues

Table C.1. continued

Key	Hex Code	Decimal Code
Return	&IID	13
Shift	&H10	16
Control	&H11	17
Menu	&H12	18
Pause	&H13	19
CapsLock	&H14	20
Esc	&H1B	27
Spacebar	&H20	32
PageUp	&H21	33
PageDown	&H22	34
End	&H23	35
Home	&H24	36
LeftArrow	&H25	37
UpArrow	&H26	38
RightArrow	&H27	39
DownArrow	&H28	40
Select	&H29	41
Print	&H2A	42
Execute	&H2B	43
SnapShot	&H2C	44
Insert	&H2D	45
Delete	&H2E	46
Help	&H2F	47
ScrollLock	&H91	145

Keypad Keys

Key	Hex Code	Decimal Code
0	&H60	96
1	&H61	97
2	&H62	98
3	&H63	99
4	&H64	100
5	&H65	101
6	&H66	102
7	&H67	103
8	&H68	104
9	&H69	105
*	&H6A	106
+	&H6B	107
Separator	&H6C	108
-	&H6D	109
.	&H6E	110
/	&H6F	111
NumLock	&H90	144

Function Keys

Key	Hex Code	Decimal Code
F1	&H70	112
F2	&H71	113
F3	&H72	114
F4	&H73	115

continues

Table C.1. continued

Key	Hex Code	Decimal Code
F5	&H74	116
F6	&H75	117
F7	&H76	118
F8	&H77	119
F9	&H78	120
F10	&H79	121
F11	&H7A	122
F12	&H7B	123

Scan Code Chart

The INKEY$ function and the KEY statement need the scan codes listed in Table D.1. These key codes identify the physical key on the keyboard that was pressed, rather than the character that the key represents. Thus, they don't differentiate between shifted and unshifted keys, and keys on the keypad return different key codes than the same keys on the main keyboard. Not every keyboard supports all these codes.

Table D.1. The scan code chart.

Main Keyboard Keys

Key	Scan Code
Esc	1
! or 1	2
@ or 2	3
# or 3	4

continues

Table D.1. continued
Main Keyboard Keys

Key	Scan Code
$ or 4	5
% or 5	6
^ or 6	7
& or 7	8
* or 8	9
(or 9	10
) or 0	11
+ or =	13
Backspace	14
Tab	15
Q	16
W	17
E	18
R	19
T	20
Y	21
U	22
I	23
O	24
P	25
{ or [	26
} or]	27
Enter	28
Ctrl	29
A	30

Key	Scan Code
S	31
D	32
F	33
G	34
H	35
J	36
K	37
L	38
: or ;	39
" or '	40
Left Shift	42
| or \	43
Z	44
X	45
C	46
V	47
B	48
N	49
M	50
< or ,	51
> or .	52
? or /	53
Right Shift	54
Print Screen or *	55
Alt	56

continues

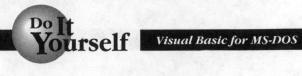

Table D.1. continued

Main Keyboard Keys

Key	Scan Code
Spacebar	57
Caps Lock	58

Function Keys

Key	Scan Code
F1	59
F2	60
F3	61
F4	62
F5	63
F6	64
F7	65
F8	66
F9	67
F10	68
F11	133

Keypad Keys

Key	Scan Code
Num Lock	69
Scroll Lock	70
Home or 7	71
Up or 8	72
Page Up or 9	73
Gray -	74
Left or 4	75

Key	Scan Code
Center or 5	76
Right or 6	77
Gray +	78
End or 1	79
Down or 2	80
Page Down or 3	81
Ins or 0	82
Del or .	83

Visual Basic Toolkit Libraries

Visual Basic for DOS comes with several libraries of software tools for you to use in your programs. To use these libraries in programs in the Programming Environment, you must load the Quicklib library file (.QLB) by using the /L switch, followed by the library name, when you start Visual Basic. In addition, each library, except the ISAM library, has an include file (.BI) to register all the functions. You should attach the include file to a program (using the $INCLUDE metacommand) before using the library functions. To create the compiled version of a program, you need the .LIB version of the library file.

Visual Basic comes in two editions, the standard edition and the professional edition. Many of these toolbox libraries are only available in the professional edition. The professional edition includes many more functions for financial and database calculations, plus a charting module for producing presentation-quality charts.

The Common Dialog Toolkit

The common dialog toolkit is a library of the most commonly used dialog boxes, such as File Open and File Save. None of these dialog boxes actually does the operation specified, they just supply the visual interface to get information from the user. For example, the File Open dialog box does not actually open a file, it merely returns the filename and path selected by the user.

To use these dialog boxes in an application, use the **Add** File command of the **File** menu to attach the CMNDLG.BAS code module and the CMNDLGF.FRM form module to a project. You also can attach the common dialog toolkit to a program by starting Visual Basic with the /L switch followed by CMNDLG.QLB to load the library, and then including the file CMNDLG.BI in your program with the $INCLUDE metacommand. The file CMNDLG.LIB is also available for compiling programs that use these functions. The following functions are available in the common dialog toolkit:

About	Creates an about dialog box for author's name, program version, copyright, and so forth
ChangeText	Creates a dialog box to return a string to search for and a second string to replace every occurrence of the first string
ColorPalette	Creates a dialog box to select a color palette visually
FileOpen	Creates a file open dialog box to locate and return the name and path of a file to open
FilePrint	Creates a dialog box to select the printer, and the number of copies to print
FileSave	Creates a file save dialog box to select a directory and path for saving a file
FindText	Creates a dialog box to return a string to search for

The Help Toolkit

The help toolkit is a library of tools for creating, displaying, and searching a help file (see Chapter 14, "Advanced-Language Features," for more information). To use this toolkit in an application, use the **Ad**d File command of the **F**ile menu to attach the HELP.BAS code module and the HELPF.FRM and HELPUTIL.FRM form modules to a project. You can also attach the help toolkit to a program by starting Visual Basic with the /L switch followed by HELP.QLB to load the library, and then including the file HELP.BI in your program with the $INCLUDE metacommand. The file HELP.LIB is also available for compiling the programs. The following functions are available in the help toolkit:

HelpClose	Closes the Help file
HelpRegister	Initializes the Help toolkit and loads the file containing the Help information
HelpSearch	Displays the Search dialog box to locate a topic
HelpSetOptions	Sets the display options for Help
HelpShowTopic	Displays a specific Help topic

The Mouse Toolkit

The mouse toolkit is a library of procedures you can use for accessing the mouse when you draw graphics with all forms hidden. When forms are visible, Visual Basic itself provides mouse support. To use this toolkit in an application, use the **Ad**d File command of the **F**ile menu to attach the MOUSE.BAS code module and the MOUSE.FRM form module to a project. You also can attach the mouse toolkit to a program by starting Visual Basic with the /L switch followed by MOUSE.QLB to load the library, and then including the file MOUSE.BI in your program with the $INCLUDE metacommand. The file MOUSE.LIB is also available for compiling the programs. The following functions are available in the mouse toolkit:

MouseBorder	Sets the boundaries for mouse movement on the screen
MouseDriver	Mouse interface procedure; checks for the presence of a mouse, and sends commands to it
MouseHide	Hides the mouse pointer
MouseInit	Reinitializes the mouse driver
MousePoll	Gets the location of the mouse pointer and the status of the buttons
MouseShow	Displays the mouse pointer
ScrSettings	Gets the current screen mode and width
SetHigh	Switches to the highest resolution video mode available

The Setup Toolkit

The setup toolkit is a customizable program for installing an application onto a hard disk from floppy disks. To create an installation program, copy the setup files, SETUP.BAS, SETUPMSG.FRM, SETUPOPT.FRM, SETUPPTH.FRM, SETUPSTS.FRM, SETUP.BI, and SETUP.MAK. Open the SETUP.MAK file in Visual Basic for DOS, and edit the InitSetup procedure to indicate the number of files, disks, and so on to install. You can then compile the Setup program and use it to install your files. The following functions are available in the setup toolkit:

InitSetup	Sets the number of files, disks, and so on needed to install your program
Setup	Does the actual installation

The Financial Functions Toolkit (Professional Edition Only)

The following financial functions are contained in the financial toolkit available in the professional edition of Visual Basic for MS–DOS. To use these functions, start Visual Basic with the /L switch followed by FINANCE to load the library, and include the file FINANCE.BI in your program with the $INCLUDE metacommand. FINANCE.BI defines the functions so they can be used in your program. When you compile a program that uses these functions, the FINANCE.LIB library file must be available. The following functions are available in the financial functions toolkit:

DDB#	Calculates and returns depreciation by using the double-declining-balance method
FV#	Calculates and returns the future value of an annuity
IRR#	Calculates and returns the internal rate of return
MIRR#	Calculates and returns the modified internal rate of return
NPer#	Calculates and returns the number of periods for an investment
NPV#	Calculates and returns the net present value of investment
Pmt#	Calculates and returns the payment for an investment
PPmt#	Calculates and returns the principal payment for the given period of an annuity
PV#	Calculates and returns the present value of a series of payments

Rate#	Calculates and returns the interest rate per period for an annuity
SLN#	Calculates and returns the depreciation by using the straight-line method
SYD#	Calculates and returns the depreciation by using sum-of-years' digits method

The Presentation Graphics Toolkit (Professional Edition Only)

The presentation graphics toolkit creates professional quality graphs and charts on the screen. The toolkit is included only with the professional edition of Visual Basic, and requires the font management toolkit. To use these functions, start Visual Basic with the /L switch followed by CHART.QLB to load the library, and include the file CHART.BI in your program with the $INCLUDE metacommand to define the functions in your program. Because you cannot draw graphics on the screen when any forms are showing, hide all the forms first by using the HIDE method. When compiling a program using these functions, the CHART.LIB library file must be available. The following functions are available in the presentation graphics toolkit:

AnalyzeChart	Prepares a single series bar, column, or line chart without drawing it. Draw it with Chart
AnalyzeScatter	Prepares a single series scatter (x,y) chart without drawing it. Draw it with ChartScatter
AnalyzePie	Prepares a pie chart without drawing it. Draw it with ChartPie

AnalyzeChartMS	Prepares a multiseries bar, column, or line chart without drawing it. Draw it with ChartMS
AnalyzeScatterMS	Prepares a multiseries scatter chart without drawing it. Draw it with ChartScatterMS
Chart	Draws a bar, column, or line chart
ChartMS	Draws a multiseries bar, column, or line chart
ChartPie	Draws a pie chart
ChartScatter	Draws a single series scatter (*x,y*) chart
ChartScatterMS	Draws a multiseries scatter chart
ChartScreen	Sets the screen mode to use when drawing charts
DefaultChart	Defines default properties for different chart types
GetPaletteDef	Returns a copy of the internal chart palette
GetPattern$	Returns a pattern from a list of patterns
LabelChart	Prints a horizontal label on a chart
LabelChartV	Prints a vertical label on a chart
MakeChartPattern$	Sets the fill pattern and color used in a pie, column, or bar chart
ResetPaletteDef	Resets the chart palette to the default
SetPaletteDef	Changes the internal chart palette

The Font Management Toolkit (Professional Edition Only)

The following font management functions are part of the presentation graphics toolkit. They are used to select, load, and print bitmapped fonts. To use these functions, start Visual Basic with the /L switch followed by the FONT.QLB switch to load the library, and include the file FONT.BI in your program with the $INCLUDE metacommand. FONT.BI defines the functions in your program. When you compile a program using these functions, the FONT.LIB library file must be available. The following functions are available in the font management toolkit:

GetFontInfo	Gets information about the active font
GetMaxFonts	Gets the maximum number of fonts that can be registered and loaded
GetRFontInfo	Gets information about a registered font
GetTextLen%	Returns the length of a string, in pixels, using the active font
GetTotalFonts	Gets the total number of loaded fonts
GTextWindow	Gets the logical coordinates of the text window
LoadFont%	Loads a registered font
OutGText%	Prints some text using the current font, color, and position
RegisterFonts%	Registers a font by using the font header information in a font file (.FON)
RegisterMemFont%	Registers the font information for fonts stored in memory
SelectFont	Sets the active font from the list of loaded fonts

SetGCharSet	Selects the graphics character set (IBM or Windows) to use
SetGTextColor	Sets the color used for graphics characters
SetGTextDir	Sets the text direction (horizontal or vertical)
SetMaxFonts	Sets the maximum number of fonts that can be registered and loaded
UnRegisterFonts	Removes all font registration from memory

ISAM Database (Professional Edition Only)

The following functions allow programs created with Visual Basic for MS-DOS to create and access an ISAM (Indexed Sequential Access Method) database. Although you can create database files with the standard Visual Basic functions, the following functions make it much simpler. These functions are also contained within the Visual Basic language, so you don't need to load any library files to access them.

BEGINTRANS	Marks the beginning of an ISAM transaction
BOF	Returns True if the current position is at the beginning of a file
CHECKPOINT	Writes the open ISAM database buffers to disk
CLOSE	Closes ISAM database files
COMMITTRANS	Adds current operations to the database
CREATEINDEX	Creates an ISAM index to a table of records
DELETE	Deletes the current record from the database
DELETEINDEX	Deletes an ISAM index
DELETETABLE	Deletes a table and its index from a database

EOR	Returns True if the current position is at the end of a file
FILEATTR	Gets the type of access allowed for an open file
GETINDEX$	Returns the name of the current index of an ISAM table
INSERT	Adds a new record into an ISAM table
LOF	Returns the number of records in an ISAM table
MOVEFIRST	Moves to the first record
MOVELAST	Moves to the last record
MOVENEXT	Moves forward one record
MOVEPREVIOUS	Moves back one record
OPEN	Opens an ISAM database file
RETRIEVE	Stores the current record into a variable
ROLLBACK	Restores the state of the database
SAVEPOINT	Marks save points within a transaction log
SEEKEQ	Searches for a record equal to a key value
SEEKGE	Searches for a record greater than or equal to a key value
SEEKGT	Searches for a record greater than a key value
SETINDEX	Changes indices in a database
TEXTCOMP	Compares two strings
TYPE	Defines the types and sizes of the variables stored in a record
UPDATE	Updates the current record in an ISAM table

Matrix Functions Toolkit (Professional Toolkit Only)

The matrix functions, which are available in the professional edition of Visual Basic, directly manipulate matrices and vectors. To use these functions, start Visual Basic with the /L switch followed by MATH.QLB to load the library, and include the file MATH.BI in your program using the $INCLUDE metacommand. MATH.BI defines the functions in your program. When you compile a program using these functions, the MATH.LIB library file must be available. Each of these functions is prefaced with an I, S, C, L, or D, to specify the data type (INTEGER, SINGLE, CURRENCY, LONG, or DOUBLE) of the elements of the matrix. That is, MatAddD is a function that adds two matrices of double-precision numbers. The following functions are available in the matrix toolkit:

MatAdd	Adds two matrices
MatDet	Calculates and returns the determinant of a matrix
MatInv	Calculates and returns the inverse of a matrix
MatMult	Multiplies two matrices
MatSEqn	Solves a system of linear equations
MatSub	Subtracts two matrices

E

Program Command Lines and Options

This appendix contains the command lines for the main programs in the Visual Basic package. In most cases, you will need to use only the command line for the VBDOS application. After you start VBDOS, it will automatically run the other programs (except FT.EXE), as needed, with the correct command lines.

VBDOS.EXE: The Programming Environment

Purpose   VBDOS is the programming environment for Visual Basic for MS-DOS. Everything but form design takes place within this environment.

Syntax   **VBDOS** [*options*] [[**/RUN**] *program*] [**/CMD** *string*]

Arguments   *options* is any of the options listed in Table F.1.

program is the name (and path if necessary) of a program to load automatically. If you use the /RUN option, the program is run after it is loaded.

string is a command string to pass to the program that can be retrieved with the COMMAND$ function.

Table F.1. Command-line options for the Integrated Development Environment.

Option	Description
/?	Displays a list of the available command-line options.
/AH	Allows dynamic arrays, fixed-length strings, and numeric data to be larger than 64K each.
/B	Allows the use of monochrome with a color graphics card.
/C:*n*	Sets the size of the COM buffer to *n* bytes.
/Ea	Allows the use of expanded memory for array storage.
/Es	Allows expanded memory to be shared with non-BASIC procedures.
/E:*n,m*	Limits the amount of expanded memory used by Visual Basic code to *n* Kbytes, and overlays to *m* Kbytes.
/G	Updates the screen in a CGA system as fast as possible; may cause snow.
/H	Uses the highest resolution possible on your hardware.
/L library	Loads a .QLB library file (a Quick library), included with VBDOS or created with the Make Library command of the Run menu. See Chapter 14, "Advanced-Language Features," for more information on libraries.

Option	Description
/MBF	Enables conversion of IEEE-format numbers to Microsoft Binary Format numbers.
/NF	No Forms; saves memory by disabling forms support.
/NOF	No Frills; saves memory by disabling the **Help** and the **Options** menu.
/NOHI	Allows you to use a monitor that doesn't support high intensity.
/RUN	Runs *program* instead of displaying it.
/S:*n*	Sets the maximum size of the programming environment to *n* Kbytes.
/X:*n*	Sets the maximum size of the overlay cache in extended memory to *n* Kbytes.

Description   The programming environment is the base for Visual Basic programming. You can run all the other programs in the Visual Basic package from within this environment, including the forms designer, the compiler, the linker, and the library manager.

For example   The following command line starts VBDOS and loads the Quick library file MYLIB.QLB:

```
VBDOS /LIB MYLIB.QLB
```

BC.EXE: The BASIC Compiler

Purpose   BC is the BASIC compiler that creates linkable object modules from BASIC statements.

Syntax   **BC** [*options*] *source* [*object*] [*list*] [;]

Arguments   *options* is any of the options listed in Table F.2.

source is the name (and path if necessary) of a program file (.BAS or .FRM) to compile.

771

object is the name (and path if necessary) of the object file (.OBJ) to create.

list is the name (and path if necessary) of a listing file (.LST) to create for assembly code.

; signifies that default names should be used for any remaining fields; otherwise BC will prompt the user for the names.

Table F.2. Command-line options for the BASIC compiler.

Option	Description
/?	Displays a list of the available command-line options.
/A	Creates an assembly language listing.
/AH	Allows dynamic arrays, fixed-length strings, and numeric data to be larger than 64K each.
/C:*n*	Sets the size of the COM buffer to *n* bytes.
/D	Enables Ctrl-Break and runtime error checking in the compiled program.
/E	Enables error trapping (ON ERROR/ RESUME) in the compiled program.
/Es	Allows expanded memory to be shared with non-BASIC procedures.
/FPA	Specifies that the compiler use the alternate math library for floating-point operations. This option does not provide math coprocessor support and is available with professional version only.
/G2	Specifies that the compiler use the 80286 command set. Programs created with BC will require an AT class machine or better. This option is available with the professional version only.

Option	Description
/G3	Specifies that the compiler use the 80386 command set. Programs created with BC will require an 80386 class machine or better. This option is available with the professional version only.
/IB:*n*	Sets the minimum number of buffers to *n* for the ISAM database software. This option is available with the professional version only.
/IE:*n*	Sets the amount of expanded memory that is not available to ISAM to *n* K-bytes. This option is available with the professional version only.
/II:*n*	Sets the maximum number of non-null ISAM indices to *n*. This option is available with the professional version only.
/MBF	Enables conversion of IEEE-format numbers to Microsoft Binary Format numbers.
/O	Creates a stand-alone .EXE file that does not need the runtime file.
/R	Stores arrays in memory by rows rather than by columns.
/S	Sends quoted strings directly to the object file.
/T	Suppresses compiler warnings.
/V	Enables communications event trapping for the compiled program.
/W	Enables event trapping and check for existing events.

continues

Table F.2. continued

Option	Description
/X	Enables support of RESUME, RESUME NEXT, and RESUME 0 statements in the compiled program.
/ZD	Enables limited CODEVIEW support. This option is available with the professional version only.
/ZI	Enables CODEVIEW support. This option is available with the professional version only.

Description   The BASIC compiler converts BASIC statements into object files compatible with the LINK linker. Object files must be linked before they can be run. You can combine object files into libraries of procedures by using the LIB Library Manager.

For example   The following command line compiles MYPROG.BAS and uses default names for the object and list files:

```
BC MYPROG.BAS ;
```

FD.EXE: The Forms Designer

Purpose   FD is the Forms Designer, which creates the visual aspect of forms.

Syntax   `FD [options][form]`

Arguments   *options* is any of the options listed in Table F.3.

form is the name (and path if necessary) of a form file (.FRM) to load for editing.

Description   The Forms Designer creates and manipulates the visual aspects of forms. All objects are drawn on forms in this program, much like a graphics drawing program.

For example   The following command line starts FD and loads the form in FORM1.FRM:

```
FS FORM1.FRM
```

Table F.3. Command-line options for the Forms Designer.

Option	Description
/?	Displays a list of the available command-line options.
/B	Allows the use of monochrome with a color graphics card.
/NOHI	Allows you to use a monitor that doesn't support high intensity.

LINK.EXE: The Linker

Purpose   The linker combines object modules and libraries into executable programs or Quick libraries.

Syntax   **LINK** [*options*] *objs* [,[*exe*][,[*map*][,[*libs*]]]][;]

Arguments   *options* is any of the options listed in Table F.4.

objs is the names (and paths if necessary) of the object files (.OBJ) and libraries (.LIB) to load into an executable program or a Quick library. Separate multiple files with blanks or plus signs.

exe is the name of the executable file to create.

map is the name of a linker map file to create.

libs is the library files (.LIB) to combine with the object files.

; signifies that default filenames are to be used with any remaining entries.

Table F.4. Command-line options for the linker.

Option	Description
/?	Displays a list of the available command-line options.
/BA	Batch mode: prevents LINK from asking for a path if it can't find a file. The program will generate a warning or error instead.

Table F.4. continued

Option	Description
/CO	Enables CODEVIEW support.
/DO	Forces a special ordering of segments. Don't use this option with custom runtime modules.
/DY:*n*	Changes the maximum number of inter-overlay calls to *n*. The default is 256, the maximum is 10,922. An interoverlay call is a procedure call from one of a program's overlays to another.
/E	Packs executable files.
/F	Optimizes calls to procedures in the same segment. Use this option with /PACKC to improve the performance of a program.
/HE	Same as /?.
/INF	Displays linker-process information.
/LI	Includes line numbers in the linker map file.
/M	Lists public symbols defined in the object files.
/NOD	Tells LINK to not use default libraries when linking a program. The user must then supply all procedures.
/NOE	Tells LINK to not use the extended dictionary when looking up symbols. Use this option to redefine a symbol and not get a multiply defined symbol error.
/NOF	Disables far calls.
/NOI	Makes procedure names case-sensitive when searching for procedures in a library.

Option	Description
/NOL	Suppresses startup logo.
/NON	Same as /DO, but no null bytes are inserted.
/NOP	Disables segment packing (enable with /PACKC).
/NOPACKF	Tells LINK that, when linking a program to a library, not to remove unreferenced functions from the library. This option results in larger programs filled with unused procedures. Use /NOPACKF to create libraries.
/O:n	Specifies n as the interrupt for passing control to an overlay. The default is 0x3F.
/ON:N	Tells LINK not to create an output file if there is an error.
/PACKC	Packs contiguous code segments.
/PACKD	Packs contiguous data segments.
/PACKF	Removes unreferenced functions. This is the default option.
/PAU	Causes the linker to pause before writing the output file.
/Q	Produces a Quick library file.
/R	Prevents LINK from using extended memory. If you use this option, it must be the first option.
/SE:n	Sets to n, the maximum number of segments a program can have.
/W	Causes the linker to issue warnings. Use this option with /NOP to test link a program.

F

Description   The linker combines multiple object files and libraries into executable programs or Quick libraries. The linker combines the object files into a single executable file and then adjusts addresses so all procedure calls point to the correct procedures. The linker then searches the libraries for any remaining procedure calls that were not satisfied by procedures in the object files. The procedures from the library files are also included in the executable file.

For example   The following command line starts the linker and combines the MYPROG1.OBJ and MYPROG2.OBJ object files and the MYLIB.LIB library file. The command line produces an executable file and a Quick library file.

```
LINK MYPROG1.OBJ+MYPROG2.OBJ,MYPROG.EXE,,MYLIB.LIB
```

LIB.EXE: The Library Manager

Purpose   The Library Manager combines one or more object and library files into a new .LIB type library usable with the linker.

Syntax   **LIB** *oldlib* [*options*][*cmds*][,[*list*][,[*newlib*]]][;]

Arguments   *oldlib* is the name (and path if necessary) of an existing library file to edit.

options is any of the options listed in Table F.5.

cmds is one or more symbols indicating what is to be done to the library:

+	Add
*	Copy
-	Remove
-*	Move
-+	Replace

list is the name of a file to contain a cross reference list.

newlib is the name of a file to contain the modified library.

; signifies that default filenames are to be used with any remaining entries.

Table F.5. Command-line options for the Library Manager.

Option	Description
/?	Displays a list of the available command-line options.
/I	Ignores case when comparing symbols. This is the default option.
/NOE	Don't create an extended dictionary. This option makes linking with a library slower, but saves memory.
/NOI	Causes the library manager to be case-sensitive when comparing symbols.
/NOLOGO	Suppresses the startup logo.
/PA:*n*	Sets the library page size to *n* bytes. The default is 16 bytes.

Description The Library Manager combines multiple object files into a .LIB-type library of executable procedures. You can use libraries of this type with the linker to produce executable applications. The programming environment requires a Quick library (.QLB), which is different from a .LIB library. The linker creates Quick libraries.

For example The following command line starts the Library Manager and converts all the procedures in MYPROG.OBJ into a library named MYLIB.LIB:

```
LIB MYPROG.OBJ,,MYLIB.LIB;
```

FT.EXE: The Forms Translator

Purpose The Forms Translator converts forms between the Visual Basic for Windows and the Visual Basic for DOS formats.

Syntax `FT [/?] source destination [list]`

Arguments `/?` lists the command-line options.

source is the name (and path if necessary) of the source file to convert.

779

destination is the name of the new file to create

list is the name of a file for warnings and errors.

Description The Forms Translator converts binary form files between Visual Basic for Windows and Visual Basic for DOS. The source file type determines which conversion is done. If the source file is a Visual Basic for Windows file, the result is a Visual Basic for DOS file, and vice versa. The Forms Translator does not convert any BASIC procedures included in the form files. You must save the BASIC procedures as text files and then attach them to the form in the new environment.

For example The following command line starts the Forms Translator and converts the Windows form in FORM1.FRM to a DOS form in FORM1D.FRM.

```
FT FORM1.FRM FORM1D.FRM
```

Index

Symbols

& (ampersand), 201
* (multiplication)
  operator, 117
+ (addition) operator, 117
+ (concatenation operator), 90
– (negation) operator, 117
– (subtraction) operator, 117
/ (division) operator, 117
< (less than) operator, 118
<= (less than or equal to)
  operator, 118
<> (not equal to)
  operator, 118
= (equals) operator, 118
> (greater than) operator, 118
\ (integer division)
  operator, 117
^ (power) operator, 117

A

About (Help menu)
  command, 40-41
ABS( ) function, 120, 394
accelerator keys, 171
access argument, 219
access keys, 171-172

accessing
  Caption property, 50
  Forms Designer, 33
  objects displayed on
    screens, 717
  properties, 652
ACCESSKEY_FORECOLOR
  property, 282
actions, initiating, 142,
  709-710
ACTIVE_BORDER_BACKCOLOR
  property, 282
ACTIVE_BORDER_FORECOLOR
  property, 282
ACTIVE_WINDOW_SHADOW
  property, 282
ActiveControl property,
  653

Do It Yourself Visual Basic for MS–DOS Examples Disk

If you want to use all the examples in this book, but don't want to type them yourself, you can obtain them on disk. Complete the following order form and return it to the address below with a check or money order for $20.00, U.S. currency only. For countries outside of the United States and Canada, please add $1.00 for overseas shipping. For California orders, please add state sales tax (7.25%). The Visual Basic examples disk will be sent to you by first-class mail. Please specify the disk size.

Visual Basic for MS–DOS
William J. Orvis
226 Joyce St.
Livermore, CA 94550

Name: _____

Address: _____

City/State/Zip: _____

Disk Price $20.00

    Overseas shipping $1.00   _____
    (outside of the U.S. and Canada)

    State sales tax (7.25% = $1.45)   _____
    (California only)

Total   _____

Enclosed is my check or money order for $_____
(Make checks payable to William J. Orvis.)
Please send me the Visual Basic for MS–DOS Examples Disk.

I prefer: ___5 1/4-inch disk

            ___3 1/2-inch disk

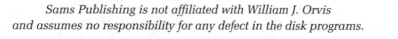